THE PUBLIC EYE

THE PUBLIC EYE:

Television and the Politics of Canadian Broadcasting
1952-1968

Frank W. Peers

UNIVERSITY OF TORONTO PRESS

Toronto Buffalo London

79

Canadian Cataloguing in Publication Data

Peers, Frank W., 1918–
The public eye

Includes index.

ISBN 0-8020-5436-6

1. Television broadcasting – Canada – History.
2. Canadian Broadcasting Corporation – History.
1. Title.

HE8700.9.C2P43   384.55'4'0971   C78-001562-2

PREFACE

THIS BOOK traces the development of the broadcasting system in Canada from the inception of television in 1952 to the passing of the Broadcasting Act of 1968. It pays particular attention to the policy decisions made by governments and by broadcasting authorities, and to the circumstances under which those decisions were made. During the period surveyed, there took place several public investigations of the broadcasting system and its performance. These investigations and their outcomes form part of the story. Necessarily, the study deals with the relationships between the CBC, the private broadcasters, government, and the regulatory authority, and also with events that affected the perceptions of politicians and the public – such as the French network strike in 1959, the Preview Commentary affair of the same year, and the controversies surrounding the CBC television program 'This Hour Has Seven Days' in 1965–6.

The volume presents a good deal of material that has not appeared previously in published form. Much of the new information is based on original source material – government documents, CBC records, a manuscript written by one of the chief participants, records kept by other principals in the story, and interviews with a number of the key figures.

The book concludes with a survey of policy changes in Canadian broadcasting over a span of fifty years, and an appraisal of the system as it has evolved.

The preparation of the book was made possible by the good will and generous assistance of many persons, some of whom I shall mention now. I should especially like to acknowledge the assistance and encouragement of two of the principal figures in Canadian broadcasting – Andrew Stewart, former chairman of the Board of Broadcast Governors, and Alphonse Ouimet, former president of the CBC. Dr. Stewart gave generously of his time, and made available to me a manuscript he had begun to prepare for possible publication soon after his retirement from the BBG, but eventually abandoned. It contained much documentary material I would otherwise not have found. A special word of thanks goes to Alphonse Ouimet, a pioneer in television technology and, if any one man can be so credited, the founder of the Canadian television venture. Mr. Ouimet talked with me at length on several occasions, put information from his records that I requested at my disposal, and checked some of my manuscript for factual errors and misstatements. For my interpretation of developments and events, of course, neither he nor Dr. Stewart bears any responsibility.

Others who read sections of the work in manuscript form include Dr. Eugene Forsey of the Canadian Senate, Bernard Trotter, Graham Spry, Professor William Morton, and Vincent Tovell, all of whom offered much valued criticism. Graham Spry in particular placed his voluminous records and papers at my disposal and imposed no limits on their use.

Among those who shared their recollections with me and who contributed their assessment of events were Davidson Dunton, former chairman of the CBC; T. J. Allard, for many years chief executive officer of the Canadian Association of Broadcasters, who since our conversations has published *The C.A.B. Story: Private Broadcasting in Canada*; Robert M. Fowler, chairman of the Royal Commission on Broadcasting in 1955–7 and of the Advisory Committee on Broadcasting in 1964–5; Finlay MacDonald, former president of CJCH and CJCH-TV in Halifax; R.L. Dunsmore, former chairman of the CBC board of directors; Jacques Landry and Marc Thibault of CBC Montreal; Fernand Quirion, former president of l'Association des Réalisateurs; Mel Jacks, at one time executive assistant to the minister of transport; James Baldwin, former deputy minister of transport; Reeves Haggan, former general supervisor of public affairs at CBC Toronto; Ernest Steele, former undersecretary of state and a member of the Advisory Committee on Broadcasting in 1964–5; Henry Hindley, secretary of that committee; and Hugh Laidlaw, former CBC counsel.

I owe much to discussions with academic colleagues and to their written work. I am thinking of William Hull of Brock University, Thelma McCormack of York University, Paul Thomas of the University of Manitoba, Helen Carscallen of Ryerson Polytechnical Institute, and Roger Rickwood of the University of Lethbridge. The three last mentioned wrote masters or doctoral dissertations at the University of Toronto from which I gained both information and insights.

I was fortunate in having access to collections in several libraries and in the Public Archives of Canada: the records of the Massey and Fowler commissions; those of the Glassco Commission and the Fowler Committee; the E.A. Weir papers; the CBC papers of J.A. Corry; the A.R.M. Lower papers; the Grant Dexter papers; and the papers of Brooke

Claxton. To the librarians and archivists at Queen's University, the Public Archives of Canada, the CBC Historical Section in Ottawa, the CBC reference library in Toronto, the archives section of Radio-Canada in Montreal, and the library of the University of Toronto, my grateful thanks for assistance and many kindnesses.

The research and writing were facilitated by a leave fellowship and a research grant from the Canada Council, and by assistance rendered by colleagues in the department of political economy, University of Toronto.

This book has been published with the help of grants from the Social Science Federation of Canada, using funds provided by the Social Sciences and Humanities Research Council of Canada, and from the Publications Fund of the University of Toronto Press.

F.W.P. University of Toronto

CONTENTS

CHRONOLOGY

Canadian broadcasting: the first fifty years

1919 Station XWA, Montreal (later CFCF) began broadcasting in September

1924 Canadian National Railways opened its first station in Ottawa

1926 Canadian Association of Broadcasters was formed

1927 First nation-wide hookup of radio stations to broadcast special programs marking Diamond Jubilee of Confederation, July 1

1928 Royal commission on radio broadcasting appointed

1929 Aird Commission's report recommended publicly owned system

1932 Federal government's jurisdiction established by appeal case before Privy Council in London
Act establishes Canadian Radio Broadcasting Commission

1936 Act establishes Canadian Broadcasting Corporation
Two radio networks formed: Trans-Canada (English) and French networks

1944 Second radio network in English established, the Dominion network

1949 Government announces interim policy for television and loans for CBC television development
Royal Commission (Massey Commission) begins hearings on broadcasting

1951 Massey report recommends continuation of CBC's authority over broadcasting, and 'single-station' policy for television

1952 Two CBC stations begin television service in Montreal and Toronto

1953 Microwave network connected CBC television stations in Montreal, Ottawa, Toronto; later extended to private station in London
First private TV stations began operations (Sudbury and London)

1957 Royal Commission on Broadcasting (Fowler Commission) reported

1958 Microwave network extended from Victoria to Halifax and Sydney to become longest television network in the world
Broadcasting Act passed, establishing Board of Broadcast Governors

1959 Strike of CBC employees in Montreal
Parliamentary hearing over 'Preview Commentary' incident
BBG sets 'Canadian content' standards for television

1960 Eight 'second' TV stations authorized
1961 CTV formed, linking private television stations in eight cities
1962 Dispute over Grey Cup coverage between CBC and BBG
1963 The 'Troika' committee asked to advise government on policy
1965 Report of Advisory Committee on Broadcasting (second Fowler Report)
1966 CBC's 'Seven Days' crisis, parliamentary investigation and the Keate
    report
    Government issues White Paper on Broadcasting
1967–8 Broadcasting Act, and creation of the Canadian Radio-Television
    Commission

INTRODUCTION

WHEN CANADIAN TELEVISION BEGAN in 1952, it was grafted to the system of radio broadcasting that had evolved over a period of thirty years. The structure of that system was ungainly. Its foundations were set in the 1930s, when national objectives were declared and a public agency created to carry them out. But compromises were built into the system, not only in the governing act passed in 1936, but more strikingly in the policy choices and operational decisions taken in the years between 1936 and the early 1950s. In those years the government had perforce to decide how broadcast services would be organized, financed, produced, and distributed.

The central problem was to decide how much to rely on the public agency, on private entrepreneurs, or on regulation carried out by an instrument of the state. The government seemed unwilling to make any clear choice among the several options that were theoretically open to it. The broadcasting system as a result was a peculiar hybrid. Was it a system in which a government-chartered public corporation would provide the national service, as in Great Britain with the BBC? Not exactly. Was it a system in which privately owned stations and networks would determine what programs the public would receive, acting in response to market considerations and calculations of advertising revenues, as in the United States? Not exactly. Was it a system whose central purpose would be to enable Canadians to communicate among themselves, without bending to pressures from the mass media of another country? Hardly. Was it a dual system in which parallel services were offered by private and public broadcasters, as in Australia? It was not that either.

The government's indecision was perhaps a response to uncertainties among the public at large. Broadcasting in Canada engendered continuing controversy. Nothing seemed settled. There was a public corporation in existence, the Canadian Broadcasting Corporation, modelled in many respects on the BBC. It provided the largest share of original programming in Canada, nearly all of the nationally distributed programs, and the only programs making extensive use of Canadian creative and performing talent. Private radio stations existed primarily to offer local services to the communities in which they were situated. But their applications for licences were referred to the CBC board of governors for that body's recommendation; the general standards of service were set by the CBC's board under powers delegated to it by Parliament; and many of the private stations, though not all, were expected to carry CBC radio services during some hours of the day. This arrangement, by which private stations became CBC network affiliates, was intended to allow the distribution of CBC programs to the entire country, without incurring too much cost to the public treasury. With the same economical objective, the government did not even consider setting the radio licence fee high enough so that the CBC could be fully financed by its proceeds. The CBC was expected to raise a portion of its revenues from advertising, so that even in the publicly owned sector of broadcasting commercial considerations impinged on the choice and scheduling of programs. A second justification for this arrangement lay in the fact that the commercially supported programs were especially attractive to the CBC network's private affiliates. As a result, the CBC and many of the private stations seemed inescapably bound together, even when their differing interests and objectives might have impelled them to separate.

The CBC and its supporters saw the central position of the public agency as crucial to the success of the system and its national and public service objectives. Many private stations, their trade organization, some business interests, and an undefined proportion of the concerned public saw the existing system as stifling private enterprise. They argued that removal of the CBC's regulatory authority and its dominant position within the system would allow a fuller choice of programs and particularly more programs with mass appeal. Unfettered, they would 'give the public what it wants.'

The private stations had fought many skirmishes in years past to gain recognition of their demands that the CBC's control be loosened or its regulatory authority removed. They had made some gains, but had not succeeded in their objective to have the broadcasting act of 1936 replaced. Now, as the television story begins, a royal commission headed by Vincent Massey was completing its investigation of broadcasting in Canada, having heard the representations of the CBC, the private broadcasters, and a myriad of voluntary groups. Its 1951 report recommended against removing the CBC's regulatory powers – indeed, the CBC was asked to exercise them more fully. The commission did not favour changing the system in any of its essentials. In general, the CBC was praised for its program performance, the commission saving most of its strictures for the 'relatively low commercial standards' of the private stations.[1]

A House of Commons committee accepted the Massey Commission's recommendations against changing the CBC's powers substantially, or altering its dominant position within the system. Moreover, it reasserted the principle that CBC operations should be free from partisan influence, and it accepted the commission's recommendation that they should be financed mainly from the licence fee, supplemented by a new statutory grant.[2] The intention was to prevent the CBC's dependence on annual appropriations that would have to be recommended by the government and then voted by Parliament. In other words, the CBC's independence from the government of the day was to be preserved.

Parliament's acceptance and approval of the existing system, however, was by decision of the Liberal majority, supported by the third strongest party, the CCF. The official opposition, the Progressive Conservatives, were sympathetic to the demands of the private broadcasters for a separate regulatory board, as were members of the fourth party, Social Credit. It was therefore apparent that a change in party fortunes in another election might well lead to a transformation of the broadcasting system, and particularly in the method of control. Another possibility was that the technological innovation represented by television might also induce a substantial change. Governments in the past had been uneasy in providing for even the modest costs of radio. Since television would be six or seven times as expensive, the government might be tempted to throw the field wide open to private investors, leaving the CBC to play a minor role. If this happened, the balance between public and private broadcasting would be drastically changed.

If the broadcasting structure in 1951 was ungainly and hard to categorize, nevertheless it had evolved as a response to the Canadian environment, and it met the most discernible of Canadian needs. The principal features of the system were a product of Canadian history, geography, economic conditions, and elements of the political culture. Canadian broadcasting was a service, or rather a variety of services, that spoke to the two principal language groups, French and English. Against

1 / Royal Commission on National Development in the Arts, Letters and Sciences, 1949–51, *Report* (Ottawa, 1951), 286. A more complete summary of the Massey Commission's recommendations is in F.W. Peers, *The Politics of Canadian Broadcasting, 1920–1951* (Toronto, 1969), chap. 16.
2 / Canada, House of Commons, Special Committee on Radio Broadcasting, 1951, *Proceedings*, 471–3.

difficult odds provided by the tremendous expanse of Canadian territory, the radio services reached the overwhelming majority of Canadians, whether they resided in urban centres or in small, widely scattered communities in the hinterland. Broadcasting was a service that
most households could easily afford – in 1950 the radio licence fee was
still $2.50 a year per household, although this amount was clearly in-
sufficient to meet the CBC's costs much longer. National programs were
provided in the hours when most people had a chance to listen, and
performance standards were reasonably high, according to foreign observers and the Massey Commission itself. The system was a combination of public and private ownership, of private initiative and state
intervention, a pattern that was fairly common in Canadian transportation and public utilities. The commercial ethos that was generally pervasive in the Canadian economy had not been abandoned but public
ownership was also employed, partly as a defence against domination of
the airwaves by broadcast services from the United States. The
influence of American entertainment, however, could not be denied, and
the Canadian broadcasting system responded to its popularity. The
commercial operations even of the CBC networks made it easy for the
national service to import and distribute American commercially sponsored programs, and thus to meet demands from Canadian listeners that
American originations not be excluded.

The system was untidy, but still manageable. Television would be an
unsettling factor, and with its arrival the stakes for Canadian broadcasting, and for the country, far higher. Television imagery, the facts and
fancies it would purvey, would deeply influence the next generation.

In the late 1940s, the question that had to be decided was how television would begin. Policy choices at that critical time might resolve the
issue as to which principle would have priority – the principle that
broadcasting is an industry, and should be based on private ownership
and governed by the market; or the principle that broadcasting is a public
service, fulfilling nationally stated objectives. If policy were to evolve
according to one or other of these principles, a more coherent structure
might be possible. If policy were to continue responding to pressures,
first from one side (the CBC and its supporters) and then from the other
(the private broadcasters and their supporters), the strangely mixed
system would persist, tilted perhaps to one side or the other. Without
clarification, and some resolution, the controversies would continue,
and the arguments would be central in the greater struggle for national
survival.

THE PUBLIC EYE

1 CANADIAN TELEVISION: BEGINNINGS

IN 1952 TELEVISION ARRIVED in Canada's two largest cities almost simultaneously – the Canadian Broadcasting Corporation opened its Montreal station, CBFT, on September 6 and its Toronto station, CBLT, on September 8. Programs were transmitted in English and (over the Montreal station) in French as well to an area that contained about a fifth of Canada's fourteen million inhabitants. Two years later, by the end of 1954, television service was available to three-quarters of the Canadian population, through seventeen privately owned stations and seven CBC stations. All carried a complement of network programs in Canada, as well as imported programs, chiefly from the United States. Canada was at that time the second nation in the world in terms of both live television production and the number of television stations. Once the start had been made, Canada extended TV coverage in share of population faster than had any other nation in the world, including the United States.[1] Yet, to judge from comments in the press and in Parliament, Canadians were overwhelmed with a feeling that they had lagged far behind; that if the television system was their own, it was but a poor thing. Why? One of the reasons was no doubt that the birth of Canadian television had been long, protracted, even painful, leaving scars that did not heal.

1 The Background

Television was talked about in the 1920s as early experimental work was

1 / In 1957 the Fowler Commission wrote: 'The growth of television in Canada has been the fastest of any country in the world up to the present time.' Royal Commission on Broadcasting, 1957, *Report* (Ottawa, 1957), 217. Hereafter cited as *Fowler Commission Report*. The United States after the war had had three years of television development before a 'freeze' was imposed at the end of 1948. In this period stations were established in forty-one cities, covering a potential audience of 40 per cent of the population. See speech by George E. Sterling, member of the US Federal Communications Commission, June 8, 1949, reprinted in *Industrial Canada* (July 1949), 187.

carried on in the United States and Great Britain.[2] It was envisaged for Canada in the report of the first royal commission on radio broadcasting in 1929 (the Aird Commission).[3] The first distinct television pictures were produced in England by John Baird in October 1925.[4] His system, however, used a mechanical means of scanning, incapable of providing high definition. BBC experimental broadcasts, using the Baird 3-line system, began in 1929, and the synchronization of sound and vision was achieved the following year. These transmissions came to an end in 1935.

Meanwhile, progress was being made in the development of other systems of television, principally in America. The results of these experiments were brought to Britain by the giant Electric and Musical Industries Ltd. – EMI, through its business links with RCA – the Radio Corporation of America. EMI developed an all-electronic system of scanning which would allow a standard of 405 lines and 25 pictures per second. It was this standard that the BBC adopted soon after starting its regular television service in November 1936 – the first high definition system in the world.

In Canada there were also modest experiments. The first successful television pictures, it is said, were shown in 1930 at l'Ecole Polytechnique in Montreal by Professor Bernier. The next year the newspaper *La Presse* began experimental transmissions, using first a 45-line system and then a 60-line system, with equipment supplied by the first Canadian television manufacturing company, Canadian Television Limited.[5] One of the research engineers working for this company was J. Alphonse Ouimet, who was to have a central part in the first twenty-five years of Canadian television. With the deepening of the Depression, experimental telecasts ceased, Canadian Television Limited collapsed, and Ouimet found a job in 1934 with the two-year-old Canadian Radio Broadcasting Commission.

Canada did not seriously consider initiating a television service before the outbreak of the Second World War, although in the United States NBC inaugurated television in April 1939 as a feature of the New York

2 / For the early history of television, see Asa Briggs, *The Golden Age of Wireless: The History of Broadcasting in the United Kingdom*, vol. II (London, 1965), 519–94. See also Erik Barnouw, *A Tower in Babel: A History of Broadcasting in the United States*, vol. I (New York, 1966), 154, 210–11, 231; vol. II, *The Golden Web* (New York, 1968), 38–9, 42, 126–8, 130.

3 / Royal Commission on Radio Broadcasting, 1929, *Report*, 8.

4 / Briggs, *The Golden Age of Wireless*, 525.

5 / J.A. Ouimet, 'Report on Television,' *The Engineering Journal* (March 1950), 172.

World's Fair.[6] The Canadian Broadcasting Corporation, charged with carrying on a national broadcasting service, was in no doubt that it was the agency that would bring television to Canada at an appropriate time. The Canadian Broadcasting Act, 1936, had carefully defined broadcasting to include 'the wireless transmission of writing, signs, signals, pictures and sounds of all kinds by means of Hertzian waves, intended to be received by the public either directly or through the medium of relay stations.'[7]

L.W. Brockington, first chairman of the CBC Board of Governors, had been shown NBC's experimental telecasts, and told the 1939 parliamentary committee on radio broadcasting something of the difficulties at that stage of television's technical development:

A television transmitter can radiate only within a limited area, the radius of satisfactory service being about 30 miles ...

There is the further difficulty that, at present, television cannot be carried from point to point on wire lines in a manner similar to that in which our present broadcast networks function. This is due to the prohibitive cost of the special coaxial cable required. ... There is an experimental coaxial-cable installation between New York and Philadelphia and it is understood that one is being made between London and Birmingham. ...

Thus, national coverage in television could be achieved only by the separate operation of an immense number of individual transmissions, each serving only a very small area. ...

Standards of transmission and receiving equipment are still in a state of experimental development. ... The cost of one unit of television transmitter and incidental equipment, apart from buildings and antenna, would be in the vicinity of half a million dollars. ... Unless moving picture film can be made available cheaply for use as television programme material, the cost of supplying daily different programmes with live talent will be highly expensive. ... Taking into account the high costs, both of equipment and production ... it is safe to say that it is not economically feasible in Canada at the moment.[8]

---

6 / Barnouw, *The Golden Web*. 125–6. Initially transmissions were on 441 lines.
7 / Canada, *Statutes*, Canadian Broadcasting Act, 1936, 1 Edward VIII, c. 24.
8 / Canada, House of Commons, 1939 Special Committee on Radio Broadcasting, *Minutes of Proceedings and Evidence*, 17–18 (March 2, 1939); hereafter cited as *1939 Proceedings*. Committees struck by the Commons to review broadcasting will often be referred to as 'the parliamentary committee on broadcasting,' or as 'the broadcasting committee.'

Brockington added that the present policy of the CBC board of governors was 'not to alienate from the public domain any broadcasting rights in television to privately-owned stations or other profit-making concerns.' He explained that this policy was not intended to prevent scientific research, as had been charged, but was "to prevent a wrong type of exploitation taking place under the guise of experimentation.' He continued:

The American and British investing public have already suffered severely because of premature and inadequate exploitation of the great new medium. ... If I rightly interpret the advice of the B.B.C. authorities and of the American authorities it is briefly this: they have been forced into building expenditures perhaps somewhat in advance of the economic and practical feasibility of the enterprise of television. ... Their advice to us ... is this: Wait; Canada is in a favourable position; share the results of our experience, but do not be so foolish as to try to share the cost of our experiments. I think that is good advice for us to follow.[9]

In Britain, television was immediately suspended with the outbreak of war, and work on television development almost ceased until the war was over. In the United States, development continued, at least until Pearl Harbour. CBS and Dumont established stations in New York, and the FCC authorized fully commercial television in 1941. Six stations hung on throughout the war, offering a limited program service to the owners of 7000 receiving sets.[10] At the end of the war, when the standard of transmission changed from 441 to 525 lines, the old receivers became obsolete.

By 1946, RCA was ready with a new postwar model, and taverns quickly acquired sets to attract customers. By July of that year, the FCC had licensed twenty-four new stations. Boxing matches, baseball games, and other sporting events were especially popular; and in 1947 the opening of Congress was televised for the first time.[11]

With all this activity in the neighbouring country, Canadian broadcasters, promoters, and newspaper writers became eager for similar excitement on their side of the border. The CBC at various times seemed intent on dampening such enthusiasm. For example, in 1944 the CBC's general manager, Dr. Augustin Frigon, was quoted as saying that television probably would not be available to the public generally for another

9 / *Ibid.*
10 / C.A. Siepman, *Radio, Television and Society* (New York, 1950), 318.
11 / Barnouw, *The Golden Web*, 244.

fifteen or twenty years.[12] In 1946 he told the parliamentary committee on broadcasting:

We hear a lot about television and there has been an extraordinary amount of publicity designed to make listeners television-conscious. Notwithstanding the millions spent in research and promotion, this new art is not developing with the rapidity that some people would like. ...
   The fundamental fact remains that television is a very costly affair, not so much in capital cost as in operating cost. We believe it would be a mistake to encourage the introduction in Canada of television without sufficient financial support and, therefore, take the risk that unsatisfactory programs would, at the start, give a poor impression of this new means of communication. ...
   We refuse to be stampeded into premature action by publicity directed to the general public and really meant for things to come. ... We are sure only a small proportion of those who have applied for television permits would be prepared to go through with their plans.[13]

Eighteen applicants mainly from the private radio stations, who were in any case resentful of the paramount position accorded the CBC in the broadcasting system, had indeed submitted applications for television broadcasting licences.[14] They hoped by applying early to get in on the 'ground floor' before the CBC could establish its own stations with public funds. Since there was no government policy on television, the applications remained on file in the radio division of the Department of Transport, with no action taken.
   A year later, the minister of national revenue, Dr. J.J. McCann, in outlining the position of the government, expressed himself in terms much like those used by Dr. Frigon:

I was at the Columbia Broadcasting Company and the N.B.C. in January and I was told by both these companies that they had spent something in the neighbourhood, in company with the Victor, DuPont [Dumont] and the others, around $50,000,000 on television to date. Along with some of the officials of the Canadian Broadcasting Corporation, we felt, on behalf of Canada, it was not prudent for us to spend a lot of money as a corporation or to encourage private companies to spend money on this until there has been some further development. ...

12 / *Canadian Broadcaster* (Sept. 23, 1944).
13 / *1946 Proceedings*, 60 (June 11, 1946).
14 / *Ibid.*, 265.

I submit, Mr. Chairman, that the idea in making application for a licence to do television work is that the private corporations may, in the early stages, get some vested interests in that particular type of broadcasting.[15]

The counsel for the Canadian Association of Broadcasters, Joseph Sedgwick, under questioning by the broadcasting committee, argued that private broadcasters should be encouraged to proceed. 'After all radio broadcasting was not invented by the government. It was not pioneered by the government. It was pioneered by private individuals, by private companies.'[16] Frigon told the committee that in the United States, TV stations existed only in cities of more than 1,500,000 population – New York, Philadelphia, Washington, Chicago, Detroit, Los Angeles, San Francisco, and Schenectady.[17] This last city, even with nearby Troy and Albany, was much smaller than the population figure Frigon cited, but the other cities were larger than Montreal or Toronto.

Not surprisingly in view of the government's stand, the 1947 committee expressed approval of the CBC's cautious attitude, adding that private applicants should not be able to obtain television broadcasting rights 'merely with a view to holding them against the time it may become profitable to put them in use.'[18]

Frigon may have thought that television in Canada was some years away; others in the CBC were more optimistic. Late in 1945 A. Davidson Dunton had been selected by the prime minister as the first full-time chairman of the CBC. Dunton was thirty-three, a native of Montreal, bilingual, with a background as a journalist, editor of the Montreal *Standard*, and general manager of the Wartime Information Board. He would be more inclined than Frigon to listen to the young men on staff who were eager to make a start in television. In the fall of 1946 Dunton took the initiative in discussing with directors of the Canadian Association of Broadcasters an idea by which the CBC might establish facilities in Montreal and Toronto through which the staff of CBC and private broadcasters might both get some training. And Frigon, responding to the same spirit, asked for authorization to approach the government for a grant to establish transmitters, studios, and a mobile unit in two cities – Montreal first, and Toronto as soon as the problem caused by 25-cycle electricity could be solved. In their November meeting the board of governors formulated the principle that the corporation should exercise

15 / *1947 Proceedings*, 229 (June 12, 1947).
16 / *Ibid.*, 235.
17 / *Ibid.*, 490 (June 27, 1947).
18 / *Ibid.*, third and final report, 627.

control in this new field from the beginning, and they asked management to work out estimated costs.[19]

The CBC assigned its assistant chief engineer, Alphonse Ouimet, to make a survey of television's progress in Britain, France, and the United States and, taking into account technical, economic, and artistic factors, to come up with recommendations on how television should be established in Canada. He was joined, on the program side, by H.G. Walker, manager of the CBC's Dominion Network. Meanwhile, talks were begun with the Department of Transport on technical standards and the allocation of frequencies among the various provinces and cities.

Without waiting for the completion of Ouimet's report, Frigon proposed to the board of governors that the CBC build a television transmitter in Montreal for experimental purposes. He estimated capital and operational costs (for two years) at $900,000, and proposed that the CBC ask for this amount in a government grant. He argued that if nothing was done, 'strictly American television networks will sooner or later invade the south-western peninsula of Ontario up to Toronto and possibly further east.'[20] On November 27, 1947, the governors authorized Frigon to make such a submission to the cabinet. He was also asked to seek the support of television manufacturing companies for the construction of the required facilities. It was hoped they might make representations to the government in support of the grant.

Ouimet's report was ready by December 1947, but a serious setback came with the government's refusal to provide a grant during the 1947–8 session. These were the last few months of the ministry headed by Mackenzie King, and the prime minister may have hesitated to embark on such a new and costly venture. And no doubt some ministers in the cabinet preferred that private enterprise take the risks in television's development.

In its meeting of May 17–19, 1948, the board heard three applications for television licences. It deferred two applications from Toronto to give others a chance to apply, and rejected the application from Ken Soble (CHML in Hamilton), noting that there was only one channel for Hamilton which the board felt should be reserved for the national system.[21]

19 / Extract provided by the CBC from Minutes of 50th Meeting, CBC Board of Governors, Nov. 18–19, 1946.
20 / Appendix to Agenda of the 56th meeting, CBC Board of Governors, Nov. 27–9, 1947 (supplied by CBC).
21 / Minutes of 59th meeting, CBC Board of Governors, Montreal (information supplied by CBC, Ottawa). Strictly speaking, the board only made a recommendation to the minister of transport that the applications be deferred or rejected.

The governors took the occasion to announce their general policy for the development of television, and their interest in pushing ahead:

The Canadian Broadcasting Corporation ... sees great potentialities in television ... and believes that Canada should not lag behind. ...
   The Board believes that in line with fundamental radio policies laid down by parliament for radio broadcasting, television should be developed so as to be of benefit to the greatest possible number of people; so that public channels should be used in the public interest; and with the over-all aim of stimulating Canadian national life and not merely of providing a means of broadcasting non-Canadian visual material in this country. The Board will strive for the maximum provision of Canadian television for Canadians.

The governors recognized that national television would be very expensive in Canada, but said revenue could be derived from television licence fees and from commercial income. They promised that the CBC would proceed 'just as soon as necessary' financing can be arranged,' by which they meant a government grant or loan, coupled with action to establish a licence fee. The board said that it would consider applications from private broadcasters and forward recommendations to the licensing authority (the minister in charge of the radio division of the Department of Transport). But it also gave notice that it was recommending that the channels necessary be reserved for the national (that is, the public) system. It added that it would follow a policy of not granting permission for individual private stations to become outlets for non-Canadian (that is, American) systems.[22]
   At their meeting in Halifax in September, the governors formally requested that a television licence fee be established equal to the radio licence fee ($2.50), to be increased later when the national system was in a position to undertake television operations.
   The government rebuffed the CBC in its request for a loan and for a licence fee. According to Blair Fraser, the cabinet took up the two requests 'one day in October, without inviting any views from the CBC, and turned them down.'[23] The cabinet considered the matter in the absence of the prime minister, with C.D. Howe acting as chairman. Howe expressed the view that the CBC should not embark on any operational program at present in view of the high cost involved and the

22 / CBC Public Announcement No. 15, Montreal, May 17, 1948.
23 / 'Why They Won't Let You Have Television,' *Maclean's* (Jan. 15, 1949).

substantial progress still to be made in the technical field.[24] Fraser quoted one senior minister as saying, 'I don't know anything about television, but it costs money, so my instinctive reaction was against it. We're into too many things already.' C.D. Howe, the minister of trade and commerce, thought television a proper field for private enterprise. Not for years, if ever (he told Fraser) could it be brought to a majority of Canadians – for a long time to come only the larger cities could hope to have it. 'If private operators think it worth while to risk that much money, let them go ahead,' said Mr. Howe. 'Some of them, like Canadian Marconi, can hope to get it back by selling TV sets. For the Government it would be a dead loss. If I were living in my own town of Port Arthur, I'd kick like a steer at paying taxes to bring television to Montreal and Toronto.'

The rest of the cabinet apparently took their cue from Mr. Howe. The government let it be known that the present role of the CBC should be similar to that of the US Federal Communications Commission, namely, general licensing and regulation of private development, although they did agree to the reservation of television channels for future development by the CBC.[25] The problem in deciding in favour of private development was that neither of the two applicants best able to proceed and to stand the attendant financial losses was a Canadian-owned company. Canadian Marconi, which held the licence for radio station CFCF in Montreal (Canada's first station), was a subsidiary of a British company. Famous Players Limited, which was applying for a television licence in Toronto, was controlled by Paramount Pictures in the United States.

The board of governors held formal hearings for six applicants on October 28, 1948 – four applying for a station in Toronto, two for Montreal. The governors decided to defer action on all these applications. They noted the uncertainty of most of the applicants regarding the kind and quality of the service they would be able to broadcast. One of the best presentations had been made by Famous Players, but the legal counsel for the Canadian Association of Broadcasters had expressed emphatic objection to the granting of a licence to motion-picture theatre interests and to a corporation controlled by non-Canadians. The governors felt they must keep in mind the need, within the shortest possible time after television was to start, of network connections between

24 / Roger Rickwood, 'Canadian Broadcasting Policy and the Private Broadcasters: 1936–1968' (Doctoral thesis, University of Toronto, 1976), 289–90, citing a letter from A.D.P. Heeney, secretary to the cabinet, to Dr. J.J. McCann, October 21, 1948.
25 / Interview with A.D. Dunton, Sept. 13, 1972.

Canadian centres. The implication of this observation was that to grant any of these applications would not further that objective. Their statement continued:

The Board does not feel that it is its function to be concerned with the monetary risks which private investors in broadcasting may run. But it must weigh prospects of service to the public over the public air channels; it must be concerned with the millions of dollars which members of the public would invest in receiver sets even at the first stages of television broadcasting. ...

It is convinced that the soundness of future development will be profoundly affected by the first steps taken ... and feels that care should be taken at the present in establishing monopoly positions that will likely be of great importance in the future.[26]

The statement pointed out that in the United States the FCC had recently imposed a 'freeze,' deferring all pending television applications to allow for a thorough investigation of technical questions relating to the allocation and use of frequencies. (Originally, stations occupying the same channel had been allowed to be too close to one another geographically. The freeze, lengthened by the Korean War, lasted from 1948 to 1952. No new American stations were licensed during this time.) The CBC governors said that the American investigation might well influence the technical aspects of television development in Canada, and deferment similar to that in the United States was also wise in this country. The board proposed using the time to examine the possibilities of 'initial co-operative development under which private organizations would participate with the national system.'[27]

The deferment infuriated private applicants, electronic manufacturers, and television enthusiasts. Other delays had been caused by lack of government policy, though the CBC tended to get the blame. Now the manufacturers and some of the broadcasters knew, through their Ottawa contacts, that the government had been prepared to hand the ring to private developers, and the CBC had balked. In *Saturday Night* a columnist wrote: 'The CBC cannot block the aspirations of private enterprise indefinitely without earning for itself a reputation for capriciousness and tyranny.'[28] This was a fairly typical comment.

26 / CBC Public Announcement No. 22, Ottawa, Nov. 3, 1948. Other applicants for Toronto were CKEY, CFRB, and Al Leary (manager of former station CKCL); and for Montreal, radio stations CFCF and CKAC.
27 / A proposal of this nature had been placed before the board by Corey Thomson of CKVL, Verdun, in opposing the two Montreal applicants, CFCF and CKAC (La Presse).
28 / John L. Watson, 'Radio,' Nov. 27, 1948.

The chairman of the CBC undertook discussions with four of the more prominent television applicants – Famous Players, Canadian Marconi, and two Toronto radio stations, CFRB and CKEY. His idea was to plan a development program so that television would not grow so haphazardly in Canada as radio had done prior to 1936. In such a development program, the private interests and the CBC might share facilities. The four applicants expressed some interest in the idea of a co-operative scheme but, in Dunton's words, they were not 'over-enthusiastic.' Dunton concluded that it would be preferable for the CBC to go ahead on its own, make another representation to government, and if private industry were to have a part in the initial stages of television develop-ment, possibly they could work out some scheme of co-operative de-velopment among themselves. The board authorized the chairman to submit a statement to the government, outlining their views and incor-porating a plan for television development (considerably scaled down from the one Ouimet was suggesting).

The CBC's statement (approved by the board on January 20, 1949) tried to impress on the government the importance of television, which 'multiplies the impact of broadcasting more than five times,' and which would be 'a very great social force.' The effects could be positive or they could be harmful, either a means of enriching the national life, or of projecting non-Canadian ideas and material into Canadian homes in a very forceful way. Direct financial support was needed if there was to be any worthwhile amount of Canadian television provided for Canadians. Admittedly, for some time it could serve only a part of the population; but through a licence fee, only those who directly benefited would contribute. Public pressure was growing, particularly as southern On-tario was within range of American transmitters. Canadian manufactur-ers were beginning the production of sets, and the whole electronics industry would be curtailed unless television came to this country.

There were dangers, the CBC representation continued, in private control. The Aird Commission had found that private stations left to their own resources became chiefly a means of pumping American material into Canadian homes. Commercial considerations would result in the formation of links between Canadian stations and American sources. The situation would be difficult to control by regulation, be-cause the operators would say they could meet the high costs only if allowed freedom to use material from the United States. And it would be very difficult for the national system to enter the field once the whole development was established on purely commercial lines. It was argued that private interests could have little real cause for complaint if they did not invest at all, or if they came in at the same time as the national system, knowing the conditions under which they would operate.

The CBC plan was to establish stations in Montreal and Toronto, and to expand the service later with stations in other areas. It was suggested that the financial basis should be a $10 licence fee, with an advance of $5.5 million for the Montreal–Toronto operations. If the government decided that private interests should have a part in the initial development, CBC would be willing to explore a co-operative arrangement; but before further discussions were possible, CBC had to have some assurance of financing.[29]

Ouimet's report had suggested that a television service could start off with a $10 licence fee, plus a $15 million loan, the licence fee to go up to $15 after the first ten years. Alternatively, if a $15 licence fee could be established at the beginning, the amount of the loan might be reduced to $6 million. The CBC governors, appointees of a Liberal government, many of them businessmen or academic administrators, decided to put forward only the first phase of the Ouimet program which incidentally involved only the lower figure of each alternative.[30]

Ouimet had also advocated a CBC monopoly in at least the initial stages of television, rather than the system of 'dual ownership' (public and private) that obtained in radio. He argued that the 'contribution of the large centres of wealth to the service of less favourably situated areas can only be achieved by the greatest possible economy of operation in all centres, including large cities – *that is, by monopolistic operation.*' Dual ownership, he continued, would greatly complicate the job of the CBC, and it would actually give little if any advantage to the public. At a time when the CBC would need every cent it could get to do the job properly, dual ownership would decrease its revenues and increase its expenditures.[31]

The governors did not advance these arguments for CBC monopoly, regarding the choice as one for government to make, although it is clear they preferred sole CBC ownership of at least the first two stations to any shared system.

29 / The submission was approved during the 63rd meeting of the CBC board of governors, January 20–2, 1949. J.A. Ouimet's recommendations were in his 'Report on Television' (Dec. 1947), (CBC Hist. Sec., Ottawa).
30 / Governors in addition to Dunton were: Vice-chairman, René Morin of Montreal, a trust company executive; Adrien Pouliot of Quebec, a dean at Laval University; Mary Sutherland of Parksville, BC; Frederick J. Crawford of Toronto, a stockbroker; G.D. Steel of Charlottetown, principal of Prince of Wales College; John J. Bowlen, a Calgary lawyer and Liberal politician, and W.H. Phillips of Ottawa, a trade union leader.
31 / CBC Hist. Sec., 'Report on Television,' Part II, 3.

From the record, it is obvious that the delay in deciding the shape of Canadian television and in making a start was mainly the responsibility of government, but in the trade journals and the public press, the CBC was getting the blame. For example, a writer in *Canadian Business* complained: 'Television programs have been filtering in from the United States to a few Canadian-owned television sets in Ontario within fifty or sixty miles of Detroit and Buffalo for some time now. ... Elsewhere in Canada television is still unknown, and the question millions of Canadians are asking is: "When will it be here?"' The writer urged the CBC to declare its own policy, and to decide between the claims of various interests that had presented their own plans for Montreal and Toronto.[32]

In October 1948 Buffalo and Detroit were linked by coaxial cable with Chicago and other midwestern cities – just in time for World Series baseball. In Toronto people flocked to see the only barroom television set at the Horseshoe Tavern, on Queen street near the corner of Spadina. Canadian General Electric was producing sets for this 25-cycle area, although it was not pushing sales, according to a reporter for *Time* magazine.[33] In January 1949, Buffalo and Detroit were linked to New York and the eastern network. The pressure for some Canadian action increased as more households in Toronto, the Niagara peninsula, and southwestern Ontario bought sets and erected rooftop antennas. The Buffalo station, WBEN-TV, was in a particularly happy position: it could select programs from three networks, and Toronto was within its viewing range.

The government was in a quandary. Pressure to declare its policy in television was building, exerted not only by the CBC, but by radio equipment manufacturers, private broadcasters, opposition party spokesmen, and members of the general public, particularly in the metropolitan centres. With an approaching election, the new government headed by Louis St. Laurent hoped to shift the burden of decision somewhere else. Besides, there had long been agitation from the private radio broadcasters and their allies to change the system by which the CBC was not only a programming agency but regulator too. Perhaps a single inquiry could suggest solutions to these problems and others that were

32 / Joseph W. Crampton, 'Canada's Television Tease,' *Canadian Business* (Jan. 1949). The Toronto *Evening Telegram* editorialized in similar vein: 'The Canadian people will not be satisfied with the CBC attitude of "wait and see"' (Editorial reprinted in *Canadian Film Weekly*, Feb. 9, 1949).
33 / Conversion of hydro-electric power in the Toronto area did not get under way generally until 1955, but in 1952 the CBC television station was provided with 60-cycle power.

vexing the government. The minister of national defence, Brooke Claxton (who as an executive member of the Canadian Radio League had helped to draft the Broadcasting Act of 1936), was very interested in promoting cultural activities. In the first month that St. Laurent was prime minister, Claxton sent him a memorandum urging that a royal commission investigate ways of assisting the arts, but St. Laurent at first resisted the suggestion. According to Jack Pickersgill, St. Laurent was persuaded 'largely because the Commission was to deal with broadcasting and federal aid to the universities.'[34]

At the end of January 1949, the speech from the throne announced the government's intention to establish a royal commission on broadcasting and encouragement of the arts and sciences, among other things.[35] In the debate that followed, St. Laurent said:

It may be that the installation of television is very costly; it may be that its range is not very wide, that it will be difficult to provide it for the outlying districts of Canada. But I do not think that these frequencies, allocated to the Canadian public, should be lightly turned over to private ownership and exploitation unless we come to the conclusion that there is no better way in which the Canadian public can be provided with this new form of entertainment and education.[36]

The prime minister's statement indicated that the government might be moving from its earlier position that television should be developed by private interests, and that the CBC's role should be that of adjudicator between such interests. Some of St. Laurent's ministers were sympathetic to the representations Dunton and his board had been making – these probably included L.B. Pearson, Brooke Claxton, J.J. McCann, and the prime minister's assistant and adviser, J.W. Pickersgill (who had not yet been appointed to the cabinet). As important, perhaps, was the pressure from radio manufacturers to get television under way somehow. Their expressed concern to establish a strong electronics industry in Canada may have been the telling factor with C.D. Howe, the most senior of St. Laurent's colleagues.

34 / J.W. Pickersgill, *My Years with Louis St. Laurent: A Political Memoir* (Toronto, 1975), 139. For an account of the agitation leading up to the appointment of the royal commission, see F.W. Peers, *The Politics of Canadian Broadcasting, 1920–1951* (Toronto, 1969), chaps. 15 and 16; hereafter cited as Peers, *Politics of Canadian Broadcasting.*
35 / House of Commons *Debates,* Jan. 26, 1949, 3; hereafter cited as *Debates.*
36 / *Ibid.*, Jan. 28, 1949, 80. St. Laurent buttressed his argument by quoting from a Conservative prime minister, R.B. Bennett, who was speaking at the time his government introduced the first system of public broadcasting in 1932.

The impression that things were moving at last was confirmed on March 20 when the government, even before it had appointed the royal commission, announced an interim policy on television. The minister, Dr. McCann, said the government was concerned that Canadians should have the opportunity to receive Canadian programs, and to have a television system of their own. It had concluded that a large measure of public participation in television would be necessary. Television would therefore be developed through a combination of public and private enterprise, in a manner which radio broadcasting had shown feasible. Action now would provide a 'large new outlet' for the electronics industry, and would eventually provide a means 'of encouraging Canadian talent, of expressing Canadian ideals, of serving the the needs of the country as a whole, and of stimulating and strengthening our national life and consciousness.'[37]

In specific terms, the government had decided that the CBC would establish two national television production centres in Montreal and Toronto, a station in each city, and a service of television programs for broadcasting by stations that might be established in other areas of Canada, which would form part of their programming. On the licensing policy, the statement said: 'In any city or area in Canada, including Montreal and Toronto, a licence to establish one private station will be granted to a private organization giving adequate assurance of financial means and of service. In view of the high cost of television operations, it is felt that individuals or groups interested in establishing a private station in any city may wish to form an association for the purpose of applying for a licence.' In network arrangements, 'whether by tele-transcriptions or direct physical hookups, the same principles will apply as in the case of radio broadcasting.' This meant in practical terms that stations would have to seek CBC approval for network links, and connections with American networks would be arranged only by the CBC.

The government announced that Parliament would be asked to provide the CBC with a loan of $4 million – not the $5.5 million the CBC had said was necessary – but before Parliament could act on the request, the house was dissolved and a general election called for June 27.

Following announcement of the government's interim policy, the CBC governors recommended further deferment of the existing applications for licences in Montreal and Toronto to allow time for those interested to 'associate themselves' in an application and to consider operating a station jointly.[38]

37 / McCann, minister of national revenue, in *Debates*, March 28, 1949, 2050–1.
38 / CBC Public Announcement No. 26, Ottawa, April 11, 1949.

The attitude of the disappointed applicants was probably summed up by an editorial in the *Canadian Broadcaster*, April 27: '[The CBC] wants to impede 'business' from getting started with television, so it cooks up this ridiculous merger plan, knowing full well that it is hopelessly impractical, but knowing also that it will provide a splendid means of stalling the issue until a more propitious time arrives.' This allegation was perhaps not far off the mark. Four months earlier, Dunton had told an audience in Montreal that stations established on a straight commercial basis in that city or in Toronto would be driven by economic necessity to bring the great bulk of their programming from American centres. He concluded, 'It adds up to this. If Canada wants to have a television system in this country which will be of great benefit to the country, it must be publicly subsidized, must have some form of direct contribution from the viewing public. I think it also must have contribution or participation of commercial programming.' He recommended a plan that would combine and concentrate public and private resources as the best way to get Canadian television established.[39]

The government's interim policy on television evaded the issue of which element in the broadcasting system was to have primacy. At the time the 1936 legislation was passed, the intention had been that the CBC would be dominant and the private stations local and auxiliary. While the CBC had succeeded since in establishing national and regional program services and its own high-powered radio transmitters, the private stations – multiplying even faster – had become increasingly popular. The CBC governors, as the regulatory authority, were still in control of the system, but the exercise of their authority tended to be light. The private interests had consolidated their support among politicians and the general public, and the sounds of dissatisfaction that most people heard concerned the dual role of the CBC as programmer and regulator, rather than the weaknesses of the private stations as creative broadcasters. Under these circumstances, it is not surprising that the government refused to emphasize the formerly accepted principle that the national service of the CBC was to be paramount. Canadian radio had held its own in the face of competition from the United States, and even the threat of the imposition of American values seemed to have receded – except now, through television. The prospective high costs of television confirmed the government's attitude of caution. If Canadian television could begin and be brought to the public with a commitment for only two

39 / A.D. Dunton, speech to the radio-press branch of the Canadian Legion, Montreal, Dec. 11, 1948. Reprinted in a CBC publication, *Let's Look at National Radio* (n.d.), 31–6.

or three publicly owned stations, that seemed the expedient program to adopt. The relations between the CBC and private stations could be worked out in due course. In any event, a royal commission's advice could be sought in the meantime. This appears to have been the government's rationale for making the limited number of decisions it did in 1949.

Also in that year, the government decided against giving the CBC assurance that it would receive the proceeds from a licence fee imposed on the owners of television sets, or indeed any other assured source of income. The promised loan for capital expenditures on television had not been authorized by the date of the election. The CBC's task was to start planning a television system without the loan, or indeed without any guarantee that a government favourable to the interim policy would be returned at the end of June.

2 Getting the Picture

Although funds were not assured, the CBC in the summer of 1949 had to make plans to order equipment and plan the construction of two television production centres. The Department of Transport had already decided on the standards to be used, after consultation with the CBC: black and white, 525 lines, two to one interlacing, 60 fields a second – the same standards as in the United States. 'Any other standard,' Alphonse Ouimet wrote, 'would have erected a television curtain between Canada and the United States.'[40]

In order to get transmitter construction off to a fast start, the CBC governors decided not to advertise for tenders, but to place orders with the Canadian subsidiaries of two American manufacturers – RCA and Canadian General Electric. These two companies were tooled to produce according to American standards, and they had said that the CBC could have access to their books so that there would be an assurance that prices were competitive. When it was announced at the end of the year that RCA was to build the Montreal transmitter and General Electric the Toronto transmitter, British companies protested that they had not had a fair chance to bid; there were questions in Parliament and critical comments in the newspapers. All companies got a chance to bid on the provision of studio equipment, and the Canadian Marconi Company, offshoot of a British firm, submitted the successful tender.[41]

40 / J.A. Ouimet, 'Report on Television,' *Engineering Journal* (March 1950).
41 / 'Television Order for Britain,' *Saturday Night*, May 9, 1950, 6–7.

After the Liberal government was returned at the end of June, the CBC chairman and general manager again pressed for a larger allocation, and the government agreed to ask Parliament for a loan of $4.5 million instead of $4 million. The government was fairly frank in its warning that a lot more would be needed. The minister through whom the CBC reported, Dr. J.J. McCann, told the committee of supply:

> I might as well truthfully tell the committee that $4,500,000 is not going to cover all the costs of putting television into operation in this country. ...
> When we project this over a period of years we believe that the total cost will be somewhere in the neighbourhood of $10,700,000 ... up to 1955. ...
> We believe that in Canada in the first year there might be 2,250 receiving sets. In the next year we expect that that will go ten times as high, or 22,000 sets. By 1952–3, it will be probably 56,000 sets, by 1953–4, 111,000 and by 1954–5, 168,000.
> If we count on the revenue from those sets, they should bring in a revenue of $3,600,000, and from commercial operation revenue $1,817,000. So that total revenue in that period we estimate would be in the neighbourhood of $5,420,000. Our total expenditures would run as high as $14 million over the years ... leaving a net capital cost in the neighbourhood of $10 million.[42]

By relating the number of sets mentioned to the revenue anticipated, one finds that the minister was assuming a television licence fee of $10, rather than the figure of $15 which the CBC had advised would be necessary (in addition to commercial revenue) if the service was to be self-sustaining.[43]

George Drew, leader of the Progressive Conservative opposition, and E.G. Hansell, speaking for the Social Credit group, argued that the estimate should not be passed until a committee on broadcasting could meet in the New Year and bring in its report. Drew voiced objections that Howe had expressed privately a year before:

> Experimental development could be carried out without any expense to the people of Canada. There are private operators who are ready to risk their money to carry on through the experimental stages. ...
> Why should public money in Canada be allocated for the purpose of giving

42 / *Debates*, Dec. 7, 1949, 2893–4. In that year expenditures on radio were about $8 million.
43 / In 1950 Dunton told the broadcasting committee that CBC estimates were based on income representing $10 per television home. That was no doubt after the government told the CBC they must cut their cloth a little shorter, *1950 Proceedings*, 83.

telecast programs to the areas of Toronto and Montreal, or for that matter ... for the larger cities such as Winnipeg, Regina, Calgary, Vancouver, Halifax and Saint John? ... I suggest that no sound reason has been put before the house for allocating one cent at this time.[44]

The loan was approved in December, but the CBC had already ordered the transmitters. McCann told the Commons that the first two stations would be on the air about September 1951. Other preparations were also going ahead. Alphonse Ouimet was appointed chief engineer and co-ordinator of television. In the partial absence of Frigon, who was suffering from a circulatory ailment, Ouimet became the chief adviser to the board. E.L. Bushnell, the director-general of programs, was sent on a tour of British and American production centres to study their programming methods.[45] He was followed by others from the program and administrative staff who were tentatively selected for the Montreal and Toronto centres. In December 1949, Fergus Mutrie was appointed director of television in Toronto, and Aurèle Séguin in Montreal. The recruiting and training of television staff began.

Applicants for private stations still hoped to be awarded channels in Toronto and Montreal, and other applications were filed for Vancouver, Hamilton, Windsor, and Winnipeg. A tentative allocation agreement had been negotiated between Canada and the United States by which three VHF channels (9, 11, and 13) were assigned to the Toronto area, and five channels to Montreal. In Toronto channel 9 was allocated to the CBC, leaving two channels for other broadcasters. In Montreal, two of the five channels (2 and 5) were earmarked for the French and English services of the CBC, although temporarily one channel would be used for both.

When the private applicants pressed for a decision, the CBC refused to resume hearings pending the report of the Massey Commission, or the submission of joint applications according to what the CBC interpreted as government policy. In May 1950, Dunton told the broadcasting committee that it was still not known how a nation-wide system would be developed, 'whether it is to be done only through private stations or through public stations or through a combination of the two.'[46] The answer would depend partly on the outcome of the royal commission's study.

The private broadcasters might have put CBC intentions to the test if

44 / *Debates*, Dec. 7, 1949, 2895–6.
45 / See Peter Stursberg, *Mister Broadcasting* (Toronto, 1971), 142–4.
46 / *1950 Proceedings*, 81 (May 26, 1950).

two or three interests in any city had been able to combine in support of an application. But initially they were not willing to do so.[47] S.M. Finlayson, speaking to the annual meeting of the Canadian Manufacturers' Association, gave the reasons. First, each applicant must have the hope that, after the initial period, he would have the channel in his own right. Second, no plan had been found that would permit the partners to disengage their financial and personal commitments on an equitable basis. Third, after disengagement, one or more of the partners would have largely to duplicate much of the thought and effort that went into the original operation. Fourth, if policy had to be the result of agreement among erstwhile rivals, the operation could not proceed with the same zest and effectiveness as would characterize competing stations.[48]

The royal commission did not report until June 1, 1951. Until the government had considered its recommendations, there was no action to extend television beyond Montreal and Toronto. It was a common impression, sedulously promoted, that as John Diefenbaker said in the House of Commons, 'Television has been held back ... in this country by the policy of the c.b.c.'[49]

While the dispute was thrashed out before the Massey Commission, progress towards getting the Montreal and Toronto stations on the air seemed to be at a snail's pace. There were troublesome holdups such as the delay of Premier Duplessis of Quebec in signing the order-in-council authorizing the erection of a transmitter for Montreal on Mount Royal. But the chief reason for the delay was shortage of steel during the Korean War, and the slow delivery of equipment from Great Britain because of defence pressures there. In June 1951 it was recognized that the two stations would not be in operation until late in 1952.[50] Meanwhile, Bell Telephone was awarded a contract to provide a relay for television programs by microwave from Buffalo to Toronto and from Toronto to Montreal, with a provision for Ottawa along the route. A systematic training program for producers and technicians started in January 1952, but even before this a full-dress studio production of a play by Len Peterson had been produced as a dry run.[51] During one

47 / Somewhat later, competing radio stations did join together to apply for television licences, as in Calgary (1953).
48 / Speech reprinted in *Industrial Canada* (July 1949), 191–3.
49 / *Debates*, March 31, 1950, 1466. See also report of addresses in Winnipeg and Edmonton by Don Henshaw, an executive of MacLaren Advertising, *Canadian Broadcaster* (Feb. 22, 1950), 3.
50 / *Debates* June 29, 1951, 4926; *Financial Post*, July 7, 1951, 3.
51 / *Ibid.* Nov. 10, 1951, 24. The play was 'The Landlady,' with Jane Mallett in the leading role.

week in March, television programs were shown for two hours a night in Montreal. The programs went by microwave link from studios in the Radio-Canada building to an exhibition of receivers in the Merchandise Mart. The sale of television sets began to accelerate. About 30,000 sets had been sold in 1950, 40,000 in 1951, and 75,000 more by the time the two Canadian stations went on the air in September 1952.[52] Of course most of these sets were in Toronto and southern Ontario where American stations could be received.

3 Deciding the One-Station Policy

The Royal Commission on National Development in the Arts, Letters and Sciences (the Massey Commission) took two years to investigate the various matters under its purview, listen to views and representations across the country, and write its report. Most of the commissioners had university associations, and many of the organizations appearing before them had educational interests. But the broadcasting stations were out in force, as was their national organization, the Canadian Association of Broadcasters, joined by the Radio Manufacturers Association, the Association of Canadian Advertisers, and the Canadian Chamber of Commerce – as well as the CBC and its allies. The commission must have heard every significant view on television that existed in the Canada of 1950.[53] In addition, some of the commissioners visited television organizations of other countries, particularly the United States and Great Britain, to talk to the authorities and sample the programming.

The main point at issue in the field of broadcasting was whether the CBC should continue not only to produce programs but to act as the regulatory body as well. Four of the five commissioners concluded that it should. Their report described television in the United States as 'essentially a commercial enterprise, an advertising industry,' and argued that in Canada the CBC must be the prime instrument for program production and national control of broadcasting.

Recalling the two chief objects of our national system of broadcasting, national unity and understanding, and education in the broad sense, we do not think that

52 / Figures for 1950 and 1951 from estimates of the Radio-Television Manufacturers Association, *Financial Post*, March 8, 1952. Figure for September 1952 (total of 146,000 sets in Canada) from *Fowler Commission Report* (1957), 217.
53 / For a summary of the views expressed before the commission, and of the recommendations in the Massey Report, see Peers, *Politics of Canadian Broadcasting*, 400–18.

American programmes, with certain notable exceptions, will serve our national needs (p. 47).

The pressure on uncontrolled private television operators to become mere channels for American commercial material will be almost irresistible. ... It seems desirable to use appropriate American television programmes, and to make suitable agreements with the Canadian private stations. These arrangements, however, should follow and should depend on the organization of a national system of television production and control. ... It seems necessary, therefore, in our interests, to provide Canadian television programmes with national coverage as soon as possible. ... In the national interest, the Board of Governors should not yield to pressure to advise the licensing of any commercial station before it is ready with national programmes which all stations may carry (pp. 301–3).[54]

Here it was, then: the CBC should direct and control television broadcasting; it should produce television programs in English and French and distribute them to all stations; and it should not recommend licensing private stations until national television programs were available by kinescope recordings or direct connections between these stations and the CBC.

But would the government accept these recommendations? Television under public auspices would be costly, and so far the government had shrunk from establishing a television licence fee. It had not even raised the radio licence fee from its prewar level of $2.50, and the CBC could no longer make ends meet from the licence fee and commercial revenues.

There were powerful elements in the Liberal party that were opposed to the recommendations of the Massey Commission dealing with broadcasting, but the prestige of the chairman, Vincent Massey, was high. (In the next year, 1952, he was selected as the first Canadian governor-general.) Moreover the government, through the announcement of its interim policy in 1949, had already committed itself to the expenditure of public money for the construction of at least two television stations, and the production and distribution of a national television service in two languages.

The tipoff on the government's attitude came within four weeks of the report's publication. On June 29, Dr. McCann called it a 'splendid report,' and praised 'particularly that section of it which deals with

---

54 / Royal Commission on National Development in the Arts, Letters and Sciences, 1949–1951, *Report* (Ottawa, 1951): hereafter cited as *Massey Report.*

television.'[55] He introduced in the House an appropriation to provide a further loan of $1.5 million to the CBC for television development (which raised the total of advances for television to $6 million).

In the fall session, the government adopted the recommendation of the Massey Commission to raise the CBC's revenues for radio purposes up to the figure of one dollar per capita. Significantly, the government did this by supplementing the revenue from the existing radio licence fee with a statutory grant that would run for five years, thus accepting the Massey Commission's conclusion that a $5 licence fee would be 'generally unpopular.'[56] This action did not bode well for the imposition of a television licence fee.

The government drafted amendments to the Canadian Broadcasting Act to carry out the recommendations of the Massey Commission, and these were referred to a House of Commons broadcasting committee for study. The committee hearings gave the usual opportunity for arguments to be expressed about the desirability of a separate regulatory board, for complaints about CBC radio programs, and so forth, but the amendments were passed.[57] Dunton told the committee that the CBC felt that it should have television stations in Ottawa, Winnipeg, and Vancouver, as well as a second station in Montreal so that the language services could be separated.[58] He and Alphonse Ouimet (the new assistant general manager) also said that a licence fee of $15 would take care of the operating cost and eventually contribute to capital. Dunton explained that the earlier figure based on a cost of $10 per television household was arrived at before costs had gone up.[59] (Fifteen dollars was of course Ouimet's figure from the beginning.) The broadcasting committee (or at least its majority) supported the royal commission's recommendations on television, and asked the CBC to proceed as soon as practicable with the extension of television coverage.[60]

Not only did the broadcasting committee approve the recommendations of the Massey Commission, but the minister, Dr. McCann, continued his glowing praise of the report. 'This government has been glad to have the assertions from this great commission report supporting the principles of the present system in Canada.'[61] But there was a difference

55 / *Debates*, June 29, 1951, 4925.
56 / *Massey Report*, 294.
57 / See Peers, *Politics of Canadian Broadcasting*, 432–8.
58 / *1951 Proceedings*, 447–8, 456.
59 / *Ibid.*, 461–3.
60 / *Debates*, Dec. 10, 1951, 474.
61 / *Ibid.*, Nov. 9, 1951, 869.

between what the Massey Commission had recommended with regard to the licensing of private television stations and the interim policy announced by the government in March 1949. According to that policy, one private station could be established in any city or area in Canada, including Montreal and Toronto. In other words, the existence of a CBC station would not preclude the licensing of a private station. But the Massey Report put the emphasis on a national program service to be supplied by the CBC. All private stations were to be 'required to serve as outlets for national programs.' Obviously there would be little point in licensing private stations in Montreal or Toronto so long as this single-station concept endured. It also appeared that private stations would be approved only *after* the CBC was in a position to distribute programs to all stations. McCann was clear about this:

Some of the hon. members opposite appear to be in a great hurry to see some private operators get television licences. It seems to be there are things that are much more important than the establishment of monopoly positions on television channels by private interests, from which they might hope to make a good deal of money in the future. Far more important to this country is the building up of a television broadcasting system which will help to link the country together in a new way; which will use a large amount of Canadian talent; and which, while bringing in some material from outside the country, will be essentially a Canadian operation carried on in the national interests. Into this system I expect later it will be possible to fit private operations co-ordinated under the over-all system serving community interests, and also acting as outlets for national program service.[62]

For the Conservatives, Donald Fleming asked how the government hoped to justify denying entry into the field of those who 'are quite prepared to come in and take their chances.'[63] John Diefenbaker argued that Canadian companies should be given an opportunity to establish television in Canada, and that the policy granting priority to the CBC should not deny rights to the kind of service given in the United States by private enterprise.[64]

The Massey Report had also recommended that capital costs of the national broadcasting system should be provided by parliamentary grants (rather than loans), and that operational costs be provided by

62 / *Ibid.*, Nov. 20, 1951, 1206.
63 / *Ibid.*, Dec. 12, 1951, 1847.
64 / *Ibid.*, Dec. 13, 1951, 1886–7.

licence fees, commercial revenues, and 'such statutory grants as may be necessary.'[65] The government did not commit itself on this in 1951.

Early in 1952, A.D. Dunton was reappointed chairman of the CBC board of governors, this time for a ten-year term as provided by a recent amendment to the broadcasting act. The board put forward a plan for the second stage of television development which called for CBC stations in Ottawa, Vancouver, Winnipeg, Quebec City, Windsor, and two others in southwestern Ontario. From their experience in radio the governors thought it almost impossible to maintain adequate coverage for national programs through private stations – that is, by relying on the powers of regulation. The stations they were asking for, added to those in Montreal and Toronto, would reach half the Canadian population and, they argued, would help provide a sound financial base for the public system through commercial revenue. The main revenue source would still be the proposed $15 licence fee; according to CBC estimates, 75 per cent of the Canadian population could be served by a system built up on this basis of financial support.[66]

In July 1952 the government announced that the CBC would construct a television station in Ottawa. McCann told the Commons that the CBC had asked for the construction of seven stations in addition to Montreal and Toronto, but for the present the government had decided on Ottawa only. A loan of $2 million was provided to cover initial operating expenses of the service and to begin construction of the Ottawa station.[67]

But pressure had also been building in Vancouver where, as Arthur Laing said in the Commons, 'the invasion is on today.' Viewers were receiving programs from Seattle and Bellingham, and a Norris cartoon in the *Vancouver Sun* showed a leader of the boy scout troop out with the boys, telling them: 'We will never get lost because there are enough television aerials in the area, and thanks to the C.B.C. they all point south.' McCann replied that he thought he could assure Mr. Laing there would be television in Vancouver.[68] Prime Minister St. Laurent confirmed this in a Vancouver press conference at the beginning of September when he said Parliament would be asked at the next session to authorize a loan to the CBC for stations on both east and west coasts and on the prairies.[69]

65 / *Massey Report*, 304.
66 / 'No Room Yet for Private TV,' *Financial Post*, Aug. 23, 1952; also interview with A.D. Dunton, Sept. 13, 1972.
67 / *Debates*, July 4, 1952, 4252.
68 / *Ibid.*, 4255.
69 / *Montreal Star*, Sept. 4, 1952.

The CBC now had in prospect stations in five of the nine locations they had asked for, plus one in the Maritimes they had not included in the 'second stage.' Nothing was said about Quebec City or the three locations in southwestern Ontario.

Three days after St. Laurent spoke in Vancouver, CBFT opened in Montreal, marking the beginning of Canada's television age. This was also the signal for private broadcasters to redouble their efforts to get a share of the action.

2 A NATIONAL SERVICE

I *How Canadians Welcomed Television*

The Montreal and Toronto television stations opened on schedule, but hardly to the huzzahs of the press. The newspapers sensed a good deal of popular interest, and some (for example, the Toronto *Telegram*) published a special section before the station's opening. But the editorial writers and columnists of the English-language papers were cool. In Montreal the news pages of the *Gazette* trumpeted, 'Montreal First to Get "Home-Grown" Television' (a slight condescension there?), but the lead editorial on the day of CBFT's opening was suspicious of the new arrival:

In Canada the coming of television has been unusual. From the start it became the policy of the Government to clamp a state monopoly upon it. Though private bodies were ready to enter the field, they were held back. ...

The results of this policy have already been felt. For one thing, the coming of television has been much delayed. For years the citizens of the United States, just over the imaginary border, have had television in their homes ... [And] the monopoly has proved, and will prove, terribly costly to Canadian taxpayers.[1]

This editorial, and similar ones in two Toronto papers, the *Globe and Mail* and the *Telegram* (both owned at this time by George McCullagh) may have been prompted by opposition to the Liberal government, or opposition to public broadcasting, or hostility to a new medium of advertising. But it also seems that to many publishers and businessmen of the day, the southern boundary (as the *Gazette* said) *was* imaginary. If television had been expanding rapidly in the United States, why shouldn't Canada just hook on? Any separate policy, any separate development, was artificial, smacking of state monopoly.

1 / *Gazette*, Sept. 6, 1952.

The structures built to house the new studios were not very impressive. The government had shaved off a million dollars from the amount the CBC had said it would need ($5.5 million), and that estimate had been kept purposely low so that government would not be frightened off. In Toronto the CBC offices and radio studios were in a former girls' school on Jarvis Street. The cheapest way to add television facilities was to construct a building at the back of the lot, and place the transmission tower right next to it. On the day the station opened, a reporter wrote:

CBLT begins business in a five-story yellow brick building next to the CBC studios on Jarvis street. And all the flowers in the world can't hide the fact that it is still far from complete. Visitors won't get to see the top floor which is barren and bleak and will stay that way until money is found to fill it with offices. Elevator shafts gape, and workmen took the wraps off the front entrance (it seems to me it's in the rear) this very weekend. The lofty transmitting tower will not be ready for at least a month.

The place is a warren of small offices, corridors, stairs, and scenery-littered studios. And it's too small already.[2]

The two afternoon papers in Toronto, the *Daily Star* and the *Telegram*, always competitive, established radio-television columns to review the programs seen and heard. Neither Gordon Sinclair in the *Star* nor Ron Poulton in the *Telegram* liked the opening entertainment on CBLT very much, although they admitted the difficulty of making a satisfactory show from official greetings and samples of programs to come.

In Montreal, Dr. McCann gave viewers the good news that no licence fees would be imposed for the remainder of the fiscal year – that is, until April 1, 1953. He added that Mr. St. Laurent had especially asked him to say that the government was 'making provision for the expansion of television service by private interests.'[3] St. Laurent himself, still on his western trip, had filmed a message that was characteristically paternal. Television, he said, should contribute to the 'full development of an enriched family and national life in Canada.' In addition to the official greetings, CBFT's opening night program (September 6) included a newsreel summary of the highlights of the past summer, a tour behind the scenes of TV operation, a variety show, and Jean Cocteau's 'Oedipus Rex.'

In Toronto, the opening programs (September 8) showed per-

2 / Ron Poulton, Toronto *Telegram*, Sept. 8, 1952.
3 / *Gazette*, Sept. 8, 1952.

sonalities and performers whose voices were already familiar through radio – Lorne Greene, John Fisher, Jane Mallett – or performers who were to become much better known through television: the weatherman Percy Saltzman, Don Harron, Wally Koster, Joyce Sullivan, the puppet Uncle Chichimus, and a young pianist, Glenn Gould, who was yet to make his reputation. But an unscheduled event got much of the publicity. Several hours before the station officially opened, three members of the notorious 'Boyd Gang,' wanted for bank robbery or murder, broke out of prison. CBLT made news by flashing their pictures on the screen during the opening day.

Commenting on the reception accorded by the newspaper critics, Mavor Moore, chief television producer in Toronto, told the Canadian Club:

Take our Opening Night. One of our Toronto critics ... said: 'CBC television was not triumphant in its opening. It was not really good. There was little worth sitting through and nothing you would want to endure a second time.' Another wrote of our entrance into television in a way which delicately suggested a posture both vulgar and vulnerable. But the *Buffalo* paper – untroubled by national psychoses – called it 'three hours of unusual, interesting and highly professional entertainment. ... Their pattern could well be followed by the u.s. television industry. All in all a very refreshing evening.'[4]

Beyond the hazards that followed from inexperienced but eager production teams, there were in both Toronto and Montreal real obstacles to attracting audiences and developing their loyalty. In each city television was scheduled for only three hours a day. In Toronto, audiences were accustomed to a full day's schedule on WBEN, Buffalo, which brought in high-budget programs from three networks boasting performers whose names were known right across the continent. In Montreal, just over half the programs were in French, the others in English, and this alternation did not satisfy either part of the audience. Nevertheless, sales of television sets began to boom in each city. But the big years were yet to come.

A great disappointment for Canadian viewers in 1952 lay in the fact that they had expected to see a number of highly rated us shows on the CBC stations, but at the last minute negotiations between the CBC and the American networks broke down. For years the CBC radio networks had carried some US programs. This had been one of the ways in which

4 / CBC Hist. Sec., 'Canada and Television,' address to the Toronto Canadian Club, Nov. 17, 1952 (mimeo.).

Canadian radio listeners had been weaned from their earlier dependence on American stations. The usual arrangement was that the CBC paid the originating American network about 15 per cent of the advertising revenue received from Canadian sponsors. In television, the three US networks decided to ask for 70 per cent of the CBC's card rate. Their tactics may have been related to a fight that was going on in Canada between the CBC and the combined forces of the advertisers and agencies, essentially over the CBC's attempt to retain control of its own programming, whether sponsored or not. Four months after its stations went on the air, the CBC reached an agreement with the American networks by which they received 50 per cent of the station-time rate (after discounts and agency commission had been deducted).[5] During those four months, CBC was unable to bring in such programs as 'Studio One' for Canadian Westinghouse, 'The Aldrich Family' for Campbell Soup, 'Television Playhouse' for Goodyear and Philco, or 'The Jackie Gleason Show.' In Toronto viewers wanting these or other series from the big studios switched to Buffalo.

The attempt of the CBC to develop a new commercial policy for television is another example of its wish to avoid mistakes of the past, as was its determination that this time it would precede the private operators in setting up stations (in radio, private broadcasting had been established first). To take another example, the CBC thought that in television it would maintain creativity by hiring producers on contract, rather than bringing them on to permanent staff.

The change in commercial policy shows how many difficulties there can be when the usual procedures worked out by North American business are interfered with. The CBC determined that it must take responsibility for all programming over its stations and that all television programs, except for those originating from other countries, must be produced in CBC studios. This had not been so in radio. For example, 'Ford Theatre,' originating in Toronto, was produced by someone from the advertising agency, Cockfield Brown; the daytime serial 'Laura Limited' was produced by a Montreal agency, and so on. Even when a CBC staff producer directed a commercial program, such as 'The Canadian General Electric Show' (with the Leslie Bell Singers), the producer was hired by the agency, which retained control of the content.

Even the American networks regarded the system as wrong, but they felt unable to change the system. Erik Barnouw points out that as early as the 1930s:

In the United States the advertising agencies... were achieving an extraordinary

5 / *Financial Post*, Sept. 6, 1952 and Jan. 3, 1953; *Time*, Canadian edition, Jan. 12, 1953.

position. ... In relation to network radio they were not mere time brokers and writers of advertising copy; they built and produced programs and – subject to only perfunctory network review – determined content. Thus they had in a few years come to control radio to an extent they would not have dared to attempt with other media.[6]

With American television, the same system persisted and led to an extraordinary number of taboos.[7] Not until the quiz scandals in 1959–60 did the networks announce that henceforth they would determine scheduling and themselves deal with sponsors.[8]

Because CBC decided to concentrate production in its own studios, it developed commercial program rates that included not only time charges but charges for the use of the studio facilities. It announced these as $1600 for an hour program or $960 for a half-hour program on CBLT, Toronto; and $500 for an hour, $300 for a half-hour on CBFT, Montreal. (The difference was due to the smaller number of sets in the Montreal area.) The Association of Canadian Advertisers formed a joint committee with the Canadian Association of Advertising Agencies to study these rates and more particularly CBC's new policy on production and direction of shows. A report submitted in July 1952 was highly critical of the rates and the policy. 'In effect,' it said, 'advertisers will be subsidizing CBC sustaining programs as well as live-talent, Canadian-produced, sponsored shows.' Few advertisers, the report argued, would be able to afford the high costs of live talent programs, even if subsidized and produced by the CBC on a multiple sponsorship basis. 'At the present stage it would seem rather hazardous for any national advertiser to rob other media to pay for TV.'

The advertisers and agencies saw nothing but danger in the production policy the CBC was implementing. The move was contrary to the dictates of experience in the United States, where 72 per cent of all sponsored network shows were 'outside packages.' The CBC's policy would make the position of the advertisers 'one of sufferance rather than participation,' they argued, and might well result in 'situations where advertisers will be forced to bear the brunt of responsibility for mistakes in the eyes of the public.'[9]

6 / *The Golden Web*, 16.

7 / Barnouw, *The Image Empire: A History of Broadcasting in the United States*, vol. III (New York, 1970), 22–4, 33–6.

8 / *Ibid.*, 150.

9 / Joint chairmen of the committee were J. Lawrence, Borden Co. Ltd., Toronto, and G.C. Clarke, Standard Brands Ltd., Montreal. *Financial Post*, July 5, 1952; *Broadcasting*, July 14, 1952; *Time* (Canada), July 21, 1952.

As it turned out, the advertisers did not boycott CBC television, because it was the only game in town, and was after all an attractive and compelling medium. But they (and the US networks) forced the CBC to modify its rates, and to set separate scales for time charges and production charges.[10] When shows from the United States became available, the CBC retained some sponsorship for its higher-cost Canadian productions of drama and light entertainment by making package deals: for example, an advertiser might be allowed one film series or one American network program if at the same time it sponsored a Canadian origination. And the CBC never gave up its principal point that it must retain production control.

2   *Towards a Mixed System: Public and Private*

With the opening of the two CBC stations, the private broadcasters redoubled their efforts to secure a modification of government policy on television. The Massey Commission had recommended that private stations be licensed only after the CBC had national television programs 'available' in French and English, by kinescope recording or any other practicable means. Since the CBC was now in production, the private stations saw no reason that their claims should any longer be denied, even if the Massey Report continued to be the government's guide.

The private owners already had two political parties on their side, the Progressive Conservative official opposition, and the smaller Social Credit group. These parties had supported the demands of the Canadian Association of Broadcasters for a separate regulatory agency, a demand which was shunted to one side by the Massey Commission. The CAB also had allies in the Canadian Chamber of Commerce, local boards of trade, and many private members of Parliament who relied on radio stations to keep them in touch with their constituents. Their newspaper allies were also important. The three largest chains – Southam, Sifton, and Thomson – all had radio interests,and the CAB could count also on a number of metropolitan dailies that opposed the government – the *Gazette* in Montreal, and the *Telegram* and the *Globe and Mail* in Toronto. But to win their point, the private stations had to win support *within* the government.

The most vigorous and persistent newspaper campaign carried on in 1952 against the CBC and Canadian television policy was in the *Van-*

10 / *Financial Post*, Aug. 29, 1953.

couver Sun, a paper that on many other issues supported the Liberal government. For seven years it had flailed away at CBC's control over private radio stations. The *Sun* was the principal owner of a small station in Nanaimo, CHUB, and this may have increased its interest in broadcasting matters. From 1949 to October 1952 it ran some thirty editorials urging the government to let private broadcasters into TV. At the end of October, it carried three articles by its investigative reporter, Jack Webster, on television as handled by the CBC. The first front-page article was headed: 'CBC's Culture Bund Alien to Canada; Canadians Pay Out Millions for CBC's Television Fumbling.' Editorially, the *Sun* accused the CBC of 'hewing to its dog-in-the-manger line which stifles all development while Canada is far behind what may be the most significant development of the century in mass entertainment and information media.' It railed against an 'assumption of intellectual superiority in operating the arrogant CBC culture trust attitude that televiewers should be confined to what the CBC considers good television for Canadians.' On October 31, the *Sun* summed up its position:

Private networks could bid [for talent] against the CBC – but the CBC outlaws their existence. Radio is socialized in Canada and free enterprise is verboten, even for the very talent which CBC claims to be fostering. So we lose the best of Canadian radio artists to Great Britain or the United States. Precisely the same thing will happen to television performers when and if CBC permits Canadians to see it. The Sun expects the CBC-loving highbrows to howl to high heaven about our philistinism in smashing their idol's clay feet, but we are positive there's nothing like competition to keep any industry functioning at its best – including the radio and television industry.

According to a correspondent for *Time*, George Drew, leader of the opposition, had been fed the *Vancouver Sun* material by British Columbia Conservatives, and the *Sun*'s Ottawa correspondent was quoted as saying that the government was changing its mind as to the part private stations would be allowed to play.[11]

In Toronto, the owner of radio station CKEY, Jack Kent Cooke, was active in promoting not only his own application for a television licence, but the claims of private broadcasters generally. For some years he had been the publisher of *New Liberty* magazine; in the autumn of 1952 he bought *Saturday Night*, a less popular but more prestigious magazine. The novelist Hugh Garner became an associate editor and *Saturday*

11 / Material on the *Sun*'s campaign was found in a file on broadcasting in the library of Time Canada Ltd., Montreal.

Night's television critic. Cooke had him prepare a five-page memorandum entitled 'The Case for Private Television Broadcasting,' which was sent to a broadcasting associate in Ottawa, Duncan K. MacTavish, a lawyer, son-in-law of one of the Southams, and head of a company that owned CKOY, Ottawa.[12] (Cooke had a management contract with CKOY, and MacTavish on occasion represented CKEY in hearings before the CBC Board of Governers.)

MacTavish was active in the Liberal party, and in 1952 became the president of the National Liberal Federation. One of the three vice-presidents was a Winnipeg lawyer, C. Irving Keith, who had also acted as legal counsel for private stations. At the annual meeting of the advisory council of the National Liberal Federation, held in Ottawa at the end of October 1952, Keith introduced a resolution proposing 'the development of television in Canada by private enterprise along with the CBC.' It was adopted in a closed meeting, according to press reports, over the objections of the minister of national revenue, Dr. McCann.[13]

The effect on Liberal party policy was regarded as a highly significant development by private broadcasters,and the CAB sought to press their advantage. On November 11, a twelve-man delegation met with the prime minister and some members of the cabinet, including Howe, Chevrier, and McCann; the report was that their brief had been 'sympathetically received.'[14]

Parliament met nine days later. The speech from the throne promised that the CBC would establish stations in Halifax, Winnipeg, and Vancouver; it also said that the government had indicated to the CBC that it was now prepared to consider applications by private stations to serve areas which the public stations at that time could not serve. The new policy was spelled out in more detail by McCann:

The objective will be to make national television service available to as many Canadians as possible through cooperation between private and public enterprise. Under this plan the private stations licensed will carry national program service, besides having time for programming of their own. ... It is desirable to have one station in as many areas as possible before there are two in any one area.[15]

12 / MacTavish forwarded a copy to Brooke Claxton, minister of national defence. Public Archives of Canada (PAC), Claxton Papers, MG 32, B5, vol. 50.
13 / *Globe and Mail*, Oct. 29, 1951.
14 / *Canadian Broadcaster*, Nov. 19, 1952.
15 / *Debates*, Dec. 8, 1952, 409.

This statement ended any immediate hope of Jack Kent Cooke or any other private applicants in six cities, including all the larger ones, of establishing a commercial station in competition with the CBC. On the other hand, it shut the CBC out of any city in which a private licence would be granted. George Drew complained:

Surely it should be the purpose of the C.B.C. to provide television broadcasts in those areas where private broadcasting will not find it economically convenient to do so. ... Then may I also point out that there has been no reason placed before us at this time as to why there should be only one station in any one centre.[16]

Among the private members, support for the role assigned the CBC was expressed mainly by Quebec representatives. For example, Maurice Breton said:

Commercial experience has shown that it is hardly possible under a solely private system to better the quality of the programs and especially to build up a national system for the great majority of the Canadian people.

May I add that, without the C.B.C., the French-Canadian group would necessarily be at the mercy of American programs, which are less costly than our own.[17]

André Gauthier added:

The present government cannot repeat the mistake committed in the early days of radio. I for one would not want to see a menace of cultural annexation by the Americans threaten once again the present generation. ...

Mr. Speaker, we from Quebec have particular reasons to resist the threat of American cultural assimilation. We have a profound devotion to our language, our religion and our traditions. ... In short, we must have a positive and constructive television policy. There is the whole difference, Mr. Speaker, between the policy put forward by the Progressive Conservative party and that expounded by the Liberal party.

The former favours a policy of abstention, a purely negative or passive one, whereas the latter demonstrates in this connection, as in others, foresight, realism and patriotism.[18]

16 / *Ibid.*, 410.
17 / *Ibid.*, Dec. 2, 1952, 269–70.
18 / *Ibid.*, Dec. 3, 1952, 313.

But there was probably not as much difference between the parties as the Commons debates suggested. The Conservatives would have liked more scope for the private stations, but no doubt realized that the CBC would have to have some production facilities in the larger cities if there was to be a substantial amount of Canadian programming. By this time both parties favoured some form of co-operative or mixed system; it was left for the CBC to make it work. In fact, George Drew took time during the debate to complain about the immorality of a "disgraceful play' by Lister Sinclair on CBC television called 'Hilda Morgan,' about the problem of a Toronto school teacher who was pregnant and whose fiancé was killed before the scheduled wedding day. Drew declaimed, 'Mr. Speaker, I know what my feeling would be if I came into a room in my own house and found my twelve-year-old daughter looking at a picture of that kind. ... I can only hope, if the dominion government is unwilling to take any action ... that the provincial governments right across Canada will take action to prevent filth of that kind going out over television stations of this country.'[19] Indeed, in Quebec the Duplessis government was proclaiming its intention to censor television, a threat that was never put to the test.

The federal Conservatives were weak in Quebec, and may not have had as much concern as the Liberals (or some of them) for programs that were distinct from the American. Or at least the Liberals tried to appropriate the patriotic label. Lionel Chevrier, minister of transport, told the House:

The essential reason for public development of television in this country is that we want ... both popular programs and cultural programs to be produced in Canada by Canadians, about Canada. ... We want programs from the United States. ... But we do not want, above all, that these programs will come over and be in a position to monopolize the field. ...

It is perfect nonsense for anyone to suggest that private enterprise in Canada, left to itself, will provide Canadian programs. People who invest their money ... will certainly invest [it] where they will make the profit – by importing American programs. ...

Our view is that the private station ... has a place in the broadcasting field, not as a competitor of the c.b.c., but as a complement to the c.b.c. ... For the present, at least, we are proposing to grant only one licence in each centre.

Why this policy? ... We feel that there is only a limited amount of capital available in Canada for investment in television stations, and, since television

19 / *Ibid.*, Dec. 10, 1952, 522–3.

stations can be established only by use of the public domain, that they should be situated so as to provide service to the largest possible number of Canadians, from one station, before anyone is allowed to provide the people in any community with two stations. ...

I am sorry to say that the Tories have abandoned the enlightened and patriotic policy which Mr. Bennett adopted twenty years ago. They have gone back to the traditional Tory policy of handing over the exploitation of the public domain to their wealthy political friends. ...

If the policy of the Conservative party is such as was laid down by the Leader of the Opposition ... then there is to be no regard for regional or minority rights. I go a step further and say that there is to be no French-language television station. ... Does my hon. friend [Mr. Fleming] think that private broadcasting and television firms will originate French-language programs? Of course they will not, because these programs are the ones that cost more money.[20]

For the Conservatives, Davie Fulton replied that no one among them was attempting to eliminate the CBC or to end public regulation of broadcasting. What they were criticizing was government policy, 'the policy of monopoly which in fact is depriving the Canadian people of Canadian coverage in the field of television broadcasting.' The people of Quebec would realize that it was the Liberal government's policy that even now was preventing the licensing of French-language television stations. Fulton went back to the point that what the system needed was an independent regulatory body to adjudicate between the CBC and the private stations.[21]

The Liberals tried to shake the opposition charge that they favoured a television monopoly. McCann first showed how the government's policy flowed from the recommendations of the Massey commission:

The royal commission emphasized the almost irresistible pressure on uncontrolled private television operators to become mere channels for non-Canadian commercial material. It recommended particularly that all private stations established should serve as outlets for national service. Of course, for some time at least, the C.B.C. will not be able to supply the national service to two stations in one area. That would leave any second station under the almost irresistible pressure to carry largely non-Canadian material.[22]

He later gave a glimpse of the government's policy for the longer term.

20 / *Ibid.*, March 17, 1953, 3010–12.
21 / *Ibid.*, 3034–7.
22 / *Ibid.*, Jan. 27, 1952, 1360–1.

Referring to the government's enunciation of the 'single-station' policy on December 8, he said:

These words make it clear that it was not the policy of the government to create monopoly in television or to limit any one area indefinitely to one television station.

The principle of one station to an area is to apply only until an adequate national television system is developed. At the rate that applications for stations are now being received it may not be long before there is a sufficient degree of national coverage to justify the government and the c.b.c. giving consideration to permitting two and in some cases more than two stations in certain areas. ...

The ultimate objective of the c.b.c. is to have at least one station in every province of Canada where that is practicable. We understand that private applications have been under development in the five provinces where no c.b.c. station is now under way, and the government does not want to discourage immediate establishment in these areas of private stations which will further extend national service coverage.[23]

The CBC in November 1952 had renewed its request for stations in southwestern Ontario and Quebec City, which the governors argued would serve large populations for a comparatively small operating cost. And the linking of Quebec City with Montreal would form the nucleus of a French network. A second transmitter was needed in Montreal as soon as possible, so that French and English programs could be separated. Then there should be CBC stations in other main areas of Canada – Edmonton, Regina, Saint John (New Brunswick), and St. John's (Newfoundland). This would provide at least one CBC station in every province except Prince Edward Island.[24]

The implication of the government's policy statement of December 8 was that CBC stations would be authorized *only* in the six locations announced (Montreal, Toronto, Ottawa, Vancouver, Winnipeg, and Halifax), and that applications for private stations would be considered for all other areas. In effect, the government had turned down the CBC request for stations in Quebec City and the other cities on the list. Pickersgill recalls that St. Laurent had not been enthusiastic about expanding the number of CBC-owned stations, and he suggests that it was Howe who 'gave the impetus to the wider development. His main interest was not in television, but in stimulating the electronics industry.'[25] In the House of Commons, George Drew asked what had hap-

23 / *Ibid.*, March 30, 1953, 3393.
24 / Interview with A.D. Dunton, Sept. 13, 1972.
25 / Pickersgill, *My Years with Louis St. Laurent*, 187.

pened to the idea of one station for every province. McCann replied, 'That is the ultimate objective, and that along with private stations, will constitute the national coverage.'[26]

Pickersgill writes that the government's statement on television policy received widespread approval; but among the broadcasters, neither side was very happy with the government's compromise. The CBC governors were disappointed, but did not say so publicly. They were sufficiently on the defensive over the CBC's 'monopoly' position. The *Vancouver Sun* said that 'in return for a crumb, the few private TV stations permitted must submit body and soul to CBC dictation.'[27] The British Columbia Association of Broadcasters passed a resolution hotly criticizing the single-station policy, and decided to send an open letter to all members of Parliament, all newspapers, and all radio stations.[28] In Toronto Jack Kent Cooke described the new policy as a 'faltering, fumbling step and not in a precise direction.' Foster Hewitt, another station owner, said that private operators had been tossed a bone after the CBC had picked it clean.[29] Joseph Sedgwick, just ending his long-held position as counsel for the CAB, wrote critically of the Massey Report and the policy stemming from it: 'Why can't we have privately operated TV stations, in Toronto, in Montreal, in every centre in Canada where entrepreneurs can be found willing to risk capital in such a venture? Clearly the people, the mass of the people, the ones who pay the taxes and have a right to be heard, would like it so, and would like private stations to be licenced not one, two or three years hence, but now.'[30]

T.J. Allard, general manager of the CAB, was at first very critical of the government's policy:

This policy places staggering power in the hands of the Canadian Broadcasting Corporation, permitting it not only to maintain its present regulatory powers but to decide for itself in what area it will have a complete television monopoly. ...

This policy will set back by years the provision of television programs that Canadians will look at, and the general development of the television industry. It also means that taxpayers in all parts of Canada will be subsidizing development of the CBC monopoly in large metropolitan areas carefully selected by the CBC itself for their commercial advantage.[31]

26 / *Debates*, March 30, 1953, 3393.
27 / *Canadian Broadcaster* (Dec. 3, 1952), 34.
28 / *Ibid.*, (March 4, 1953), 19.
29 / *Globe and Mail*, Nov. 21, 1952.
30 / *Saturday Night*, (Feb. 28, 1953), 30.
31 / Quoted in *Montreal Star*, Nov. 21, 1952.

As time went on, however, the radio station owners realized that the CBC was not being allowed to decide for itself the areas in which it would establish TV stations, and that in fact many more cities were open to private development than to public. They may even have realized that the public subsidies were a means of bringing programs to the private stations at little cost to them. When Allard appeared with his board of directors before the 1953 committee on broadcasting, his brief set quite a different tone: 'With respect, we should like to congratulate and commend the government on its present television policy ... [The announcement by Dr. McCann on March 30] brings government policy into line with the recommendations of the Massey Commission and at the same time reaffirms the general Canadian distaste for monopoly.'[32] Asked by Donald Fleming about the CAB's commendation of government policy, Allard explained that the policy announcement of March 30 was very different from the government's earlier statements.[33]

The complaints of the private broadcasters exasperated some of the supporters of the public system. After Joseph Sedgwick's article appeared in *Saturday Night*, the historian Arthur Lower wrote the editor:

There is no doubt in my mind that if we Canadians allow television to pass under American control and with American programs providing the determinative element in the items offered, we may as well sooner or later shut up shop: our future will be American. Persons who deny this are blind when they are not worse. They were characterized in Parliament as 'virtually traitors.' With this description I agree. It is not a matter of public vs private ownership – at least that is a secondary aspect of the controversy. The point is that private ownership means American control. No amount of subterfuge can whittle that statement away.

Who is willing to join in an association for the defence of Canada through the defence of Canadian Television? I shall be glad to receive names.[34]

Lower had been in correspondence with John Diefenbaker and M.J. Coldwell, leader of the CCF party, and Coldwell replied, agreeing with his views on the CAB:

32 / *1953 Proceedings*, 260 (April 29, 1953).
33 / *Ibid.*, 293. In an interview on July 22, 1975, Allard explained the wording of the CAB's official statement as an endeavour to 'help remove the issue from partisan politics.' He added that this endeavour failed, as Progressive Conservative and Social Credit members extended their opposition to the regulatory system to criticism of CBC programming and alleged inefficiencies.
34 / *Saturday Night*, April 18, 1953.

Step by step over the years they have encroached on the area Parliament designated as exclusively the responsibility of the C.B.C. The Conservatives have for years been their mouthpiece in Parliament and I am afraid that the Board of Governors has been weak, although I believe, too, that Dunton and others around him have tried to stem the tide which has flowed against them. ... One of the troubles is, of course, that ... newspapers or their proprietors now own a number of local stations and the propaganda in the press and through the C.A.B. itself is, of course, intense. ... The Minister, Dr. McCann, ... is not at all friendly with C.A.B. ... However, I am afraid that there is a strong element within the Liberal party here, directly interested – some of them personally interested – in private radio and television and I feel there is indeed grave danger of temporary success for C.A.B. ...

To my mind there are no more serious problems facing Canada than the gradual control of the press and radio, especially when taken into conjunction with economic control by the United States. Unless the tide can be stemmed or reversed, another generation or two will witness the absorption of our country by our powerful neighbour. One safeguard is, singularly, and this many English-speaking Canadians do not realize, the French-speaking Canadians in Quebec.[35]

Lower's efforts led to the organization of the Canadian Radio and Television League in 1954, which remained in existence until the Fowler Commission hearings in 1956. The organization was reconstituted in 1958 as a successor to the old Canadian Radio League (1930–6) under the name of the Canadian Broadcasting League.

Carrying out the government's direction to proceed with private applications, the CBC board heard applicants for stations in eight cities at the end of March 1953. Seven licences were recommmended, for Hamilton, London, Windsor, and Sudbury in Ontario; for Quebec City; and for Saint John and Sydney in the Maritimes. The Hamilton station, CHCH-TV, using a channel originally assigned to Toronto, was owned jointly by Southam and Sifton newspaper interests and by Kenneth Soble, owner of radio station CHML. The London applicant was the owner of both the *London Free Press* and radio station CFPL. The applicants for Sudbury and Sydney were the owners of the local radio stations, and for Saint John, the owner of a radio station and newspaper. In Quebec City two radio stations, with overlapping ownership, joined Famous Players (a subsidiary of Paramount Pictures) to apply for the television licence.

35 / Queen's University Archives, A.R.M. Lower Papers, Coldwell to Lower, March 12, 1953.

In Windsor the applicants were the owners of radio station CKLW, which previously had a large share of American participation. At the time of applying for the television licence, control was held by Canadians, particularly by men associated with the Toronto radio station CFRB: members of the Rogers family, and Harry and Joseph Sedgwick. In 1955 application was made to transfer control to Paramount Windsor Theatres Ltd., the same interests as Famous Players. This application was denied on the grounds that Famous Players already had a half-interest in the Quebec City station and also in a station that had been established in Kitchener.[36] Several months later, the CBC governors approved a transfer of one-third of CKLW's shares to another American-owned company, RKO Distributing Corporation of Canada Ltd. The recommendation was made 'on provision that there be no further transfer of share ownership, directly or indirectly, to non-Canadian control.'[37]

But the policy for licensing was far too loose, with no discernible ground rules with reference to concentration of ownership among the communications media in any locality or in relation to foreign ownership. If the governors themselves provided little leadership, they at least asked for policy direction:

The Board finds some difficulty in the fact that there has been no rule, statutory or otherwise, to which applicants, such as the present one, could turn for assistance in establishing the basis upon which their applications will rest. ... It recommends that the Licensing Authority give consideration to this matter and to the desirability of a provision relating to the degree of non-Canadian control, direct or indirect, in the use of a Canadian air channel, possibly along the lines of the United States provision limiting the amount of alien interest in a licensed station in that country to 20 per cent.[38]

No action was taken regarding foreign ownership until the new broadcasting act in 1958, and even then there were loopholes. When a later licensing authority, the CRTC, moved in 1970 to force the sale of CKLW and CKLW-TV, the stations were entirely owned by RKO-General Tire and Rubber of Akron, Ohio.

The station in Sudbury was the first private television station on the air, in October 1953, and CFPL-TV in London followed in November. By

36 / CBC Public Announcement No. 95, Dec. 2, 1955.
37 / Extract from minutes of 100th meeting, CBC board of governors, Ottawa, March 29, 1956.
38 / CBC Public Announcement No. 99, March 29, 1956.

the end of June in that year, two more stations had been licensed (Regina and Rimouski), and the CBC met with the nine successful applicants to plan network service. Members of the CAB executive sat in on the meetings.[39] By the end of March 1954, the national TV network comprised nine stations, five of them CBC stations, and four privately owned affiliates. At the outset, ten and a half hours of programming a week were provided to the affiliates by kine recordings; at the end of the season, the network service to these affiliates averaged twenty-four hours a week. This included a daily ten-minute news package.[40]

The biggest television attraction in 1953 took place before any private stations were on the air, and that was the telecasting of the coronation of Queen Elizabeth II in London. There was a race among all the North American networks to show the film of the event first. This led to the use of a new 'hot kine' process to develop the film within minutes of the recording, and rushing the seven-hour program across the Atlantic by jet plane and helicopter. In the end, CBC had the film on the air before either CBS or NBC, and the ABC network in the United States, taking its feed from CBC, scooped its rivals by minutes. The *New York Times* wrote: 'It was the CBC, with the co-operation of the British and Canadian air forces, that quietly and unostentatiously took the blue ribbon.'[41]

The coronation event persuaded many Canadians to buy television sets, as did the coming of television to Ottawa. The CBC's station there opened just in time to see the coronation. During 1953, about 560,000 sets were sold, more than doubling the number in operation. The successes of 1953 were a feather in the cap of the new general manager of the CBC, Alphonse Ouimet, who had succeeded to that position at the first of January. E.L. Bushnell, the former director-general of programs, became assistant general manager.

The peak years for the sale of television sets were 1954, 1955, and 1956, with sales in 1955 reaching 765,000 sets. It was estimated that by March 1957 2.5 million homes were receiving television, over 60 per cent of Canada's total. A year later, the figure had gone up to 71 per cent; and at the beginning to 1960, 78 per cent of Canadians had television sets in their home. The figures are set out in Table 2.1. There was also a very rapid increase in the number of television stations in these years, particularly of private stations (see Table 2.2).

In 1954 the microwave network linking Montreal, Ottawa, and Toronto was extended to Quebec City and Windsor, allowing the private

39 / *Canadian Broadcaster*, July 1, 1953.
40 / *CBC Annual Report*, 1953–54, 31.
41 / *Ibid.*, 6–7. See also Barnouw, *The Image Empire*, 44–5.

TABLE 2.1

Statistics relating to television coverage for each fiscal year

Fiscal year ending March 31	Cumulative sale of TV sets ('000)	Percentage of homes with sets	Percentage of population within range of Cdn. stns. (A & B contours)
1953	310	8	26
1954	728	17	43
1955	1423	34	66
1956	2169	51	72
January 1	Number of TV homes ('000)		
1957	2306	57	78
1958	2796	67	82
1959	3111	73	85
1960	3444	78	87

Sources   *CBC Annual Reports, 1954–55* and *1956–57*
CBC statistics department

TABLE 2.2

Number of TV stations each fiscal year

Fiscal year ending March 31	CBC English	CBC French	Private English	Private French
1953	1	1 (bilingual)		
1954	4	1 (Fr.)	4	
1955	6*	1	17	2†
1956	6*	2	22	3†
1957	6‡	2	26	4
1958	6	2	31	5
1959	6	2	34	7
1960	7	4	37	8

*Includes CBOT, Ottawa which until June 1955 was bilingual
†Includes CFCM-TV, Quebec, which was then bilingual
‡Excludes two armed forces stations in Newfoundland (1957 and thereafter), managed by CBC
Satellite stations, CBC and private, have not been included. In 1960, CBC had four of these, private stations had eight.

Source   *CBC Annual Reports, 1952–53* to *1959–60*, and revisions made by CBC Director of Statistics, R.L. Lewis

stations there and in London, Kitchener, Hamilton, and Kingston to become part of the 'connected' network. 'Unconnected' stations in 1954 included CBC stations in Vancouver, Winnipeg, and Halifax, and private stations in Calgary, Edmonton, Saskatoon, Regina, Port Arthur, Sault Ste. Marie, Sudbury, Rimouski, Moncton, Saint John, and Sydney. This rapid development forced the CBC into an enormous film and kine-recording operation. The English network service had risen to about fifty hours a week and the French network service to forty hours; distributing these programs to so many stations by film and kinescope was in itself a formidable task. During 1954 agreements were made with the communications companies to extend the direct relay facilities from the Atlantic to the Pacific. Winnipeg was connected to the network by microwave in 1956, and on July 1, 1958, a television program 'Memo to Champlain' marked the opening of the longest television network in the world, as Vancouver and Victoria were connected with Halifax and Sydney. The following year the connected network was extended even further as St. John's and other Newfoundland stations were joined to it.

The development of television program service in the 1950s and its distribution, in two languages, over so many miles was a phenomenal feat of building, and one for which governments, private companies, and the CBC all deserve credit and recognition.

3 Paying the Bill

When television began, the government had agreed in principle that the main source of revenue should be a licence fee. This had a two-fold advantage: during the years of development, the burden would fall on those who actually received television programs; and, traditionally, a broadcasting licence fee had been a visible guarantee of the independence of CBC from government. If the CBC had the proceeds of an annual licence fee that did not change from year to year, it would not be dependent on the government for annual appropriations and would not be so vulnerable to influence from the party in power.

The minister, Dr. McCann, said in July 1952 that a decision on the amount and details of the licence fee was imminent, but the announcement never came.[42] In the first year, television licences would not have produced an appreciable amount of revenue, and viewers who depended

42 / Globe and Mail, July 10, 1952.

so much on American programs would have thought it an outrageous tax. And 1953 was an election year – not a good time for a new imposition, especially when the radio licence fee was so unpopular. Canadians always found it hard to understand why, if broadcasting was 'free' in the United States, it should not be the same in Canada. At the same time, many Canadians (and particularly those in French Canada) wanted their own program services, whether or not advertising revenues would support them.

The government, indeed, had shrunk from raising even the radio licence fee to keep pace with increased prices in the postwar period. The Massey Commission in 1951 noted that a proposal to raise the licence fee to $5 was generally unpopular, particularly since there was a widespread impression (not unjustified) that the $2.50 licence fee was not effectively collected – that it was, in fact, evaded by many householders. Nevertheless, the commission thought it important enough to tie the cost of the service to those benefiting that they recommended continuing the radio licence fee at its old level. Because this was insufficient to meet current expenditures, the commission recommended also a statutory grant for a five-year period so that the total revenue of the CBC for radio could be brought up to the equivalent of one dollar per head of the Canadian population each year. The government acted on this recommendation in the fall of 1951, and the CBC received an annual sum of $6,250,000 for five years.[43]

Once this measure had been taken, it no longer seemed so important to retain the unpopular radio licence fee. Nearly everyone had a radio, so why worry about the principle of 'them who gits, pays'? And the device of determining the corporation's income for a period of years through a statute, it was argued, offered sufficient protection of the CBC's independence.

For some years the question of how to pay for Canadian television had been tossed around in the columns of the press and in meetings of broadcasters and electronics manufacturers. The CBC was almost alone in advocating a licence fee. Some of the manufacturers preferred a form of public subsidy – for example, the general manager of Canadian Marconi.[44] To others who did not think about it very deeply, the remedy was simple – turn over the development of television entirely to private enterprise, as in the United States. This ignored not only the sizeable losses sustained during the first few years by the large networks (who

43 / Peers, *Politics of Canadian Broadcasting*, 412–13, 415–16, 432.
44 / S.M. Finlayson, 'The Institution and Operation of Television in Canada,' *Industrial Canada* (July 1949), 192.

because of their radio revenues could afford it), but also the vastly different conditions in Canada which made television per capita much more expensive.

In November 1949, the president of Stromberg Carlson, a radio manufacturing firm, put forward his solution. There was in existence a 15 per cent excise tax on radios sold in Canada, and there would be on television sets too. President Hackbush estimated that $50 million worth of TV sets would be sold, and if the sales and excise taxes on these sets were handed over to the CBC, there would be no need for a $10 or $20 licence fee.[45]

As time went on, the proposal of Mr. Hackbush was forgotten. But at the beginning of 1953, television sets were selling faster than anyone had predicted, and the boom was just beginning. Someone in government may have remembered the excise tax suggestion, or have had the same thought himself. At any rate, in his budget speech on February 19, the minister of finance, Douglas Abbott, announced not only the abandoning of the radio licence fee, but also a new way to finance television operations. The objective, he said, was to give the CBC a direct source of revenue, but not to have the CBC dependent on annual appropriations. 'We wish to emphasize that it is a separate corporate body, under the general control of parliament but not a part of the government.'[46]

The plan was to amend the Canadian Broadcasting Act so that the CBC would receive from month to month the amount of revenue yielded by the 15 per cent excise tax on television sets and parts and would apply this to television; it would also apply to radio the revenues from the tax on radio receivers. In the case of radio, the statutory grant still determined the total revenues.[47] There was no such ceiling or minimum in the case of television. The tax could therefore provide a feast in one year, a famine in another. McCann explained that the tax on an average set (with tubes) should bring in about $39 – the 'equivalent of a $15 tax for $2\frac{1}{2}$ or 3 years.'[48] Obviously the government would have to think again when the country became more or less saturated with television sets, but by then another election would be out of the way.

45 / 'Use Sales Tax to Finance TV Proposes Manufacturer,' *Financial Post*, Nov. 19, 1949.
46 / *Debates*, Feb. 19, 1953, 2133.
47 / An amendment to the Radio Act abolished the radio licence fee, and an amendment to the Canadian Broadcasting Act required the minister of finance to transfer to CBC an amount equivalent to the proceeds from the excise tax. See Canada, *Statutes*, 1–2 Eliz. II (1953), c.48, s.3 and c.22, s.1.
48 / *Debates*, March 18, 1953, 3155.

4 *The State of Television, 1953–7*

The years between 1953 and 1956, when the Royal Commission on Broadcasting was appointed, were satisfying ones for television broadcasters in Canada, both public and private. All indices showed that the public interest was great, and the principal demand was for an extension and expansion of the service. Television sets were being bought faster than anyone had predicted. Then, in spite of the fact that a typical station was on the air only in the late afternoon and evening, the average viewer was watching his set for almost four hours a day – nearly as much as his counterpart in the United States where the television day was considerably longer.[49] Advertisers were buying more time, particularly for spot announcements and for imported programs that were cheaper than Canadian productions. Commercial revenue for CBC television went up as follows (year ending March 31): 1954, $1,334,766; 1955, $4,157,325; 1956, $7,403,438; 1957, $9,841,638. (These were net figures, after deductions for agency commissions, payments to private stations, and production costs of commercials.)

In 1955, of fourteen private stations on the air for the full year, nine operated at a profit and five at a loss.[50] Their net sales were over $6 million. It had been expected that a station would take at least two years to break even. Stations were beginning to show a profit after only one year of operation.

There were harmonious relations between the CBC as a network program service and the private television affiliates. The CBC made an effort to consult the affiliates as the service developed, hoping to engender a better atmosphere than had characterized its relations with the private radio stations. Regular meetings were held, and the operational rules discussed. For example, in December 1953 Canadian Press reported:

Under the agreement made by the publicly-owned corporation and fourteen private broadcasters, the CBC has exclusive rights to import live of kinescope-recorded programs. If the private stations want them, they must get them through the CBC.

The only programs from outside Canada which the private stations are free to obtain themselves are syndicated films. The CBC has agreed not to distribute such films in its network service, but may do so under special circumstances and only if a majority of private stations agree.[51]

49 / Max Rosenfeld, 'How TV is Changing your Life,' *Maclean's* (Dec. 1, 1954), 35.
50 / *Fowler Commission Report*, 151–2.
51 / *Montreal Star*, Dec. 10, 1953.

The successful applicants for private stations were glad to be engaged in such a growing enterprise, and pleased that for some years, at least, they would be protected from competition in their localities as a result of the government's 'single-station' policy. The CBC was not a competitor but a source of programs, its own and mass entertainment programs from the south, all delivered free of line charges or other costs.

For the CBC, times were easier than they had ever been. Even for its radio service, the $2.50 licence fee had never been really adequate, and it had become less so after the war years. The Massey Commission recommendations had given an effective remedy for that worry. Then the television service had started with an uncertain financial base. The turning over of the excise tax on television sets and parts provided enough money for about three years. There was even an operational surplus until 1956. Then the sale of sets began to slow down, and the costs of operating an expanded network continued to rise. After provision for depreciation, the television service showed an excess of income over expense in two years – a surplus of over $5 million in 1954, and of $4.5 million in 1955. There was an operational deficit of $1 million in 1956, and of $1.75 million in 1957. The total expenditures in these four years had increased from $13 million to almost $35 million. The spending had reached large proportions, and to the layman it looked as if there might be a considerable amount of waste. The 1955 broadcasting committee commented on the 'remarkable developments' in the national television service and agreed with Dunton that it could not be operated on a purely commercial basis. But it recommended that the existing system of financing television should be thoroughly reviewed.[52]

The government continued to finance capital installations for CBC television by loans authorized by Parliament. By 1955 there had been six of these:

1949	For construction of Montreal and Toronto stations	$ 4,500,000
1951	For production facilities, Montreal and Toronto	1,500,000
1952	For Ottawa station and initial television operations	2,000,000
1953	For beginning construction of stations in Vancouver, Winnipeg, Halifax, and second transmitter in Montreal	4,750,000
1954	For completion of projects listed above	3,000,000
1955	For second Ottawa transmitter, further studios, technical facilities, offices etc.	8,500,000
		$24,250,000

These expenditures were near the amounts forecast by the CBC general manager, but compressed in much less time. The operational costs were still within the projected figure of $15 per television household.

On the whole, the television program service seems to have met with a fairly good reception in these early years. It is remarkable how few complaints were voiced in Parliament: most of the grievances had to do with radio commentaries, lack of opportunity accorded the private stations, or the CBC's position of regulator as well as operator.

In his appearances before parliamentary committees, Dunton emphasized how big a job it was to bring television to the Canadian people, and how expensive. More transmitters were needed per million persons in this country than in most. The distances were long. It was estimated in 1953 that a network by microwave from coast to coast would cost about $3 million a year, and, including duplicate facilities, might run to $4 million. Television production was inherently expensive, and even more so in Canada with its need for program services in two languages. The economic pressures to use mostly imported programs were heavy. These pressures increased not only because more and more Canadians and Americans shared many common interests, but because Canadians had developed expensive tastes. Advertisers who paid full advertising card rates (station and network) made a substantial contribution to the costs of Canadian production, but advertising alone would not cover the full costs of such production. Moreover, the CBC considered it a public responsibility to achieve a 'sensible balance' in its television programming, and to appeal to a variety of interests. It was not CBC policy to offer its news, public affairs, religious, or education broadcasts for sponsorship.[53]

In cities where viewers had a choice between American and Canadian programs, such as Toronto and Vancouver, there was a hard struggle to make the public aware of the less well publicized Canadian programs. In Toronto, for example, station CBLT started off in its first year with about a quarter of the viewers during the evening, on average. As more stations were licensed in Buffalo, the audience was fractured into more pieces, and it would have been possible for CBLT's share to have gone down. Instead, it rose gradually, averaging about 35 per cent in 1954.[54] The following year Dunton told the broadcasting committee that CBUT in Vancouver was 'well in the lead,' with an average of between 50 and 55 per cent of the average viewing.[55]

53 / See *ibid.*, 11–17, 301–5, 323–5.
54 / Scott Young, 'Let's Stop Monopoly Television,' *Maclean's* (May 1, 1954).
55 / *1955 Proceedings*, 307.

The CBC stations in competitive areas held their share of audience partly by scheduling popular American programs in prime time (as the sponsors wished), and placing Canadian productions around them. Indeed, as the number of hours of program service went up, the percentage of Canadian programs went down, until in 1955 it was just about 50 per cent on the English network, as contrasted with 80 per cent on the French network.[56]

Some programs of course had enormous audiences even in competitive areas. Saturday night hockey, special events such as the Grey Cup football finals, a variety program such as 'Holiday Ranch,' the national television news at 11:00 PM – such programs swamped the competing channels. Many other series had very impressive audiences – for example, 'GM Theatre,' whose best known production in the 1956 season was Arthur Hailey's 'Flight into Danger,' shown on television systems throughout the world, and later made into a movie. Interview programs such as 'Tabloid' and 'Almanac,' public affairs programs such as 'Close-Up,' and the weekly 'News Magazine,' all had big national audiences, much larger than serious radio programs had ever attracted, and larger too than the readership for national publications.

But the most amazing impact of television was in French Canada. The CBC produced the same variety of programs in Montreal for the French network as it did in Toronto and the other English-language production centres, but more of them, because not so many programs could be drawn from other sources. The people of Quebec became fascinated viewers. Although Toronto had had a head start in acquiring television sets, by the end of 1954 more sets had been sold in Montreal than in Toronto. The programs represented a life that the people of the province recognized as theirs; they had always had a strong sense of identity, of their common history, traditions, and outlook: television only strengthened it. Artists appearing on programs became stars, and had strong personal followings in a way that English Canadian performers never achieved.

In Montreal the locally produced 'Music Hall' outdrew one of the most popular American imports seen on the English channel, the Ed Sullivan Show. Even personalities in more instructional programs dealing with international developments could develop a mass following, such as René Lévesque in his popular program, 'Point de mire.'

In an article in *Maclean's* magazine, Ken Johnstone gave English-Canadian readers a glimpse of how Quebec viewers regarded one of their

56 / *CBC Annual Report, 1954–55*, 5. The annual report for the previous year stated that 67 per cent of CBC's national television service was Canadian (p. 31).

favourite programs, 'La Famille Plouffe,' which was scheduled at 8:30 on Wednesdays. 'Hockey schedules in St. Jerome, Joliette and Quebec City have been shifted to avoid games on Wednesdays. In Valleyfield the start of games is delayed until after 9 p.m. Throughout Quebec, theatre owners complain that attendance drops when the Plouffes are on the air. ... In Montreal eighty-one per cent of all TV sets owned by French-language viewers are turned to the Wednesday night show, according to the Elliott-Haynes survey. Fifteen per cent of English set owners also watch the French language show.'[57] The scripts were by a best-selling novelist, Roger Lemelin, but the actors performing leading parts became even better known: Denise Pelletier as Cécile, Jean-Louis Roux as Ovide, Jean Duceppe as Stan Labrie, as well as the actors playing Mama and Papa Plouffe. An English-language version with the same performers was scheduled on the English network two nights later, but although it drew respectable audiences, it never had the same impact.

In the provinces with an English-speaking majority, there was some complaint that programs were too dull, or too serious, or too self-conscious, and complaints by a smaller number of people that the programs were too light in content, or too commercial, or that the schedules were dominated by American entertainment. But these expressed opinions were not the main reason that the government decided in 1955 to launch a full-scale investigation of broadcasting in Canada. Rather, it was the old quandary of how much to pay for television, how to pay for it, and what the appropriate agency should be for regulation and control.

57 / 'Meet Quebec's Most Famous Family,' *Maclean's*, (Feb. 1, 1955).

3 THE FOWLER COMMISSION, 1955-1957

I *Uncertainty about the CBC's Authority*

When the Massey Commission reported in 1951, the government of Louis St. Laurent may have assumed that the position of the CBC as regulating authority for Canadian broadcasting would be settled for some years ahead. After all, the commission's report had merely recommended continuance of the set-up that had been in existence since 1936, and it did so in laudatory terms. The majority of the commission were 'convinced that the existing Canadian system of broadcasting has served the country well in the past and offers the greatest hope of national unity and enlightenment in the future.' They urged only that it be given 'the power and resources sufficient for its great national responsibilities.'[1]

True, one member of the commission, Arthur Surveyer, had dissented, but the government expressed wholehearted support for the recommendations of the four commissioners constituting the majority. The first parliamentary committee to review the report (1951) rejected out of hand the claim put forward by the Canadian Association of Broadcasters that broadcasting was merely another form of publishing, and that therefore only technical regulation was needed. The committee added that all other parliamentary committees, as well as the royal commission, had considered the principles underlying the laws governing broadcasting and found them sound. The committee felt that those principles were 'becoming sufficiently established to enable the Canadian Broadcasting Corporation to concentrate on its essential national functions and the privately owned stations to pursue their important community functions.'[2]

But if this was a sign that Parliament was weary of the old debate about a 'single system' versus an independent regulatory authority outside the

1 / *Massey Report*, 300.
2 / *1951 Proceedings*, 473.

CBC, the opponents of the existing system refused to take the hint. The CAB maintained its campaign, reflected not only in the pages of the *Canadian Broadcaster*[3] and public relations news sheets such as *The Printed Word*, but in radio editorials by some of the member stations (for example, the editorials of Sam Ross over Station CKWX, Vancouver) and in 'Report from Parliament Hill,' a series distributed from Ottawa by the CAB's Radio Bureau, with speakers such as Chester A. Bloom, who was billed as 'editorial commentator for Canadian newspapers and non-government owned broadcasting stations.'[4] The CAB won the right to send a delegation to meet directly with the cabinet in 1952, and was delighted with the impact it was having on such Liberal bodies as the National Advisory Council and the Federation of Young Liberals.[5]

When the CBC was established in 1936, most of the country's newspapers supported the public system of broadcasting, the Canadian Broadcasting Act, and the CBC.[6] But by the 1950s most of the principal newspapers had shifted their position. Some of the newspapers supporting the Conservative party in the metropolitan areas, such as the *Gazette* in Montreal or the *Telegram* or *Globe and Mail* in Toronto, had always been opposed to the CBC, even though the Conservative party in the 1930s had been a proponent of public broadcasting. During the war, the CBC's role in disseminating government information, and the wartime restrictions on political broadcasting, had alienated some of this Conservative support, for example, the old leader and former prime minister, Arthur Meighen.[7] More Conservative newspapers were now prepared to attack the CBC, although the *Ottawa Journal* and (in a modified way) the *London Free Press* remained friendly. After the war, however, the number of critics of the CBC among the publishers accelerated. Some of this opposition was due to the making of common cause with the

---

3 / The trade magazine edited by R.G. Lewis (which had no official connection with the CAB) was published for some years after 1951 under the name *Canadian Broadcaster and Telescreen*. The CAB from 1953 to 1958 operated under the title 'Canadian Association of Radio and Television Broadcasters' (CARTB), but ordinarily it will be referred to in these pages as the Canadian Association of Broadcasters.

4 / The Social Credit MP, E.G. Hansell, cited a pamphlet by Chester Bloom, 'The Threat of Thought Control,' reprinted from a talk broadcast over sixty-seven radio stations. *Debates*, June 4, 1954, 5529. For an example of station editorials, see 'Sam Ross Reports,' *Canadian Broadcaster* (Jan. 20, 1954), 16–17.

5 / 'Freedom in Sight,' *Canadian Broadcaster* (Feb. 18, 1953); 'Radio-TV Loom as Hot Potatoes,' *ibid.*, (Nov. 19, 1952). See also the speech by the Liberal member for Dollard, Guy Rouleau, *Debates*, Jan. 28, 1955, 651.

6 / For the earlier position of newspapers, see Peers, *Politics of Canadian Broadcasting*, 66–7, 74–7, 189–91.

7 / *Ibid.*, chap. 13; also pp. 386–8.

private broadcasters – particularly by newspapers whose proprietors also owned or had interests in radio and television stations. The Sifton, Southam, and Thomson newspaper chains were all station owners. Among their newspapers, only the *Ottawa Citizen*, a Southam paper, retained its twenty-year-old position of support for the national broadcasting service and the role of the CBC as regulating agency.[8]

The *Winnipeg Free Press*, a Sifton newspaper, had won a national reputation under its long-time editor, John W. Dafoe. After his death, Victor Sifton personally directed the editorial policy. He and his brother, Clifford, were very much aware of their broadcasting interests; their newspapers campaigned incessantly for diminished regulation and for repudiation of the Massey Report.[9] And they were supporters of the Liberal party, as was the *Vancouver Sun*, which ran a more strident campaign. The *Toronto Daily Star* remained (with the *Ottawa Citizen*) among the few Liberal papers supporting the party's traditional position on broadcasting; *Le Soleil* in Quebec City was perhaps another. But in the larger cities – Vancouver, Calgary, Edmonton, Regina, Saskatoon, Winnipeg, Windsor, Hamilton, Toronto, Montreal, Halifax – most of the newspaper voices criticized the system or damned the CBC's performance. The controversies over television only added to the din.

Public opinion polls and program rating services added to the uncertainty over how much support there was for the CBC and the public system. According to the Canadian Institute of Public Opinion (the Gallup Poll of Canada) in November 1949 – the first year of the Massey Commission – 45 per cent of those surveyed thought the CBC was 'doing a good job,' 24 per cent a 'fair job,' and 16 per cent a 'poor job' (15 per cent were undecided).

A question asked by the Canadian Gallup Poll in 1954 was not strictly comparable to that asked five years earlier, but from the standpoint of the CBC was moderately reassuring. The question asked was this: 'It has been suggested that the publicly owned CBC should suspend operations and leave all radio broadcasting to private stations. Do you agree with this suggestion or not?' Fifty-three per cent of respondents thought CBC operations should not be suspended; 24 per cent agreed with the sugges-

8 / The former editor of the *Ottawa Citizen*, Charles Bowman, had been a member of the Aird Commission and had much to do with establishing the public system.
9 / In 1951 the *Winnipeg Free Press* reprinted fifteen of its articles in a pamphlet entitled *The Report on Radio*. In 1953 the two Siftons split their newspaper and broadcasting interests. Victor Sifton became the sole owner of the *Winnipeg Free Press*. Clifford Sifton, who had newspapers in Regina and Saskatoon and radio stations in Winnipeg, Regina, and Hamilton, became a particularly vigorous spokesman for private broadcasting.

tion that they should; and 23 per cent had no opinion. People in the prairies took the strongest exception to the idea that the CBC should be discontinued (58 per cent). British Columbia (perhaps reflecting the *Vancouver Sun*'s vigorous campaign) had the highest minority agreeing that the CBC's operations should be suspended (32 per cent), as compared with only 21 per cent in Quebec and the Maritimes.[10]

The principal company engaged in producing program ratings in the early 1950s was Elliott-Haynes Limited, which conducted most of its surveys by telephone while programs were in progress. From time to time it also conducted more general surveys. The credibility of its surveys tended to be high among the private stations, and lower with the CBC. Private station representatives often quoted Elliott-Haynes ratings in appearances before the House of Commons broadcasting committee; the CBC spokesman usually refused to discuss them, holding that the rating services provided their figures to subscribers on a confidential basis.[11]

Elliott-Haynes conducted a 'continuing survey' of attitudes to ownership and operation of radio in Canada, and found in three successive years, 1949 to 1951, that 60 per cent of Canadians favoured 'all private ownership and operation,' 19 or 20 per cent favoured 'all government ownership and operation,' and only about 14 per cent favoured 'part private, part government ownership and operation' – a description which presumably was applied to the existing Canadian system. According to other Elliott-Haynes figures produced by the CAB, listeners in the principal cities overwhelmingly preferred the programs of private radio stations to those of the CBC. For example, in 1951 CBR Vancouver (the CBC station) was said to have only 11 per cent of the audience, as compared with 20 per cent for CJOR, 15 per cent for CKNW, and 23 per cent for CKWX. In Winnipeg, CBW had a smaller audience than any of the three private stations. In Toronto, CBL with 11 per cent and CJBC with 13 per cent (both CBC stations) were hardly in the running with CFRB which was said to have 28 per cent, or CKEY which had 21 per cent. Similarly in

10 / Canadian Institute of Public Opinion, Toronto, Release or Saturday, March 13, 1954.

11 / Dr. McCann, perhaps reflecting advice he had received from the CBC, told the 1953 committee: 'My own experience ... is that an awful lot of people and private stations have been deluded into the opinion that the appraisal that you get from Elliott-Haynes and all those people are really accurate. It has never been proven that it has been.' *1953 Proceedings*, 431. Harry Sedgwick of CFRB countered that the Elliott-Haynes survey had been 'carefully drawn,' and could be relied upon (437).

Montreal, the two CBC stations, French and English, were rated below four private stations (CKVL, CKAC, CFCF, and CJAD).[12]

Dissatisfied with the existing ratings services, the CBC in 1951 commissioned two other firms to measure audiences (particularly for commercial programs) using other methods than the coincidental telephone survey. International Surveys used a diary method, and Gruneau Research Ltd. developed a 'radio panel' which was supposed to be more representative of the Canadian population than a sample reached by telephone calls at random. Although the CBC did not publicize the findings, the results were generally more favourable to their programs. The commercial manager, E.A. Weir, wrote to CBC personnel in October 1951: 'Most *five* a week programs, daytime or evening, on both the Trans-Canada and French networks showed ratings approximately twice as great as those usually shown by coincidental telephone ratings. There were also wide variations in the ratings of many night-time or once-a-week programs.[13]

With the arrival of television in 1952, Elliott-Haynes was at first dominant in providing rating services for the newer medium as well, but because of the single-station policy competitive positions of television stations were not so important except in Toronto and Vancouver where American stations were available. The CBC established its own audience research division in 1954, and it employed a variety of commercial survey companies to measure television audiences – particularly International Surveys and, at a later date, the A.C. Nielsen Company of Canada.

With the growth of television, radio audiences declined, especially in the evening hours. As the Fowler Commission began its hearings in 1956, reports by International Surveys showed that in competitive areas Canadian stations had won an important segment of the audience, if they were still out-distanced somewhat by the older American stations. For example, in September 1956, the average share of audience in the evening hours (between 6:00 PM and 00.00) for the Canadian stations in the Toronto area was 34 per cent (CBLT averaged 21 per cent and CHCH-TV, carrying many CBC programs, averaged 13 per cent). WBEN-TV had 46 per cent of the audience, WGR-TV 15 per cent, and other

12 / *1951 Proceedings*, 168–71, Appendix A to submission by the Canadian Association of Broadcasters.
13 / CBC research department, Toronto, 'Summary of a Study of Radio Panel of Canada Ratings, as made by Gruneau Research Ltd.' A memorandum by E.A. Weir, dated Oct. 22, 1951, accompanied the report.

stations 5 per cent. In the Vancouver area, CBUT had 36 per cent of the audience, and four United States stations the remaining 64 per cent (KVOS-TV 35 per cent, KTNT-TV 4 per cent, KOMO-TV 11 per cent, and KING-TV 14 per cent).[14] In other large cities (except Windsor), Canadian stations had a near-monopoly of viewers – although perhaps half the programs carried by the English-language stations were of American origin.

Canadians were more aware of the CBC than ever before, because of television, but at the same time there was still a popular preference for the big American entertainment programs; and in cities with only one station, people longed for more choice, and many blamed the CBC for the restricted options.

With public support for the existing system so hard to gauge, the Liberal party became less sure of its position in respect to broadcasting control. The reports of the 1953 and 1955 broadcasting committees were hesitant in affirming support for the form of regulation embodied in the Canadian Broadcasting Act. Having referred to the proposal for a separate regulatory body as advocated by the CAB, the 1953 committee said: 'The Committee was unable to study this subject with the care which it would appear to merit in the light of the continued interest which is expressed therein and which would be necessary in view of the concept of a national system with control vested in a single body responsible to Parliament, the Canadian Broadcasting Corporation.'[15] The 1955 committee seemed to half make up its mind, but ended its report on an inconclusive note:

Your Committee took note of a brief presented by the Canadian Association of Radio and Television Broadcasters with respect to a separate regulatory board having minimum essential regulatory powers over radio and television broadcasting in Canada. The Canadian Chamber of Commerce forwarded your Committee a resolution supporting that view. On the other hand a communication from the Canadian Federation of Agriculture supported the present system of national control of radio and television. Your Committee is of the opinion, however, that the evidence adduced does not warrant the establishment of such a regulatory board at the present time. ...

Your Committee commends the private stations for the part they are playing in the development of the national service and for their efforts to give better

14 / CBC Bureau of Audience Research, 'Facts on Radio and Television in Canada and Data on Listening and Viewing Patterns,' June 1957.
15 / *1953 Proceedings*, 450.

community service by way of discussion of matters of local interest, and other public service broadcasts.

Your Committee has carefully considered the single service coverage policy which now governs television broadcasting. It is of the opinion that the policy has proved to be a desirable one. It finds, however, that its application involves certain technical and other difficulties which would warrant further study of the whole question.[16]

After the committee had reported in 1955, the minister, Dr. McCann, made it clear that he personally saw no need for a separate regulatory board. He quoted with approval two editorials from the faithfully Conservative *Ottawa Journal*, no doubt to embarrass the opposition critics, particularly Donald Fleming, the party's spokesman on broadcasting. The *Journal* referred to a 'well-organized campaign of private interests against the supervisory authority of c.b.c. ... aimed at putting c.b.c. and private interests on an equal footing.' The *Journal* agreed with the Massey Commission that the private broadcaster had been granted a privilege, but no vested interest; and said that the private station was not on an equal footing with the cbc, that it was not in competition, and that 'private broadcasting should be subordinate to a national service, as is now the case.'[17]

McCann told the Commons he subscribed '100 per cent to those views,' and then announced that a special inquiry would be set up: 'One of the recommendations of the Massey commission was that the whole subject of television and radio broadcasting in Canada be reconsidered by an independent investigating body not later than three years after the commencement of regular television broadcasting. ... I am prepared to announce, on behalf of the government, that there will be either a commission or a board of inquiry set up some time within the near future to study the whole situation.'[18] The Massey Commission had indeed suggested a further investigation, but only for television. Presumably, it thought that, with the commission's proposed changes in effect, radio and the general broadcasting structure would be reasonably stable, but that the course of television's development would need further checking.

McCann's announcement came during a debate – once again – over the regulatory authority of the cbc. Yet Grant Dexter (whose sources

16 / *1955 Proceedings*, 814, 816.
17 / *Ottawa Journal*, April 1 and 2, 1955.
18 / *Debates*, July 26, 1955, 6875.

were good) wrote in the *Winnipeg Free Press* that the government's chief concern was the high cost of television:

The long controversy as to the wisdom of the Government dominating radio and television seems not to disturb the cabinet. There are apparently no doubts on this ground. Likewise, no importance appears to be given to the argument that an independent regulatory tribunal should take over these functions of the CBC.

... Expenditures are rising very rapidly. Much the larger part of the revenue is public money. ... The present structure cannot endure because the very large tax yield from sales of television sets and parts will not continue.[19]

The emphasis in the inquiry would be financial, but no one believed that the old battles over ownership and control would not be fought again.

2 *The Commission and Its Task*

The government did not announce that it had decided on a royal commission, nor name the members, until December 1955. The order-in-council appointing the commission said that it was to examine television and its financing, but also aspects of sound radio broadcasting which were related to television broadcasting. Two paragraphs outlined broad objectives which were to be included in the commission's frame of reference:

1. Canadian broadcasting must give expression to Canadian ideas and aspirations and reach the greatest possible number of Canadians; and
2. The grant of frequencies or channels should continue to be under the control of Parliament; and the broadcasting and distribution of Canadian programs by a public agency should continue to be the central feature of Canadian broadcasting policy.[20]

Specifically, the commission was to review the CBC's policies in television broadcasting, its finances, the measures necessary to provide an adequate proportion of Canadian programs, and the licensing and control of private stations in the public interest.

The commissioners chosen also reflected the government's concern over financing. They seemed not to resemble the members of the Mas-

19 / First of two editorials, Sept. 28, 1955.
20 / Pc 1796, Dec. 2, 1955. Reprinted in *Fowler Commission Report*, 293–4.

sey Commission in background or primary interest. The chairman, Robert M. Fowler of Montreal, had been a lawyer, but had spent most of his life in business and in public service. Between 1937 and 1939 he was a staff member of the Rowell-Sirois Commission on dominion-provincial relations. During the war he served three years as general counsel and secretary to the Wartime Prices and Trade Board. In 1945 he became president of the Canadian Pulp and Paper Association, a position in which he continued until 1972. Politically, he was a Liberal, and had many friends in government circles in Ottawa.[21]

The second commissioner was Edmond Turcotte, Canadian ambassador to Colombia, who had previously been editor of the Montreal daily *Le Canada*, a newspaper supported by the Liberal party. During the war Turcotte also had worked for the Wartime Prices and Trade Board.

James Stewart, the third commissioner, was president of the Canadian Bank of Commerce (as was the chairman of the first royal commission on broadcasting in 1929, Sir John Aird). Stewart lived in Toronto and his politics were unknown, but the CCF leader in Ontario, Donald MacDonald, charged that the commission was loaded against the publicly owned broadcasting system. Fowler, he said, had been chairman of the executive council of the Canadian Chamber of Commerce when that body had passed resolutions attacking the CBC, and Stewart who had also been active in the Chamber 'could not be dissociated from the attempts of the business world to undermine the CBC.'[22]

Business interests, including those in broadcasting, were better satisfied. An editorial in *Saturday Night* (owned by Jack Kent Cooke of CKEY) called the CCF's criticism 'not only a childish show of bad manners but a characteristic display of prejudice.' The inquiry was needed, it maintained, because in 1955–6 the CBC would spend up to $42 million and the following year about $50 million. Was the spending to go up and up each year 'while the CBC continues to throttle private competition'? *Saturday Night* said the commission must find the answer.[23]

Chester Bloom, a veteran reporter who wrote for the Sifton and Bell newspapers and broadcast over the private stations, welcomed the practical experience of the men chosen for this commission. He con-

21 / 'Fowler: stepping down, but not retiring,' Montreal *Gazette*, Jan. 25, 1972. In an interview, Jan. 27, 1976, Fowler said that the first approach to him regarding the commission was made by Brooke Claxton. Claxton was also the one who had suggested Massey as the head of the royal commission in 1949 (Pickersgill, *My Years with Louis St. Laurent*, 139). By 1955 Claxton had left the government, but remained active in Ottawa's political circles.
22 / 'CCFer Scores "Anti-CBC Radio Survey,"' Toronto *Telegram*, Dec. 7, 1955.
23 / 'A Needed Inquiry,' Dec. 24, 1955.

trasted them with the members of the former commission, who had made the error of 'inviting every obscure organization in Canada to make suggestions on public control of radio and television.' Bloom continued:

The new Commission's first task will be to recapture CBC's radio and television management and policies from the influence of the first Commission of the phony pseudo-intellectuals. These people rushed in from all quarters under the guise of hastily formed organizations. Actually, a large number were make-believe leagues, associations, societies, councils and groups. ...

The vociferous slogan of these minority groups was ''Save Canadian Culture from Vulgar American Radio.' This patriotic outcry carried the day against the more sensible mature organizations and experienced broadcasters.[24]

In February 1956 the commission published newspaper advertisements asking for the submission of briefs by April 15. There was little fear, apparently, that it would be inundated by material from the 'make-believe leagues, associations and societies' that worried Chester Bloom. (The commission did ask for thirty copies of each brief: was this perhaps to discourage the shadow organizations?) Fowler announced that public hearings would be held in cities across Canada, beginning with a week of hearings in Ottawa when the CBC, the CAB, and others with a direct interest in broadcasting might be heard. After the regional hearings, the commission would return to Ottawa to receive briefs from national organizations wishing to be heard there and, some weeks later, the final submissions of the CBC and CAB. The government nominated Paul Pelletier, assistant secretary to the cabinet, as the commission's secretary, and the commission engaged two legal counsel: John M. Coyne of Ottawa and A.J. de Grandpré of Montreal.[25] G.C.W. Browne, recently retired as controller of telecommunications, became technical adviser, Guy Hoult, a senior partner in P.S. Ross and Sons, financial adviser, and Dallas W. Smythe (an economist with the University of Illinois formerly on the staff of the FCC) was engaged as program analyst.

Meanwhile, a number of voluntary associations began to compile their briefs, some of them stimulated or encouraged by CBC personnel or by private broadcasters. The CBC, for example, assembled a bulky 'information kit' containing items such as annual reports, speeches, a copy of

24 / Reprinted in *Canadian Broadcaster*, Jan. 19, 1956.
25 / In 1963 John Coyne became a member of the Board of Broadcast Governors; and in 1973 A.J. de Grandpré became president of Bell Canada, the largest component in the Trans-Canada Telephone System.

the broadcasting act, reports of parliamentary committees, and so on. The kits were handed out to organizations showing interest in the submission of briefs.

Some broadcasters remembered the important part played two decades earlier by the Canadian Radio League, which had exerted a perhaps decisive influence in shaping the first two broadcasting acts of 1932 and 1936.[26] They watched for signs that a similar organization might be rallying support for the public system of broadcasting in 1955. Following the lead suggested by Professor Arthur Lower of Queen's University, Kingston, a group in Toronto had formed the Canadian Radio and Television League, which issued a leaflet called 'Dial' and began recruiting members. The president was E.A. Corbett, former director of the Canadian Association for Adult Education (who had been on the executive of the old Radio League), and the treasurer was Albert Shea, who was engaged privately in communications research. In Halifax, George Douglas, a professor at Dalhousie University and a friend of Lower, enlisted members of the league, with some unexpected results. The president of the Canadian Association of Broadcasters was at this time Finlay MacDonald, of radio station CJCH. On March 17, 1955, the *Halifax Chronicle-Herald* reported:

The President of the Canadian Association of Radio and Television Broadcasters warned a Halifax audience last night to beware of organizations whose apparent purpose is one thing and whose real purpose is another. Finlay Mac-Donald ... directed his attack against the newly formed Canadian Radio and Television League. ...

He said the newly formed organization lists a membership sparked by a charter membership of academic socialists, members of the CBC, the C.C.F. party, and what he called 'intellectual egg-heads.' ...

He said that fifty per cent of these people did not know the aims or purposes of the League. Recently the League held a general meeting in Toronto ... [with] an address by Professor Lower of Queen's University, one of the best known socialists in Canada.[27]

MacDonald's address won some attention in other cities, but he received an editorial rebuke from the home-town paper. The

---

26 / For the role of the Canadian Radio League in 1932 and 1936, see Peers, *Politics of Canadian Broadcasting*, chaps. 4 and 7. An article in *Canadian Broadcaster*, Jan. 17, 1957, 'Radio League of Canada Influences All Government Inquiries,' illustrates a fear of the league's revival.'

27 / *Halifax Chronicle-Herald*, March 17, 1955.

Chronicle-Herald objected particularly to his statement, 'I do not infer that such an organization is Communist dominated.'

That is one of the oldest of propaganda devices: it is known as 'setting up a straw man and then knocking it down.' ...

Let him not name such men and then hint at 'the political undertones involved' in their efforts. They have a right to their own opinions and their own attitudes in matters of public concern.

George Grant, a professor of philosophy at Dalhousie, in a letter to the editor wrote:

Professor Lower is not a socialist. ... It has always been easy to find out what his opinions were from his many writings, as for instance, his recent defence of the liberal democratic tradition, 'This Most Famous Stream.' ... During the last years in the u.s.a., we have watched the appearance of misrepresentation, guilt by association and false insinuation. ... Mr. MacDonald's misrepresentation is just an example of this sort of demagoguery. ...

Having listened to the radio station of which Mr. MacDonald is the manager, I can well understand why he objects to the intellectual.[28]

The Canadian Radio and Television League prepared and submitted a brief to the Fowler Commission, but as an organization it never had much strength. The mass organizations holding a similar position on broadcasting matters preferred to make their own submissions (the Canadian Federation of Agriculture, and the Canadian Labour Congress, for example – two organizations which had not been in existence during the heyday of the Canadian Radio League). Lower had written a draft submission for consideration by the executive of the league; when they attempted to reshape it, or to water it down so that it would be agreeable to everyone, Lower decided to make a personal submission, one in which the chairman of the Royal Commission showed special interest.[29]

Since the Fowler Commission had only one subject of investigation – broadcasting – and the Massey Commission had many more (not only broadcasting, but films, periodicals, galleries and museums, libraries, universities and scholarships, and support for the arts), one might have expected that the number of organizations appearing and the number of

28 / *Ibid.*, March 19, 1955.
29 / Queen's University Archives, A.R.M. Lower Papers, Fowler to Lower, Aug. 6, 1956.

briefs presented would be very much smaller. The surprising thing is that so many responded again in 1956. The Massey Commission had held hearings in sixteen Canadian cities, the Fowler Commission in twelve. The Massey Commission received 462 briefs; Fowler, a surprising total of 276.[30] The broadcasting system was still a subject of lively interest to articulate Canadians.

Those who presented the 276 briefs may be classified as follows:

Broadcasting organizations:	
Private broadcasters	30
CBC	1
Citizens' groups, other interests	18
Private citizens	30
Educational interests:	
Universities and colleges	11
Voluntary associations	18
Professional associations (including librarians)	19
Voluntary associations, citizenship and welfare	21
cultural	18
ethnic and language rights (French Canadian)	8
Women's associations	10
Business interests and associations	27
Trade unions and associations of artists	13
Farm groups, co-operatives	15
Churches and church-centred groups	18
Political groups	9
Provincial governments, municipalities	6
Newspapers, publishers	4
	276

3 Views on the Regulating Authority

The sharpest differences expressed before the commission were over the regulating power of the CBC. In general, we can say that the CBC and the majority of voluntary groups, excluding the business associations, favoured the existing system, or a variation of it. On the other hand, an overwhelming majority of the private broadcasters, supported by chambers of commerce and a few other associations, wanted the CBC stripped

30 / *Massey Report*, 8; *Fowler Commission Report*, 2.

of its regulatory power which, they said, should be assigned to a completely separate body, one that was not itself engaged in broadcasting.

Through several of their meetings, the CBC governors discussed the presentation to be made by the chairman to the Fowler Commission, reviewed draft statements prepared by management, and indicated what they felt the answers should be to questions that might be raised in a number of contentious areas. In addition to compiling a main brief, the CBC prepared sixteen special studies at the commission's request. Eight of the ten governors (including the chairman) were in Ottawa for the first public meeting held by the commission on April 30, 1956, when the chairman made an oral presentation and answered questions from the commissioners and their legal counsel.[31]

Dunton told the commission that the CBC was submitting a memorandum rather than a brief, adding in explanation, 'We do not in fact hold a brief for any national aspect of broadcasting in Canada.'[32] In spite of this disclaimer, it was evident from his testimony that he saw very many advantages to the CBC's having a co-ordinating role – and certainly he mentioned few drawbacks. He argued that much more than a simple transfer of powers was involved, as was implicit in the arguments of those advocating a separate board. The CBC had the responsibility of providing a broadcasting service to the entire country, and this could only be done in some sections through private stations. To have access to these facilities for distribution of programs, the CBC must have power of co-ordination. A co-ordination by others, such as a separate board, would leave the CBC with the responsibility, but without the corresponding authority. Co-ordination was carried out not only by the board of governors but through the day-to-day operations of the corporation. How would a separate board deal with this?

He argued that the justification for a separate board was often premised upon the idea of competition between CBC and private stations. But this was not supported by the facts, which showed a great deal of co-operation between the CBC and private stations, and very little com-

31 / The members of the CBC board of governors at this time were: A.D. Dunton, Ottawa, chairman; Dean Adrien Pouliot, Quebec City, vice-chairman; Gordon A. Winter, St. John's; Dr. G. Douglas Steel, Charlottetown; Gérard Gingras, Montreal; Dr. J.A. Corry, Kingston; F.J. Crawford, Toronto; R.J. Fry, Winnipeg; K.G. Montgomery, Edmonton; and Roland K. Gervin, Vancouver. The eleventh position on the board was vacant, and was filled shortly thereafter by Mrs. J.E. Houck of Brampton, Ontario. During the meeting of the board in Ottawa, Fry died suddenly on May 1st; A.M. Shinbane of Winnipeg was appointed to complete his term.
32 / Canada, Royal Commission on Broadcasting, 1955–7, transcript of hearings, April 30, 1956, 13. Hereafter cited as *Hearings*.

petition. The CBC was spending millions of dollars in program service, which in television went out through and to twenty-five different private stations, in addition to corporation outlets. There was a lack of direct commercial competition, and a lack of competition between CBC network programming and the local programming of private stations.

The situation in broadcasting was not analogous to that in railway transportation. Critics had said that a publicly owned railway (Canadian National) and a privately owned railway (Canadian Pacific) were both subject to regulation by a 'separate' Board of Transport Commissioners: why, therefore, should there not be a separate board in broadcasting? Dunton said that both railways carry out the same function, but in broadcasting the functions of the CBC and private stations are quite different – the CBC must use private facilities in some sections of the country to bring its service to everyone. Nor did the Canadian situation have a parallel in any other country. In Australia, for example, the public and the private radio systems each had its own network, and the public system did not have to rely at all on private stations for distribution of the national service. Dunton admitted that 'if the CBC and private stations are told not to work together but to behave like competitors, then there is plenty of reason to have a separate Board.'[33] If it were decided that the CBC was to operate only from publicly owned facilities, its task would be much clearer than it was now. But it would also be more costly for the Canadian people.

As the hearings proceeded, and the charge was heard again and again that the CBC board was acting unfairly as prosecutor, judge, and jury – or cop and competitor – the governors privately re-examined their position, to decide what minimum powers they must have if they were adequately to carry out their responsibilities. They felt if the national objectives were the same, and the CBC had to continue working through private stations to distribute the national service, then the powers to control such distribution must remain with them. It was not so essential, in their view, to retain the power of making general regulations respecting the character of programs and advertising, or to rule on Canadian content or the use of live talent, or to make recommendations to the Department of Transport on station licences. These powers, if necessary, could be transferred to a separate board.[34]

This position was reflected by Dunton in his final testimony in early

33 / *Ibid.*, 100, 105. Dunton's discussion of the licensing and control of private stations is on pp. 96–114.
34 / Interview with J.A. Corry, former member of CBC board of governors, Kingston, July 8, 1973. The discussion in the CBC board took place on Sept. 21, 1956.

October when the CAB and the CBC were each provided some days for rebuttal. Dunton then said:

I would just like to sum up. We feel there are two different main courses possible for Canadian broadcasting: one, a separation – not just the establishing of a separate body, but the separation of public and private elements into two compartments, presumably the public element continuing to have responsibility for carrying on a national service – that is, a service reaching right across the country. The other, for the continuation of the present kind of integrated system we have; in this case, we believe it is essential that the body responsible for the national service must have corresponding authority over the carrying of the national service on private facilities. Further, Mr. Chairman, we don't think it is essential, but we do think that experience has proved it practical for the same body to have other regulatory powers over programmes or recommending responsibilities about licences.[35]

To some observers, this represented an about-face. *Le Droit* of Ottawa wrote on October 13: 'At first, Mr. Dunton was uncompromising and asked that the status quo regarding broadcasting be maintained in Canada. But today, he testified in the opposite direction and asserts that the Governors are ready to give up their positions to members of a control board independent from state enterprise and he believes that the time has come to allow two TV stations in each city of the country.' On the same day, the *Globe and Mail* wrote that the Fowler Commission had now 'received the high-sign to strip from the CBC some of the absolute power which this crown corporation wields over Canadian radio and television.' The *Globe* added that while policing the airwaves, the CBC had been 'cowed by private station operators into overlooking obvious infractions.' An independent tribunal could be tougher in ensuring that the private stations carried programs 'of a Canadian character,' and the CBC could fulfil its prime function of 'producing those Canadian programs.' For its part, the *Financial Post* saw a chance that the long dispute between the CBC and the private stations could be brought to an end. It quoted Dunton as saying that the CBC would be glad to get the private stations out of its hair. 'Now that this point is cleared up, it should be feasible to devise a system that will make everybody happy.'[36]

35 / *Hearings*, Oct. 9, 1956, 7552–3. Dunton said the minimum powers necessary for the national service were to be found in Section 20 and Section 21 (a) and (b) of the Canadian Broadcasting Act. The less essential regulatory powers were contained in other sub-sections of Section 21, namely, (c), (d), (e), and (f). *Ibid.*, 7546–7.

36 / 'The CBC and its competitors,' Oct. 20, 1956.

Throughout the course of the hearings, Dunton had played down the CBC's role in regulating the content of programs and the amount of advertising, perhaps because of criticism that the CBC was regulating its competitors, or the opposite kind of criticism, that the board was too passive in correcting abuses or in ensuring that the private stations carried more Canadian programs or employed more Canadian talent. Or it may have been that Dunton just did not believe that regulation was an effective means for getting better programs. He explained his position this way: 'I think our Board has not very great faith in what you can do to obtain good broadcasting through written regulations. ... I think the CBC is not particularly interested in detailed controls and direction of other people's activities. We think essentially good broadcasting comes from the exercise of a sense of responsibility by broadcasters who do their best within their means. ... I think the experience of broadcasting around the world shows that bodies who are not responsible but try to tell somebody else what to do to obtain good programming have not been very successful.[37]

The record of the CBC as a somewhat inactive regulator made it hard for the private broadcasters to convince the commission and the public that they were the victims of an unjust system, but they went ahead in their presentations with characteristic vigour. In their first appearance the main spokesman was James Allard, executive vice-president, assisted by the president, Fred Lynds, and twelve members of the board of directors. They submitted their main brief and twelve other documents on the first day, and two more the next day.

Allard made it clear that the private station members of the CAB objected not so much to the regulation of the stations by a public authority, but to the agency entrusted with that power:

We are not even suggesting that it is improper for these functions of Parliament or the Government to be delegated under certain circumstances to an appropriate administrative tribunal. We are suggesting only that such an administrative tribunal should represent third-party judgment, that it should be a tribunal in no way connected with any body which operates broadcasting stations or networks. ...

The Corporation competes with the non-government stations for both audience and business, yet it is a board of regulation in relation to this group of individual stations with whom it is so competing. ...

We suggest this places the Corporation in an unenviable position. No matter how fair or proper, no matter how just any regulation which it may promulgate or no matter how fair its administration thereof, it is always difficult for the public ... to divide the Corporation into its regulatory and operating functions.[38]

In discussion, it appeared for a time as if Allard were not willing to admit that broadcasting required any special regulation of content, as he introduced an argument that he had expounded before parliamentary committees, that broadcasting was merely another form of publishing and thus should be subject only to the general laws of the land. However he finally admitted that there may properly be *some* regulation of content.[39] Fowler asked whether there were any particular regulations that the stations objected to. Allard suggested that a certain amount of fear had inhibited expression of complaints, but that he would consult his colleagues and answer the question the next day.[40]

The commissioners asked several times for examples of cases in which the CBC had acted as both plaintiff and judge, or cases in which the CBC had regulated in its own interests as a broadcaster. The evidence adduced was not very impressive, but from the standpoint of the CAB this was somewhat beside the point. It was the principle that was important. Allard explained: 'The Commission will find ... that a significant element of the public feels there is something basically unfair, something wrong, something to be a little fearful of in a situation where the executive, legislative and judicial bodies are combined and a working board is forced into the position where it is making recommendations on situations which concern themselves as an operating body.'[41]

Restrictions on the formation of networks were cited (in CAB's Exhibit 312) as the most substantial grievance. After quoting the CBC regulations requiring CBC consent for any station to operate as part of a network, the CAB stated categorically that 'in practice, the conditions surrounding permission for networks have made operation of these impossible.' In their report, the commissioners commented:

On the evidence, this is not a correct statement of fact. ... There was no evidence of a concrete proposal for the formation of a private national radio or television network since 1945 and there were a number of instances of quite extensive network arrangements on a regional basis that have come into existence without difficulty ...

38 / *Ibid.*, May 2, 1956, 507, 517, 519.
39 / *Ibid.*, 540.
40 / *Ibid.*, 553–4.
41 / *Ibid.*, May 2, 1956, 698.

At our final hearings, the spokesmen for CARTB were at pains to disclaim any submission to this Commission seeking the right to establish private networks ... No one seemed very interested in the subject of networks, except as an example of some supposed restrictions by the CBC.[42]

In the early stages of the commission's hearings, newspaper writers watched for indications of which way the commissioners were leaning. A reporter for the *Toronto Telegram* wrote (May 11, 1956) that while Fowler and Stewart might have been expected to be sympathetic to a private enterprise group, 'the CARTB brief was so loaded with irrelevancies and unsubstantiated charges against the CBC that the legitimate case the private broadcasters have was lost.' The *Globe and Mail* (May 14) described Fowler's cross-examination of Allard as 'so intensive and critical that it seemed to border on hostility.' The editorial concluded that there could be no objection to the commission's putting the methods and motives of the private operators under the microscope, but that the CBC should be given 'identical treatment.'

In their final appearances before the commission, the CAB's rebuttal was presented, not by Mr. Allard, but by their legal counsel, W.J. Estey of Toronto and Gordon Henderson of Ottawa. Several new documents were filed, including 'A Draft Act for a Canadian Telecommunications Board.' This draft bill was new so far as the public was concerned, but it had previously been presented to the cabinet.[43]

The CAB suggested a board that in some ways would have been a Canadian equivalent of the FCC. The board would have five members, and the chairman and the vice-chairman were to be full time. One of them was to be a judge or experienced lawyer, and the other an engineer. The board would deal with all the uses of radio waves, would handle technical standards of all telecommunications, allocate frequencies and channels, recommend the granting of broadcast licences, regulate the operation of networks, and control the proportion of advertising time. It was apparently to be removed from parliamentary control 'except by changes in the board's constitution or by its abolition.'[44] Otherwise its dealings would be with the governor in council through the minister of transport. The board could order periods reserved for CBC programs on private stations which, apparently, were to be paid for carrying them. No mention was made of over-all program regulation apart from the

42 / *Fowler Commission Report*, 121–2.
43 / Evidence of F.H. Elphicke, a past president of CAB. *Hearings*, 1701.
44 / *Fowler Commission Report*, 132. The draft bill became the commission's Exhibit 311.

stipulation that the board would not have the power of censorship, and that no regulation could interfere with the right of free speech.

The unveiling of the draft bill came so late in the hearings that it did not receive a great deal of discussion, and the suggested removal of parliamentary supervision, in the interests of a more 'independent' board, almost guaranteed that none of the major political parties would espouse it. The bill's provisions may have had some appeal for a governing party, because on closer examination it appeared that the board was not really 'independent.' According to section 17, the governor in council would have the power at any time to 'vary or rescind any order, decision, rule or regulation of the Board.' For twenty-five years, Canadians had been trying (with limited success) to remove broadcasting from partisan politics. This bill would surely have had the opposite effect.

If the CAB had not quite made its case, at least part of its argument had registered with the public. The distinction between the radio service provided by the CBC and by the private stations was becoming blurred. In the 1930s and 1940s, the private stations were thought to provide essentially a local or community service, except in so far as they served as outlets for national programs from the CBC. They were stations of limited power; at the end of the war, only two or three exceeded a power of 5000 watts. After 1948, an increasing number of private radio stations were authorized to go up to 50,000 watts – the same power as the CBC's regional stations. The distinction between local and regional service was being obliterated; and if radio networks declined in importance, as had already happened in the United States, would the distinction between community service and national service also disappear?

The CBC argued that there was still an insignificant element of competition between CBC and private radio stations, because of the difference in the quality of their programs and the declining commercial emphasis on CBC stations. Following the advice of the Massey Commission, the CBC had discontinued local advertising, leaving this lucrative field for the private stations. The number of sponsored network programs in radio was also declining as advertisers turned to television, or alternatively to local radio on a selective basis. The net commercial revenue of CBC radio had declined from $2,903,000 in 1952–3 to just over half that figure in 1956–7 ($1,564,000).[45]

In television, the CBC could justifiably say that there was even less competition with the private stations, since as a result of the single-station policy, each station, whether a CBC or a private station, was in

45 / CBC, 'The Commercial Activities of the Networks and Stations of the Canadian Broadcasting Corporation, 1936–1965,' (Ottawa, 1965, mimeo).

effect assigned its own exclusive territory. On the other hand, this meant that the stations were developing in much the same way, if one excludes for the moment the CBC's production capacity. In other words, each station in its non-network hours provided a local service, sold local commercials, arranged to carry syndicated films, and broadcast to as large an area as its transmitters could reach. The old distinctions in radio of local, regional, and national service hardly applied, except that the CBC was assumed to be the originator of most national programs.

Even this distinction would be lost, perhaps, when the single-station policy of the government was abandoned. It had always been regarded as temporary, and now the public demand for second stations was rising. When a CBC and a private station were licensed for the same area, would there not be a truly competitive situation? Then how could it be argued that the CBC as the regulating authority was not in control of its competitors?

Obviously much depended on the nature of the policy governing the development of second stations – whether or not the CBC was expected to provide some of their program service to those stations, and whether the CBC would be asked to reduce its commercial role.

The CAB asked for 'competitive television broadcasting,' that is, they wanted additional channels opened for private development. When Fowler asked the representatives of the association whether they wanted to 'remain part of the national system,' the question took the broadcasters by surprise. Finally those present seemed to agree with Geoff Stirling (who had recently won a television licence for St. John's, Newfoundland, over an opposing application from the CBC) when he replied, 'The only thing I would like to see is better shows in the system so we have a greater interest, but I want to remain part of the national system.'[46] The broadcasters did not speak as if a privately owned network of television stations was an immediate possibility. The commissioners concluded, 'no one suggested that a national network was today a practical proposition; no one offered to establish a network on any extensive scale with any substantial content of Canadian programmes; no one seemed very interested in the subject of networks, except as an example of some supposed restrictions by the CBC.'[47]

The force of the CAB presentation was partly blunted when, in subsequent sessions, certain members of the association took a different or an opposing stand on the question of a separate regulatory board. The individual station representatives supporting the unified system in which

46 / *Hearings*, May 3, 1956, 604–5.
47 / *Fowler Commission Report*, 122.

the CBC board of governors was the regulating authority were not numerous, but they were prominent in the industry. They included Murray Brown of CFPL and CFPL-TV, London, and Corey Thomson of CKVL, Verdun, one of the most successful radio stations in the Montreal area. More surprising was the defection of Finlay MacDonald, of CJCH, Halifax, and past president of the CAB. His brief accepted the concept that 'from the beginning up to the present time private stations ... exist not as equal elements but as links' in the national system. He agreed that the CBC must have sufficient authority to achieve distribution of its product. He regarded the CBC 'as the licensing body in Canada for all practical purposes, and we have no quarrel to find with the policy.' If a separate body were set up, and the original concept retained, 'then the separate regulatory body would only have to turn around and transfer all its powers to the c.b.c.' MacDonald acknowledged that he had once supported the idea of a completely separate board. Now he appeared to suggest merely a greater distinction between the CBC as an operating body and the regulating authority of the board of governors.[48]

On the question of regulation and control, most of the organizations not directly involved in broadcasting repeated the position they had taken before the Massey Commission six years earlier, with the exception that a number of those supporting a 'one-board' system were more sharply critical of the CBC for not exercising stricter supervision and enforcing their own regulations (on limitations in advertising, for example.)

The Canadian Chamber of Commerce, a national federation of 750 boards of trade and chambers of commerce, said it took its stand on a principle that had been formulated as many as eight years ago: 'The Chamber believes in the principle that no person or organization in any field should be both competitor and regulator and urges the establishment of a separate regulatory body having minimum essential regulatory powers over radio and television broadcasting in Canada.' The chamber's quarrel was with a system 'under which no one can do a proper and conscientious job.' Some of the CBC's regulations were extremely sweeping, 'and stations had a very limited right of appeal. Fowler asked, 'Would you not think that if it were so bad – this evil you are so worried about – that we would have had a lot a people wanting to get out of this network arrangement? ... We have had twenty-five years' experience with this.'' The spokesman for the chamber replied that he could not point to particular grievances, but that 'is not proof that they do not exist.' Fowler said the commission had asked everyone the same

48 / *Hearings*, June 19, 1956, 3317–21.

question, and so far they had been unable to find examples of this unfairness.[49]

The other large national association of businessmen, the Canadian Manufacturers' Association, did not make a submission. A smaller association, though an important one, the Association of Canadian Advertisers, supported the principle of more competitive broadcasting and believed that more commercial stations should be licensed. But surprisingly it failed to address itself to the question of a separate regulatory board. It did not think that an all-commercial system was possible; for example, there would have to be special financial support for French-language broadcasts in Canada.[50] The Radio-Electronics-Television Manufacturers Association also appeared before the commission, and advocated a separate regulatory board. It held that the CBC had retarded the development of television in Canada because of its dual function in regulation and operation. When Fowler suggested that the delay after 1949 had been a government decision, the president of the association replied that it must have been with the advice of the CBC. Had that advice been from people 'representing industry and commerce and the various arts,' the recommendation would have been different.[51]

Excluding business groups, a large majority of the organizations submitting briefs favoured the continued regulation of broadcasting by the CBC board of governors. Of the national associations, only two supported the idea of a separate regulatory board: the Imperial Order, Daughters of the Empire, and the Canadian Federation of Mayors and Municipalities (which submitted a brief but did not speak to it). Four national organizations, because of a division of opinion among their membership, took no position: the National Council of Women, the Canadian Association of Consumers, the Canadian Citizenship Council, and the Canadian Welfare Council. Among organizations favouring CBC regulatory powers were these: Canadian Arts Council; Canadian Council of Authors and Artists; Canadian Federation of Agriculture; Canadian Labour Congress; Confédération des Travailleurs catholiques du Canada; Canadian Association for Adult Education; Société canadienne d'Education des adultes; Association Canadienne des Educateurs de langue française; Canadian Association of University Teachers; Canadian Home and School and Parent-Teacher Federation; Canadian Library Association; Co-operative Union of Canada; and the United Church of Canada.

The report of the commission (p. 130) speaks of 'the vagueness of the

49 / *Ibid.*, Sept. 10, 1956, 4542–77, 4586–8.
50 / *Ibid.*, June 4, 1956, 2945–56, 2976, 2980.
51 / *Ibid.*, Sept. 15, 1956, 5812, 5822–4.

arguments both for and against the proposal' for a separate regulatory board:

Opponents of the idea said 'It will destory the CBC' or 'It will result in two independent groups of broadcasters, two systems of broadcasting, one public and one private', without any proof as to why these results would necessarily come about. Those who favoured such a board were equally vague and seemed unable to define what factual changes would result from an acceptance of this proposal. They ... resorted to general and subjective arguments. They said it was contrary to 'democratic principles' to have a body acting as both regulator and competitor. They argued that the Canadian constitution required executive, legislative and judicial functions to be kept quite separate, but failed to recognize that this suggested rule was less firmly established in Canadian than in American constitutional practice.

It was indeed true that many who voiced support for the existing system did so in the terms stated by the Massey Commission, which by inference Fowler was declaring to be too vague and general.[52] But in fact, some of the organized groups did make concrete proposals, a number of which may have influenced the final recommendations. Several organizations, such as the Canadian Council of Authors and Artists and the Canadian Labour Congress, suggested that there should be a greater and more visible separation between the over-all regulating and controlling body (the regulating division perhaps reporting to the chairman of the CBC board) and the program and operational part of the CBC – but they did not want to 'divorce' the two.[53] A number of groups, for example the National Association of Broadcast Employees and Technicians and the General Faculty Council of United College, Winnipeg, scored the CBC for not enforcing regulations, and gave examples.[54] The University of British Columbia Television Committee had a suggestion not unlike that of Finlay MacDonald, of station CJCH: that the CBC Board of Governors be renamed the 'Board of Governors of Canadian Radio and Television Broadcasting,' to make it clear that it was concerned with the entire system, and not just with the operations of the CBC. Dean G.C. Andrew of UBC told the commission:

The single change we would suggest considering is that the present Board of Governors at the C.B.C. might be tied less closely to the Canadian Broadcasting

52 / See *Massey Report*, 285–6.
53 / *Hearings*, 793–4, 802–5, 6041–3.
54 / *Ibid.*, 978–9, 6328–33.

Corporation operationally, this for the purpose of making it more apparent, than it currrently is, that the Board of Governors is in a position to ensure that standards in broadcasting and television are maintained both by the national system and by the private outlets. We do not think that the Board of Governors as they currently exist have lacked impartiality, but they have been put in the position of appearing to be the spokesmen and defenders of the national public system in their dealings with the independent stations, and for this reason their full effectiveness may have been in some degree inhibited.[55]

The most ignominious retreat by the CBC as regulator, although it did not receive much attention in the press, had occurred in 1953 when the CBC attempted to carry out a recommendation of the Massey Commission that the board of governors 'investigate ways of ensuring that private radio broadcasters employ more Canadian talent.'[56] In October 1952, the CBC announced proposed changes in the regulations for radio stations that would require them to devote a percentage of their broadcast time to Canadian programs. After resistance from the private stations, the board of governors backed down. The revised regulations, promulgated in June 1953, abandoned the attempt, and in fact met the private stations' demands that they should be allowed more time for advertising.[57]

4 Views on the Licensing of Stations

General attitudes expressed on the licensing of radio and television stations depended very much on the stand taken in relation to the regulating authority. Those organizations that wished the CBC board of governors to continue its regulating functon approved of existing licensing procedures, by which the Department of Transport acted as the licensing authority on the decision of the cabinet, so far as new stations were concerned, and on the decision of the minister in relation to other matters, such as power increases, changes in frequency, transfer of ownership, and so on. Such applications in every case were to be referred to the CBC governors for their recommendation, and it was the CBC that arranged public hearings of the applications.

Few of the witnesses had any precise suggestions about licensing policy. A group of professors at Laval University in Quebec City suggested that the establishment of new private television stations should

55 / *Ibid.*, May 14, 1956, 1594.
56 / *Massey Report*, 298.
57 / *Canada Gazette*, Part II, SOR/53–235, June 24, 1953, 569–74.

be reduced to a minimum. They said that private stations left to themselves soon became the puppets of sponsors.[58] The General Faculty Council of United College, Winnipeg, would have preferred a system that was entirely publicly owned. But these representations were exceptional; the majority seemed to prefer the mix about as it was. And pleas were heard in many communities for additional service: for more CBC service in areas served primarily by private stations, and for private television stations in the areas where CBC had a Canadian monopoly.

A number of witnesses were worried about the 'chain' ownership of stations. On the other hand it was argued by Jack Kent Cooke (who was not himself the owner of a chain of stations) that such multiple ownership increased efficiency.[59] Stronger opposition was expressed to a concentration of ownership in the various media of communication, especially in instances where the same owner had a newspaper and a radio station, or a newspaper and both radio and television stations, in the same locality.[60] Two publishers who were in broadcasting – Clifford Sifton and St. Clair Balfour, Jr., of the Southam company – felt that this question should be left to the working out of the anti-combines legislation, although in the ensuing discussion it appeared doubtful that the Canadian statute applied to radio and television.[61]

The Canadian Association of University Teachers advocated that private stations be licensed on the understanding that they were agents to carry out public policies, that they existed to supplement the national service or to carry it to areas in which the CBC did not establish its own stations. The relationship between the CBC and the private station should therefore be that of principal and agent rather than that of equal competitors.[62]

It is difficult to determine what the CAB's attitude was to the licensing, or indeed the existence, of CBC stations. An article published in the *Toronto Star* after the first round of the commission's hearings, and attributed by the *Star* to the Canadian Association of Radio and Television Broadcasters, says this:

58 / *Hearings*, June 29, 1956, 4397–8.
59 / Brief, Toronto Broadcasting Co. Ltd. (CKEY), Exhibit 123.
60 / Brief, National Association of Broadcast Employees and Technicians (Exhibit 216); Arthur Lower, *Hearings*, 5968. Leslie Wismer of the Canadian Labour Congress cited Peterborough, Kingston, Hamilton, Regina, London, and Saint John, NB, as one-newspaper cities in which the publishers controlled radio and TV stations. *Hearings*, 839.
61 / *Ibid.*, 1078, 2802, 2838, 2842. A regulation under the Radio Act – 31A (1)(d) – attempted to guard against extension of multiple ownership of stations.
62 / *Ibid.*, 5260–1.

It cannot be successfully argued, in our view, that the CBC is necessary in order to provide entertainment, newscasts, sports events, imported programs on film, whether disc or tape. ...

We suggest that the CBC might get out of the ownership and operation of stations and networks completely, and become a program production body, producing and purchasing from any available source, including the National Film Board, such programs as were envisaged when the broadcasting enterprise of this country was placed under the control of the various broadcasting control bodies starting with the days of the late Hector Charlesworth. These programs should be made available for sale to all radio and TV stations, to be used whenever deemed advisable. If sufficient distribution was not thereby achieved, compulsion could be exercised by an authority directly responsible to the majority of the elected representatives of the people. ... i.e., Parliament itself. ...

The CBC, under these conditions, would have very little expense other than straight program expense.[63]

This position was advocated by two or three organizations that appeared before the Fowler Commission, other than by broadcasters themselves, notably by La Chambre de Commerce de Québec, and La Fédération des Chambres de Commerce des Jeunes de la Province de Québec.[64]

The CAB's brief and supplementary memoranda were not as definite about CBC withdrawal from station operation as was its publicly released statement. The discrepancy was probably a sign that members had disagreed on this crucial question. Indeed, on May 2, Jim Allard, the CAB's general manager, told the commission (p. 507), 'We should like to make it unmistakably clear that this Association and its members have no wish whatsoever to destroy or emasculate the CBC as an operating body.' What was left unclear was whether the CBC as an operating body should own stations, or do more than produce programs. Malcolm Neill, of CFNB, Fredericton, who in the early 1950s had been CAB president or chairman of the board for three years, while fully endorsing the CAB brief, said that the CBC did not need its transmitters, because private stations could be leased for the distribution of its programs. The CBC should merely supply the connecting facilities and the programs required for national service.[65] Geoff Stirling advanced the same proposal,

63 / 'Would Have CBC Scrap Stations, Fire Staff; Make Radio, TV Private,' July 5, 1956.
64 / *Hearings*, 4359, 5514–6. La Chambre de Commerce de Québec thought it would not be practical for CBC to withdraw from television operations, but could do so in radio.
65 / *Hearings*, 3742–3. This was essentially the proposal advanced by the CAB in 1932, and rejected by Parliament at that time.

suggesting that CBC stations be leased or sold to private enterprise on the understanding that they carry four hours a day of national service.[66] Other private broadcasters who were not so prominent in the counsels of the CAB, such as Jack Kent Cooke, supported the idea that the CBC should be a program-producing body only, and should operate like the National Film Board.[67]

Against this concept, there were broadcasters who, while specifically endorsing the CAB's brief, saw a continuing role for the CBC as the operator of stations and networks. For example, A.M. Cairns of CFAC, Calgary, said the public system was necessary and desirable, though not to the exclusion of others. Robert Large of CFCY, Charlottetown, seemed to favour separte CBC and private networks.[68]

Because of the diversity of the CAB's membership – radio and television stations, large stations and small, stations that were financially secure and those that were marginal, stations that were network affiliates and those that were independent – it is understandable that on some issues there could not be complete agreement. In television, the private stations were distributing a good share of the network service; in radio, because of declining sponsorship of network programs, the tendency was to take only programs in 'reserved time.' The prosperity of the television stations was very much bound up with the success of the network; not so in radio. The larger radio stations in particular felt that they could now survive on their own. On the other hand, they sensed that there was a good deal of public support for the CBC, and that all-out opposition would be tactically unwise. There was also the problem posed by the terms of reference given the commission, which said that 'the broadcasting and distribution of Canadian programmes by a public agency shall continue to be the central feature of Canadian broadcasting policy.' It seemed that the CBC was not to be reduced to an agency for the production of public service programs.

There were at least two suggestions that the government as such should not have any part in deciding who should have, and who should not have, a broadcasting licence. The brief of La Société Canadienne d'Education des Adultes (exhibit 194) asked that the CBC board of governors handle applications directly in order to avoid any political interference with the broadcasting system. In presenting a personal brief, a Liberal member of the Manitoba legislature, Jack St. John, suggested that an independent regulatory board should be established

66 / *Ibid.*, 4797–8, 4804–7.
67 / *Ibid.*, 3077–8, 3113–14.
68 / *Ibid.*, 2178–9, 3610–12.

that would have power to license under the act.[69] Fowler replied, 'We cannot make the recommendation. The terms of reference make it explicit that the exclusive use of certain frequencies or channels for broadcasting shall continue to be under the control of the Parliament of Canada.' This may have been a somewhat narrow reading of the terms of reference, but it at least indicated that the commission was unlikely to recommend that decisions on new licenses be removed from the cabinet.[70]

The private broadcasters generally wanted as few licence restrictions as possible, although Allard suggested that licences should go only to Canadian citizens, and people of substance, integrity, and repute in the community, preferably with some related experience.[71] Clifford Sifton, owner of Station CKRC, Winnipeg (and some other stations), thought the government should issue as many licences as they could find people ready and willing to use them.[72] Gerry Gaetz of CJCA, Edmonton, contended that licensing should be in perpetuity, adding that a broadcaster would 'feel better' if he were dealing with a body that had no interest in broadcasting.[73] The president of L'Association Canadienne de la Radio et de la Télévision de langue française (an association of thirty-two stations) pointed out that private station applications went to the Department of Transport, which in turn sought the advice of the CBC. On the other hand, when the CBC made application for licences to the Department of Transport, the applications were dealt with in secret session without any reference to the private stations.[74] The Chambre de Commerce de Québec supported the contention of many private operators that, in the granting of television licences, a certain priority should be given to the applications from sound broadcasting stations.[75]

The draft act submitted by the CAB would have transferred the responsibility for the technical examination of applications from the Depart-

69 / *Ibid.*, May 9, 1956, 1278. Mr. St. John and another Liberal MLA had recently introduced resolutions in the Manitoba legislature, passed with a large majority, calling for more TV stations in the province, favouring competitive television in Winnipeg, and urging the setting up of an independent regulatory board. *Debates*, July 28, 1956, 6647.
70 / The Broadcasting Act of 1968 makes the regulatory board (the Canadian Radio-Television Commission) the licensing authority, while granting a right of appeal to the governor in council. Presumably it can be argued that final control of the allocation of frequencies is still with the Parliament of Canada.
71 / *Hearings*, 655.
72 / *Ibid.*, 1055.
73 / *Ibid.*, 2108–9.
74 / *Ibid.*, 4321–33, evidence of D.A. Gourd, who was also vice-president of the CAB.
75 / *Ibid.*, 4386.

ment of Transport to a new Canadian Telecommunications Board, and also given the board the right to recommend to the governor in council through the minister of transport on the granting of broadcast licences. Mr. Henderson, one of the lawyers representing the CAB, emphasized that it was to be an independent board, 'unresponsive to Parliament, because they have to be exercising judicial functions.' Fowler asked, 'So Parliament is divorced from any control?' Henderson replied, 'Well, I would not say divorced from any control; it can change the structure but it is divorced from its day to day judicial determinations, yes, that is right.'[76]

If the contemplated board was to be independent of Parliament in its licensing policies, it is not so clear that it was to be independent of the government. As previously noted, the draft act said the governor in council might either with or without petition 'vary or rescind any order, decision, rule or regulation of the Board.' There was no appeal from such a decision, although an appeal from decisions of the board could be made to the Supreme Court upon questions of law.[77]

In supporting the objective of 'maximum growth in the private broadcasting industry,' the CAB's second counsel, W.J. Estey, pointed out that whereas the United States had 2964 authorized AM stations, Canada had only 175; and while the United States had 485 commercial television stations in operation, Canada had only 36. This was evidence that 'our Canadian industry is being held back' by CBC control. Fowler interjected, 'The system of which you complain very vigorously has, in fact, enabled the private broadcasters to do very well.' Estey replied, 'The station owner is doing all right, but the public suffers.'[78]

During the CBC's 'rebuttal' appearance, Dunton said that the board of governors had made recommendations for scores of private station licences, including those for fourteen private stations within the coverage area of CBL, Toronto. 'This,' he added, 'is the Corporation that is trying to keep down the circulation of private stations.'[79]

There was some discussion of the procedure by which the CBC held a public hearing for an application after the technical aspects had been considered by the Department of Transport. Dunton said that the practices surrounding the licensing of private stations had arisen from the concept of one system, reinforced by the strong powers of recommendation assigned to the board by the broadcasting act. The licensing author-

76 / *Hearings*, Oct. 3, 1956; quoted in Fowler Commission Report, 132.

77 / 'A Draft Act for a Canadian Telecommunications Board,' Exhibit 311, submitted Sept. 28, 1956.

78 / *Hearings*, Oct. 3, 1956, 7115–17.

79 / *Ibid.*, Oct. 9, 1956, 7530.

ity (that is, the minister of transport) found it useful to have a board drawn from all across the country that would make recommendations from the national standpoint. Such a function for the board, Dunton declared, was not essential to CBC operations, but it had been found to be a practical arrangement. He added, 'It is not the most interesting part of our work' and 'not the most essential.'[80]

The CBC, Dunton said, would not object to public hearings for CBC applications. When private applications were being considered by the board, members of staff were not usually present. He felt that it would not be useful to have a sub-committee of the board deal with licence recommendations because the important part of this was the public interest aspect. It was most useful to have the full board expressing its views and 'intuition' in arriving at an appreciation of the public interest. The board would like to see financial statements of the stations, in order to help it in its deliberations, but had so far been refused by the licensing authority.[81]

Turning to ownership of broadcasting stations, Dunton said that an opportunity for different groups and individuals to take part in broadcasting was desirable, and so in general the board did not recommend an extension of 'chain ownership.' Nevertheless, keeping in mind various circumstances that could arise it was usually better to have statutory provision for flexibility, providing the principle to be followed was clear. Since 1947 applications for broadcast licences from newspapers had been considered on the same basis as other applications, following a parliamentary committee recommendation to that effect. Applications for television licences from radio station owners were considered on the same basis as others, although radio experience might help an applicant. In applying the general policy against an extension of chain ownership, the board considered radio and television as separate media. On the question of foreign ownership, Dunton said there should be a policy decision at a higher level. There was no statutory provision covering the percentage of control of Canadian stations allowed foreign interests, although the board had recommended a limit of 20 per cent.[82]

5 Views on the CBC, Private Broadcasting, and the Mixed System

Although the emphasis varied from group to group, nearly all the submissions supported the system in which CBC and private stations broad-

80 / *Ibid.*, Oct. 10, 1956, 7632–9.
81 / *Ibid.*, 7660–9.
82 / *Ibid.*, 7679–89.

cast side by side, and in which the CBC took the main responsibility for the national service, and the private stations for local and community service. There were a few who regarded the CBC's operations as far too expensive, and who thought its operations should be reduced or curtailed – for example, the Retail Merchants' Association of Canada, and the Canadian Legion for Manitoba and North Western Ontario.[83] A number of private broadcasters, such as Geoff Stirling and Don Jamieson of St. John's, contended that CBC production costs were too high, that its programs were too narrow in appeal, and that substantial savings could be realized if the CBC had more showmanship, ingenuity, and commercial sense.[84] But many others, including most of the farm organizations, labour groups, women's organizations, home and school associations, universities and educational groups, testified to the value they placed on CBC programs, and accepted the costs without complaint. This was true of both English- and French-language organizations. In fact, the commission found that the sentiment of French Canada was 'virtually unanimous' in its commendation of CBC programming.[85]

Across the country, a number of briefs mentioned specifically that the CBC was not only a strong unifying force, but one of the principal bulwarks against the domination by American media of Canadian entertainment and mass communications.[86]

Many of these organizations emphasized that the CBC should have adequate sources of revenue, probably from the general taxation funds, and a number suggested statutory grants for a fixed period of years so that the CBC would not be dependent on the good will of the party in power. Often they seemed to be less interested in economy than were the members of the commission, who tried to impress upon them how much the extension of services might cost. In fact the commission was disappointed that it received so little help on financial proposals, which it regarded as the main purpose of the whole inquiry.[87]

In the CBC's presentations, Dunton emphasized that regardless of who carried out the broadcasting function, some means of financing other than advertising was essential to meet stated Canadian objectives and to

83 / *Ibid.*, 1086, 1356.
84 / *Ibid.*, Sept. 11, 1956, 4748–83.
85 / *Fowler Commission Report*, 237.
86 / For example, merely from briefs heard in Western Canada, the Manitoba Federation of Agriculture, the Canadian Federation of University Women, a group of citizens in Nanaimo, BC, the Television Committee of UBC, the Alberta Federation of Agriculture, the Saskatchewan Farmers' Union, and provincial committees of the Labor-Progressive [Communist] Party.
87 / *Fowler Commission Report*, 247.

allow the production and distribution of Canadian programs. Commercial support was necessary to broadcasting in Canada, but public interest had to be first. An assured basis of income was required, since there must be freedom from program control by others. There should be a relationship between the number of people watching and the amount and kind of service. Regular assessment of the work of the CBC should be made, both qualitatively and financially, but these assessments should be spaced so that the CBC would have time to concentrate on its main job of broadcasting.

National television service to Canadians, the CBC said, could be maintained at about the present level for an annual cost of $15 per television home. This was the scale forecast by the CBC in 1952 on the basis of the development authorized at that time. Actual CBC expenditures had kept well within that ratio, the CBC memorandum added. The CBC did not ask for any specific financial arrangements or amount, but press reports tended to interpret the CBC's discussion of the $15 figure as a request for a $15 television licence fee.

The $15 'base for calculation' would not cover any appreciable increase in the amount of Canadian programming, further extension of TV to areas not covered, any daytime extension of programming, colour television, or additional service if some areas were to have a choice of Canadian TV stations.[88]

In the final hearings, the CBC's general manager, Alphonse Ouimet, said that consistently people had tended to underestimate television's costs, popularity, rate of growth, and long-range impact on the minds of people. He suggested that this pattern should not be repeated. Television was just beginning and was not anywhere near complete development. Canadians could afford television; they had spent more per capita in four years to buy receivers than the people of any other country. The problem was not one of 'affording' but of collecting for the program service. Compared with the costs of other information or entertainment media, television was an inexpensive commodity. And Canadians wanted as good a service as any other people. For example, they would not be satisfied with black-and-white when the United States had colour. Nor would the present hours (late afternoon and evening) be acceptable in the future. Similarly there would be expectations for an improvement in the quality of service. Inability to keep up in these respects could mean the difference between success and failure in the objective to keep Canada Canadian.[89]

88 / CBC, Memorandum to the Royal Commission on Broadcasting, 1956 (Exhibit 2).
89 / *Hearings*, Oct. 11, 1956, 7848–59.

6 *Views on an Alternative TV Service and a Private Network*

Many people in addition to the broadcasters expressed a desire for a second TV station, and some demanded an immediate reversal of the 'single-station' policy. A few, such as the Toronto and District Trades and Labour Council and the Nova Scotia Federation of Home and School Associations, suggested that the extension of existing program service to other areas should take priority.[90]

In their brief, the Association of Canadian Advertisers held that the economy could not support two national television networks, but that advertising could well support second stations in major areas. And this seemed a fairly common assumption among those who expressed a view on the viability of a second service. A number of organizations asked that the 'second stations' be integrated with the existing system. For example, the Winnipeg city council, which was strongly in favour of a second station, thought that it should carry some CBC-produced programs.[91] The briefs of the labour organizations in Winnipeg and Toronto said that the second stations should be operated by the CBC, even in areas where the CBC had the first station. The general manager of stations CFPL and CFPL-TV, London, urged that second stations be required to reserve certain periods in their schedules for Canadian programs produced by the CBC or by themselves.[92] But the president of the Canadian Marconi Company (owners of CFCF, Montreal) thought that even the existing situation was made 'incongruous' and 'incompatible' by the attempt to bring together a public and a private system. He much preferred the Australian system, where the lines were clearly drawn.[93]

The CAB's representatives were sure that the possibility of forming national networks should be open to the private stations, and that CBC should not be the authority to whom they would have to apply. They were not so sure that a private television network, on a national scale, was economically feasible. But Estey told the commission that the CBC wanted an atmosphere created where private enterprise could grow to a stature enabling it to operate national networks.[94]

Dunton replied that for years it had been possible for private stations to share costs through subsidiary networks. He saw nothing in the

90 / Brief, Nova Scotia Federation of Home and School Associations; *Hearings*, 2427–8.
91 / *Ibid.*, 889.
92 / *Ibid.*, 4931.
93 / *Ibid.*, Sept. 13, 1956, 5209–11.
94 / *Ibid.*, Oct. 3, 1956, 7150–2.

regulations to stop any group from coming to the present board with a concrete plan for a regular network operation.[95] (This was surely a little ingenuous, because the assumption throughout the years, and as late as the Massey Report, was that the CBC provided the national service, and private stations were to be essentially local or regional services.)

Dunton also asserted that the business facts of 'second stations' must be faced. Radio provided the picture of what could happen in television. In Montreal and Toronto, English-language radio was prosperous, but if the commission examined the actual studio production of the private stations, it would see that the live program content did not exceed 3 or 4 per cent, excluding news and the reporting of local events.[96]

Dunton said the CBC was not against second stations that would provide an alternative service, but he felt the possible results should be outlined. He foresaw a probable increase in the use of syndicated (or 'canned') programs, and imported programs placed on a spot basis, with a tendency for stations to use these rather than network programs. Advertising business would tend to flow to stations carrying these cheaper programs, rather than to the stations distributing a fair measure of the national service. Since the main argument for alternate stations was increased choice for the viewers, one could offer the same justification for having two kinds of stations, one CBC and the other private. The kind of station had a definite bearing on the choice of programs the viewer would have. He suggested that even in Toronto, Vancouver, and Winnipeg the commission consider CBC ownership of the alternate station, with the CBC renting out the facilities to private program producers as ITA did in Britain; or perhaps ownership by a community group which would put profits back into live production.[97]

Stewart asked whether the government's single-service policy was adopted on the recommendation of the CBC. Dunton said CBC had put the various factors 'as we saw them' before the government. When Fowler asked whether the point had now been reached where the policy might be re-examined, Dunton said the CBC would like to see alternative service developed where economics allowed. If a substantial amount of Canadian programs were required for these stations, then the national service would have to supply them. This might amount to an hour a day, but in any case, some element of national service should be provided. He thought it would be worthwhile to use some public funds to make sure of a reasonable amount of Canadian content.

Fowler again posed the question whether the time had come for

95 / *Ibid.*, Oct. 9, 1956, 7518–27.
96 / *Ibid.*, Oct. 11, 1956, 7792–3.
97 / *Ibid.*, 7807–13.

abandoning the single-service policy. Dunton agreed that it had, subject to the considerations they had been discussing, such as Canadian content and program standards. He added, 'We think the time has come for the CBC also to have second stations in the proper places.' The CBC's interest in having its own stations in additional centres was based on a look ahead: the CBC knew that more national service would go out if it had its own transmitters.[98]

There was little comment on Dunton's proposal that the system of independent television devised in Britain might be adapted for Canada – perhaps because Dunton did not elaborate, and few Canadians understood the structure of ITA anyway.[99]

After the hearings had concluded, the commission spent a few days in Chicago and New York, but as a commission it did not travel to Britain or any other country outside Canada and the United States. Fowler himself had visited England before the start of the public hearings; the fact that he or other members did not return was perhaps a sign that the British system was not being considered for Canada.

As the Fowler Commission proceeded with its financial studies and its program analysis, observers tried to assess the effects of the evidence presented in the hearings, and to predict the possible outcome. There was fairly general agreement that the CBC had done a better job in setting forth its position than had the private broadcasters. *Maclean's* magazine wrote editorially:

Time after time he [Fowler] demanded, and failed to get, examples of the tyranny and persecution by the CBC that elicited such heart-rending screams from the private stations. Some of the examples submitted were palpably false, like the 'grievance' of a station compelled to give up a channel that it had received on a strictly and explicitly temporary basis. Others were nearly twenty years old. Quotations of CBC regulations were given with large and relevant chunks omitted that didn't happen to fit the CARTB's argument. Fowler didn't hesitate to give this sophistry the drubbing it deserved.

With the CBC he had fewer complaints. This disparity has been cited to prove Fowler's 'bias.'

It doesn't seem to occur to these critics that the CBC, as usual, made a vastly better job of putting its case. A.D. Dunton, chairman of the CBC board of governors, is one of the most persuasive advocates in Canada. ... He knows the

98 / *Ibid.*, 7814–24, 7839–40.

99 / The *Financial Post* was one newspaper that supported Dunton's suggestion that the ITV structure in Britain might be adapted for Canada. 'The CBC and its Competitors,' Oct. 20, 1956.

value of understatement. ... He seldom makes the mistake of abusing, or mis-representing, or even patronizing those who disagree with him.[100]

While the report was being written, an important political change was taking place. George Drew stepped down as leader of the Progressive Conservatives, and a party convention in December – the first to be televised in Canada – selected John Diefenbaker as the new leader. The commission would have to make sure that its report appeared before the election was called in 1957.

100 / 'Advice to private broadcasters: stop shouting – talk facts,' Nov. 24, 1956.

4 A TURNING POINT

'WITH THE PUBLICATION of the Fowler Report, we have reached an important turning point.' Don Jamieson was speaking in Halifax to a meeting of the broadcasters of the Atlantic region, but his words proved applicable to the broadcasting system as a whole.[1] Dated March 15, 1957, the report was tabled in Parliament on March 28, a day when Prime Minister St. Laurent was in trouble with opposition parties over a critical letter he had written some months previously to the CBC chairman, A.D. Dunton. The propriety of St. Laurent's action received much more attention in the House of Commons than the recommendations of the royal commission. Alistair Stewart, a CCF member, asked whether the minister of national revenue was not delighted with the Fowler Report. McCann replied, 'From what I hear it is very good.' On the same day, the prime minister said there would certainly be no attempt to introduce legislation to implement any of the report's recommendations before the prorogation of the parliamentary session.[2] In fact, Parliament was dissolved in April, and an election called for June 10.

The report of the commission won praise from unexpectedly diverse quarters. In Britain, Sir George Barnes, in an article in *The Listener* headed, 'A Classic Statement on Broadcasting,' wrote of the report: 'It is frank; it is self-confident; it is not assertive. Although it is concerned only with Canada, it will, I believe, long remain a classic statement on broadcasting, for it is more deeply thought about, better argued and more clearly expressed than any British or American document on the subject that I have read.'[3]

---

1 / Keynote address to the annual convention of the Atlantic Association of Broadcasters, carried in digest form by *Canadian Broadcaster*, May 16, 1957. Jamieson was co-owner and general manager of CJON and CJON-TV, St. John's.

2 / *Debates*, March 28, 1957, 2766, 2773.

3 / *The Listener*, (May 2, 1957), 709. Barnes at this time was principal, University College of North Staffordshire, but before that had been director of talks for the BBC and, from 1950 to 1956, director of television.

The *Canadian Broadcaster*'s summary of reaction was headed, 'Report is Favored by Business and Labor,' and quoted a 'quite favorable' statement from the Canadian Association of Broadcasters, and one from Raymond Dupuis, president of the Canadian Chamber of Commerce.[4] This body issued a press release which said, 'Generally speaking, the Fowler Commission's main recommendations appear to be in line with the Canadian Chamber's policy as expressed in its submission to the Royal Commission on Broadcasting.' As for the Canadian Labour Congress, the *CLC News* (April 1957) had this to say: 'Recommendations of the Royal Commission on Broadcasting and proposals made by the CLC and its affiliates bear a remarkable similarity. ... A preliminary study of the 518-page document showed that the Commission agreed with labour's viewpoint on many more points than it disagreed.' So two organizations, with almost contradictory views on broadcasting, felt the commission's report reflected their thinking! One could only marvel, and wonder whether a Solomon had come to judgment, or whether the Fowler Commission was speaking with forked tongue.

1 *Broadcasting as a Canadian Phenomenon*

At the outset the commission recognized that in the prosperous Canada of the 1950s, radio and television had become necessities in the home, and that their influence would continue to grow. Although all the long-term effects were hard to predict, the report suggested the national community should, by wise foresight, try to ensure that these media became, on balance, agencies for good.

In the larger groupings of the community, the region and the nation itself, radio and television may be able to perform unifying and cohesive functions for our society. They may perhaps narrow the gap in outlook between urban and rural life; they may increase knowledge and understanding of regional problems throughout the whole country; they may even make good many of the deficiencies in an individual's education by the information and enlightenment that radio and television can bring.[5]

Here was a re-statement of the faith expressed by the Massey Commission in the national potential of Canadian broadcasting, or, many years before that, by the Aird Commission and by the first prime minister to

4 / *Canadian Broadcaster*, April 18, 1957.
5 / *Fowler Commission Report*, 6.

introduce broadcasting legislation, R.B. Bennett. The Aird Commission in 1929 had said, 'In a country of the vast geographical dimensions of Canada, broadcasting will undoubtedly become a great force in fostering a national spirit and interpreting national citizenship.'[6] Bennett had said that without national control, 'broadcasting can never become a great agency for communication of matters of national concern and for the diffusion of national thought and ideals ... never be the agency by which national consciousness may be fostered and sustained and national unity still further strengthened.'[7]

The Fowler Commission emphasized that the good things broadcasting could bring would not come easily or automatically. Radio and television, it said, 'can be dehumanizing forces, tending to make all men conform in thought, action and aspiration to the lowest common denominator of their kind.' Much would depend on the leadership in both the public and the private elements of the Canadian broadcasting system.

This system, responding to special Canadian conditions, was unique. It could not be the same as broadcasting in the United States, in England, or in Australia. The commissioners contrasted a situation in New York, where seven television transmitters could reach four and a half million receiving sets – double the number in all of Canada; or in Chicago, where any of the four television stations could reach a market of the same size as would be reached by all of Canada's thirty-eight stations taken together. Aside from the factor of the widely dispersed population, resulting in much higher costs, was the Canadian duality: the fact that the Canadian population was divided into about 11,000,000 English-speaking and about 5,000,000 French-speaking people.

Even these were not the factors most crucial for the success of the broadcasting system. That was, the adjacency of the United States. 'The central, unique fact about Canadian broadcasting is that we are here in North America, a nation of 16 million people living beside a nation of 168 million which speaks the language of our majority and is rich, inventive, with a highly developed broadcasting system of its own. No other country is similarly helped and embarrassed by the close proximity of the United States' (p. 8).

The Fowler Commission restated, a little more elegantly, the central proposition of the Aird Report of 1929, that Canadian listeners must have Canadian broadcasting. 'As a nation, we cannot accept, in these powerful and persuasive media, the natural and complete flow of

6 / *Report of the Royal Commission on Radio Broadcasting, 1929*, 6.
7 / *Debates*, May 18, 1932, 3035.

another nation's culture without danger to our national identity. ... Assuming, as we must, that their broadcasting system is satisfactory and suitable for Americans, this is no basis for thinking it is desirable for Canadians.' The commission said this was not a new problem for Canada, and recalled previous responses to pressures from the United States – Confederation itself, the first transcontinental railway, the chartered banking system, the protective tariff, and the national airlines. Most of these had been at an added cost, borne nationally. 'However, if the less costly method is always chosen, is it possible to have a Canadian nation at all? The Canadian answer, irrespective of party or race, has been uniformly the same for nearly a century' (p. 9).

The effort to distribute radio and television services across Canada requires a public agency to spend the money and administer the system. 'This is an undertaking of considerable difficulty. ... No politician in his sane mind could want to encounter the difficulties and criticisms and headaches of supervising a public broadcasting system if he could possibly avoid it. The fact is that for Canada there is no choice' (p. 10). Then came an elaboration of a slogan employed in 1932 by the Canadian Radio League: 'The State – or the United States':

We cannot choose between a Canadian broadcasting system controlled by the state and a Canadian competitive system in private hands. The choice is between a Canadian state-controlled system with some flow of programmes east and west across Canada, with some Canadian content and the development of a Canadian sense of identity, at a substantial public cost, and a privately owned system which the forces of economics will necessarily make predominantly dependent on imported American radio and television programmes (p. 10).

These statements had no novelty, but they came with extra force from men who were themselves among the captains of industry and finance. They stated that the volume of advertising revenue available was not sufficient to pay for a Canadian broadcasting system. The commissioners had learned that Canadians wanted a system of their own, that they wanted to keep some part of their broadcasting fare Canadian, and that they were willing, within reason, to pay for it. What had developed was a typical and traditional Canadian pattern of combining public and private ownership in one system. And this system was not merely a compromise:

We believe it should be regarded as another of Canada's unique and positive achievements. It is, we believe, a better system for Canada than either a completely state owned system or an entirely privately owned system. In the combination of public and private enterprise, Canadian broadcasting has had variety and flexibility which an all-public or all-private system could not have achieved. ... If the union of public and private elements produces clashes of opinion and controversy within the system, it is all to the good in an institution engaged in public information and the formation of public opinion.

The general conclusion, very much in the spirit of the Massey Report, was: 'Our broadcasting system is a distinctive and valuable achievement in which Canadians can take pride' (p. 13).

2 *Thoughts on the CBC*

Under the Canadian Broadcasting Act, the CBC was charged with carrying on a national broadcasting service within Canada – but nowhere was that defined. The commission, however, was satisfied with the interpretation of the mandate offered by the CBC's chairman, A.D. Dunton. The commission suggested that, from the weight of evidence, it appeared that 'Canadians like the programme fare they are getting.' The performance of both the CBC and the private stations had a substantial measure of support, although more criticism was voiced of the private stations' programming. Dr. Dallas Smythe's analysis of the program fare, although purely quantitative, indicated a good balance among types of programs offered by the CBC to the Trans-Canada and French radio networks, and a less satisfactory balance in the Dominion network (the alternative English radio network).[8] Unaffiliated private stations had a less satisfactory balance of programs than did the network stations, public and private. In television, where network programs had a more important place than in radio, the commissioners found a better program balance than in radio (p. 63). This in spite of television's youth, and the 'perhaps excessive' predilection of English-language stations for western and private-eye programs, and of the French stations for quiz programs, games, and contests.

The commission was generally satisfied with the percentage of Canadian programs on CBC radio stations, both English and French. In television, it recognized that it was difficult to match the better American programs, but it found some evidence that on many occasions, the

8 / Smythe's analysis, Appendix XIV, was printed in Volume 2 of the report under the title, 'Canadian Television and Sound Radio Programmes.' The page references in the text above, however, refer to the main report (Volume 1).

Canadian public was listening to or viewing 'the best that can be found anywhere' (p. 68). The CBC had stimulated and encouraged Canadian creative and interpretative talent, and contributed significantly to the cultural growth of Canada. The commission took pains not to define culture too narrowly. It embraced, said the University of British Columbia television committee, 'everything from hockey and lacrosse to the Group of Seven and Andrew Allan's radio drama ... Foster Hewitt, Barbara Ann Scott, 'Rocket' Richard, are all important in developing the Canadian concept of Canadian culture. So also are Lawren Harris, Lister Sinclair, Earle Birney, Sir Ernest MacMillan. ... The development of Canadian culture is not the perquisite of a few. It should embrace the whole way of life of the Canadian people, and should offer something for everyone in the country.'[9]

In 1946, there were 977 CBC employees; in 1956, the total was 5,022. The commission found the increase was almost entirely due to the rapid growth of television. A comparison with American networks seemed to indicate that the establishment was not out of line (p. 163). Both Dunton and Ouimet, the commissioners said, were 'able, experienced and competent' – Canada was fortunate to have them. But they had the general impression that 'the development of senior administrative personnel has not kept pace with the growth of the functions and activities of the CBC,' and the general manager was overworked. There was also some confusion in the public mind about the distinction between the responsibilities of the board of governors and the operating officials of the CBC (p. 166). The greatest administrative deficiency, the commission believed, was lack of a qualified financial executive near the top of the organization.

The CBC's physical plant, they found, was something of a patchwork, and could not be as efficient as desired (p. 170). This may have been caused by piecemeal methods of capital financing, but they suspected some of it could have been avoided by better long-term planning. In the major network centres, operations were carried on in a variety of scattered locations – sixteen in Toronto, and twenty in Montreal. This jumbled growth of physical facilities for television was perhaps unavoidable, but now some consolidation in the two principal cities was necessary. That would mean new plant.

The commission regarded the CBC's commercial activities as quite legitimate. The mixture of public and advertising support had led to a more varied and interesting program fare than would result from an all-public or an all-commercial system (p. 174). Advertising had its place

9 / Quoted in *Fowler Commission Report*, 76.

in broadcasting, and the CBC when engaging in commercial activities should do so vigorously. The Fowler Commission did not agree with the Massey Commission in recommending that the CBC eschew local commercial business. Television development had removed whatever logic there had been in cutting back on commercial revenues. Where the CBC and private stations are engaged in the same type of operations, competition should be 'open and vigorous.' After suggesting a number of measures the CBC could take to increase its commercial revenues, the commission cautioned that it was not recommending the abandonment of basic CBC policies or the sudden expansion of its commercial activities. It had no desire to see the CBC become 'more commercial' or to have program production slanted to attract greater advertising support (p. 186). Nevertheless, there was more emphasis on this phase of CBC operations than in the reports of other bodies reviewing the CBC's performance, whether royal commission or parliamentary committees.

The commission believed there were great advantages in the CBC's owning and operating radio and television stations across Canada, primarily because such direct experience in station operation facilitated its task of producing a national program service. But the commissioners also felt that station operation should be profitable for the CBC – arguing that in the United States, NBC and CBS drew most of their profits from station operation rather than from network operation. CBC stations, because of their added program responsibilities, could not be as profitable as private stations, but at least CBC should know more than it did about the profit or loss on each station, and thus try to reduce the drain on the public treasury (p. 190).

As for the pattern of station ownership, the commission found the existing distribution of private and publicly owned stations 'generally satisfactory.' It did not believe that the CBC should attempt to gain complete national coverage through its own stations (p. 186).

The Fowler Commission was more critical of the CBC in its regulatory role than as a programming and broadcasting organization. The existing regulations for radio stations were minimal, and it was doubtful if they were even applicable to television stations. All of them needed review, and new controls should be introduced to require progressive improvement in the program content of some private stations. The regulations that remained in the books should be enforced; the CBC had not been vigorous enough in such enforcement (pp. 110–14).

The commission reiterated the principle that, in broadcasting, it is of primary importance that the operating agency be independent of control and interference from the government of the day (p. 276). It did not try to assess the amount of independence of government that the CBC had enjoyed in its operational and programming activities, perhaps because there had been very little complaint on this score (in spite of the CAB's references to private stations as 'non-government' stations). Further, the commission recommended that the CBC retain its paramount network position with the necessary authority to assure distribution of the program service (pp. 120, 123).

The CBC was thought 'too timid' in bringing to the attention of the Canadian public the vital function it was performing in Canadian life, and in giving an account of itself. The commission suggested that with a more careful definition of its role by Parliament, the CBC could afford to 'speak up' in a bolder public relations policy (pp. 137–8).

Summing up, the commission said (pp. 287–8) that the CBC was the central factor in the Canadian system, and that for its support public money must be spent in quite large quantities.

In the past twenty years the CBC has made some mistakes and has, on occasions, been left in somewhat impossible situations. But its mistakes have largely been mistakes of over-enthusiasm, a certain clumsiness and lack of practical experience, and a little uncertainty both as to where it was going and where it would be allowed to go. Perhaps others will think, as we do, that these are rather typical Canadian faults.

3 Assessing the Private Stations

The Fowler Commission reaffirmed the principle stated by the Massey Commission and by parliamentary committees that private broadcasters were integral parts of a single system. This understanding should be a term of each television and radio licence, and henceforth it should be accepted that the presence of private elements in broadcasting was a permanent part of the Canadian pattern. If this were placed beyond doubt, it would then be reasonable to expect a high level of performance to justify the grant to them of valuable public rights – 'higher in fact than it has been, with some notable exceptions, in the past' (pp. 144–5).

In television, the performance of the private stations did not differ markedly from that of CBC stations. During the evening hours, network programs dominated the schedule. In radio, however, the standards were much more variable. Private stations as a group offered a substantially lighter and less diversified fare than did CBC stations. What they did offer was a valued local and community service.

From an analysis of financial statements, the commission concluded, 'Whatever the disabilities under which the private broadcasters labour, they are not difficulties of financial distress and lack of profits. Of 144 radio stations reporting for 1955, 111 operated at a profit and 33 at a loss. For all stations, total net income before taxes was 20 per cent of net sales. Results were not so clearly established in television, because many stations had just gone on the air in 1955. Of fourteen stations, five operated at a loss. Of those reporting a profit, some were already showing a high return (pp. 148–52).

Of the 144 radio stations included in the study, only 100 showed any expenditures for 'artists' and other talent fees.' The average expenditure by the 100 stations for talent fees was about $18,000 per station in the year, of which $8,600 was paid by the station itself, and the rest billed to sponsors. In television, remarkably, the results were no better. Twelve of the nineteen stations included in the study showed some expenditure for talent fees, and the average expenditure for each of the twelve was about the same as for the radio stations (pp. 152–3). The commission concluded: 'We have been forced to the conclusion that free enterprise has failed to do as much as it could in original programme production and the development of Canadian talent, not because of a lack of freedom, but because of a lack of enterprise.'

The regulatory authority should play a more vigorous role in ensuring the greater use of Canadian talent by the private stations, but a voluntary improvement in program content was also called for. The commission suggested that the CAB itself give a lead to its members. This, it said, would be a 'welcome change' from its antagonistic and uncooperative attitudes to the public authority in the past.

In his speech to the Atlantic broadcasters, Don Jamieson, who a few years later was to become president of the CAB, admitted that not all the criticism of private broadcasters had originated with 'misguided egg-heads or bribed stooges of those who advocate state control.' The private broadcasters had failed to make their case with ordinary, respectable Canadian citizens. He continued:

Within this industry we have too many operators who have grown fat and complacent. They have abdicated control of station programming to advertisers and agencies and to crew-cut youngsters, masquerading as program directors. ...

Quantity has become the determining factor in most radio advertising. Consequently programming has to be geared accordingly. ... There is no other advertising medium of which I am aware, that has permitted itself to be dissec-

ted, mauled and mutilated by every questionable rating study that comes along.
...

We are not mere salesmen, or manufacturers. We are broadcasters, and, whether we like it or not, we have a serious responsibility in what has been called, with considerable truth, the struggle for men's minds.

He called upon the association to adopt an enforceable code of ethics, and he suggested that private broadcasters go along with the Fowler Commission in supporting the concept of a national system, provided to some extent out of public monies, in which the private stations would have an important role.[10]

No new departure was announced, however, until the industry saw what kind of legislation would emerge after the 1957 election.

4 A New Regulatory Authority

The biggest departure from existing policy lay in the commission's recommendations for a new regulatory authority. This was the new element that allowed the CAB and many private broadcasters to conclude that the report taken as a whole was perhaps not so bad. It did not give what the CAB had asked for, but at least it would remove the regulatory authority from the CBC.

The commissioners argued that regulation included four kinds of state control over broadcasting, and these need not be exercised by the same agency. The four kinds of control were listed as follows: (1) licensing regulations and procedures, and selection of licensees; (2) regulations of general application as to station performance and program content; (3) operational decisions and actions to provide a national broadcasting service, partly through public and partly through private stations; (4) supervision of the policies, performance, and financial affairs of the public broadcasting agency producing and distributing programs; and general supervision of the performance of private stations (pp. 87–8).

The first two, the commission said, were what are usually thought of as broadcast regulations; the last two should not be confused with the regulatory process.

The commission did not propose any fundamental change in the amount of delegation that Parliament would give to broadcasting agen-

10 / *Canadian Broadcaster* (May 16, 1957).

cies created by statute, nor in its over-all supervision of the broadcasting system. It did suggest that there were two public elements involved, and that this factual separation of powers be more precisely defined in law. One of these should be the operating agency, engaged in the production and distribution of a national program service. The Canadian Broadcasting Corporation, with 'minor' changes in its statutory powers and organization could be this agency.

The other should be a board, responsible to Parliament, to direct and supervise the entire broadcasting system. This new board would not be part of the CBC and should not be identified with the CBC. Rather, the CBC (as well as private broadcasters) should be responsible to the board. To emphasize the separation, and the new relationship, the commission suggested it be given the name, 'The Board of Broadcast Governors' (p. 91).

In spite of the attempt to make their proposal new and fresh, when one looks at the suggested composition of the board, its functions and responsibilities, one has the impression that the old CBC board of governors could have been renamed without a substantial departure from the report's recommendations. It was perhaps the CBC as an operating body that would be affected most by the new proposals, in spite of the earlier description of these changes as 'minor.' For example, the head of the operating agency would no longer answer directly to Parliament, but to the new board. There would be no council of men and women, drawn from the public in various parts of the country, to review program plans and month-to-month performance, or to supervise operational relationships between the network centres and the private affiliates. These would surely have been more than minor changes in statutory powers and organization.

But to return to the proposed regulatory board: it should be fairly large, have experience and competence in business affairs, have a broad knowledge of Canada, have sufficient diversity to reflect public opinion, and be selected from the several regions of the country. So far, almost the prescription one hoped the government had been following in its selection of the board of the CBC.

The commission suggested, however, that the number of governors be increased from eleven to fifteen, perhaps to reflect the growth in the size of broadcasting activity; and meetings should be held monthly, rather than about five times a year. The governors should be appointed for five years, rather than three; and should be removable only on a joint address of the Senate and House of Commons, instead of being subject to removal for cause by the governor in council. These proposals were intended to shield the governors from the possibility of interference from the government of the day.

The chairman of the board, in the commission's view, need not be a full-time member. He could perhaps discharge his responsibilities in eight or nine days of the month. Yet the chairman (assisted by an executive committee of the board) would be responsible for 'general supervision of the whole Canadian broadcasting system, the preparation and enforcement of general broadcasting regulations, the determination of broadcasting policy for the CBC and supervision of its financial affairs, and relations with Parliament and the public on broadcasting matters generally' (p. 97). Surely the commission did not have a realistic appreciation of the complexity of broadcasting in Canada, or else they were willing to have a system which would be run largely by public servants who would not be appointed directly by elected representatives, that is, by the government.

The commission explained its preference for a part-time chairman of the board by referring to the confusion that existed between the duties of the full-time CBC chairman (Dunton) and of the CBC general manager (Ouimet). It was true that there was a good deal of confusion, particularly in the public mind (as reflected in the commission's hearings), but surely the fact that the CBC chairman was a full-time member of the board was not a fundamental cause of the confusion that existed. It had much more to do with historical circumstances, the abilities and interests of the incumbent chairman, and the dual role of the board of governors in supervising CBC operations and the system generally.

The board of broadcast governors should be financed through votes on the annual estimates of one of the government departments, probably the Department of Transport. This would provide an annual occasion when 'parliamentary scrutiny and debate might be focused on the operations and activities of the Board to which in our opinion it can be more usefully directed rather than on the detailed activities of the CBC.' The commission was delicately suggesting that parliamentarians in the past, by their preoccupation with programs and the conduct of business by the CBC, had violated the principle that day-to-day operations should be delegated to a public authority which had been purposely placed outside the partisan arena.

Not only should the board of broadcast governors have the power to regulate and control program content, it should have the duty to do so – more vigorously, it was made clear, than the CBC board had attempted. It should do this by general regulations and, if necessary, by a specific directive to a particular station. It would be as concerned with the program performance of the CBC as with that of the private stations. (One wonders how it could realistically exercise this concern, and still maintain its distance from the CBC.) Enforcement of regulations should be entrusted to a separate branch or office under the Board of Broadcast Governors (p. 114). The broadcasting legislation should provide for penalties short of the suspension of a station's licence, through a summary proceeding in court.

The commissioners admitted, in the last paragraph of the chapter on regulation (p. 136) that the changes they were proposing were perhaps more of form than of substance:

We do not pretend that any of these suggested steps makes any fundamental change in the arrangements for regulation and control of Canadian broadcasting that have existed in the past. These arrangements have, in general, worked well and have served the Canadian people well and we believe it would be foolish to change them materially. At most, our suggestions for change may reduce possible misunderstanding of the system we have in Canada – a single system in which both public and private stations are all integral parts and which is regulated and controlled by a single public board, representing the public interest and responsible to Parliament. ... It is to be hoped that this long and frequently bitter argument about a separate regulatory body will come to an end and private broadcasters will accept their true role as valued and essential partners with the CBC in the single Canadian broadcasting system.

5 Licensing of Stations and Establishment of Networks

Under the commission's proposals, the Board of Broadcast Governors would act very much as did the CBC board in hearing applications for broadcasting licences and making recommendations to the government. The difference would be that the CBC would appear as a party before the hearings to state how the grant of the application would affect its position and argue for or against the application. Similarly, the board would hear CBC applications in public sessions, and other interested parties, including private broadcasters, would have the right to be heard (pp. 102–3). Licences would continue to be granted for five years, and before renewal the station's performance would be reviewed by the board before it advised the minister of transport. Less critical matters in licensing, such as routine transfers of shares, would not need to go to the board, and even more important licensing applications could be handled by committees of the board, rather than by the full board.

It was recommended (as advocated by the CBC board) that a statutory provision prohibit any future acquisition of more than 20 per cent of the ownership of a station by non-Canadians. But the commissioners were against any absolute prohibition of chain ownership of stations, or of the common ownership of several media of communication (pp. 106–8). The commission thought a preference should be given to the completely independent applicant, but that the regulatory authority should be able to use its discretion in deciding particular cases.

The amounts of the licence fees paid by private stations were reviewed by the commission (from $100 paid by the smallest stations to $6,000 by the largest). The commission recommended that in the upper part of each bracket, the fee be raised somewhat, and that the proceeds go, not to the CBC as was then required, but to the Consolidated Revenue Fund of the government (pp. 155–7).

Networks should be established under the authority of the Board of Broadcast Governors, but not through a licensing procedure. The five existing networks operated by the CBC (three in radio and two in television – English and French) were to be confirmed by the new broadcasting act. If a private station wished to disaffiliate, it would apply to the board. If the CBC sought a change, through adding a station to the network or dropping one, it too would apply to the board for approval. With CBC networks established, the operation of that network should be the responsibility of the CBC, subject only to the general supervision of the board. In other words, the CBC could prescribe the periods to be reserved by its affiliates, or on infrequent occasions require stations to carry particular programs (pp. 119–20).

Applications for new networks or hook-up arrangements would be made to the Board of Broadcast Governors, in very much the same way that they had previously been made to the CBC. In speaking of the statutory provisions, the commission said, 'In theory, at least, they would govern new national networks, but in practice they would likely apply mainly to various types of regional and local networks' (p. 121). The commission apparently was convinced that in the foreseeable future a national network offering satisfactory service could not be established on a purely private basis.

6 Television for the Future

The commission discussed three elements of growth in the television system as they attempted to discover whether Canadians could, or should, afford it.

First, extension of the television broadcast day. Canadian stations were on the air for an average of sixty-two hours a week, little more than half the hours of neighbouring stations in the United States. Private stations were free to broadcast as many hours as they found profitable; the question was, how fast the CBC should extend its broadcasting day. The CBC had suggested adding two hours of service per day each year until 1962, but this would cost an extra $17 million each year. The commission recommended (p. 220) a slower rate of growth, at an annual cost of about $9.5 million, which would give some increase in the network 'package,' but an even greater increase in local and regional programming.

Second, new stations for areas not served. The commission remarked on the creditable record of extending service to 80 per cent of the population in less than five years, and recognized that henceforth service would be much more costly for each thousand of population added to the total. The CBC had proposed adding 51 small transmitters across Canada, which would raise the figure to about 90 per cent. The commission thought this too costly, but believed the same result might be achieved by expecting private broadcasters to serve perhaps 24 of these localities through low-power repeater stations. It recognized that CBC operating costs would increase at the same rate under this plan, but capital expenditures would be lower (p. 223).

Third, new stations for areas that were being served – the contentious issue of second stations. The commission stated that in their opinion, the 'single channel' policy had been a wise one, and had resulted in a more rapid and more even development of television facilities across Canada than would otherwise have occurred (p. 226). But that had been an interim policy, and now there was strong public demand for the granting of licences for second stations. The commission had concluded that 'the time has come, or is near at hand' when the single-station policy should be abandoned. The question was how to do this without repeating the mistakes in radio, where some of the poorest programming was to be found among the unaffiliated stations. The economic practicalities would mean new stations for only a small number of localities – Montreal, Toronto, Winnipeg, Vancouver, and possibly Calgary, Edmonton, Halifax, Regina, and Sudbury. This small number would hardly form the basis of a second national television network, 'even on the doubtful assumption that the Canadian economy can support a second national network' (p. 228). It was desirable that second stations be integral parts of the single Canadian broadcasting system, with the same purposes and obligations as existing stations.

Nevertheless, the commission did not think it reasonable for the CBC to provide these new stations with a program service; it would involve heavy additional expense . If the CBC had surplus productive capacity, some programs might be sold at a profit to the non-network stations. (This was surely an unlikely possibility unless the CBC programs were heavily subsidized.)

How to resolve the dilemma – because, as the commission said,

Left to their own devices for providing programmes, operators of second television stations will be subject to strong economic pressures. There will be the pressure to take as much advertising as possible. There will be the pressure to obtain programmes at the lowest possible cost and, in practice, this would mean a high content of filmed American programmes and little original production or use of Canadian talent. Finally, there will be heavy economic pressure on these new independent stations to become outlets of United States networks (p. 230).

The commission concluded that the principal safeguard would have to be 'clear-cut regulations defining the minimum standards of programme performance' required of such stations. The commissioners left it to the new regulatory authority to frame the detailed regulations for any new second stations, but offered some general guidelines. If the board concluded that the level of performance would still be lower than desirable, then, the report said, 'Canada would do better to wait for alternative television service' (p. 235).

The commission said it was working under the assumption that most of the second stations would be privately owned, because the most likely locations were already being served by CBC stations. But looking to the future, it should be part of the licensing policy to authorize CBC stations in cities where private stations were now located.

7 How to Finance the CBC

In the last chapter was reached 'the main objective and culminating point of this whole inquiry' (p. 247). To buttress their conclusions, the commissioners placed in their main volume an appendix of nearly one hundred pages, the report of their financial adviser, Guy E. Hoult (p. 423 ff.).

For the fiscal year ended March 31, 1956, CBC operating expenditures totalled $44.5 million. Total income was $43.2 million, including $13 million from the CBC's commercial activities. The deficit was therefore $1.3 million, and this would go up rapidly as television expanded but as revenues from the 15 per cent excise tax on receiver sets and parts failed to keep pace. The problem was to find a new basis for determining the allocation of public funds which would be consonant with the desired rate of growth in broadcasting, particularly in television.

First, to provide for capital requirements. Until the arrival of television, and the subsequent abandonment of the radio licence fee, the CBC had met both its capital and current operating requirements out of revenues from the licence fee (including costs of amortizing the loans extended for capital expenditures). Television required a new and larger source of revenue, but the government refused to entertain the proposal for a television licence fee.

The Massey Report had recommended that capital for television development be provided by parliamentary grants – outright grants, and not loans. The government did not act on this recommendation and continued to make loans that were theoretically repayable.

The Fowler Commission also favoured grants rather than loans for capital purposes, and said it would be neither reasonable nor logical for the government to increase the amount of its grants 'merely to be able to get back the amount of the increase in the form of interest on, or repayment of the loans' (p. 267). The capital budget for the CBC should be approved and provided annually by the federal treasury, having been included in the appropriate estimates considered by Parliament. An annual examination of the capital requirements was the thing that the government and Parliament could do best, since these requirements effectively determined the course of future activities. 'This is the surest way, we believe, to carry out the intent that the broadcasting system should be directly subject to Parliamentary control and supervision' (p. 271).

The commission found that the estimated proceeds from the excise tax for the next six years would almost exactly balance the estimate of capital requirements, and it suggested earmarking the proceeds from this tax as a fund for the CBC's capital purposes.

Turning to the provision of operating funds, the commission did *not* consider that the annual voting of funds was a suitable method of financing a public broadcasting agency. This would leave the corporation 'dependent on the chance that as the estimates come up for consideration, the broadcasting agency is in temporary favour with the majority of members, or on the chance that the members are, for the moment, irritated with some series of programmes or some policy of the agency.' In broadcasting, it was of primary importance that the operating agency be independent of control and interference from the government of the

TABLE 4.1

Net operating expenditure: television and radio combined (thousands of dollars)

Year ending March 31	Forecast expenditure			Actual net expenditure
	Gross expenditure	Commercial revenue (net)	Net expenditure	
1958	$62,610	$18,372	$44,238	$47,125
1959	71,188	21,058	50,130	55,221
1960	78,362	22,600	55,762	55,877
1961	86,948	25,106	61,842	63,351
1962	93,824	26,312	67,512	74,701
1963	101,559	27,650	73,909	77,519

Sources Forecast from Fowler Commission Report, p. 263
Actual expenditures calculated from *CBC Annual Reports*

day. This was not merely a theoretical point. The history of the Canadian Radio Broadcasting Commission, between 1932 and 1936, suggested that the system of annual votes was one of the weaknesses which led to the extensive changes of 1936 when the Canadian Broadcasting Act was passed (p. 276).

It would be much better that the CBC's operational needs be assessed over a period of years, and that Parliament make provision for funds over the period through some financial formula. Then the CBC would be expected to manage its affairs within that income. In this way the CBC could make the necessary long-range operating plans.

On the basis of submissions from the CBC, the commission drew up forecasts for a six-year period, scaling down the estimates to cover what it considered the most necessary services. Its forecasts of net operating expenditure are shown in Table 4.1 and, for purposes of comparison, the actual net expenditure for each of these years is set down in the column on the right.

The forecasts included in the Fowler Report are reasonably close to what actually took place in the years 1958–63, and would have been closer if we had subtracted from the gross expenditures not only the commercial revenue, but miscellaneous revenue from sources other than parliamentary grants. The chief discrepancy arose from a slower growth in commercial revenue than had been expected, related perhaps to an economic recession in the years under review, or to a more rapid development of second stations than had been anticipated. The total of net expenditures forecast for the six years would have required public grants of $353,393,000. The actual grants in these six years totalled $347,270,000 – a figure remarkably close to the forecast.[11]

There was still the problem of arriving at a formula as a basis for parliamentary grants over an extended period. Three suggested methods were outlined. Fowler and his fellow commissioners preferred a method which would calculate the annual grant during a five-year period as a percentage of a statistical measure of national economic activity – specifically, 'the Personal Expenditure on Consumer Goods and Services.' They calculated that a share of about .3 per cent would bring in the desire revenues, with some provision for a progressive rise in the percentage to allow for future developments or expansion of the service (including colour television). Whatever formula was adopted, they emphasized that 'it should be applied by statute for the full five-year period and not altered unless some really serious change occurs in the Canadian broadcasting situation' (p. 284).

8 Assessment of the Fowler Report

The Fowler Commission produced a report that was thorough, well expressed, closely argued, and in keeping with majority opinion as reflected in the submissions made to it. It almost persuaded the contending interests to accept its recommendations as a workable compromise – but not quite. This may have been due to some ambiguity in the concept of a 'single system' which the commission did not entirely resolve, despite an ingenious attempt to introduce a regulatory board which would supervise the activities of the CBC, and yet be separate from it.

The problem was that the old system, established by the broadcasting act of 1936, had worked well in terms of practical results, but had never been accepted by the private broadcasters and their allies as fair to them. The single system depended on their co-operation, and on an individual station basis this was sufficiently forthcoming to make the system work. But the organized effort was made constantly to change the system and, as the resources of the private stations grew, support from other elements in society increased – business organizations, newspapers, local MP s, political parties.

All this was accompanied by the strong determination of the CBC – its chairman, board of governors, and general manager – to establish a program service that would be less dependent on the private stations for

11 / J.A. Ouimet explains that the Treasury Board in these years insisted on using the Fowler Commission forecasts as a basis for the CBC estimates, so the close relationship between the two sets of figures is not so surprising. Interview, Feb. 14, 1977.

its success. More than this, there was among them a growing distaste for the regulatory role, a distaste that was expressed frankly by Davidson Dunton in the commission's hearings, and that had led in 1953 to the abandonment of the attempt to enforce provisions for Canadian content in the radio programs of the private stations.

Added to this, the system had developed beyond the point envisaged in 1936. A growing number of radio stations had only a peripheral connection with the national service – they were essentially commercial operations providing a local or regional program service, and autonomous in their day-to-day decision-making. The private television stations were all within the national system because of the one-channel policy, but this situation would soon end. If the majority of second stations were to be privately owned, with the further possibility of a private network, the logic of having the CBC board of governors as the regulatory authority disappeared. With the business assumptions natural to at least two of the commission's members (and to a Liberal government in which the most important figures were Louis St. Laurent and C.D. Howe), not much time would be spent in conceiving a second broadcasting agency that would be, like the first, publicly owned.

The Fowler Commission saw, as did the Massey Commission before it, the danger in having two government-appointed boards, one to run the CBC and the other to regulate the private stations. This would be possible if the private stations and the CBC stations were quite separate, but the Canadian system had not developed that way. It would be quite a shock to the system to divide them now, as well as an expense of considerable magnitude. Canadians by this time expected a broadcasting service of their own, in English and French, both radio and television; and in 1957 they could not have this at a reasonable cost except by a combination of the existing private and public facilities.[12]

There were weaknesses in the commission's proposal for a board of broadcast governors that would be the single board in the broadcasting system, but there were even greater difficulties in continuing the pattern established in 1936, and real disadvantages in substituting a two-board system. If there were two boards, appointed in the same manner, and both responsible to Parliament, rivalries would be almost inevitable, and how would conflict be resolved except by government intervention? One board or the other would be almost certain to be regarded by the public as relatively unimportant. There would even be the danger that

12 / However, as we shall see, Ouimet was soon to conclude that the separation of public and private broadcasting could be effected over a period of time without undue strain.

one board would work in the interests of the CBC, and the other in the interests of the private stations, reinforcing the conflicts that existed, and making more difficult the task of distributing the national program service.

The central recommendation for a new public authority, with responsibility over the entire system, was therefore worth proceeding with, and the second principal recommendation, for a stable means of financing the CBC, was also eminently sensible.

Some of the weaknesses in the report have been mentioned in the discussion of its various phases. The commission underestimated the size of the job which would have to be undertaken by the new board. Part-time members would not be adequate. Not enough thought was given to how the CBC could be kept as a responsible public agency. It might become cut off from the community it served, or find itself completely subservient to the Board of Broadcast Governors – whose knowledge of broadcasting would be very limited for many years.

Some doubtful recommendations sprang from the commissioners' concern for economy. They had a tendency to regard the CBC as having developed far enough. In a country with strong regional interests, the CBC would have to develop a production capacity in most of the provinces, and the Fowler Commission put this off into the future. They talked as if nearly every CBC station could become self-sustaining, on the model of the private stations, while recognizing (truly enough) that network service was the least economically viable aspect of Canadian broadcasting. CBC stations could not always pay for themselves, however, unless they delivered a primarily commercial service, and from the standpoint of the public, what would be the sense in that? If a second commercial service was desired, it would be more logical to license another private station.

In fact, the commercial policy recommended by the Fowler Commission was at least doubtful. E.A. Weir, the CBC's former commercial manager, provides a good analysis in his book, *The Struggle for National Broadcasting in Canada*:

It is doubtful if the Commission fully understood all the implications of an intensified commercial policy – that, carried to its logical conclusion, such a policy meant little short of a new orientation. ... The salability of programs now became a prime consideration, and the thinking of the program staff consciously or unconsciously, but inevitably, was directed very largely to the production of salable programs. ... The Fowler recommendation sparked this intensified drive and was notably reinforced by the specific recommendaton of the Parliamentary Committee of 1959 which said: 'Your Committee is of the opinion that increased efforts should be made to ensure the emergence of vigorous commercial policies.'[13]

In 1957, however, it was not the commercial policy recommended by the Fowler Commission that attracted the attention of commentators. It was the proposal for a new regulatory board. Newspapers that welcomed this included traditional friends and opponents of the CBC: the *Winnipeg Free Press*, the *Hamilton Spectator*, the *Globe and Mail* of Toronto, the Montreal *Gazette*, the *Halifax Chronicle-Herald*, the *Vancouver Province*, the *London Free Press*, the *Winnipeg Tribune*, the *Montreal Herald*, the Victoria *Colonist, Le Droit* of Ottawa, and the *Kingston Whig-Standard*. Others, while not endorsing the specific recommendation, welcomed the emphasis on continued public control of broadcasting, such as the *Toronto Daily Star*, the *Ottawa Journal,* the *Victoria Times*, the *Montreal Star*, the *Calgary Herald*, and *Le Devoir* of Montreal.

The *Vancouver Sun*, the *Regina Leader-Post* (owned by Clifford Sifton), the *Lethbridge Herald*, and the Fort William *Times-Journal* (a Thomson newspaper) were disappointed that the CAB's proposal for an independent regulatory board had not been followed. These newspapers, together with the *Toronto Telegram*, would have preferred a specific recommendation for a private network. The *Winnipeg Free Press*, the Montreal *Gazette*, and *Le Droit* were alarmed about the size of the financial projections. In the *Winnipeg Free Press*, Grant Dexter faulted the commission for not insisting that the public subsidies to the CBC be devoted to 'programs with a Canadian cultural content,' rather than to programs of popular entertainment.[14]

A number of newspapers, of both political persuasions, were warmly congratulatory. The *Ottawa Citizen* considered the report eminently realistic, and said the Fowler Commission had been at great pains to work out a system that would reduce the danger of political pressure to a minimum. The *Ottawa Journal* called the report 'a warm, civilized, perceptive document addressed as much to owners of radio and TV sets as to the Government and Parliament.' The *Montreal Star* referred to the report as 'a landmark in the history of Canadian communications comparable only to the Aird report of 1929.' The *Vancouver Province* complimented the commission on the detail and close reasoning of their report and thought they were deserving of public thanks.

In *Queen's Quarterly*, George Ferguson, the editor of the *Montreal*

13 / E.A. Weir, *The Struggle for National Broadcasting in Canada* (Toronto, 1965), 312–3.
14 / April 12, 1957.

Star, revealed something of the commission's strategy (Ferguson was a close friend of R.M. Fowler). The government, he reported, had seen little need for prolonged public hearings in centres across the country. Fowler wisely decided otherwise. He had formed the conclusion that private broadcasting interests proposed to make a bold and intensive effort to invade, to weaken, and if possible to destroy the field occupied by public broadcasting. His strategy was to hear from all the broadcasters, and from a variety of less interested organizations as well. 'The strategy proved successful. The Canadian Association of Radio and Television Broadcasters were heard, collectively and individually, at almost interminable length.' If as a result of the hearings, the private broadcasters concurred in the major findings, the Fowler Commission would have achieved one of the objectives it set itself – 'to write "Finis" to the acrimonious and stultifying criticism which has been such a feature of the prolonged debate on Canadian broadcasting.' Ferguson concluded: 'The Report as a whole is an impressive document, so well constructed and thought out that it is unlikely another Royal Commission on broadcasting will be needed for a long time, if ever. ... The Report, in its central thinking, bears the deep impression left by the brief presented personally by Professor A.R.M. Lower, of Queen's University.'[15]

With so much laudatory attention, and the encomiums from both Liberal and Conservative newspapers, the commissioners could perhaps hope that, after a decent pause for the election, the new government would proceed to implement their suggestions.

15 / 'The Fowler Commission Report,' *Queen's Quarterly* (Summer 1957), 178–85.

5 A NEW GOVERNMENT, A NEW BILL

1 Party Criticisms of the CBC

Before the Fowler Report, it often appeared that two of the four parties represented in Parliament – the Liberals and the CCF – supported the existing broadcasting system, and the other two parties, the Progressive Conservatives and Social Credit, opposed it. From this divergence in party positions, some made the rough translation that the Liberals and the CCF supported the CBC, and that the other two opposition parties supported the CAB. In 1953, during discussion of the broadcasting act, one of the CCF members, Joe Noseworthy of Toronto, said of the Conservatives and Social Credit: 'The two political parties who are today supporting this amendment, through the years have supported C.A.B. just as intently as if they had been directly sent here to do that. You will find that any recommendations which have been put forward by C.A.B. as opposed to C.B.C. have had the support of the two groups which today are supporting the amendment now before the committee.'[1]

In fact, there was some division of opinion within each of the two major parties on the most desirable form of public control, and particularly within the Liberal party – to some extent within the cabinet, even more among the backbenchers. This strain of criticism of the existing system, and particularly of the CBC which seemed to personify it, grew more evident as the 1950s wore on, and CBC became embroiled in political controversy. Many of the CBC's difficulties arose from programs carried on either the radio or television networks.

A degree of tension is not uncommon between a communications medium and the public authorities, especially government leaders, because while the media give an advantage to those in office by displaying them prominently in the news, such prominence is at times unwelcome. It can be especially unwelcome when issues receive extended treatment

1 / *Debates*, April 22, 1953, 4726.

outside the news summaries and the government refuses to speak out, or does so ineffectually. By the spring of 1957 when the Liberals called an election, their nerves were frayed and their attitude to the CBC distinctly cool or unfriendly, although the tensions were partly hidden from view.[2]

Private broadcasters did not run the same risks because their coverage of national events was minimal. In general, they took their news from the wire services or they carried CBC programs; they originated very little of their own. The principal radio series they received from Ottawa (organized through the CAB) was 'Report from Parliament Hill,' a vehicle for local MPs to use in speaking to their constituencies. Between the MPs appearances, the series offered commentaries supporting the position of the private stations.

The CBC, however, considered that one of its functions was to arrange programs reflecting a variety of viewpoints on contentious issues, to expose minority as well as majority positions, and to make the public aware of issues arising as new subjects of debate. In the selection of a subject or in its treatment, the CBC sometimes offended one group or another, and MPs heard all the complaints.

By 1957 there had been numerous programs and program series that aroused public criticism; and, while opposition parties were quicker to make public protests, in the end it was perhaps the Liberal party that was more deeply wounded.

In 1951, three series of radio programs offended certain Roman Catholic listeners, Holy Name societies, and other groups attached to the church. Those programs included a series of talks by the English astrophysicist, Fred Hoyle; a series by contemporary psychiatrists; and several talks by the philosopher, Bertrand Russell.[3] About the same time, the CBC's International Service was under attack for being insufficiently militant in the politics of the Cold War. Throughout the early 1950s, commentaries heard on the national network (particularly 'Capital Report') were accused of being slanted to the left, especially the broadcasts of the CBC's resident correspondents in London and Paris – Matthew Halton and Douglas LaChance. Halton often dealt with the decline of European influence in third-world countries, and the coming to power of social democratic parties in Europe. LaChance was pessimistic about the French position in Algeria. The MPs who voiced these

2 / During the period, a few Liberal MPs spoke in defence of the CBC, for example, A.M. Hollingworth (March 8, 1955) and Elmore Philpott (July 28, 1956), but as a rule they left defence of the CBC to the minister, Dr. McCann.

3 / See Peers, *Politics of Canadian Broadcasting*, 421–3, 433–4, 436–7.

criticisms most were Conservative or Social Credit – George Drew, Donald Fleming, E.G. Hansell, John Blackmore – but their views were to some extent shared by conservative-minded Liberals. There was some resentment over the commentaries of Charles Woodsworth, editor of the *Ottawa Citizen*, particularly when he criticized the NATO policy of German rearmament (a position which later cost him his job with the *Citizen*).[4] There was criticism in the House of Commons (although chiefly in Social Credit ranks) of 'The Investigator,' a clever satire on Senator Joseph McCarthy, broadcast in Andrew Allan's Stage 54 series.[5] In 1953, there was a proposed Citizens' Forum broadcast on the report of the Currie Commission and the supposed irregularities in the Department of National Defence ('horses on the payroll'), a topic that was cancelled on the insistence of the CBC chairman.[6]

With the arrival of television, there was a dispute between the ministers in the government responsible for the CBC and the National Film Board over which agency should have control of the filmed material prepared for television. The minister answering for the Film Board, Robert Winters, had already attempted to purge that agency of leftist sympathizers, and had succeeded in replacing the government film commissioner, who he thought was not sufficiently co-operative.[7]

In 1954, the government expressed opposition privately to CBC management about a program that was intended to deal with the unemployment situation. The minister of labour, Milton Gregg, was asked to make a statement, and refused. According to Blair Fraser's report, the television program was 'mostly films of textile towns and Unemployment Insurance Commission pay lines.'[8] The program, as it happened, was scheduled at the same time that the Conservative opposition decided to stage a debate on unemployment. C.D. Howe was acting prime minister, and when he heard of the planned program, he 'blew up.' According to a *Winnipeg Free Press* correspondent sending background information to his editor, Howe 'denounced Davie [Dunton] as a Tory, said that if the C.B.C. persisted in this act of sabotage he would fire everybody, from Davie down.' Other members of the cabinet finally talked Howe out of

---

4 / Information given the author by Woodsworth, who later joined the Department of External Affairs.
5 / *Debates*, June 4, 1954, 5531; *1955 Proceedings*, 116–17.
6 / Question by John Diefenbaker, *Debates*, Jan. 29, 1953, 1434.
7 / Information from J. Ross McLean, former government film commissioner, who later joined the staff of the BBG.
8 / 'Are we headed for an Unemployment Crisis?' *Maclean's*, May 15, 1954, 9.

persisting in his threat, and the CBC refused to back down. The *Free Press* writer added, however, 'Davie is very much in the Cabinet's black books.'[9]

The year 1954 also offered the only occasion when the government refused to accept a CBC recommendation regarding the licensing of a station.[10] It will be recalled that in December 1952 the government had refused to accept the CBC's plan for its own television stations across Canada except in six locations. One of the cities that the CBC had included in its list, but where a CBC station had not been authorized, was St. John's, Newfoundland. However, on March 30, 1953, McCann told the Commons that the ultimate objective of the CBC was to have at least one station in every province, implying that it was only a matter of time.

In Newfoundland, the only city that was of a size to support a production centre was St. John's. In 1954, two young entrepreneurs who owned a newspaper and a radio station in that city, Geoff Stirling and Don Jamieson, applied for a television licence. Don Jamieson was a very popular broadcaster, and the two men had good connections with the Liberal party, and especially with the premier of the province, Joseph Smallwood. One writer on Newfoundland politics has it that 'two cabinet ministers were confidential shareholders in Radio Station CJON, co-owned by Stirling and Jamieson, which got its licence through good Liberal offices.'[11]

The CBC had received requests that it establish a television station in St. John's and, after deferring the Stirling–Jamieson application, it held one of its board meetings in St. John's 'to size up the whole situation on the spot.' A week before the meeting in June, Dunton believed he had unofficial word that the cabinet would be prepared to consider the establishment of a CBC station in Newfoundland.[12] The board made the somewhat curious recommendation that the CBC be authorized to establish a station in St. John's 'which would be one of the key centres of the national system,' but added that if this was not approved, the private application should be approved.[13]

9 / Grant Dexter Papers, Queen's University Archives, memorandum of May 23, 1954. Dunton has confirmed the broad lines of the story that was recounted (Interview, Sept. 13, 1972 and Aug. 24, 1976). In 1961, a Conservative government was equally unhappy with a television program related to unemployment. See *Debates*, March 8, 1961, 2783; March 15, 1961, 3015, for complaints by the minister of Labour, Michael Starr.
10 / *1955 Proceedings*, 284–5.
11 / Richard Gwyn, *Smallwood: The Unlikely Revolutionary* (Toronto, 1968), 135.
12 / *1955 Proceedings*, 284–5, and interview with A.D. Dunton, Sept. 13, 1972.
13 / CBC Public Announcement No. 81, June 21, 1954.

The government delayed its decision on the CBC's recommendation until October. The minister who represented Newfoundland in the cabinet, J.W. Pickersgill, secretary of state, provides this explanation:

In my opinion, there were at least a dozen better ways to spend a million dollars of public money for the benefit of Newfoundland. I knew that Geoffrey Stirling and Donald Jamieson, the owners of a private radio station, were prepared to finance a private television station without any cost to the Treasury. I went to Newfoundland to explain to a few influential advocates of a CBC station in St John's my reasons for opposing it on the grounds that the money was needed more for other purposes and that the private station would, in any case, be obliged to broadcast CBC network programs.

McCann, as Minister for the CBC, pressed their case vigorously, but the cabinet decided the issue in my favour.[14]

The government announced that the company of Stirling and Jamieson had been granted the licence.[15]

It was not until after the Fowler Commission had been appointed, however, that the public could detect important signs of strain between the CBC and prominent Liberals. One *cause célèbre* was a proposed television discussion of a controversial new book, *The Mackenzie King Era*, by H.S. Ferns and Bernard Ostry. This book had aroused the ire of some of King's old associates, among them Brooke Claxton, and after consideration the CBC program authorities, prompted by Davidson Dunton, cancelled plans for the program.[16]

The most permanent damage to their party, the Liberals thought, was through the news reports, commentaries, and other programs that discussed the pipeline debate in 1956. Members of the press gallery and other journalists in Ottawa were overwhelmingly opposed to the conduct of the government in this affair, and the CBC found it impossible to achieve anything like a numerical balance in the views expressed over

14 / *My Years with Louis St. Laurent*, 225.
15 / 'CJON Bests CBC for St. John's TV,' *Broadcasting* (Nov. 1, 1954).
16 / See *Debates*, Feb. 6, 1956, 881; Feb. 7, 911, 945–55; Feb. 15, 1196–7; Feb. 17, 1334. Claxton wrote J.A. Corry, Jan. 16, 1956, 'Neither the authors nor the publishers should be given the satisfaction of having the book purchased or read.' He wrote his brother-in-law, T.W.L. MacDermont, March 28, 1956, that he had told Dunton of the proposed program: 'I could not conceive of Dave passing on this. ... He had not yet heard of the project. It reached his desk in the ordinary course the next morning and he killed it.' PAC, Claxton Papers, MG 32/B5, Vols. 71, 81.

the air. In Parliament the Liberal resentment was expressed by a private member from Hamilton, Russell Reinke.[17]

Dunton was so conscious of Liberal ill-feeling that he advised not going ahead with a proposed press conference on television with George Drew, the leader of the official opposition. Dunton was fearful that any Liberal invited to the program the next week would refuse to take part, with the result that the CBC's 'balance' would be all the harder to defend. The program staff in public affairs sought an interview with Alphonse Ouimet, the general manager, to discuss the decision, and learned that he had not been consulted. After their appeal, the general manager, with Dunton's concurrence, decided to let the invitation be extended to Drew, and, fortunately, C.D. Howe accepted the invitation to appear in the series the following week.[18]

The Liberals went into the 1957 election campaign suffering from the opposition criticism of its conduct over the pipeline issue, and of the rough treatment the opposition parties had received in Parliament. Some Liberal members could hardly restrain their fury at the interpretation given events by the newspapers and especially by the CBC – the CBC, which many of them had thought of as their own creation, but which now seemed to have betrayed them.

On two other occasions, members of the government showed their impatience with the CBC, but it may be surmised that the pipeline broadcasts were at least part of the reason for their annoyance. In August 1956, Solon Low, the leader of the Social Credit party, complained about 'We Shall Not Be Moved,' a radio play about the labour martyr, Joe Hill. He said to the minister, 'I say you had better look inside the C.B.C. to find out those who are selling the Canadian people down the river,' implying that anyone interested in the subject of the play was a communist.[19] McCann apologized for the production, said it was not always possible to avoid errors, and added, 'Apparently there are Communists everywhere and they infiltrate into organizations of government as well as into places of industry.'[20] A Progressive Conservative member, George Nowlan, protested: 'I think criticism has gone to the

17 / *Debates*, July 28, 1956, 6626–32. In reply to Reinke, George Hees, a Progressive Conservative, said that CBC, in common with the wire services, had reported the pipeline debate fairly, and that to single out the CBC was 'whining on a very large scale,' *ibid.*, 6648. Reinke asked for copies of all scripts reporting the pipeline debate. These were tabled in seven volumes, at an estimated cost to the CBC of $1750. *Debates*, Jan. 22, 1957, 555.
18 / *1959 Proceedings*, evidence of F.W. Peers, June 30, 1959, 538.
19 / *Debates*, Aug. 13, 1956, 7553–5.
20 / *Ibid.*, Aug. 14, 1956, 7564–5.

extreme limit when we have the suggestion here that the C.B.C. apparently is an organization for the propagation of communism in this country. ... I did not want this opportunity to pass without saying that in my opinion the C.B.C. is trying to carry out a difficult task. ... Speaking for myself and I think for many more associated with me here ... we feel that the C.B.C. has done a reasonably balanced job in the work it has accomplished.'[21]

McCann later issued a prepared statement clarifying his remarks. 'I was just making a general remark about the possibilities of Communist infiltration everywhere. I do know, in fact, that the Corporation takes great care in the selection of its personnel, with full co-operation, as required, of the proper security authorities.'[22]

The final incident took place in the autumn of 1956, but it was not revealed until March 25, 1957, in a story by Arthur Blakely for the Montreal *Gazette*. Blakely wrote of the 'growing hostility' on the part of the government to the CBC, and said that after the election it planned to exercise much tighter control over the corporation. He traced the hostility back to the pipeline debates in the previous year: 'Ministers were pained to discover that they had ceased to rate a top spot in news broadcasts, with their announcements of departmental developments. They also found that they fared poorly in CBC commentaries on pipeline news. And opposition spokesmen tended to take top billings. ... Vigorous interventions from the Cabinet have been coupled with more violent ones from the permanent secretariat of the National Liberal Federation.' He referred to a 'determined bid' by Prime Minister St. Laurent to interfere in CBC public affairs broadcasting, and mentioned several other ministers who allegedly had 'tried their hands at direct intervention.'

A storm arose in the Commons, and St. Laurent made a statement in reply to a question from Howard Green. He admitted writing a letter to Dunton the previous October, objecting to the tone of two broadcasts by John Conway, a young professor from England who was at the University of Manitoba. In his talks, Conway had been critical of Canadian foreign policy as it related to areas of the Commonwealth. St. Laurent defended his action by saying that he had written, not as prime minister, 'but as a Canadian citizen.'[23]

A CCF member, Hazen Argue, asked the minister of national revenue,

21 / *Ibid.*, 7579.
22 / BUP dispatch from Ottawa, Aug. 16, 1956.
23 / *Debates*, March 28, 1957, 2769. There was extended debate the next day, followed by a series of questions to other ministers in the attempt to discover other instances of interference with CBC programming.

Dr. McCann, about representations he might have made to the CBC about particular programs broadcast or proposed to be broadcast by the CBC. McCann replied:

I am the minister responsible to parliament for the C.B.C., and ... I have the duty to make representations to the Canadian Broadcasting Corporation with reference to any matter. ...

I have made those representations as an intermediary and directly. As an intermediary I receive hundreds of letters from people throughout Canada, some of them commending programs and others severely criticizing them. Those are either passed on by my office or I take them up directly. All the conversations I have had with reference to programs and the like have been personal conversations with the chairman of the board, his general manager and his director of programs. ...

Throughout the years many of the representations which I have made have been not with reference to programs but with reference to business matters such as the buying of sites. I am continually admonishing the C.B.C. that they are too expensive; that they are employing too many people; that I think a lot of these things ought to be cut down; that their spending program ought to be curtailed as much as possible.

Let me say with reference to the C.B.C. and its development that we are away ahead of the schedule we originally started to carry out, with television particularly. We have gone ahead because of public demand, but that has required expenditures that we did not contemplate at the time.[24]

Dunton was disturbed by the implication in the first part of the minister's remarks. He wrote McCann, with a copy to each member of the board of governors:

Suggestions or criticisms about program matters addressed to you and sent to the Corporation have been considered by the Corporation just as though they had come to it directly, and given no more or no less weight because they had come in this way. I have always understood you were in agreement with this. ...

It has always been our understanding that under the Canadian Broadcasting Act the Corporation is itself responsible to Parliament for its broadcasting. Thus, in all matters of its programming the Corporation has always acted according to its own best judgment, impartially, as seems required by the oaths taken by the Governors under the Act.

Our understanding has not been that you were responsible for the CBC, or the

24 / *Ibid.*, April 3, 1957, 3005.

CBC responsible to you. ... We have noted what we thought were a number of clear statements by you of this position on previous occasions. ...

I do wish to say categorically that to the best of my knowledge and memory all decisions of the Corporation regarding programming, for the eleven and a half years of which I can speak, have been taken solely according to the judgement of the Corporation, without any sense of fear or favour. I am not suggesting in any way that the judgement has been perfect; I do say it has been independent.

Two days later (April 6), Dunton made some of the same points in a luncheon address given to the Royal Montreal Curling Club on the occasion of its 150th anniversary.[25]

Parliament was prorogued on April 12, and more immediate issues of the election campaign engaged the attention of all the politicians. Most observers, perhaps from force of habit, expected the Liberals to win handily. But during the televised coverage given to the Progressive Conservative leadership convention in December 1956, the new leader, John Diefenbaker, had made a powerful impact. Prime Minister St. Laurent was always uneasy with television, and was a stiff and stilted performer in front of a camera. Officials of the Liberal party organization were also suspicious of the newer medium, and tried to restrict party broadcasts on television to a minimum. But the free-running telecasts from the Conservative convention in Ottawa had been a revelation to many Canadians, and there was evidence that millions had watched the convention proceedings with great interest. Canadian politics would never again be quite the same.

2 *Conservative Victory*

If the Liberals, after their mauling over the pipeline debate, were cool to the CBC, for their part the Progressive Conservatives were still distrustful. For a dozen years they had championed the idea of a separate regulatory board. George Drew, as premier of Ontario and later as the leader of the opposition in Ottawa, had often tilted at the CBC. John Diefenbaker, his successor, was on friendlier terms with program personnel, and sometimes expressed his admiration for their work, both in private letters and in the Commons. But he had been one of the early champions of the separate board, even at a time when the party had not decided to abandon its earlier support of the broadcasting act of 1936.[26]

25 / Interviews with Dunton, Sept. 13, 1972, and Aug. 24, 1976.
26 / Peers, *Politics of Canadian Broadcasting*, 359–60.

More recently, he had complained of 'hog-wild spending' in the CBC, and expressed bafflement as to why the CBC with the best outlets in Canada was continually in the red, while private stations made money.[27]

Before the federal election date was set, the Conservative premier of Ontario, Leslie Frost, initiated an argument by correspondence with Davidson Dunton, charging that the CBC's newscasts were heavily weighted in favour of the Liberal government in Ottawa. As an example, Frost cited the television newscast of March 5, which included coverage of L.B. Pearson's activities at the United Nations, the visit of the minister of mines to Ghana, and an announcement from Paul Martin, minister of national health and welfare about a federal–Ontario hospital insurance conference in Ottawa. In reply, Dunton defended the selection of items on the basis of news interest, and suggested that a representative of Mr. Frost and a representative of the CBC sit with an independent and experienced newsman to examine the relevant CBC news coverage of recent months.[28] The substance of the correspondence was leaked from the premier's office to the *Globe and Mail* early in April, and Dunton responded by releasing the texts of the letters exchanged.

Broadcasting did not become an important issue in the election campaign, which centred rather on the Liberals' long period in office (twenty-two years), levels of taxation and credit restrictions, old age pensions, the government's record in maintaining prosperity, the arrogance of the Liberal cabinet, especially toward Parliament, and Diefenbaker's vision of a greater Canada.[29] In some of his campaign speeches, however, Diefenbaker charged that Ottawa's current policies on radio and television were 'an unjustifiable challenge to freedom of speech.'[30] The Liberals were attempting to bring about a one-party state, but a Conservative government would recognize the role of private radio and TV by setting up a semi-judicial board to deal with all broadcasting matters. Both Prime Minister St. Laurent and Revenue Minister McCann, he said, had tried to tamper with the CBC, and their actions threatened freedom of speech in Canada.

In the campaign broadcasts on television, the Liberals did not fare as well as the Conservatives. Aside from the fact that St. Laurent was an uncomfortable performer, the party organization decided to film the

27 / *Debates*, July 28, 1956, 6624–5.
28 / *Montreal Star*, April 4, 1957.
29 / John Meisel, *The Canadian General Election of 1957* (Toronto, 1962), 44–62, 273–7.
30 / Toronto *Telegram*, May 5, 1957.

majority of Liberal telecasts, rather than producing them live in a television studio. The effect, as one reporter wrote, was a 'hazy' visual quality as the prime minister appeared on the home screen.

On election night, CBC's television coverage was regarded as 'a fine job of reporting the best drama of the year.'[31] The Canadian Gallup poll had indicated a comfortable majority for the Liberals, but when the results were in the Conservatives had 112 seats to the Liberals' 107, although the Liberals had obtained almost 130,000 more votes than the Conservatives.[32]

A week later, John Diefenbaker took office as the head of a minority government. George Nowlan of Nova Scotia, a former president of the Progressive Conservative Association of Canada (1950–4), became minister of national revenue and the minister through whom the CBC answered to Parliament. He had also been president of the Evangeline Broadcasting Company, which owned small radio stations in Windsor and Kentville, and therefore had some knowledge of broadcasting. He was regarded as more friendly to the CBC than, for example, the minister of finance, Donald Fleming, who for many years had been the Conservative party's principal spokesman on broadcasting in the House of Commons.

Neither party had been forced to express itself on the major recommendations of the Fowler Commission. A rumour circulated that certain radio and TV interests were offering $50 million for the CBC. This brought a statement from the new prime minister that the CBC was not for sale: 'No offer has been received or will be considered.'[33]

L.B. Pearson was chosen as leader of the Liberal party to succeed Louis St. Laurent in January 1958. The nominating convention was given coverage on radio and television similar to that when Diefenbaker succeeded George Drew. A report had it that some in the Conservative caucus had objected to the appearances of Pearson on television. Stanley Knowles of the CCF reminded Diefenbaker of his objections in March 1957 to government interference with CBC programming, and Diefenbaker replied, 'There should be no interference and will be no interference with the C.B.C.'[34]

On January 20, 1958, an ill-considered challenge from Pearson to the government to resign and allow the other minority party (the Liberals) to

31 / Montreal *Gazette*, June 12, 1957.
32 / Meisel, *Canadian General Election of 1957*, 238–40.
33 / *Canadian Broadcaster* (Oct. 3, 1957).
34 / *Debates*, Jan. 23, 1958, 3666.

take over the reins led to the precipitate dissolution of Parliament and another election.[35] On March 31, the electorate truly 'caught the vision,' and returned Diefenbaker and the Conservatives with 208 members in the house. Now the party could implement its policies in every important field without fear of reversal.

3 *Level of Performance in Broadcasting, 1956–8*

During the period when the Liberals were most critical of the CBC, and while the new Conservative policy was in the making, there were many signs that the broadcasting system was functioning as well as it ever had, and that there was growing public acceptance and appreciation of its performance.[36] It may have been partly that unrealistically high expectations had been moderated – viewers had learned that not every program would fascinate them equally, and that this was as true of the big budget programs from the United States as it was of Canadian productions. One sign of the mellow public mood was the very friendly reception given the Fowler Report, and its statement that 'The Canadian viewer need not feel that Canadian radio and television is second best. It often is, of course, but on many occasions the Canadian public is listening to or viewing the best that can be found anywhere' (pp. 67–8).

An independent film and television producer, Paul L'Anglais, told the Montreal Chamber of Commerce that the CBC had gone 'all out' to give Canadians a TV network that had no equal in the United States. (L'Anglais would soon be associated with the company that became the CBC's competitor in Montreal.) He went on to say that CBC had effectively developed technicians, directors, writers, and other artists, and that some of its major productions like Hamlet, La Bohème, and Monserrat 'could be shown in any part of the world.'[37]

The veteran theatre critic in Montreal, S. Morgan Powell, in December 1957 wrote a year-end appraisal of the state of the performing arts in which he paid tribute to radio and television for training many actors, making them more secure, and contributing to the success of various theatrical enterprises. He pointed out that some 15,000 performers had

35 / *Mike: The Memoirs of the Rt. Hon. Lester B. Pearson*, vol. III, ed. J.A. Munro and A.I. Inglis (Toronto, 1975), 31–4.

36 / Early in 1957, the board of governors felt that 'public reaction in the last six months had been better than at any time in the past.' Extract from minutes of 103rd meeting, supplied by the CBC.

37 / *Montreal Star*, Nov. 27, 1957.

taken part in CBC productions during the year, and that $11 million had been paid out to Canadian talent. 'What is more surprising still,' he continued, 'is that the great majority of the plays shown on Canadian television were either written or adapted by Canadian authors, following the example of the plays presented by radio.'[38] New writers such as Arthur Hailey ('Flight into Danger,' 'Shadow of Suspicion,' 'Course for Collision,' 'Time Lock') and Bernard Slade ('The Prizewinner') made a reputation which opened the international market to them. Experienced dramatic writers, such as W.O. Mitchell, Tommy Tweed, Joseph Schull, George Salverson, and Len Peterson wrote as successfully for television as they had for radio. Many English-language productions were shown on other networks, particularly the BBC and the Australian broadcasting system. In French Canada the main dramatic feature, 'Téléthéâtre,' was highly successful, and it, too, brought along new writers such as Marcel Dubé and Jacques Languirand. In popularity, nothing could match the dramatic serials, particularly Roger Lemelin's 'La Famille Plouffe,' or 'Les Belles Histoires des pays d'en haut.' One of Quebec's best journalists, André Laurendeau, became also a skilled writer in television drama.

Some of the most elaborate (and expensive) productions were presentations of opera and ballet, though these never won the size of audience that variety and dramatic programs would attract. Nevertheless, they were important to the young companies of singers, dancers, and musicians that were establishing themselves in the principal Canadian cities. The series on the English network which encompassed many of these productions, 'Folio' (and later 'Festival') won some critical acclaim, but was also the target for those who objected to the CBC broadcasting 'above people's heads,' or 'stuffing culture down their throats.' The Vancouver writer, Eric Nicol, commented that the typical newspaper critic of TV was 'a sort of skin-diver in his peculiar element, ready to spear anything that is too deep to be caught by a six-year-old standing up to his knees in shallow entertainment.' He was amused by their occasional about-face: 'All Canadian critics fired their barbs into the CBC program Scope, for instance, including the first performance by a French mime named Marcel Marceau. Marceau went to New York where he received both popular and critical acclaim, and appeared on Ed Sullivan's program. As soon as Marceau showed up on Sullivan's program, the Canadian TV critics knew he was terrific. That's how sharp they are. They know a big fish the minute he swims into an American

38 / 'Gentlemen, the Players,' *ibid.*, Dec. 21, 1957.

channel.'[39] The most quoted criticism was of a National Ballet production by a Liberal member of Parliament from New Brunswick, Henry Murphy. He complained of 'long-haired nut boys cavorting around in tight, long underwear,' and asked when the CBC was going to stop trying to cram culture down the throats of Canadians.[40]

In programs of lighter entertainment, 'Front Page Challenge,' Wayne and Shuster, Juliette, 'Holiday Ranch,' hockey and football broadcasts all became established programs on the English TV network. The same could be said for 'Music Hall,' 'Au P'tit Café,' and sports broadcasts on the French network. 'Close-Up' with Frank Willis, 'Point de mire' with René Lévesque, and 'Fighting Words' with Nathan Cohen made each of these men celebrities. The regional interview programs, of which 'Tabloid' was an example, had the same effect. Producers and writers of the light entertainment programs on the English network were already getting offers from production companies in New York and Hollywood (Norman Jewison, David Greene, Frank Peppiatt, and John Aylesworth were examples), and some were drawn to British films or television (Sidney Newman, Silvio Narizzano, Elaine Grand).

One of the more constant critics of the broadcasting system and the CBC, the *Canadian Broadcaster*, was moved to comment:

People can say what they like about the political structure of the CBC, but no one can deny that since TV came to Canada some five years ago, its mechanics have improved remarkably. ... After five years of flubs, boobs and mistakes, the average show now has originality of idea and polish in presentation. ...

Not long ago, in the border areas, it was a common thing to hear: 'Oh, that show's on Canadian TV. It'll be terrible. Turn to something else' Now, a frequent remark is, 'Let's see what's on Canadian TV. I'm sick of American quiz shows and whodunits.'[41]

There were always large audiences for the national news on television, and even more for special events such as the Liberal and Conservative leadership conventions, or the Grey Cup and the Grey Cup parade. The biggest audience in Canadian television history watched Queen Elizabeth (with Prince Philip) open a new Parliament in 1957 on Thanksgiving Monday. Elliott-Haynes estimated the cumulative total as 7,600,000.[42]

39 / In a column for Southam newspapers, July 1956.
40 / *Debates*, Jan. 14, 1957, 167.
41 / Feb. 21, 1957.
42 / CBC internal memorandum, 'For Your Information,' Nov. 19, 1957.

These accomplishments did not bring a sudden cessation of editorial criticism. The *Edmonton Journal* (September 25, 1957) called for 'a thorough going-over for the CBC ... on the grounds of finance, good taste, entertainment value, and other aspects.' The *Regina Leader-Post* wrote (October 5, 1957): 'It is fair to say that the new Conservative government would be going contrary to the basic principles of Conservatism if it fails to seek effective ways of curbing the costly aggrandizement of the state radio and television quasi-monopoly.' It is also fair to say that each of these newspapers was associated with broadcasting interests in the same city.

It was still quite clear, of course, that viewers in English-speaking Canada, on the average, preferred to watch United States programs in most light-entertainment categories. But the evidence was solid that they wanted Canadian programs as well.

3 The Government's Intentions

In the election campaign of 1958, George Nowlan told a radio audience in Halifax that competing television stations would be permitted in various centres in the near future.[43] Prime Minister Diefenbaker followed with a more precise statement while speaking at Kenora: 'We intend to bring in legislation for a semi-judicial body similar to the Board of Transport Commissioners so that radio and television will have that justice which is the essence of our system. The time is long overdue for private stations that their cases shall be judged by an independent body, instead of as in the past by those in national competition acting as both judge and jury.'[44]

This speech, as the *Ottawa Citizen* pointed out, was in a spirit contrary to the Fowler Commission's findings, which had rejected the parallel with the railways and the concept of private and public broadcasting as equal competitors. Trying to dramatize the change in Conservative policy since the time of R.B. Bennett, the *Citizen* reprinted extracts from the House of Commons debate of May 18, 1932.[45]

The CAB was jubilant. Its president, Vern Dallin of Saskatoon, told the orgnization's members that Ottawa's recognition of the need for a new regulatory structure was due mainly to 'the consistent and vigorous information campaign conducted by your association over the years.' He added, 'Let us not forget that we are one of the biggest, most

43 / *Canadian Broadcaster* (March 27, 1958), 5.
44 / Quoted in *Ottawa Citizen* editorial, March 24, 1958.
45 / *Ibid.*, March 20, 1958.

important and influential groups in Canada and not merely a collection of individual stations meeting together once a year.'[46]

When the 24th Parliament assembled on May 12, the speech from the throne promised 'a new agency to regulate broadcasting in Canada and to ensure that the Canadian Broadcasting Corporation and the privately owned broadcasting stations work effectively together to constitute a national system to provide satisfactory television and radio services to all Canadians within reach.'[47]

Meanwhile, CBC finances were in a perilous state. Expenditures had risen as forecast during 1957 because of the larger number of stations receiving service, the extension of the microwave, rising program standards, and the effects of collective bargaining agreements with performers and staff. But the revenue received from the excise taxes had actually declined – from about $19 million for the year ended March 31, 1957, to less than $17 million for the year following. The total deficit at the end of March 1958, was nearly $5 million. Before the 1958 election, Dunton and Ouimet had to acquaint Nowlan and the Treasury Board with the situation, and try to make sure that the estimates submitted to the House would be sufficient to meet the requirements for the year 1958–9. The government responded positively, and as Nowlan told one of the members asking for an extension of CBC service, 'This government this year has provided several millions of dollars more to the Canadian Broadcasting Corporation than has ever been provided before.'[48]

CBC expenditures at this time were rising about $12 million each year, and for many Conservative MPs the costs were excessive. A Nova Scotia member, Lloyd Crouse, said the appropriations were too high for a nation of only 17 million people. Some CBC productions, he added, were very good, but others although 'lavish in the extreme' were neither educational nor entertaining.[49] The exuberant J.C. Van Horne, a member from New Brunswick, took the gloves off: 'If this government ever inherited a mess, it was when we took over the C.B.C. The whole top echelon of the C.B.C. seems to be blinded by the wrong kind of liberalism. The C.B.C. is a source of more complaints than any other branch of this government. I suggest that the government sell the C.B.C. and make it completely independent. ... So far as the men at the C.B.C.

46 / *Canadian Broadcaster* (May 22, 1958).
47 / *Debates*, May 12, 1958, 6.
48 / *Ibid.*, May 14, 1958, 65.
49 / *Ibid.*, May 22, 1958, 366.

are concerned, they seem to want to go out of their way to make the
c.b.c. unpopular and a source of irritation for many Canadians.[50]

Dunton told the board of governors that the television operating
budget was about 15 per cent over that of the year previous. Reciting
figures that he must have used to impress the government, he said that
United States drama costs were approximately four times those of the
cbc. In fact, the general range of cbc costs was from one-half to one-
tenth of us network costs. The cbc, he said, produced more television
programs than either nbs or cbs, and cbc did this with about one-fifth of
the budget.[51]

The *Winnipeg Free Press*, which had long worried about cbc costs,
had Grant Dexter send them an analysis from Ottawa. Dexter found that
the votes in the estimates corresponded closely to the budget figures in
the Fowler Report, although the capital grant had been cut, presumably
because the cbc was not ready to start colour transmission. Dexter
concluded, 'The cbc Board of Governors and the management may be
fired and the form of the administrative organization may be changed.
But the publicly-owned radio and television service is going to be generously financed ... for this year at least.'[52]

A year had gone by since the Progressive Conservatives were first
elected to office, and Nowlan was aware of a growing unease within the
cbc and among its supporters. On June 3 he found an occasion to explain
his position:

When we came into office we faced a situation in which the c.b.c. would have
ground to a full stop last October because their estimates were exhausted. ...

As a result, the first thing that had to be done last fall was the provision of a
vote to enable the c.b.c. to carry on for the balance of the year. This we did. ...
We have provided several million dollars more this year than has ever been
provided before for the c.b.c. The service is being expanded as rapidly as
possible. ... There has been criticism of the government for having made too
much money available to the c.b.c. I do not subscribe to that criticism for one
moment. ...

In the United States of America ... 55 per cent of the area, not the population
but 55 per cent of the area ... has available to it only one television station. ... In
the United States of America there are three television networks and according

50 / *Ibid.*, May 20, 1958, 302.
51 / Extract from minutes of meeting of cbc board of governors, held March 24, 1958
(information supplied by cbc).
52 / 'The cbc Gets What It Asked For,' May 23, 1958.

to the financial reports none of them, as networks, are making much money, if they are breaking even. ... We have a national network for television and we also have a French network for television. In other words, we are maintaining two television networks with a population of 16½ million whereas the United States of America is finding great difficulty in maintaining three networks with a population of roughly 170 million. I say therefore that on the whole we are not doing too badly in extending the services under the circumstances which exist today. I think it is generally recognized in so far as our radio is concerned or our radio programs, that the standard and quality of the c.b.c. will compare favourably with any radio network or any radio system in the world.[53]

4 *Nowlan's Preparations*

During this time, Nowlan had his officials considering alternative lines of policy that might form the basis of new legislation, and he was learning as much as he could himself about the complexities of the broadcasting system. In this he relied mainly on Davidson Dunton, for whom he developed great affection and respect.[54] In the summer and autumn of 1957, Dunton sent him a series of background papers on such topics as methods of financing used heretofore, Fowler's recommendations and possibilities for the future, the relation between the CBC, the government, and Parliament, the Conservative party's statements on broadcasting, the regulation and licensing of broadcasting stations, and future possibilities for 'second' television stations.[55]

Within the government ranks, there were a number of officials with experience in evaluating proposals and recommendations in the area of broadcasting. In 1955 there had been a cabinet committee on broadcasting, chaired by Dr. McCann, to consider long-term policy for television, and its financing.[56] It was assisted by an interdepartmental committee of officials, under the chairmanship of Paul Pelletier, who later became secretary of the Fowler Commission. Other members of the committee represented such departments as finance, external affairs, and the Privy Council Office. Dunton or Ouimet sat in on each of their meetings.[57]

53 / *Debates*, June 3, 1958, 812–13.
54 / Interview with Finlay MacDonald, Toronto, Oct. 1, 1975.
55 / Information from A.D. Dunton, who referred to memoranda dated July 30, August 27, and September 4, 1957.
56 / Other ministers included L.B. Pearson, Stuart Garson, Hughes Lapointe, and James Sinclair.
57 / Information from Dunton and Ouimet. The committee met five times before reporting to the minister.

Soon after the election of March 31, 1958, Nowlan asked Finlay MacDonald to head an informal committee of officials, drawn principally from the same group that had met in 1955, to advise him on policy proposals that he might put before the cabinet.[58] Finlay MacDonald as a private broadcaster would be able to bring another perspective to the consideration of the questions needing decisions. He was a friend and political associate of the minister in Nova Scotia, and Nowlan knew that, although he had been a president of the Canadian Association of Broadcasters for one year, he had differed with the association on its position expressed before the Fowler commission. In fact, MacDonald tended to support Fowler's main recommendations, although he was a Progressive Conservative and Fowler a Liberal. According to MacDonald's recollection, Nowlan also agreed substantially with the Fowler Report.

MacDonald went to Ottawa for two or three weeks and met with a committee of officials that he describes as 'having no status whatever.' A special committee of cabinet had also been established, and Nowlan would presumably use the report he received from the informal group in drafting his proposals to the cabinet committee.

The officials whom MacDonald consulted included R.B. Bryce, secretary to the cabinet, Paul Pelletier, John Baldwin, deputy minister of transport, and G.W. Stead of the Department of Finance, as well as A.D. Dunton.[59] The cabinet committee consisted of Nowlan, George Hees, minister of transport, and Donald Fleming, minister of finance.

In the discussions, John Baldwin argued the advantages of having a separate regulatory board. He was familiar with the situation in transport, where both the railways were subject to the authority of the Board of Transport Commissioners, and the publicly owned railway, the Canadian National, had its own board of directors.[60] This argument, of course, had been considered by the Fowler Commission, but regarded as less practical than its own proposal for a single board that would be somewhat removed from the management of the CBC.

On May 2, MacDonald and three members of the committee (Baldwin was not present) drew up a report that was forwarded to Nowlan. MacDonald reported that the meeting was unanimous that the type of board recommended by the Fowler Commission was the one better suited to meet Canadian broadcasting needs. The group felt that Canada had had one system of broadcasting in Canada, and a single system should

58 / MacDonald interview.
59 / Information from MacDonald and others.
60 / Interview with John Baldwin, Ottawa, Dec. 1, 1975.

continue, at least for some time to come. They rejected the suggestion that the CBC should have a board apart from the board responsible for the entire system. Neither did they support an alternative suggestion put forward that the regulatory board should consist of five full-time or 'professional' members.[61]

MacDonald believes that Nowlan shared these views, and advanced them in cabinet, but it is clear that he met opposition from George Hees, and no doubt Donald Fleming as well.[62] Fleming had been the broadcasting critic for his party in opposition; he was concerned about the level of expenditures of the CBC and advocated strict parliamentary control through annual appropriations. Presumably he did not want a semi-autonomous board, of the Fowler model, interposed between the CBC and the ministry. Both he and George Hees represented Toronto constituencies, and were well aware of the strong desire of business interests, including two newspapers, to secure a licence for a second Toronto television station.[63] Hees was a close friend of the Bassett and Eaton families, who were the owners of the *Telegram*.[64] As minister of transport, furthermore, Hees was influenced to some extent by officials in his department, who tended to favour a separate regulatory board.[65]

In a memorandum to cabinet, Hees wrote that he could not support the Fowler Commission's recommendation for a single board. The CBC and private radio stations, he said, were in a competitive relationship and the same kind of relationship was likely to develop in television. A single board would give rise to the criticism that members of the new government had made in the past as to the impropriety of having the same board responsible for the CBC as an operating agency as well as for the licensing and regulation of stations including the CBC's competitors. He pointed to the analogies in the field of transport, and suggested there

61 / Information from F. MacDonald and A.D. Dunton.

62 / Members of the cabinet from Toronto were thought to be particularly friendly with private interests. Interview with Davie Fulton, former minister of justice, June 14, 1975.

63 / Mel Jack, executive assistant to Hees as minister of transport and minister of trade and commerce, recalls that ministers from Toronto were receiving representations from newspapers and other Toronto hopefuls. Interview, Dec. 4, 1975.

64 / Grant Dexter, Ottawa correspondent for the *Winnipeg Free Press*, reported late in 1954 that there was a close connection between Hees and John David Eaton. He said that Eaton wanted Hees, who was then president of the Progressive Conservative Party of Canada, to succeed Drew as party leader. Dexter's informant was Grattan O'Leary, editor of the *Ottawa Journal* and a friend of Drew. Dexter Papers, Queen's University Archives, File 44.

65 / John Baldwin thinks Hees' memo to cabinet reflected the views of officials in the department, but suggests that the more inportant influences were the position taken by the Conservative party and Hees' own preferences. Baldwin interview, Dec. 1, 1975.

was no conflict between the CNR and the Board of Transport Commissioners, or between Trans-Canada Airlines and the Air Transport Board. Hees favoured a regulatory board of three or five full-time members, rather than a part-time board of fifteen members. Licensing should continue to be done by the minister of transport, on the recommendation of the new regulatory board. The policy should be established of permitting competition between television stations, as economic conditions permitted, the timetable and procedures for implementation to be left for the new board to determine.[66]

As secretary to the cabinet, R.B. Bryce undertook to draft a memorandum setting forth the main problems in broadcasting policy and suggesting alternative solutions. The draft was circulated among members of the interdepartmental committee that had met with Finlay MacDonald six weeks earlier. The principal alternatives discussed were in relation to the new board, who should have the licensing powers, and how the CBC should be financed. As for the new board, the first alternative was a single comprehensive board, as recommended by the Fowler Commission and Finlay MacDonald; the second alternative was a small full-time regulatory board and a separate board of directors for the CBC, as recommended by the minister of transport; and the third alternative was a single comprehensive board with a full-time nucleus. On licensing, there were two alternatives: recommendation by the new board to the government, or legislation to allow the new board to grant licences with the approval of the governor in council. As for the financial arrangements, the two alternatives were a statute every five years outlining a formula through which the CBC would receive annual grants for operating purposes; or annual appropriations, as in the case of most government departments and agencies.

Paul Pelletier, who had become a member of the Civil Service Commission, replied in a memo explaining and defending the recommendations of the royal commission on broadcasting. He suggested, that properly understood, the commission's proposals were not inconsistent with the stand taken by the present administration when in opposition. It was an

uncontrovertible fact that the vast majority of Canadians are not interested in seeing any change whatsoever made in the present system. This was established over and over again during the course of the Royal Commission hearings [when] the only people who pressed for a change were a very small but very vocal group

66 / Substance of the memo given me by a confidential source.

– a certain number (but by no means all) of the private broadcasters, some newspapers and a few chambers of commerce. What these people really want is not to be freed from what they describe as the 'shackles' of the CBC but to be freed from any kind of control at all. In fact, these people want to import into Canada the American system where a great deal of attention is paid to licences, wave-lengths, areas of coverage, but precious little to programming.

The fundamental and very serious defect of the small permanent Board is that it will almost certainly destroy the national broadcasting system. ... With this kind of organizational structure, the division between the two groups will almost certainly become more marked as time goes by and the silly quarrels which have flared up in the broadcasting field during the past several years, for from being quietened, would likely increase and become more bitter. ... In practice, I think this proposal would eventually result in playing into the hands of the relatively few private broadcasters and newspapers who would like to control broadcasting themselves.

Pelletier did not think the analogies between broadcasting and transport stood up to critical examination.

The CNR and CPR do not constitute a single national system. The CBC and the private broadcasters do. The CNR and CPR, generally speaking, both serve the same markets. The CBC, by and large, serves the national market while the private broadcasters cater more particularly to local needs. Where the analogy really breaks down is when one considers that the railways deal in passengers and freight, both of which are very tangible and measurable items. On the other hand, broadcasters are dealing in such imponderables as education, entertainment, information and the lively arts, to which it is virtually impossible to apply anything resembling a slide rule technique.

Pelletier hoped that the letter would be drawn to the attention of the prime minister, Fleming, Hees, and Nowlan.[67]

With the principal views now before it, the cabinet was ready to make its policy decisions early in July. But meanwhile, interest groups outside the government were trying to exert an influence on the outcome.

5 *Interest-Group Activity*

For several months, CBC supporters had been trying to find out in what direction the government was preparing to move. Even before the 1958

67 / Copy of memorandum from Pelletier to Bryce, June 20, 1958, shown to the writer by A.D. Dunton, Aug. 24, 1976.

election, Graham Spry, the founder of the Canadian Radio League in 1930 and a 'father' of the broadcasting system that emerged, had made two trips from England to Canada to make a reconnaissance and to beat the bushes for supporters of his position.[68] He wrote Professor Arthur Lower in December 1957 that, from his talks with important Conservatives, 'the dangers to the CBC are not those of extinction but emasculation.' The cabinet were divided among themselves. Nowlan was a strong and well-informed supporter of the CBC; Hees had absorbed a good deal of the Toronto outlook, and favoured a regulatory board along CAB lines; Fleming was most dubious about five-year grants, and wanted to cut down expenditures. The prime minister's position was less clear. Spry remarked on 'the extraordinary influence and power of local station owners in constituency and regional politics, through their impact on local opinion and the publicity accorded politicians.'[69]

Spry set about re-establishing something like the old Canadian Radio League – the small organization that E.A. Corbett headed in 1955–6 had withered away after presenting a brief to the Fowler Commission. Spry had found out that some of the private station owners liked the recommendations of the Fowler Report, and even their official organization, the CAB, had made no strong statement against it.

Spry's earlier trips to Canada (in which he combined discussions on broadcasting with work connected with his position as agent general for the province of Saskatchewan) were in the autumn of 1957 (October 14 to December 14), and in February 1958. During the height of the election campaign in March, Spry was back in London, but news of the speech made by Diefenbaker in Kenora on a separate regulatory board prompted him to arrange another visit for May. This time he decided to ask his employer for a formal leave of absence, since he proposed to stay for three months, in an attempt to have some influence on the shape of the new legislation. He had two contacts among the prime minister's advisers – Derek Bedson, Diefenbaker's executive assistant, and Merril Menzies, a Winnipeg economist whose ideas for a northern vision had impressed first Alvin Hamilton and then Diefenbaker. Spry told Bedson who was in London for the Commonwealth Conference that he would soon be asking to have a delegation meet the prime minister to discuss broadcasting policy.[70]

Establishing himself in Ottawa for the three-month period, Spry ral-

68 / Spry Papers, entries in diary.
69 / Lower Papers, Spry to Lower, Dec. 26, 1957. At this time Spry represented the government of Saskatchewan in London, England. On his work with the Canadian Radio League, see Peers, *Politics of Canadian Broadcasting*, chap. 4.
70 / Interview with Spry, July 17, 1972.

lied support from organizations that had submitted briefs to the Fowler Commission in support of public broadcasting. After meeting private broadcasters, Robert Fowler, L.B. Pearson, and others, he telephoned the minister, George Nowlan, and arranged an appointment for the next morning. Nowlan was cordial, and said he would give his support to the proposal for a delegation to meet with the prime minister. By the end of May, a statement had been drafted announcing the formation of the Canadian Broadcasting League.[71] The news was made public through a letter sent out to MPs and senators on June 11, 1958. The letter was signed by the honorary secretary of the league, E.L.R. Williamson, MBE, of Ottawa; Spry was not mentioned in it. Those listed as endorsing the league's preliminary statement included: Dr. Nancy Adams, past president, Federated Women's Institutes of Canada, Ethelton, Saskatchewan; Mrs. C.T. Armstrong, president, Farm Women's Union of Alberta, Calgary; Dr. Marius Barbeau, ethnologist, author and musician, Quebec and Ottawa; Dr. E.A. Corbett, Canadian Association for Adult Education, Toronto; Professor Donald G. Creighton, historian, University of Toronto; Merrill Denison, industrial historian, Bon Echo, Ontario; Mrs. H.M. Ellard, president, Quebec Women's Institutes; Alf Gleave, president, Saskatchewan Farmers Union, Saskatoon; David Kirk, secretary-treasurer, Canadian Federation of Agriculture, Ottawa; Professor A.R.M. Lower, Kingston; Donald MacDonald, secretary-treasurer, Canadian Labour Congress, Ottawa; Dr. John E. Robbins, secretary, Humanities Research Council, Ottawa; J.W. Wesson, president, Saskatchewan Wheat Pool; and Father Henri St. Denis, OMI, Ottawa (a member of the original executive of the Canadian Radio League, together with Corbett).

The signatories hoped that the issue of broadcasting regulation could be resolved without any political controversy 'by separating regulation from CBC management and conferring regulatory powers upon some public authority such as the Board of Broadcast Governors recommended by the Royal Commission of 1957.' They opposed a supervisory board 'such as that urged, on the United States model, by the Canadian Association of Broadcasters in their draft telecommunication bill.' Two boards would be cumbersome, inefficient, and one or the other unnecessary. They hoped the CAB would withdraw that older suggestion and endorse the principle of a single board, responsible to Parliament and free from political interference. 'Any weakening or interference with CBC network operations would injure not only the CBC as the east-to-

71 / Lower Papers, Spry to Lower, May 30, 1958.

west national influence in Canadian broadcasting but deprive private stations of most of their Canadian programmes and an important part of their income.'[72] When the letter was sent out, the names of four university professors were added to those sponsoring the statement: G.C. Andrew and Roy Daniells of Vancouver, George Grant of Halifax, and W.L. Morton of Winnipeg.

What the league hoped to do was to show the prime minister and his supporters that their often-expressed insistence on a separate regulatory board could be met without abandoning the concept of a unified, integrated system giving primacy to the national program service of the CBC. The Fowler recommendations might be accepted even by a government that had not appointed the commission. Many private broadcasters were out for something closer to the model of the FCC in the United States, but not all agreed on this position.

The CAB found that their representatives had very ready access once the Conservatives came to power.[73] Jim Allard, the executive vice-president, explains that although Nowlan was the most pro-CBC member of the cabinet, he was open to the CAB also. Allard advanced the proposal of a regulatory board with three to five full-time members, and he reports that the Conservatives at first agreed, but then concluded that it was not practical. Allard felt that part-time people were too vulnerable to political pressure, that they were too likely to be in the pocket of the prime minister or other ministers, who did not even have to say out loud what it was they wanted. Nowlan told a Senate committee that the CAB 'were very strongly at one time in favour of a small professional board, and they worked on me and urged it be done. I put it to them, did they want a small board per se, or did they want an independent board, and they said they wanted an independent board regardless of the size.'[74] By an 'independent' board, the CAB did not mean a board of the type proposed by Fowler – one that would take responsibility for the CBC and answer for it before Parliament. Although there were different ideas among CAB's members about the nature of an independent board, a prevalent notion was that the board should make only very general regulations, but whatever decisions were made should apply to CBC stations in exactly the same way as to privately owned stations.

The CAB's preparations for the hearings of the Fowler Commission had revealed that several important members supported essentially the

72 / Lower Papers, copy of league's printed statement, June 11, 1958.
73 / Interview with T.J. Allard, Ottawa, July 22, 1975.
74 / Senate of Canada, *Proceedings* of the Standing Committee on Transportation and Communications, Sept. 2, 1958, 14.

status quo. They included Murray Brown and Walter Blackburn of CFPL and CFPL-TV in London, as well as Finlay MacDonald. Taylor, Pearson and Carson, operators of a number of stations, mainly in western Canada, were (according to Allard) 'split down the middle.' Harold Carson, who had great respect for Dunton, also opposed the concept of a separate regulatory board, although he did not show the dissension within his organization publicly.

These members, and some others, were concerned about the criticisms of their organization that were contained in the Fowler report. The CAB had been chided for issuing 'much onesided or misleading information on the true nature and functioning of the present system of broadcasting in Canada.' The commission added:

It is fervently to be hoped, for the sake of the healthy growth of the Canadian broadcasting system in the years to come, that the private broadcasting interests, insofar at least as the CARTB is the expression of their collective will – we know there are dissenting opinions among them as to the wisdom of their past attitudes – will steer a different course in the future. Should they continue, however, to put their stake on devious propaganda wrapped in colourful verbiage, as they have the undeniable right to do, they should then be rebutted with clarity and vigour. [75]

In April 1958 a group of influential members of the association met in Toronto to discuss organizational matters, and especially the role of the executive vice-president. According to the United States periodical, *Broadcasting*, those attending were: F.A. Lynds of Moncton, past president; J.M. Davidson of Northern Broadcasting (the Roy Thomson interests); W.J. Blackburn of the *London Free Press*; Clifford Sifton; Finlay MacDonald; William Guild, of the Taylor, Pearson and Carson stations and, like Finlay MacDonald, a former president of CAB; and H.R. Carson.[76] The group agreed to recommend to the association's board of directors that the services of Allard be replaced with those of a full-time president. Allard was only subsequently informed of the meeting, and he immediately sent a letter to all CAB members informing them that he did not plan to resign.

Allard had a good deal of support, particularly among the smaller member-stations. D.A. Gourd, president of the French-language section, fired off a telegram, saying that if Allard were to go, so would the French-language members of the association. At the next meeting of the

75 / *Fowler Commission Report*, 139.
76 / 'CARTB's Allard May Be Let Out,' *Broadcasting*, April 28, 1958, 30.

board of directors, he asked for a vote of confidence, which he says was unanimous. At the annual meeting in May held in Montreal, none of these who had been at the Toronto meeting were placed on the board of directors (Lynds and Davidson had been members of the previous board). Vernon Dallin, of CFQC, Saskatoon, continued as the association's president, although he resigned in June to be succeeded by Malcolm Neill of CFNB, Fredericton – who was regarded as a 'hard-liner' in his opposition to the CBC. Neill's family had long-time Conservative connections; his father, who had established the station, was a brother-in-law of a former Conservative leader, R.B. Hanson.

Back in the other camp, the newly formed Canadian Broadcasting League was ready by the beginning of July to ask for an appointment with the prime minister. A delegation met Diefenbaker and Nowlan on July 18. Their representation was reinforced by a statement sent to members of Parliament by the Canadian Federation of Agriculture, and a brief submitted to the cabinet by the Council of Broadcasting Unions, a federation of six unions representing 30,000 members employed or engaged from time to time in broadcasting.[77]

The delegation from the Canadian Broadcasting League was a large one, whose members appeared as representatives of organizations with a total membership of over ten million people. The organizations included the Canadian Federation of Agriculture, the Canadian Council of Churches, the Canadian Labour Congress, the National Council of Women, the IODE, the Catholic Women's League, the Federated Women's Institutes of Canada, and the Canadian Association of Consumers.[78] The delegation was headed by Donald Creighton, a historian in the Conservative tradition, and the biographer of John A. Macdonald. After Creighton introduced the delegation and made a general statement, Spry discussed the particular objectives of their presentation. The league emphasized the single system of broadcasting, asked for a large rather than a small board, and stressed the need for independence from the interference and pressures exerted by government or by political parties.

The league supported the plan put forward by the Fowler Commission by which the CBC would be the operating public authority, responsible to the independent board. Their brief called for an early decision 'along the broad lines already so widely accepted,' and suggested this could pro-

77 / CBC internal memorandum, 'For Your Information,' July 22, 1958.
78 / Press release, Canadian Broadcasting League. CP reported a delegation of forty members, but Nowlan told the Senate committee (Sept. 7, 1958) there were 'about 75 of them from all over Canada.'

duce another unanimous vote in the House of Commons in support of a single, integrated, firmly Canadian system of national broadcasting.

Prime Minister Diefenbaker said that it was perhaps the most representative group that had ever met with him, but did not indicate what sort of bill the government was preparing. In reality, the delegation was too late to affect policy in any substantial way, although it may have strengthened Nowlan's hand in trying to preserve some of the CBC's autonomy in its network operations.

6 *The Resignation of Dunton*

While the organizational representations were proceeding, the CBC was marking completion of its television network from sea to sea – from Sydney, Nova Scotia, to Victoria, British Columbia. July 1, the date on which the connected network went into operation, was not only Canada's birthday, but also the 350th anniversary of the founding of Quebec by Samuel de Champlain. An elaborate television program, 'Memo to Champlain,' was arranged to celebrate the inauguration of the coast-to-coast network, with multiple pick-ups across the country, and with two television personalities as hosts, Joyce Davidson and René Lévesque. The occasion brought statements in the House of Commons by George Nowlan and the leader of the opposition, L.B. Pearson.

A less happy event was announced by Nowlan three days later – the resignation of A.D. Dunton from the CBC, effective July 15. Dunton was leaving to become president of Carleton University in Ottawa. Nowlan spoke most warmly of him in the Commons. He said that in one of the most difficult positions in the public service, Dunton had shown 'a combination of tact, firmness and ability which has characterized his term of office and placed the administration on a high level of efficiency. ... The high standard of C.B.C. radio and the tremendous growth of C.B.C. television culminating in the inauguration of the national microwave system on July 1 will serve as monuments to his record of service to Canada.'[79]

Although some reporters in their stories on Dunton's resignation speculated, 'Did he fall, or was he pushed,' there is no evidence that his resignation was other than voluntary. It is true that some members of the government, and the prime minister in particular, felt that too many senior public servants had become identified with the former Liberal administration. Several important officials, such as Mitchell Sharp, had

79 / *Debates*, July 5, 1958, 1907.

already resigned. But Dunton is certain that there was no pressure on him to resign, and recalls that when he made his intention known, Nowlan tried to persuade him to stay. As for his reasons, Dunton explains that he was aware of the general shape of the legislation that was in process and, while he felt that the new system could perhaps work, he did not particularly want to spend his life battling to make it work.[80]

The comment everywhere on Dunton's record as chairman was most laudatory, even in the publications that had opposed him every inch of the way. The *Vancouver Sun* (July 5) conceded that he had 'expertly guided the national broadcasting system through a period of immense expansion.' The *Winnipeg Free Press* (July 7) called his service to Canada exceptional, and said he must have been aware that 'a coming war would be fought out in wearying and frustrating battles of attrition with the enemies of the CBC nibbling away little bits here and tiny chunks there.' The *Ottawa Journal* (July 5) thought all would agree that 'Mr. Dunton was a brilliant CBC head, that his brains, temperament and civilized outlook made it a great broadcasting institution.' The *Montreal Star* (July 17) emphasized Dunton's view that the CBC urgently needed to be given some assurance of its finances over a period long enough to permit it to plan effectively.

Following his resignation, Dunton characteristically said very little, but his sudden departure caused considerable alarm among the CBC staff, who did not know what kind of system was in the making, what the CBC's place in it would be, or who would be at the head of it. Dunton's departure, although it was not the main cause, signalled rougher times ahead, a decline in morale and in the smoothness of the CBC's operation. The difficulties of the next year and the decade of the sixties did not arise as a result of the change in CBC leadership. Rather they were a consequence of rapid social and political change – in Quebec, in the country as a whole, in the social mores, and in public expectations of television. Their effects were complicated by a substantial change in the structure and control of the broadcasting system, by a less sympathetic political leadership in Ottawa, and by the increased scale of the television operation itself. Nevertheless, many persons within and without the CBC associated the more difficult times with the loss to the corporation of Davidson Dunton. It can also be said fairly that Dunton, the public spokesman, strategist, and policy leader, and Ouimet, the organizer, manager, and builder of the public television system in Canada, made a

80 / Interview with Dunton, Sept. 13, 1972.

more effective team than any who succeeded them in the next dozen years.

The Liberal leader took the occasion of Dunton's departure to press the government to announce its broadcasting policy. Pearson introduced a resolution deploring the government's failure to make such an announcement, 'thereby removing the uncertainty as to the future of public and private broadcasting in Canada.' He maintained that 'the dangers to which our cultural and non-material life are being exposed today are as great if not greater than those facing control of our economic development. Indeed, the two fears and the two results are closely connected.' The present broadcasting system had not worked too badly in practice; 'it would be a mistake if we changed our broadcasting policy so that we had two boards.' Two boards would be 'wasteful and over-lapping. On the other hand, one small full-time board ... with all the power to regulate and control might ... prejudice the national system, based as it is on the special responsibilities of the c.b.c. and the prior position of the c.b.c.'[81] Pearson declared that in general he approved of the recommendations of the Fowler Commission.

H.W. Herridge, for the CCF, complimented Pearson on his 'excellent hour and twenty minutes speech,' and termed Nowlan's speech of June 3 'the best speech made by a Conservative member of the House of Commons on radio broadcasting and television for a good many years.' He moved an amendment to Pearson's motion regretting that the government had not declared itself in support of the maintenance and expansion of publicly owned facilities.[82]

For many years past, most Quebec MP s had been Liberal, and they were often the strongest supporters of the CBC, no doubt because without public funds French-language broadcasting would have been minimal in the predominantly English-speaking North American continent. But now there was a contingent of fifty Conservative MP s from Quebec, contributing to Diefenbaker's sweep, but elected in part by the efforts of the Duplessis political machine. As premier of Quebec and leader of the Union Nationale party, Duplessis had feuded for many years with Radio-Canada (the CBC in Quebec) as an emanation of the federal authority and an instrument of centralization. The temper of some of the new members was shown in a speech by L.J. Pigeon, the MP for Joliette-L'Assomption-Montcalm. He wanted Nowlan to order strict supervision of programs of all types, and to censor them if necessary in the interests of morality:

81 / *Debates*, July 14, 1958, 2215–16.
82 / *Ibid.*, 2216–21.

There could be nothing more pernicious or destructive of the spiritual strength of the nation, than this repeated spectacle, in the very heart of the family circle, and before so many innocent young eyes of impressive scenes of pleasure, of passion and of sin that can permanently upset and destroy all that had been done to make youngsters upstanding. ...

Let the c.b.c. do away with smutty stories, and with daring costumes. ... A cleanup job is necessary. ...

Let us throw out these people with warped ideas, leftist ideas, who grab half the television programs, such as, for example ... Pierre Elliott Trudeau, Gerard Pelletier and Jean-Louis Gagnon, who should be permanently kept away from the national network ...

Let these gentlemen be replaced by people imbued with democratic and Christian ideas.[83]

Closing the debate, Nowlan indicated that although there had been delays in its preparation, the new legislation would soon be ready for introduction in the House. He did not want to leave anyone in doubt that this government was 'in favour of support for and maintenance of the publicly owned facilities in the field of radio and television.' His next statement was more puzzling: 'With every committee of the House of Commons regardless of the political party, unanimously recommending in favour of maintaining such a system, with three royal commissions recommending the same thing, any political party that would seek to depart from that would certainly not be worthy of the confidence of the people and would not get the confidence of the people and would be politically inept and politically stupid.'[84]

On the single-channel policy, Nowlan said that had been laid down by the preceding government, 'and I think properly at that time.' (This statement was certainly not in accord with his party's stand in 1952.) He added that if any changes were now thought to be advisable, they should wait until the new broadcasting legislation was in effect.

7 *The Drafting of the Bill*

Once the cabinet had taken the basic decisions concerning the revision of the broadcasting act, the usual procedure was for the clerk of the Privy Council (the secretary of the cabinet) to outline the nature of those decisions in a memorandum to the associate or assistant deputy minister

83 / *Ibid.*, 2226–8.
84 / *Ibid.*, July 15, 1968, 2263.

in the department of justice who normally attended the meetings of the legislative committee of the cabinet. In the case of the broadcasting bill, this legal officer was E.A. Driedger (who subsequently became deputy minister of justice). His task was to draft clauses of the act in accordance with the cabinet's instructions, but to make sufficient investigation of the subject area to ensure that the suggested provisions would be workable. For this purpose, he had to consult officers of the agency or departments concerned – the CBC and the departments of national revenue, finance, and transport – and refer points on which there was no agreement to the legislative committee of the cabinet for decision. In this instance, Nowlan and Hees met with the cabinet committee on legislation to iron out any problems.[85]

It seems probable that the cabinet took its main decisions in a meeting held on Saturday, July 11. It decided, for example, that henceforth the regulation of broadcasting would be undertaken by a board of broadcast governors – the name taken from the recommendation of the Fowler Commission – but, contrary to Fowler's advice, the chairman and two other members of the board would be salaried and full-time personnel.

The board would have powers along the lines proposed by Fowler, except that it was not to be charged with the management and detailed supervision of the CBC. Its powers over the CBC were to be as close as possible to those that it would exercise in respect to private stations, except that in so far as it was the regulator of networks, it would have special powers over the CBC as an operator of networks.

There was to be a separate part of the act outlining the establishment, objects, and powers of the CBC, which would be subject to regulation by the board of broadcast governors, and which would be required to secure its licences for new stations in the same way as private broadcasting companies. Licensing would continue to be a function of the minister of transport, but acting henceforth with the advice of the board of broadcast governors rather than of the CBC.

In regard to finance, it was decided that the CBC's operating and capital requirements should be met out of parliamentary appropriations, and that there should not be a statutory grant as the Fowler Commission had recommended. And to avoid prolonged debate it was hoped that the replacement of the broadcasting act could be accomplished without amendments to the radio act.

With Dunton gone from the CBC, the burden of protecting the CBC's interests in the discussions that attended the drafting of the new act fell

85 / Information from the Hon. E.D. Fulton, and from confidential sources within the government.

on Alphonse Ouimet, the general manager, and Hugh Laidlaw, counsel for the corporation. Laidlaw had worked in the department of justice until he joined the CBC in 1955.[86]

Driedger was given only about two weeks to produce a first draft of the bill.[87] During this time, the CBC tried to make the point that the regulatory authority should not be expected to supervise in any detailed way the programming functions of broadcasters. Laidlaw wrote, 'It seems obvious that no authority can exercise control of an administrative nature in the creative aspect of programming. ... It will be necessary to delineate in some pretty specific terms ... the limitations of this sort of control if the program function is not to be inhibited.' He also argued that if the CBC, like the Canadian National Railways,, was to have a board of directors responsible for its own operation, 'consistency would require the submission of the Annual Report and the responsibilities attendant thereon to Parliament through the appropriate Minister' – not through the BBG, as Fowler had recommended.[88]

Ouimet pressed for the delegation of power to the CBC to exercise authority over the operation of CBC networks. He pointed out 'the difficulties that could arise were the new Board ... to some extent ... divorced from the day to day operational aspects of broadcasting, to attempt to administer network connections, releases and so on.'[89] He and Laidlaw also raised the question of a possible conflict in the authority of the two boards on matters such as the licensing of a new CBC station, or an increase in power of an existing station. If the governor in council authorized the expenditure, would it be after or before the BBG had made its recommendation? In other words, what authority was to make the initial decision?

A memorandum for the legislative committee of the cabinet was drafted by the secretary of the cabinet, after the CBC's views had been ascertained, and the first draft of the new bill appeared on August 1. Section 10, containing a general statement of the objects and purposes of the regulatory board, was cause for alarm within the CBC. It read: 'The Board shall supervise, regulate and control broadcasting in Canada so as to ensure the provision of a varied and comprehensive broadcasting service, and to ensure the existence and efficient operation of a national broadcasting system.' Ouimet and Laidlaw expressed a concern that

86 / Interview with Laidlaw, Ottawa, June 24, 1974.
87 / *Ibid.*
88 / 'Notes Re Revision of Broadcasting Act,' July 15, 1958, memorandum drafted by Laidlaw (J.A. Ouimet Papers).
89 / *Ibid.*

this section was capable of an extremely broad interpretation that conceivably could result in the virtual control of the programming function of the CBC, and suggested removal of the words 'supervise' and 'control.' The board's power, they suggested, should be to 'regulate' within the framework of regulations which would be of general application.[90]

In the next draft of the bill (August 8), section 10 was changed to read: 'The Board shall regulate broadcasting in Canada and co-ordinate the activities of broadcasting stations in Canada so as to ensure the continued existence and efficient operation of a national broadcasting system and to ensure the provision of a varied and comprehensive broadcasting service being of a high standard and basically Canadian in content and character.'

When the legislation was given first reading in the House of Commons on August 19 as Bill C-55, section 10 had been further amended. The CBC had suggested that the wording indicate that the board's purpose was to 'ensure that the CBC and private stations work effectively together to constitute a national broadcasting system to provide varied and comprehensive television and radio service with a reasonable proportion of Canadian content and character.' In Bill C-55, section 10 read:

The Board shall, for the purpose of ensuring the continued existence and efficient operation of a national broadcasting system and the provision of a varied and comprehensive broadcasting service of a high standard that is basically Canadian in content and character, regulate the establishment and operation of networks of broadcasting stations, the activities of public and private broadcasting stations in Canada and the relationship between them and provide for the final determination of all matters and questions in relation thereto.

In later years, some dispute arose between the BBG and the CBC on the meaning of this section. Ouimet did not consider that this section was intended to give the BBG full and detailed authority in all matters affecting the relations between stations and between networks and stations. The BBG's more specific powers, he suggested, were contained in the subsequent section outlining the matters on which the board could make regulations. The chairman of the BBG, Andrew Stewart, believed that it had been the government's intention that the board have such final authority. He had been told that section 10 had been drafted after the other more specific powers were in the bill, and that the concluding

90 / Laidlaw interview, and memoranda on file in the J.A. Ouimet Papers.

words, 'have the final determination of all matters and questions in relation thereto' were added by the prime minister himself.[91]

The CBC's interpretation is supported in part by a modification that was made to the wording of section 11(a). In the original draft, the BBG was to have power to regulate 'respecting the establishment and operation of networks of broadcasting stations in Canada and the broadcasting station operating as part of a network.' In Bill C-55, subsection (a) was changed to read, 'respecting the minimum broadcasting times to be reserved for network programs by any broadcasting station operating as part of a network.' The board's powers, it seems, were to establish minimum standards, rather than to supervise detailed operational arrangements between networks and stations. This was amplified in subsection (g): 'prescribing the terms and conditions for the operation of broadcasting stations as part of a network and the terms and conditions for the broadcasting of network programs.'

According to information provided to Ouimet, it was not the government's intention that the BBG should have the power to make specific orders as to the broadcasting performance of particular stations, 'despite the recommendations of the Royal Commission'' (pp. 112 and 113, and draft section 21 on p. 413). The government had concluded instead that it was better to proceed by general regulation and perhaps by exhortation and persuasion backed by the possibility of refusing renewal of a licence.[92] It was originally their intention to allow the board to establish various categories of stations, related to revenues and other resources, for which expectations would be different; but no practical way was found to implement this, and all versions of the bill were silent on this matter.

8 *Introduction of the Bill*

By the middle of August, the government was ready with its bill. Nowlan's resolution that the house go into committee gave nothing away, except that the new regulatory board would be called the Board of

---

91 / Interview with Andrew Stewart, Victoria, June 10, 1975. He said his information came from E.L. Bushnell, who was assistant general manager while the legislation was being prepared. J.A. Ouimet has commented that the additional words probably came from the Privy Council Office or the Prime Minister's Office, but he does not know whether the prime minister added them personally.

92 / J.A. Ouimet interview, quoting from a memorandum dated July 28, 1958.

Broadcast Governors and that the cbc would continue to operate the national broadcasting service in Canada.[93] Could this be an act based on the Fowler recommendations? In his opening speech, Nowlan spoke of the commission's report as 'one of the most interestingly written reports that has ever been written by any royal commission.' He referred to the fears and doubts expressed as to the attitude this government might take to the publicly owned broadcasting system in Canada: surely those doubts had been 'dissipated before this.' He mentioned the large delegation that had appeared before the prime minister and himself, and quoted 'that distinguished Canadian scholar and historian, Dr. Creighton':

Canadian strength and Canadian unity ultimately depend upon Canada's maintenance of her autonomy and spiritual independence on the North American continent. Throughout our history we have persistently followed national policies devised to strengthen our unity from ocean to ocean and to maintain our separateness in North America. Our defences against the 'continentalism,' which has so often threatened us from the south, have been based on the east-west axis provided by nature, the strong line of the St. Lawrence–Great Lakes and the Saskatchewan. Confederation gave us our trans-continental political union. Sir John Macdonald's national policy provided the framework for an integrated trans-continental economy. A national broadcasting system can do for us, in the realm of the mind and the spirit, precisely what these old and tested national policies have done for the political and the economic sphere. A steady flow of live programs along the east-west lifeline will express Canadian ideas and ideals, employ Canadian talent, and help unite our people from sea to sea and from the river unto the ends of the earth.[94]

Pearson said it was unfortunate that the bill was being introduced in the dying days of the session, and asked that it be referred to a select committee for fuller consideration. Douglas Fisher, for the ccf, was not convinced that such detailed consideration was needed.

The Liberals, Pearson and Jack Pickersgill, outlined provisions they wanted to see in the new act – recommendations taken from the Fowler Report, and ones that had been supported by the Canadian Broadcasting League: the concept of a single system, a regulatory board responsible to Parliament that would ensure quality of service, the cbc to have the power of control over its networks, high and enforceable standards for any private network that might be formed, and financial support for the

93 / *Debates*, Aug. 16, 1958, 3651–2. At this time in the Canadian House of Commons, a resolution stage preceded first reading of a bill.
94 / *Ibid.*, Aug. 18, 1958, 3749.

CBC that would be made secure on a long-term basis.[95] Pickersgill said he wanted to see a board that would be clearly independent of the government, with a chairman appointed for a rather long term – 'what we have had in the past under the Canadian Broadcasting Corporation under Mr. Dunton, namely a board that could not be pushed around by anybody. That is what we want.'[96] It was essential that the CBC should not depend on annual appropriations: 'The best and most effective way of controlling the operations of a government department is through the financial control. But that is precisely what we do not want in this field.' Instead there should be a financial provision based on a formula that could not be changed by the government from year to year.

Douglas Fisher argued that committee consideration should not be necessary because broadcasting in all its aspects had been pretty well covered by parliamentary committees and by royal commissions. He mentioned receipt of a communication from a private station attacking the views of the Canadian Broadcasting League. He wondered whether many people realized how powerful a lobby the private stations had carried on, in co-operation with the Sifton newspaper interests, the Thomson newspaper interests, and others. He wanted to see the new regulatory board more vigorous than the CBC had been in going after the private stations for their level of performance, and he wanted to see the CBC a bit more free in its programming.[97]

Nowlan in closing debate on the resolution told the members there was no long-term financial program set out in the bill. He remembered that the government had given an undertaking to have the bill go to committee, but he hoped the house would not insist on it. The bill was then given first reading.[98]

95 / *Ibid.*, 3751–2.
96 / *Ibid.*, Aug. 19, 1958, 3764.
97 / *Ibid.*, 3757–9.
98 / *Ibid.*, 3766.

6 THE BROADCASTING ACT, 1958

THE BILL REVEALED to the House of Commons in first reading on August 19, 1958, was to effect a fundamental change in Canadian broadcasting policy – the first substantial change since the CBC was established in 1936. Indeed, the policy change was more fundamental than that of 1936. In that year the national broadcasting agency had changed in form from a government commission to a crown corporation with increased guarantees that it could act independently of the government of the day. But the Canadian Radio Broadcasting Commission (CRBC) established in 1932 and the CBC established in 1936 had similar functions, so that the 1936 legislation represented an important but still incremental change from the legislation of 1932. In each instance a single national agency was at the heart of things. Whether constituted as the CRBC or the CBC, that agency was expected to control the entire broadcasting system, including stations without network affiliation, through the regulatory powers delegated to it by Parliament. The assumption underlying both the broadcasting act of 1932 and the succeeding act of 1936 was that the public agency should predominate in providing programs for national audiences in Canada's two principal languages, in setting and maintaining program standards, in preventing foreign domination of Canadian networks, and in devising ways to extend program services to all parts of the country. The private stations, by this rationale, were to play a supplementary part, helping to distribute national and regional network programs to individual communities, and providing local program and advertising services in areas for which they were licensed.

Although nowhere clearly stated, the implication of the new bill in 1958 was that the publicly owned CBC should have considerably reduced stature, and that the private broadcasters should have a status approaching that of the CBC.[1] A new regulatory agency would be set up and, for the purposes of its regulations, the CBC and private stations would be

---

1 / Interview, Hon. E.D. Fulton, Vancouver, June 14, 1975.

equally subordinate to it. The CBC was to be limited in another way: it was deprived of independent funding, with no provision for either licence fee or statutory grant. Nor was it to be the sole operator of national networks. Since the new bill contained more explicit provisions for the authorization and regulation of networks, it could be assumed that the government expected that a private network would be formed to compete with the CBC.

Because the Progressive Conservative party had been committed for the past ten years to introducing a regulatory board separate from the CBC, no one was surprised that the bill did provide for a new regulatory system for Canadian broadcasting. What was more extraordinary was the speed with which the legislation was introduced, debated, and passed. After first reading on August 19, the bill received second reading on August 25. Committee consideration and third reading were completed the following day. The Senate proposed two amendments that the Commons agreed to after a few minutes' debate. The bill received royal assent on September 6, and came into force by proclamation on November 10, 1958.

In such a contentious field as broadcasting, the House of Commons would ordinarily spend more than two or three days in discussing even minor amendments or routine appropriations. But here was a fundamental policy change that Parliament seemed to take in its stride. The bill's speedy passage was partly a result of timing; it was introduced in late summer, when the public's attention was not so likely to be on affairs of state. The members of Parliament were looking forward to their own recess (prorogation took place on September 6). Outside Parliament, the Canadian Broadcasting League sent a delegation to the minister to protest the creation of a second public board apart from the board responsible for the CBC, and the financial provisions of the bill. But Nowlan told the delegation and confirmed in a telephone call to Spry that the minister of finance (Fleming) was adamant, and had strong support within the government. He said the bill was the best he could get from cabinet or caucus.[2]

The lack of fight in the Commons was not entirely a product of the bill's timing. It reflected a realization by the opposition parties that they

2 / Information from Graham Spry. His diary shows conversations with Nowlan or Nowlan's office on August 14, 15, 20, and 23. He also had discussions with Liberal leader L.B. Pearson, CCF leader Hazen Argue, and private broadcasters such as Murray Brown (CFPL, London). Nowlan referred to the league's criticisms and to their meeting with him when he discussed the bill before a Senate committee. Senate Committee on Transport and Communications, *Proceedings*, Sept. 7, 1958, 8–9.

had been soundly trounced in the recent election, the Liberals having been reduced to forty-nine seats, the CCF to eight. The members were also constrained in their tactics by the high regard in which they held George Nowlan, who received their representations with every courtesy, but who in effect said, 'Let's see how it works out before we make a change.' The opposition was aware of conflicting views within the cabinet, and assumed that Nowlan had worked hard to prevent the weakening of the CBC. All his statements had marked him as a supporter of public broadcasting, and he had even gone out of his way to pay tribute to the Liberal record in the broadcasting field. In neither opposition party did members want to embarrass Nowlan.

1   *Provisions of the Bill*

The new Broadcasting Act made provision for two boards, one regulatory, and the other to operate a national broadcasting service.[3] The bill was in three parts, the first establishing a fifteen-member Board of Broadcast Governors, the second an eleven-member board of directors for the CBC, and the third repealing the Canadian Broadcasting Act of 1936, and providing for a transitional period while the new act was coming into force.

The Board of Broadcast Governors (BBG) was to have three full-time members, appointed by the governor in council. One of them was to be designated chairman, and one the vice-chairman of the board. Each of the three was to be appointed for a seven-year term, and could be re-appointed for additional terms. They could be removed from office only by the governor general on address of the Senate and House of Commons – a procedure that would also be necessary for the removal of any part-time member.

The part-time members were to be appointed for a term of five years; their appointments could be renewed for two consecutive terms of office. They, like the full-time members, were appointed 'during good behaviour.' The full-time members were to be paid a salary determined by the governor in council, and the part-time members an honorarium during attendance at board meetings.

The board was to have an executive committee of three full-time and four part-time members, so that if all members were in attendance the part-time members would be in a majority. The quorum, however, was five.

3 / Canada, *Statutes*, Broadcasting Act, 1958, 7 Elizabeth II, c. 22.

The board's authority and purpose were described in section 10:

The Board shall, for the purpose of ensuring the continued existence and efficient operation of a national broadcasting system and the provision of a varied and comprehensive broadcasting service of a high standard that is basically Canadian in content and character, regulate the establishment and operation of networks of broadcasting stations, the activities of public and private broadcasting stations in Canada and the relationship between them and provide for the final determination of all matters and questions in relation thereto.

These objects and purposes were extensive, if somewhat ill-defined. But some other provisions in the act cast doubt on how broadly section 10 was to be interpreted. For example, under section 13 (4)(b), the board could grant permission for a station to carry programs from a network with which it was not regularly affiliated, but only for a period up to one month; and if that station was an affiliate, for example of the CBC, it could not be affiliated temporarily with another network, except with the CBC's permission.

The licensing procedures (described in section 12) were as under the old act, except that instead of the CBC board of governors it was now the BBG that would hold hearings and make recommendations to the minister of transport. For the licensing of new stations, the minister of transport must secure the approval of the cabinet before issuing the licence. The board could attach as a condition of licence the requirement that the station be operated as an affiliate of a CBC network. The board could also grant permission to other persons to operate a network, although it could not insist that any station join such network.

For the first time there was now a statutory provision respecting foreign ownership. Stations and networks were to be operated only by Canadian citizens, or by a Canadian corporation with at least three-quarters of its voting shares held by Canadian interests, and with at least two-thirds of its directors Canadian.

The board's specific powers included these: control over program standards, the character of commercials, and the time devoted to advertising; control over the minimum time a station must set aside for network programs if it was operating as part of a network; setting of regulations to promote and ensure the greater use of Canadian talent by broadcasting stations; authority to compel any station to broadcast network programs of public interest or significance; and authority to scrutinize all operations, including finances and programs, as the regulations of the board might specify.

As penalty for a station violating a condition of its licence, the board could, after a hearing, suspend the licence for a period up to three months, although the licencee could appeal to the courts on any question of law.

The board was to be financed through parliamentary appropriations, and was to report to Parliament through a minister designated by the governor in council. Its staff was to be employed under the Civil Service Act.

As for the CBC, it lost not only its general regulatory powers, as recommended by the Fowler Commission, but its authority over network relationships as well. It could make operating agreements with private stations, but any mandatory provisions for the distribution of programs through such private stations would have to be imposed by the BBG.

The 1958 legislation abolished the former CBC board of governors, but continued the CBC as an institution to maintain and operate broadcasting stations and networks. Under its new structure, the CBC was to consist of a president, a vice-president, and nine other directors – all to be named by the cabinet. The president and vice-president were to be appointed for seven years 'during pleasure.'[4] The other directors were appointed for three years, with the possibility of re-appointment for another term, and they were to hold office 'during good behaviour.' The president and the vice-president could be removed by the cabinet 'for cause' at any time; the other directors could be removed only on a joint address from Parliament.

The CBC held its former powers over the operation of its own stations. Cabinet approval was still required for the establishment of a station, and in addition the CBC's application for a station had to go before a public hearing arranged by the BBG (as outlined in Part I of the act).

The president was to be the chief executive officer of the CBC. He and the vice-president were to be paid a salary to be fixed by the cabinet. The other directors were to be paid honoraria during attendance at meetings. As before, the corporation could hire its own staff without going through the procedures of the Civil Service Act.

The flexibility allowed the corporation in its business transactions was increased. Under the previous act, the cabinet's approval was needed to acquire or dispose of property worth more than $25,000, or to enter into any agreement to spend more than that sum. In the new act, this figure was changed to $100,000, and the limitation did not apply at all to program material. The changes took into account the vastly increased

4 / This provision was changed as the result of an amendment introduced in the Senate. See below, pp. 167–8.

costs of television, and made it unnecessary for CBC officials to run back and forth in their negotiations for films, television series, and other contracted programs.

Except for the statement that the corporation was established for the purpose of operating a national broadcasting service, and could maintain and operate stations and networks, the act was silent as to the CBC's special responsibilities. The objectives of the *entire system* were stated in Part I, section 10, but they applied equally, it seemed, to the CBC and the private stations. It could probably be assumed that the CBC had particular responsibilities, to provide a nearly complete coverage for network programs, to broadcast in English and French, and to provide a wide range of programs meeting different needs and tastes. Yet the CBC was to be dependent on another public board in any move to extend its service through additional stations, either its own or private stations; and it lost control over the licensing of private stations that might cut into its audiences or revenues.

The act left it quite uncertain how the BBG could effectively ensure 'the continued existence and efficient operation of a national broadcasting system,' or determine all matters in relation to 'the activities of public and private broadcasting stations in Canada and the relationship between them.' Apparently the board had to operate by general regulations; it had no more authority over the national broadcasting service, the CBC, than it had over the private stations. The CBC under the new act continued to report directly to Parliament, in exactly the same way the BBG did. If the BBG attempted to act as an over-all co-ordinator of public and private broadcasting activities, the CBC could point to provisions in the act that spelled out its own powers and its own reporting line. The question was therefore open as to how much was left of the 'integrated, single system' which had never been formally renounced.

The creation of two separate boards, and the uncertain relation between them, marked one important departure from the recommendations of the Fowler Commission. The other principal reversal of the commission's recommendations was in respect to CBC financing. Under the new act, the CBC was to be financed by direct annual appropriations, in respect to both operations and capital needs. Its budgets were to be approved by the cabinet on the recommendation of the designated minister and the minister of finance (who was also chairman of the Treasury Board). The only concession to the idea of a secure source of income for a period of years was in a provision, under section 35, that the CBC should submit, each fifth year, a five-year capital program for approval by the cabinet, 'together with a forecast of the effect of the program on the Corporation's operating requirements.' But this procedure had no binding effect on any yearly appropriation.

Under the 1958 legislation, the CBC did not have the independence from government that it had when it was assured proceeds from radio licences, or that it had under the statutory arrangements enacted following the Massey Report. The Diefenbaker government, wishing to hold in check the expenditures of the CBC, deliberately refrained from adopting the Fowler Commission's recommendation that a formula should be set to provide the CBC's operational requirements for a five-year period. Because of tradition, and of understood 'rules of the game' that applied to the CBC and other crown corporations, the CBC continued to act in accordance with its own judgment with respect to programming decisions, the letting of contracts, and so forth. But the possibility was always there that the government would try to exert pressure. Dependence on an appropriation voted annually would leave the CBC ever-anxious, and that too may have been what the government intended.

2   *Debate in the Commons and Senate*

When Nowlan moved second reading on August 25, his short speech suggested that the legislation had been favourably received almost everywhere. He said it created 'a framework and nothing else' which divorced the operating and regulatory functions, as had been promised. He argued that because there did not seem to be objections to the bill in principle, any consideration by a select committee might better be left for another session. He reminded the House that there had been a long period of investigation and discussion; now it was only necessary to pass the legislation and thus remove uncertainty.[5]

Nowlan's reference to general acceptance of the bill in the press was based on a somewhat selective reading of editorials. Most newspapers did give cautious approval, but a number of them, including the *Montreal Star*, the *Ottawa Journal*, the *Ottawa Citizen*, and the *Toronto Star*, urged that Parliament should not act with undue haste, and should give the bill a thorough examination. Indeed, the *Toronto Star*'s editorial (August 20) was headed, 'Weak Bill for Broadcasting.'

Through Nowlan's frequent references to the Fowler Commission in his statements to the House, he left the impression that the government's bill was carrying out the principal recommendations of the Fowler Report, and that it differed only in less essential details. Even the

5 / *Debates*, Aug. 25, 1958, 4044–6.

Ottawa Citizen wrote on August 20, 'The bill itself follows in essentials the recommendations of the Fowler commission.' Three days later the associate editor, Frank Swanson, in a signed column tried to correct this impression.

In spite of criticisms made in the Commons by Pearson and Pickersgill, the impression persisted that the Fowler Report was the main inspiration for the bill. For example, Donald Cameron, independent Liberal senator from Alberta, said on August 28, 'Unquestionably from the administrative point of view, two boards functioning in such closely related fields are cumbersome and clumsy. Nevertheless this was the recommendation of the Fowler Commission.'[6] In some degree, the Fowler Report itself may have contributed to the confusion in men's minds. Nowhere did it contain any summary of recommendations, as was to be found in the Massey Report, for example. It was therefore difficult for legislators and others to check the recommendations one by one, and to discover which had been followed and which changed or ignored. It is true that the Fowler Report contained a draft bill, but few would go through the exercise of comparing the legislation, clause by clause.

Nowlan's impression that the bill was receiving general acceptance was probably based on the responses within the broadcasting community. The majority of the private broadcasters, and the CAB, had won the 'independent regulatory board' they had so long sought. The CBC was mollified by the changes in the draft bill that were thought to safeguard its position as a national program service.[7] And in spite of the misgivings of some supporters, such as Eldon Wilcox of the Council of Broadcasting Unions, the Canadian Broadcasting League decided to accept Nowlan's word that this was the best bill he could get, and to heed his advice that an attempt to apply further pressure might result in something being lost.

After Nowlan had made his brief statement in the Commons, Pearson made a lengthy speech which was obviously the result of a careful briefing. He mentioned again the importance of broadcasting for national development: 'In no sector of our national life more than in the field of broadcasting is there a greater and more continuing need for strong and independent public service and public control.' He recalled that the broadcasting acts of 1932 and 1936 had each received detailed

6 / Senate, *Debates*, Aug. 28, 1958, 725.
7 / Spry's diary for Aug. 19–20, 1958, reports that Donald Manson, former general manager of the CBC, and Hugh Laidlaw, CBC legal counsel, both considered that it was a 'good bill,' because 'position saved.'

study by Commons committees with dozens of witnesses appearing before them to give evidence. He spoke of the never-ceasing pressures from private interests, and recalled Bennett's warnings in 1936, of the broadcasting system coming 'under the power of the government,' and of the pressures from private broadcasters.[8] Over the years, Pearson said, we had become careless in maintaining the accepted doctrine of public control. 'What was at once, for instance ... a privilege for private broadcasters had gradually become a vested interest and eventually has been invoked as a right. As soon as this privilege could be put forward in public discussion as a right, which of course it was not, then the position of the c.b.c., the public corporation, could be attacked on the ground that the public agency was at the same time a judge and competitor. ... Those stations did not have separate rights to claim but rights which were merely an extension and complement of the national system'[9]

Pearson found three major defects in the bill. It would tend to create two national broadcasting syetems rather than one. Its administrative set-up was cumbersome. And it weakened the Canadian Broadcasting Corporation.

Section 10 of the bill mentioned the continued existence and efficient operation of the national broadcasting system as an aim and objective of the new regulatory body, but Pearson feared the bill would have the opposite effect. The CBC, although subject to the general regulations of the BBG, would not report to that body, but through its own minister to Parliament, and it would be conducting its activities separately. For their part, the private stations would now appear as equals with the public sector of broadcasting. The new board would regulate their separate activities and their relationship. This board would report to Parliament through its minister independently of the CBC board. While there was an attempt in the legislation to assign equal rights to the two elements in the broadcasting system, in fact they did not have the same purposes or equal responsibilities.

The CBC, Pearson agreed, had not always exercised adequate control over the private stations. But would the new board do better? Would it not have as a major consideration the financial problems and costs when determining the program standards? In its attempt to apply uniform standards, it would probably fit them to 'the financial situation of the weakest private station, even if it is part of a c.b.c. network and is subsidized in the same way as now happens by the c.b.c.'[10]

8 / Bennett's warnings were in *Debates*, June 15, 1936, 3710.
9 / *Ibid.*, Aug. 25, 1958, 4049.
10 / *Ibid.*, 4050.

Pearson forecast that the new board would 'tend to become a regulatory body for private stations only, influenced increasingly by the financial situation of those private stations.'

The second basic weakness was that the bill provided for two boards of a generally comparable character. 'If these two boards do not get into each other's way, or indeed into each other's hair, with resulting confusion and conflict, it will be because one of them – more likely perhaps the c.b.c. board – will become more or less useless.'[11]

The third weakness was that the bill would seriously weaken the CBC. It did not give the CBC clear control of its own networks. It might prevent it from getting the channels it needed, since the power to recommend on this went to the other board. And not only would the CBC be subject to the general regulations of the BBG, but it would have to submit its activities for approval to the responsible minister, the minister of finance, the government, and finally to Parliament. 'It will readily be seen that in this procedure there will be opportunities to restrict the c.b.c.'s activities, to discourage leadership and enterprise within the c.b.c. and to tamper with its independence.'[12]

The CBC, Pearson believed, would now be more than ever exposed to the possibility of political interference. In the past, the operating personnel, from the general manager down, had been insulated from direct political pressure and interference by the presence of a board of governors and a full-time chairman. By the terms of the new legislation, the senior executive of the corporation would be the president, who would also function as chairman of the board of directors. This would mean that government ministers would deal directly with the senior operating officer of the corporation, instead of with a chairman removed from day-to-day operation. The new board, consequently, would no longer be able to act, as it did formerly, as a protective shield for those who developed and produced programs.

Finally, the CBC would be weakened by the financial provisions of the bill. The Fowler Commission had recommended a high degree of financial independence, and had suggested three possible methods of financing, 'designed to preserve the prerogatives of parliament, to maintain the independence of the c.b.c. and to meet the need of the corporation for funds.' The government had rejected all of these. The CBC would now have to depend on the discretion of the minister of finance and other ministers. Under a government 'not too enthusiastic about the c.b.c.' the power of the purse could be used annually to impose the views of

11 / *Ibid.*, 4051.
12 / *Ibid.*, 4052.

government 'in a field where this kind of interference could be damaging to the right of the people to be informed objectively.'[13]

Pearson criticized the manner in which the president and vice-president of the CBC were to be appointed. In the BBG, the three full-time members would be secure from any threat of sudden dismissal, and with their powers they were likely to become 'the czars of broadcasting in Canada.' In the CBC, the president and vice-president were to hold office 'during pleasure for a period of seven years.' They could be removed almost at whim.

Having offered such fundamental criticisms, Pearson announced that his party would vote against the second reading of the bill.

Pickersgill complained that the bill did not live up to advance notices, and that Nowlan had 'misled me ... and a good many others in the country into thinking what the government was going to do was substantially to implement the recommendations of the Fowler report.' The bill would result in a mixed system 'where nobody is to blame and where nobody has clear responsibility. Who is going to govern the C.B.C. if this bill is adopted; the board of broadcast governors, as Fowler recommends; or this board of directors ... or the minister to whom the board of directors and the C.B.C. would be responsible?'[14]

For the CCF, Douglas Fisher offered a much milder criticism of the bill, and said again that his group did not want a special committee at this stage of the session. He felt, with the Fowler Commission, that the CBC should report to the BBG. Mainly, he wanted 'more guidance from Ministers about interpretation of the bill,' and 'assurance from the government at this time, in this debate, that they agree the bill is not a victory for the private broadcasters but that it represents a victory for national broadcasting in the public interest.'[15]

Before the vote on second reading, Nowlan replied to the Liberal criticisms that in providing for an independent regulatory board, 'This bill simply carries out one of the main fundamental recommendations of the Fowler commission, and a fundamental policy of this party through the years.' The government had done nothing whatsoever to interfere with the CBC as an operating unit: 'let us not have any nonsense on that score whatsoever. The C.B.C. still has its own network; the C.B.C. still operates that network and the C.B.C. will continue to do so.' In his 'able and careful speech,' the leader of the opposition had only been able to express 'forebodings.' The only material point seemed to be that the CBC

13 / *Ibid.*, 4053.
14 / *Ibid.*, 4071.
15 / *Ibid.*, 4055–8.

would report to Parliament and not to the board. Did that make any great difference? Reporting through the board would not insulate the cbc from parliamentary criticism. Members could always use the report of the bbg as the basis for talking about or criticizing the cbc. So the cbc might as well report directly.

On the matter of supplying funds through annual appropriations, Nowlan said that during all the years the Liberals were in office, the cbc's estimates were submitted to the Treasury Board after having been recommended and approved by the minister of finance. Pickersgill, to set the record straight, interjected: 'Only in the last two years. ... That is precisely why we appointed a royal commission.' Nowlan said that in any event there had been loans and grants since 1954. This bill merely faced the situation realistically, that the cbc would continue to require substantial funds, and it maintained the supremacy of Parliament.[16]

Nowlan defended the two-board system by saying that the Board of Broadcast Governors was to be the overriding agency, and that there was no thought of 'destroying the single system, or anything of that kind.' He was convinced that when the bill was passed 'the c.b.c. will find itself in a stronger position than ever before' because the criticism that had originated with the private stations would be removed. The bill would solve 'this fundamental problem which has bedevilled broadcasting for fifteen years.'[17]

Douglas Fisher announced that the ccf group would vote with the government. He said it would be too damaging to open up six or eight months of propaganda and warfare. Twenty-five votes were cast for the Liberal resolution of giving the bill a six-months hoist, and 122 votes against.[18] Before the final vote on second reading, Nowlan denied once again that the bill would result in government control of the cbc. 'This great public agency, whose worth and the need and necessity for whose independence I appreciate just as much as any man sitting on the other side of the house or any man in Canada, will be preserved and maintained.'[19]

Consideration of the clauses of the bill proceeded immediately in committee of the whole, and was finished the following day. In spite of Liberal objections, no change was made in the provision that the cbc president and vice-president were to hold office 'during pleasure.' Nor would the government agree that they should be appointed on the

16 / *Ibid.*, 4073–6.
17 / *Ibid.*, 4077.
18 / *Ibid.*, 4080.
19 / *Ibid.*, 4089.

recommendation of the Board of Broadcast Governors, and that the provision be eliminated for nine other CBC directors. Nowlan argued that with a separate board of directors, the CBC would be better insulated from political pressure. He added, 'I at least want the committee to give us an opportunity to try it and see how it works. We can then change it if it should be necessary.'[20] The Conservative majority also voted down an amendment which would have had the CBC report to the Board of Broadcast Governors rather than to Parliament. Nowlan explained again that he could not accept any suggestion for a change in the method of financing the CBC – that insistence on annual appropriations was a matter of government policy.

CCF members, quoting a press release from the Canadian Broadcasting League, moved an amendment to section 10, making it clear that the BBG should be charged with the supervision, regulation, and control of all broadcasting in Canada in the public interest. (This sentence was one of the clauses in the Fowler Commission's draft act.) Nowlan said that the wording of section 10 had been very carefully considered by the draftsmen of the Department of Justice, and refused to accept the added sentence. The Liberals supported the CCF amendment, which was defeated.[21]

The bill moved on to third reading and was carried by a vote of 124 to 31, the CCF supporting the government. But even the short debate in Parliament and elsewhere led a few newspapers to reconsider their editorial position. The *Globe and Mail*, for example, on August 22 had welcomed the central provisions of the bill, and said that they needed only wise implementation. On August 25, it condemned the bill's financial provisions for the CBC:

How hesitant these measures are and how vague! They ask the CBC to plan five years in advance and to get its plans approved, but offer no assurance that approval, once given, will be backed by cash.

They do nothing, really, but perpetuate the unsatisfactory arrangement whereby the CBC goes to Ottawa every year, cap in hand, asking for money – an arrangement which not only invites inefficiency in its operations, but begs political interference in its affairs.

Another Conservative newspaper, the *Ottawa Journal*, had earlier suggested that there might be flaws in the legislation, which it was Parlia-

20 / *Ibid.*, Aug. 26, 4136–7.
21 / *Ibid.*, 4108–14.

ment's job to detect. On August 26, it again asked for fuller discussion, adding:

Mr. Pearson fears, and we think with reason, that the 15-man board of broadcast governors and the 11-man board of CBC directors will get in each other's way to the detriment of the national service. ... In spite of the minister's reassurances the bill leaves unanswered the question of whether the C.B.C. is to have authority and freedom to maintain a good national service.[22]

On the other hand, the *Toronto Telegram* and the Montreal *Gazette* continued to express satisfaction with the bill. And the *Canadian Broadcaster* called it 'a matter of rejoicing for the industry. The years-long battle to free private enterprise broadcasting from domination from its nationalized competition has been brought to a reasonably satisfactory conclusion.'

When the bill reached the Senate, the Liberal senator from Windsor and Toronto, David Croll, sharply criticized its main provisions:

The bill, in my interpretation, will create two national broadcasting systems, and it will weaken the C.B.C. There are two bodies set up, the Board of Broadcast Governors and the Board of Governors of the C.B.C. There must be conflict between them. One will represent the public interest, and the other will represent, in the main, the private interest. ...

And so, by this bill, for the first time in 32 years we are handing over the exploitation of the public domain to other bodies, and will find, as in radio, that these TV licences and franchises, will fall into the hands of great controlled empires, and what we will have instead of a public monopoly will be a private monopoly. ... In the past private stations have been competing with one another but never with the C.B.C. The C.B.C. was a senior partner and the private stations were junior partners. Now, under this bill, they have equality ... and the pendulum will swing the other way.[23]

The opposition leader in the Senate, W. Ross Macdonald, referred to critical statements issued by the Canadian Federation of Agriculture, the Canadian Labour Congress, and the Canadian Broadcasting League, and reiterated many of the arguments that Pearson had advanced in the Commons. He quoted the league in particular on the financial provisions

22 / Quoted by J.W. Pickersgill, *ibid.*, 4159.
23 / Senate *Debates*, Aug. 27, 1958, 683–4.

for the CBC, and on the appointment of the two senior officers 'during pleasure.'[24]

The government leader in the Senate, W.M. Aseltine, said the object of the legislation was to implement the Fowler Report as far as possible. He referred to Croll's 'more or less socialistic speech,' and said there was nothing to back up his forebodings. The Fowler Report had been generally accepted in principle, and he believed the bill would similarly be accepted. He quoted from the introductory paragraph of the statement issued by the Canadian Broadcasting League: 'The Canadian Broadcasting League ... welcomes the Government's statements on the intention of the new legislation. It welcomes also the fact that the bill preserves the Canadian Broadcasting Corporation, and appears to provide for a single national broadcasting system, under the control of a large representative Board of Broadcast Governors.' He added that nothing in the bill would impair the CBC, and 'if I thought anything was being done in that direction I certainly would not vote for the bill.'[25]

The Liberals in the Senate were in an overwhelming majority, and if they had felt strongly about the bill, they could have defeated it, but perhaps at some peril for their own future. Instead, they referred it on second reading to the standing committee on transport and communications. The aspect of the bill that led them to this action was no doubt the clause that forbade ownership of stations by companies that were controlled outside Canada. The Senate usually displayed a tender regard for property interests, as John A. Macdonald had clearly intended.[26]

The chairman of the Senate committee was Adrian K. Hugessen, a Montreal Liberal, who (as he told the committee) was also on the board of the Canadian Marconi Company, and of Canmar Investment Company, a holding company which was owned by the English Electric Company. Hugessen remained in the chair, but said he would abstain from voting on any matter that directly affected Canadian Marconi. Representatives of the Canadian Marconi Company were there the first morning, having come from Montreal to appear before the committee, while it seemed that other organizations with a less direct interest may not have been notified of the hearings.[27] A Conservative senator from

24 / *Ibid.*, Aug. 28, 1958, 716–21.

25 / *Ibid.*, 723–4.

26 / In speaking at the Quebec Conference in 1864 on the functions of the Senate, Macdonald said, 'The rights of the minority must be protected, and the rich are always fewer in number than the poor.' Robert A. MacKay, *The Unreformed Senate of Canada*, rev. ed. (Toronto, 1963), 47–8.

27 / Senate of Canada, Standing Committee on Transport and Communications, *Proceedings*, Sept. 2, 1958, 8.

Ontario, William Brunt, who was a close friend and adviser of the prime minister, said he would speak for station CFRB in Toronto, and the TV stations in Kitchener and Windsor, which were also vitally concerned with the same provision in the bill.[28] Station CFRB was owned by Standard Radio Limited, the shares of which were sold in the open market. An undetermined portion of them were held outside Canada. The directors of CFRB had a part interest in CKLW and CKLW-TV in Windsor, but control of those two stations had passed to an American company, RKO Teleradio Pictures. The station in Kitchener, CKCO-TV was (according to Senator Brunt) owned principally by Famous Players Limited, an American-controlled company; and although this was not mentioned, Famous Players also had a half-interest in the two television stations in Quebec, CFCM-TV and CKMI-TV.

The problem was in section 14 of the bill that had been passed by the House of Commons, which had restricted foreign ownership by providing that at least three-quarters of the shares in a broadcasting company must be held by Canadians. The president of Canadian Marconi, Stuart M. Finlayson, told the committee that the English Electric Company, a British firm, owned about 51 per cent of Canadian Marconi. About 8 per cent of the shares were owned by individual Canadians, and about 40 per cent were 'widely distributed,' mostly in the United States. His company had received the first broadcasting licence in Canada (for CFCF, Montreal), and it was hopeful of receiving a television licence. If the bill were amended to allow ownership by Canadians or Commonwealth citizens, he said his company would still not qualify, since only 58 or 59 per cent was owned in Canada or England.[29] He felt it could not have been the intention of the government to deprive a company such as his of the right to apply for and gain a television licence and, as the bill now stood, there would be a question even of their retaining a radio broadcasting licence.

The senators agreed with him, and asked Nowlan for his views. Nowlan said he had never thought of the restriction applying to existing stations; 'indeed, we have no intention of applying it to stations which have been authorized heretofore.'[30] Mr. Thorson of the Department of Justice was with him, and they offered an amendment which the Senate eventually passed.

A second matter pursued by the senators was the question of why the CBC president and vice-president were to be appointed 'during pleasure,'

28 / *Ibid.*, 24.
29 / *Ibid.*, 20.
30 / *Ibid.*, Sept. 3, 1958, 54

and the other nine directors were to hold office 'during good behaviour,' with their removal possible only upon a joint address of the Senate and the House of Commons. The explanation was that since the duties to be performed by the two full-time officials were partly administrative, the government might want to replace them without undue delay. Nowlan finally said the resolution of this question was in the senators' hands, implying that he did not feel strongly one way or the other.[31] The result was that the Senate passed another amendment, this time to section 22 of the bill, providing that the president and vice-president (like the other directors) should hold office during good behaviour, but in their case, removal could be effected at any time by the governor in council for cause. These two amendments were accepted and passed by the House of Commons on September 6.[32]

The question of the CBC's annual appropriations was discussed again, and on this the minister was not so accommodating. He tried, however, to give a measure of reassurance: 'The Government's feeling was, and my feeling still is, once you get an undertaking from the Government on a five-year capital program, together with a forecast of its effect on the operating revenue, that the CBC has an implied guarantee from the Government that moneys will be provided within that framework for the operations during the five-year period.'[33] Besides, he said, it was not really possible to forecast a five-year current operation budget when costs were going up so rapidly and expansion taking place.[34]

So the new broadcasting act was on the statute books, and a new era in broadcasting was about to begin. Frank Flaherty, writing for *Canadian Business* in October, said that in his handling of the bill, Nowlan had displayed 'qualities of firmness, agility and tact which rank him among the abler occupants of the treasury bench in the present or any recent government.' The only criticism that could be made was that the bill appeared so late in the session. That, Flaherty continued, was not Nowlan's fault. It was due to the difficulties the cabinet had in making up its collective mind about what should be in the bill. Nowlan probably performed 'even greater feats of persuasion and diplomacy behind the scenes than he did on the floor of the house.'

A calm appraisal of the new legislation was offered by the political scientist, Alexander Brady, writing in the *Canadian Forum*. He did not believe that public debates on broadcasting were at an end, nor should

31 / *Ibid.*, 53.
32 / *Debates*, Sept, 6, 1958, 4761.
33 / Senate Committee *Proceedings*, 46.
34 / *Ibid.*, 48.

they be. 'Broadcasting and television remain crucial issues for debate because they are basic in fostering Canadian nationality. ... Without the CBC the Canadian people would today be more deeply engulfed in the cultural influences of the United States.' There were dangers in more sharply dividing the dual elements in Canadian broadcasting, as the Liberals had claimed, and the CBC and the BBG might be brought into 'fruitless rivalry.' But the dangers were not inevitable, said Brady, provided the government and the two public bodies acted in good faith and with good sense.

Brady thought the Liberals were on solid ground in complaining that the new structure was needlessly elaborate and cumbersome. The Board of Broadcast Governors was probably larger than it need be; and the government might have been wiser to forgo the additional board of directors for the CBC. Since the CBC would now be concerned primarily with operating decisions, it could be better administered simply by a small corps of permanent officials accountable to the BBG.

The ultimate success or failure of the new system, Brady continued, would rest primarily with the BBG, and would depend upon the imagination, integrity, and resolution of the members of the board: 'If their grasp of the major significance of broadcasting in the national life is feeble, we need expect little from them. We need also expect little if they fail to receive the strong backing of a Government anxious to see that the purposes of the act are achieved. Behind them is needed a vigilant public opinion determined that the struggle for Canada's cultural growth is worthy of exacting effort and adequate funds.'[35]

3 *The Two Boards*

As soon as the legislation revealed that there would be twenty-six positions to be filled, suggestions began to flow into the government on who might be appointed. The decision was that of the cabinet, but Nowlan had to co-ordinate and recommend. When the composition of the boards was announced, one could perhaps recognize the nominees of particular ministers: there was, for example, the prime minister's dentist on the Board of Broadcast Governors, as well as the brother-in-law of the minister of trade and commerce, George Hees; and on the CBC board, a campaign director for the minister of justice, Davie Fulton. But the general intention was, seemingly, that the Board of Broadcast Gov-

35 / 'Broadcasting and the Nation,' *Canadian Forum* (Oct. 1958), 150–1.

ernors should start with a clean slate, that it should be independent of organized interests, and with no special knowledge of or experience in broadcasting. The emphasis in choosing the CBC board of directors was on an understanding of financial and business matters, which it was thought would enable it to ensure efficiency in CBC operations, particularly in view of the fact that the CBC would be spending $65 million in public money during the current year. Experience in broadcasting was considered an asset for the CBC directors.

The appointments were made on November 10, to coincide with the proclamation of the broadcasting act. The three full-time members of the BBG were: Dr. Andrew Stewart, who upon becoming chairman, left his position as president of the University of Alberta; Roger Duhamel, vice-chairman, who had been editor of the Montreal weekly, *La Patrie*; and Carlyle Allison, editor-in-chief of the *Winnipeg Tribune*, a Southam newspaper.

Duhamel and Allison were regarded as Conservatives, while Stewart had no party affiliation. He had a good reputation as a fair-minded university administrator, and had maintained good relations with the Social Credit government of Alberta. By profession he was an agricultural economist, and he was currently chairman of the Royal Commission on Price Spreads. Before that, he had been a member of the Royal Commission on Canada's Economic Future (a commission chaired by Walter L. Gordon). He had come to Canada from Scotland at the age of twenty, and had graduated from the University of Manitoba. He took two years of graduate work at the University of Edinburgh, before taking an appointment in the economics department of the University of Alberta. The university for many years had held a licence for a radio station, CKUA, but in the years when Stewart was president the station was operated and financed by Alberta Government Telephones, and the university's responsibility was to program a certain number of hours a week.

Of the other twelve members of the BBG, perhaps the only one with a national reputation was Dr. Eugene Forsey. He was an expert on the Canadian constitution, the author of a book on the royal power of dissolution, had been active in the founding of the CCF, and indeed had run as a candidate opposing the Conservative leader, George Drew. He was employed as research director for the Canadian Labour Congress, but was known as a man of strong principles and independent views. Although he remained within the CCF party until it was superseded by the New Democratic party (at which time Forsey resigned over the 'bi-national' policy the new party adopted), he had been a great friend of a former Conservative prime minister, Arthur Meighen, and he was often thought to be a socialist of a very conservative stripe (or 'red Tory'). Forsey, who lived in Ottawa, became a member of the BBG's executive committee.

The other part-time members were: Joseph F. Brown, a Vancouver florist; Dr. Mabel G. Connell, a Prince Albert dentist; Dr. Emlyn Davies, a Baptist minister in Toronto; Edward A. Dunlop, director of the Canadian Arthritis and Rheumatism Society; Guy Hudon, Dean of the Law Faculty at Laval University, Quebec; Yvan Sabourin, a Montreal lawyer; Mrs. R.G. Gilbride, a leader of welfare work in Montreal; Colin B. Mackay, a lawyer, and president of the University of New Brunswick, Fredericton; Roy Duchemin, managing director of the *Cape Breton Post* in Sydney, Nova Scotia; Lieut. Col. J. David Stewart, shipping executive and former mayor of Charlottetown and president of the Canadian Federation of Mayors and Municipalities; and Robert S. Furlong, a lawyer in St. John's, Newfoundland.

The slender representation of business on the Board of Broadcast Governors was surprising. Only two – Brown and J.D. Stewart – were businessmen, and their business interests were modest in size. Lawyers, journalists, and university professors were among them, but they were not the most eminent in their field. Most were Conservatives, as in the past membership in the CBC board of governors had been mainly Liberal.[36] The board was geographically representative, with at least one member from every province, and most governors had been active in welfare or other community work. With so many of them untried on the national scene, much rested on the leadership given by the three full-time members, Andrew Stewart, Roger Duhamel, and Carlyle Allison.

The CBC in many Conservative eyes was an agency that had helped the Liberals maintain themselves in office. Accordingly, there was much curiosity as to whether the government would appoint the general manager, Alphonse Ouimet, and the assistant general manager, Ernest Bushnell, as president and vice-president (and thus directors) of the reconstituted CBC. The announcement of November 10 confirmed that indeed they would remain as the two senior officers – Nowlan's recommendation had been accepted by the cabinet. Ouimet had been the principal motivating force behind the development of television in Canada, and by this time he had six years' experience as the corpora-

36 / Looking back in 1967 at the composition of the board, the *Globe and Mail* wrote (Aug. 2): 'Unhappily the BBG has never, under either Liberal or Conservative governments, been what could be described as non-political. Most of its members have been noted for nothing other than loyal service to the party in power.'

tion's chief executive. Bushnell, who at 58 was eight years older than Ouimet, had been with the CBC and its predecessor, the CRBC, since 1933, and for most of that time he had been directly in charge of programming. Before joining public radio, he had been a private station manager, and he was known and liked throughout the industry. It was thought that his interests and experience nicely complemented Ouimet's professional and engineering expertise.

The nine part-time directors of the CBC were: G. Alexandra Carter, of Salmon Arm, British Columbia, who was active in community affairs, and who had worked for the Calgary *Albertan*; Ellen Armstrong, of Calgary, who had been president of the Farm Women's Union of Alberta and had also been associated with the Canadian Broadcasting League; William L. Morton, chairman of the department of history at the University of Manitoba, and author of 'The Progressive Party in Canada'; Kate Aitken, a broadcaster for twenty-three years over CFRB, Toronto, and a well-known radio personality on network programs as well; Charles W. Leeson, of Stratford, Ontario, a businessman associated with a manufacturing firm and an insurance firm; Raymond Dupuis, president and managing director of a large department store in Montreal, and past president of the Canadian Chamber of Commerce; Robert L. Dunsmore, of Montreal, a civil engineer, and retired president of Champlain Oil Products Ltd., a subsidiary of Imperial Oil; R.W. Ganong, of St. Stephen, New Brunswick, president of Ganong Brothers Ltd., a chocolate manufacturing firm, and former president of the Atlantic Provinces Economic Council; Professor C.B. Lumsden, of Acadia University, Wolfville, Nova Scotia, an active leader in the Canadian Legion.

The Board of Broadcast Governors was the more important board, because of its overriding authority and its responsibility for the development and carrying out of new policies, but its members were distinctly less well known than the CBC directors. Only one of them had any experience in broadcasting administration – R.S. Furlong, who had been a governor of the old Broadcasting Corporation of Newfoundland from 1939 to 1949. In charge of the CBC were two experienced broadcasting administrators, and four members on its board had substantial business experience. In its selection of directors for the CBC, the government demonstrated not only a concern for economy and efficiency in the public agency, but an attempt to answer charges from the opposition that it wanted to weaken the corporation.

Now it remained to see how the two boards would work together in the interests of a national broadcasting system and 'the provision of a varied and comprehensive broadcasting service.'

4 Policy Changes Effected with the New Act

By separating the CBC from the regulatory structure, the Progressive Conservative government brought about a policy change that, clearly, the party leaders had long intended. As a party with a strong mandate won at a recent election, it was in a position to move decisively and to claim that it had public backing. Popular sentiment was hard to assess. There is no doubt that in many areas of the country viewers wanted a second television service, and if this could be provided with private capital and supported by advertising revenue few people would worry about possible long-term effects on the existing system. Such desire for an additional program service was whetted and stimulated by a number of existing broadcasters and other entrepreneurs who hoped to share in what was turning out to be an increasingly lucrative industry.

On the other hand, the most recent study of Canadian broadcasting had expressed some doubt that second private television stations could be established in the near future without injury to the 'single broadcasting system' that was designed to be responsive to Canadian needs and adapted to Canadian conditions. The Fowler Commission concluded that if a newly established board of broadcast governors did not see ways of maintaining adequate Canadian content and reasonable program standards, 'Canada would do better to wait for alternative television service.'[37] The government had not undertaken any new study as a basis for modifying this conclusion, but most people assumed that the new legislation heralded the establishment of second television stations and possibly a second television network.

The Diefenbaker government wanted to demonstrate its devotion to free enterprise by increasing the opportunities for ownership in private broadcasting, but it wanted to do so while retaining the CBC, partly as a way of ensuring that broadcasting would remain predominantly Canadian, and partly as a way of bringing a national service to regions and communities that could not support stations that depended entirely on commercial revenue. The prime minister and other members of the cabinet recognized also that the CBC in its twenty-three years of existence had won strong support among many elements of the population, and the government did not wish to be accused of weakening or destroying the CBC. This twin desire, to open the field of broadcasting more freely to private enterprise, yet to do so without visibly damaging the CBC, led to some of the ambiguities in the legislation. The CBC was to lose

37 / *Fowler Commission Report*, 234–5.

its authority as adviser to the government on broadcasting policy, its power to command stations to carry CBC programs, and its control of the number of station outlets and the conditions under which they could broadcast. Those powers were to go to a second public board, the BBG; but the CBC was to be only partially responsible to the BBG, since it would continue to report directly to Parliament through a minister of the crown. It was also uncertain whether effectively the decisions about where the CBC should establish stations should come from the BBG, the government, or the CBC itself (with the government's approval). The broadcasting act would require a testing period before anyone could be certain how in fact it would be interpreted and applied.

The change in broadcasting policy in 1958 was a fundamental one, but its significance was not realized at the time by most Canadians. One explanation, as we have seen, lay in George Nowlan's skill in presenting the government's legislation as a slightly modified version of what the Fowler Commission had recommended. And in truth none of the structures that the public saw disappeared over night: there was the CBC, still in place, its networks intact, there were the affiliated private stations, drawing programs from the CBC; and there were the unaffiliated stations, to this point existing only in radio, continuing to inform and amuse local audiences.

If the changes that were about to take place were masked, a more important explanation was that the broadcasting system devised in the 1930s had already been modified by so many expedients and compromises that the statutory change of 1958 seemed but one more of the same kind as the others. The CBC was still the dominant force in program production and network distribution, in both radio and television, French and English. But the private sector had been developing and growing faster than the public sector in number of stations and accessibility to audiences. Under CBC leadership, the growth of television in Canada had been the fastest of any country in the world, as the Fowler Commission (p. 217) reported; and the live-production output of the combined English and French TV networks in 1958 was greater than that of any other network in the world.[38]

But because of the former government's decision to provide this national service in the most economical way possible, the CBC had eight television stations compared with forty-four stations operated by private enterprise. If, as seemed promised, further private television stations were to be licensed after 1959, it looked on the surface as if this

38 / *CBC Annual Report, 1957–58,* 17.

were a mere extension of the policy already in effect. The difference would be that the additional programming would have to be supported either by advertising revenues generated in the limited Canadian market; or by importation from external, mainly American, sources. There seemed little doubt which alternative would be selected in the hours when most Canadians were watching their television sets.

It could also be predicted that the CBC, already under considerable pressure from its private affiliates to schedule programs that would attract the largest audience, would be forced into a competitive position by second stations that were freer to operate according to market considerations. The CBC, in other words, might become a declining force in furthering Canadian communications, even on its own stations and networks. The commercial ethos was being accorded a recognition greater than it had ever received in the past.

This was not necessarily the policy objective that government leaders intended – or at least not all of them. The prime minister himself had often voiced support for the CBC as a national agency of communication and unification, and his nationalist stance in relation to industry and commerce was well known. The provisions for the Canadian ownership of broadcasting stations in the 1958 bill were perhaps an instance of this concern. But with a preference for private enterprise in as many field as possible, there was probably an unduly optimistic faith that the national objectives of the broadcasting system could be achieved by the setting of general regulations, rather than by the direct provision of services financed by the Canadian public. The confidence in the beneficial effects of stronger regulation was discernible in the recommendations of the Fowler Commission, although Fowler and his colleagues were cautious about diminishing the dominant position of the CBC in Canadian broadcasting. The policy actually adopted in 1958 put the emphasis rather more on levelling the position and status of the CBC and the private stations, providing more formal procedures for all broadcasters, public and private, to follow in seeking benefits or resolving disputes, but leaving open the question of who should decide when the proliferation of outlets and services would threaten the system's objectives given such general statement in section 10 of the new act.

7 A 'SEA OF TROUBLES': THE CBC FROM 1958 TO 1963

FROM THE PASSING OF THE BROADCASTING ACT to the defeat of the Diefenbaker government, the CBC had an uneasy time. The standards of programs did not change markedly, though tight budgets restricted the number of television variety and drama programs, and a number of highly skilled writers, performers, and directors left Canada to pursue their careers in other countries, particularly England and the United States.[1] Some would have done so regardless of the opportunities in Canada – artists often want to win an international reputation, or work where the challenges are greatest, or earn higher fees. In the early sixties, the arrival of second stations meant that trained technicians and production personnel were in more demand, and the CBC lost some of these to the private stations and the second network. The competitive situation also meant that, increasingly, Canadian television was judged by a commercial standard and by the share of the audience that could be won for each station's programming. The temptation was always present, even in the CBC, to rely on the scheduling of popular American programs in the evening hours. To the private stations affiliated with the CBC network, such decisions could mean the difference between profit and loss, or between higher and lower profit margins.

In spite of changes in personnel and the loss of some artists, CBC programs maintained a high standard, particularly in what was regarded as its 'serious' television programming. On the French network, public affairs programs such as as 'Premier plan' and 'Tribune Libre,' the long-standing music program, 'l'Heure du concert,' the variety progràm 'Music-Hall,' and 'le Téléthéâtre' provided a level of information and

---

1 / Those who went to British films or television included: Silvio Narizzano, Elaine Grand, Ted Allen, Jackie Rae, Ted Kotcheff, Sidney Newman; and to American films or television, Lloyd Bochner, Lorne Greene, Robert Goulet, Leslie Nielsen, Don Harron, among performers, and Arthur Hiller, Harvey Hart, Norman Jewison, David Greene, Frank Peppiatt, John Aylesworth, and Bernard Slade among writers and directors.

entertainment that was generally recognized as commendable. The same could be said for Close-Up, Newsmagazine, Festival, General Motors Presents, and 'The Wayne and Shuster Hour' on English television.

Nevertheless, the CBC did experience a number of difficulties in this period that had unfortunate results, some of them political in nature, or having political consequences. One or two of these were internally generated, although still related to the social and political atmosphere of the Canada at that time.

George Nowlan was under a variety of pressures. Not only the ordinary members of the Conservative caucus, but many of his cabinet colleagues were suspicious that the previous CBC board and management too had become too closely identified with the old Liberal administration. They wanted a completely new board of directors and, if possible, new management. They also had the feeling that the CBC had been far too costly and extravagant. Nowlan consulted the chairman of the recent Royal Commission on Broadcasting, and Fowler told him that although he had great respect for Ouimet as an engineer and as second in command, he did not think Ouimet had the right qualifications to head the national programming agency.[2] As against this advice, Ouimet's experience and undoubted capacity, and the respect he had won in broadcasting circles, suggested that he should not be passed over, particularly when he was one of relatively few French Canadians who had risen to a top position in the public service and the new government's sensitivity to French-Canadian aspirations was being watched very closely. Finally, the cabinet made its decision on November 9, and Nowlan called Ouimet and Ernest Bushnell to the minister's office to let them know that they were being appointed president and vice-president of the CBC.[3]

1 *The Succession to Dunton*

After the passing of the 1958 broadcasting act, the fact that the government did not decide who to put in charge of the corporation until the very

2 / Interview with R.M. Fowler, Jan. 27, 1976. Fowler received the impression that Nowlan was in favour of bringing in someone else as president, but that the prime minister was reluctant to pass over a qualified French-Canadian candidate.
3 / Interview with J.A. Ouimet, June 30, 1975. Ouimet became convinced later that he was not the government's first choice, but he said he did not know that at the time of his appointment. Bushnell, who was director-general of programs until 1953, had moved in that year from Toronto to Ottawa to become assistant general manager.

last day before the act was proclaimed (November 10) was itself an ill omen. Dunton had resigned in July, and the new legislation did not take effect until four months later. The Conservative government had time to arrange an orderly succession – to choose someone from outside the CBC as president, if they wished, or to accept Dunton's recommendation of Alphonse Ouimet, who had worked with him as general manager for over five years. Ouimet had a greater part in planning and building the television service than any other single individual; through his long experience in the CBC be was imbued with the traditions of broadcasting as a public service; he had an unparalleled knowledge of the financial and technical aspects of Canadian broadcasting; and he was highly respected within the CBC and by broadcasters generally. He did not have experience as a member of the governing board, was not nearly so well known nationally as was Dunton, and his ability to assess currents of opinion within society and to work within a broadly political context was unknown. Also untested was his capacity to lead and inspire the creative and program staff of the CBC, since Dunton (after consultation) had tended to make the more important program decisions himself, as well as to explain them to Parliament and the public.

Inside the CBC, the appointments of Ouimet and Bushnell brought relief: the resignation of Dunton and the uncertainties in the new legislation had created fears about the corporation's future independence. Newspaper assessments were mixed. The *London Free Press*, owner of radio and television stations, suggested (November 12) that the two appointments 'should enable the publicly-owned agency to go forward in confidence.' John Bird in the *Toronto Star* (November 12) wrote that 'both these full-time salaried executives represent straight, deserved and almost inevitable promotion.' But on the same date the *Star* said editorially, 'With all respect to the technical and professional ability of Alphonse Ouimet and Ernest Bushnell, they are primarily administrators who have spent most of their career as CBC employees. Can they be expected to give the CBC the leadership or defend it against its enemies with the same authority as such former strong chairmen as Leonard Brockington and A. Davidson Dunton? Both Mr. Brockington and Mr. Dunton were able to withstand powerful political pressures.' The *Winnipeg Free Press* (November 12) warned, 'The danger in leaving the operation of the CBC to managerial personnel is that it may have no clear-cut policies, and that the BBG, with its very wide powers, may go beyond the area of general prescription and become involved in more detailed direction of the CBC. ... The system will work only if the BBG interferes as little as possible with the working of the CBC.' *L'Action Catholique* in Quebec (November 17) wrote concerning the appointments to the two boards, 'The government made a laudable effort and took the French-Canadian cultural element into account, but it did not go far enough.'

Although Ouimet and Bushnell had been close associates for five years, they were not an ideally matched pair. Ouimet, an engineer, was rigorously trained and logical, highly intelligent, interested in rational methods of organization and administration, and abstemious in his habits. Bushnell, who had started as a private broadcaster, was primarily a program man, gregarious, emotional, convivial, and (in 1958–9, by his own statement) hard-drinking. He displayed a lack of interest in aspects of administration, such as budgets and financial controls, and a suspicion of formal organizational principles and techniques.[4] There was a further complicating circumstance in that Bushnell for over fifteen years had occupied a more senior post than Ouimet, and indeed in 1953 he had felt 'passed over' when he had not been appointed general manager.[5] Now the two were in charge, each on the board of directors, and working under the eye of a watchful government which each year had to approve the amount of appropriations requested. And before even approaching the government, they would need the support of nine other members of the board, all of them new to their responsibilities, and all aware of which members of cabinet had put forward their names.

The board of directors held their first meeting in Montreal on December 4–6, 1958. The government's limited confidence in Ouimet was shown when, before the board met, Nowlan called him in to warn that the government was very upset by what they believed to have been the corporation's extravagance in the past. He wanted someone with business experience to oversee the budget, and said he hoped the board would elect R.L. Dunsmore as chairman. When Ouimet replied that the act made no provision for this, Nowlan suggested that Dunsmore should at least be chairman of the executive committee. Ouimet countered that it would be anomalous for himself as president and chairman of the board not to be chairman of the executive committee.[6] Nowlan was not satisfied, and asked that Dunsmore and Ouimet discuss the matter. As a result of their conversation, Dunsmore agreed to forgo the chairmanship

4 / Peter Stursberg, *Mister Broadcasting: the Ernie Bushnell Story* (Toronto, 1971), chap. 19, esp. 165–72, 219.
5 / *Ibid.*, 165.
6 / Ouimet interview, June 30, 1975.

of the executive committee, and to accept Ouimet's suggestion that he be the chairman of the finance committee.[7]

On the first day of the board meeting, Nowlan was introduced and told the directors this was an historic event, marking the first major change in the Canadian broadcasting system since 1936. Because of the size and importance of the CBC and the amount of money involved, careful direction and control were essential.[8] What was unusual was that Nowlan requested another appearance on the second day, when he said even more frankly that the government was worried by the possible extravagance of the CBC and that it was the directors' responsibility to watch over this. The finance committee, he suggested, should be centred near Ottawa and have financial talents in its membership. In reality Nowlan was asking the 'outside' directors to keep an eye on the 'inside' (fulltime) directors; he specifically asked them not to identify themselves too closely with management. He said he wanted to be able to speak with assurance in cabinet or Parliament on the subject of CBC financial controls, and this assurance should be based on the scrutiny given by the finance committee.[9]

The government was suspicious not only of the CBC's spending, but also of possible lingering connections between the CBC and the Liberal party, or Liberal predilections on the part of CBC personnel. But more substantive difficulties faced the new management team. They had to familiarize the new board with the CBC's operations, role, and traditions. There was the question of the CBC's autonomy with respect to the BBG, and the working relations between the two bodies. In particular, Ouimet and the CBC board felt they must exercise constant vigilance to prevent an inexperienced BBG from impairing the capacity of the CBC to carry out its mandate – a capacity that would suffer if the BBG made too many concessions to new TV stations experiencing financial difficulty. The board had to decide how to maintain or establish CBC presence in some of the important regional centres opened to second TV stations. They had to be concerned about the effects that second television stations would have on the CBC's revenues and the CBC's place at the heart of the broadcasting system. Management had to deal with the consequences of

7 / Interview with R.L. Dunsmore, Kingston, Aug. 11, 1974. Dunsmore had had previous discussions with William Hamilton, the postmaster general (and his member of Parliament) on the role he was expected to play in the CBC.
8 / Information from Ouimet, who read from minutes of the CBC board of directors, Dec. 4, 1958.
9 / CBC board of directors, Minutes, Dec. 5, 1958. When references are made subsequently to such minutes, in each case they are to extracts shown the author at his request by J.A. Ouimet.

an extremely rapid growth in CBC personnel during the preceding five years, and see that policy within the CBC was subject to unified direction. Traditionally, the CBC had a very small headquarters staff in Ottawa, with the vast majority of its personnel in the production centres, and particularly in the two network centres, Toronto and Montreal. There was some feeling, particularly strong on Parliament Hill, that these two centres were too autonomous, too powerful, and needed to be brought under firmer control. Ouimet as general manager had transferred some network executives to Ottawa from Montreal and Toronto, including the head of programs, but supervisors in particular areas of programming remained where they had been, next to their production personnel.

The circumstances at this time in which the CBC was asked to carry out its responsibilities were therefore unusually difficult. The CBC was to operate under a new act that had its own ambiguities. The system that had developed as a result of history and the new legislation was complex, and not easy to make effective. A new an inexperienced regulatory board was in control of the system as a whole. There were new elements of competition in television, in addition to the continuing competition offered by United States networks and border stations. CBC morale was not as high as it had been, due not only to the sudden departure of Dunton, but more especially to the CBC's altered position and prestige. Outside the realms of broadcasting and of politics, the social changes of the 1960s were beginning to have their effect. Those changes provided the setting for some of the more spectacular of the troubles experienced by the CBC not only in the Diefenbaker years, but continuing throughout Canada's 'tenth decade.'

At the end of December 1958, when Ouimet had been able to meet only once with his board of directors, a dispute arose in Montreal which erupted into a strike, assumed grave political dimensions and damaged the CBC as a functioning, bicultural institution.

2 The Montreal Strike

In Montreal, the CBC director for the province of Quebec was Gérard Lamarche. All television personnel, including the producers, reported to André Ouimet, also in Montreal, who was the younger brother of Alphonse, the corporation president in Ottawa. André Ouimet was a strong and forceful administrator, who had won promotion to his position on the recommendation of the then director for Quebec with the concurrence of a panel in head office from which Alphonse Ouimet had

carefully remained aloof.[10] He had been in charge of television operations in Montreal almost from the beginning, and under his direction
Montreal became one of the largest production centres in the world. He
was used to making his own decisions, partly because the director for the
province, Lamarche, had come from radio, and partly, no doubt, because he did not want to seem to be relying on his brother in Ottawa.

The dispute in the Montreal studios arose in a time when Quebec
society was undergoing rapid transformation, characterized by a growing distrust of established authority, development of a new form of
French-Canadian nationalism, increased labour militancy, and in particular an ambition on the part of the Canadian and Catholic Confederation of Labour (CCCL) to organize professional workers, with the communications field offering a welcome opportunity to engage public attention.

The strike arose from various dissatisfactions felt by Montreal television producers with their workload, the increasing number of controls
placed on them and their budgets, the step-by-step removal from them of
a number of important functions such as casting, script selection, and fee
negotiations, and especially a feeling that their views and representations were being summarily dismissed by André Ouimet and the director
of television production, Jean-Paul Ladouceur.[11] In November, one of
the producers, Pierre Lebeuf, refused an assignment that he regarded as
arbitrary, and when Ladouceur warned him that this refusal would be
remembered when it was time to renegotiate his contract, Lebeuf replied
that his next contract would be a collective agreement.[12] Lebeuf met
with some colleagues who felt similar grievances, and consulted Gérard
Picard, a leader in the Catholic syndicates – the CCCL. A general meeting
of producers was held in the Windsor Hotel on December 5 and a
provisional committee formed, with Lebeuf as president. André Ouimet
met with the producers on December 11, but in accordance with CBC
policy and head office instructions, refused to recognize the association
for bargaining purposes. Both sides agreed to review the situation, and
gave themselves until March 12 to reach an agreement. In a second

10 / André Ouimet had been named director of television by Aurèle Séguin as director
for the province. Séguin had formerly been director of television himself, and André
had been his executive assistant.
11 / For a description of working conditions and grievances felt by the producers, see
Guý Parent, *Sous le règne des bruiteurs* (Montreal, 1963), esp. 114 ff. Also, a mimeo-
graphed statement (5 pp.) released on Jan. 7, 1959, the English text of which was
headed, 'The Producer Association: It's Origins; It's Story' (*sic*).
12 / Parent, *Sous le règne*, 116.

general meeting a week later, the producers formed 'L'Association des Réalisateurs' and authorized the executive to seek incorporation under Quebec law as a professional syndicate. A new executive was elected with Fernand Quirion as president. The producers seemed to be abandoning their agreement to take some time in exploring a settlement, perhaps because of advice they were receiving from the leadership of the syndicates.

In discussions that ensued, André Ouimet put forward the corporation's position that the management functions of producers were incompatible with union affiliation and the right to bargain collectively.[13] In 1959 the principle of bargaining by fully independent employee associations affiliated with labour organizations was not recognized in the public service except in crown corporations such as the Canadian National Railways and the CBC. Even in these organizations, such bargaining was restricted to personnel who were deemed to have no management functions. As a programming agency the CBC had to maintain a reputation for being non-partisan and fair in presenting different points of view on highly controversial questions. Dangers were obviously posed for this neutrality if those who exercised editorial control in programs were affiliated to an organization pursuing its own political interests even if unaligned to any party. At that time, probably no one in public life, certainly none of Ottawa's political leaders, conceived of groups within management being certified for collective bargaining purposes. André Ouimet's response should have been expected. But some producers thought his manner indicated he was treating them with contempt.[14]

At a general meeting of the association on December 23, the producers authorized their executive to call a strike at an appropriate time. Only when things seemed to be getting well out of hand did André Ouimet suggest that the producers meet with Gérard Lamarche, the director for the province. Lamarche telephoned Bushnell for advice and assistance – Alphonse Ouiment was on holiday in Florida.[15] Bushnell arranged for James Gilmore, controller of operations, to join Lamarche in Montreal,

13 / CBC summary, 'History of Dispute between the Montreal Television Producers' Association and the Canadian Broadcasting Corporation,' prepared in mid-January 1959 (mineo., 13 pp.).
14 / Interview with Marc Thibault, Montreal, March 29, 1972.
15 / Nowlan, perhaps reflecting Bushnell's view, later told the Commons that the strike 'never should have happened.' The difficulties between management and producers were 'minor' and 'should and could have been dealt with in half an hour if they had been brought to the attention of the management here in Ottawa.' *Debates*, Feb. 6, 1959, 776.

together with a lawyer nominated by the Department of Justice. The meeting with Lamarche and Gilmore took place on December 29.[16] The producers reiterated their demand that the association be recognized as a bargaining unit, as authorized under the Professional Syndicates Act, passed by the Quebec legislature in 1941, and that they should have the right to affiliate with the CCCL. The CBC replied that as a federal agency the legislation that governed their collective bargaining agreements was the Industrial Relations and Disputes Investigations Act. Lamarche and Gilmore proposed several alternatives, such as an in-house professional association without collective bargaining rights, or an application for certification to the Canada Labour Relations Board (which would almost certainly be denied), or that the producer function be redefined to establish a new job category of 'director' which would not carry the existing management functions of a producer. The spokesmen for the producers were not interested in these proposals, and the CBC officials said that any further consideration of their demand would require a formal written request which if necessary would have the immediate attention of the executive committee of the board of directors.

Informally, the producers had been in touch with the leaders of other unions, especially of the performers, and had received assurances that in case of a strike their picket lines would be honoured. Precipitately, the association's leaders called the strike to begin at 5 PM the same day, December 29, and seventy-four of about eighty-five producers responded.[17] That night, a mass meeting was held in the Canadian Legion Hall, addressed by Jean Marchand, general secretary of the CCCL, and other union leaders, who publicly honoured the pledge to observe picket lines.[18]

In Ottawa, Bushnell had been consulting with Dunsmore, and on

16 / The events of the strike have been drawn from the CBC Industrial Relations Newsletter, circulated among employees at the time, from CBC Archives in Montreal, and from a Chronology of the Montreal Strike, prepared by Alphonse Ouimet (15 pp.).
17 / A list of producers who received letters of dismissal, Jan. 22, 1959, is on file in CBC Archives, Montreal, file IT3-1-4-1, vol. 3.
18 / According to Fernand Quirion, the association's most important outside advisers were Marchand and Jean-Paul Geoffroy, counsel for the CCCL. When the strike vote was taken (Dec. 23), Marchand advised against calling a strike. Gérard Pelletier, Marchand's associate and also a regular broadcaster, tried as an intermediary to warn Lamarche that the situation was at the flashpoint. According to information given to Alphonse Ouimet, Geoffroy told the producers that the only way they would be recognized was to walk out, and within two days the CBC would give them the recognition they wanted. At any rate, Quirion and the other leaders assumed that the strike would be of short duration. Interview with Fernand Quirion, Montreal, March 20, 1972.

December 31 he telephoned the president in Florida to advise him of the strike. Ouimet arrived in Montreal that evening, immediately met with CBC management, and on New Year's Day talked with Quirion and with Gérard Pelletier. Formal meetings between the CBC and the association resumed on January 3, 4, and 5, without substantial progress. During this time, and for the remainder of the strike, supervisory personnel kept the stations on the air. On the French television station, the main fare was feature films and, at the beginning of the strike, newscasts.

On January 8, Quirion and Marchand sent a telegram to the minister of Labour, Michael Starr, requesting his intervention and a meeting with the prime minister. The dispute, Marchand told Starr, affected 'the whole population of Quebec.'[19]

This claim was only a slight exaggeration. As the strike wore on, television viewers tired of the steady diet of films, and wanted to have their favourite programs back. The unions organized a series of mass meetings and benefit concerts at which some of the most popular performers and authors appeared – Felix Leclerc, Jean-Louis Roux, Jean Duceppe, Gratien Gélinas, Roger Lemelin, André Laurendeau, Denise Pelletier, Ginette Letondal, Paul Guèvremont, Monique Leyrac, and – rising to increasing prominence – the television news analyst, René Lévesque, who toured with a variety show throughout the province. Prominent members of the Liberal opposition at Ottawa were often careful to sit in the front rows. French-language journalists in Montreal, especially in *Le Devoir*, gave the strikers most sympathetic coverage.

In the middle of January, there was still an impasse, in spite of efforts made by Claude Jodoin, president of the Canadian Labour Congress, to get the two sides to agree. (Seven unions supporting the strike were affiliated with the CLC.) A new session of Parliament opened on January 15, and the Montreal strike soon became a subject of debate. The CBC executive committee directed its efforts to getting the union personnel back to work.[20] In the middle of these meetings, the CBC president had a heart attack (January 18), and for the next six months. Ernest Bushnell was acting president. As Bushnell's biographer explains, in any top-level negotiations that followed, 'the discussions had to be conducted in English since neither the acting president nor the chairman [Dunsmore]

19 / In a second telegram dated Jan. 9, 1959.
20 / Both Ouimet and Dunsmore thought as a matter of principle the CBC could not recognize a producers' association as a bargaining unit. Another member of the executive committee, Raymond Dupuis, whose department store had lost a strike, was less certain of the CBC's position.

could speak French, and that was resented by the Quebec nationalists and trade unionists on the other side.'[21]

On January 20, the CBC notified the producers that unless their position substantially changed, it could no longer deal with the association, and on January 22 all employees not at work were told that unless they returned within twelve hours they would be presumed to have resigned. Marcel Carter, who had been placed in charge of the Montreal negotiations, and Ronald Fraser, director of public relations, explained the decisions in a press conference, and were quoted as saying that if the producers and other employees stayed out, the CBC was 'prepared to start from scratch if necessary to rebuild the French network.'[22]

Whatever happened next, it was debatable whether the CBC would be able to win its point, and if it did so it might be at some cost to its image in French Canada and its internal working relationships and morale. The government had maintained a 'hands-off' policy, and some of its supporters in Parliament who had been elected with the help of the Union Nationale party of Maurice Duplessis may have been rather glad that Radio-Canada (the French network) was in difficulty. It had long been accused of being leftist, of giving too much time on the air to critics of the Duplessis government, such as André Laurendeau, Maurice Lamontagne, Gérard Pelletier, and other liberal academics and journalists. But as the Liberal opposition in Ottawa began to hector the government for its inactivity, cabinet unity seemed to crack. Nowlan, in answer to Lionel Chevrier, told the House that the strike was 'entirely in the hands of the management of the corporation.'[23] A few days later, however, Léon Balcer, the solicitor-general, told Chevrier, 'I do not believe that the strike is illegal.'[24] Cardinal Léger was qoted in the debate as saying, 'Everyone has the right of association. The C.B.C. strike is nothing else than that. That right, and we have examples of this every day, must be asserted.'[25] The government was undoubtedly becoming more annoyed that the CBC had been unable to resolve its difficulties.

The threats of dismissal by the CBC created a rash of activity on all fronts. In Toronto, four national and international unions held a Saturday afternoon emergency meeting 'to discuss the mass dismissal of our

21 / Stursberg, *Mister Broadcasting*, 182.

22 / Montreal *Gazette*, Jan. 23, 1959. Carter answered questions in French, Fraser in English.

23 / *Debates*, Jan. 16, 1959, 11, and Jan. 22, 1959, 173.

24 / *Ibid.*, Jan. 26, 1969, 308.

25 / *Ibid.*, Jan. 27, 1959, 367; quoted by Maurice Bourget (Lévis).

members in Montreal.'[26] The speakers in addition to their own leaders included Fernand Quirion and Gérard Pelletier. Also in Toronto, the Association of Television Producers and Directors (representing Toronto's forty producers – half the number in Montreal) wired Bushnell on January 23 that it was 'opposed to any move that might extend to other television production centres ... the dispute between the CBC and some of its employees in Montreal.' It urged immediate resumption of negotiations and, presumably for the benefit of the press, went on to declare that it was a 'professional group,' not affiliated with any union, adding that since its formation some months previously it had had 'regular and useful discussions with the corporation on matters affecting the professional stature of its members.' Apparently the Toronto producers did not want anyone to get the impression that they were about to walk out.[27] La Presse commented that they had the kind of association that the Montreal producers had characterized as a 'club de pêche.'[28]

In Montreal, twenty-one supervising producers and supervisors (about half of them from public affairs, including two English-language producers) met to protest the corporation's action.[29] Marc Thibault, the public affairs supervisor, accompanied by Roger Rolland, program director for the French network, travelled to Ottawa on January 24 to urge Bushnell to defer sending out the letters of dismissal. At the University of Montreal, forty professors, including the deans of two faculties, appealed for the resumption of the negotiations, and urged a review of the situation by a royal commission.[30]

26 / Wording from a dodger circulated before the meeting. The four unions, ANG, ARTEC, IATSE, and NABET, were all affiliated with the Canadian Labour Congress, and belonged to the Council of Broadcast Unions. The union that remained determinedly aloof throughout (although in Montreal its members contributed to the strike fund) was the American Federation of Musicians.

27 / Television development in Toronto and Montreal had proceeded independently in each centre. The Toronto producers had almost no communication with Montreal, knew very little of the grievances felt by their Montreal counterparts, and did not want any union affiliation.

28 / 'Toronto n'est pas Montréal!' Jan. 26, 1959.

29 / On January 26, Le Devoir referred to approximately twenty-five supervisory personnel. The next day La Presse listed twenty-one signatories. Roger Rolland did not sign their statement, but was instrumental in arranging Thibault's interview with Bushnell.

30 / Le Devoir, Jan. 28, 1959. Among the signatories were André Raynauld, subsequently a member of the CBC board of directors, and later chairman of the Economic Council of Canada; and Marc Lalonde, in 1965 a member of the Advisory Committee on Broadcasting (the Fowler Committee), and later a cabinet minister.

Some of the national and international unions, aware that their Montreal members in staying off the job were violating the terms of their contracts, instructed them to go back to work. In response to such instructions from IATSE (the International Alliance of Theatrical Stage Employees), their Montreal business agent replied that in a secret vote, 93.3 per cent of the members decided to continue their support of the Producers' Association.[31] From Toronto, the president of the CCAA (Canadian Council of Authors and Artists), Neil LeRoy, announced that after several warnings the two member associations in Montreal had been suspended – the Union des Artistes and the Société des Auteurs.[32] These two associations represented not full-time employees but actors, writers, and singers who were on contract or who were engaged on a per-occasion basis. Another national union, ARTEC (Association of Radio and Television Employees of Canada), which included office workers and announcers, had already advised their members to return to work.[33]

The advice from the national offices of the unions had some effect. On

31 / *Globe and Mail*, Jan. 24, 1959, 'Stage Union's Order May Crack Solidarity.'

32 / *Ibid.*, Feb. 3, 1959, 'LeRoy Says Quebec Unions Stay Suspended.'

33 / CBC Archives, Montreal, File IT3-1-4-1, vol. 2, confidential letter dated Jan. 13, 1959 from Eldon Wilcox, executive vice-president, ARTEC, Ottawa, to all Montreal members. This letter reflects the divisions felt within and between the employees' unions, and also the growing conflicts based on language and national sentiments. Some extracts follow:

'It is necessary to say at the beginning that ARTEC has no criticism to offer of the producers, their leaders, or their cause. But some persons (who are not officially connected with the producers or the CCCL) have seized this struggle as a means to increase their own power. They have made speeches to divide English-speaking Montrealers from those who speak French. We have been reliably informed that the CCCL had no desire to have employee unions respect their picket lines. With the artists and producers alone they could have achieved all they now have. ... Meanwhile our members could support the producers with money and public support and demonstrations.

'Such a strike by producers, supported by artists, was to be aimed at recognition – a sacred trade union principle. But others have introduced new principles – the autonomy of Quebec, division of local unions from their national and international unions. ... They have said anything, true or untrue, to hold power.

'In this situation the principle is still recognition. And ARTEC members and officers have given support from the first day. ... The response of ARTEC was almost 100 per cent solid. Both local and national officers issued statements backing the producers' cause and stating we could not cross the line. ... All this time out national officers were being attacked and insulted by local officers of other unions who tried to divide ARTEC leaders from their local members. ...

'The union was not on strike. Members were advised to respect picket lines to avoid violence and disorder, but otherwise our contract was in force. ... No other orders were

January 30, the cbc estimated that 95 per cent of their 714 ARTEC employees were at work, as compared with 9 per cent of NABET members (from a group of 446 engineers and operators), and 39 per cent of ANG members (the American Newspaper Guild, representing 56 editors and news writers who worked for French and English radio and television and for the International Service).[34]

The most important pressures were being applied in Ottawa, on government, and on the cbc administration. On January 23, the prime minister and eight members of the cabinet heard the annual submission from the cccl, which asked that the minister of labour intervene. The prime minister made no promises, but agreed that the officers of the cccl should confer with the minister of labour, Michael Starr, and with Nowlan.[35] A day later, the deputy minister of labour telephoned Bushnell to suggest mediation.[36] On January 25, a delegation from the Council of Broadcast Unions, headed by Neil LeRoy, also urged mediation, and won from Bushnell an agreement to withhold action on the letters of dismissal.[37] On January 27, a special train took a thousand strike supporters from Montreal to Ottawa to stage a noisy but gay and colourful demonstration on Parliament Hill.[38]

As the strike dragged on, some Quebec Conservatives were aware that increasingly the federal government was receiving the blame in French Canada. Roger Lemelin, the author of the popular television serial, 'The Plouffe Family,' wrote in Le Devoir: 'When you consider with what almost serene eyes, approaching indifference, the heads of cbc at Ottawa and the central government itself are letting the situation grow worse, you ask yourself if the federal political play is not to see the means of expression of French culture weakened.'[39]

---

possible, lest ARTEC lose its certificate, and our members lose bargaining rights for 2000 in a battle for 74 – a battle we were never asked to join. ...

'Our people in Montreal, beginning to learn the truth, were drifting back to work. It was essential that we take action to preserve our own union and break the control of unauthorized persons who were recklessly using our union. No choice was left. On the night of January 11 we issued a joint statement by the national and local executives advising you to return to work.'

34 / Ibid., telex from P.A. Meggs, cbc Ottawa, to regional representatives, Jan. 30, 1959. Figures quoted were for those employees at the Radio-Canada Building, the broadcasting centre in Montreal.

35 / Globe and Mail, Jan. 24, 1959, 'pm Won't Intervene.'

36 / J.A. Ouimet, Chronology of Montreal Strike.

37 / Globe and Mail, Jan. 26, 1959, 'Meeting Defers cbc Ultimatum, Strike Averted.'

38 / Toronto Star, Jan. 28, 1959, report by John Bird.

39 / Quoted by John Bird, ibid., Jan. 27, 1959.

One Montreal Conservative MP decided to step into the breach – Egan Chambers, the member for St. Lawrence–St. George, a downtown constituency in which the Radio-Canada building was located, and in which many of the strikers lived. According to Chambers, he took his action as a private member and 'did not even discuss the matter with any member of the cabinet beforehand.'[40] However, he had sent a note to Nowlan, expressing his intention, and was not discouraged from carrying it forward.[41] The CBC board of directors was meeting in Ottawa (its second meeting) on Monday, February 2. On Sunday, Chambers met for three hours with representatives of the producers' association. On Monday, Bushnell advised the CBC board that Nowlan might like to meet with them informally. Later that morning, Bushnell received a call from Egan Chambers saying he had seen the producers the night before, and had a simplified proposal for settlement. Chambers met with Ron Fraser and other members of CBC management for four hours. The directors later met with Nowlan and, after more discussion the following day, adopted a suggested formula for settlement that was nearly identical to Chambers' formula.[42]

During the next several days, Chambers presided over the discussions of his suggested formula, with the two sides meeting usually in separate rooms, and Chambers moving from one group to the other. When it seemed that agreement might be found on recognition of the association as a bargaining unit, without union affiliation, he quickly got that article initialed by the principal CBC negotiator, Marcel Carter, before it could be discussed at CBC headquarters the next day.[43] Bushnell was brought into the negotiations on one occasion (February 6) and agreed to an arbitration clause the producers had wanted – Chambers thought that because of the number of drinks being poured that this part of the agreement might not hold. In the event, what stalled the negotiations was the producers' insistence that they could not sign any agreement until conditions satisfactory to union heads had been agreed upon regarding return-to-work arrangements for union employees.[44]

Negotiations with the unions dragged on, with Chambers still acting as

---

40 / Announcement by Egan Chambers to Press Gallery, Feb. 3, 1959. Sent by telex from R.C. Fraser to G. Lamarche. CBC Montreal Archives, file IT3-1-4-1, vol. 4.
41 / Interview with Egan Chambers, Montreal, March 24, 1972. Chambers became president of the Progressive Conservative Association of Canada in 1963.
42 / Ouimet, Chronology of Montreal Strike.
43 / Chambers interview.
44 / CBC Industrial Relations Newsletter, Feb. 17, 1959.

mediator. Agreement with the industrial unions was reached on February 22, and with the authors and artists on February 28. Meanwhile, there had been an increasing number of acts of violence in Montreal, beatings of non-strikers and intimidation of their families, cars damaged and houses splattered with paint, and a union official from Toronto, Neil LeRoy, was attacked by two assailants following a mass meeting held in Montreal.[45] On March 2, there was a 'near-riot' in front of the Radio-Canada building on Dorchester street, and twenty-nine strike supporters were arrested, including Jean Marchand and René Lévesque.[46] What held up the final settlement with the producers was the CBC's charge that, in spite of the understanding negotiated, the producers still intended to affiliate with the CCCL.[47] Finally, on March 7 the producers and the CBC agreed to a pledge that Chambers worded by which the association would not 'become affiliated directly or indirectly or through the intervention of a third party with the CCCL, or any union, group of unions or federation of unions.'[48] All strikers returned to work on Monday, March 9. The unresolved issues between the producers and the CBC eventually went for arbitration by Professor H.D. Woods, of McGill University, whose report was handed down on January 20, 1960.

In the dispute and its resolution, everyone suffered substantial losses. The CBC lost on its main point of principle that, as part of management, producers should not engage in collective bargaining on the specifications of their job and the conditions of work (they had never intended to negotiate individual salaries through the association.) The CCCL lost the chance to recruit a professional syndicate in a key communications field and in a federal agency; some observers had regarded this as an exciting prospect presaging the development on the European model of unions of management personnel and *syndicats de cadres*.[49] Many technicians, stagehands, writers, and performers, as well as the producers them-

45 / UPI dispatch, Ottawa, Feb. 5, 1959.
46 / *Montreal Star*, March 3, 1959. Lévesque and Marchand were charged with disturbing the peace.
47 / CBC Industrial Relations Newsletter, March 3, 1959, 'Return to work obstructed by producers' intent to affiliate contrary to settlement understanding.'
48 / *Ibid.*, March 7, 1959.
49 / 'Les pays européens, beaucoup plus avancés que nous en ce domaine, ont créé il y a déjà longtemps des syndicats de cadres. ... L'association des réalisateurs de Radio-Canada est, croyons-nous, une des premières tentatives d'organisation de salariés qui participent à la fois à l'autorité et à l'exécution. ... L'association des réalisateurs de Radio-Canada peut être le premier syndicat de cadres à prendre forme au Canada.' Lead editorial by Gérard Filion, *Le Devoir*, Jan. 10, 1959.

selves, lost two months' salaries, and returned to work in an atmosphere of hostility and suspicion between themselves and those who had stayed on the job.[50]

But there were equally serious effects on the CBC as an institution and serious implications, too, for the country as a whole. The CBC suffered a loss of respect from many articulate groups within the country, from intellectuals, parliamentarians, and members of the government. The sense of grievance among many French Canadians, that their needs and interests were unheeded by the English-speaking majority, and particularly by the government in Ottawa, was heightened.[51] Some who had not thought of themselves as nationalists before, like René Lévesque, came through the experience with bitterness. After his arrest at the beginning of March, Lévesque wrote in an open letter:

The CBC ... quite predominantly in its higher echelons, is English. ... In Ottawa, there is also a House of Commons controlled by a political party in which the overwhelming majority of MPs are English. ... They are the final authority over public radio and television. And three ministers, almost exclusively, have had to answer recent questions about the CBC. All three are English [Michael Starr, George Nowlan, Prime Minister Diefenbaker]. ...

Some of us, and maybe many, come out of this with a tired and unworthy feeling that if such a strike had happened on English CBC, it would – as the hon. George Nowlan said, and on this occasion not erroneously – have lasted no more than half an hour. To this day, ours has lasted 66 days. Of such signal advantages is the privilege of being French made up in this country![52]

During the strike, the English programs of the CBC were not interrupted, except for the English version of 'The Plouffe Family'; and English-language employees almost without exception had remained on the job. Soon after the strike, the artists' and performers' unions in Montreal withdrew from the Canadian Council of Authors and Artists,

---

50 / To ease the task of reconciliation, the CBC in April transferred André Ouimet to a staff position as director of planning. Within a few months he left the CBC to join the company that established the second French-language TV station in Montreal.

51 / After the strike had ended, Gérard Filion wrote: 'Nous avons assisté à un phénomène qui s'est répété fréquemment depuis deux ans: l'incompréhension des Canadiens de langue anglaise vis-à-vis des problèmes canadiens-français. ... Il s'est fait une plus grande consommation de slogans nationalistes sur les lignes de piquetage et dans les assemblées qu'en aucun autre moment et aucun autre lieu du Canada français.' Lead editorial, *Le Devoir*, March 11, 1959.

52 / *Ibid.*, March 7, 1959. Part of the open letter was quoted by Ken Johnstone, 'The war that nearly wrecked the CBC,' *Star Weekly*, Toronto, June 13, 1959.

and the 'two solitudes' seemed once again in being. Bernard Trotter, reviewing the implications of the strike six years later, concluded: 'It provided the occasion for the coalescing of disparate interests among the liberal left and strengthened their resolve in the cause of a conscious nationalism. It had, without doubt, separatist implications – but these were felt rather than stated on both sides. It was, in a very real sense, the first crack in the dam that broke with Duplessis' death a few months later.'[53]

3 The Cancellation of 'Preview Commentary'

During the months that followed, the French network of the CBC had to pick itself up and re-establish its television service under new directors, meanwhile allowing time to heal some of the serious breaches in working relationships occasioned by the strike. In its haste to restore a full service and working morale, at least one serious error in program judgment was made: the scheduling of a television play, 'La plus belle de Céans,' to mark the beatification of Mother Margaret d'Youville, the founder of the Grey Nuns. This turned out to be a racy drama that included scenes depicting the 'fast life' of her husband in their early married years.[54] Religious groups were horrified and sent bitter complaints to the CBC and to members of Parliament. Some of the convents, they said, had rented television sets especially for the performance, and had allowed students and young nuns to stay up to see the play. The first broadcasting committee appointed by the Conservative government was just getting under way, and inevitably, the Mother d'Youville drama became a focus for complaints and questions as to who should bear the responsibility for it.[55]

It was a very rough time for the CBC in Parliament. First the Montreal strike, then the Mother d'Youville program. In the parliamentary committee, complaints were raised about the cost of CBC television and about its commercial policy – in particular, the inability (as it was deemed) to recover all expenditures on sponsored programs from advertising revenues. Then a totally unexpected issue became headline news.

The CBC's acting president made a sudden decision to cancel a daily

---

53 / In a seminar presentation, Queen's University, March 1965.
54 / 'Disputes Threaten Operations of CBC,' *Montreal Star*, May 13, 1959.
55 / Rémi Paul (PC) said the program was 'an insult to Catholics and French Canadians,' *Debates*, May 7, 1959, 3412. Jean-Noël Tremblay (PC) demanded that the committee be given the names of all those responsible for approving the script and the production.

four-minute radio talk ('Preview Commentary') on its English network, and this was followed by an even more sudden decision to reinstate the program. The series had been on the air for more than two years. During the parliamentary session, four of the five morning commentaries had each week focused on political developments in Ottawa, with members of the press gallery giving their interpretations of government actions and policies and of the events unfolding in Parliament. Correspondents for a number of newspapers and periodicals took turns in broadcasting the commentaries; it was the responsibility of the CBC public affairs department to see that a reasonable variety of viewpoints was maintained. On June 23, the day after 'Preview Commentary' ended, four public affairs supervisors resigned, to be followed within forty-eight hours by some thirty radio and television producers. The CBC refused to accept their resignations and the program went back on the air. During the next ten days, the acting president was replaced as chairman of the board of directors; the minister answering for the CBC in Parliament appeared before the broadcasting committee that investigated the circumstances surrounding the cancellation; and the future of the CBC vice-president was in jeopardy.[56]

The whole incident was extraordinary. Such a peremptory command from the chief executive to kill a series, without consulting the programmers concerned, was unprecedented.[57] Some speculated that the attitude of the prime minister was a key to the explanation for what had happened.[58] Although he does not refer to 'Preview Commentary,' journalist Patrick Nicholson, who in 1959 was a confidant of Diefenbaker, has written in his book *Vision and Indecision* of the

disastrous disenchantment of the press with its former favourite. Throughout his long lone wolf years in the Opposition, John Diefenbaker had created and enjoyed a warm relationship with the Press Gallery, such as no other politician could boast in living memory. ... But this free and easy relationship and the ever-open door subtly changed when he began – in the journalists' phrase – to walk on the water. ... From journalists, Mr. Prime Minister seemed to demand an uncritical – perhaps even adulatory – press as of right. He even began to call individual writers onto the carpet in his office, and dress them down over petty

56 / Because of the writer's personal involvement in this incident, references will be made only to what appears in the records or in the accounts of others.

57 / *1959 Proceedings*, June 30, 1959, 529 and 543.

58 / Peter C. Newman, *Renegade in Power* (Toronto, 1963), 234–6; Peter Dempson, *Assignment Ottawa* (Toronto, 1968), 105–7.

little points which he testily rated as unjustified criticism. The alert and free-wheeling Press Gallery, accustomed to the dignified silence of criticized Liberal ministers, was shocked by this unbecoming reaction as much as it was offended by the interference.[59]

Whatever unease may have been expressed about 'Preview Commentary' in high political circles, practically no criticism of the series, of the choice of commentators, or of the texts of individual broadcasts had reached the public affairs department of the CBC, either from listeners or from the program heads. The supervisor, Frank Peers, was therefore astonished to be handed a sheet of paper by the controller of broadcasting, Charles Jennings, on June 15, announcing the replacement of the program by a news report on parliamentary developments each day, the change to be effective June 22.[60]

Bushnell, the acting president, denied at the time (and since) that criticism from political figures occasioned the change:

Never at any time has an order or a directive been given to me, or to my president, Mr. Ouimet, by the Honourable Mr. George Nowlan or by any member of parliament, or by anyone else who could be said to wield political influence. ... To close an ear completely to criticism, regardless of its source, would in my view clearly indicate irresponsibility on the part of management. ...

Why then did I choose to change this particular program Preview Commentary and substitute one format for another? Because it seemed to me that it had somehow changed from the original intention and was not doing as good a job. Having made up my mind, I moved quickly to substitute a factual news report of the Ottawa scene.[61]

Peers and his departmental colleagues became convinced from inquiries made of other corporation officials that the decision was politically motivated. Emergency meetings of the senior program directors in Toronto were held on June 20 and 21, and a statement drawn up protesting the decision. The second evening the group met with Bushnell, who made no promise except that the decision would be reviewed by the board of directors which was meeting in Toronto the following day. At the conclusion of the meeting, Bushnell asked the group to put their

59 / (Don Mills, Ont., 1968), 103–4.
60 / *1959 Proceedings*, evidence of Peers, 520–1.
61 / *Ibid.*, evidence of Bushnell, 555–6; see also Stursberg, *Mister Broadcasting*, 189–98.

confidence in him and in the action he had taken regarding 'Preview Commentary.'[62]

In an attempt to make sure that the 'Preview Commentary' decision received full discussion by the board the next day, three representatives of the senior program group (E.S. Hallman, Peter McDonald, and Peers) asked for a meeting with the historian, W.L. Morton, a member of the board.[63] When on the next evening, June 22, Morton told Peers and Hallman that the board had confirmed Bushnell's decision to cancel the program, Peers and his immediate deputies, Hugh Gillis and Bernard Trotter, decided to make their case in public, and submitted their resignations.[64] They explained that the decision to make a program change because of external pressure, real or anticipated, threatened the integrity of public affairs programming, and they felt they had taken every step open to them within the corporation to have the decision seriously reconsidered, but had failed.[65]

On the same day, H.G. Walker, director of English networks, had sought the intervention of Alphonse Ouimet, who was at his home in Ottawa, recuperating from gall bladder surgery. On June 23, Bushnell returned Ouimet's call in the presence of Walker and Charles Jennings (who as controller of programs was Bushnell's close associate in Ottawa). Bushnell told Ouimet that the decision was necessary, otherwise he and the president might both be removed from their jobs.[66] (A week earlier, Jennings had told Walker that Bushnell had said, 'heads were to roll ... if we did not remove Preview Commentary by June 22 ... Specific heads mentioned were, Mr. Bushnell and Mr. Nowlan.'[67]) Ouimet recalls that he advised Bushnell to tell their fellow directors everything, reminding Bushnell that the CBC had never given in to political interference, and warning him that it would be disastrous if he did so now.[68]

Bushnell told the broadcasting committee that he had indeed used the phrase, 'heads will roll,' but what he had meant was that 'with this rather tragic series of unfortunate circumstances that we have had in the last six

62 / *1959 Proceedings*, evidence of Peers, 523–6. Eight English network officers signed the protest, including the director and program director of radio (J.M. Kannawin and E.S. Hallman), the program director of television (P. McDonald), and the chief news editor (W.H. Hogg).

63 / Peers had met Morton earlier in the day to outline the situation as he saw it.

64 / Helen James, the other assistant supervisor, was on tour in western Canada. She wired her resignation from Edmonton.

65 / *1959 Proceedings*, 526.

66 / *Ibid.*, evidence of Walker, 549.

67 / *Ibid.*, 548.

68 / Interview, Feb. 13, 1977.

months, that if we did not pull up our socks, certainly somebody's head would roll – and quite properly.'[69] To his biographer he explained that Walker and Jennings may have misunderstood the conversation with Ouimet because they had heard only one side of the telephone conversation. He added, 'No one in my presence had ever said or implied that "heads would roll." '[70]

Ouimet, who supports Walker's version, has written of Bushnell's explanation in the book by Stursberg, 'As to his version of the 'Preview Commentary' incident, he forgets that if Walker and Jennings did hear only one side of the conversation, I heard it all – since the telephone call he made was to me. He clearly told me that "heads would roll, Nowlan's, yours and mine." '[71]

The resignations were reported with banner headlines on the front pages of English-language newspapers, and a number of organizations and prominent educators made public statements or wired the CBC board of directors protesting the decision and asking that the CBC's independence be reaffirmed.[72] Davidson Dunton was quoted by The Canadian Press as saying, 'If the board of directors of CBC do not put Preview Commentary back on the air they are selling out the principle of national broadcasting in Canada.'[73]

Opposition leaders in Parliament pressed for an immediate debate on the charge that 'clandestine political influence had been brought to bear on the Canadian Broadcasting Corporation management.' Pearson quoted a statement made two years earlier by the minister of finance, Donald Fleming, when he had been in opposition: 'If the Canadian Broadcasting Corporation is to function in a manner free of government influence, then there must not be attempts on the part of the Prime Minister or other members of the government to influence the programming activities of the Canadian Broadcasting Corporation, and above all opinion broadcasts on public issues.'[74] Speaking for the government, Davie Fulton, the minister of justice, and George Nowlan denied the charge 'so baselessly brought in this house by the Leader of the Opposition.' Nowlan said the decision to cancel Preview Commentary was the

69 / 1959 Proceedings, 557.
70 / Stursberg, Mister Broadcasting, 198.
71 / J.A. Ouimet Papers, Pointe Claire, Que.
72 / For example, the Canadian Association for Adult Education, Canadian Association for Civil Liberties, Ontario Federation of Labour, Canadian Federation of Agriculture, a group of Montreal educators and journalists, and the broadcasting committee of the General Synod of the Anglican Church of Canada.
73 / Globe and Mail, June 25, 1959.
74 / Debates, June 23, 1959, 5037.

management's, and that he 'knew nothing about it until this morning (June 23), when I heard on the radio that this decision had been made.'[75] The next day, the prime minister gave a delphic reply to another question from Pearson: 'Mr. Speaker, the honourable gentleman and the representatives of his party are taking a strong stand, as have members of this party, against any government interference with the c.b.c. I think that constitutes a complete answer to the hon. gentleman's question.'[76]

On June 23, the parliamentary committee on broadcasting was in Toronto to tour the radio and television facilities of the CBC, together with members of the CBC's board of directors. Although there was an effort to insulate them from the commotion caused by the resignations in the public affairs department,[77] the *Globe and Mail* reported that they 'bumped headlong into ... writers and producers wth books, pictures and personal papers under their arms.' The next day the front page headline of the *Toronto Star* reported, '35 More Ready to Join CBC Walkout; Quit Coast to Coast Unless Settlement.'

All this agitation – the headlines, the growing number of resignations, the representations being made to Ottawa – prompted the CBC board of directors to reconsider their position on the third day of their meeting (June 24). Several directors met Nowlan informally while he was on his way through Toronto to a taxation conference at St. Catharines.[78] The board decided to hear several program executives – Jennings, Walker, McDonald, and Hallman. Hallman did most of the talking. He read from a handwritten report prepared by Peers, and discussed with the board the list of press gallery commentators who had appeared on the program. At the conclusion of their discussions, the board 'unanimously' agreed to reinstate the program as of Monday morning, June 29.[79] It was also decided to ask those who had resigned to return to work. Most did, but Peers, Gillis, and Trotter did not, since they had received an invitation to testify before the parliamentary committee on June 30.[80]

On the evening of June 24, the board took yet another decision. They agreed that in future a chairman and a vice-chairman, other than the

75 / *Ibid.*, Fulton, 5037–8, Nowlan, 5400.

76 / *Ibid.*, June 24, 1959, 5086.

77 / 'M.P.'s on CBC Tour 'Detoured' From Strife,' *Toronto Star*, June 24, 1959.

78 / *1959 Proceedings*, 605, evidence of Nowlan.

79 / Bushnell was quoted in the *Toronto Star*, June 25: 'The decision was unanimous. ... So unanimous, in fact, that we didn't even have to take a vote.'

80 / Hugh Gillis left the CBC later in 1959 to direct a communications program at Boston University. Later he became academic vice-president of St. Mary's University, Halifax, and president of the Canadian Broadcasting League. Bernard Trotter left the CBC in 1963 to become director of academic planning for Queen's University, Kingston. In 1975 he was appointed to the board of directors of the CBC.

president and vice-president, should be elected by the directors annually, and the by-laws of the corporation were amended to permit this.[81] R.L. Dunsmore and C.W. Leeson, who were not present at this evening meeting, were elected chairman and vice-chairman respectively. No public announcement was made regarding these changes. When a newspaper reported on July 14 that a new chairman was to be appointed, Nowlan replied to a questioner in the Commons that he had not read the report and could not comment on it, adding that the government had taken no action in that connection.[82] When Pickersgill complained nine months later that the House had been misled, Nowlan explained that the board of directors had amended its by-laws to permit these changes, but said that he had not received any formal communication on the matter, and did not remember hearing about it until 'a considerable time later.' Dunsmore remained chairman of the board until the legality of the CBC by-law was challenged in 1963, immediately after the Liberals returned to office.[83]

The program committee of the board met on June 25, and proposed informally that the board should consider giving Bushnell leave of six to eight weeks, and that as soon as feasible he should be retired. The executive committee met the following week, on June 29–30, with Ouimet in attendance the first day. On that day Nowlan was invited to meet with them for a discussion of witnesses' scheduled appearances before the parliamentary committee on June 30.[84]

After Bushnell had appeared before the broadcasting committee, the executive committee of the board granted leave to him for a period of two months, and 'as an emergency measure' named a management committee to carry on CBC operations in the absence of both the president and the vice-president.[85] Ouimet returned to his office on August 4, and took a full part in the next meeting of the board of directors. Bushnell was not present, and his leave was extended to September 21.[86]

81 / Minutes, CBC board of directors, June 22–24, 1959.
82 / *Debates*, July 14, 1959, 5959.
83 / *Ibid.*, March 30, 1960, 2608; June 6, 1963, 726–7. See below, chapter 11, p. 309.
84 / Information from two former members of CBC board of directors.
85 / *Debates*, July 7, 1959, 5579; announcement read by J.M. Macdonnell, acting for the minister of national revenue. The chairman of the management committee was Col. R.P. Landry, assistant to the CBC president. Other members were Marcel Carter, controller of management planning and personnel; Charles Jennings, controller of broadcasting; J.P. Gilmore, controller of operations; Max Henderson, comptroller; W.G. Richardson, director of engineering; and R.C. Fraser, director of public relations.
86 / Bushnell resented the suggestion that he should not attend the sixth directors' meeting, which met in Ottawa and Halifax September 9–12, 1959. Stursberg, *Mister Broadcasting*, 220.

Bushnell resigned from the CBC early in December. A reporter asked Nowlan, 'Did he fall or was he pushed?' Nowlan replied, 'He fell, and I tried to grab him as he fell over the precipice. That's the honest-to-God truth.'[87]

4 *The CBC and Parliament*

The disasters that befell the CBC during the illness of its president damaged the corporation in the eyes of the press and public, but the situation was compounded by the hostility shown by some of the Conservative members of the Commons. A member from Quebec, J.-N. Tremblay,[88] was perhaps the most bitter critic, but others who seemed determined to humble the CBC included Arthur Smith, of Calgary South, James McGrath of St. John's, and Jack McIntosh of Swift Current – the latter two with private station backgrounds. With a hugh majority in the Commons, the government was inclined to give parliamentary committees more scope than in the past, and the broadcasting committee in particular seemed free of any pronounced government restraint.

The 1959 committee, under the prodding of Arthur Smith, insisted that the CBC disclose in detail the production costs of programs offered to sponsors, and the amounts paid by particular advertisers. Bushnell tried to persuade the committee that it was unwise for the CBC in a competitive position to provide this information, and he found support for his position from opposition members, from the Association of Canadian Advertisers, from the CBC board of directors, and indeed from Nowlan himself. In spite of all these representations, the majority of the committee, in Pickersgill's words, 'took it upon themselves to disregard his (the minister's) advice and to insist upon asking for this information.'[89]

Although the 1959 committee went farther than any other in requiring the CBC to disclose details of its commercial and program operations, it did not have adequate resources to evaluate the information received, and the result was probably to blur the distinction between questions of broadcasting policy and decisions that were administrative and operational.

Both in the House and before the committee, Nowlan extended to Bushnell his personal support. On June 29 he told the Commons: 'The

87 / *Winnipeg Tribune*, Dec. 3, 1959, report by Charles King.
88 / Tremblay later became Quebec's minister of cultural affairs.
89 / *Debates*, July 18, 1959, 6323. See also *1959 Proceedings*, 64–70, 77–8, 151–67, 238–53, 567–8, 591–8, 630–4.

last six months have been probably the most hectic in the history of the corporation. I can say of my personal knowledge that during this period Mr. Bushnell has worked tirelessly and given himself wholeheartedly and solely to the corporation. I know that on many occasions he worked 17 or 18 hours a day throughout the strike. Although I am not a doctor I can tell hon. members ... that Mr. Bushnell is completely and totally exhausted.'[90] To the committee, the minister explained: 'Mr. Bushnell and I have been very close. We have talked freely and met two or three times a week in discussing the affairs of the corporation.'[91] Members of the committee may not have realized how unusual it was for a minister to meet this often with the head of a crown corporation, although Pearson commented on it some days later.[92] Nowlan was well liked within the committee, on both the government and the opposition sides. They were probably sympathetic when he voiced a mild complaint, 'I have no power with the c.b.c. I am in the unfortunate position of receiving a lot of the blame and having no responsibility for anything.'[93]

In their investigation of 'Preview Commentary,' the committee heard Bushnell's denial that he had any political reason for cancelling the program, but then decided against hearing from any who had been instrumental in reversing Bushnell's decision. Pickersgill complained: 'We wanted two further witnesses. The steering committee agreed to have one of those witnesses, but the hearings were terminated abruptly before that witness could be heard. We wanted to have another witness, a member of the board of directors ... but we were turned down by every member of the majority voting against extending an invitation to those witnesses who might have been able to solve the problem.'[94] Instead, the committee elected to hear Nowlan as the next witness, who denied again that he had given any specific directions to Bushnell, although he added, 'I may have given my own personal opinion, and may have said: my colleagues are sore about this or irritated about that, or did appreciate that, or something of that kind.' He said that doubtless he had mentioned the program 'Preview Commentary' to Bushnell from time to time, but he could not recall any specific comment he had made.[95]

In its report to the Commons, the committee included only one sentence on the 'Preview Commentary' matter: 'Your Committee investi-

90 / *Debates*, 1959, 5200.
91 / *1959 Proceedings*, 603.
92 / *Debates*, July 18, 1959, 6302.
93 / *1959 Proceedings*, 604.
94 / *Debates*, July 18, 1959, 6325.
95 / *1959 Proceedings*, 604, 612.

gated the charge that "clandestine political influence" was responsible for the removal of the program, "Preview Commentary" and found no evidence to support the charge.' In other sections of the report, the committee affirmed its support of the basic aims and objectives of the CBC, but said there should be an administrative reorganization and 'the restoration of clear authority and responsibility to the central headquarters in Ottawa,' with one senior official at headquarters responsible for the supervision of all production. The board of directors must assume full responsibility for policy, and the committee recommended that 'the person occupying the position of Chairman of the Board shall not hold other executive offices in the Corporation.' Concerned about the costs of television, the committee suggested the adoption of 'some formula whereby limits may be set on the annual contribution of the federal government to the Corporation,' and an effort 'to ensure the emergence of vigorous commercial policies.'[96]

In the Commons debate on the CBC estimates, J.W. Pickersgill for the Liberals and Douglas Fisher for the CCF made it clear that they did not agree with the tone of the committee's report, or some of its specific recommendations. Pickersgill thought the committee was trying 'deliberately to usurp the authority of the board of directors' in recommending that a senior officer in Ottawa have clear authority over all program production. He agreed that weakness had been showed at the very top, but did not agree that the whole administrative structure had been found wanting. As for the observation that the board of directors should be responsible for policy, Pickersgill felt that the BBG should make policy for the whole national system.[97]

Douglas Fisher criticized the report for its very sketchy references to the purposes for which the CBC was created, and for its preoccupation with commerical revenues. He wanted the government to clarify its position: 'We would welcome nothing more than a statement, not from the minister but from the Prime Minister himself, on what he believes and thinks about the C.B.C. and its position in the future. I think that would do more to handle what concerns me most within the framework of this house, that is the niggling, nasty desire among Conservative members to junk the C.B.C. I believe there is a great need for the Prime Minister to lay it on the line so that all members of his party will realize that junking the C.B.C. is not Conservative policy.'[98]

Pearson thought the three chief needs of the CBC were financial se-

96 / *Ibid.*, 807–9.
97 / *Debates*, July 18, 1959, 6322–4.
98 / *Ibid.*, 6312.

curity so that it would not be 'forced to go each year to the Minister of Finance and beg for the means of its existence,' administrative efficiency, and maximum freedom from political pressures. He argued that the CBC, 'partly because of the new set-up, is now under greater ministerial and political influence than before and there is, consequently, more ministerial contact with it than before.' Pearson restated five points in Liberal party policy: the CBC was an essential and vital element in Canada's existence and survival; the private stations were a part of the single system; the CBC must be financed for a period longer than a year; the CBC must be free of political intervention; and the CBC should be a major contributor to the sense of national identity.[99]

Nowlan confessed to the broadcasting committee that, as the minister answering for the CBC, he had almost hoped his 'head would roll': 'I must say that I wondered if that was a threat or a promise, because certainly there is nothing I would rather do, frankly, than be rid of the responsibility of reporting to parliament for the C.B.C.' He reported telling Bushnell, 'I was sick and tired of these criticisms coming in from all over the country, from members of parliament, from my colleagues, and from the public generally.'[100] But in the Commons debate, he spoke more positively on behalf of the government: 'No party has a monopoly of affection for the C.B.C. ... In my opinion the C.B.C. is one of the great national organizations of this country. ... For anyone to suggest that the Prime Minister, directly or indirectly, interfered with this corporation through me or through anyone else is absolutely untrue and unwarranted.'[101]

In 1960 another broadcasting committee was appointed but too late in the session to proceed with hearings. There were two debates in the Commons on the CBC, with the usual variety of opinions expressed, but Nowlan reiterated his position: 'Certainly as far as this government is concerned I want to say again ... we believe in the C.B.C.; we support the corporation, and as long as this government is in power – and, I hope, as long as any government is in power – that policy will be maintained; because I am quite certain that if any government attempted to destroy that principle they would be heaved out of office so rapidly that they would never know what struck them.'[102]

During 1960, much of the attention was diverted from the CBC to the BBG, the licensing of the second television stations, and the new regula-

99 / Ibid., 6301–7.
100 / 1959 Proceedings, 604.
101 / Debates, July 18, 1959, 6328 and 6330.
102 / Ibid., July 12, 1960, 6194.

tions prescribing minimum quotas of Canadian content for all television stations and networks. With the prospect of more competition, the CBC was concerned with maintaining its share of commercial revenues, and with its uneasy relations with the BBG. After the violent criticism the CBC had received in 1959, some program supervisors tried to exercise extra caution in 1960: too much caution for the television critic of the *Globe and Mail*, or for an editorial writer of the *Winnipeg Free Press* who asked whether it was coincidence or something more that, since the Diefenbaker government came to power, the CBC had shown 'all the independence and courage of a rabbit confronted by a tiger.'[103]

More important than any efforts to avoid provoking its critics, the CBC management undertook a complete reorganization of its administrative structure. But these efforts had little effect on the broadcasting committee in 1961, which again undertook its examination of the CBC with a special zeal.[104]

The committee's central purpose was to examine the working of the broadcasting act of 1958 to determine what changes might be recommended, and to this end it questioned representatives of the BBG, CBC, and CAB. But even more time was spent examining CBC operations, sometimes in the finest detail. Of some 744 printed pages reproducing evidence before the committee (excluding appendices and minutes), 437 pages represent testimony from CBC officers (mainly Alphonse Ouimet), 182 pages testimony from the BBG (Andrew Stewart), 35 pages evidence from the CAB, and 35 pages the auditor general's examination of CBC accounting methods and financial organization. The CBC was called before the committee on twenty-two different days, as compared with seven for the BBG and two for the CAB representatives.

In 1959, the broadcasting committee had been angered by Bushnell's attempt to withhold certain kinds of information never made public previously. In 1961, Ouimet provided the committee with a plethora of

103 / *Winnipeg Free Press*, May 24, 1960; also Dennis Braithwaite in the *Globe and Mail*, May 21, 1960.
104 / The CBC's reorganization included the appointment of three general managers, H.G. Walker (English networks), Marcel Ouimet, who was no relation to the president (French networks), and Charles Jennings (regional broadcasting). Five vice-presidents were appointed as staff advisers to the president: assistant to the president (R.P. Landry); programming (E.S. Hallman); administration and finance (Marcel Carter); corporate affairs (R.C. Fraser); and engineering and operations (J.P. Gilmore). In the main, these were not so much new jobs as new titles; a reshuffle to clarify lines of authority. On January 26, 1960, the government appointed Captain W.E.S. Briggs as vice-president to succeed E.L. Bushnell (see below, p. 211). *Debates*, Jan. 26, 1960, 323; *CBC Annual Report, 1959–60*, 11.

information, to the point where the veteran member for Toronto-Greenwood, J.M. Macdonnell, complained that a kind of 'paper curtain' was being imposed between committee members and the corporation itself.[105] The members asked for and received information about the committees of the board of directors and their membership, the number of board meetings, the percentages of meetings attended by each director, the size of the production staff, the numbers of employees belonging to unions, television operating costs per home per year, the administrative organization, the names and experience of the heads of divisions, the use of management consultants, the methods by which the network and other production centres reported, the operation of script bureaus, the methods of supervising controversial broadcasting, the overtime costs, the number of performers given employment and how much they earned, staff expenditures compared with operating expenditures, the costs of cbc publications, operating expenditures by location, the number of employees earning over $10,000 a year, costs of cbc productions compared with those of the bbc and us networks, statements outlining program standards to be observed, coverage statistics, sponsorship arrangements, advertising rates, rights for football telecasts, film inventory and film purchases, plans for consolidation of facilities in Toronto and Montreal, and the operation of the cbc international service. As a result of rotation of members on the committee and their spotty attendance,[106] some questions were asked several times. The Liberal member, Jack Pickersgill, observed:

I think of the amount of time and energy of the members of the higher administrative staff, the chief executives of the c.b.c., that we are absorbing here ... when they ought to be spending their time directing the corporation and not answering endless trivial questions. ... It seems to me that a few members of this committee are taking the view that this committee was set up to substitute itself for the board of directors of the c.b.c. ... The idea that we should go over all the details of the operation is just ridiculous. It is a misuse of the time of parliament, and a misuse of the time of the committee.[107]

Looking back at the committee's proceedings, one reporter wrote:

Three Conservatives accounted for a large proportion of the anti-cbc questions

105 / *1961 Proceedings*, 429.
106 / For example, only 16 of the 35 members were present on April 11, when Ouimet presented his major report on cbc operations.
107 / *Ibid.*, 528.

and comments: Art Smith (Calgary South), J.H. Horner (Acadia), and James A. McGrath. ...

Smith ... mercilessly rode J.A. Ouimet, the CBC president. He attacked the acting on CBC television ('still very much in the little-theatre stage'), accused the CBC of being taken in by a phony political correspondent, suggested that the CBC's function might be carried out better by private interests in some places. ...

J.H. Horner managed to build a mountain of Canadian nationalism out of the molehill of one incident – the CBC hired an American to broadcast a Calgary rodeo.

But it was J.A. McGrath who put forward, in the most articulate way, what many enemies of the CBC have been thinking in the last year. ' ... we now have second television stations in major cities and there is the possibility of a second network which takes the exclusive national service away from the CBC; in other words, there are other people who are now capable of providing a national service ... with no cost to the taxpayer.'[108]

For the first time, a report of a parliamentary committee on broadcasting failed to affirm the value of public broadcasting. There was no hint that the members believed in the value of the CBC, and there were sections of the report that criticized or called into question the CBC's operations, its planned capital investments, its inventories of films, and its supervision and control of scripts and programming.[109]

In addition to its criticisms of CBC operations, the committee recommended amendments to the broadcasting act which would have had the effect of removing the president and vice-president from the CBC board of directors. Another suggested amendment would have divested the CBC of its power to prevent affiliated stations from joining a temporary network, thus allowing the new private network to distribute some of its programs through CBC affiliates.

Some of the traditional supporters of public broadcasting rushed out statements opposing the committee's recommendations. The secretary-treasurer of the Canadian Labour Congress said, 'The three most important proposed amendments to the Act are all bad, and the other main recommendations are almost equally sinister. ... the report as a whole is a private broadcasters' report. It should serve as an alarm signal to all those who believe in maintaining a national system of broadcasting 'basically Canadian in content and character' and the free and independent CBC without which the national system would cease to be national,

108 / 'The P.C.s Fear the CBC 'Is Out To Get Them',' Robert Fulford, *Toronto Star*, Nov. 1, 1961.
109 / *1961 Proceedings*, final report, 989–92.

and become nothing but a carbon copy of the cheapest and shoddiest American radio and TV.'[110]

In a similar statement, H.H. Hannam, president of the Canadian Federation of Agriculture, said that the report weakened the application of the principles of a national broadcasting system operated in the public interest. 'As a document dealing with the problems and policies of broadcasting in Canada the Report is one that conveys little information and no inspiration to the public. Its effect is negative and tends to be unjustifiably destructive of the nation's confidence in the performance of the Canadian Broadcasting Corporation.'[111] The *Montreal Star* (July 3) headed its editorial, 'A Biased Report on Broadcasting.'

More surprising was the hostile assessment of a newspaper and a radio station neither of which had the reputation of supporting the CBC – the Toronto *Globe and Mail* and the independent radio station with perhaps the largest listening audience in the country, CFRB, Toronto. The *Globe and Mail* (June 30) wrote:

There may have been an element of spite in the manner in which the Commons committee on broadcasting conducted its inquiry this year into the affairs of the Canadian Broadcasting Corporation, and the resulting report is hardly a helpful document. Some of the questioning of CBC officials before the committee was needling of a distasteful sort, and the management changes recommended in the report are of dubious origin.

The committee proposes a reorganization of the CBC's command structure which would have the effect of demoting President Alphonse Ouimet and his deputy by removing them from the board of directors. A change of this nature, clearly, could only be justified by compelling arguments, and the committee has none to offer. ...

It is not the role of Parliament, in our view, to harry and chase the CBC with minor questions about the details of management and minor criticisms about program policy. ... Certainly there are many things to be criticized in the CBC – and this newspaper has not been slow to point them out – but when its over-all work is compared with that of other broadcasting systems, the CBC does not take a second place.

110 / Press release, June 29, 1961. The CLC sometimes turned for information on broadcasting matters to Eugene Forsey, who at this time was a member of the executive committee of the BBG. Letter, Forsey to Peers, March 23, 1976.
111 / News release, Ottawa, June 29, 1961. Hannam followed with a four-page letter to Nowlan on August 1, a letter which he said had been approved by the CFA board of directors.

Radio station CFRB broadcast an editorial of its own four times on June 30 and July 1 under the title 'Politics and the Canadian Broadcasting Corporation.' It claimed that although the station had frequently been critical of the sums spent on the CBC, the proposal to remove the president and vice-president from the CBC board of directors would 'make the CBC nothing more than a department of government.' It said that as broadcasters with more than a third of a century experience, CFRB was conscious of the grave dangers of any political party controlling broadcasting, and added: 'Notwithstanding its shortcomings the CBC does a good and necessary job for Canada and despite the fact that for some years now Parliament has controlled the purse strings of the corporation it has remained relatively free of political domination. This is undoubtedly due to the high quality of its top executive officers, the same officers this committee now wants to remove from a voting position on the board.' The radio editorial urged listeners 'to tell your member of parliament to keep the CBC free of political control.'

This was the last broadcasting committee to meet while the Conservatives held office, and for whatever reasons the government took no steps to implement any of the committee's recommendations. The government did, however, have the Glassco Commission make a special study of the CBC's organization and operations with the objective of increasing its efficiency.

5 The Glassco Commission's Investigation

In its sixth recommendation, the parliamentary committee made reference to the Royal Commission on Government Organization (the Glassco Commission), suggesting that after the commission had reported, the CBC board of directors should consider 'the advisability of commissioning management consultants to inquire further into the operation of the Canadian Broadcasting Corporation.'[112] The Glassco Commission had been appointed in September 1960 to report on the organization and methods of operation of the department and agencies of the government of Canada, but it had not intended to investigate the CBC.[113] Before the CBC directors had time to review the parliamentary committee's recommendation, the government decided that the Glassco Commission itself should undertake an inquiry into the CBC.

The broadcasting committee's suspicion that all was not right with the

112 / *1961 Proceedings*, 992.
113 / *Ibid.*, 732, evidence of A.M. Henderson; also information from J.E. Hodgetts.

CBC's organization had been heightened by the testimony of the auditor general, Maxwell Henderson, who appeared before the committee on the initiative of a Progressive Conservative member from Winnipeg, Gordon Chown. Henderson had been auditor general for fifteen months. Before that he had been the CBC's chief financial officer (comptroller) for two years. Prior to that he had been in private business, notably with the firm of distillers, Seagram of Canada, and during that period he had for a time been chairman of the executive committee of the Canadian Chamber of Commerce – an organization that had often expressed criticism of the role of the CBC in Canadian broadcasting. While with the CBC, Henderson did not establish close relations with Ouimet, who felt that the others in the management group did not accept Henderson as a member of the team.[114] Consequently, when the CBC's management structure was revised in the fall of 1959, Henderson, although remaining comptroller, was not promoted, but rather he reported to the vice-president, administration and finance (Marcel Carter). Henderson resented this and enlisted the support of the finance committee of the board of directors in his effort to establish a reporting line direct to the president.[115] He coupled this with a recommendation that the corporation's organizational structure should have an 'independent evaluation,' that is, that it should be reviewed by a firm of management consultants. This recommendation had not been accepted by Ouimet.

Testifying before the parliamentary committee, Henderson did not hesitate to criticize CBC management policies, although he admitted that it was 'traditional under our constitutional system' that the auditor general should not do so. He had transgressed this rule, he explained, because of his first-hand knowledge and experience within the corporation. 'Until these very fundamental questions of organization, management and internal control are settled, it is difficult to make recommendations intelligently in other areas of the corporation's activities.'[116]

Ouimet's relations with the government were sufficiently cool that it needed no more than Henderson's publicly stated criticisms and possibly the broadcasting committee's report for the government to decide

114 / Interview with Alphonse Ouimet, July 1, 1975. Henderson had been hired by the CBC in December 1957 at the insistence of Dunton and on the recommendation of the deputy minister of finance, K.W. Taylor. Dunton (in an interview, Aug. 24, 1976) speculated that Taylor may have been acting on the suggestion of the minister of finance, Donald Fleming. If so, Henderson's appointment may have reflected the government's concern about the mounting costs of television, or about the 'uncontrollable' CBC.
115 / *1961 Proceedings*, 722–6.
116 / *Ibid.*, 739–40.

that Glassco should undertake a full-scale investigation. Ouimet, in contrast to Bushnell, often found the minister (Nowlan) inaccessible and frequently had to deal with him through his secretary and executive assistant, Ruby Meabry.[117] His first meeting with Diefenbaker, on the occasion of the prime minister's appearance at a television studio, had been disastrous. The teleprompter did not work properly, and Diefenbaker was furious, blaming Ouimet and everyone else within earshot.[118] The government did not dare to try directly to get rid of Ouimet, but for over five years his salary was held stationary – at $20,000, the amount he had received as general manager in 1954.[119]

To understand what developed during the Glassco and succeeding investigations, it is necessary to be aware of attitudes within the CBC, at the head office in Ottawa and in the network centres of Toronto and Montreal. The general climate was, of course, determined largely by broadly political considerations – relations between the government and the CBC, public opinion about the CBC program service,[120] relations between the CBC and the regulatory board – and the economic conditions affected by the licensing policy of the government and the BBG. But beyond this, there were the working relationships within the CBC itself. In the main, the president received the support he needed from the board of directors, in spite of a degree of tension between him and the chairman, R.L. Dunsmore, whose position he regarded as of doubtful legality. Ouimet gave very full information to his directors, and over a period of time they identified themselves with the CBC, its objectives and traditions.

There was a rather greater problem in personnel of the head office. To use a gross simplification, the president's assistants and advisers could be placed in two groups. There were the practical men, whom Ouimet could count on to carry out corporation decisions quickly and decisively, who were hard-working and devoted lieutenants – typified by vice-presidents such as J.P. Gilmore, R.C. Fraser, H.G. Walker, Marcel Carter. There were other persons whom Ouimet considered as less than helpful, obstructive, non-compliant, or procrastinators – and these were often persons with a programming background.

117 / Ouimet interview, July 2, 1975.

118 / The date was July 14, 1958. Information from personnel at television station CBOT, Ottawa.

119 / Ouimet interview, June 30, 1975.

120 / A survey in 1962 of public attitudes to the CBC, carried out by Canadian Facts Limited on behalf of the CBC research department, showed that a large majority of Canadians supported the CBC's objectives and thought that the CBC was carrying them out well. CBC Ottawa, *What the Canadian Public Thinks of the CBC* (1963).

Both groups admired Ouimet's drive, intellectual ability, and integrity, but the second group felt that he had a limited understanding of how programs were conceived and produced; they cited statements indicating his belief that programs could be analysed and 'audited' for shortcomings in the same manner as other facets of the operation. This group tended to be critical of some of the directions in which the CBC was moving, and also more outspoken. They had contacts among journalists, senior civil servants, university faculties, and sometimes politicians.[121] The first group, predictably, had more direct responsibility for operations and policy implementation than did the second group, who often felt that their views and suggestions went unheeded.

The vice-president during these years, Captain W.E.S. Briggs, had previously been the CBC representative in the Maritime provinces, and thus had not been in a central policy position. He owed his appointment in 1960 to George Nowlan, who was also from Nova Scotia. (Ouimet had recommended against Briggs for this position.[122]) Briggs was a simpler man than the president and believed in the military virtues such as loyalty – loyalty to country, to the Navy, the corporation, and probably the minister. As vice-president, he had the responsibility for shorter-term operations, particularly of the English networks. Neither of the groups described above considered that Briggs had the intellectual grasp or the executive abilities of the president. He had little communication with the French program service because he did not speak French at all, and in accent seemed more British than Canadian.

When the Glassco Commission was asked to review the organization and operations of the CBC, the commissioners felt they already had enough to do, and turned the job over to G.H. Cowperthwaite, of an accounting firm in Toronto. He knew little about broadcasting, and to assist him Glassco assigned a research co-ordinator from the central staff of the commission, Henry Hindley, whose name is to reappear in the story of the later period, 1963–7. Hindley, who had occupied senior management and government posts in Britain before coming to Canada in the 1950s, was a man of no little cultivation, and an excellent writer. In assigning Hindley to the CBC project, Glassco specified that he was to pay particular attention to the programming aspect of CBC, since that was the area in which Cowperthwaite felt deficient.[123] No formal terms

121 / Their criticisms later found reflection and amplification in the second Fowler report (the *Report of the Committee on Broadcasting, 1965*) and in the book by E.A. Weir, *The Struggle for National Broadcasting in Canada*, published in 1965.
122 / Ouimet interview, February 13, 1977.
123 / Interview with H.O.R. Hindley, Ottawa, August 25, 1976.

of reference were given Cowperthwaite, but rather a verbal briefing by Glassco; and Cowperthwaite's team was given only two months (September–October 1961) to complete their interviews in the CBC – later extended to three months.[124] Cowperthwaite, Hindley, and their associates in the project submitted a report from the project team to the commissioners. Some months later Hindley prepared a first draft of the commission report, which Glassco rewrote himself.[125] The report, dated January 21, 1963, but released on April 17, appears in volume 4 of the commission's reports, *Special Areas of Administration*.[126] Soon after the report had been completed, the government of John Diefenbaker was defeated in the Commons, and the responsibility for possible implementation went to the new government of L.B. Pearson.

In their general conclusions, the commissioners observed that 'a complete assessment of performance would necessarily pay high tribute to many of the Corporation's accomplishments in providing Canadian audiences with radio and television services of high quality. Nevertheless, there can be no doubt but that the Corporation is in need of extensive reorganization to secure efficiency and economy in its operation' (p. 49). The tone of the report was highly critical of CBC management and direction, and especially of what it said was a failure to develop positive goals.

The report argued that because the board of directors must assume responsibility for the CBC's broadcasting operations and for the integrity of its programs, the board's membership should be carefully chosen, and the directors themselves should determine how long the chief executive should remain in office. At the same time, there would on occasion be need for policy direction from the government, and this right could be protected by giving the minister responsible the power of formal direction (p. 51).

The commissioners were critical of the heavy workload assumed by the president. The Fowler Commission in 1957 had recommended that under the chief executive there be a senior manager responsible for day-by-day management. The changes in the organization instituted in 1959 had failed to accomplish this purpose (p. 36).

As for the headquarters organization, the commissioners commented:

If it be accepted that the primary business of the Corporation is to produce and broadcast radio and television programmes, the most striking feature of the

124 / Ouimet interview, and Minutes, CBC board of directors, Sept. 18–21, 1961.
125 / Interview, H.O.R. Hindley. His draft was reduced in scope by Glassco to meet criticisms from another commissioner, Watson Sellar, that it went beyond the formal terms of reference.
126 / Royal Commission on Government Organization, *Report*, vol. 4 (Ottawa, 1963).

headquarters organization is that fewer than twenty people are directly concerned with programming while over 800 in Ottawa and at engineering headquarters in Montreal are engaged in ancillary operations. It is therefore difficult to resist the conclusion that the headquarters organization is excessively preoccupied with secondary matters, and that the generally high standard of the national programme service is largely attributable to the enterprise and initiative of the network and regional managements (p. 37).

When after the criticisms of the 1959 broadcasting committee the corporation took action, instead of instituting any substantive reorganization, 'a whole new level of management was superimposed on the existing organization, but the effective management of broadcasting remained where it had always been – in Montreal and Toronto' (p. 38). The report said it was necessary to centralize the formulation of policy, but not the conduct of primary and secondary operations. 'Many of the present troubles and difficulties would be resolved, and the speed of business accelerated, by an extensive decentralization to the regions and a more rational distribution of the control of ancillary operations at headquarters and throughout the organization' (pp. 39–40).

(It might be said parenthetically that the question of centralization and decentralization is a recurring one for the CBC. Canada, unlike many other countries, has required an organization allowing for several production points, and Montreal and Toronto are inevitably the French and English network centres. Program pressures force the making of many decisions on the spot. On the other hand, the head office must answer for those decisions, and must control costs. Solutions are not easy, and the Glassco Commission's recommendations are general and almost too facile.)

The report went on to say that the salary levels of the senior officers were too low in relation to their responsibilities – $20,000 for the president and $16,000 for the statutory vice-president, both figures set by the governor in council.[127] These low salaries had led to an undesirable compression in other salaries at senior levels, and prevented flexibility in recruiting suitable persons for responsible positions.

The commission was critical of the provisions for financing the corporation:

Each year Parliament is asked to vote the funds necessary to bridge the gap between corporate income and outgo. The scrutiny of these budgets is carried

127 / The board of directors more than once had recommended raising the salaries of the president and vice-president, but the government always refused to take action on their request.

out by the staff of the Treasury Board, the outcome being usually an arbitrary reduction in the operating budget of three or four million dollars. ...

In these circumstances, forward planning becomes extremely difficult. The Fowler Commission recommended that certainty of financing for five years ahead should be provided to permit an orderly development of activities and your Commissioners agree that dependence on annual votes by Parliament seriously complicates the task of management. If, as appears quite possible, the Corporation is fated to lose much of its commercial revenue to private competition, management should know now whether or not it may count on increased appropriations of public funds so that it can plan accordingly (p. 28).

The recommendations for a more secure system of financing, as well as for changed relationships between the president and the board of directors, and between the corporation and the government, would have required changes in the broadcasting act. There was in addition the unsolved problem of the amount of jurisdiction the BBG had over the CBC.

Ouimet's immediate reaction to the Glassco Report was to reiterate a call he had been making for another royal commission on broadcasting. The report, he said, 'underlines the need for the full-scale inquiry into broadcasting which the Corporation has been requesting for some time. This is obviously a question for Parliament to decide.'[128] He wrote this nine days after a general election had resulted in a Liberal victory over the Conservative government of John Diefenbaker. Pearson would assume office on April 22, and a new era would begin.

128 / J.A. Ouimet, letter to staff, Ottawa, April 17, 1963.

8 THE BBG's 'MOST PRODUCTIVE' YEARS: 1958-1963

REVIEWING HIS TEN YEARS as chairman of the Board of Broadcast Governors, Andrew Stewart has described three periods in the life of the BBG: the first from November 1958 to April 1963; the second to mid-1966 and the issuing of the government's White Paper; and the third from July 1966 to March 1968, when the BBG prepared for the new dispensation.[1] It was the first period that he regarded as the 'most productive.' It was also the period when the BBG and CBC seemed most combative.

Following the proclamation of the 1958 legislation, the board, unlike the CBC, began its work without permanent offices, without staff, and without traditions – except those borrowed from the former governors of the CBC. And unlike the CBC, which as a crown corporation could find its own quarters and hire its own staff, the BBG always had to go through 'official channels.' It took the Department of Public Works ten months to find any adequate space, and even then there were no proper facilities for public hearings. Stewart recalls the 'incredible delays,' under Civil Service Commission procedures, in appointing a few senior officers. Still, by early 1960 an organization had been fashioned and a budget set, with the work organized among five branches: secretariat, legal, technical, economics, and program. But the total staff consisted of only five senior officers and twenty-three others, mostly secretaries and clerks.

Important decisions had to be taken by the full board – under the act, the twelve part-time members of the BBG had the same powers as the three full-time members. The chairman and his two associates in Ottawa did the work preparatory to the decisions of the board, and administered the regulations in force. The first vice-chairman, Roger Duhamel, continued to live in Montreal and did not get deeply involved in the work of the board. When he resigned in July 1960 to become Queen's Printer, Carlyle Allison, the third full-time member, made it known that he

1 / Interviews with Andrew Stewart, Sidney, BC, June 11–13, 1975; during the interviews, the writer had access to an unpublished manuscript of some 434 pages, prepared by Stewart. This will be cited as Stewart MS.

wanted to be appointed vice-chairman. He was a man with political connections (he used to say that Stewart was a 'political eunuch').[2] As editor of the *Winnipeg Tribune*, he had been a friend and adviser to Diefenbaker, to whom he felt a continuing loyalty. Allison was a hard-working member of the board, increasingly knowledgeable about broadcasting as time went on, blunt in manner, and quick to form opinions. Stewart thought the government would have been wiser to appoint another French-speaking person as vice-chairman,[3] but instead Bernard Goulet of Montreal was appointed to the third position. A native of Winnipeg, Goulet had had considerable experience in private broadcasting in Winnipeg and Montreal, and in more recent years had his own production agency. Although some felt that he did not carry much weight in the French-Canadian community, his appointment was welcomed by the private broadcasters. Goulet, who was warmly regarded by Stewart and other colleagues, died after an operation in December 1964. Allison was vice-chairman from January 1961 to November 1965.

The board's public meetings were held to hear applications for new stations, for transfers involving a change of ownership or control of stations, sometimes for applications to form networks or to disaffiliate from a CBC network, and also to hear representations on proposed amendments to the regulations. The *in camera* meetings usually occupied more days than the public hearings; not only did decisions have to be made on the matters discussed in the open hearings, but other applications as well, such as for share transfers not involving a change in ownership or control. The chairman and his associates had to consult frequently with private broadcasters and the CBC, sometimes through two consultative committees that were established, one on public and the other on private broadcasting; with advertisers who were affected by regulations; and with the minister designated as responsible for broadcasting matters, who needed to be kept informed. During the period up to 1963, Stewart never discussed broadcasting issues with the prime minister, although Allison may have done so.[4] Of the three ministers Stewart had most to do with (Nowlan, Pickersgill, LaMarsh), it seems evident that he had the warmest regard for Nowlan, who he recounted was 'anxious to be informed, courteous in receiving opinions, always conscious of the humour of a situation, and had the successful politi-

2 / Stewart MS, 1.
3 / *Ibid.*, 21.
4 / Stewart interview.

cian's skill for avoiding direct and potentially disastrous confrontations.'[5]

It is plain that there was more dissension within the Board of Broadcast Governors than among the directors of the CBC. Partly this resulted from a lack of established traditions, the newness and inexperience of the staff, the varying interests displayed by members coming from different regions, and partly, perhaps, their connections with different members of the government. The lack of unity may also have been due to a difference in the style of leadership. Stewart was a fair-minded man, gentle in manner and considerate of the feelings of others, but with fixed principles that sometimes made him unyielding even in matters of detail.[6] He expected the government to decide policies on the larger questions, and believed that regulatory boards should assume the relatively more modest task of interpreting and applying those policies so formulated.[7] But broadcasting was a touchy and potentially explosive subject for governments to deal with; they did not like to take strong and clearly defined positions unless forced to do so by events. The part-time members of the board may therefore have lacked some elements of the required leadership if they were to perform their roles consistently and with recognized public objectives before them. They were also left in some doubt by the terms of the broadcasting act about how extensive their powers should be in relation to the CBC.

Stewart has said quite frankly that it was frequently impossible to get unanimity, even among permanent members of the board. Some important decisions were made by a margin of one vote. His experience left him dubious of the concept of a large, representative board, as recommended in the report of the Fowler Commission in 1957. He was not convinced that the part-time members represented a cross-section of public opinion, nor that they necessarily acted as Parliament might have done.[8] Although he respected a number of the individual members, he was critical of the method of their appointment. The chairman was not consulted as vacancies occurred. The practice of loading boards with

---

5 / Stewart MS, 14.

6 / An associate in the BBG wrote privately (April 19, 1962), 'Nothing could be purer or more admirable than Andrew's intentions ... [but] his rage for tidying everything up, and planning every detail of an indefinite future ... may lead him into all kinds of things that he has no conception of at the moment' (correspondence shown to the writer).

7 / Stewart MS, 58, 80, 206–7, 222; also 'Statement by Andrew Stewart' as member of the advisory committee appointed by the secretary of state (the 'Troika'), May 1964, 2–4 (mimeo.).

8 / Stewart interview, June 10, 1975.

the supporters of one political party could only bring administrative tribunals and administrative law into disrepute. The board, he felt, failed to create the necessary public confidence, mainly because of the extent of the known political associations of most of the appointees.[9]

The board soon began processing applications for new AM and FM radio stations, and for TV rebroadcasting stations, and in its first period particularly showed an inclination to grant more licences than had the CBC board of governors. It also began almost immediately a review of existing regulations for radio stations (there were no separate regulations for TV stations at the time the BBG took office.) Hearings were held on proposed amendments to the radio regulations, and the result for the private owners was somewhat more favourable advertising limits. For example, 'the Board acceded to requests of private broadcasters and made the daytime limit on advertising content apply on a 24-hour basis.' Previously, there had been stricter limits on night-time advertising.[10]

But the big concern was television. It was generally assumed, as Nowlan had earlier suggested in the Commons, that second television stations would be authorized for the larger centres, but that first the regulatory board must announce the regulations under which all TV stations would operate.[11] Stewart, in his first address to a CAB convention, went further than this. He said that the act clearly provided for networks other than those of the CBC, adding that 'the Board would, in principle,' favour the extension of networks which serve to link separate stations together ... [if] they contribute to the objectives of the national system.'[12]

On July 18, 1959, Nowlan announced in the Commons that the government had decided that from September 15 it would be prepared to consider applications for additional television stations in areas alredy provided with television service.[13] The BBG announced 'basic principles' that it proposed to apply to television after second stations were licensed, and public representations on the principles were heard in November 1959. The new television regulations were announced later the same month; hearings on applications began early in 1960, and by June 1960 recommendations for second television station licences were in the hands of the Department of Transport. Hearings on television

9 / *Ibid.*

10 / 'Radio Regulations Simplify Advertising Limits,' *Canadian Broadcaster* (June 11, 1959).

11 / *Debates*, May 22, 1958, 338; July 15, 1958, 2262; April 30, 1959, 3226.

12 / *Canadian Broadcaster*, 'CAB Daily No. 2,' (March 24, 1959).

13 / *Debates*, 6300. The minister's decision was on the advice of the BBG.

network regulations were held in September 1960, and an application to operate a private TV network was heard in April 1961. Things were moving very fast. The new board certainly could not be accused of being dilatory.

1 *Regulating Canadian Content*

The single factor that would most affect the profitability or even the viability of second television stations was the amount of Canadian programming they would be required to carry. The BBG's decision on this question would have implications for the possible formation of a second network, and also for the competitive conditions under which the CBC and its private affiliates would operate.

Past royal commissions and parliamentary committees had set Canadian programming as a key objective of the broadcasting system. In 1958 two sections of the act gave the BBG a broad mandate to prescribe minimum standards for such programming.[14] Section 10 required that the board 'for the purpose of insuring the continued existence and efficient operation of a national broadcasting system and the provision of a varied and comprehensive broadcasting service of a high standard that is *basically Canadian* in content and character, regulate ... the activities of public and private broadcasting stations in Canada' (italics added). By section 11, the board could regulate respecting program standards to promote and ensure 'the greater use of Canadian talent.'

In the summer and fall of 1959, the BBG, after preliminary discussions with the CBC and CAB, explored two possible approaches.[15] The first was to be abandoned as the result of opposition expressed in the formal hearings; the second, establishing a quota of 'Canadian content,' was to be incorporated into the television regulations.

The first approach was based on a clause in the act by which the BBG could require licensees to carry network programs of public interest or significance. As a 'basic principle' for its proposed television regulations, the board announced on July 28, 1959, that it intended to reserve a maximum of two hours during the period 8 PM to 11 PM 'for purposes to be prescribed by the Board of Broadcast Governors.' The intent was to

14 / For a fuller discussion of the BBG's record in program regulation, see Peter Stewart Grant, 'The Regulation of Program Content in Canadian Television,' *Canadian Public Administration*, XI:3 (Fall 1968), 322–91.
15 / Stewart as a precaution had sent the minister (Nowlan) an advance copy of the proposed ground rules for the regulation of television. Stewart MS, 370.

ensure that worthwhile programs, many of them Canadian, would find a place in the hours of prime viewing, even if the programs were not commercially attractive. The Canadian Association of Broadcasters, with support from the Association of Canadian Advertisers and the Canadian Association of Advertising Agencies, was wholly opposed to this regulation.[16] More surprising was the evident suspicion voiced by Alphonse Ouimet. He said in the public hearing, 'As the regulation reads, its application to existing network stations could seriously affect or even disrupt the entire programme schedules of the CBC.'[17] Ouimet feared that the BBG's plan could not be carried out without their involvement in CBC programming.[18] He also thought that this proposal was linked with the suggestion that the CBC provide some of its network service to second TV stations when licensed. Ouimet was opposed to this, although R.L. Dunsmore was not.[19]

The *Canadian Broadcaster* sensed the rift devel9ping between the CBC and BBG. Describing the hearings, the magazine wrote (November 12):

Perhaps the biggest upset came from President Alphonse Ouimet of the Canadian Broadcasting Corporation. It had been known the BBG had ideas about maintaining a single national television broadcasting system by dividing some of the top shows on the CBC networks between the established CBC affiliate and the competitive station to be licensed shortly. In many quarters it was a foregone conclusion that the present CBC network shows – American and Canadian both – would be divided between the old and the new stations. ...

But Mr. Ouimet made it clear the CBC does not plan to split its present network programs with anyone; that they are essential to the network; and that it intends to keep the network intact.

Finlay MacDonald, of CJCH Halifax, who hoped to be an applicant for a second television station in that city, was 'appalled' by Ouimet's statement. 'Surely I would think the Canadian Broadcasting Corporation would be the first to encourage or look into or investigate any avenues which would see certain programmes of value.' He said it

16 / BBG Public Hearings, *Proceedings*, Nov. 2, 1959; CAB at 5 ff., ACA and CAAA at 65 ff.
17 / *Ibid.*, Nov. 3, 1959, 222–3.
18 / Ouimet interview, June 30, 1975. The Canadian Labour Congress and the Canadian Broadcasting League, on the other hand, supported the proposed regulation. *Ibid.*, Nov. 2, 1959, 89 and 107.
19 / Dunsmore interview, Aug. 11, 1974.

struck his company as strange 'that the concept of the distribution of public values over the last quarter century, with respect to private stations, has been so invalid and useless that it would not appear to be logical that 8 or 10, 12 or 20, new licensed television stations would not be the obvious receptacles for at least some of what we have come to regard as a national broadcast product.'[20] However, Ouimet reasoned that the corporation did not have the productive resources at that time to provide service to another network. He also felt certain that the private stations would not accept such a proposition, in spite of Finlay Mac-Donald's views.[21]

The other approach put forward by the BBG, the proposal of a minimum percentage of Canadian content, had a mixed but essentially more favourable reception. The president of the CAB, Malcolm Neill, argued in principle against any particular quota of Canadian programming:

A wrong turning at the outset may make it more difficult to get back to the right road since it involves the risk of reducing the effectiveness of television service, of the reputation of Canadian performers in the minds of viewers and of making the phrase 'Canadian content' synonymous with 'mediocre.' ...

Quality broadcasting ... cannot be achieved by percentage requirements, but only in an atmosphere of deliberate encouragement. ... Good broadcasting, however defined, cannot be achieved by regulation.

The desired objective cannot be met by what is essentially a tariff against the United States. ... Our combined experience shows it would be possible to meet the percentage requirements, but that this could be done only by marked reduction in quality.[22]

Neill went on to suggest that if a percentage formula was applied, 35 per cent should be set as the minimum for the first year, progressing to 45 per cent in three years.

The BBG's announcement had suggested that 'the total Canadian content on any station shall not be less than 55 per cent of the total program content during any week.' Ouimet thought this proposal rather unrealistic for some of the stations in a weak financial condition, and suggested that a 50 per cent figure might apply to networks, and 50 per cent also to individual stations between 6 PM and midnight. He also

20 / BBG Hearings, Nov. 3, 1959, 306–9.
21 / Ouimet interview, Feb. 13, 1977.
22 / BBG Hearings, Nov. 2, 1959, 9–17.

suggested that the averaging should be done over a period longer than one week.[23]

The opposition of the broadcasters to the proposed regulation was encouraged by advertisers who feared that the provision for Canadian content would increase costs. The president of the subsidiary of a large American company wrote to an applicant for a television station in Winnipeg:

While we cannot speak for other advertisers, I can confidently assure you that if new regulations force up the already high cost per thousand of television, Canada's biggest television advertiser will not hesitate to switch into media that offer better value for money.

I am, of course, implying that the Board of Broadcast Governors' proposed regulations may seriously damage the economic health of the television broadcasting business; and I, therefore, believe that it is vitally in your interest to put up, individually or through c.a.b., the strongest possible fight against the b.b.g's proposals. And in this respect I can assure you that through a.c.a. and through our contacts with c.a.b. directors, this Company is devoting a great deal of time and energy to the task of helping independent broadcasters to ward off this major threat to their economic well being.

This last paragraph obviously grinds our own axe as well as yours (i.e. 55% Canadian content is impossible and will be unduly expensive).[24]

 The letter indicated clearly that Canada's largest advertisers had no interest in having Canadian broadcasting develop other than as an extension of the commercial system of the United States.

The regulations as promulgated (November 15, 1959) kept the figure of 55 per cent as an objective, but made several important modifications. Stations were allowed until April 1961 to reach a figure of 45 per cent Canadian content, and they did not have to reach 55 per cent until April 1962. Also, Canadian content could be calculated on the basis of a four-week average rather than weekly, as originally proposed. Further,

23 / *Ibid.*, Nov. 3, 1959, 219–20. Carlyle Allison told an interviewer, Sept. 10, 1971, that the figure of 55 per cent had been suggested by the minister, George Nowlan. Allison said that on its own the BBG would have opted for a lower figure. Hugh Saunderson, 'Broadcasting and Regulation: The Growth of the Single System in Canadian Broadcasting' (MA thesis, Carleton University, 1972).

24 / This letter, signed by W.W. Williams, president of Procter and Gamble Company of Canada, Sept. 17, 1959, was attached to the brief of the Red River Television Association (a company formed by the Siftons and other Winnipeg interests). It was read into the proceedings of the BBG hearing, Jan. 14, 1960 (201–5) by the chairman, Andrew Stewart.

Canadian content was so defined as to include not only Canadian productions, but news broadcasts and commentaries, broadcasts originating outside Canada in which Canadians were participating, and broadcasts 'featuring special events outside Canada and of general interest to Canadians.' The BBG's announcement (November 18) explained, 'Such events might include, for example, the World Series, an Address by the President of the United States, a meeting of the General Assembly of the United Nations.' Moreover, up to a certain maximum, one-half the time devoted to programs from other Commonwealth countries, or from French-language countries, could also be classified as 'Canadian.'

To control direct hook-ups with United States television networks, the BBG had originally proposed that no Canadian television station should have any direct program connection with a United States network without the BBG's permission. This proscription was modified to prohibit Canadian television stations from operating as a part of a network inside or outside Canada without the BBG's permission, or to affiliate with any such network. The BBG's permission would still be required for microwave or line connections with United States networks or stations, but Canadian stations could still bring in programs on videotape or film without reference to the BBG.

As the CBC was operating in 1959–60, its networks would have no difficulty meeting and indeed exceeding the minimum requirements for Canadian content: Ouimet had told the BBG that the percentage of Canadian content on the English network was about 66 per cent and on the French network about 85 per cent. On individual stations, even those that were CBC-owned, the percentage of Canadian content was much closer to the 50 or 55 per cent figure, since non-network hours tended to be programmed with American television and feature films. The real test of the new regulations would come with the second television stations about to be launched.

Over the years, all aspects of the Canadian content regulation came under heavy fire, and amendments were made from time to time. The classification of special events outside Canada as 'Canadian' perhaps drew the most derision. In 1965 the report of the Fowler Committee on Broadcasting stated that 'if the present format of regulations is continued, they could be simplified by eliminating such artificial rules as those applied to the World Series and other events of wide interest. ... It would be better to state the *true* Canadian content even if at present levels this is less than 55%' (pp. 63–4). But to any regulation universally applicable, the Fowler Committee preferred that particular conditions of licence be imposed on each station and network.

2 *Licensing Second Stations*

With the decisions on how much Canadian programming would be required of television stations, the way was now prepared for the hearing of applications for second stations in the principal cities. Hearings were announced for eight cities, to start in Winnipeg on January 11, 1960, and to conclude in Ottawa during the week of June 23. The other six cities from which applications were expected were Vancouver, Montreal, Toronto, Edmonton, Calgary, and Halifax.

The scramble for licences began. Many hoped that the well-known aphorism of Roy Thomson was true, that a television licence was a permit to print your own money. It was becoming well known that radio in Canada had been, on average, a very profitable enterprise. Although there were wide variations among the radio stations reporting in 1956, for all stations the total net income for the 1955 fiscal year had been over 20 per cent of net sales.[25] The Canadian Bank of Commerce Letter of June 6, 1960, 'placed broadcasting third in profitability among some 140 leading industries in 1957.'[26] Graham Spry's conclusion after examining these reports was that broadcasting 'was and probably is one of the quickest roads to fortune in Canada, provided that syndicated programming is freely permitted and a good advertising market is available.'

But as business enterprises the majority of radio stations were small. Television, as a much more costly medium, presented greater risks, but if the market was large enough and management sufficiently skilful, the rewards could be commensurately larger, too. Again, much would depend on the amount of program fare that could be imported cheaply, and whether program production costs for the more expensive programs could be shared among several stations.

With the announcement that eight cities were likely to receive additional television licences, as one magazine writer reported, 'most of the biggest names and bankrolls in Canadian broadcasting and publishing have been engaged in mutual jockeying for position – and talent, equipment and political influence.'[27] Hopeful contenders drew their backing from other big businesses as well: for example, the richest department store owners in Toronto and Vancouver, a giant lumber company in British Columbia, shipping and grain interests in Winnipeg, and film distributors in several cities. There were wide variations, even in the

25 / *Fowler Commission Report*, 149.
26 / Quoted in Spry, 'The Decline and Fall of Canadian Broadcasting,' *Queen's Quarterly* (Summer 1961), 216.
27 / Ray Gardner, 'Backstage in private TV,' *Maclean's* (Feb. 27, 1960), 3.

same centres, in the estimates of revenues and expenditures and in projected capital outlays. Fairly typically, losses were predicted for the first year of operation, and profits beginning about the third year.

Initial expectations were over-optimistic. Andrew Stewart summarized the experience up to 1963:

In 1961 the new stations obtained $15 million in gross revenues, but in their first full year of operation aggregate losses, before depreciation and taxes, amounted to $4.8 million. In 1962 the aggregate revenue of the stations increased 57% and aggregate losses were reduced to slightly over $1 million. By 1963 aggregate profits, before depreciation and taxes, reached $1.4 million. In the case of particular stations losses greatly in excess of those anticipated led to departures from the program pattern proposed, in an effort to cut costs, and in some instances, there was substantial reorganization. The most disturbing case of reorganization was that of CFTO-TV, Toronto.[28]

Stewart discreetly minimizes the 'departures from the program pattern proposed'; the discrepancies between the forecasts made in the hearings before the board and what materialized later on the television screens were often noted. The Fowler Committee commented in 1965:

When applications were made for licences of new stations – especially the so-called 'second TV stations' – the contestants for these valuable rights made detailed and glowing promises to the BBG about the performance they would give. These undertakings were assessed by the BBG and undoubtedly influenced the choice of the applicant to receive a licence. ... In fact, the program performance of the private stations – in particular the second television stations – bears very little relationship to the promises made.[29]

In each city visited, the BBG hearings on the second-station applications generated both press attention and a measure of popular excitement. Particularly in centres such as Winnipeg, Calgary, Edmonton, Ottawa, and Halifax, where only one station had been available to most viewers, the public was eager for alternative programming.[30] Even if the

28 / Stewart MS, 150–1. After 1963, the financial position of the new stations rapidly improved. Aggregate profits increased from over $4 million in 1964 to about $8.5 million in 1966. In the latter year, all second stations reported profits.

29 / Report of the Committee on Broadcasting, 1965, 106–7, hereafter cited as Fowler Report II.

30 / In Winnipeg and Ottawa, there were actually two stations, since the CBC had a French-language TV station in addition to the more widely viewed English-language station. Winnipeg viewers were soon to have another choice, with the construction of a TV station at Pembina, North Dakota, as well as the new 'second' Canadian station.

programs originated by the new stations turned out to be disappointing, the additional choice was valued sufficiently that few would henceforth speak of a possible return to the system existing before 1958. The question of one board or two was of interest mainly to specialists, but in many minds a suggestion that the CBC should be restored to a dominant position in Canadian broadcasting would be looked on as a return to the days of the single television service.

In Winnipeg and Vancouver, the first two cities in which hearings were held, the applicants chosen for licences by the BBG were unexpected. In Winnipeg, the successful applicant was associated with radio station CKY (Lloyd E. Moffat), with financial backing by the president of Investors' Syndicate, T.O. Peterson, and by the man who became president of the television company, Ralph S. Misener, member of a wealthy shipping family, but best known locally for his interest in a football team, the Winnipeg Blue Bombers. Two other groups applied, both with radio interests, and one of them seemed more representative of the Winnipeg 'establishment.' Joining in this application were Clifford Sifton, owner of several radio stations and newspapers, his brother, Victor Sifton, publisher of the *Winnipeg Free Press*, James A. and Kathleen Richardson, members of the prominent family of grain merchants, and others almost as well known. The local radio station owned by Clifford Sifton, CKRC, was older and more respectable than CKY, which was regarded as a 'rock 'n' roll' station. But according to one reporter, the expected contrast in style between the existing CBC station in Winnipeg and the new private station, CJAY-TV, would prove most welcome to viewers in that city.[31]

As the BBG moved across the country, its public sessions continued to attract audiences. The hearings were attended by a large group of broadcasters and advertising men, as well as by those hoping to apply successfully at some other location. Everybody wanted to decipher what factors would bring success. Did the Siftons lose out in Winnipeg, they asked, because they were well known Liberal party supporters, or because they had too many media interests? Did Misener and Moffat succeed because of their program promises, or the slickness of their presentation? Was it important to have a smooth lawyer with the right political connections? So the discussions went after each hearing and the announcement later as to which applicant had received the nod.

When the Vancouver hearings began, the board's recommendation for Winnipeg was still unknown. Vancouver had five applicants. The

31 / Ted Byfield, *Globe and Mail*, Aug. 13, 1960.

first represented a powerful concentration of media interests, including Frank A. Griffiths of radio station CKNW; William Speers of radio station CKWX, partly owned by Selkirk Holdings (Taylor, Pearson, and Carson); the *Vancouver Sun*, and the Southam company, owners of the *Vancouver Province*. CKNW and CKWX were usually rated as the first and second radio stations in the area.[32]

A second applicant had a different combination of media interests – radio station CJOR, Associated Television (ATV) in Britain, and Sovereign Film Distributors of Toronto. Directors from the business community included the president of Macmillan-Bloedel and the head of Woodward department stores. A third applicant had an equally impressive roster of businessmen, including Victor Spencer, another department store owner, Walter C. Koerner, whose fortune had been made in wood products, and Frank McMahon, an oil tycoon.

The winner was none of these, but a young man named Art Jones, who some ten years before had started a photo and advertising illustration business, that had turned to the production of television films and commercials. Although he had backers from the investment community, there were fewer 'big names' associated with his application than with any other.[33] The board seemed impressed with his personal initiative – although as it turned out, Jones soon lost control of his company.

The *Vancouver Sun* columnist, Jack Scott, reflecting on the hearings, wrote (January 27) that Canada was incapable of supporting commercial television of quality. 'By bowing prematurely to the pressure of the private interests [for second stations] we have become fated – doomed is a better word – to a corruption of TV's potential role.' Of the five applicants in Vancouver he said, 'any neutral observer could see, naked to the eye, that all five were exactly the kind of people who will set television right back into its infancy.' But not many expressed Scott's foreboding.

In announcing its decisions for Winnipeg and Vancouver the BBG listed thirteen factors to which it gave weight in reaching its decisions. These included coverage, facilities, location of effective control in the company, financing, experience of both the directors and management personnel, expected revenue and capacity of the market, program com-

32 / BBG Hearings, Jan. 18, 1960, 73. A witness from the Retail Merchants Association complained, 'This group has far too much control of the advertising and communications media in the city.'

33 / After the decision was made, Eugene Forsey was told by another member of the BBG that two different cabinet ministers had wanted two other applicants to get the licence. Letter, Forsey to Peers, March 23, 1976.

mitments, and 'association of the applicants with other media of communication.'[34]

The applicants in the next city visited, Montreal, showed that connections with other media were not so easy to escape. There were two applicants for the French-language station. One was Jack Tietolman, owner of a successful bilingual radio station in Verdun, CKVL. Tietolman's radio station had a good record in its use of Canadian talent, and he had financial backing from a theatre chain (United Amusements Corporation). The other applicant was Paul L'Anglais and associates. L'Anglais had experience as a radio and television producer and as a packager of films for television. The principal owner of the company was J.A. DeSève, an importer of French films. André Ouimet had recently left the CBC to become a vice-president and assistant general manager of the new company. Another CBC alumnus was Jean-Paul Ladouceur, who would be production supervisor.

The French-language station in Montreal would have to do more original production than any English-language private station in Canada, and the BBG in recommending DeSève and L'Anglais for the licence were no doubt influenced by the amount of production expertise they had assembled.

There were also two applicants for Montreal's English-language station. Mount Royal Television was a company grouped around the talents of Geoffrey Stirling and Don Jamieson, although Jamieson was to have no financial interest in the Montreal operation. Stirling and Jamieson were co-owners of the television station in St. John's, Newfoundland, and Stirling was the principal owner of radio station CKGM in Montreal. The other applicant was Canadian Marconi, owner of the first radio station to be licensed in Canada, CFCF Montreal. Canadian Marconi was controlled by a British company, English Electric, and only about 8 per cent of Canadian Marconi shares were owned in Canada, although its board of directors included such business luminaries as the president of the CPR, a member of the Timmins family, the president of Canadair, and Senator Hugessen of Montreal.[35]

The lack of precision in the financial forecasts provided to the board was well illustrated in Montreal. For the English-language station to be established, Canadian Marconi estimated commercial revenues of $3.5 million; Mount Royal (Geoff Stirling) in contrast estimated only $1.6 million. Another concern that the BBG must have discussed was that of foreign ownership. The government had obviously intended in 1958 that

34 / BBG Annual Report, 1959–60, 19.
35 / BBG Hearings, Montreal, March 8, 1960, 230–1, 477.

radio and television stations should be owned by Canadians, but by an order in council dated August 18, 1959, the Canadian Marconi Company had been exempted from the operation of section 14 of the broadcasting act.[36] The question was, should this exemption apply to a future television station, or was it intended to apply only to the existing radio station, CFCF. The board decided not to exclude Canadian Marconi from consideration, and in fact recommended it for the Montreal television licence.

The Toronto hearings, held from March 15 to 19, attracted the largest number of applicants, in spite of the fact that the successful firm would have to compete not only with the key station of the CBC's English network, but with Hamilton and with three Buffalo stations affiliated with the three US networks. Toronto after all was in Canada's richest market, was the largest commercial and advertising centre, and a centre for publishing and English-language performing talent. Nine contenders vied for the use of the last VHF channel available in the city.

Most of the applicants had impressive credentials in the field of mass communication, or if the principals did not, well-known directors, writers, and performers were recruited for the lists of company directors. The three daily newspapers in Toronto all submitted applications: the *Globe and Mail* (in collaboration with the J. Arthur Rank film company), the *Toronto Star*, and the *Telegram* – although the *Star* undercut its own application by suggesting that 'in the ordinary course of events newspapers should not control any other form or medium of communication.'[37] (The *Star* proposed to limit profits to 7 per cent, and to direct any profits in excess of this to community services through a foundation.)

Two radio stations applied: CFRB, Canada's largest station, owned by a holding company, the Argus Corporation; and CKEY, owned by Jack Kent Cooke, who was also the owner of Consolidated Press, which published two magazines, *Saturday Night* and *Liberty*. Canada's largest magazine publisher, Maclean-Hunter, also submitted an application.

The other three applicants had a more mixed ownership. S.W. Caldwell, the head of an agency handling syndicated film, applied on behalf of a number of shareholders. Stuart Griffiths, a former program director of CBC television in Toronto, applied on behalf of a group of Toronto investors and Granada Television, a British company for whom Griffiths had also worked. Henry Borden, nephew of a former prime minister, applied for another group of investors, including Southam Press which would have 30 per cent of the initial share capital.

Although most of the applications were well-prepared and made the

36 / *Ibid.*, 267.
37 / *Ibid.*, March 15, 1960, 193.

right kind of promises, three in particular were thought to have a reasonable chance of winning the board's favour: CFRB (Rogers Radio Broadcasting Co.), the Toronto Telegram (Baton Aldred Rogers Broadcasting Ltd.), and Stuart Griffiths and associates (Upper Canada Broadcasting). But well before the hearings, reports began to circulate that John Bassett, publisher of the *Telegram*, was boasting that as a result of his political connections, he had the licence sewn up.[38] Bassett's chief financial backer was John David Eaton, 'reputedly the most generous of all Tory campaign bankrollers,'[39] and the *Telegram* had been the most vigorous supporter of the Conservative government in power in Ottawa. Bassett's chief associate in the applicant company was Joel Aldred, a well-known radio and television announcer who had become a prominent party worker. Their lawyer was Edwin Goodman, third vice-president of the Progressive Conservative party of Ontario. Other applicants had Conservatives in prominent positions, too – for example, Joseph Sedgwick for CFRB, Anthony Adamson for Upper Canada, Henry Borden for Southam, J.S.D. Tory for the *Globe and Mail*. But none of them seemed so close to the government in power as Baton Aldred Rogers.

Within a few days of the conclusion of the Toronto hearings, the board announced its decision in favour of Bassett's group. Immediately, charges of political favouritism were heard. In the Commons (March 29) Diefenbaker denied 'with all emphasis' that any communications had gone from any cabinet minister to the BBG expressing preference for any applicant.[40] On the same date, Joseph Sedgwick, former counsel for the CAB, and also counsel for the unsuccessful applicant, CFRB, published an extraordinary letter in the *Globe and Mail*:

As the Board gives no reasons for preferring the Baton-Aldred-Rogers application (the Telegram group) over the other eight, one must guess, although there are some indicia, not completely helpful. ...

(1) The Board does not favor any monopoly of media of communication, and thus in Winnipeg preferred the independent Misener group to the Southam-Sifton group with its other publishing interests.

(2) The Board prefers the young and ambitious applicant, even though not

---

38 / For example, a lawyer who became connected with one of the applicants told Graham Spry in London on Oct. 9, 1959, that Bassett had let it be widely known that the government had promised him a licence for Toronto. Spry Papers, memorandum to his file, dated October 9. See also *Debates*, July 13, 1960, speech by J.W. Pickersgill.
39 / *Time*, Canadian edition, 'Switching Channels' (April 11, 1960).
40 / *Debates*, 2551.

much experienced in the broadcasting or TV field, nor too well financed. This would explain the success of the Vantel application in Vancouver.

(3) The Board prefers well established and experienced applicants even though they already have an AM license. This explains the success of Marconi (CFCF) in Montreal, though it does not explain the failure of CFRB and CKEY in Toronto.

(4) The Board has no objection at all to a monopolistic situation, and thus did not consider the *Telegram* group handicapped by their ownership of a newspaper, an AM station, 25 per cent of the Hamilton TV station, and a film distributing agency. This explains the *Telegram*'s success, but does not explain the failure of other publishing interests in Winnipeg, Vancouver and Toronto. ...

If the result is not to be explained by any ordinary process of thought or reason, a clue may be found in some lines from Kipling:

'Ere they hewed the Sphinx's visage
Favoritism governed kissage,
Even as it does in this age
And it will do evermore.

Pickersgill for the Liberals and Douglas Fisher for the CCF complained about the decision in the House of Commons, and Fisher outlined the Conservative connections of members of the board:

You have to go a long way and search extensively to find a metropolitan daily as bad in almost every way as the Toronto *Telegram*. If the standards of the Toronto *Telegram* are going to be transferred to the television station all I can say is, God help the Toronto listeners and watchers. ...

[On the board] we have a brother in law of the Minister of Transport. ... We have Mr. Sabourin who is known as a Conservative organizer in Montreal. We have Mr. Brown, who I understand is a prominent Vancouver Conservative. We have Mr. Duhamel, who again is a well known Conservative. We have Mr. Duchemin, who is the publisher of a newspaper ... [that] seemed to take the Conservative line. ... Another member of the board is a former leader of the Conservative association in Newfoundland, and another was secretary of the Conservative association of Prince Edward Island.[41]

(A story was later told of one unsuccessful applicant for a station who placed an advertisement reading, 'For Sale, One Cadillac convertible, one bunch of sour grapes, one Conservative Party membership card.')

41 / *Ibid.*, June 21, 1960, 5196–7.

When Joseph Sedgwick again appeared before the BBG as counsel, one of the members of the board, Eugene Forsey, refused to stay in the room to hear him, and the chairman gave Sedgwick a mild reproof, referring to his 'regrettable lapse.'[42]

Most of the BBG's other choices were received more calmly. The exception was Edmonton, where the BBG awarded the licence to the CBC rather than to a private station applicant.[43] In Calgary, the owners of radio station CFCN became the owners of the second television station (the other station was also privately owned). In Halifax, Finlay Mac-Donald was the successful applicant on behalf of radio station CJCH. In Ottawa, a company newly organized by E.L. Bushnell, former vice-president of the CBC, competed successfully against radio station CFRA and two other applicants. Bushnell and MacDonald were known to be friends of the minister of national revenue, so some people were suspicious that political influence may have played a part in these decisions. There was probably less division within the board on these two applications. Stewart has let it be known that personally he was unhappy with the Toronto decision.[44]

While the new stations were building their transmitters and ordering their studio equipment, the BBG turned its attention to the problem of ensuring that the new stations would provide a reasonably satisfactory standard of program service and meet the requirements set by the BBG as the guardian of the 'single system' contemplated by the act. A second network seemed to offer one practical way of accomplishing these objectives.

3 Licensing the CTV Network

When the television regulations were being discussed in 1959, and subsequently during the second station hearings, numerous references were made to the desirability of sharing or exchanging programs among these stations. Three possibilities were discussed, although never in any systematic way: the provision of CBC programs to the newly licensed stations; arranging a simple program exchange by tape or film; or the operation of a full-fledged second network, privately owned.

The first possibility, CBC participation, was introduced into the dis-

42 / BBG Hearings, Nov. 30, 1960, 363; *Debates*, Feb. 26, 1962, 1242, question by Douglas Fisher.
43 / The Edmonton decision is discussed below, pp. 249–51.
44 / Stewart MS, 151.

cussions only to be quickly abandoned. In November 1959, Edward Dunlop, a member of the BBG, asked Ouimet whether the CBC might divide its network service between existing affiliates and potential second stations. This had a precedent in radio, where the CBC operated two English-language networks: one for its own stations and a number of private affiliates, the second for private stations serving essentially the same communities as were reached by the first network. But the CBC president was opposed to any similar development in television:

Frankly, we don't think that as a matter of principle or as a matter of practice it would be an easy thing to do. As a matter of principle the operation of a network, ... the unity of a network, its presence in a city, its integrity as a working and operating entity is very, very important to its successful operation.

Furthermore, I believe that with time, although I don't think it is possible now, there will be ... an opportunity for a competing network. ... And I think it is essential that these networks keep their separate identities.[45]

Six months later Ouimet restated the same position in Edmonton.[46]

Finlay MacDonald of Halifax had thought the CBC should provide program service to a second television network. But the owners of the other second stations did not share this view. In a private meeting arranged with the BBG on May 30, 1960, they warned that they would oppose any move to establish a second CBC TV network.[47] That option was now dead. The other two options, however, were being pursued simultaneously, one on the initiative of the second stations, the other through the encouragement of the chairman of the BBG and the willingness of Spencer (Spence) Caldwell to become the entrepreneur.

In the 1950s Caldwell had formed an agency to distribute syndicated television programs, had prospered, and now longed to become a television station owner. As he pleaded in applying for the Toronto licence: 'We have spent a lifetime getting ready for this moment. We have experience in radio, and film, and television. ... We have heard today of the largest radio station in Canada, by its own admission, the largest magazine publishing company – the largest everything – even the richest man in Canada is involved. Surely they have enough! Is it not time that somebody else had a chance? Isn't it our turn now at success?'[48]

Caldwell had not been awarded the Toronto station licence, but now

45 / BBG Hearings, Ottawa, Nov. 3, 1959, 229.
46 / Ibid., Edmonton, May 10, 1960, 187.
47 / Stewart MS, 164.
48 / BBG Hearings, Toronto, March 21, 1960, 1024.

he was persuaded there was still another opportunity for him – the second television network. After discussions with Stewart, he kept together the company he had formed to apply for the Toronto station, and announced that he would now seek to form a network.[49] Stewart reported to his board on the conversations with Caldwell, and the board issued a release after its hearings in Calgary indicating that it was prepared to hear applications for the operation of a second network at its September meeting, and that it would issue guiding principles in June.[50]

About the same time, the five second stations that had so far been licensed (CHAN-TV, Vancouver; CJAY-TV, Winnipeg; CFTO-TV, Toronto; and CFCF-TV and CFTM-TV, both of Montreal) met in Toronto to discuss methods of program interchange, including the possibility of a new network.[51] They were cool to the idea of a second network not controlled by the stations themselves, and preferred, at least for the time being, a less formal method of program exchange.[52] In July 1960, the nine newly licensed stations formed the Independent Television Organization (ITO), with headquarters in Winnipeg, to allow stations to co-operate in the buying and selling of programs and films and to develop an exchange of Canadian programs. R.E. Misener of CFCF-TV, Montreal, became the first president.[53]

Before announcing its 'guidelines,' the board had to decide in principle whether the station affiliates would be allowed majority ownership in any private network that was formed. The board decided that it did not favour a 'mutual' company because of potential domination by the Toronto station.[54] Because of the reluctance of the stations to 'sign up' with Caldwell, he was not ready to proceed with his application, and the board decided that its meetings scheduled for September 1 and 2 would be used only to discuss the proposed guidelines, not to receive applications.

In his first discussions with the BBG, Caldwell had proposed that affiliated stations might hold up to 49 per cent of the equity of his company.[55] This provision was included in the twelve conditions for a network announced on June 30. The BBG specified that the private network should have at least six 'second-station' affiliates, but the stock

49 / 'His TV Bid Failed, Now Seeks Network,' *Toronto Star*, May 18, 1960.
50 / Stewart MS, 161–2.
51 / 'Second TV Network,' *Canadian Broadcaster* (June 2, 1960).
52 / Stewart MS, 165–6.
53 / 'New TV Body Is Organized to Rival CBC,' *Globe and Mail*, July 19, 1960.
54 / Stewart MS, 167 (insert).
55 / *Fowler Report II*, 235.

held by the stations should not exceed 49 per cent of the voting stock in the network company.[56]

At the BBG hearings on September 1 and 2, representations on the proposed conditions for a network were made by four organizations: the CBC, the ITO, S.W. Caldwell, and the Canadian Broadcasting League. Much of the discussion focused on the definition of a network. According to the broadcasting regulations issued the previous year, a network was defined as 'an organization or arrangement employing electronic connections ... between two or more stations for the presentation of programs, but does not include the operation of a licenced satellite station.' This obviously would not include an arrangement for the distribution of programs by film or videotape, which was the immediate objective of ITO. Richard Misener, appearing for the nine stations in ITO, said no one could prove to the board that any group could obtain microwave connections on any practical basis except on a most limited regional basis. In any case, microwave costs were 'probably beyond our purse at this moment.' The operation of a television network was in itself not a profitable investment. The member stations of ITO were unanimous in their conviction that any privately owned television network must be 'controlled by its member stations – that is, member stations own the controlling stock and that it be operated as a mutual network.'[57]

The Canadian Broadcasting League asked that no action be taken immediately on the licensing of a second network, or the formulation of regulations, to allow time for a more informed public discussion. Graham Spry, speaking personally, added that market forces ran counter to the national purposes set out in the broadcasting act to such an extent that the board could not achieve its objectives 'solely through the regulation of private broadcasting operations, local or network.' The primacy of the CBC must be maintained for its national purposes; no private network should be allowed to provide unfair competition to the CBC, or to reduce revenues and the Canadian programming provided to CBC affiliates. He preferred that the private network should be set up as a public trust.[58]

Caldwell argued that microwave connection was essential, and claimed that microwave facilities were available to his organization 'right now' from Quebec City to Windsor. If a network licence were granted, the common carriers would speed up further installations. Microwave costs, he said, were lower than the costs of videotape

56 / BBG Hearings, Ottawa, Sept. 1, 1960, 11.
57 / Ibid., 119–20.
58 / Ibid., Sept. 2, 1960; league statement, 243–8; Spry, 249–94.

distribution. The stations should have participation without having control. An applicant should not be dependent on securing affiliation agreements in advance. As for the viability of a commercial network, 'it does not take a giant to figure out that it can be profitable.' Speed was necessary for the setting up of this private network; the stations were selling out their time in advance of going on the air, and it would be difficult to extract from them reserved time periods for national programs. 'The later we leave it the tougher it will be.'[59]

Ouimet said the CBC was not opposed to a second network so long as it was not allowed to damage the national service or the partnership between the CBC and its affiliates. 'We are in favour of competition ... in programming, in service, but certainly not in favour of two organizations competing together for the essential means of providing that service, and that is our affiliates.' A station, he argued, must not be affiliated with more than one network, or operate as part of more than one network.[60]

The definition of a network in the regulations, he suggested, missed an essential characteristic. Electronic connection was important but did not of itself define a network. 'What happens actually, in a network operation, is that for a certain important segment of the broadcast day, the affiliated stations turn over to the network operator their responsibility for what that station will broadcast.' The contractual arrangement was therefore important; that was what differentiated a network from a mere program exchange.[61]

Ouimet said the CBC was not directly concerned in the question of ownership in respect to the private network. The network should have a close connection with the stations, and probably should own stations, 'because network broadcasting is not the profitable element in broadcasting.' The condition of affiliation was the most important; the network, not the affiliated station, must determine the use of reserved time.[62]

The hearings did not resolve the question as to whether Caldwell would be able to enlist the second stations as affiliates of his proposed network. What did follow immediately was a clarification of what was meant by a network. The BBG regulations were altered to define a network as 'a person having affiliation agreements with two or more stations to broadcast ... within specified periods ... a specified program

59 / *Ibid.*, Sept. 1, 1960, 183 ff.
60 / *Ibid.*, Sept. 2, 1960, 333–6.
61 / *Ibid.*, Sept. 1, 1960, 27.
62 / *Ibid.*, 32.

or package of programs in a manner determined by such person.'[63] Ouimet's point had been made: the essence of a network was a contract or affiliation agreement through which the network company within specified periods of time would control the programs to be broadcast.

Once the regulations had been announced, the BBG was ready to deal with any application to form a network. That permission having been granted, the network company would still have to file affiliation agreements with the board before it received permission to begin operations.

In the hearings set for the beginning of December 1960, the only applicant was S.W. Caldwell. The company he proposed to incorporate would be capitalized at $1,800,000, of which up to 49 per cent could be held by affiliated stations. It would have a board of sixteen – eight members nominated by the stations, four by Caldwell, and four by other investors. His company would not build production facilities, but would use the facilities of the stations and private production companies. Reserved time would begin at ten hours a week.[64]

With no production facilities of his own, and with the slight interest shown so far by the second stations, Caldwell was in a weak bargaining position. This is seen in the financial terms of the proposed affiliation agreement. Caldwell was claiming for his network only 25 per cent of the revenue from time sales, as compared with 50 per cent received by the CBC and 70 per cent by networks in the United States.[65] On the other hand, he would not be providing the stations with sustaining programs as did those other networks.

Speaking for himself and John Bassett, Joel Aldred said that CFTO was 'basically opposed to joining any network.' He saw no need to give up 25 per cent of the station's income 'on the easy-to-sell types of programming.'[66]

Soon after the hearing, the board granted Caldwell his 'hunting licence.' He needed six affiliates, but the key would be CFTO. Football made it happen. Bassett was then chairman of the Toronto Argonaut Football Club, and he became the successful bidder for the rights to broadcast the games of the 'Big Four' in eastern Canada. The CBC had

63 / The amended regulations were announced Oct. 14 and appeared in the *Canada Gazette* on Oct. 26, 1960.

64 / BBG Hearings, Ottawa, Dec. 1, 1960, 401–14.

65 / *Ibid.*, 421.

66 / *Ibid.*, 449. Ouimet's information was that the BBG approached CHCH-TV Hamilton to see whether it would become the flagship station of CTV if CFTO did not finally accept. The implication that CHCH was not needed as a CBC affiliate encouraged that station to seek and obtain disaffiliation a short time later. Ouimet interview, Feb. 13, 1977.

paid $325,000 for these rights in 1960; Bassett raised the bid to $750,000 for the next two seasons. As he explained, 'I am also Chairman of the Toronto Argonauts and a substantial shareholder in that football team, and therefore I am familiar with how football works, and there is no question that this knowledge was of value to me.' He went on to say that he had told the other owners that he could cover only Montreal, Toronto, and Ottawa, through the other independent stations in those cities that were unaffiliated with the CBC. But he would offer the games to the CBC affiliates (in northern Ontario, for example), so long as they accepted his sponsors.[67]

There were two or possibly three obstacles to this plan. The first was that the CBC would not release its affiliates from their reserved time. The second was that Spencer Caldwell had taken an option with Bell Telephone on the necessary microwave connections. The third was that Bassett would have to apply to the BBG for permission to form a temporary network.

The result was that Caldwell found himself, for once, in a strong position. On March 10, 1961, Bassett's newspaper, the *Telegram*, reported that Bassett had signed a 'letter of intent' with Caldwell. And when Caldwell reappeared before the BBG on April 13 for permission to operate the television network, Bassett was there to support him. The BBG announced its approval on April 21, and the CTV television network began its operations on October 1, 1961.[68]

Surveying the situation in the summer of 1961, after Caldwell's network was licensed but before it began operations, Graham Spry tried to assess the impact of recent developments on the CBC and the broadcasting system as a whole.[69] The total CBC expenditure in 1960–1 was $100.9 millions. 'Of this, $88.9 millions was spent on programming including $9.2 millions for network distribution and programme operational services of $2.8 millions. That is, at least 88 percent of CBC expenditures was on programmes, even allowing in the $100.9 for depreciation of $3.5 and a refund of $2.7 millions to the government out of surplus. Five-eighths of the programme expenditure was for non-advertising, sustaining programmes and three-eighths for advertising programmes. The latter produced for CBC some 38 per cent of its total revenue. The contribution of the taxpayer to CBC ... was some 59 percent.'

Spry calculated further that with the $162 millions spent on advertis-

---

67 / BBG Hearings, April 13, 1961, 307–18.
68 / BBG Annual Report, 1961–2, 11.
69 / 'The Canadian Broadcasting Corporation, 1936–1961,' *Canadian Communications*, II:1 (Autumn 1961), 13–25.

ing over both CBC and private facilities, plus the $59 millions spent by the taxpayer on the CBC, the gross expenditure on Canadian broadcasting as a whole was about $221 millions. Of this, $124 millions went to private broadcasting, and (after refunds to the government) about $97 millions to the CBC. But he estimated that whereas 88 per cent of CBC expenditures went toward producing, acquiring, and distributing programs, less than half of the expenditures of the private broadcasters were for such purposes.

The effect of second stations and of CTV, Spry argued, would be to 'cream off the easiest advertising revenues in competition with the CBC in the major Canadian markets, with some 65 percent of the population.' Unlike the CBC which had about forty private affiliates, the new network would not pay for further affiliates in smaller centres that could not earn a revenue for the network.

Spry was not sanguine about CTV's future as a money-making enterprise if it did any substantial proportion of live, original programming. But he admitted that Caldwell had 'some odds in his favor. They are increased by the initial 10 hour service weekly compared with the CBC's two networks supplying together some 110 hours weekly, and by the fact that more than half of the CBC programmes are sustaining non-commercial programmes. ... It will therefore be some time in the future before the private network of eight stations and ten to 28 hours weekly commercial programming only in English can be compared with the CBC's two networks, one English and one French, serving in all at least 60 CBC and private stations and 30 relay stations with programmes in both languages, a total of 110 hours or more each week.'

Spry concluded, 'I wish Mr. Caldwell's experiment well, though I would prefer a very different corporate structure, such as a trusteeship, with defined statutory obligations laid down by Parliament, more share ownership by the network company itself with less local station ownership, and less ownership through the local stations or individuals by American and British film and television interests.' Here Spry was referring to recent changes in the share distribution of some of the second stations.

4 *CTV and the Private Stations*

CTV (the Canadian Television Network) began operations with affiliates in eight cities: Vancouver (CHAN), Calgary (CFCN-TV), Edmonton (CFRN-TV), Winnipeg (CJAY), Toronto (CFTO), Ottawa (CJOH), Montreal (CFCF-TV), and Halifax (CJCH-TV). At the outset, only three cities received programs live by microwave – Montreal, Ottawa, and Toronto. For the other five stations, CTV programs were transmitted on the same microwave facilities leased by the CBC, but in hours the CBC was not using microwave. Those stations put the programs on videotape and then released them at the scheduled time. However, CTV contracted with the telephone system to extend the microwave westward to Vancouver by September 1962, and eastward to Halifax by the summer of 1963.[70]

Andrew Stewart, whom the network might have claimed as at least its godfather, declared on the opening program that the inauguration marked 'an important step in communications and another tie binding Canada together.'[71] From the CBC, Michael Hind-Smith moved to CTV as program director; the new network's other principal program officer was Ross McLean, the originator of the CBC public affairs series, 'Close-Up.' In its first year, the network provided eight and a half hours of programming a week, including three quiz or game shows, two hour-long detective programs, two westerns, and football and other sports telecasts. Fewer than half the programs were Canadian – football, the quiz shows, a barn dance program – and these were relatively inexpensive productions. The most expensive program, a variety show, was cancelled after a few weeks. CTV did not have an exciting schedule, and most of the television reviewers expressed disappointment.

In public, Caldwell expressed great confidence: 'Every one of our eight stations is equipped to produce shows. We've got $30 million worth of equipment at our disposal and we plan originating shows right across the country. ... But ours is going to be *commercial* TV, an *advertisers*' network. We'll carry no unsponsorable programs, except for occasional public-service specials – like royal visits, or something like that. I think we'll *make* millions some day, and give fifty-two percent of it to Donald Fleming (the minister of finance.'[72]

Privately, Caldwell was worried by the extent of CTV's losses in the first year, which he expected to exceed $600,000; and this figure might

70 / *Canadian Broadcaster* (Aug. 3, 1961).

71 / *Ibid.*, Oct. 5, 1961. Spry had written on May 3 to a member of the BBG, 'The BBG is creating this network. It rushed the dates, it encouraged Caldwell, it defined the conditions, it made no serious demands for qualifications among the directors or shareholders. ... This will be the BBG network ... though with such limited capital it could fail and fall into the hands wholly of some or all the stations and the film interests, primarily non-Canadian,' Spry Papers. To compare Spry's forecast with what happened to CTV, see chapter 10, p. 298, and chapter 12, pp. 359–60.

72 / Quoted by Trent Frayne, 'How Spence Caldwell got a TV network by the tail,' *Maclean's* (Feb. 10, 1962), 46.

increase when the extended microwave circuit came into use. On January 10, 1962, he and representatives of the affiliated stations met with the full-time members of the BBG to explore measures that would assist the network.[73] He proposed some delay in applying the 55 per cent content requirement; classifying Commonwealth programs as 100 per cent Canadian content; relaxing the commercial restrictions; and disaffiliating some CBC affiliates so that they could join CTV.

Caldwell also complained about the intense competition from the CBC and its commercial practices. The BBG raised these points with the CBC in a regular meeting of the consultative committee on public broadcasting, and Stewart came to the conclusion that CTV's troubles were not caused by CBC commercial practices. The problem was that CBC had more extensive coverage, could command more revenue and therefore could pay more for the programs it acquired. 'The problems which the network and the stations were encountering were inherent in their position in the market rather than being engineered by the CBC.'[74]

Part of CTV's difficulty was that, especially in the first two years, some of the stations were having their own financial woes, and were highly critical of CTV and the revenues they felt were drained away by the network centre. The stations never took up the amount of stock in CTV that was offered them; their share of ownership was only about 20 per cent.[75] Furthermore, the same stations that were affiliated with CTV refused to abandon their own mutual company for the purchase of programs, ITO. In its second year of operation, CTV increased the number of hours in its schedule to twenty-four, instituted a nightly news program, and one public affairs program, 'Telepoll.' But ITO continued to operate, and was used by the stations as a bargaining counter whenever negotiations with CTV took place.[76]

Not all the second stations were in financial difficulty in 1961 and 1962. Those in Winnipeg, Edmonton, and Calgary, where there was little or no competition from the United States, were achieving their expected revenues, or so it was reported. And in Ottawa, 'CJOH was showing an operating profit within a few months of beginning broadcasting.'[77] But

73 / Jeremy Brown, *Toronto Star*, Jan. 11, 1962; Stewart MS, 182–3.
74 / Stewart MS, 185.
75 / The BBG announced changes in 1962 that met some of CTV's requests. See *Canadian Broadcaster* (June 7:) 'BBG: TV Regulations Are Relaxed,'; also, *ibid.* (Sept. 6, 1962), 'Move Gives Moose Jaw CTV Outlet in Regina.'
76 / Nathan Cohen, 'Last-minute talks save CTV network,' *Toronto Star*, Jan. 17, 1964; Jon Ruddy, 'Canada's official private network (CTV) and the unofficial one (ITO ...) are engaged in a subtle but fierce struggle,' Toronto *Telegram*, March 27, 1965.
77 / Stursberg, *Mister Broadcasting*, 239.

three stations that had been most ambitious in their plans, and in the promises made before the BBG, were in deep trouble: CHAN-TV, Vancouver, CFCF-TV, Montreal, and CFTO, Toronto. In Vancouver, the young man whose imaginative presentation had caught the attention of the governors, Arthur Jones, was removed from his position as the top executive, to be replaced by J. Ray Peters, who had started with the company as station manager. Its staff, originally projected at 120 employees, was reduced in the summer of 1961 to fewer than 90. To bolster its shaky financial position, the BBG allowed Famous Players (a US-controlled company) and British ATV each to buy 12 per cent of the equity.[78]

CFCF-TV, Montreal, also went through a reorganization, but the most dramatic changes occurred at CFTO, Toronto. There was much hoopla when it opened on New Year's Day, 1961, with a large and modern physical plant, well-equipped studios capable of handling elaborate productions, a good-sized staff, and the announced intention of producing programs not only for local audiences, but for a national audience, and indeed, through co-production arrangements, for network audiences in the United States. The public first got some intimation that there was trouble in CFTO's executive suite when early in March the station dismissed fifty-eight employees, and when it was reported that twenty-five more releases were planned.[79] The station had started with 310 employees, and the number had gone up to 370. In May, a new general manager was brought in.

To understand the next development, one has to look at the arrangements for control of the voting stock. The chairman of the board, John Bassett, and his financial backer, John David Eaton, held 40 per cent of the equity in CFTO in the name of their newspaper, *The Telegram*. The next largest block of stock, 34 per cent, was held by Joel Aldred and E.S. Rogers through their company, Aldred Rogers. But through another arrangement by which the *Telegram* held all the Class B preference shares, the *Telegram* held 51 per cent of the voting stock.[80]

During the summer of 1961, Bassett decided that Aldred, the president of the company, must vacate his executive post.[81] This made for good gossip – Bassett and Aldred were both well-known figures in Toronto, especially Aldred who appeared in television commercials on both sides

78 / Dick Lewis, 'Birth Pains,' *Canadian Broadcaster* (March 9, 1961).

79 / *Broadcasting* (March 13, 1961), 82.

80 / BBG Hearings, Toronto, March 17, 1960, 430, 450.

81 / *Canadian Broadcaster* (Aug. 17, 1961). The story was broken by Nathan Cohen in the *Toronto Star*, Aug. 11, 1961.

of the United States–Canada border. But the report of their disagreement and splitting up developed a policy dimension when it was learned what buyer Bassett had found for Aldred's share of the stock. The intended purchaser was a US network, the American Broadcasting Company, owned by ABC-Paramount.

The BBG had to approve transfers of stock for all broadcasting stations, but under the general procedures they had adopted, public hearings were not held unless effective control was involved. So a private meeting was held with the representatives of CFTO's chief stockholders on August 24 to consider the application that had been made to the minister of transport for the sale of shares to ABC-Paramount.[82] The board was told of the heavy losses so far incurred, and the need for additional capital. CFTO had explored the possibility of interesting other purchasers, such as Southam and Thomson interests,[83] but the control position of the Telegram Publishing Company was not negotiable. ABC-Paramount was prepared to provide the capital without demanding control. An added advantage would be an outlet for some of the station's productions in the United States. Under the proposed arrangement, ABC-Paramount would own 25 per cent of the equity, but only 18.8 per cent of the voting stock. The company would also invest $2 million in debentures, and would be entitled to name three directors on a board of twelve.

Although Stewart expressed his concern about an American network having such an influential position in an important Canadian station, a majority of the governors voted to approve the transfer, but only after a deferment of thirty days to allow CFTO time to try to find an equivalent offer from 'experienced Canadian broadcasting interests.'[84]

In the House of Commons, J.W. Pickersgill directed a question about the proposed transfer to George Nowlan, who was back in the house after a period of illness. Nowlan replied, 'Having had a heart attack, I have been prevented by the doctors from reading fantastic stories, so I have not seen the one to which the hon. member refers.'[85] A week later, Pickersgill asked whether the minister had drawn to the BBG's attention 'the fact that the transfer of a substantial ownership in this station to the American Broadcasting Company would be contrary to the sentiments

82 / Stewart MS, 153–6.
83 / Spry reported Roy Thomson as telling him that CFTO owed over $9 millions, to RCA, to the banks, to Eaton's, and to the Telegram. Spry to E.A. Forsey, Oct. 3, 1961 (Spry Papers).
84 / BBG announcement, Aug. 28, 1961.
85 / Debates, Sept. 7, 1961, 8058.

expressed in this house at the time the Broadcasting Act was passed, and would certainly not be in the national interest.' Nowlan answered, 'I am sure the members of the board of broadcast governors read *Hansard*, and they will notice the remarks made by the hon. member, which I suspect may express the sentiments of this house.'[86]

In fact, Nowlan talked to Eugene Forsey, who as a member of the BBG had strongly opposed the board's decision, and to Andrew Stewart, who summarized the discussions of August 24.[87] Forsey also sent a letter to his colleagues on the board, restating his views:

The mere transfer of Mr. Aldred's shares would not provide one copper of additional capital. It follows that A.B.C. must be doing a lot more than simply buying out Mr. Aldred. This transaction is like an iceberg: what the public can see, the share transfer, is only a hidden fraction of the whole. Much the larger, and more dangerous, part lies hidden. If CFTO is losing money on an impressive scale, and if A.B.C. is providing it with a substantial amount of loan capital ... then it must follow as the night the day that A.B.C. will have effective control. ... The result will be a flood of A.B.C. programmes, and A.B.C. 'experts,' experts at making a 'fast buck.' ... A.B.C. will run the show. ...

Approval of this deal means turning over to an American network control of the largest private TV station in Canada ... the key station in the private network. ... Pressure to let in the other American networks will become irresistible; and before we know where we are, the Americanization of Canadian private TV will be an accomplished fact. ... To me, approval of this proposal is an evasion of the declared will of Parliament, and can end only in a complete reversal of a whole generation of Canadian broadcasting policy.

It may be argued that we still have the C.B.C. and the B.B.G., the sure shields of Canadianism in its hour of trial. But the C.B.C. is under constant attack, constant pressures to go more and more commercial, which means almost certainly less and less Canadian. The more money an Americanized private TV makes, the more C.B.C.'s private affiliates, on which it depends for most of its distribution, will want to cash in by cutting down what they take from the C.B.C., the more the welkin will ring with protests against the C.B.C.'s 'deficits'; the heavier will be the pressure to take the C.B.C. out of broadcasting altogether and make it a mere auxiliary National Film Board. ... The Board can at best maintain only minimum standards; and the pressure on it to lower the minima and to relax the Canadian content requirements, will be almost intolerably severe. ...

I am more than ever convinced that we ought to have a public hearing on this

86 / *Ibid.*, Sept. 13, 1961, 8289.
87 / Spry Papers, Forsey to Spry, Sept. 20, 1961.

transaction. It is not, as some suggested at our August meeting, merely a matter of public curiosity. It goes to the very root of the public interest. ...

I need hardly say that I still hope an acceptable Canadian offer will be forthcoming, and that if I have to resign, I shall do so most reluctantly.[88]

From London, Spry sent a letter to the prime minister, with copies to three other ministers (Nowlan, Harkness, and Fulton) and to Andrew Stewart. In it, he set out a list of television stations in which there was either American or British participation: Quebec (the English and French stations), Kitchener, Windsor, Vancouver, Ottawa, Pembroke, Cornwall, Montreal (English and French), Halifax, and now the proposal in Toronto. 'As no one of any party in the Commons or, so far as I know, any newspaper has summarized these tendencies towards the dependence of Canadian television stations upon non-Canadian ownership, I take this occasion, with due respect, to put the emerging situation before you. In the United States, no foreign ownership of this key instrument for influencing public opinion is by law permitted. Australia has acted to restore greater Australian control. Canada, however, the most vulnerable, is somewhat blindly accepting both the multiplication of non-Canadian interests in private television and the weakening, through disaffiliation or other steps, of the CBC Networks which alone serve the electorate in centres, small as well as large, French as well as English, throughout the Canadian nation. ...'[89]

From Kingston, Arthur Lower, in that year president of the Royal Society, wrote the prime minister also:

I plead with you to step in and prevent the Board of Broadcast Governors selling out our television to one of the American 'chains.' This is the result I have foreseen from the beginning of allowing private 'enterprise' significant entry into our broadcasting system.

In my opinion, men who are willing to sell out and those who are parties to selling out are little better than traitors to their country. Without national broadcasting, there can be little future for Canada.

And let us not forget that it was Mr. Bassett's predecessors in Montreal, the commercial group of that city, who tried to sell us out a century and more ago. 'Tout ça change, tout c'est la même chose.'

Please step in: it will be as big a thing almost as your Bill of Rights.[90]

88 / Copies of this letter were sent to Nowlan and to Graham Spry.
89 / Spry Papers, Spry to Diefenbaker, Sept. 15, 1961.
90 / Queen's Archives, Lower Papers, Lower to Diefenbaker, Sept. 21, 1961.

When the BBG met again on September 25, Stewart read to the other members a letter he had received from Lower:

From the first I have foreseen that private radio and television in Canada ultimately must mean simply American radio and television. The crisis has come sooner than I had expected.

I think that it is up to you as an honourable man and to those of your Board who are genuinely Canadians to resign rather than permit the American company to come in. You must face this. You surely do not wish to go down in Canadian history as the man who sold out our major instrument of nationalism to the Americans, that is, who sold out his country.

I cannot make it too emphatic: that is what you and your Board are facing – betrayal. You have to choose.[91]

Forsey wrote Lower that the board listened 'in what the Indians call "pin-drop silence".'[92]

On September 26 the BBG reversed the decision taken a month earlier, stating that it was 'not prepared to recommend any transaction involving financial participation of American networks in Canadian television stations.' There was some dissent, and Edward Dunlop of Toronto asked that his disagreement be recorded. He argued that the board should not refuse a transaction that the terms of the act allowed, and also that the board without any new evidence should not reverse a decision previously taken.[93]

Since CFTO was prevented from transferring stock to ABC, the directors of the company rearranged the shares among themselves, the net result being that the *Telegram* held a larger part of the equity, and that Aldred no longer had any financial interest in the station. CFTO subsequently entered into an agreement with ABC for a larger loan than had previously been arranged (it was now reported to be $2.5 million).[94] ABC would have three directors on the board, would participate in the profits of the station, and would have a hand in its management. Donald Coyle, an ABC vice-president, spent considerable time at the station, and even attended meetings of CTV on behalf of CFTO.[95]

After the fact, the BBG passed a resolution, effective April 1, 1962,

91 / *Ibid.*, Lower to Stewart, Sept. 21, 1961.
92 / *Ibid.*, Forsey to Lower, Sept. 28, 1961.
93 / CRTC Library, copy of letter, Stewart to Leon Balcer, minister of transport, Sept. 27, 1961 (microfiche).
94 / *Canadian Broadcaster* (Oct. 19, 1961).
95 / *Broadcasting*, Dec. 11, 1961, 9; Stewart MS, 159–60.

requiring stations, on request, to reveal such details of their financial structures as outstanding loans, debentures, and management services.[96]

Very soon the financial position of the second stations registered an improvement, as a larger share of advertising flowed their way. In the 1961–2 fiscal year, the CBC reported that its gross revenues were between $10 million and $12 million less than they would have been under the single-station policy.[97] Advertising revenues of the CBC in that year were reduced by 12.5 per cent, and by a further 6.3 per cent in 1962–3.[98] In the latter year, the government attempted to improve the economy by mid-term budget cutbacks, and the CBC like other federal agencies was asked to reduce its planned expenditures.

The results of the increased competition and of government austerity were predictable: the CBC's own productions, especially those not offered for sponsorship, tended to be reduced, or to be pushed out of prime time. In spite of the talk about a single system of broadcasting, in which national objectives should be realized, what was developing in fact was a substitution of a more thoroughly commercial system, in which private broadcasting was becoming the dominant element. And even the CBC was forced to compete largely in these terms, for its own survival, and also to allow its private affiliates to compete on equal terms with the private stations that were not linked with the CBC. It was quite a different system than the one Canada had in 1945 or even 1957.

5 CBC versus BBG

It was not the troubles of CTV or of stations such as CFTO that claimed the greatest amount of attention in the press, but rather the disputes between the CBC and the BBG in the early 1960s, which reached a climax in the struggle over the Grey Cup coverage in 1962.

The 1958 act, by providing for a corporation responsible to Parliament, with its own reporting line, and with the responsibility of operating 'a national service,' obviously intended the CBC to continue as a key component in the national broadcasting service. The minister answering for the CBC in Parliament said repeatedly that it was not the government's purpose to weaken the CBC, and estimates put before Parliament each year included provisions for the extension of its service through the

96 / *Canadian Broadcaster* (April 12, 1962).
97 / *CBC Annual Report, 1961–62*, 16.
98 / *Ibid.*, 1962–3, 20.

construction of additional stations. The regulations of the BBG were to apply to the CBC only in the manner they applied to private stations; in neither case was the BBG to make operational decisions, or to intervene in the decisions of the broadcasters unless they contravened some general regulation.

On the other hand, by section 10 of the act, outlining the board's objects and purposes, the BBG was to regulate 'the establishment and operation of networks of broadcasting stations, the activities of public and private broadcasting stations in Canada and the relationship between them and provide for the final determination of all matters and questions in relation thereto.' The BBG believed that unless it was given specific information by the CBC on their budgets and future plans, it would not be possible for the BBG realistically to determine 'all matters and questions' governing relationships between the public and private elements. They were strengthened in the conviction that adjudicating matters between the CBC and the private stations and networks was an essential part of their job on being told (by Ernest Bushnell) that the last clause of section 10 had been added to the draft act in 1958 in the office of the prime minister, probably by Diefenbaker himself.[99] The CBC's directors, on the other hand, saw no reason why they should submit detailed projections to the BBG, and then again to the Treasury Board. They were not responsible to the BBG, they argued, but to Parliament; if the BBG had to consent to their plans and operational decisions, what was the role of the directors, who had been appointed by the government in exactly the same way as the board of broadcast governors? To the BBG, the CBC's attitude appeared one of intransigence; the CBC, they said, had not adjusted to its new and reduced role under the legislation of 1958. Because so often it was Alphonse Ouimet who argued against BBG positions, he became the personification of CBC 'intransigence.' But from a reading of CBC records, and interviews with CBC officials and former directors, it seems evident that Ouimet's position was fully shared by his board. In fact, in any representations to the BBG, he acted with the authorization of the CBC directors, and often on their specific instructions.

The CBC–BBG relationship assumed an importance whenever the CBC applied for a licence against a competing application from a private owner; and when CTV tried to increase its coverage for a program by adding to its network certain stations that were formally affiliated with the CBC television network.

The BBG could not but be aware that the CBC was having its difficulties

99 / Stewart interview, June 10, 1975; Stewart MS, 206.

with the Diefenbaker government, which regarded it as too costly and extravagant, and which was frequently unhappy with its programs. The governors knew, too, that the CBC was the object of more than one critical investigation, and that it was frequently under attack in the columns of the newspapers. On the other hand, there were always demands for more CBC service in communities where the corporation did not have its own stations. Sometimes, no doubt, the government, while approving estimates for capital projects, was not averse to the BBG's taking the responsibility for denying or postponing the CBC's request for a new station.

As early as 1959, the question of how the BBG would handle a CBC application for a station licence was posed by James McGrath in the broadcasting committee. Stewart replied, 'I would say we recognize that the corporation has a national responsibility to provide a national network and therefore, if the corporation applies for admission to a particular situation on this ground, and there is an application from a private station, I would think that in such cases the board would approve the application of the corporation because of the national responsibilities.'[100] This answer received some unfavourable press comment, and Stewart considered that he had made a mistake.[101]

The first important test of the board's interpretation of the CBC's role or 'mandate' was when the CBC applied in May 1960 to establish the 'second' television station in Edmonton. CFRN-TV, owned by the pioneer broadcaster G.R.A. Rice, had been a CBC affiliate since its opening in 1954. The CBC, in applying for a station of its own, argued that it should have production facilities between Winnipeg and Vancouver, and that Edmonton as the largest centre in this area was an appropriate site. The CBC was also asserting the long-term objective of establishing stations in every province, and preferably in the provincial capitals. CFRN-TV was willing to become an independent TV station, and tacitly supported the argument that a combination of a private and a publicly owned station would provide a greater variety of programs, a better 'mix,' than two private stations.

Edmonton was a rapidly growing city, and a prosperous one. Not unexpectedly, there were others who wanted to grasp the opportunity to secure a licence while there was still time. There were four other applications, including one from Selkirk Holdings (successor to the well-established firm of Taylor, Pearson, and Carson, with extensive broadcasting interests in Edmonton and other western cities).

The majority of the board voted to recommend that CBC be granted the

100 / *1959 Proceedings*, 483.
101 / Stewart MS, 50.

licence, but the next day, the chairman learned from Allison that the government was unhappy with the decision, and wished to see the decision reversed. The board refused to re-open the question, made its recommendation to the minister of transport, and the government went ahead with the necessary order-in-council authorizing the CBC to proceed with the station.[102]

Eugene Forsey showed an awareness of attitudes in the Conservative party when on May 29 he wrote Spry, 'I was staggered to find how many colleagues regarded the CBC as immensely powerful, and expressed dread of our being attacked for knuckling under to it! They seemed to have no notions of its being beleaguered. ... I've been told 'all' the newspapers will be against us. ... I dare say my name will be mud with the Government; if they only knew it, our Edmonton decision has saved them from a bad mess.' But not only Conservative politicians were critical of the board's decision. In the Commons J.W. Pickersgill said that it was 'an unnecessary waste of the taxpayers' money to have a public television station established in the city of Edmonton, which is very well served at the present time by a private station, when there are all kinds of outlying points like places in Newfoundland and northern Manitoba ... and in northern Ontario which are not served.'[103]

Nowlan agreed that it was 'rather unfair to have private applicants making application at the same time as publicly-owned applicants, particularly if the publicly-owned one gets the application in the end.' But he did not offer any solution if a similar situation occurred in the future. 'There is a difficult area there, one which was certainly not foreseen when the act was drafted.' In defending the BBG from charges of political favouritism, he added: 'If there are any political rewards which could be recognized, if this board is an organization which considers politics at all, I cannot conceive of any applicant who might be more deserving than some of the applicants in Edmonton in view of their record of service and co-operation with the Conservative party throughout the years.' And he pointed out that while the BBG had approved the CBC's application for Edmonton, it had refused the CBC's application for Pembroke, granting it instead to a private firm. He had been 'the most surprised man in the world' when the BBG made its recommendation for Edmonton.[104]

Pickersgill countered: 'Now surely the minister is not telling us, as he seems to be, that the C.B.C. can blithely make an application to the B.B.G. without satisfying the B.B.G. that it has the financial competence to carry it out? ... I ask the minister ... did the government give ... assurance to the c.b.c. before they made that application that the money would be made available before they got the licence?'

Nowlan admitted that the allocation for the Edmonton station was 'included in the capital budget of the c.b.c. which had been passed months before,' but said that only after the event did Ouimet inform him that the CBC had submitted its application. Then, somewhat belatedly, he defended the CBC's decision to apply: 'It should be borne in mind that the c.b.c. has no transmitting facilities between Winnipeg and Vancouver. If this is to be a national system, then certainly the corporation needs transmission facilities somewhere on the prairies over this vast expanse of 2000 miles, and Alberta was the logical place where such facilities should go.'[105]

The Edmonton station came out of the CBC's capital budget for 1960–1 and 1961–2, and no other large capital expenditures had been planned for these two years. But late in 1960, the CBC learned that a private company was applying for a second French-language TV station in Quebec City, where a single company, half-owned by Famous Players, owned both the French and English TV outlets. Quebec City, as far back as 1952, had been in the corporation's list of recommended locations, but the Liberal government of the day had not agreed to the CBC's request. When it seemed that the BBG was likely to open Quebec City to other applicants, the CBC board of directors decided to apply for the Quebec channel, reasoning that 95 per cent of the construction costs would occur during the 1962–3 fiscal year.[106]

Two applications to establish the French station were heard in Quebec City in February, 1962. The other applicant was Jacques LaRoche, operator of Quebec radio station CJLR, joined by the novelist Roger Lemelin, and the principal owners of the Montreal French-language TV station, J.A. DeSève and Paul L'Anglais.[107]

As in Edmonton, the CBC application was supported by important local officials and the larger community organizations, including the mayors of Quebec and Lévis, the rector of Laval University, the Société Saint-Jean Baptiste de Québec, and the regional office of the Confederation of National Trade Unions.[108] The CBC argued that Quebec City would be better served by a combination of public and privately owned

105 / Ibid., 6228–9.
106 / CBC board of directors, Minutes, 15th meeting, Quebec City, Feb. 14–16, 1961. The decision was made known through a public announcement.
107 / BBG Hearings, Quebec City, Feb. 9, 1962, 847–912. LaRoche and associates had first applied at a previous hearing in Ottawa, June 20, 1961, when the decision was deferred.
108 / Ibid., 765–90.

stations than by two private stations. A CBC station would be able to provide programs of better quality, would be prepared to spend 25 per cent of its annual budget on talent, and would be able to serve minority interests as well as more popular tastes. Ouimet said that the owners of the present station in Quebec had indicated several times that they would prefer to have a second station operated by the CBC to one that was privately owned. A CBC television presence in Quebec City was necessary to 'properly reflect and interpret the character of the people of French Canada.'[109]

But this was late in the winter of 1961, when the political situation in Ottawa was becoming most delicate. The support for Diefenbaker's government in the province of Quebec, expressed in 1958 when fifty members were returned to the House of Commons, had been leaching away. A general election was expected in 1962. In an attempt to recover Quebec support, the prime minister made 'a much-publicized pilgrimage to Quebec City' on December 28, 1961, to announce cabinet changes, but the posts granted French Canadians still did not satisfy the Quebec wing of the party.[110] Jacques Flynn, the member for Quebec South, was made minister of mines. The other cabinet minister from the Quebec City region was Noel Dorion, commonly identified with the provincial Union Nationale party, and never a friend of the CBC. Both ministers were anxious about their diminishing chances of re-election, and did not want any decision of the BBG to 'rock the boat.'

The hearings in Quebec City ended on February 16, 1962, but for an unusually long period there was no word on the board's decision. An announcement on some other matters was made on February 19, and a second announcement listing the board's decisions was made on March 21, but still no mention of Quebec City.[111] One of Spry's correspondents (a member of CBC staff) speculated, 'The delay over Quebec City must indicate a really sharp cleavage in the Board.'[112]

For his part, Stewart at this time was worrying about the procedure to be followed whenever the CBC applied for a station that would involve a substantial outlay of capital. He felt that the CBC's role in extending a second program service to additional communities should be the matter for a government policy declaration, and should not be decided by the BBG on an ad hoc basis. But the government was obviously unwilling to make such a statement, or indeed to give any policy guidance. In the

109 / *Ibid.*, 712–64.
110 / Newman, *Renegade in Power*, 132.
111 / *Canadian Broadcaster* (April 12, 1962).
112 / Spry Papers, letter dated March 22, 1962.

absence of a defined government position, Stewart advocated that the board itself draw up a statement of longterm policy, and that it not deal with further applications from the CBC until that policy was established.[113]

In its closed sessions, the board considered various proposals and resolutions on the Quebec applications, but there was an obvious lack of consensus. The BBG member from Quebec City was Guy Hudon, dean of law at Laval University. He opposed any further delay in arriving at a decision, let it be known that he favoured the CBC's application, and said he might have to resign if the Quebec decision was unduly deferred.[114] When the board met again in Winnipeg (during the hearings of April 3–6), Hudon, supported by Eugene Forsey, pressed for a decision. No majority could be found for approving either the CBC or the LaRoche application. Another announcement was made by the BBG on April 18, and again there was no mention of Quebec City. About this time, the 1962 election campaign got under way, with the polling date set for June 18.

When the board met again in Ottawa at the end of May, Stewart learned the reason some members were so reluctant to make an immediate decision and to announce it. The member of the cabinet from Quebec City (Jacques Flynn) had let it be known to some board members that any decision would be an unfortunate one, because the city was divided in its support for the two applicants. After discussions on three different days, a motion was finally approved to deny the LaRoche application, but to reserve decision on the CBC application.[115] On the same day, Hudon and Forsey submitted their resignations to Nowlan, who was campaigning in his own Nova Scotia constituency. The letter of resignation was made public on June 7.[116]

In Montreal, the 250,000-member Quebec Federation of Labour called for an end to the BBG, and a return to the regulatory authority of the CBC.[117] From Quebec City, the *Globe and Mail*'s correspondent reported that the BBG's disagreement and indecision had probably hurt the chances for re-election of the four Conservative members representing the Quebec district.[118] When the election took place on June 18, both

---

113 / Stewart MS, 58.
114 / *Ibid.*, 58; Spry Papers, Forsey to Spry, March 21, 1962.
115 / Stewart MS, 61–2; BBG Announcement, June 11, 1962.
116 / 'Rejection Protested; Two Quit over Quebec TV License,' *Toronto Star*, June 8, 1962.
117 / *Globe and Mail*, June 12, 1962 (CP dispatch).
118 / Thomas Sloan, 'Blow to 4 PCs Seen,' June 9, 1962.

Flynn and Dorion lost their seats to Social Credit candidates, and Conservative representation in the province as a whole was reduced to fourteen.

Both boards were feeling the strain. On June 26, a Canadian Press dispatch quoted Stewart as confirming that difficulties existed between the two agencies. He said that if the boards could not get together, and if the BBG could not override the CBC, then there must be 'a reference to Parliament to resolve the difficulties.'[119] But Canada had a minority government, one that was unlikely to resolve difficulties in so controversial a field.

So far as the Quebec City situation was concerned, LaRoche resubmitted his application later in 1962, and the two applications were heard again in January 1963. On this occasion, the CBC application was 'approved unanimously,' and the LaRoche application was denied.[120] In the meantime, another even more explosive controversy had arisen between the CBC and the BBG, involving as well the CTV network and Toronto station CFTO. That controversy was over the telecasting of the 1962 Grey Cup football game, and on this issue the CBC and BBG joined open battle.

6 *The Grey Cup Fiasco*

The background to the dispute over the network coverage of the football championship game lay in the BBG's effort to promote 'cross-programming' between the two networks, and the CBC's insistence upon control of its network and the maintenance of separate network identities.

In December 1961, the BBG stated its view that 'cross-programming,' by which affiliates of one network could carry programs supplied by another network, was desirable and 'consistent with the concept of the single broadcasting system.' Using the example of a CBC affiliate, the board explained that although such a station could not carry a CTV program during the CBC's 'reserved time' periods, it could carry programs up to four hours a week directly from the CTV network in periods other than 'reserved time.'[121]

The BBG's announcement was made in spite of opposition to the

119 / 'Report BBG-CBC Dispute May Go Before Parliament,' *Toronto Star*, June 26. 1962.
120 / BBG Announcement, Jan. 30, 1963; Stewart MS, 62.
121 / BBG Public Announcement, Dec. 7, 1961.

concept of 'cross-programming' expressed on numerous occasions by the president of the CBC. Ouimet held that cross-programming was equivalent to the 'splitting of networks,' which would occur if CTV used the CBC network's private affiliates to round out its own national coverage. (The CBC had over thirty-five English-language affiliates, as compared with the CTV's eight or nine.)[122]

The BBG's announcement on cross-programming had little effect: the CBC continued its opposition, and its private affiliates showed little interest in carrying CTV originations. The broadcast arrangements for the 1962 Grey Cup, however, exacerbated the hard feelings developing between the BBG and CBC, and led to an open confrontation in which the BBG was not the winner.

The previous year, CFTO Toronto had outbid the CBC for the rights to telecast the football games played in eastern Canada, and also for the final east–west game, the Grey Cup championship. The eastern games were carried on the CTV network, but because it still did not have microwave connections in western Canada, CTV could not realistically be expected to handle such a national event as the Grey Cup final. John Bassett of CFTO therefore sold the rights to the sponsors, who approached the CBC to broadcast the game. Bassett then asked that his station and the other two 'second' stations in Ottawa and Montreal be added to the CBC network for the occasion. The sponsors were not interested in paying for such duplicate coverage, and the BBG refused to order the CBC to make the telecast available to the three stations.[123]

In 1962, CTV owned the western portion of the football rights, and Bassett the eastern. Bassett, with the option of first refusal, matched the CBC's bid of $175,000 for exclusive rights to the Grey Cup game. The advertisers, however, still wanted wider coverage than CTV could provide.

The BBG was aware of the proposals and counter-proposals made by the owners of the rights and the CBC and met with Caldwell and Ouimet on May 30 to hear their views. Following the meeting, a letter was sent to CTV with a copy to CBC which said, 'The Board is not prepared, even if it were in a position to do so, to require the Corporation to release its affiliated stations for the purpose of carrying a broadcast of the game by

---

122 / For the CBC's objections, see *1961 Proceedings*, May 23, evidence of Ouimet, 618–21; also June 15, evidence of Stewart, 923–5. The right of an affiliate to use a program on film or videotape from another network in local time was not in dispute.
123 / BBG Press Release, Nov. 28, 1961. In an earlier statement (March 9, 1961), the BBG had recommended that the Grey Cup game be carried by the CBC, but that it 'be made available to all stations wishing to broadcast it.'

CTV network.'[124] This statement referred to the provision in the act which forbade stations affiliated with the CBC from operating as part of another network without the approval of the BBG, and this in turn required the permission of the CBC.[125]

Bassett then addressed a letter to the BBG, with a copy to the CBC, offering the Grey Cup game to the CBC, sponsored or unsponsored, but hoping that the CBC would reach agreement with the sponsors. The CBC quickly expressed willingness to accept the broadcast – without sponsors. Four weeks later, July 5, the BBG informed the CBC that the television rights were owned by Bassett and Caldwell, and that Bassett's offer of June 7 was 'not acceptable to the other owner of the television rights.'[126] The board then decided there was an impasse, and advised Ouimet and Caldwell that under a section of the BBG's regulations, 'the Board will require both networks to distribute the broadcast without addition or deletion, and the broadcast will be so carried on all stations of or affiliated with both networks.'[127]

The CBC expressed strong opposition to the proposed regulation which would force it to take the CTV broadcast of the game, complete with commercial announcements. The BBG called a special hearing for Saturday, August 18, to hear views on the proposed course of action, and afterward published the amendment to the regulations in the *Canada Gazette* (November 7). The CBC, having sought legal advice from the federal Department of Justice, concluded that the board's regulation contravened the broadcasting act and announced that it was refusing to abide by the BBG's decision.

In its press release of November 15, the CBC said it did not intend to allow 'CTV or any unauthorized person or organization, either directly or indirectly, to use the national broadcasting service as a sales tool.' It quoted from the legal opinions it had received from E.A. Driedger, the deputy attorney general, and from a Toronto lawyer, C.F.H. Carson, both of whom doubted the validity of the board's regulation.[128]

124 / BBG Hearings, Aug. 18, 1962, 937.

125 / Stewart MS, 396.

126 / BBG Hearings, Aug. 18, 1962, 938.

127 / *Ibid.*, 943.

128 / In his letter dated July 24, 1962, Driedger referred to the power of the BBG under section 11 (1)(f) to order licensees to broadcast programs of public interest or significance. He did not think the advertising messages could be considered 'of public interest or significance,' and therefore the BBG was going beyond its authority in ordering the CBC to carry the advertising portion of the broadcast. Carson advised that through Bassett's letter to Stewart, and Ouimet's letter to Bassett on July 11, 'mutual promises were given which would constitute a binding contract' – that is, for a 'clean' feed of the pick-up of the game. The letter to Ouimet from CTV on June 13, Carson said, was evidence that CTV had joined in the offer made by Bassett.

Throughout the controversy, the private affiliates supported the CBC's stand, as did most newspaper comment.

The CBC remained adamant in refusing to accept CTV's commercials, but in mid-November it offered to make five courtesy announcements mentioning CTV's advertisers. According to Andrew Stewart, the responsible minister at the time, Secretary of State Ernest Halpenny, decided to back the CBC solution. Negotiations had to be conducted between the CBC and each of CTV's advertisers, because the broadcast rights had been transferred to them at the beginning of October. In the end, CTV and all the advertisers agreed to the CBC's proposal.[129]

The game itself on December 1 was an anti-climax. A fog rolled in from the Toronto lakeshore, obscuring the players and much of the action. As Andrew Stewart wrote, 'It seemed a fitting climax to the events that the 1962 Grey Cup Game ended prematurely in a fog.'[130]

When the CBC and CTV reached their agreement on the coverage of the Grey Cup, there was no need even to attempt to apply the BBG's especially enacted regulation. It was quietly withdrawn in January 1963.[131]

It was a mystery to many observers why the BBG had gone to such lengths to ensure national coverage for the Grey Cup game, to the point of ordering the CBC to carry CTV's commercials. Those who took the CBC's side in the dispute interpreted the BBG's actions as evidence of a tender regard for the new network it had licensed, and an anxious concern about its survival. The directors of the CBC were more than ever determined to exercise the greatest possible degree of autonomy with regard to the BBG. The CBC president, moreover, pursued a campaign to promote the notion that the 'single system' of broadcasting was outmoded, unwieldy, confused, and too complex, and that a new investigation of broadcasting in Canada was needed, preferably through a royal commission. He felt this would point the way to a dual system in which the public and private elements would be more clearly demarcated, and he believed that if the CBC were more nearly self-sufficient, it could be largely independent of the regulatory authority.[132]

Meanwhile, in the discussions of the BBG advisory committee on public broadcasting, the CBC had been urging the reservation of televi-

---

129 / Ouimet interview, 1 July, 1975. After the initial agreement on Grey Cup coverage, the CBC and CTV went on to work out an agreement for sharing rights on all Canadian professional football, including the Grey Cup, for a five-year period. *CBC Annual Report, 1962–63*, 14.

130 / Stewart MS, 412.

131 / BBG Announcement, Jan. 30, 1963.

132 / The most complete statement of Ouimet's position was in his speech to the Ottawa Canadian Club, Dec. 5, 1962. But he had been advocating a royal commission for several months before this.

sion channels for CBC use, and the board of directors of the CBC authorized management to undertake the work preparatory to additional licence applications.[133]

As a result of discussions with the CBC and private broadcasters, and its own studies of the situation, the BBG came to the conclusion that the national advertising revenues would not support further 'second stations' in more than one or two additional cities. However, the board accepted the CBC's argument that within the 'two stations' policy, additional licences should be issued to the corporation to enable it to operate at least one station in each province, preferably in the capital city. To this end, the BBG announced on December 20, 1962, that it would be prepared to hear applications from the CBC for the reservation of channels in four cities – St. John's, Newfoundland; Saskatoon; Fredericton–Saint John; and Sudbury. A fifth possibility was mentioned, a channel for Prince Edward Island.

But before action could be taken on these channel reservations, a spring election in 1963 had resulted in the defeat of the Diefenbaker government, and the return of the Liberals to power under L.B. Pearson. The new government might well have its own ideas on the proper course to be pursued.

7 The BBG's Reputation in 1963

By the time the Liberals assumed power, the BBG had been involved in several controversies, some of them with damaging results, but none with the political or public relations impact of certain misfortunes that had befallen the CBC – the Montreal strike, for example, or the resignations over 'Preview Commentary.'

There were, however, a number of incidents that left an impression that the BBG was not a strong body, or that it was too likely to be swayed by political considerations and other circumstances of the moment. The BBG's first important decision had been to set a quota for Canadian content in television, but that had subsequently been weakened by the board's interpretation and application of the regulation. To many critics, the recommendations for second station licences seemed politically partisan. The decision to favour the creation of a private television network despite indifference or opposition from the second stations appeared to identify BBG too closely with the fortunes of CTV. On the other hand, the BBG's decision in favour of the CBC in Edmonton was

133 / CBC board of directors, Minutes, meeting of Feb. 5–6, 1963.

regarded by other interests as showing too much deference to a big-spending public corporation. A lack of unity within the BBG was publicly demonstrated during the hearings of the parliamentary committee on broadcasting in 1961, when Andrew Stewart, on instructions from the full board, had to withdraw a proposal that he had formally made for an amendment to the broadcasting act.[134]

The three most serious incidents were the tentative approval of CFTO's application for share and management participation by an American network, ABC, and the subsequent reversal of that decision under pressure; and the two issues involving the CBC, the indecision over the granting of the Quebec City licence, and the attempt to dictate the terms under which the CBC would carry the Grey Cup game. The Grey Cup controversy got more public attention, certainly in English Canada, and much of it unfavourable to the BBG. As Stewart subsequently admitted, 'The BBG lost the round.'[135] The other contest of wills with the CBC, over the television licence for Quebec City, showed the susceptibility of a predominantly part-time board to political influence. It was damaging in French Canada, and the resignation of two members from the board further weakened the BBG's moral authority.

At the same time, the BBG had its successes and sources of strength. In a very short time, it had presided over a considerable transformation of the broadcasting system from a condition in which the public element was dominant to one in which the public and private elements were regarded as equal components, with equal rights if not responsibilities. The BBG had established procedures for hearing representations and for making its decisions known that were generally commended. It had done so with a tiny staff, a small outlay of public funds, and a great deal of hard work on the part of Andrew Stewart and Carlyle Allison particularly. In March 1963 the BBG's total staff, including the three full-time members of the board, numbered only forty, and the BBG's expenditures were just over $350,000.

If the BBG had made some awards and decisions that were thought to be politically motivated, no one was inclined to place the blame on Andrew Stewart, who was generally regarded as an independent and fair-minded man. He certainly had the confidence of George Nowlan,

---

134 / The amendment would have delegated authority to the chairman to deal with station applications to carry or refrain from carrying network programs outside of 'reserved time,' and also would have removed the necessity to secure the permission of the network concerned. The amendment was opposed by the CBC president in a meeting of the BBG attended by all board members, part-time and full-time. *1961 Proceedings*, 864–6, 883, 917, 923–4, 945–6.
135 / Stewart MS, 394.

the minister to whom he reported during most of this period. Nowlan told the Commons in 1960 that when he had approached Stewart in 1958 to become the chairman, his colleague, Dr. Sidney Smith, former president of the University of Toronto, had said, 'If you get him you will have the best man in Canada.' Nowlan added that he was more convinced of this now than ever before.[136] The minister did indicate a difference of opinion with the board on the policy of admitting American networks to a share of ownership in Canadian television stations, but he would have found out in discussion that Stewart was opposed to this decision also.[137]

It was with the private broadcasters that the BBG had established a particularly high reputation. The CAB and the majority of stations had argued against the Canadian content provisions and some of the BBG's regulations, but they were generally satisfied with the structural changes in the system resulting from the 1958 legislation, and with the BBG's interpretation of its role.

When the regulations governing television stations were first announced in November 1959, the CAB took that early occasion to demonstrate support for the BBG. The executive committee of the CAB went on record as complimenting the CAB for the careful study it had made, adding, 'It appears that the new regulations offer sufficient realistic flexibility to make a practical trial of them possible.'[138] The *Canadian Broadcaster*, usually critical of any controls placed on station owners, editorialized, 'Regulation by the BBG is a long haul from the old regulation-competition of the CBC. Besides the undemocratic structure of the old system, it is an improvement because the BBG is headed by a group of people blessed with a rare combination of intelligence and understanding.'[139]

After Don Jamieson was elected president of the CAB in 1961, for what turned out to be a four-year term of office, relations between the CAB and the BBG became even closer, since Jamieson spent more time on the business of the CAB than had his predecessors. The CAB representatives told the parliamentary committee in 1961 that the BBG was providing responsible and effective leadership, and the amendments to the 1958 act that the CAB proposed were designed to strengthen the BBG's authority at the expense of the CBC.[140]

136 / *Debates*, July 13, 1960, 6230.
137 / Stewart MS, 155; Forsey to Spry, Sept. 2, 1961, Spry Papers.
138 / 'CAB Approves BBG Regulations,' *Canadian Broadcaster* (Nov. 26, 1959).
139 / *Ibid.*, Aug. 3, 1961.
140 / *1961 Proceedings*, 133, 143, 947. Stewart, in discussing the amendment he had proposed which was repudiated by the full board, told a questioner (Fisher) that he had

The CAB's friendliness toward the BBG helped confirm the opinion of some others (for example, the Canadian Broadcasting League and its allies) that the BBG was over-protective of the private broadcasters, too concerned about the viability of their stations and of the second television network, CTV. The dilution of the Canadian content regulations, the hesitation to approve a CBC television licence in Quebec City (leading to two resignations from the board), the rather strange position taken during the Grey Cup controversy, the lack of reproof to station owners who ignored promises of program performance when applying for licences – all this led some to conclude that, as so often happens, a regulatory board tends to become identified with those whom it regulates.[141]

While generally supporting the BBG, the CAB still favoured a smaller, full-time board, such as it had proposed to the Fowler Commission in 1956. At the time Hudon and Forsey resigned, the *Canadian Broadcaster* wrote that in setting up a board with twelve part-time members, the government had overlooked the fact that 'it would be impossible for these part-time governors to have the same understanding as the full-time governors.'[142] Speaking more officially for the CAB, Jamieson told a group of broadcasters that the three full-time members had acquired a sizeable knowledge of the economics and operational problems of the industry. But it was 'increasingly difficult to get the real picture across to the part-time members.' He favoured another inquiry into the structure of broadcasting, but not the royal commission that Ouimet had asked for. 'At this stage in the game, another Royal Commission, with the usual entourage of pressure groups and screwballs, could end in chaos. There should be an examination by people who are in the field. The BBG could create the auspices for any enquiry which is necessary.'[143]

Since it had been reported in the mid-summer of 1962 that Don Jamieson was advising the Liberals on broadcasting policy and techniques for use in the next election campaign, it was of some interest to see how closely the new government in 1963 would follow Jamieson's recommendations.[144]

'mentioned' the proposal to the CAB president (Jamieson). The amendment was one that the CAB had also put forward. *Proceedings*, 917.

141 / This appraisal of the BBG appears in this writer's article, 'The Nationalist Dilemma in Canadian Broadcasting,' in Peter Russell, ed., *Nationalism in Canada* (Toronto, 1966), esp. pp. 260–2. See also E.A. Weir, *The Struggle for National Broadcasting in Canada*, chap. 25.

142 / *Canadian Broadcaster* (June 21, 1962).

143 / *Ibid.*, Sept. 20, 1962.

144 / Barbara Moon, 'The Back-room Conspiracy,' *Maclean's*, (July 28, 1962).

9 ADVICE TO THE PERPLEXED LIBERALS

THE ELECTION on April 8, 1963, again resulted in no party having a clear majority, but the Liberals now had the largest representation, with 129 seats in the House of Commons compared to the Conservatives' 95. The NDP won 17 seats and Social Credit 24, but with evident disunity among the Social Credit members, John Diefenbaker delayed his decision to resign. Eventually, Lester Pearson was called to Government House, and on April 22 his cabinet was sworn in.

The 1958 broadcasting legislation had carried out the Progressive Conservative party's pledge to remove private stations from the control of the CBC and to institute a separate regulatory board. Under Pearson's leadership the Liberal party had remained an advocate of a single broadcasting system in which the public element should be dominant. In the Commons, the Liberals had argued that the Conservative government's legislation would lead to confusion and conflict between the two boards, to a weakening of the CBC, and to a situation in which the BBG would become concerned primarily with the private stations.[1] In the light of developments and the seeming accuracy of his earlier predictions, one might have expected the new prime minister to move with confidence to provide his own remedies.

Aside from his party's position, Pearson had had a long personal interest in broadcasting issues. For years he had had friendly associations with Graham Spry, dating back to their days as students at Oxford. During the 1930s, he kept in touch with Alan Plaunt who wrote him about the struggle to establish a public corporation in charge of Canadian broadcasting, and who later tried to recruit him for a senior position in the CBC.[2] Pearson's memoirs describe his attitude: 'I had been interested in the Canadian Radio League in the thirties and my views did not change in principle during the intervening years, though certainly they had to be modified in practice. My general view was that broadcasting

1 / See above, chapter 6, pp. 160–2.
2 / Peers, *Politics of Canadian Broadcasting*, 210, 297.

should be treated as education and that there should be the greatest possible public control; that the emphasis should be on the public system and private broadcasting should be very much a subsidiary.'[3]

It was not unprecedented for a prime minister to intervene in deciding broadcasting policy. In 1932 the action by Parliament to establish the Canadian Radio Broadcasting Commission followed R.B. Bennett's persuasion by supporters of public broadcasting, especially through the influence of two close advisers, W.D. Herridge and R.K. Finlayson, who were in sympathy with the Canadian Radio League.[4] Bennett was sufficiently dominant that when he made up his mind, others within the cabinet followed. Even Mackenzie King, who in dealing with his ministers was more careful to obey the conventions of collegiality, overrode the advice of the department charged with the control of radio frequencies and of its minister, C.D. Howe, when he requested the chairman of a Commons committee on broadcasting to change the tenor of its report. King wanted the committee to recommend undivided control of broadcasting by a public corporation, which he was persuaded was in the spirit of 'the Aird Report brought up to date.'[5]

But of course the situation in 1963 was not as simple as that in either 1932 or 1936. The prime minister's party did not have a majority in 1963, although if it had moved to restore control of broadcasting by a single board, following perhaps the Fowler Commission's recommendations, it presumably could have counted on the support of the NDP in Parliament. Furthermore, the Liberals had promised a great number of policy initiatives in the 1962 and 1963 campaigns, and to show their determination to act, Pearson in 1963 had promised 'sixty days of decision' – 'more constructive things will be done in the first sixty days of a new Liberal government than in any similar period of Canadian history.'[6] The government could not move rapidly on all fronts at the same time.

Aside from the difficulties of pushing through a legislative program in a divided House, there were extra-parliamentary pressures that weighed on the government. The private component in broadcasting had grown enormously in size, profitability, and influence since the 1940s and 1950s when the Liberal leadership had supported the dominant position of the national broadcasting service in the mixed system. The private broadcasters had reason to be grateful to the Conservative party since it was a

3 / *Mike: The Memoirs of the Rt. Hon. Lester B. Pearson*, vol. 3, ed. John A. Munro and Alex I. Inglis (Toronto, 1975), 189.
4 / Peers, *Politics of Canadian Broadcasting*, 65, 68, 76, 89.
5 / *Ibid.*, 172, 182–3.
6 / *Mike*, vol. 3, 81.

Conservative administration that had granted them the long-sought separate regulatory board, but publicly their trade association, the CAB, took care not to become identified with one party or the other.[7] There were a few private broadcasters in elected positions in each party. Indeed, the current president of the CAB, Don Jamieson, was reputed to be an adviser to the Liberal Party of Canada; it was more widely known that he was a friend and supporter of the premier of Newfoundland, Joseph Smallwood, and of the federal cabinet minister who held a Newfoundland seat, J.W. Pickersgill.[8] As CAB president, Jamieson did not take any public part in the Liberal campaigns. However, his sympathies and connections were known in political circles. Even in the years when Louis St. Laurent was prime minister, some Liberals had expressed publicly their dissatisfaction with the government's broadcasting policy. Among the critics was a young Torontonian, Keith Davey, who emerged in 1962 and 1963 as the Liberal campaign director, and very much part of the inner circle. Davey later described his attempt to secure a modification of what had been traditional Liberal policy:

I spent eleven years at radio station CKFH in Toronto, which was then and still is owned and operated by one of the truly great pioneers of Canadian radio, Mr. Foster Hewitt. ...

It was at this period of my career that I attended a Young Liberal Convention and there moved, sponsored, worked for, and ultimately saw carried, a resolution asking the Government of the day to change this situation which allowed the C.B.C. to control its own competition. This was finally done, but not until after the Government of the day was changed. So, today, we have the Board of Broadcast Governors and the regulations for which, by and large, they have been responsible.

Davey recalled the regulatory system before 1958 as 'an unhappy situation at best, and it became intolerable with the explosive postwar growth of private broadcasting in Canada.'[9]

No one was publicly advocating a return to the situation in which the

7 / As an illustration of this concern, T.J. Allard explained to the author that in 1952–3 the CAB had modified its originally expressed opposition to the Liberal government's announced policy for television development to avoid becoming identified with the Conservative party's opposition to that policy, as expressed by George Drew. Interview, Toronto, July 7, 1975.

8 / According to Richard Gwyn, 'Two [Newfoundland] cabinet ministers were confidential shareholders in Radio Station CJON, co-owned by Stirling and Jamieson, which got its licence through good Liberal offices.' Gwyn, *Smallwood: The Unlikely Revolutionary*, 135.

9 / Senate *Debates*, Feb. 13, 1968, 821

CBC board of directors would become also the regulatory board. But the Liberals had expressed approval of the Fowler Commission's recommendation that there be one board as a regulatory authority to whom also the president of the CBC as chief executive officer would be responsible 'for the conduct and direction of the affairs of the Corporation.'[10]

In 1958 Davidson Dunton had accepted this proposal as superior to an arrangement with two boards. At that time Alphonse Ouimet had not expressed his preference, but in 1962 it became clear that he regarded the best line of evolution to continue the two boards, but to separate their functions so clearly that they would have little to do with one another. In his speech to the Canadian Club of Ottawa on December 5, 1962, he complained that the Canadian system of broadcasting had become so complex that it confused the public, many parliamentarians, and even the public bodies concerned with its operation. It was especially complex because the CBC had to depend on private stations for the distribution of its programs: 'Today, with the addition to radio of public and private TV networks and with two Boards, the lack of CBC self-sufficiency is becoming more of a problem not only for the Corporation, but I believe also for the BBG and many of the private affiliates and I am afraid it will get worse as time goes on.' He believed that over a period of ten to twenty years, with the addition of more CBC stations and repeaters, the public and private sectors could be completely separated:

If this were done, the private stations and the CBC could eventually operate entirely independently of one another as do the public and private sectors in Australia and Britain. This separation would in turn greatly simplify the relations between the two Boards. ... Eventually, the main concern of the BBG would be to regulate and recommend regarding private stations, as is the case in Australia, with the CBC continuing to answer directly to Parliament on all its activities but without the present complex inter-relationships between BBG and CBC. Thus, this single basic step of providing the CBC with its own outlets would by itself eliminate over the years the major complexities of the Canadian system.

Ouimet indicates that his views were widely shared among the CBC board of directors, but there was probably not complete unanimity among his senior staff.[11] The speech was well reported and received

10 / *Fowler Commission Report*, 417: Appendix XI, draft statute, 'An Act Respecting Broadcasting,' sec. 41(1). For the statements of Liberal party concurrence, see *Debates*, Aug. 25, 1958, 4050 (Pearson), and 4083–4, 4087 (Pickersgill).
11 / The writer's observation at the time as an employee of the CBC was that at least some of Ouimet's assistants at head office were doubtful of the wisdom of putting forward his proposals under the existing circumstances. The writer's own reservations were outlined in a letter to Ouimet on Dec. 7, 1962.

extensive comment on the nation's editorial pages.[12] It seemed to surprise some of the CBC's most constant supporters, such as the Canadian Broadcasting League. Early in 1963 the league released a statement that said a divided system with the CBC on one side and a purely commercial sector under the Board of Broadcast Governors' authority on the other would be unacceptable. The league held that a dual system would not solve the problem of continuing controversy and conflict between the public and private sectors of the Canadian broadcasting system. It supported Ouimet's suggestion that ultimately the CBC should have a network composed entirely of CBC-owned stations, but it reiterated its view that the CTV network organization should also be a public body, with access to some public funds, so that it could resist a too heavy influence from United States commercial enterprises.[13]

The CBC board supported Ouimet's view that 'the public is better served through a combination of one CBC station and one private station than by other means,' and the objective of providing the complete national service through CBC-owned stations.[14] It was unlikely, however, that a board of Conservative appointees would carry much influence with the new minister who would report for the CBC in Parliament, Secretary of State Jack Pickersgill. He was thought to have been one of the ministers who in 1954 was influential in turning down the recommendation of the CBC board of governors that a CBC television station be established in St. John's Newfoundland. Instead, the government had authorized the issuing of the St. John's licence to a company headed by Geoff Stirling and Don Jamieson.[15] As a member of the opposition in 1960, Pickersgill explained: 'The [Liberal] government in its wisdom decided that there should not be a C.B.C. station at St. John's, as it also decided there should not be one at Saint John, or Fredericton, or Regina, or Saskatoon. ... We decided that if we established public

12 / For example, in the Vancouver *Province*, *Calgary Herald*, *Edmonton Journal*, *Kitchener Waterloo-Record*, Toronto *Globe and Mail*, Toronto *Telegram*, *Peterborough Examiner*, *Ottawa Journal*, Ottawa *Citizen*, *Montreal Star*, *La Presse*, and *Quebec Chronicle-Telegraph*. The CBC director of public relations (Jan. 16, 1963) summarized majority reaction as: support for a new comprehensive study of broadcasting; opposition to CBC exemption from BBG control; tentative support for CBC being provided with its own outlets; and grudging agreement that CBC could not vacate the commercial field.

13 / 'CBC Suggestion Opposed,' Montreal *Gazette*, Jan. 4, 1963 (CP dispatch).

14 / *CBC Annual Report, 1961–62*, 18, 27; *ibid.*, 1962–3, 15.

15 / Interview, A.D. Dunton. Pickersgill has confirmed that in cabinet he led the opposition to accepting the CBC's request. Pickersgill, *My Years with Louis St. Lourent*, 225.

stations in Vancouver, in Winnipeg, in Toronto, in Ottawa, in Montreal and in Halifax, we would have enough stations to provide national network coverage and that the rest of the field should be left to private initiative.'[16]

During that debate Pickersgill was by inference questioning the wisdom of granting the CBC the 'second station' in Edmonton on the grounds of the additional public expense. But if he had not changed his mind on this, he had on the question of a private network: 'I think it is a very sensible thing to have a private network if we are going to have this competitive group of stations. I know all the objections there were in the old days of radio to a private network and that it was prohibited for many years. But after all, as the newspaper points out tonight, we are supposed to have 17,814,000 people in this country ... an increase of two-thirds over ... 1936.'[17] A few months later, he told the Commons, 'Quite frankly, if we lived a thousand miles from any other country, if Canada were an island with 18 million people on it, I am not so sure, taking everything into account, that I would feel that public broadcasting was necessary at all.'[18]

There were signs that other Liberals as well had accommodated themselves to a situation in which private broadcasting would be the more dominant element in the system. The Council of the National Liberal Federation met in Ottawa at the end of January 1962. Bernard Trotter has provided this account of how a resolution dealing with broadcasting was modified before it was adopted:

The original draft of a policy resolution on National Cultural Institutions presented to that meeting described 'Canadian broadcasting with its combination of public and private stations in a *single system*' (italics mine). Dr. Pauline Jewett (later M.P. for Northumberland) met with less than an enthusiastic response from her fellow delegates when she objected to the failure of the draft resolution to offer any concrete support of the CBC and moved an amendment pledging the Party to 'determined moral and financial support of the Corporation.' The resolution was sent to a sub-committee for further work. When it emerged again in the form which was unanimously approved by the Council without further debate, the resolution promised continued 'moral and financial support' for the CBC. But it included the following additional clause: '... a new Liberal Government will give full scope for the parallel development of both public and private initiative in broadcasting under an independent and truly non-partisan agency of

16 / *Debates*, July 13, 1960, 6218.
17 / *Ibid.*, 6235.
18 / *Ibid.*, Jan. 18, 1961, 1186.

control.' Perhaps most significant in retrospect was the deletion of the reference to 'a single system' from the sentence quoted above. The rest of the sentence remained. This deletion was therefore hardly an accident. The final resolution was moved by Mr. Walter Gordon (on behalf of Miss Jewett) and seconded by Mr. Baxter Ricard, owner of CHNO, Sudbury, one of those who had been named to the sub-committee as a spokesman for private broadcasting.[19]

At the end of his article (written in 1966) Trotter asks whether it is fair in the light of subsequent events to suggest that the Liberal party was prepared to 'sell out the national system of broadcasting to private interests.'[20]

This question may have been too starkly put, but it was soon clear that the Liberals after the 1963 election were not interested in reviving their former policy, emphasizing one system and one public board in control of that system, at least not without further inquiry.

1 *Pickersgill's Appointment of the 'Troika'*

On the subject of broadcasting, Jack Pickersgill was one of the most knowledgeable ministers in Pearson's new cabinet. After joining the civil service in 1937, he had become a private secretary and confidant to Prime Minister Mackenzie King, and an even more important adviser to Prime Minister St. Laurent. He entered politics in 1953, 'under the combined pressures of Mr. St. Laurent and Joey Smallwood,' to become secretary of state in the St. Laurent government and member for the Newfoundland constituency of Bonavista-Twillingate.[21] During the Liberal party's lean years, from 1958 to 1962, Pickersgill, Lionel Chevrier, and Paul Martin were Pearson's chief lieutenants in the House of Commons, and Pickersgill undertook to advise Pearson on staff, policy positions, and tactics in the House – not always with happy results.[22] The portfolio of secretary of state which Pearson assigned to Pickersgill in 1963 may not have seemed a very senior one for such an experienced colleague, but Pickersgill was asked also to act as leader of the House.

Until August 1962, the minister of national revenue had reported to

19 / 'Canadian Broadcasting Act IV: Scene '67, or, Double Talk and the Single System,' *Queen's Quarterly* (Winter 1967), 468.
20 / *Ibid.*, 480–1.
21 / *Mike*, vol. 3, 39.
22 / Grant Dexter Papers, Dexter to Tom Kent, May 8, 1958, Queen's University Archives.

the Commons for both the BBG and the CBC, but when in that month George Nowlan succeeded Donald Fleming as minister of finance, the newly appointed secretary of state, Ernest Halpenny, took over the broadcasting responsibilities. Since Pickersgill had been the broadcasting critic for the Liberals, it was perhaps natural that the secretary of state would remain the parliamentary spokesman for the BBG and the CBC. Some of those clustered around the Broadcasting League were not entirely happy with the choice of Pickersgill. George Ferguson, editor of the *Montreal Star*, wrote Spry, 'I do not believe that the change in government necessarily lessens the threat to public broadcasting. No prime minister has ever made a high priority out of its protection, and I am appalled by Pearson appointing Pickersgill as the minister to report on CBC to Parliament. ... [A friend] remarks that Don Jamieson was TV advisor to Pearson during the campaign, and Jamieson is president of the CAB. It will be interesting to note whether the BBG recommendation that CBC establish a TV station in St. John's will now be accepted.'[23] Spry had similar doubts, and wrote Forsey that he hoped other ministers would provide a counterweight, and that a reasonable policy would emerge after full inquiry, preferably by a royal commission.[24]

Within ten days of taking office, Pickersgill decided on a tactical move that would at least give the government time to formulate its policy, and that would appeal to a prime minister who by training and temperament favoured negotiation and consensus. Immediately before the election, Andrew Stewart had addressed a letter to 'the office of the Prime Minister' asking for a thorough review of broadcasting policy and the broadcasting act, and had mailed it on April 8 before the outcome of the election was known.[25] Stewart told a service club meeting the next day of the difficulties in interpreting the 1958 legislation and insisted, 'It is essential to have a piece of legislation which means what it says and which leaves no dispute as to how the board is to behave administratively.' Questions needing clarification included the definition of broadcasting and the growth of cable systems, political broadcasting, the licensing of new CBC television stations, affiliation of stations with the CBC, and conflicts between the CBC and the private television network.[26] But the problem that most concerned the BBG was the CBC's desire to extend its television service. As Stewart explained to the annual meeting of the CAB:

23 / Spry Papers, Ferguson to Spry, April 24, 1963.
24 / *Ibid.*, Spry to E.A. Forsey, April 27, 1963.
25 / *Globe and Mail*, 'BBG Asks Federal Review of Broadcasting,' April 10, 1963 (CP dispatch).
26 / *Ibid.*

Difficulties with regard to the allocation of frequencies and extension of the public service came to a head when it became known to the Board, that the Directors of the Corporation were committed to a policy of applying for all second television licences, and of opposing private station licences in centres now served by private affiliates of the CBC. The Corporation took the position that as the Directors considered these stations 'necessary and desirable' [Section 29 (1) (b)], the Board should recommend favourably on applications by the Corporation, leaving it to the Governor-in-Council to decide whether to provide the necessary funds and to pass the necessary order. The Board felt that, if it were committed to the procedure, and by inference to the policy, it should be on the basis of a statement of policy, and not as a result of a decision by the Directors of the Corporation. ... The Board believes, and has held this view for some time, that the only solution to this problem is a statement of public policy on the licencing of additional television stations to be owned and operated by the Corporation.[27]

At the same CAB meeting, Jamieson had kind words for the BBG, and supported its stand:

It is surprising, and yet I suppose not so surprising, that there are those organizations and those creatures of government which tend to take unto themselves power and authority which never was intended to be theirs at the time of their creation.

I have been impressed by the manner in which the permanent members of the Board of Broadcast Governors and its chairman have recognized that theirs is an administrative body, not a policy-making body. ... It should enforce the law; it should not determine the law or policy.

I commend the board for the manner in which it has taken this stand. ...

I have evidence that editorial and other print comment concerning the Grey Cup controversy reflected an almost total lack of knowledge on the subject by the majority of those who chose to write about it. ...

But there is another element here, and that is the propriety of a public agency, and specifically the Canadian Broadcasting Corporation, engaging in what amounts to a propaganda or public relations campaign on behalf of some specific matter of policy in which it happens to be engaged.[28]

The most important announcement before the CAB meeting in Toronto was from the secretary of state. Pickersgill told the convention that, with the prime minister's concurrence, he was asking Stewart, Ouimet, and

27 / Speech of May 1, 1963, quoted in Stewart MS, 80.
28 / Digest of Address to the CAB Convention, *Canadian Broadcaster* (May 23, 1963), 6.

Jamieson to have a series of discussions 'with a view to preparing for the consideration of the government a statement of those areas of public policy on which all three are in full or substantial agreement and those points on which there is a divergence of view.' The government would then be able to decide whether a further public inquiry was needed.[29]

The private broadcasters were delighted that their association had been accepted by the government as a policy adviser on a basis of equality with the two public bodies, the BBG and the CBC.[30] They were no doubt gratified also that the minister had chosen to make his important statement just nine days after taking office before the assembled broadcasters.

In his statement Pickersgill went on to specify three 'fixed points of public policy to which the present government is already committed.' The first was that there should be 'scope for the parallel development of both public and private initiatives in broadcasting, with an impartial agency of control.' (This ruled out a return to the board of the CBC as the controlling agency, but did it mean also that the government would not favour the BBG taking responsibility for the CBC, as the Fowler Commission had recommended?) Then, a prime objective should be 'to bring broadcasting in both official languages within the range of all Canadians as rapidly as circumstances and finances permit.' Finally, it was the government's view that 'the budget for public broadcasting should be determined by Parliament for a period of years in such a fashion that it cannot be changed or influenced by the government of day in order to preserve public broadcasting from partisan political pressure.' (This was one of the Fowler Commission's recommendations.)

Stewart, Ouimet, and Jamieson were invited to tender their advice as the three men 'with the greatest experience in broadcasting,' and they became known as the 'Troika.' Stewart was the first to use the name, and wrote the following limerick:[31]

The 'Troica' is surely a 'queer'
Three horses, no lead and no rear,
   A stud, CAB
   And a mare, CBC
But the BBG's gelded, I fear.

29 / Statement of May 1, 1963, *Canadian Broadcaster* (May 9, 1963), 8.
30 / The *Canadian Broadcaster* wrote that the government's move came 'as the result of a lot of campaigning on the part of Don Jamieson,' who after two years of dedicated service had staunchly behind him 'a united industry.' Editorial, 'Dawn of a New Day,' (May 9, 1963). Jamieson was elected to a third term.
31 / Stewart MS, 256.

The Troika met the week after their appointment, and at irregular intervals after that, usually only for a day or two at a time. The most urgent problem was to respond to the pressure for alternative television service in areas that had only one station. On September 24, an interim report was made to the minister, but nothing further was submitted until May 1964.

The interim report recommended 'in principle, that the extension of alternative Canadian television service when it occurs should proceed through the extension of transmission facilities of the Canadian Broadcasting Corporation,' but recommended a 'freeze' on applications for second service until July 1964. It also expressed support for the principle contained in the minister's statement of May 1 that the budget for the CBC should be determined by Parliament for a period of years. In Pickersgill's letter of acknowledgement, he said that he and his colleagues had found the recommendations sensible, and the government applied the freeze that had been recommended.[32]

The two principles agreed upon, extension of CBC facilities to provide alternative television service and statuatory funding for public broadcasting, were obviously two matters that the CBC had been advocating for some time. The interim report may therefore have been regarded as a triumph for Ouimet. But the government did not take any steps to implement its 'fixed position' on financing the CBC, nor did it publicly endorse the Troika's recommended policy in relation to the extension of alternative television service. Stewart understood that Pickersgill, and at least some of his colleagues, were reluctant to approve capital expenditures for additional 'hardware' for the CBC.[33]

In fact the concept of providing two television services in most communities through a combination of CBC and private facilities, rather than by two private stations one of which would be affiliated with the CBC, had been discussed at length by the Board of Broadcast Governors, and had found acceptance there. Stewart explains:

The position which eventually emerged from the BBG's consideration of the problem was that there would be established a tier of second outlets on top of the structure of first stations which would preserve and extend the public national service and would maintain the local service in the smaller centres. As we saw it this would be accomplished by allowing the CBC, intially, to install rebroadcasting stations in the smaller centres. This would have the effect of extending,

32 / Stewart MS, 256; BBG Annual Report, 1963–4, 16–7. The interim report was tabled in the House of Commons on Oct. 1, 1963 (*Debates*, 3075).
33 / Stewart MS, 234.

gradually, a full public service to all Canadians. ... The private stations would become affiliated with CTV network, on terms which would enable them to continue a local service to their communities. Structurally, there would be a separation of the public sector from the private sector, which would reduce the problem of the relation between the two parts. The audience would have a choice of the public service and the private service; and we believed that this would offer the public the best choice of programming. We thought it was a good design to guide the extension of 'second' service.[34]

Stewart admits that the BBG was slow to come to this position: 'The CBC was first to commit itself to the extension of second service through the facilities of the CBC. Later the Board came to adopt the same position.'[35]

Aside from the government's reluctance to grant the CBC more capital funds, there was a difficulty in persuading CTV to extend its service to stations in the smaller markets that would be disaffiliated from the CBC. Stewart believed the net earnings of CTV stations in the major markets were high enough to make it possible for them to 'absorb losses associated with gradual extension of the network service.' But the station owners may have seen things differently. A manager of one of the private television stations associated with CTV wrote Spry:

My assessment is that CTV, even with increased coverage composed of stations dis-affiliated from the CBC, as the CBC was able to replace them with satellites, would still not provide a sufficient amount of money to enable the CTV network to provide any basis of sustaining programs as well as sponsored ... [or] any sort of a balanced program schedule. If you complicate this by the reluctance of sponsors to underwrite almost any kind of Canadian production the job becomes almost impossible. These are the reasons why I think that financially some kind of public funds will be needed for CTV operation.[36]

2 Report of the Troika

When in May 1964 the Troika reported to the minister, it submitted a 'combined statement' of nine pages, and as well each member of the Troika submitted a statement of his own: Stewart's statement was twenty-three typed pages, Ouimet's about the same length, and

34 / *Ibid.*, 233–4.
35 / *Ibid.*, 235.
36 / Spry Papers, letter dated May 16, 1963.

Jamieson's about as long as Stewart's and Ouimet's statements combined.[37] On the surface, it seemed that they disagreed on more matters than they had agreed upon. By this time, Pickersgill had moved from the Department of the Secretary of State to Transport, so he was no longer the minister to whom the two agencies reported, although his department as the licensing authority still had an interest in broadcasting. Maurice Lamontagne, formerly president of the privy council, succeeded Pickersgill as secretary of state. As an adviser to the leader of the opposition, Lamontagne had helped draft Pearson's speech in 1958 criticising the broadcasting act, and Spry thought his appointment good news.[38] Lamontagne had an interest in establishing a cultural policy for Canada, bringing together under the secretary of state the principal cultural institutions relating to broadcasting, film, galleries, and museums, and support for the arts. But he did not have Pickersgill's seniority, and he did not carry authority in either the caucus or the Commons.[39]

During the discussions of the Troika, Ouimet felt that he and Stewart were very close to agreement, but that Jamieson made it impossible for the three men to reach a consensus. Jamieson kept saying, 'What you, Ouimet, are proposing is that the BBG regulate only the private stations,' and he would not be regulated by anyone who did not also regulate the CBC. Ouimet had already conceded that the CBC should receive channel allocations through the BBG. And, according to Ouimet, Pickersgill was never able to bridge the last differences of opinion before he shifted portfolios. After Lamontagne succeeded to the office, he appointed a second deputy minister specializing in cultural affairs, Ernest Steele (the other deputy minister continued to be concerned with patents, copyright, etc.), and Steele appointed Henry Hindley as his assistant. Ouimet thought that with these moves, the CBC president to a considerable extent lost access to the minister.[40]

Stewart's summary of the positions taken in the discussion mentions some points on which he was closer to Ouimet, and some on which he and Jamieson were in agreement. Because it is impossible to trace the influence this document had on the outcome of the policy discussions in cabinet (Ouimet is not sure that the reports were even read by Pickersgill

37 / The combined statement in an introductory section included Pickersgill's statement of May 1, 1963. It was tabled in the House of Commons, May 25, 1964, together with the individual statements of the 'troika.'
38 / Spry Papers, letter written to a correspondent in the CBC, Jan. 24, 1964.
39 / Newman, *The Distemper of Our Times*, 247–9.
40 / Ouimet interview, July 2, 1975.

or Lamontage), it does not seem necessary to summarize them in detail. Ouimet calls the Troika's discussions 'an exercise in futility';[41] by the time the reports were submitted, the government had already decided on a more formal inquiry.

In their separate statements, each member of the Troika abandoned use of the term, 'the single system,' or 'the single, mixed system' that the Fowler Commission in 1957 had regarded as a basic assumption for Canadian broadcasting,[42] and which by inference was incorporated in the existing broadcasting act (section 10). Jamieson wrote that the concept had for years been rendered 'virtually meaningless.' Stewart wrote that the public and the private sectors were increasingly separate and distinct, and the principal question was what authority must be delegated to ensure that the whole system served common ends. Jamieson was completely opposed to any one-board system, and Ouimet had reservations about it 'on practical grounds,' although in principle it offered such advantages that it deserved thorough re-examination by another inquiry. Ouimet added, 'I would say that I am firmly of the opinion that any two-board system under which one board would be required to report to a second board is neither desirable or practical.' Stewart noted that the private broadcasters were irrevocably opposed to being placed under a board that might even have the appearance of being the board of the CBC, and he did not see why it should be necessary to require the private broadcasters to accept a solution to which they were implacably opposed.

In their combined statement, the three therefore concentrated on suggestions for the improvement of the two-board system. For most purposes, they suggested, 'the Corporation should report to Parliament, annually, on the performance of the public sector; and the Board should report, annually, on the performance of the private sector.' The roles of each sector should be defined in the legislation, and should be amplified in a White Paper on broadcasting.

The three were agreed that Parliament should determine the structure of the system, and give direction on the extension of the facilities and service. They reiterated the principle recommended in the interim report, that the extension of alternative television service should proceed through the extension of CBC transmission facilities. Before the CBC moved to install its own facilities in any particular area, negotiations should proceed with the existing private affiliate, and the BBG (as the body responsible for the performance of private stations) must concur

41 / *Ibid.*
42 / *Fowler Commission Report*, 13.

with any arrangement arrived at. When a private station was needed to distribute the public network service, conditions of its affiliation agreement with the CBC should also have the concurrence of the BBG.

Efforts of the BBG and the CBC to co-ordinate policies and procedures should be made through a Joint Committee on Broadcasting, with representatives from each board, and questions of jurisdiction that could not be resolved should be referred to the proper court.

Recommendations on matters of over-all broadcasting policy should be made to the government of the day by the public broadcasting agencies – the BBG, and CBC, and the Department of Transport. Such recommendations would be preceded by public hearings conducted by the BBG.

The 'combined statement' went a considerable distance towards a separation between public and private broadcasting, but left unclear how much authority the BBG should have over decisions that trenched upon the CBC. Ouimet favoured 'maximum separation of the two groups of trustees in terms of responsibilities.' Stewart's position on this matter was close to Ouimet's, although he wanted the areas in which co-ordination was needed more clearly spelled out. Jamieson, on the other hand, supported an allocation of responsibilities that approached the existing one. Although he favoured a minimum of regulation, he felt that such conditions as were imposed by the BBG should apply to the CBC as well as to private broadcasters. Parliament he argued, should more carefully define the CBC's responsibilities, including the commercial revenues it was authorized to raise. The BBG should have a strengthened role in spectrum management, should have a board of full-time members, and should have the power to arbitrate in case of conflict between the private and public sectors. Thus, in Jamieson's view, the BBG should *not* become, in effect, the 'Board of (Private) Broadcast Governors.'

The combined statement did not mention the CBC's part in commercial broadcasting, though obviously this was one of the reasons for the tensions between the CBC and the private broadcasters, particularly the second TV stations and the CTV network. In his report Ouimet conceded that the current gross commercial revenue of over $30 million a year was too high, since that amount could be achieved only at the expense of restricting time available for Canadian programs. But he said any cutback must be compensated for by an increase in public funds, and this should be realized on a planned basis and over a period of years. It was not practical under present and immediately forseeable circumstances for the CBC to operate on a completely non-commercial basis.

Stewart expressed the opinion that 'in principle, the public service should be operated on a non-commercial basis, leaving the market for advertising revenue as the means to support the private service.' He realized, he said, that it would be impossible to move to this position immediately.

Towards the end of May, when the reports were tabled in the House of Commons, Lamontagne commented, 'While the work done by the so-called 'troika' will certainly prove to be most useful, the reports show quite clearly that there are still important areas of disagreement.'[43] The newspapers chose to report mainly on some of those areas of disagreement, especially Stewart's recommendation that the CBC should become non-commercial. The two afternoon newspapers in Toronto (the *Star* and the *Telelgram*), for example, headed their front-page stories, May 26, 'Drop commercials from CBC-TV, Dr. Stewart urges,' and 'BBG Chief advises CBC Give Up Ads.'

Spry wrote Stewart suggesting that his proposal would simply mean more money for the wealthy stations in the major markets, and little or no help for the smaller stations. Stewart replied that in part the way he had stated his position on CBC commercial policy 'was designed to make the strongest possible case against a repetition of the directive that the CBC become more aggressively commercial.'[44] Presumably he had in mind the most recent parliamentary committee (of 1961) and possibly the report of the Fowler Commission.

Lamontagne had not waited for the formal submission of the reports from the Troika to announce another inquiry into broadcasting. Rather than serving as advice to the minister, the reports of the Troika became background reading for the Advisory Committee on Broadcasting, whose members were announced on May 25, but which had been in the making for three or four months.

3 The Advisory Committee on Broadcasting: Fowler II

The committee announced by Lamontagne comprised three members, Robert M. Fowler, Marc Lalonde, and Ernest Steele, with Fowler as chairman. Constituted as an advisory committee to the secretary of state, it had the usual powers of a body appointed under the inquiries act. It became known as the Fowler Committee on Broadcasting, but because of Fowler's role in the royal commission of 1955–7, his second inquiry has sometimes been referred to mistakenly as a commission as

43 / *Debates*, May 25, 1964, 3520.
44 / Spry Papers, Spry to Stewart, June 1, 1964; Stewart to Spry, June 5, 1964.

well. The committee's report of 1965 is almost the same length as the Fowler Report of 1957, and is sometimes cited as 'Fowler II.'

Fowler had not made comment publicly on the changes the 1958 legislation had made in departing from the recommendations of the royal commission. He had a long talk with Nowlan in the fall of 1957, was convinced of his desire to do the best he could, and did not wish by anything he said to weaken Nowlan's hand.[45] He wrote and talked to Pearson from time to time, and Pearson has recorded that in the efforts to rebuild the Liberal party, 'Bob Fowler was extremely useful in proposing new ideas, whether for policy or organization.'[46]

Fowler was disappointed with the 1958 legislation, but considered that there were some common features to the legislation and his report: an integrated system, a stated objective for programming, and recognition of the necessity for publicly supported, Canadian broadcasting. When Lower asked for his comment on the appointments to the Board of Broadcast Governors, Fowler replied:

Privately, I can tell you I was greatly disappointed. ... We asked for an improvement in the status and representative character of the membership and have got something no better and probably much worse.

The basic fault seems to lie with the legislation rather than with the appointments. ... It is defective in several ways, notably in the financial provisions which are probably fatal to real independence and vigour of the c.b.c. This weakness could only have been offset by having a really strong Board of Broadcast Governors and that became hopeless when they decided to have three full-time members. My real complaint is not that they ignored our advice but rather that they accepted most of it but destroyed the intended result by a few small, but vitally important changes. ... The Board we described has no similarity to the one we how have – except that both number fifteen. ...

I don't want to weaken Nowlan's position as he is the best friend in the government the c.b.c. has. On the other hand, I can't whitewash what has been done.[47]

After the new governors had taken office, Fowler wrote Stewart a few times, suggesting, for example, that the CBC was the most potent educational force Canadians had, and encouraging him to take an active interest in the kind of programming that was done, both public and private, and also in the stations' advertising practices.[48] As the BBG

45 / Interview with R.M. Fowler, Montreal, Jan. 27, 1976.
46 / *Mike*, vol. 3, 54.
47 / Letter dated Nov. 24, 1958, with copy to Spry, Lower Papers.
48 / Letters dated Dec. 15, 1958, Jan. 21, 1959, copies to Lower.

proceeded with its hearings and began to formulate and administer its own regulations, Fowler formed the opinion that Stewart as chairman was 'too nice and too modest,' and did not really exercise the powers given him. Fowler was appalled by the inadequacies of the BBG's office space on Rideau Street, and the lack of facilities, even for the showing of video tape. The top board, he felt, had accepted a secondary position.[49]

At the end of December 1963, Pickersgill approached Fowler to ask whether he would take a look, not too extensive, at the broadcasting structure and give his assessment. Pickersgill was concerned about bringing cable TV under public control, about long-term financing for the CBC, about too much commercialism. He thought the question of a single or a dual system (and of one or two boards) was of lower priority, and could be deferred. (Here he was perhaps reflecting the discussions he had had with the Troika.)

Fowler prepared a twenty-page memorandum and forwarded it to the minister, January 13, 1964. In it he argued that the choice of a dual or a single system was fundamental to nearly every other decision. He continued to favour a single, mixed system, but said either choice, so long as it was definite, would be better than the confusion created by continued ambiguity. He thought there were ways in which the two existing boards might be modified to give one board the over-all responsibility and authority, although he still preferred a one-board structure. Other matters touched on in Fowler's memorandum were cable television, commercial activities, extension of coverage, program content, efficiency of CBC operations, and financing of the CBC.

Fowler was still not sure whether this sort of quick assessment was what Pickersgill had in mind, or whether he intended a more formal assignment. In any case, within a few days Pickersgill had been shifted to the Department of Transport, and Lamontagne was in the secretary of state's office.

Early in March the prime minister saw Fowler in Montreal and asked him to update his previous report. According to Fowler, the prime minister expressed some concern about failure of management within both the CBC and the BBG, but said he did not want a full and expensive inquiry by royal commission. Lamontagne drew up more extensive terms of reference for the committee than Pearson and Fowler had envisaged during their conversation on March 10. The selection of the two other members of the advisory committee was made by Lamontagne also; neither was known to Fowler, although they soon formed a close and harmonious team.

49 / This and the next three paragraphs based on the Fowler interview.

A public announcement that the government had decided upon another inquiry was made at the annual CAB convention in Quebec City on April 6. (The fact that both Pickersgill and Lamontagne made important policy statements at CAB conventions is testimony to the importance ministers accorded the private broadcasters.) Lamontagne expressed his concern with the lack of clarity in the broadcasting act and its other shortcomings, said it was desirable to improve the structure and financing of the CBC, and impressed upon them the need for all broadcasters to contribute collectively to Canadian cultural development. 'With this in mind and wishing to end the uncertainties in Canadian broadcasting, the government now feels that the time has come to provide for an inquiry into these matters through a committee on broadcasting to be set up by the government.'[50]

On May 25, the same day he tabled the report of the Troika, Lamontagne announced the membership of the committee: Robert Fowler, Marc Lalonde, and Ernest Steele. Lamontagne hoped they would report at the beginning of 1965, after which the government would introduce new legislation and refer that legislation to a parliamentary committee for detailed study. Spokesmen for all opposition groups welcomed the move, although Diefenbaker suggested that the CBC should also be investigated by a committee of Parliament.[51]

Marc Lalonde was a partner in a Montreal law firm, but had spent two years in Ottawa as a special assistant to Davie Fulton when Fulton was minister of justice in the Diefenbaker government. Like Lamontagne, he was an opponent of any heightened French-Canadian nationalism, and in May 1963 joined Pierre Trudeau and five others in issuing their own Manifesto for the Nation, which emphasized the federal option. Lalonde, the son of a Quebec farmer, had pursued graduate studies at Oxford after taking his law degree at the Univeristy of Montreal.[52]

G.G. Ernest Steele had been secretary of the Treasury Board for four years, and during this time he had the opportunity to learn much about the CBC's financial requirements in relation to other demands on government. Lamontagne had just recently brought him into his department as deputy minister (undersecretary of state).[53]

---

50 / Address to the Radio and Television Executives Club, whose meeting in Quebec coincided with the annual convention of the CAB. See also *Debates*, April 7, 1964, 1846.

51 / *Ibid.*, May 25, 1964, 3520–1.

52 / See Andrew Webster, 'Quebec Voice Non-Doctrinaire,' *Globe and Mail*, July 8, 1964. Lalonde later became a policy adviser to Prime Minister Pearson, principal secretary to Prime Minister Trudeau, and (after 1972) a cabinet minister.

53 / Interview with Steele, Ottawa, Aug. 23, 1976.

The composition of the committee was surely unusual, in that Steele was put into the position of sharing in the committee's public recommendations, which the government might or might not accept; after which, presumably, Steele as a deputy minister would be charged with translating the government's decisions into statutory form, possibly helping to draft an accompanying White Paper. He and Lalonde were each reported to be friends of the minister, and while their views on broadcasting were not known, Fowler's views were on public record. Indeed, in an interview with the *Toronto Star*, he reiterated some of them, reminding the reporter that his earlier report had warned against a two-board system, but that the Diefenbaker government had ignored the warning, with predictable results.[54]

The terms of reference asked the committee to study the broadcasting act and related statutes to recommend what changes should be made, appraise the studies made by the CBC of its structural organization, make recommendations on the financing of the CBC, and study and recommend ways of providing alternative telelvision services, excluding cable (CATV) systems.[55]

The committee announced in a press release of May 31 that it had decided not to hold public hearings or 'undertake the usual cross-Canada tour,' but said it would welcome written briefs submitted by October 1, 1964, with written notice by the beginning of August. Meanwhile, it began a study of the current broadcasting situation, and of various records provided by the BBG, the CBC, and other agencies and departments of government. The secretary of the commission was Gordon Sheppard, who had been brought into the office of the secretary of state as a special assistant while Pickersgill was the minister. He had the advantage of being bilingual, and also some brief experience in television and film production.

Although the advisory committee was expected to act faster than a full-fledged royal commission, there were signs that almost every interest with a stake in broadcasting – the government, the opposition parties, the BBG and CBC, the private broadcasters – could hardly wait for the situation to be clarified, or perhaps for the structure to be reordered. One element, indeed – cable television, or community-antenna television (CATV) – was regarded as so immediate a threat to conventional broadcasters that the government had already commissioned a separate study of how it should be regulated, and that subject was specifically

54 / Arnold Bruner, 'He'll guide the destiny of broadcasting,' May 30, 1964.
55 / *Fowler Report II*, vii.

excluded from the Fowler Committee's terms of reference.[56] All signs pointed to quick action on the broadcasting front, if the Liberal minority government could command support in the House, or if through another election it could gain the majority denied it in 1963.

56 / *Debates*, May 25, 1964, 3520 (Lamontagne); July 22, 1964, 'Statement on Community Antenna Systems,' 5799–800 (Pickersgill).

10 THE SYSTEM IN THE MID-SIXTIES

THE BROADCASTING SYSTEM that the Fowler committee investigated in 1964 and 1965 was considerably changed from the one that had come under Fowler's scrutiny in 1955 and 1956. Aside from the different agency of control and regulation, the balance had shifted between the public and the private components. This becomes evident from an examination of statistics relating to the number of radio and television stations in 1956 and 1965, their network affiliation, and operating expenses for the CBC and the private sector in 1955 and 1963. By 1965 the dominance of the public sector, which had been a cardinal principle of Canadian broadcasting since the legislation of 1932 and 1936, had all but disappeared (see Table 10.1).

At first glance, the statistics in Table 10.1 do not indicate much change in the relative positions of private and public broadcasting. The CBC's share of television stations declined in these years from 23.7 per cent to 21.3 per cent, and the CBC's share of radio stations even went up marginally, from 11.6 per cent in 1956 to 11.8 per cent in 1965. But the numerical increase in each instance is important. In television, there were nearly thirty communities served by private stations where no private stations had been before. Only seven centres without a CBC television station in 1956 had one in 1965, and these included two Newfoundland communities with low-power stations (Corner Brook and Harmon Field). In radio, private broadcasting had gained sixty-four AM stations, an increase that was double the *total* number of CBC AM radio stations in 1965. In the nine intervening years, both broadcasting sectors had grown rapidly, but the increase was more significant for private broadcasting than for the CBC.

The number of stations in each sector do not tell the whole story, since from examining them one might conclude that the CBC had not been dominant even in 1956. But in that year the CBC television stations were to be found in Canada's largest cities, whereas most of the private stations were in the smaller cities. By 1965, every large Canadian city had a private television station as well as a CBC station. Furthermore, as

TABLE 10.1

Television and am radio stations in Canada (originating programs)

	Television		Radio	
	1956	1965	1956	1965
CBC stations	9	16	22	31
Private stations	29	59	167	231
	38	75	189	262

Sources   1956, Report, Royal Commission on Broadcasting, 32–4
1965, Report of the Committee on Broadcasting, 72
Table excludes FM stations and unmanned relay stations

TABLE 10.2

Television and AM radio stations, by network affiliation
(originating programs)

	Television		Radio	
	1956	1965	1956	1965
CBC stations	9	16	22	31
Private stations,				
affiliates of CBC	29	44	98	84
Total	38	60	120	115
Stations with no CBC connection				
Unaffiliated				
private stations	—	4	69	147
CTV affiliates	—	11		
Total		15	69	147

TABLE 10.3

Television and AM radio stations (originating programs)
1965, by language

	Television	Radio
English-language stations		
Owned by CBC	11	25
Private, CBC affiliates	36	55
Private, unaffiliated	1	123
Private, CTV affiliates	11	—
Total	59	203
French-language stations		
Owned by CBC	5	6
Private, CBC affiliates	8	29
Private, unaffiliated	3	24
Total	16	59

Source   Report of the Committee on Broadcasting, 72

the principal producer of programs in Canada, and the sole network operator in 1956, the CBC was clearly the dominant force in the decade of the 1950s, particularly in television. Classifying the stations by network affiliation shows the pattern of change in more detail.

In Table 10.2 we see that in 1956 only a third of Canadian radio stations had no CBC connection, whereas in 1965 the stations without a CBC connection (147) exceeded by a good margin the stations that were a part of CBC networks (115). In television, CBC continued to provide programs to four out of every five Canadian stations, so in this respect it was still dominant. Affiliates of the CBC depended on the network for most of their quota of Canadian content. But in terms of what the television audiences saw and heard, the CBC's dominance was not so firmly established. Evening hours, especially 'prime time,' tended to be filled with more American programs than Canadian programs, both in network time and in the hours the individual stations scheduled for themselves. In the hours not optioned to the network, the stations usually ran films or syndicated television programs produced in the United States.

In terms of coverage – that is, share of the population that could receive broadcast signals if they had sets – the CBC had achieved a satisfactory result in reaching over 90 per cent of the Canadian population. In fact, the CBC was already exceeding what the Fowler Commission had suggested was a practical limit for coverage in the country with such a scattered population as Canada.[1] This was accomplished through the 'mixed system,' that is, through a combination of CBC and affiliated private stations. In radio, CBC programs were available to about 98 per cent of the English-speaking population, and to 94 per cent of French-speaking Canadians. In television, CBC network service was available to 92 per cent of English-language households, and to 89 per cent of French-language households. CTV coverage was potentially about 71 per cent of the English-language population.[2]

If we compare the broadcasting services available to the French and English-speaking populations, we can see that the CBC was relatively a more important presence in French Canada than in English Canada. This is true even without allowing for the fact that over half the Canadian people were within direct range of the English-language programs transmitted from stations in the United States. Table 10.3 shows the number of radio and television stations operating in English and in French.

1 / *Fowler Commission Report*, 223. In 1956 about 80 per cent of Canadians were within reach of television signals.

2 / *Fowler Report II*, 73.

The figures show that in 1965, the CBC owned 31.3 per cent of all French-language TV stations, compared with 18.6 per cent of English-language television stations. Only 18.8 per cent of French-language stations were unaffiliated with the CBC, compared with 40.7 per cent of all TV stations broadcasting in English.

In radio, the percentage of CBC-owned French stations was slightly smaller than the percentage of English radio stations owned by the CBC. But over 60 per cent of English-language radio stations did not distribute CBC programs, compared with just over 40 per cent of French-language stations that were unaffiliated with the CBC.

The growth of private broadcasting relative to the CBC is also demonstrated in the figures for operating revenue and expenses. In 1955–6, according to the Fowler Commission's report, the CBC's 'ordinary expense' for television and radio combined was $42,135,000 (p. 458). The private stations were shown (p. 485) as spending $24,621,000 in 1955.

According to the report of the advisory committee, in 1963–4 the total operating expenses, radio and television combined, were $106,725,000 for the CBC; and for the private broadcasters in 1963, $106,983,000. Because of their profits (net income before tax) of some $10 million, the private broadcasters were actually collecting about $117 million from Canadian consumers in 1963, through the advertising payments made by the sellers of goods and services. This amount slightly exceeded the parliamentary grants the CBC received for operating and capital purposes in 1963–4 (about $80 million) and in gross advertising revenues (about $31 million), for a total of $111 million.

In 1965, according to the Dominion Bureau of Statistics, the total operating expenses for the CBC and private stations were still about equal, approaching $125 million in each case, but profits (before taxes) for private stations had gone up to about $22 million, and their revenues to some $146 million.[3]

1 *Private Broadcasting*

Although the number of private radio stations greatly exceeded the number of television stations – 281 stations to 65 in 1965 – the total operating revenue in private television by then had crept past the total revenue for private radio ($75 million compared with $70 million).[4]

3 / Dominion Bureau of Statistics, *Radio and Television Broadcasting 1965* (Ottawa, 1966), 8.
4 / *Ibid.*, 10–11. In 1963 the operating revenues of private radio had exceeded those of private television by about $5 million. *Fowler Report II*, 379.

Some of the television stations were licensed to the owners of radio stations, and in that way had common interests. But in many ways, the interests of television stations and radio stations were divergent. Often they were competitors in a single market. They placed a different value on a network connection – in television it was almost essential, but in radio most stations did not actively seek an affiliation with the CBC, because few network programs were now sponsored. The most profitable kind of radio broadcasting consisted of popular music recordings interspersed with spot commercials.

The Canadian Association of Broadcasters represented the vast majority of private stations in Canada, but sometimes had to avoid taking clear positions because of the varying interests of its membership.[5] Not only were there the differences previously mentioned between television and radio stations, but sometimes there were differences between the operators in one medium. For example, during the Grey Cup controversy, many of the private television stations supported the CBC against the interests of the 'second' stations constituting the CTV network. Even among CBC television affiliates, there were differences. A few stations in areas of more concentrated population were glad to disaffiliate. CHCH-TV in Hamilton had left the CBC network in 1961 to become a profitable independent station. In 1964, CKCO-TV, Kitchener, found it advantageous to switch its affiliation from the CBC to the CTV network. But for many smaller television stations throughout Canada, affiliation with the CBC was essential for their survival. They depended on the network not only for entertainment programs, national news, and major sports events, but for the revenues from nationally sold advertising, which often made the difference between profit and loss. These stations were made uncomfortable by campaigns such as were carried on in the editorial pages of the *Canadian Broadcaster* to transform the CBC into purely a production agency for specialized kinds of programs – a proposition that sometimes found advocacy in some of the daily newspapers, such as the *Winnipeg Free Press* and the Toronto *Globe and Mail*.[6] The Canadian Association of Broadcasters never adopted this position.

5 / T.J. Allard wrote the secretary of state, Jan. 13, 1966, that CAB represented 'virtually all of the privately-owned sector in this country'; 228 radio stations and 55 television stations were members. Using the DBS figures cited above, this is about 82 per cent of the private stations.

6 / For one of many editorials in the *Canadian Broadcaster*, see the issue of April 25, 1963. A reply by Graham Spry was published July 4, 1963. In an editorial, June 18, 1964, the publisher recalled that the *Broadcaster* had been offering 'this simple solution' for the past ten years. The *Winnipeg Free Press*, May 21, 1963 ('Whither the

Of course what the public could best judge was the programming of the radio and television stations, although it was sometimes hard for the casual listener or viewer to disentangle network and locally produced programs.

In private radio, popular music, headline news, advertising, and local service in the form of information on the weather, markets, and traffic formed the usual programming pattern. With the growing number of stations, however, some specialization among stations developed. One station might seek to appeal to the mature members of the family, with 'middle of the road' music and news of community activities and events. Another might be a 'top forty' station, broadcasting repetitiously the records appearing on the charts – charts which were often drawn up by services operating in the United States. The special audience to which these stations appealed was drawn particularly from adolescents and young people, who had more spending power than in previous generations. In a centre with more than three or four radio stations, further specialization might occur, with one station broadcasting country and western music, another appealing to various ethnic groups, and another so-called 'better listening,' which often meant standards and semi-classics, performed sometimes in a syrupy adaptation for strings. The fluctuating success a station achieved might depend on the formula adopted, its novelty, and the counter-moves made by the competitive stations.[7]

Applicants for new radio stations were often chosen on their promise to provide a 'balanced' program service. In their public hearings, some members of the BBG showed an evident dislike of 'rock 'n' roll' stations and a preference for 'good music' stations, for certain localities at least. At one hearing, the vice-chairman, Carlyle Allison, complained of a station's 'raucous sound ... this constant upbeat in voice of announcer, of the music, of everything else that is done on the station.'[8] But in spite of warnings and admonitions, stations tended to continue with whatever formula they found profitable. Several stations that had been licensed in

---

CBC?') published an editorial article on similar lines, and printed Spry's letter of criticism on June 15. The editor of the *Free Press* indicated that he had not been in entire agreement with the view put forward, presumably by the publisher. Letter to Spry, June 10, 1963.

7 / The efforts of station CKEY to regain its former eminence in the Toronto market, against the depradations of CHUM, are recounted in the *Canadian Broadcaster* (Jan. 28, 1965): 'CKEY, Toronto, seeks two audiences with split personality.'

8 / A.J. Beke, 'Broadcasting and the Freedom of Choice' (doctoral dissertation, University of Michigan, 1970), 233–4.

the expectation that they would be 'good music' stations turned instead to more popular programming to increase their profit margins.[9]

Another program format that developed in this period was the 'hotline' show, in which listeners were invited to call the station by telephone to voice their opinions for broadcast on a variety of subjects. One station in particular, CJOR, in the view of the BBG violated the ethical code in arranging its interviews, and exceeded the limits of good taste.[10] After a review of the open-line programs of the station, the BBG refused to recommend a renewal of the licence to Mrs. George Chandler, widow of the station's founder. CJOR was forced to sell out to new owners.

This was the only instance in which the BBG refused to recommend renewal of the licence of an existing radio station owner. There were no such refusals in television.[11]

Generally speaking, radio stations were surviving the competition of television, and were continuing to prosper. They appealed to their listeners by providing local services and the kinds of music that made few demands on the audience. Since radio in the United States had developed similar patterns, and network radio in that country had almost disappeared, Canadian stations now had few competitors from outside their communities.

On the whole, Canadian audiences in the early 1960s accepted the radio fare provided them with few complaints. Perhaps they were merely resigned to it. In some age groups, many individuals paid little attention to radio, since they found television more entertaining, more talked about, more compelling because of its visual impact, with programs that were more recognizable and distinctive. In certain areas of the country, particularly where private radio service was limited, there were demands for the installation of CBC facilities, and these were pressed on the member of Parliament serving the constituency. The effect in Parliament was that members tended to complain of the inadequacies of CBC coverage, but said little about the service of private radio, except occasionally to commend a local station that made its facilities available to an MP for a report to the voters.

9 / *Ibid.*, 227 ff.

10 / One of the station's interviewers, Pat Burns, was often abrasive in dealing with callers who had any inclination to disagree with him, and roundly condemned persons who refused to accept his calls. Another interviewer had an extended discussion with a caller on the nature of the physical acts engaged in by female homosexuals. BBG Hearings, Vancouver, March 23, 1965, 108–48; Stewart MS, 414–26.

11 / The CBC board of governors had recommended discontinuing the licence of a radio-station owner on but one occasion also (in 1948, in the case of CJDC, Dawson Creek).

The principal complaints from the public about radio were on the theme of too much advertising. In the United States there were no government regulations limiting the amount of time that could be devoted to commercials, only the guidelines recommended by the National Association of Broadcasters. In Canada, the successive broadcasting acts gave the regulatory authority the power to set program standards, including the character and amount of advertising.

Before the arrival of television, radio stations had been allowed only up to two minutes of spot announcements in each broadcasting hour, and none was permitted between 7:30 and 11:00 PM or on Sundays. These restrictions were eased after 1954, and by 1959 radio stations were allowed five spots in any fifteen-minute period, up to a maximum of four minutes. These were indeed generous allowances, and the BBG in making them also abandoned the former CBC policy of allowing less time for commercials after 6:00 PM. The amount of time allowed for commercials in sponsored programs was somewhat less than for time segments in which spot announcements were placed: in a sponsored half-hour program, the advertiser was allowed four minutes, fifteen seconds.[12] The effect of this distinction was to encourage further the trend towards non-sponsored hours of broadcasting, but periods that seemed chock-a-block with commercials. In 1961, the distinction between sponsored programs and programs with spot commercials was removed, and the restrictions were applied on a cumulative basis: there could not be more than 250 minutes of commercial messages between 6:00 AM and midnight (about 23 per cent of the total time), nor more than 1500 minutes in a calendar week (about 20 per cent of the broadcast day until midnight).[13]

The Fowler Committee found that private radio stations had responded to the challenge from television with considerable vitality, and that the stations were in close contact with their public. The committee welcomed the program exchange initiated by the CAB in 1962, and hoped this might promote the development of Canadian artists and other creative talent. But over-all the committee was dissatisfied with private radio's performance:

In many cases, radio has become a mere machine for playing recordings of popular music with frequent interruptions to carry as much advertising as can be

12 / BBG regulation 7 (1) and (2). *Can. Gazette*, Part II, July 8, 1959, SOR/59-211, 504. See also BBG Annual Report, 1959–60, 44.
13 / BBG Public Announcement, Nov. 9, 1961, 'Statement on Amendments to the Radio (AM) Broadcasting Regulations.' Also, *Can. Gazette*, Part II, Nov. 22, 1961, SOR/61-486.

sold. This is particularly true for private stations not affiliated with the CBC. The regions served by one or a few stations are thus very far from receiving the 'varied and comprehensive broadcasting service of a high standard' that is required by the Act. ... Furthermore in emphasizing local service, many stations have neglected to offer their audiences an outlook on Canadian and international reality.[14]

The committee found that the average French-language radio station was paying $16,300 a year on artists' fees, but on average an English-language station paid only $5,900 annually. Even in the larger urban centres, 'the granting of many AM licences has often led to a general lowering of quality and a decrease in variety.' The committee concluded that the controlling authority must try to ensure that 'the performance of a private station must be a valid part of the Canadian broadcasting system. It is not good enough if one station concentrates on news and public information, another on classical music, another on rock-and-roll. Each station, perhaps with differing emphasis, must expose its listeners to the complete spectrum of radio services.'[15]

By the mid-sixties, only a few new AM stations were being licensed each year. The BBG's annual reports for 1965 and 1966 showed, for example, that seventeen applications for AM stations were approved in these two years, as compared with twenty-one applications for new FM stations. The slowing down in the growth of AM radio was related to the crowding of the frequency band, but also to a reluctance on the part of the BBG to jeopardize the profitability of existing AM stations. In theory, the private broadcasters were strongly in favour of the operation of the free market, and of unrestricted competition. But when new applications came forward in communities already served by one or more stations, it was very common for existing licensees to oppose the applications.[16]

FM radio was still growing rapidly, although nearly all of the FM stations were owned by the AM stations in the same localities, and they were often programmed along similar lines. A CAB compilation showed that there were twenty-seven privately owned FM stations operating in 1962, forty-nine in 1965, and sixty-six in 1968.[17] During this period there

14 / *Fowler Report II*, 52.

15 / *Ibid.*, 270.

16 / The situation was not very different from 1955, when Dunton told the broadcasting committee that 'in the last three years over 80 per cent of the applications for broadcasting stations in areas served by other stations had been opposed by one or more existing stations.' *1955 Proceedings*, 655.

17 / 'Privately Owned Broadcasting Stations in Canada' (unbound).

was a growing tendency for the FM station to be programmed separately from its AM twin, although in 1960 a licensee of one of the FM stations in Toronto, CHFI, opposed CFRB's application for separate FM broadcasting on the grounds that 'competition brings about a lowering of the standard of the broadcast.'[18]

2 *Private Television and CTV*

After the recession of 1961 most television stations became increasingly profitable. The BBG's annual report for 1963–4 (p. 12) showed that the aggregate net profit of forty-two stations was $652,000 in 1962 and $4,249,000 in 1963. These figures were for stations that had been established before 1960. For twelve stations established after 1959, including the nine new 'second' stations in the major markets, there was an aggregate profit of just over $1,400,000 in 1963. In the next year, the nine 'second' stations accounted for 40 per cent of the aggregate net profit of $9.8 million (this figure represented the total profit of fifty-six stations in 1964). By 1965, the aggregate profit had gone up to $13.1 million. Only six television stations recorded an operating loss, and all nine of the 'second stations' were in a profit position.[19]

According to the Fowler Committee's report, the French-language television stations were more profitable than the English. In 1963 their net income after tax exceeded the net income of the English-language stations, with only a little more than one-fifth the investment. This showed the reliance of most of these stations on the programming of the CBC French network, and also the fact that they had very much less competition from the United States. It was also noted that over half the total profits were made by the nine largest stations.[20]

The Fowler Committee also commented that, as with radio, 'the amount paid out for artists' and other talent fees is disappointingly small' – $2,435,000 in 1963, or less than 5 per cent of gross revenue. (This compared with CBC television payments of $9,280,000 in 1963 for artists' and other talent fees. This figure had dropped by $800,000 from 1961 – presumably because of the CBC's loss of revenue to the second stations.)[21]

There were perhaps only two clouds on the horizon for the private

18 / BBG Hearings, Ottawa, Nov. 29, 1960, 198.
19 / Figures in this paragraph from BBG Annual Reports.
20 / *Fowler Report II*, 302.
21 / *Ibid.*, 302 and 44.

television stations in the medium and large-sized markets. One was the competition from United States transmitters – some of them (such as at Pembina, North Dakota, and Bellingham, Washington) placed next to the Canadian border to enable them to establish higher commercial rates on the basis of Canadian viewers. Toronto (with the competition of Buffalo stations), Vancouver, and Windsor were the cities hardest hit. The other cloud, by 1965 a little bigger than a man's hand, was the rapid growth of cable television (community antenna television, or CATV). After a number of representations from the broadcasters, the BBG was asked in 1964 to undertake an inquiry into CATV with the advice of the Department of Transport. The BBG's report recommended legislative action to allow further regulation of CATV systems, but the government delayed its policy decisions.[22]

When cable television systems started in the early 1950s, they were thought of as extensions of the service that a householder could receive from a rooftop antenna. Often the CATV systems were used to bring television to smaller communities that because of terrain, or distance from transmitters, could not otherwise be served. It therefore did not seem necessary to the drafters of the 1958 broadcasting act to bring cable systems under the authority of the regulatory board. The definition of 'broadcasting' remained the same as in 1936 – that is, 'any form of radioelectric communication ... by means of Hertzian waves.' This did not include the transmission of those signals by wired systems.

By the early 1960s, it was evident that cable systems in Canada were being used chiefly to increase the number of program services available to urban residents, and especially to bring in American stations. As time went on, more and more Canadian television operators became concerned about the added competition, and the fragmenting of their market. The BBG's investigation was a response to such complaints. The Department of Transport issued licences to cable operators, paying attention to technical considerations, but did not attempt to supervise the cable company's selection of program services to be relayed. As it appeared that the government might move to regulate cable systems more closely, by giving the BBG statutory authority over them, a number of MPS expressed apprehension. For example, a member from the interior of British Columbia said:

The [cable television] industry – and it is a fairly large industry throughout Canada – is in an uproar. You can imagine why, Mr. Speaker. For the most part

22 / Stewart MS, 352–3.

these companies carry United States stations. ... Like any other industry, this industry wants to expand. It has a right to expand. ... I get a little annoyed when I think of the people in my riding who are cut off ... when throughout the rest of Canada 50 per cent of Canadian citizens can turn their dials and pick up United States programs. ...

I keep wondering what the government wants to do. Does it want to have a Canadian content on this thing? If so, it will just wipe out the whole cable TV industry.[23]

The National Community Television Association of Canada was active in lobbying members of Parliament and the cabinet. For example, in March 1964 it asked to see the prime minster, but instead saw the secretary of state and the minister of transport.[24] When the secretary of state announced the appointment of the Fowler Committee to advise the government on new broadcasting legislation, he told the Commons that the committee would not study community antenna television systems, because the government had received the joint recommendations of the BBG and the Department of Transport, and it hoped to make known its policy on cable television within a short time.[25] In the summer of 1964, the minister of transport said that, pending a formal amendment of the Broadcasting Act or the Radio Act, he was asking the BBG to assist the Department of Transport in reviewing all new CATV applications. In particular, the BBG would have to declare that it was satisfied that the service to be provided would not result in the operation of any existing television station in Canada becoming uneconomic, and would not inhibit the establishment of an alternative Canadian service in that area.[26]

This was a weak safeguard. The BBG was unsure of its authority, and did not have the information or resources to act decisively. Cable television continued to grow faster in Canada than in any other country of the world. The Fowler Committee in 1965 warned that 'the viability of the national network system could be disrupted if unrestrained or unregulated growth of CATV systems is allowed to continue.'[27] However, in its minority situation, the government decided not to proceed with separate legislation, but to bring cable television undertakings under the terms of the new broadcasting act that it intended to draft.[28]

23 / *Debates*, March 2, 1964, 407–8 (D.V. Pugh).
24 / *Ibid.*, March 25, 1964, 1459, and April 24, 1964, 2451.
25 / *Ibid.*, May 25, 1964, 3520.
26 / *Ibid*, July 22, 1964, 5799–800, and Aug. 10, 1964, 6630.
27 / *Fowler Report II*, 253.
28 / Secretary of State, *White Paper on Broadcasting, 1966*, 13–14.

In the middle 1960s, cable television was more of a threat for the future than a present danger to the financial position of the larger TV stations. All but one or two Canadian stations depended greatly on the networks to which they were affiliated for the quality of their program service, particularly in the evening hours when they had their largest audiences. Undoubtedly the most popular programs were the American entertainment programs carried by the CBC and CTV networks – at least that was so in communities where English was the language of the majority. For some, this meant that Canadian television shared in all the inadequacies, superficialities, and false values that led FCC chairman Newton Minow to characterize television in the United States as 'a vast wasteland':

When television is bad, nothing is worse. I invite you to sit down in front of your television set when your station goes on the air and stay there without a book, magazine, newspaper, profit and loss sheet or rating book to distract you – and keep your eyes glued to that set until the station goes off. I can assure you that you will observe a vast wasteland.

You will see a procession of game shows, violence, audience participation shows, formula comedies about totally unbelievable families, blood and thunder, mayhem, violence, sadism, murder, western badmen, western good men, private eyes, gangsters, more violence, and cartoons. And endlessly, commercials – many screaming, cajoling, and offending. And most of all, boredom. True, you will see a few things you will enjoy. But they will be very, very few. And if you think I exaggerate, try it.[29]

Speaking to the private broadcasters of Canada in April 1965, BBG chairman Andrew Stewart had more reassuring words:

Reorganizing the limits to what can be expected of private commercial broadcasting, it is my opinion that private broadcasters in this country are doing a much better job than they are being given credit for doing, if one were to judge only by the complaints that are heard. ...

I do not view the number or nature of the complaints received by the Board as indicating any significant degree of dissatisfaction with the service which is being provided by private broadcasters generally. ...

It seems to be the lot of broadcasting in democratic countries to operate in a turbulent atmosphere. In the words of Dr. Frank Stanton, broadcasting is 'captious, carping, cantankerous and controversial'. ...

One almost despairs of finding any issue of significance on which Canadians

29 / Speech to the National Association of Broadcasters, Washington, 1961; quoted in Erik Barnouw, *The Image Empire*, 197–8.

can display substantial unanimity ... and we seem destined at least for the moment to be engaged in a dismal orgy of self-doubt, self-criticism, and self-depreciation. ...

[When we recover the spirit of other times] Canadians will realize that despite the difficulties of distance and sparse population, and the pervasive influence of a lively and powerful competitor to the south, they have created for themselves a broadcasting system which represents an achievement with which they have reason to be content if not proud.[30]

These words of comfort may have helped brace the broadcasters for the Fowler Committee's report, which was made public just a few months later. That committee was unsparing in its critical assessment of the private stations' performance. It found too few Canadian programs on private stations, too little use of writing and performing talent, and 'poor and mediocre programming' (p. 43). 'Their program schedules are unbalanced; they do not provide sufficiently wide variety, and do little to further the development of a Canadian consciousness' (p. 230).

An aspect of private broadcasting that the Fowler Committee did not examine was the growing concentration in station ownership. In 1968 Andrew Stewart told a Senate committee:

I think there is a dilemma in this matter. Everybody is conscious of the dangers of concentration of expression of opinion. This is what we want to avoid. We want plurality of expression, and multiple ownership can go against this. On the other hand, there are considerable advantages to grouping of stations; economies that can be effected by larger scales of operation and through multiple ownership. It is certainly our view that in some of the cases of multiple owner-ship an improved level of service does in fact follow as a result of the econo-mies.[31]

But Stewart added that the BBG had never felt that concentration of ownership in the media had gone so far that the board should have called a halt to it. He said: 'We are conscious of the problem of multiple ownership, but we have never rejected an application on the basis that it has gone too far. We keep saying it can go too far, and it should be stopped, but we have not tried to devise a formula for this purpose.'

30 / Speech to CAB annual convention, Vancouver; reprinted in *Canadian Broadcaster* (April 29, 1965).
31 / Testimony before the Senate Committee on Transport and Communications, Feb. 20, 1968; quoted in *Report* of the Special Senate Committee on Mass Media, vol. II: *Words, Music and Dollars* (Ottawa, 1970), 6–7.

A.J. Beke, a Regina lawyer and student of control in broadcasting, made a detailed examination of the BBG's decisions in licensing and regulation, and concluded: 'During the Board's nine-year term there was a greater growth of multiple ownership and newspaper ownership of broadcasting facilities than at any other comparable period in Canadian broadcasting history.'[32] The growth in multiple ownership took place not so much through the licensing of new stations as through the BBG's approval of transfers of shares in existing stations. The trend towards concentration of ownership in the hands of a few companies was not so startling as it was in the case of newspapers, but it was still unmistakable.

A few of the important proprietary groups can be listed as illustration, some of them with interests in publishing as well as broadcasting. For example, by the end of the decade, Selkirk Holdings Limited, a successor to Taylor, Pearson and Carson, was a large holding company in which Southam Press had a 30 per cent interest. Alone or in partnership with Southam, Selkirk owned radio stations in Edmonton, Calgary, Lethbridge, Grande Prairie, Victoria, Vancouver, and Vernon, and television stations in Calgary and Lethbridge. Selkirk and Southam had a 50 per cent share in the Hamilton television station, CHCH-TV, a substantial interest in the Vancouver and Victoria television stations, and a minority interest in CJCH-TV, Halifax. Selkirk and Southam also had cable television interests in several cities. Southam, the owner of a large chain of newspapers, had minority interests in a radio station in Ottawa, and in radio and television stations in London. Selkirk was the owner of All-Canada Radio-Television, Limited, a media representative for over seventy stations.[33]

Moffat Broadcasting Limited owned radio stations in Winnipeg, Moose Jaw, Calgary, and Vancouver, and had a 50 per cent interest in CJAY-TV in Winnipeg, and a substantial interest in an Edmonton radio station.

Western Broadcasting Company Limited had very nearly a controlling interest in CHAN-TV in Vancouver and CHEK-TV in Victoria, with Southam, Selkirk, and Famous Players the other important shareholders. Western Broadcasting also owned radio stations in New

32 / Beke, 'Broadcasting and the Freedom of Choice,' 159. Beke has also pointed out how much more reliance has been placed on competition as a regulatory tool in the United States as compared with Canada.

33 / Report of the Special Senate Committee on Mass Media, vol. I, *The Uncertain Mirror*, 33–5; vol. II, *Words, Music, and Dollars*, 100–6. Information on station ownership that follows is from chapter 4 of the latter volume, pp. 75–115.

Westminster, Calgary, and Winnipeg, and it later secured minority interests in CJCH-TV Halifax and CHBC-TV Kelowna.

The family of publisher Clifford Sifton, through the Armadale company, owned radio stations in Regina, Winnipeg, and Hamilton, a television station in Regina, and newspapers in Regina and Saskatoon. Until 1969 the Siftons had a one-third interest in CHCH-TV in Hamilton.

A company formed by Allan F. Waters owned radio stations CHUM and CHUM-FM in Toronto, AM and FM stations in Ottawa, a half-interest in CJCH-AM in Halifax (later wholly owned), and a one-third interest in CKVR-TV in Barrie (later increased to a two-thirds interest).

In the province of Quebec, the Power Corporation, through Quebec Telemedia Inc., owned radio and television stations in Sherbrooke and Rimouski, a radio station in Trois Rivières, and CKAC, the *La Presse* radio station in Montreal. Interests associated with the Power Corporation also owned a large number of daily and weekly newspapers, including *La Presse*, the largest French daily newspaper in Canada.

In New Brunswick, companies controlled by K.C. Irving by the end of the decade owned two television stations, one radio station, and owned or controlled all five English-language newspapers that were published within the province.

If the Fowler Committee did not study the patterns of ownership in private radio and television, it did report on the 'second stations' as a group, and their relations with the private television network, CTV. The stations had maintained their mutual company, ITO, the Independent Television Organization, as a means of procuring and distributing programs for the stations' use. They were also affiliated with Spence Caldwell's CTV network. But, the committee found, a 'private hassle' was going on between these two competing groups, without regard for the public interest. CTV was in financial difficulties and, the report said, 'the essential trouble is that the CTV affiliates do not want CTV to be a success.' The committee agreed that there was a need for a private network to distribute news, actuality broadcasts, and telecasts of major sports events. But it did not wish the private network to fall into the hands of the affiliated stations. 'They have not shown themselves to be competent or responsible enough to discharge this responsibility.' The second stations had not fulfilled the program promises they made when applying for their licences; they had national responsibilities which the committee felt must be carried out. The CTV network should be reconstituted as a non-profit trust, or in the last resort, the regulatory authority itself might act as trustee of the private network.[34]

34 / *Fowler Report II*, 233–9.

3 *The CBC*

In 1965, when Dr. Stewart thought his term of office with the BBG was coming to an end, he offered his personal views on the respective roles of the CBC and private broadcasters, and also on CBC programming:

The public service should be used as a means to assist in securing a total service more varied than it would otherwise be. ... [It] should, in some definable sense, be a complete service; but the balance in the public service should be recognizably different from the balance in the private service.

In Canada, the public service must continue to be the primary instrument of the national purposes in broadcast communication. But it does not seem possible to me to effect a proper balance in the total service if the obligations at the national level rest solely on the public service operating on a single channel. It is essential that the private sector makes some contribution too. ...

As a taxpayer and as one who has had an opportunity to take a close look at broadcasting as well as a number of other areas in which public funds are expended, I do not feel that the CBC service costs more than we can afford. I am sorry if any large number of people hold this view.

The CBC is criticized for *avant garde* productions; and because, in its public affairs programming, it gives exposure to ideas against which taboos still appear to exist.

It would be a sad state of affairs if, in any sector of broadcasting or in any other media, the only permissible material was in defence of the establishment, or the established ways of doing things, or even was in support of the mores of the majority.

Hinting that some of the criticisms levelled against the CBC were deserved, he continued:

But broadcasters should keep in mind the differences between the print media and radio or television. It is true that people can turn the dial, but they should not have to do so because the manner of broadcasting, as distinct from the subject, is deliberately made offensive to them. ...

It is unfortunate that the relations between Parliament and the Corporation are no better than they seem to be. The causes, it seems to me, are not all on one side.

I have seen broadcasts over the past six years in which interviewers hardly dry behind the ears attempted to make political leaders, cabinet ministers and members of Parliament look foolish. ...

On the other hand ... some of the difficulty results from an unwillingness on the part of Parliament to come to grips itself with some of the real problems of broadcasting ... and to declare itself by setting out, at least in broad terms, what it expects of the CBC.[35]

Stewart's appraisal reflects some of the views and criticisms of the CBC commonly expressed during the mid-sixties. The CBC was bringing Canadians programs that would not otherwise be presented – but the programs too often reflected the tastes of tiny minorities. The CBC was representing various points of view – but too many speakers and programs were upsetting or inconoclastic. CBC producers were allowed freedom to experiment and to create – but some of their productions were shocking or immoral. A criticism that might have been advanced with some justice was that in many ways the CBC, on the English side, was imitative of the United States networks, in style and subject matter, and that increasingly the CBC's television schedules in prime time were dominated by light entertainment programs that would attract advertisers and please the CBC's private affiliates.[36] Such criticisms were less frequently heard, and scarcely at all in Parliament.

In the 1960s, and especially after 1962 when the English-language Trans-Canada and Dominion networks were consolidated into the CBC Radio Network, national radio programs took on rather different functions from those of national television. Television was the mass medium *par excellence*; radio was programmed for individual listeners, more numerous in the mornings, and around meal hours than at other times of the day. Network radio was not attractive to sponsors, except for a few special events, and commerical constraints therefore almost disappeared. Radio was the better medium for music, frequent newscasts, and some kinds of talks and interviews. It was more mobile, and could more readily be on the scene, in both urban areas and more remote localities. Relatively more of its production expenditures went for writing and performing talent, and radio was therefore essential in providing artists with both sustenance and professional experience. One result of such specialization, however, was the CBC radio attracted relatively small audiences in centres where private stations concentrated on popular programming.

More of CBC's radio resources were employed in reaching segments of

---

35 / 'Broadcasting is for people – different people,' address given to CAB annual convention, Vancouver, March 29, 1965; reprinted in *Canadian Broadcaster* (April 29, 1965).

36 / Weir, *The Struggle for National Broadcasting*, 402–5; Peers, 'Oh say, can you see?' in *Close the 49th Parallel etc.*, ed. Ian Lumsden (Toronto, 1970), 146–50.

the population that otherwise would not be served. For example, in 1967 the CBC's northern service was broadcasting on medium wave to twenty-nine communities in the Yukon and Northwest Territories and in the northern areas of five provinces; and on shortwave to the High Arctic.[37] In the same year, 150 isolated or thinly populated communities had English radio network service through low power relay transmitters, and French network service was similarly distributed to thirty-four such communities. The CBC also provided radio and television programs to the Department of National Defence for Canadian servicemen abroad, in northern Canada, and in ships at sea. The CBC's international service, which began operations in the last year of the Second World War, was operated on behalf of the Canadian government, and every few years during an economy wave there were reports that the service would be discontinued or curtailed. The Fowler Committee concluded that, in spite of its antiquated shortwave equipment, and its 'modest annual expenditure of only $1.8 million,' the service was achieving a satisfactory degree of success. They recommended that the service be renamed Radio Canada International, that it be integrated into the CBC as a principal division of the corporation, and that it be provided with more powerful and modern transmitters.[38]

But television was naturally the committee's principal focus of attention. Roy Faibish, a former executive assistant to Alvin Hamilton (a minister in the Diefenbaker government) and a man with some experience in television production, was commissioned to examine programming on both CBC and private stations.[39]

In a working paper Faibish prepared for the use of the committee, he wrote:

The argument put forward by CBC and private programmers that they must 'compete' in kind because that is what the majority of their audience demands usually results in a decision 'to conform'. ... So there must eventually disappear the sense of tension in living; and with it any real taste for its challenges, the power of real enjoyment, even of the pleasures which are so multitudinously offered, must decline also. ...

The strongest argument against modern mass entertainment is not that they

---

37 / *CBC Annual Report, 1967–68*, 41.

38 / *Fowler Report II*, 179–89. The International Service was absorbed into the CBC in April 1968.

39 / Faibish later became assistant to the manager and subsequently a vice-president of the private station in Ottawa, CJOH-TV. He was appointed in 1976 as a full-time member of the CRTC.

debase taste – debasement can be alive and active – but that they overexcite it, eventually dull it, and finally kill it; that they 'enervate rather than corrupt' in de Tocqueville's phrase. ... We have not reached this stage yet, but these are the lines on which we are moving. ...

The advent of competitive television in Canada has been a major goad to popular 'sensationalism.' There is not likely to be any halt if matters are left to take their normal commercial course. ...

As long as the CBC and second stations find it necessary or desirable to use a preponderance of U.S. material then we must concern ourselves with the values operative in the U.S. TV industry. ... The heaviest viewing in Canada and the U.S.A. is among the lower half, in terms of age, education, and income. The advertiser knows that ... And then there is the thrust of the CBC affiliates, who are wielding greater and greater power, and whose aim is to retain the dividends of network service and to press harder and harder ... to increase income through locally sponsored entertainment programs packed in the U.S.A. ...

The CBC English Network programmers act as if it is the size of the audience that validates the CBC's claim to be a national instrument rather than the provision of the best possible balance of Canadian programs over the widest possible range of interests.[40]

Comparing the CTV and CBC English network schedules with those of comparable countries, Faibish found that both networks closely followed the American network patterns, though the preponderance of light entertainment programs was not as extreme on the CBC's own stations as on its affiliated stations. On the BBC and the television system of France (using the 'first' channel in each case), Faibish found that a better balance was achieved in their full-day programming than in any of the North American services.

Because of the accessibility of United States stations in many parts of Canada and the scheduling of American programs by the Canadian networks in prime time, Faibish found that audience viewing of US programs was clearly predominant:

Considering all stations together, CBC, private Canadian and U.S. stations where available, the viewing of Canadian-produced programs was only 30 per cent of the total evening viewing. In our seven major cities the average CBC owned station devoted 57 per cent of its evening schedule to Canadian-produced programs and drew 53 per cent of its audience with these programs. The average Canadian 'second station' devoted about 34 per cent of its evening schedule to

40 / 'Programming, English Television,' Papers of the Committee on Broadcasting, 1965, PAC, RG 36/23, vol. 9, File 10-16-1.

Canadian-produced programs and these draw 28 per cent of its total evening audience.

Drawing on the information provided (mostly by the CBC research division), the Fowler Committee concluded that, in general, the addition of a private station in a city had *increased* the viewing of American programs. 'The advent of private Canadian stations in areas where the CBC formerly provided the only service might have been expected to increase the availability of programs of Canadian origin. In fact ... it has worked in the opposite direction' (p. 34).

As for program quality, the committee reported that the comments they had received in briefs and interviews were generally favourable about CBC programs – especially information programs, drama, and special reports. But they had received a flood of criticisms of the quality of programs produced by private stations.

Not all was well with CBC programming, however. Too many of the network programs were produced in two centres, Toronto and Montreal. The CBC had made an outstanding contribution to the development of Canadian culture both in English and in French, but it had not avoided the danger 'that each culture may isolate itself from the other. ... In fact, each of the two networks seems more interested in producing outside broadcasts in foreign countries than in studying what is going on in Canada across the cultural and language frontier.' (p. 37). And although the CBC had a much better record than private television in supporting Canadian talent, the committee found that even in the CBC the share of the budget for artists' and other talent fees was steadily declining (p. 40). On the whole, however, the Fowler committee had few recommendations for the improvement of CBC programs. Rather, the report recommended attention to the quality of programs on private stations, improvements in CBC administration and financing, and especially assumption of more responsibility by the licensing and regulating authority.

However any weaknesses of the CBC in 1965 might be assessed, it was evident that the corporation was still the prime instrument for the carrying out of the national objectives of the broadcasting system as a whole. It was still the principal means by which Canadians in the two main language groups were provided with programs that related to the life of their own national community, rather than to that of their powerful neighbour to the south. The CBC was the institution that must attempt to meet the varying demands made of the broadcasting services in Parliament and by successive committees of inquiry. Indeed, the sometimes unrealistic expectations of how much and how many things the CBC could do meant that, on a local basis, CBC stations could hardly compete with the commercial channels for an equal share of the audience at most times. But no way had been shown to provide Canadian programming in quantity to the people of all sections of the country except by a nationally supported production and distribution agency. Regulation alone could not do it.

Unless the structure of the broadcasting system were to be changed radically, with an entirely different set of institutions, it seemed clear that there would have to be renewed emphasis on the role of the CBC if Canadians were to be provided with programs of variety and of excellence, addressed to their needs and interests. The Fowler Committee, despite the critical tone of its report on many aspects of Canadian broadcasting, concluded that the interests of the CBC must be paramount within the Canadian broadcasting system.[41]

41 / *Fowler Report II*, 123–6.

11 FROM THE FOWLER COMMITTEE TO THE END OF 'SEVEN DAYS'

DURING THE FIFTEEN MONTHS of the Fowler Committee's inquiry, neither the BBG nor the CBC could stand still. Before continuing the story of the committee's investigations and report, we should review each agency's operations in the changed political conditions that followed the Liberal party's victory in the spring of 1963, how they responded to the varying demands made of them, and what kind of support they received from the government or Parliament.

1 *The BBG*

On September 24, 1964, in answer to a question from Mr. Diefenbaker, Prime Minister Pearson revealed that Dr. Stewart had notified him 'some time ago' that he did not intend to continue as chairman of the BBG. Pearson did not say whether any date of separation had been discussed.

Although not himself a partisan, Stewart was aware that the Liberals did not have much confidence in the board appointed by the previous government. When the new prime minister took office, Stewart wrote a letter to the effect that if Pearson wished to make a change, Stewart would give him his resignation at any time that it was requested. Again on May 4, 1964 (and this no doubt was the letter Pearson's statement referred to), Stewart sent another letter to mention the possibility that new legislation might be enacted before the end of his term in November 1965.[1]

In asking his question, Diefenbaker assumed that Stewart's intention to quit was related to a BBG recommendation for a station licence.[2] In February 1963, before the change of government, the BBG had recommended approving two applications for radio station licences in the

1 / Stewart MS, 3.
2 / *Debates*, Sept. 24, 1964, 8375.

Ottawa-Hull area: a French-language station for the CBC, and another French station for a private applicant. The recommendations were not given consideration by the minister of transport until after the election. The government then decided to grant a licence to the CBC, but to deny the application of the private company. The new minister of transport, George McIlraith, may have had a special interest in the recommendation, since he represented one of the Ottawa constituencies. His explanation in the Commons was plausible, although there may have been an unexpressed political consideration as well:

It seemed to me that what was being done was to destroy the whole system of French language broadcasting in Ottawa by putting two additional stations into operation at the same time, or by increasing the present coverage by three times what it was. That seemed to me a thoroughly wrong policy, and in the great many conversations which I had in Ottawa with persons of the French language, I found complete unanimity on that point. Therefore what I did was to approve one of the recommendations and decline the other.[3]

Observers wondered whether the government's rejection of this recommendation indicated an almost complete lack of confidence in the BBG, especially when they recalled that the Diefenbaker government had accepted each of its formal decisions. (Whether some members of the BBG were influenced in their deliberations by party considerations was another matter.)

Another ticklish situation for the BBG resulted from the CBC's application for the second television station in St. John's, Newfoundland. On April 5, three days before the election in 1963, the BBG recommended approval of the CBC's application, but added two rather unusual conditions. One was that the CBC refrain for two years from accepting either local commercials or 'national selective' business on their St. John's station. The other condition was that the CBC use 'its best endeavours' to assist CJON-TV in obtaining microwave facilities, presumably to bring in CTV programs from the mainland. CJON-TV was the St. John's station owned by Geoff Stirling and Don Jamieson. The conditions spelled out in the BBG's recommendations were intended to offer that station a measure of protection for at least two years.

The CBC application had already been deferred once, and an active citizens' lobby in St. John's was agitating for the CBC service to begin. For several months after the BBG's announcement nothing was heard as

3 / *Ibid.*, July 12, 1963, 2152; and June 12, 1963, 948.

to whether or not the government would accept the recommendation and allow the CBC to proceed. On August 6 the St. John's Citizens Committee had an interview with the BBG vice-chairman, Carlyle Allison, to inquire into the reasons for the delay. Several days later, the lobby published a full-page advertisement protesting statements that Allison had made, for example, his explanation that Dr. Stewart had been anxious to consult the secretary of state about relations between the BBG and the CBC, and his incautious remark that Stewart, with the change of government, 'wanted to see which way the cat would jump.' The advertisement ended with an appeal to Premier Smallwood not to 'stand by and watch Mr. Pickersgill preside over the betrayal of Newfoundland to Mr. Jamieson.'[4] In early October, 1963, the CBC received the government's authorization to proceed with the St. John's station.

In the latter part of the year, the Liberal government had made several appointments to the BBG. Their first nominee was an Ottawa lawyer, John Coyne, who had been counsel to the Fowler Commission in 1956–7. He was appointed in August, Joseph Grittani of Toronto in September, and five additional part-time members of the board in December 1963. The seven new members therefore were just short of forming a majority.

In the spring of 1964, as the Troika discussions were proceeding, Stewart came very close to Ouimet's view that the 'single system' was in part fictitious, and that possibly it should be abandoned. He was probably aware that the secretary of state and the government were unlikely to agree with him in this view. He has recorded that Pickersgill was committed to the 'mixed system' as originally conceived, and that he was opposed to further 'hardware' for the CBC – which would be entailed if the CBC were to be self-sufficient. On Pickersgill as a minister, Stewart has commented, 'I had some difficulty in following his sharp, mercurial, and as I occasionally thought, devious mind.'[5] He has not spoken about Mr. Lamontagne, Pickersgill's successor as secretary of state, who in any case was in the government for a much shorter period.

Reporting an interview with Stewart, the *Canadian Broadcaster* explained that his decision to step down dated back to the time when the Fowler Committee was appointed:

His reason for intimating he would not be available for a further term, he said, was that it may be assumed that, as a result of the Fowler investigation, there will

4 / 'An Open Letter to the Citizens of St. John's,' *Evening Telegram*, St. John's, Aug. 19, 1963. See also *Debates*, July 30, 1963, 2780–1.
5 / Stewart MS, 14.

be a great deal of change in the broadcasting industry in general, and no doubt the structure of the Board of Broadcast Governors in particular. As he would not be interested in serving another seven years under any circumstances, he felt he should advise the government on this point.[6]

Stewart was also aware that Fowler, and the Liberals in government, did not think the BBG had been sufficiently forceful, either with the CBC or private broadcasters. In 1964, for the first time, the BBG began to prosecute stations in the courts for exceeding advertising limits. The usual fine imposed was about $25; in one case, a station was fined over $300. Another station was ordered off the air for a week because of falsification of logs.[7]

Stewart told Fowler he thought the CBC did a good program job and had a good program mix, given the corporation's objectives. The BBG had made representations on occasion about the CBC's avant-garde programming, as the result of complaints from the public, but the CBC resented the board's intrusion.[8]

One of the three permanent members of the board, Bernard Goulet, died suddenly following an operation on December 1, 1964. The government took no action for over a year to restore the complement of full-time members, and indeed it allowed Carlyle Allison's term of office to expire on November 9, 1965, without nominating an immediate replacement. For three months Andrew Stewart was the only full-time member holding office, until the appointments of Pierre Juneau and David Sim effective February 7, 1966. Juneau was named vice-chairman.

Allison had been an effective board member, but for political reasons the Liberal government did not favour his re-appointment. As Judy LaMarsh has written, the manner in which he was let go was unnecessarily cruel. Allison was not advised that he would not be reappointed until the day after his term expired. Stewart protested this treatment, and the prime minister replied that when the decision was made, the minister, through a misunderstanding, had failed to advise Allison immediately.[9]

6 / 'Chairman foresees changes – will withdraw November '65,' Oct. 1, 1964.
7 / Papers of the (Fowler) Committee on Broadcasting, report of interview with Ross McLean of the BBG, Dec. 3, 1964; PAC, RG 36/23, vol. 7, file 10-7-3.
8 / *Ibid.*, interview recorded Aug. 4, 1964.
9 / Stewart MS, 22. See also Judy LaMarsh, *Memoirs of a Bird in a Gilded Cage* (Toronto, 1969), 239–40. Allison returned to Winnipeg to direct public affairs programs on CJAY-TV.

2 The CBC

If the BBG was left for a time to languish at less than full strength, at least it did not get the bumpy ride that the CBC was experiencing in Parliament. The most serious confrontation developed in 1966, after the Fowler Committee's report and due in part to it, so that story can be told later in this chapter. But the background to the CBC's serious difficulties may be sketched now.

When the Liberals returned to office, CBC management may well have assumed that their worst troubles were over. True, the Glassco Commission had just turned in a highly critical report, directed at the CBC's organization and administration, but the management was confident that many of the Glassco criticisms would prove unfounded, and the suggested reforms impractical. In any case, a new government would have to review the major steps proposed to remedy any weaknesses, and the CBC could hope for a sympathetic hearing. The Liberals were known to favour longer term financing for the CBC, and Ouimet and his officers were convinced that a change in the system of appropriations was the single most important reform that was needed. The CBC's board consisted of Conservative government appointees, but they had supported the traditional public service objectives of the corporation, and had worked together fairly smoothly in a mainly non-partisan way. For its part, if the government felt limited confidence in the existing board, it would soon have a chance to replace the directors as their terms of office expired.

One of the first things Pickersgill did as secretary of state was to refer to the justice department the action in 1959 of the CBC board of directors in naming R.L. Dunsmore as chairman. Ouimet and the CBC's legal counsel had always had doubts about that, and the board had once decided to ask for an opinion from the justice department, but the request had been routed through the minister, Nowlan, who took no further action.[10] When Pickersgill asked the justice department for an opinion, the deputy minister advised that the CBC's by-law no. 3 was invalid.[11] The corporation then amended the by-law, and the president again presided at meetings of the board of directors. Dunsmore was persuaded to remain for another month as chairman of the finance committee, but submitted his resignation effective July 3.[12]

10 / Ouimet interview, June 30, 1975.
11 / *Debates*, June 6, 1963, 726–7.
12 / Ouimet interview; and CBC press release, June 1, 1963.

On the matter of salaries for the president and the vice-president, the CBC directors in October 1963 renewed their request that those salaries be raised, commensurate with responsibilities, pointing out that Ouimet's salary had remained at $20,000 since 1954. The Conservative government had ignored similar requests, but early in January 1964 it was announced that Ouimet's salary would henceforth be $40,000, and the salary of the statutory vice-president, W.E.S. Briggs, would be increased from $16,000 to $25,000.[13]

In late 1963, Ouimet was meeting periodically with the other members of the Troika, but an even more immediate problem was how to respond to the report critical of CBC organization and management that had been written by the chairman of the Glassco Commission. Ouimet and Dunsmore were each convinced that the published report contained serious inaccuracies, although the CBC was not given access to the original studies prepared by the consultants. George Davidson had been put in charge of a Bureau of Government Organization to study and recommend appropriate responses to criticisms that the Glassco Commission had made of government departments and agencies.[14] When he received Ouimet's initial reply to Glassco's criticisms of the CBC, he wrote: 'A superb rebuttal on the whole. I do not think that it leaves very much of the Glassco criticism unanswered. That does not mean that there are not weaknesses, possibly serious ones – in the administration of the CBC. What it does mean, however, is that the Glassco Commission has failed to put its finger on them with sufficient evidence or in sufficiently convincing fashion to make them stick. Any objective and impartial jury, on reading the case for the defense, as set out in this document, could only arrive at the verdict, Not guilty as charged.'[15] CBC management went on to prepare what the Fowler committee termed a 'rather violent and certainly lengthy response ... extending to 118 typewritten pages.'[16]

Because the criticisms of Glassco tended to be general, Ouimet, with the board's approval, decided to organize a task force of six persons within the corporation and a management consultant outside to conduct its own study, and to arrive at more specific recommendations for the CBC board. The chairman of what became known as the 'president's

13 / Ouimet interview.
14 / Interview with Henry Hindley, Ottawa, Aug. 25, 1976. Hindley worked with Davidson in the Bureau of Government Organization before transferring to the Department of the Secretary of State, in which he became an assistant undersecretary.
15 / CBC Hist. Sec., Ottawa, file 14-2-6, memorandum dated June 24, 1963.
16 / *Fowler Report II*, 138.

study group' was Michael Harrison, who until that time had been executive assistant to Ouimet. Harrison had also worked for the Glassco commission, although not on the CBC project.[17]

Before the president's study group had completed its work, the Fowler Committee was appointed by the secretary of state, with one of its duties specified as 'an appraisal of the studies being made by the Canadian Broadcasting Corporation of its structural organization.'[18]

Although some members of the president's study group started out with the assumption that the existing organization was basically sound, as their study proceeded they became more critical themselves, and the report they turned in to the CBC in September 1964 made recommendations for thorough-going changes. They recommended, for example, that in addition to the statutory vice-president (W.E.S. Briggs), there should be a vice-president designated as chief operating officer. Concerned about the problem of program leadership at head office, they suggested that the vice-president, programming, should have executive authority extending to the network and production centres. These two recommendations and some others were not accepted by the CBC president and board, although other changes were made in the CBC organization and administration as a result of the report of the president's study group.[19] But the sequence of events, the direct or implied criticisms of management by the Glassco Commission, the president's study group, and later the Fowler Committee, and the seeming resentment that accompanied the CBC's responses, did not improve internal morale, particularly on the program side. This had an explosive consequence in 1966, revolving around the public affairs program, 'This Hour Has Seven Days,' which will be discussed shortly.

Throughout the period of the first minority government of L.B. Pearson, the CBC was subjected to strong criticism in the House of Commons and Senate, mainly on the score of its 'avant-garde' programs and of the corporation's rising costs. Often these criticisms were coupled with requests for an extension of its services, and sometimes with a protestation that the member voicing the criticisms was a supporter of the CBC

17 / *Ibid.*, 139–40; 1966 Standing Committee on Broadcasting, Films and Assistance to the Arts, *Proceedings*, May 24, 1966, 973–9 (evidence of Michael Harrison). This committee will henceforth be referred to as the broadcasting committee, and cited as *1966 Proceedings*.

18 / *Fowler Report II*, vii.

19 / Harrison left the employment of the CBC within a few months of completing the report, later becoming vice-president, communications, for Southam Press. For his assessment of the results of the study group's report, see *1966 Proceedings*, 980–1003. He felt (p. 983) that most of the recommended changes had not been carried out.

and of freedom of expression – so long as the programs gave no one any offence! In July 1964 the CBC president was asked to appear before the House of Commons standing committee on public accounts, which expressed its concern at the CBC's spending levels. The committee's report noted that operating expenses had increased from $40 million in 1955–6 to $108 million in 1962–3, and welcomed the appointment of the Fowler Committee which it thought must give serious attention to the problem of controlling such increases in cost.[20] The CBC president tried to impress on the parliamentarians the tremendous development of television and other services in those seven years. He pointed to the extension of television service to 94 per cent of Canadians, through CBC stations and network affiliates; the operation of many additional radio and television stations; the increase in the number of hours of television programming each year; and the unavoidable escalation of costs through price rises and increases in labour rates. (In 1964–5, the CBC estimated that 40 per cent of its $8 million increase in expenditure from the previous year was due to the higher wage rates and increased costs of goods and services, whereas 60 per cent of the increase had resulted from extensions and improvements to the national broadcasting service.)[21]

The liveliest protests in Parliament were about individual CBC programs, and these were the protests that tended to receive attention in the press. Former Prime Minister Diefenbaker was indignant about a television program called 'The Open Grave' before it went on the air. He moved adjournment of the House to discuss the showing of a program which 'will be a flagrant, scandalous and sacrilegious insult to a majority of Canadians.'[22] The program was thought to be a success by most reviewers, and was later shown on the BBC.

On the English network, the television program 'Quest' drew some criticisms for its 'immoral' presentations, as did 'This Hour Has Seven Days,' which began in October 1964.[23] In March 1965, a petition called 'The Declaration of Women,' with over 70,000 signatures, was presented to the prime minister and the secretary of state by a group

20 / House of Commons *Journals*, Aug. 5, 1964, 589–90.

21 / *CBC Annual Report, 1964–5*, 20.

22 / *Debates*, March 23, 1964, 1350–1.

23 / *Debates*, March 2, 1964, 399 (C.S. Smallwood); July 31, 1964, 6264 (H.A. Olson); Oct. 26, 1964, 9413–4, 9421–48 (Diefenbaker, Olson, Lambert, Gundlock, Nasserden, Rhéaume); Oct. 27, 1964, 9469–9502 (Klein, Macquarrie); Oct 28, 1964, 9524–38 (Danforth, Horner, Noble, Vincent); Nov. 3, 1964, 9709–23 (Thomas, Ricard, Caouette, Cantelon).

wanting to 'clean up' television.[24] The French network was under frequent attack for 'allowing fellow-traveller leftists, agnostics, terrorists and other trouble-makers to promote, on certain programs, class struggles and contempt for religious, civil and legal authorities.'[25] Social Credit members from Quebec were the most vociferous critics, but were joined occasionally by other representatives. Diefenbaker took delight in quoting from a speech made by a member of the Liberal cabinet of the province of Quebec, Bona Arsenault, who said, 'There has been left wing communistic infiltration of the French network of the Canadian Broadcasting Corporation, most of our newspapers and political organizations, perhaps even the Quebec Liberal Federation.'[26]

A program that was not shown was the subject of more debate, however, than any that was telecast in the years 1964 and 1965. This was a television film on a day in the life of the prime minister, given the title 'Mr. Pearson – the Man and the Office,' which was commissioned by the CBC but produced by an independent film director, Richard Ballentine, of Intervideo Productions Limited, Toronto. The film, which was to use *cinéma vérité* techniques, was intended for the series 'Telescope,' which was ordinarily under the jursidiction of the features rather than the public affairs department. The film producer and his liaison in the CBC had unwisely agreed to allow the subject of the film (the prime minister) full rights to veto anything contained in the program. Later, the network directors brought in the public affairs supervisor to try to modify this arrangement, as creating an unsuitable precedent, and to smooth out any difficulties that had arisen in the filming operation. But because of the nature of the material (the cameras had been set up in the prime minister's office), Mr Pearson had to have some control over what was shown to the public, and this meant in practice that a number of his colleagues and advisers attended the private screenings. Some of them expressed reservations about the finished result, and for their part the CBC program officials were uneasy about the technical quality and editing of the production. No instructions seem to have been issued from the prime minister's office, or even any informal view tendered by Pearson or his immediate assistants, except on matters relating to cabinet secrecy. Some of his cabinet colleagues, however, may not have been so circumspect.

24 / *Ibid.*, March 25, 1965, 12768; also Senate *Debates*, March 4, 1966, 254–5 (Senator Josie D. Quart).
25 / House of Commons *Debates*, May 27, 1965, 1756 (Gérard Laprise, quoting resolution passed by the supreme council of the Knights of Columbus).
26 / *Ibid.*, Oct. 26, 1964, 9414.

But the CBC, on the recommendation of the program directors of the English network in Toronto, decided not to show the film, explaining to the press that it did not meet minimum CBC standards, in that 'the camera work is distracting, the lighting and sound are of uneven quality and often poor, and the editing is inadequate.' The public affairs supervisor, Reeves Haggan, insisted, 'The decision not to show the film was made in Toronto, not Ottawa, and there was absolutely no government pressure. ... There is no question of censorship.'[27]

These statements did not still suspicions, fanned not only by the press, but by the film producer, Mr. Ballentine, who resented the aspersions cast on his film by the official CBC statement, and who had spent several months preparing the program, which he thought deserving of national exposure. He had retained the rights to show the film to film societies and to enter it in competitions, and before long screenings were arranged that were attended by correspondents and press gallery reporters in Ottawa, and by some MPs.

The opposition had a field day in the House of Commons, asking questions, raising grievances, charging ministerial interference, and ridiculing Pearson, his staff, and the CBC. The full story emerged pretty well in the explanations given by Pearson to the House, but the disclosures were so protracted that most people gained their impressions from news stories appearing in such papers as the *Globe and Mail*.[28]

The decision not to broadcast the program became an embarrassment to the government, and particularly to the prime minister. He was finally driven to declare:

Well, the Leader of the Opposition has suggested that one way of clearing up this particular allegation would be to have a showing of this film for members of parliament. I hope that can be arranged, and that this can be done without interfering with the C.B.C., who have custody of the film. I will take the right hon. gentleman's request to the C.B.C. and join in that request that this film be made available to members. ... I hope I shall not be accused of interfering with the affairs of the C.B.C. if I get in touch with the president of the corporation and express my own view that this film should be exhibited publicly.[29]

27 / Pearson gave an account of his involvement in the program arrangements in *Debates*, June 24, 1964, 4679–86.
28 / Opposition members drew on the reports in this newspaper by Dennis Braithwaite; for example, *Debates*, May 26, 1964, 3610–14 (Erik Nielsen), and 3617–8 (Douglas Fisher); June 23, 1964, 4632–4 (Nielsen).
29 / *Ibid.*, June 19, 1964, 4493.

The CBC's initial decision not to telecast the film was reviewed by the board of directors at one of their regular meetings, and they decided that the film remained 'unacceptable for showing on the basis of broadcastings standards.' They added that they were satisfied there had been 'no political interference.'[30] After Lamontagne read this response to the House, Réal Caouette, the Quebec Social Credit leader, charged that the statement 'proved once more that it [the CBC] has some entirely irresponsible governors.'[31]

3 The Fowler Committee

As the work of the advisory committee got under way, each institutionalized group with an interest in broadcasting had some reason for apprehension. In the period of the Fowler Commission, eight years before, the chairman had shown himself to be less than impressed with the performance of private stations and the CAB. In the intervening period, the industry had grown in size, power, and prestige: would Fowler and his present associates give the private broadcasters the more favourable recognition that they wished for? They had at least three assets that had not been present in 1956. The first was the existence of a regulatory structure for six years in which they were regarded as a parallel rather than a subsidiary element. Another was the leadership given their industry by the president of the CAB, Donald Jamieson, a man whom Fowler regarded favourably, and who was beginning to share with Fowler an advisory role in the federal Liberal party. A third asset was the benevolent attitude of the existing regulatory body, the BBG.

But the future of the BBG itself was by no means assured. Fowler had previously recommended one public board, and two had been created. From occasional correspondence, Stewart knew that Fowler had wished the BBG to assume more active leadership that it had, and in particular he had wanted it to show its superior position to that of the CBC board, in programming and in other matters.

The CBC had received on the whole a good report from the Fowler Commission in 1957, and as a broadcasting agency was providing very much the same kind of service that it had in that year. But its difficulties

30 / *Ibid.*, June 25, 1964, 4693, statement by Lamontagne.
31 / *Ibid.*, 4711. Some years later, the CBC showed the film on its television network. The cinéma vérité film had technical and other shortcomings, but revealed some interesting aspects of Pearson's style and personality.

in the intervening period had left it seriously weakened. For the Liberal government as for the Conservative government before it, the corporation was sometimes a political embarrassment – but that had been true in every decade. The various inquiries, so critical of management, had left the CBC vulnerable to attack from politicians, rival interests, and the press, and had injured internal morale. The program services provided by the CBC were still regarded by most articulate Canadians as necessary for the life of the country, but the reasons for the mounting costs of television were not understood, and the programs that appealed to minority groups of various kinds had been attacked repeatedly in the press and in Parliament. The increased access for the majority of the Canadian public to the entertainment programs of the United States had diminished interest in the Canadian broadcasting system, and hence support for its public component.

Still, the CBC usually emerged with credit from open inquiries, such as the two royal commissions in the 1950s, and CBC management hoped that the story would be repeated in 1964–5. But some of its experiences during the course of the investigation were disquieting. There seemed to be an unending series of requests from the secretary of the committee, Gordon Sheppard, for information on the most detailed subjects. The committee itself did not hold open hearings with community groups. Nor did it restrict itself to formal briefs and presentations, but undertook interviews with CBC personnel, individual directors on the board, former directors and ex-employees. Sheppard himself was a former CBC employee. He was released from his position before the end of the inquiry, to be replaced by Henry Hindley, also from the office of the secretary of state. But Hindley had had an important role in drafting the report of the Glassco Commission, with whose critical recommendations the CBC president was still wrestling. The person engaged by the committee to examine English-language programming on CBC and private stations, Roy Faibish, had brief experience in CBC production, but longer and more important experience as a special assistant to a former Conservative minister, Alvin Hamilton. Fowler's colleague on the committee, Ernest Steele, had been in jobs where it was his responsibility to assess and try to keep within bounds the CBC's requests for money – first as secretary of the Treasury Board, then as undersecretary (deputy minister) in the office of the secretary of state. And, as previously mentioned, it became known within the corporation that the report of the president's study group had been less favourable to the organization and administration than CBC's top management had hoped.

Despite all these considerations, no one was quite prepared for the thorough-going nature and critical tenor of the committee's report, which surfaced in the first week of September 1965, while Parliament was in recess, and only a few days before it was dissolved (September 8) to make way for another election.

4 *The Second Fowler Report*

The first sentence in the report has become its most widely quoted: 'The only thing that really matters in broadcasting is program content: all the rest is housekeeping.'[32] The committee suggested that the Canadian broadcasting system had become mature physically, and should now become mature mentally. For both public and private broadcasters, the primary emphasis must be on programming. The private sector must share in the national objectives of the Canadian system, but the CBC, having the principal responsibility, must be paramount in creating and maintaining a broadcasting system distinctively Canadian. In any fundamental conflict between the two sectors, the interests of the CBC must prevail.

Although in the committee's view the CBC's performance had certain weaknesses, such as failing adequately to foster understanding between the two main cultural groups (p. 37), in general CBC programming was commended. Private stations had a 'generally low level of performance,' and in television, the development of the second network had contributed to 'the large and growing exposure of American television programs in Canada' (pp. 30, 35).

The criticism of programming, although sharply expressed, was no more severe than in the first Fowler report. More disturbing to the private broadcasters was the contention that only by more positive action of the board or agency in control could substantial improvements be achieved. Even more alarming was the suggestion that Canada should place all authority in the hands of *one* board:

We advocate the creation of a public agency to be called the Canadian Broadcasting Authority, which should be entrusted by Parliament with the supervision, control, and direction of all broadcasting in Canada. Among its powers, it should be responsible for determining who should hold licences, and the terms

32 / *Fowler Report II*, 3. In a memorandum for Pickersgill prepared on Jan. 6, 1964, Fowler had written: 'The only thing that really matters in broadcasting is programme content. All the rest is housekeeping and technicalities.' Fowler interview, Montreal, Jan. 27, 1976.

and conditions applicable to the use of radio frequencies and television channels by all Canadian broadcasters. ... We suggest that a system of individual program undertakings should be developed by the Authority of its programming objectives and, when approved, should become formal conditions of each licence and enforceable as such either by prosecution or suspension of the licence. ... The Broadcasting Act should make it clear that no one has an automatic right to the 'renewal' of a licence (p. 58).

The report specified that the broadcasting authority should have 'direct supervision' of the CBC, and should decide the general form and content of balanced programming by the CBC. Since there would be only a single board, the CBC would lose its own board of directors. Instead, there would be a chief executive officer, the director-general, appointed by the governor in council but responsible to the broadcasting authority (CBA); and the authority would appoint, on the recommendation of the director-general, a chief operating officer, or general manager for the CBC (pp. 148–51).

In the emphasis given to the qualifications suggested for the two principal officers of the corporation, it was evident that the committee did not feel that the existing president and vice-president should remain in office much longer. The criticisms extended to other senior officers at headquarters. Because of inadequate salaries in the past, CBC management had had no choice but to appoint from within the organization; the result was 'too much inbreeding' in the headquarters group. Their experience in television was deficient; they were probably too old, and some of them were unsuitable for the tasks to which they had been assigned (pp. 152–3). The Fowler Committee, which had engaged its own team of management consultants, did not agree with the proposal of the president's study group that line authority in programming should extend to a senior officer in Ottawa. Rather, it thought that, in addition to the director-general and general manager in Ottawa, there should be two network managers, one in Montreal and one in Toronto, whose principal concern should be the procurement and scheduling of programs, from the CBC production pool and other program sources (p. 157).

As each previous inquiry had recommended, the committee felt that the CBC should be assured of its non-commercial revenues by some statutory arrangement, rather than being dependent on annual appropriations from Parliament.[33] It recommended a statutory annual grant of

33 / At least 17 of 55 written briefs submitted voluntarily to the committee supported long-term financing to free the CBC from any danger of political influence. PAC, RG 36/23, vol. 11.

$25 for each television household in Canada, with the formula to be reviewed before the elapse of the five-year period initially provided for. The committee pointed out that for each household the cost would be about the same as that of one package of cigarettes a week, and stressed that the recommendation was put to the government 'with complete confidence' (p. 313).

One of the principal recommendations of the Troika was ignored in the report of the Fowler Committee – that Canadian television viewers would be best served in each community by a CBC and a private station, or by services each provided through rebroadcasting outlets. The government had been chary of endorsing this proposal, which would have involved a considerable expenditure of public funds in extending CBC facilities to provide alternative television service, and the Fowler Committee shared the government's concern. 'Taking the whole picture of television and radio coverage in Canada into reasonable perspective, it is clearly hard to justify capital expenditures for such purposes as providing more choice of alternative programming, or of giving direct coverage from CBC stations to people who are already receiving the network service through affiliates' (p. 75). More specifically, the committee added, 'We do *not* subscribe to the view that the CBC can, or should attempt to, provide a service that is complete in the sense that it should fill the entire day and night with CBC programs and transmit them directly to all Canadians by its own stations' (p. 80). The committee therefore recommended a five-year freeze on the extension of CBC television service through its own stations, except in areas that had no service in their first language, whether English or French. 'Reservations which the CBC now holds on television channels in several locations should be dropped' (p. 82). Such a recommendation was clearly supportive of the private sector, though the report recommended also that 'a firm degree of restraint should be applied to the licensing of new private stations' (p. 84).

On the question of coverage and possible extension of the CBC service, the committee considered that the government must announce a clear policy, probably in a White Paper that should be presented for debate in Parliament. Beyond this, an act of Parliament should state 'firmly and clearly' what it expected the broadcasting system to be and do; it should set explicit goals, for both public and private sectors, and these should be amplified in a White Paper on broadcasting policy.

Having done this, Parliament should delegate the administration, control, and direction of the national broadcasting system to an independent board or authority, which would render account annually to

Parliament. If in Parliament's view the goals were not being met, it could then decide whether to change the goals, or the powers or personnel of the authority. Neither the government nor Parliament should be involved 'in the details of administration, finance, or programming.' That responsibility should remain with the authority (p. 94).

5   *Response to Fowler II*

The committee's report drew a great deal of attention in the press for a short while, and was then lost in the cacophony of a hard-fought election campaign. The Fowler Report could hardly compete for attention in the aftermath of charges that ministerial aides had been involved in a bribery offer from friends of an escaped criminal, or that the minister of justice was derelict in his duty, or that a Vancouver postal clerk had been discovered spying for the Soviet Union, or that two ministers (one of them Mr. Lamontagne) had accepted furniture without payment from a firm that went bankrupt.[34] A debate in 1964 over adopting a new Canadian flag had been one of the most protracted and emotional debates in Canadian history, but by the fall of 1965 that issue was superseded by the 'scandals' and the question of morality in government.[35] The Liberals for their part tried to appeal on the basis of the need for 'majority government.' More substantive issues, including modification of the broadcasting system, had to await the election outcome and the choice of new ministers.

The Conservatives could not be expected to welcome the main recommendation of the Fowler Committee, for a one-board system, since they had rejected a similar recommendation in 1958. No one knew whether the Liberals, if they were returned, could be persuaded to rekindle their former enthusiasm. A good deal might depend on whether or not the Liberals had a majority in the next Parliament, and also on whether those who stood to lose from the implementation of the advisory committee's report were successful in mobilizing opinion against it.

Initially, editorial opinion seemed quite divided. E.A. Weir wrote at the time that 'The report was met by a barrage of editorial criticism from the press and certain commentators. But it also met with wide commendation.' Weir examined about a hundred editorials and commentaries, and found about 60 per cent critical and 40 per cent laudatory. 'Howls of protest were loudest among those publishers heavily interested in both

34 / See Richard Gwyn, *The Shape of Scandal* (Toronto, 1965).
35 / *Mike*, vol. 3, 181–2, 204.

newspapers and broadcasting stations, particularly the Sifton–Southam, Bell, and associated groups in the West and Ontario.'[36] As Weir noted, the main attack was on the composition of the proposed Canadian Broadcasting Authority – a full-time chairman and fourteen part-time members. This was translated by broadcasters, columnists, and editorial writers as a recommendation for a broadcasting 'czar' to dictate to all Canadian stations.

Within a week of the appearance of the report, the directors of the Canadian Association of Broadcasters issued a statement outlining their initial position:

The Canadian Association of Broadcasters sees this as similar to and potentially more dangerous than the system that existed between 1936 and 1958. ... The proposed Canadian Broadcasting Authority would be assigned sweeping powers. ... Its chairman would be vitually a broadcasting czar empowered to determine what Canadians would see and hear from Canadian broadcasting stations.

CAB will insist upon a continuation of a separate regulatory body, a tribunal not involved in the operation of broadcasting stations either public or private. It is the CAB's opinion that this is the essence of the 'impartial agency of control' proclaimed as government policy by the present Minister of Transport [Mr. Pickersgill] to an annual meeting of the CAB just two years ago.

CAB believes that creation of a Canadian Broadcasting Authority as visualized in the Fowler Committee Report especially if possessed of the wide powers that report contemplates would seriously damage the ability of Canadian broadcasters to provide programs Canadians have demonstrated they want; result in an inferior and less acceptable standard of programming; and drive a majority of Canadian listeners and viewers to U.S. stations.[37]

The *Canadian Broadcaster* quoted approvingly a CBC 'Viewpoint' telecast by Charles Lynch, chief of Southam News Services: 'Mr. Fowler and his colleagues ... just took it as a general assumption that programs on public and private radio and television are mediocre, and constructed their report accordingly. ... But I don't suggest you turn off your sets to wait for these great reforms. There's the election, and it may take a while for Parliament to get around to Mr. Fowler and his new world of broadcasting. You just go on watching those mediocre programs that you love so well.'[38] The *Broadcaster* ran a series of lead editorials opposing the recommendations under the title 'Retort to the

36 / *The Struggle for National Broadcasting*, 456.
37 / *Canadian Broadcaster*, Sept. 23, 1965.
38 / *Ibid.*, 'Fowler Report indicts the low-brows.'

Fowler Report.' It quoted the new CAB president, Jean-A. Pouliot, as characterizing the committee's proposals as 'repugnant to our sense of democratic freedom.' Pouliot felt that 'the present system, under which the CBC has its own board of directors and the BBG acts as an overall impartial agency or regulation, is the best system the Canadian public has yet had.'[39]

The chairman of the BBG, Dr. Stewart, told a gathering of broadcasters in October that he had recommended a two-board system – one administering the public sector and the other suprervising private broadcasters – in 1964, and he had not changed his mind. He added that he had agreed to remain as chairman beyond the expiry of his seven-year term in November 1965, and that he intended to participate in the shaping of whatever form was given the administration of broadcasting as a result of the committee's report.[40] The BBG scheduled a special in-camera meeting on January 10, 1966, to discuss the implications of the Fowler Report. As a board it had not made any formal representation to the Fowler Committee, perhaps because it lacked a consensus.[41]

The Canadian Broadcasting League expressed the view of many traditional supporters of public broadcasting when it wrote Prime Minister Pearson (September 24, 1965), 'It is in the main a good report. ... The Report should, in its essential recommendations, be fully implemented.'[42] The degree to which it had diverged from the stand taken officially by the CBC became apparent only when the CBC released a fifty-five page document commenting on the committee's report, containing these crucial paragraphs:

The Corporation does not regard the Canadian Broadcasting Authority as proposed by the Committee to be 'properly established'. Furthermore, the proposal is so inadequately delineated that it is difficult, if not impossible, to judge its practicality. ...

The Report gives 'Czar-like power' to the Chairman of the Authority. ...

The foregoing and other considerations have led us to seriously ask whether Canadian broadcasting has now developed to a point where the responsibility is too wide and the structure too complex and too firmly established for a single public agency. ...

The Corporation agrees with the expressed views of the Chairman of the BBG and the President of CAB that if the current legislation can be clarified and the

39 / *Ibid.*, Oct. 21, 1965. Other 'retorts' on October 7, November 4.
40 / *Ibid.*, Oct 21, 1965, 'CCBA Convention: BBG's Stewart favors two-board system.'
41 / *Ibid.*, Jan. 6, 1966.
42 / PAC, RG 36/23, vol. 17.

roles of all broadcasting components amplified in a White Paper, the present two-board system can be made to work well.[43]

In the face of such unified opposition, it would have taken a single-minded and resolute government to accept the more far-reaching proposals of the Fowler Committee, including the recommendation for a single board. When the results of the election of November 8 were in, the Pearson government had been returned to office, but with a plurality very much like that given in 1963. There was still no majority. Walter Gordon, who had urged the prime minister to seek a majority, tendered his resignation from the government. In the cabinet changes that followed, Maurice Lamontagne, who had selected the members of the advisory committee, was dropped from the cabinet. His place as secretary of state was taken by Judy LaMarsh, who was moved from the more senior portfolio of minister of national health and welfare, much against her will.[44]

The election campaign had left little time for the prime minister to consider problems relating to broadcasting, or how his government (if re-elected) might respond to Fowler's recommendations for structural changes. Before the campaign concluded, the government had to make its announcement regarding the reappointment of the heads of the BBG and the CBC. The seven-year terms of Stewart, Allison, and Ouimet were all to expire on November 10 (two days after the election).

On July 14, 1965, Pearson told a questioner in the House that Stewart for some time had been contemplating retirement, 'but it is not yet a decision and we hope we may prevail on Dr. Stewart to stay for some time longer.'[45] Ouimet was also invited to stay on, the necessary orders-in-council were passed, and on October 15 the newspapers carried an announcement that Stewart and Ouimet had been reappointed to their positions for the statutory seven-year term. No mention was made of Allison, and Stewart wrote the prime minister expressing his hope that it would be possible to announce Allison's reappointment. As mentioned previously, Allison was advised that he would not be reappointed on the day after his term expired.[46]

Stewart at this time expected to retire when new legislation was

43 / 'Comments by the Canadian Broadcasting Corporation on the Report of the Committee on Broadcasting 1965,' Nov. 1965 (submitted to Lamontagne, Nov. 26, 1965).
44 / *Mike*, vol. 3, 216.
45 / *Debates*, June 14, 1965, 2334.
46 / Stewart MS, 22.

enacted, and had that understanding with the prime minister.[47] In informal discussions, Pearson told Ouimet that he wanted him to stay on, although Ouimet was also aware that new legislation could be used to terminate his appointment before the expiry of the seven-year period.[48] In spite of Pearson's expressed confidence in the CBC president, rumours began to circulate among some in the program division that Ouimet would not be in his post for long.[49]

Late in December 1965, the prime minister took the unusual step of announcing that he himself would head a special seven-member cabinet committee to study the Fowler Report. The members were not announced, but they were expected to include the new secretary of state, Judy LaMarsh, and the minister of transport, J.W. Pickersgill.[50] It soon became known that the first task of the cabinet committee was to prepare a White Paper for submission to Parliament, as Fowler had recommended.[51]

While the White Paper was in preparation, an open breach developed between CBC top management, backed by the board of directors, and a public affairs unit in the English network, over the conduct of the most popular television program concerned with current affairs – 'This Hour Has Seven Days.' One of the results was to diminish support for the CBC among parliamentarians and, potentially, for the positions the CBC directors took with respect to the new legislation in prospect. In the aftermath of 'Seven Days' a number of private members in three parties – Liberal, Progressive Conservative, and NDP – expressed impatience with CBC management and a measure of support for the 'Seven Days' producers and program hosts. It gradually became clear in Parliament, also, that the new secretary of state, Judy LaMarsh, lacked confidence in the CBC president, his immediate associates, and the board of directors, and sympathized to a considerable extent with the program personnel who were resisting or challenging their authority and program edicts.

Miss LaMarsh was an intelligent and headstrong minister, given to blunt and sometimes unfortunate statements, with a liking for 'showbiz'

47 / *Ibid.*, 3.
48 / Ouimet interview, July 2, 1975.
49 / Such speculation was passed on to the author at the time by personal acquaintances. About the same time, Pat Pearce wrote in the *Montreal Star* (Oct. 18, 1965) that the 'surprise' reappointment of Ouimet had 'opened the floodgates to a criticism of the organization that has been barely hinted at before: that of senior officers within the corporation itself.'
50 / *Globe and Mail*, Dec. 23, 1965; also statement by Albert Béchard, parliamentary secretary to Miss LaMarsh, *Debates*, March 8, 1966, 2425.
51 / *Ibid.*, 2419 (LaMarsh).

and some of the people in it. In her previous portfolio, she had taken responsibility for developing the Canada Pension Plan, a national plan for contributory pensions, but in the last stages the prime minister accepted the advice of other ministers in order to reach an accommodation with the province of Quebec. In the less important portfolió of secretary of state, she wished to take charge of the preparation of new legislation, and to make whatever new appointments were necessary to implement it. But again, she was blocked to some extent by the personal interest the prime minister took in broadcasting (as symbolized by his chairmanship of the special cabinet committee), by his insistence on having the last word in the chief appointments, and, plainly, by his lack of confidence in her judgment and discretion.[52] LaMarsh's position was further weakened by the rift that developed between her and the CBC president and board of directors, and by the feeling of Dr. Stewart also that she was critical of him and the BBG.[53]

It might be supposed that LaMarsh would gain in authority by the strength of her department, and in particular by the degree of expert knowledge possessed by her principal advisers. Ernest Steele, the undersecretary, had been a member of the advisory committee on broadcasting, and Henry Hindley had been secretary to the committee in its later stages. Indeed, each had drafted certain of the chapters in the committee's report, although some observers were sure that in its more controversial recommendations, such as the one for the Canadian Broadcasting Authority, it was very much Fowler's report.[54]

Steele and Hindley continued to work on the preparation of the legislation, formally under LaMarsh's direction, but also maintaining liaison with Pearson and the cabinet committee. Steele was in a slightly embarrasing position in that he had signed a report some of whose important recommendations were not accepted by the cabinet, and who then had the task of putting into legislative form the policy options which the government chose.

The 27th Parliament met January 18, 1966. As part of the Pearson government's reform and restructuring of the committee system in the House of Commons, there was appointed, for the first time, a standing committee to review broadcasting, films, and assistance to the arts,[55]

52 / *Mike*, vol. 3, 190–1; *Memoirs of a Bird in a Gilded Cage*, 259–60.

53 / Stewart MS, 2, 14–15.

54 / Ouimet interview, July 2, 1975. A number of the report's recommendations were foreshadowed in the memorandum Fowler had sent to Pickersgill in January 1964.

55 / *Debates*, Feb. 7, 1966, 863. On the reform of the committee system, see Robert Jackson and Michael Atkinson, *The Canadian Legislative System* (Toronto, 1974).

with twenty-five members including Gérard Pelletier, one of the three
'Wise Men' the Liberal party had recruited in Quebec to revitalize it
before the 1965 election.[56] Pelletier was a journalist (for some years
editor of the labour weekly, *Le Travail*, and for a shorter period editor of
the large Montreal daily, *La Presse*) and a regular broadcaster on the
French network (for example, as chairman of the discussion series, 'Les
Idées en Marche'). His wife was a scriptwriter for children's and feature
programs, and Pelletier was very familiar with the personnel and organization of the CBC's French-language division in Montreal, Radio-
Canada. During the French network strike in 1959, he had been an active
supporter of the strikers, and in the years following he was a friend and
associate of many who were in positions of influence in CBC Montreal,
including the general supervisor of public affairs, Marc Thibault, and the
newly appointed assistant general manager of the network, Raymond
David. Pelletier was named chairman of the 1966 broadcasting committee, with his friend, Pierre Trudeau, also a member; Ronald Basford, of
Vancouver, was vice-chairman. Both Pelletier and Basford were to
become ministers in the government of Pearson's successor, Pierre
Trudeau.

During the spring of 1966, the cabinet committee was reviewing the
Fowler Report and preparing a White Paper on broadcasting, and this
was expected to become the main business of the Commons standing
committee. But suddenly the committee was activated by an eruption
within the CBC over the management's decision regarding the program,
'This Hour Has Seven Days.' The CBC's estimates had been referred to
the committee, which under this guise was able to turn its full attention
to what Diefenbaker called a crisis of 'uncertainty and chaos in the
affairs of the Canadian Broadcasting Corporation,' and which the minister, Judy LaMarsh, told reporters was 'an iceberg symptomatic of more
fundamental problems within the corporation.'[57]

Ever since the program had gone on the air in October 1964, the series
had been a storm centre, and by the time of its demise it was clearly the
most discussed and written about program in the history of the CBC. Its
program performance and the method of its termination have implications for the study of the social role of the mass media, the ethics of
broadcast journalism, the administration of crown corporations, and the
relationships between public corporations, governments, and legisla-

56 / Newman, *The Distemper of Our Times*, 370–3; *Mike*, vol. 3, 217–20.
57 / *Debates*, April 19, 1966, 3977.

tures. Indeed, the story of 'Seven Days' is deserving of much fuller treatment than can be accorded it here.[58]

6 *'This Hour Has Seven Days'*

The dispute over the program was about several things: the freedom of programmers to select topics, personnel, and talent, and to shape their material into programs according to their own professional judgment; the right of management to manage, and the responsibility of CBC management to the public and Parliament; the lack of confidence between different levels of management; the short-circuiting of established lines of authority; the varying appraisals of when a program was in the public interest; the ethics of producers in acquiring and editing program material, and in the ways they circumvented or defied management decisions; and finally, it was about whether the men at the top of the organization were to survive, or be displaced by others, possibly by some who were carrying the fight against them.

The proposal for the program was initiated by two television producers, Douglas Leiterman and Patrick Watson; it was discussed with the general supervisor of public affairs, Reeves Haggan, and given the approval of senior management early in 1964. Leiterman and Watson had both worked on a previous program, 'Close-Up,' with considerable success. Leiterman had continued with the production of filmed documentaries, and Watson had gone from Toronto to Ottawa to produce a public affairs program from the national capital, 'Inquiry.' Haggan at that time was supervisor of public affairs for the Ottawa area, having worked previously in Toronto, and in the fall of 1963 came back to Toronto as general supervisor of public affairs for the English network.

With all their years of experience in the corporation, these men were known to the heads of the network, and even to the president and vice-president of the CBC, because of the attention their former programs had received. In the proposal that went forward to management, the two

58 / An excellent account of events in the 'Seven Days' crisis appears in Helen Carscallen, 'Control in a Broadcasting System' (MA thesis, University of Toronto, September 1966), hereafter cited as Carscallen thesis. See also her article, 'Nine Years and Seven Days Later,' *Content* (Aug. 1975), 2–9. The program became the subject of a case study (No. 3) prepared for the School of Public Administration, Carleton University ('Cases for Discussion,' May 1967, foreword by A.M. Willms).

producers set as their objective, 'On Sundays at 10:00 PM, a one-hour show of such vitality and urgency that it will recapture public excitement in public affairs television and become mandatory viewing for a large segment of the nation. ... The program will be provocative, thoughtful, the all-seeing eye. ... Items can qualify in terms of urgency, controversy, national interest, human condition, satire, beauty or art. Seven Days will range Canada and the world. Reporter–cameramen teams will pounce on significant events wherever they occur, looking not only at the news but at the reasons behind it.' The format was to be a magazine show three times out of four, with a more substantial film documentary every fourth week. Provision was made for filmed reports, investigative reports, interviews with prominent guests, audience participation through studio audiences and the reading of audience mail, and satire in comedy sketches or songs written for the occasion.[59]

The hosts in the program's first season were the well-known actor, John Drainie, and Laurier LaPierre, a professor of history at McGill University who had been a regular performer on Patrick Watson's 'Inquiry' program the previous season. The second year, 1965–6, the producers wanted to have Watson substitute for Drainie as host. CBC management finally agreed to this, on condition that Leiterman become the sole executive producer of 'Seven Days,' although Watson was allowed to assume the role of executive producer of 'Document,' the hour-long film that was inserted in the series each fourth week. So although Leiterman had the top authority within the production unit, Watson was still closely associated with it in an editorial capacity, as well as conducting interviews and presenting items on-air.

Although CBC management had approved the program and its objectives and format, it soon became clear that the Ottawa headquarters were apprehensive about the program's specific plans and mistrustful of its supervision. This was particularly true of the statutory vice-president, W.E.S. Briggs, who was being given greater authority by the president as the chief operating officer of the corporation. Briggs was particularly dissatisfied with the performance of the co-host, Laurier LaPierre, dating from his appearances on 'Inquiry.'[60] He complained frequently and bitterly about the program to H.G. Walker, the general manager of the English networks.

It should also be recalled that the CBC was under frequent criticism and

59 / Carscallen thesis, 71–4.
60 / Information from CBC personnel at Ottawa headquarters; see also comments by H.G. Walker, *1966 Proceedings*, 562, 641.

attack in the House of Commons; that it had been severely criticized by official inquiries from 1959 onward; that its status and future independence might be affected by the review process under way that would affect the contemplated legislation; and that the president and his team did not feel comfortable with the two ministers through whom they reported during this period, Maurice Lamontagne and Judy LaMarsh. They may have felt a need not to make mistakes. The fact that a controversial program that was also intended to become (and soon became) a very popular program meant that they would view it with more than usual attention and concern. When they found that their well-intentioned questions and criticisms, as well as their edicts of prohibition (both transmitted through the general supervisor, Reeves Haggan) were argued and disputed at every point by the 'Seven Days' producers, senior management's attitude hardened, and they sought to make changes in the personnel of both the supervisory structure and the production unit itself.

For their part, the 'Seven Days' producers were confident of their own ability, sometimes to the point of arrogance, delighted by the large and growing audience for the program, and made heady by the prospect of two-way communication with it. They were sure in their own minds that the program was performing as promised, and they felt that they had the general confidence of their departmental supervisors. But higher management seemed to them out of touch, obstructive, and fearful of offending society's established interests. Reeves Haggan, the general supervisor, and the producers, particularly Watson, had their own highly placed political contacts; they had reasonable access, for example, to Pearson and Diefenbaker, to Walter Gordon (finance minister until the end of 1965) and Judy LaMarsh. The program's Ottawa editor, Roy Faibish, had resumed his contract with the program at the conclusion of his service with the Fowler Committee, and he provided a good conduit for communications with political figures on both sides of the House. Other production personnel – Leiterman himself, and producer Ken Lefolii, for example – had long experience as print journalists and therefore their own contacts with the press. The program could generated its own publicity without relying on the more cumbersome machinery of the CBC organization in Toronto. Those under contract for 'Seven Days' and allied programs formed a unit of about forty persons, who because of their method of work and Leiterman's style of leadership developed a considerable *esprit de corps*.[61] In fact, to management it

61 / Carscallen thesis, 76–85.

was evident that the 'Seven Days' unit had set itself up as 'an independent separate corporation within the Corporation.'[62]

During the two seasons the program was on the air, the producers and Ottawa headquarters disagreed on the subject matter of particular program segments, on methods of presentation, on questions of taste, on ethical standards particularly in gaining access to interview subjects or film footage, on the fairness in representing diverse views on a topic, and, before long, on the refusal of the program directors to accept management decisions without argument or evasive tactics.

It should have been obvious when accepting the program proposal that production of a series intended to deal with current and fast-moving developments could not proceed on a basis of referring each item to a management group by telex or telephone in a city miles removed from the production centre. Management really had to have confidence in its representatives on the spot. Yet this seems to have been lacking from the very first broadcast.[63] Before the parliamentary committee, Ouimet expressed the view that 'people involved in the production of programs of a controversial nature should have less autonomy than those involved in non-controversial programs.'[64] His general point was sound: that CBC management must be able to intervene because it was finally responsible; but the notion of continuous review of program decisions at high levels of management is hardly practical. If supervisory personnel make too many mistakes in their program decisions, obviously they should be removed; but considerable delegation must take place.

It is fair to add that there were only a few occasions when items were prohibited from going on the air as a result of information sent in advance to senior management. Most of those occurred in the fall of 1964, during the first weeks that the program was produced. After this, the supervising and reporting line was changed, and during the second year a supervisor of special programs (Hugh Gauntlett) was placed directly over the 'Seven Days' unit to act as liaison with the general supervisor of public affairs and higher management. In this later period, most of management's objections were expressed *after* the program items had been broadcast. There were perhaps five occasions when an item was prohibited outright, and fifteen others when program components drew criticisms or objections from Ottawa-based management. That made a total

62 / *1966 Proceedings*, 499, evidence of H.G. Walker. Ouimet called it 'a little empire within the CBC.' *Ibid.*, 610.
63 / Ouimet says this assessment is incorrect. Interview, Feb. 13, 1977.
64 / *1966 Proceedings*, 609.

of about twenty items criticized, out of something like 300 items that went on the air in the fifty editions of 'Seven Days.'[65]

A few examples of items causing difficulty, with a statement of the attitudes expressed by each side to the dispute, will explain the rift that developed between the 'Seven Days' producers and the general supervisor of public affairs on the one hand, and the CBC president and vice-presidents on the other. To follow the events in the dispute, up to the non-renewal of contracts and the final resignations, it may be helpful to refer to a chart of the CBC organization as it existed in March 1966 (see Chart I).[66]

During the first season, 1964–5, when Leiterman and Watson were co-producers, an item intended for the first or second program was vetoed by the general manager (H.G. Walker) without his ever having seen it. This involved film footage of interviews with young Quebeckers about a visit by the Queen to Quebec City. Watson told the broadcasting committee that 'there was an instruction that there be no programming about this subject.'[67] Indeed, the CBC was criticized for its bland coverage of that visit, which brought out demonstrations and other signs of hostility in spite of the tightest security measures.[68] The vice-president, W.E.S. Briggs, had considerable experience covering royal tours and similar state ceremonials, and is supposed to have instructed Walker to exercise great care in what was shown on camera.[69] The producers had also planned a skit satirizing the Queen as a family woman, mop in hand, but the supervisors in Toronto did not regard this as appropriate on the day she arrived in Quebec.

Another disputed item in the first season concerned a story about a United Church minister (the Rev. Mr. Horsburgh) who was charged with contributing to delinquency because of alleged sexual activity among teen-agers in his church. The Toronto supervisors decided to allow the item, after the trial had been concluded, against advice that had been received from management in Ottawa. The latter regarded the item

65 / Carscallen thesis, 90. Leiterman mentioned fifteen items over which there were serious differences with top management. Many more had been the subject of discussion with 'middle management' in Toronto, but had been settled by agreement. *1966 Proceedings,* 255. See also evidence of Walker, *ibid.*, 504–5, 575–81, 634–7.
66 / Adapted from 'Cases for Discussion in the Study of Public Administration,' Case No. 3, School of Public Administration, Carleton University, Ottawa, May 1967 (mimeo.), 18.
67 / *1966 Proceedings,* 66.
68 / Dennis Braithwaite, 'Bland Auntie CBC,' *Globe and Mail,* Oct. 12, 1964.
69 / Carscallen thesis, 92–3, quoting Haggan.

CBC Organization, March 1966

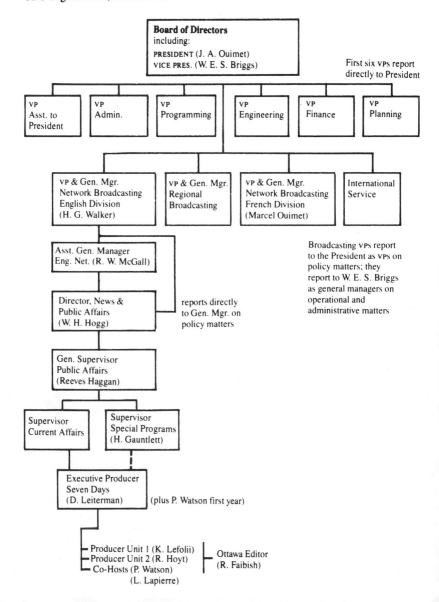

as 'sleazy,' and thought the network supervisors had acceded to pressure from the producers.[70]

By this time, attacks on the program were being made in the House of Commons. Several MPs objected to an interview that was shown with George Lincoln Rockwell, leader of the United States Nazi party,[71] and to an item dealing with the arrest of a United States presidential aide for homosexual activity.[72] Early in December, as part of a reorganization decided upon in the continuing review of administrative structures, the reporting line for the general supervisor of public affairs was changed. Instead of reporting to the network program director and the assistant general manager in Toronto on program matters, he was to report henceforward to the director of news and public affairs, a new position, occupied by the former chief news editor, W.H. Hogg. Hogg was to have direct access to the general manager, English networks in Ottawa – H.G. Walker. From one point of view, this shortened the lines whenever a question needed to be referred to Ottawa for decision. From another point of view, however, it may have indicated lack of confidence in Haggan, and this proves to have been the case.[73]

Two items shown in the first year indicate the producers' intention that the program play an 'ombudsman' role. In the first of these, 'Seven Days' interviewed a youth who as a first offender had been sentenced to seven years in prison for robbery with violence. The judge who had sentenced him complained to the CBC that not all the facts had been brought out in the program, and management forced the producers to carry an apology for this lack in the next week's broadcast.[74] The second instance concerned a farmer, Fred Fawcett, who was being kept in a hospital for the criminally insane. His family had tried unsuccessfully to gain his freedom, arguing that he was sane or had become sane. With the co-operation of his sister, the 'Seven Days' program sent in a camera crew, posing as relatives, with portable cameras concealed in picnic baskets. In the interview that was filmed, Fawcett gave all the appearances of being sane, and within the next year he was released. In this case, Haggan and Hogg shared management's concern about the ethics

70 / *1966 Proceedings*, 66, 116, Carscallen thesis, 93–5.

71 / Complaints by Diefenbaker, *Debates*, Oct. 26, 1964, 9413; Lambert, 9422; Rhéaume, 9448; Klein, Oct. 27, 9469–70; Horner, 9583, Oct 29, 1964.

72 / *Ibid.*, Oct 26, 1964, 9448 (Rhéaume).

73 / Walker told Carscallen in an interview on Jan. 17, 1966, 'Reeves Haggan had unfortunately become too identified with the Seven Days producers.' Carscallen thesis, 76. Haggan later said that there had been 'a conscious attempt over the past year to weaken the position of the general supervisor of public affairs.' *1966 Proceedings*, 484.

74 / *Ibid.*, 295–6. On appeal, the youth's sentence was reduced to three years.

of gathering program material by subterfuge, but after alerting the authorities by telephone they allowed the item to go on the air. Again, the president and his advisers held that the interview was an example of the unethical practices of the program's producers, and damaged the credibility of the CBC.[75]

The 'ombudsman' items, which pitted the little man against authority, were among the most popular in the 'Seven Days' series; one of the hosts, Laurier LaPierre, expressed a particular concern that the program deal with 'the inequities of our society.'[76] Walker, on the other hand, pressed for a limitation in the number of 'ombudsman' features, feeling that it was 'a precarious business to always champion the underdog.'[77]

Towards the end of the first season, management believed that the program had been brought under control, and the series was rescheduled for 1965–6. But the problems began all over again. One disagreement was the decision of Leiterman and Watson that Watson would himself appear regularly on camera. Management agreed but insisted that he not be a co-producer. At the very beginning of the season, there was an argument as to which men should interview the party leaders during the 1965 election campaign. Management did not want to use LaPierre, fearing his partisan connections – but the producers insisted, hinting that any other arrangement would bring LaPierre's resignation from the program, and possible reverberations in French Canada.[78]

The first program of the new season (October 3, 1965) contained a satirical sketch that stimulated an organized campaign against the program's daring, and brought an apology on behalf of the CBC president to all viewers who were offended. In turn, the producers protested that the apology was uncalled for. The satire was on the occasion of the Pope's

75 / *Ibid.*, 298, 416 (Leiterman); 608 (Ouimet); 579 (Walker). Stuart Keate of the *Vancouver Sun* later commented that 'most metropolitan dailies in Canada would have awarded their staff a bonus for such a successful exercise in social justice.'

76 / *Ibid.*, 175–6; also seen Alan Edmonds, 'The Show that Survives by Success Alone,' *Maclean's*, March 5, 1966, 26.

77 / *1966 Proceedings*, 242 (Leiterman); Carscallen thesis, 101. But it is possible that Walker meant merely what Haggan outlined as an intention to confine 'investigative reporting to matters of substance with careful and thorough research, and insistence upon accuracy and fairness.' *1966 Proceedings*, 545.

78 / *Ibid.*, 244–7 (Leiterman); 468–9 (Haggan); 572–3 (Walker). After all the argument within the CBC on who should conduct the interviews, only two party leaders accepted the invitation to appear on the program – T.C. Douglas of the NDP, and Réal Caouette of the Créditistes.

visit to the United States, and a pontifical mass that was scheduled for the following day in Yankee Stadium. In Helen Carscallen's description:

The skit according to the producers was a satire on the hard-sell commercialism of television network officials. The network executive on the telephone to His Holiness proposes an exhibition baseball game – Yankees vs Cardinals, just before pontifical mass, on the same spot to attract and hold viewers and 'win your way into their hearts.' To clinch it, the Pope would umpire the game – 'I'm sure no one would question your infallibility, and if they did you could excommunicate him.' The network official goes on to say, 'I sincerely believe, Your Holiness, you would be the biggest thing since Barbra Streisand – Thank you, Your Holiness: Anything I can do ... Tickets for 'Hello Dolly'? I'll certainly do my best, but I'll be honest with you. ... I don't think you'd have a prayer!'[79]

Walker told the broadcasting committee that it had been 'quite stupid to consider doing a satire on a visit of the Pope. It was a visit of extreme importance at that time in the context of world peace.' The sketch had been 'highly offensive and improper.'[80] According to the CBC audience survey, the program that evening was seen by 26 per cent of all English-speaking adults and teen-agers, or a total audience of some 2,370,000 people. Of this number, 53 per cent found the skit interesting, 19 per cent found it in bad taste or irreverent or an attack on the Catholic church, and 7 per cent thought the skit pointless or not funny enough.[81]

Other disputes followed: for example, over an on-camera confrontation between a Grand Dragon of the Ku Klux Klan and a Negro guest who was brought into the studio before the Klansman's interview was concluded. The Klansman had professed admiration for black men, but refused to shake hands when asked to do so. Management regarded this as an undignified gimmick. The 'Seven Days' unit also got into jurisdictional disputes with the news department, and sometimes found covert ways to show film footage of events that it had been decided should be reserved for news programs.[82]

On November 18, 1965, Walker gave notice at a meeting with Leiterman and the 'Seven Days' supervisors that the program would be discontinued at the end of the calendar year. In fact, it would go off the

---

79 / Carscallen thesis, 113. The sketch, by Stan Daniels, has since been replayed on CBC radio.
80 / *1966 Proceedings*, 541.
81 / Carscallen thesis, 114.
82 / The news department was unionized, and CBC management had to deal with grievances filed by the editorial employees in the newsroom.

air sooner if the producers did not obey instructions and stop challenging management's rules and decisions.[83] Haggan, who was not at the meeting, heard about it on his return from a trip out of town; but Leiterman and his producers had already decided they must accept management's conditions if the program was not to be summarily cancelled. One of those conditions was that they stop talking to the press.

Ouimet had recently been reappointed as CBC president, and in the minds of the producers this was a factor in the adoption of a tougher stance by management.[84] It is doubtful if this was a factor, but relations did seem to be smoother during the remainder of 1965, and Haggan heard nothing more about the proposed cancellation of the program. In January 1966, he was told that the program could continue the next season, but that 'four people had to be taken off ... Watson, LaPierre, Zolf and Faibish.'[85] Haggan discussed this announcement with his immediate colleagues, Hugh Gauntlett and Peter Campbell (supervisor of current affairs), and they agreed 'that there was no reason we could accept for cutting off these people's careers.' Haggan decided to stall. He told Hogg that passing this word along to the producers in January would be disastrous for the morale of the unit.[86] But Walker assumed that the message would be transmitted to Leiterman.[87] Haggan explained to the broadcasting committee: 'I heard nothing about the Watson and LaPierre matter, or the Faibish, Zolf matter, from January until April, and it seemed to me that as the program was doing a solider and solider job and coming on regularly every week in an efficient and workmanlike manner, the management was quite properly and sensibly altering its view from the November decision to the December decision to the January position.'[88]

During the winter and spring of 1966, 'Seven Days' reached its greatest popularity in terms of numbers of viewers and expressed audience satisfaction. According to audience surveys, it was reaching a total of three million Canadians, a much higher figure than any previous public affairs series had achieved. In fact, the ratings for March showed it as the second-highest Canadian program, next to the Saturday night hockey game. The scheduling of 'Seven Days' also delivered a large

83 / *1966 Proceedings*, 249–50 (Leiterman); 470 (Haggan).
84 / *Ibid.*, 402 (Leiterman). Haggan expressed a similar view, 447.
85 / *Ibid.*, 470.
86 / *Ibid.*, 437–8.
87 / *Ibid.*, 513 (Walker).
88 / *Ibid.*, 471.

audience for 'Document,' the rather more substantial program that took the place of 'Seven Days' once each month.[89] The CBC had been concerned with the inroads into its audiences by CTV stations; here at last was a program that outstripped its opposition, pulling far ahead not only of CTV's public affairs series, 'Telepol,' but of its light entertainment programs as well.

Audience satisfaction and the program's successes help explain the decision not to cancel 'Seven Days' outright, but management remained worried by the program's excesses, its sensational items, its frequently abrasive interviews, and what was regarded as a lack of balance in some subject areas. For example, the program had featured some effective reportage on American involvement in the Viet Nam War, including an hour-long 'Document' filmed by Beryl Fox call 'The Mills of the Gods.' Critics in the press and in the House of Commons complained that many items in the program were anti-American. (The Viet Nam intervention was still being treated as a patriotic exercise in most United States news and entertainment programs, and Canadians relied heavily on United States news sources for their information.) Walker told the broadcasting committee, 'Altogether too frequently ... there seems to have been what one might call snide pokes at the United States foreign policy. This has been done from time to time in the opening or closing lyrics in the program, one of which was about United States participation in Viet Nam. ... This is simply misleading and suggests bias.'[90] Ouimet, who in his testimony was more inclined to occupy the high ground of CBC programming policy, explained to the committee:

We have already understood, through what Mr. Walker said, that the great percentage of what was done, and some of the better items as well as some of the items most appreciated by the public were the ones with which there was nothing wrong at all, either in the method of collecting them or in terms of the policies involved. I think it is perfectly possible to have an excellent program which would keep the main strong point of 'Seven Days' without having any of its excesses.[91]

What you do not know, and I have to tell you, is that for the last two years we have had to deal with this program regularly, week in and week out, at all levels of the Corporation. ...

After a period of time the responsibility for doing what the Corporation wants

89 / *Ibid.*, 336–7 (Leiterman).
90 / *Ibid.*, 576.
91 / *Ibid.*, 684.

done must be taken by the people responsible at the level at which they are responsible. It must be done at the executive producers' level, at the supervisory level, and it must not involve the whole Corporation.[92]

If this was the way CBC management saw things, one would have expected action to be taken through disciplining or removing Haggan, or at least Leiterman. Instead, the decision was to remove the co-hosts, as if that would accomplish the modifications so long sought.

7 The Demise of 'Seven Days'

Three incidents in the closing weeks of the 1965–6 season perhaps confirmed management's judgment of the kind of remedial action it had decided to take. First, there was a dispute about what kind of attention the program should give to the affair of Gerda Munsinger, a woman of doubtful reputation who had become the friend of one or two ministers of the former Conservative government. In the end, Leiterman explained, they were able only to present one item – an interview with some boys at Upper Canada College, 'and that only after a great deal of argument and persuasion on the part of our supervisors, with management, that the program could not possibly go on the air in such a contentious situation with no reference to the subject.'[93] There was even more trouble about an item the producers were not allowed to show. A number of reporters had sought interviews with Pierre Sévigny, a former associate minister of defence who had been involved in the Munsinger affair. Leiterman sent a reporter and camera crew to Sévigny's home in Montreal, asking that the camera be turned on while the reporter, Larry Zolf, went up the walk to knock on the door. Leiterman said,

I often tell our staff that it is no good for them to come back and say 'Mr. Sévigny says that he has no comment,' that we have to have on film anything that is said. Whether we use it or not is another question which is subject to all kinds of supervisory checks, as we know. ...

I do not want to go into a great deal of detail here, but Mr. Sévigny took strong objection to this, and in fact the reporter was hit over the head a few times with a cane.[94]

92 / *Ibid.*, 687–8.
93 / *Ibid.*, 261.
94 / *Ibid.*, 417.

Management regarded the attempted interview as an invasion of privacy, and as another failure to observe CBC ethical standards.[95]

The third incident (April 3) was over the questioning of Claude Wagner, the attorney-general for Quebec, a proponent of capital punishment, which was then being debated in Parliament. Wagner's interview had been recorded some months before, and extracts from it were presented on two occasions. On this date, eight minutes were shown, containing Wagner's remarks on the question of the death penalty, and Wagner was unhappy with the result. Management was dissatisfied with the rationale provided by Leiterman: 'Mr. Wagner represented one side and Mr. LaPierre and Mr. Troyer attempted to draw him out by putting other viewpoints. But, there is no doubt where Mr. LaPierre stood.'[96] Management no doubt linked this performance in their minds with a previous program (March 20) in which LaPierre wiped away a tear from his eye after listening to a very affecting interview, conducted by Roy Faibish, with Mrs. Truscott, the mother of a fourteen-year old boy condemned to death for the murder of a school girl.[97]

On April 5, Walker told Hogg and Haggan in Ottawa that the CBC would not renew Watson's and LaPierre's contracts for 'Seven Days.' He said it might be possible for Watson to work instead on a program that Haggan, Watson, and Marc Thibault (public affairs supervisor for the French network) had put forward as a bilingual project. But this would depend on Watson's attitude to the corporation and his general views regarding Canada.[98]

Haggan did not decide at that time what his course should be. 'I did not react very strongly at that particular meeting. I said I would like some days to consider the import of these instructions and to discuss them with my colleagues.'[99] He did discuss them with Gauntlett and Campbell, but not with Leiterman, who was in Florida. Walker, however, said he would like to discuss the bilingual project with Pat Watson, to have a man-to-man chat, to get to know him as a human being. Haggan replied that the matter of the new project was urgent, and that if Watson was to be associated with it, preparations should begin immediately.[100]

---

95 / *Ibid.*, 569 (Walker). Stuart Keate, who had applauded the Fred Fawcett interview, regarded the attempted Sévigny coverage as a doubtful exercise at best.
96 / *Ibid.*, 394.
97 / *Ibid.*, 139, 209 (LaPierre); 505, 508, 642–3 (Walker).
98 / *Ibid.*, 427–9 (Haggan).
99 / *Ibid.*, 455.
100 / *Ibid.*, 427–8, (Haggan); 523 (Walker).

Walker went to Toronto, not to inform Watson of the non-renewal of his 'Seven Days' contract, but for the 'man-to-man talk' he had mentioned the day before. But inevitably, his discussion with Watson ranged over the concerns management had had with 'Seven Days,' and the challenges to its authority.[101] Walker found Watson very affable and friendly, and quite constructive in making suggestions for the bilingual program. He apparently did not realize that in dropping the information that neither Watson nor LaPierre would be rehired for 'Seven Days' he was making a tactical error on which the producers could take their case to the country.[102]

Watson immediately informed Haggan of what Walker had told him, and Haggan expressed his gloomy forebodings to Hogg.[103] Watson also reached Leiterman in Florida the next day, but agreed to continue with the program until Leiterman was back in the country, April 13. On the 14th, Walker had another meeting with Haggan, and asked him whether Leiterman was prepared to produce 'Seven Days' the following season without Watson and LaPierre. Haggan recalled:

I said to him that if he required an answer, as he did by 5:00 PM on that day, the only possible answer would be no, and this was my opinion. Mr. Walker pressed me, saying: 'Have you asked him if he will?', and I said: 'No, I have not', and I tried to explain to him that it was not a good or fruitful way in which to put a matter of this nature to a producer, and that by forcing it in this way the only conceivable answer he could get would be a negative one.

However, Mr. Walker was very firm and explained to me it was necessary to settle this matter before the directors' meeting in Halifax.[104]

The Halifax meeting was a regular meeting of the board of directors, scheduled for April 20. In the normal course of things, the directors would expect a run-down of program plans for the next season, and they had also planned a review of program policies in the area of public affairs.

After Haggan got in touch with Leiterman by telephone, Walker saw

101 / *Ibid.*, 35–6, 43, 47 (Watson); 573–5 (Walker).
102 / Carscallen thesis, 147. As late as May 4, Walker expressed confidence that 'Seven Days' could return next season with different hosts (*1966 Proceedings*, 506). On May 5, he defended his decision to talk directly with Watson (537). On May 10, Ouimet said that Walker himself now realized 'if he had not opened up as much as he did with Mr. Watson, that perhaps the whole thing would not have exploded' (740).
103 / *Ibid.*, 429 (Haggan).
104 / *Ibid.*, 456. Haggan spoke of meeting on the 13th, but it seems to have been Thursday the 14th.

Leiterman the same afternoon, April 14, and said he must have a reply by 5:00 PM (the next day was Good Friday).[105] Leiterman was not prepared to give him the assurance that he would produce the program without the two program hosts.

After that ultimatum, things rushed to a conclusion. That night, Leiterman and producer Robert Hoyt decided to leak the news to George Bain, Ottawa editor of the *Globe and Mail*.[106] Leiterman believed that Walker had violated the terms of Leiterman's own contract as executive producer in informing Watson unilaterally that he could no longer be host of the program. According to the contract, Leiterman had 'the responsibility for the selection of scripts and principal artists.'[107] Only a year before, Walker and the Toronto management had agreed, after a complaint from the Producers' Association about another program, to follow 'due process under which changes in performance and artists on a program should take place only after consultation with the producer concerned.'[108]

At four o'clock in the morning, April 15, Leiterman telephoned the news to LaPierre in Montreal.[109] The *Globe and Mail*'s story appeared the same morning. Haggan, who had not known of Leiterman's decision to talk to the press, submitted a memorandum to the president asking that he reconsider 'several head office decisions adversely affecting the responsibilities of the public affairs department,' and protesting that only chaos could result 'from attempts by head office to undertake detailed direction of particular programs and their personnel.'[110]

Helen Carscallen has written of the campaign mounted by the 'Seven Days' producers to keep the story before the public. From the time the story broke, on April 15, there were only four more programs scheduled before the summer break. The producers continued to present the program each week, but there was always the uncertainty as to whether each one might be the last. Widespread publicity in the media brought a flood of letters, telegrams, and phone calls to the CBC and to a quickly organized 'Save Seven Days Committee,' with William Kilbourn of York University as chairman. As organizer the committee employed Stephen Patrick, a free-lance writer. Committee rooms were set up in a

105 / *Ibid.*, 266 (Leiterman).
106 / Carscallen thesis, 136.
107 / *1966 Proceedings*, 307.
108 / *Ibid.*, 1096.
109 / *Ibid.*, 139 (LaPierre).
110 / 'Secret 7 Days' memo reveals conflict between CBC top brass,' *Toronto Star*, April 21, 1966. Haggan's memorandum was filed with the 1966 Committee. *Proceedings*, 348–9.

motel room on Jarvis Street in Toronto, opposite the CBC studios. Letter-writers and callers were encouraged to take their complaints to President Ouimet, the board of directors, and to members of Parliament. The committee would try to ensure that an intelligent and interested group of back-benchers was appointed to the broadcasting committee which undoubtedly would be reviewing the imbroglio. Local 'Save Seven Days' committees were encouraged in several cities, and prominent citizens invited to help the campaign. Other CBC producers would be enlisted to support their cause through the Association of Television Producers in Toronto. By midnight of Sunday, April 17, according to a count by Bell Telephone, approximately seven thousand calls had reached the CBC switchboard.[111]

The initial response of the newspapers was not so satisfying to the 'Seven Days' producers. Blair Fraser surveyed the editorial opinions expressed, and reported on CBC radio: 'Pat Watson and Laurier LaPierre may be able to out-number CBC management on the picket lines, but in the press across Canada management seems to have the edge. ... In general, the producers are getting very little editorial sympathy in the fuss over Seven Days.'[112]

But in parliament, Diefenbaker and Tommy Douglas (leader of the NDP) joined in urging an immediate review of the situation. Diefenbaker understood that 3800 or more telegrams had been received by the CBC. He suggested that 'because two officials connected with the ''Seven Days'' program, one in Ottawa and one in Toronto, gave their views to the Fowler committee, these two gentlemen have been advised that their contracts are to be terminated because they have not left a good image of the C.B.C.'[113]

The producers' association in Toronto was cautious about supporting the 'Seven Days' unit, or threatening a withdrawal of services, but was moved to take a position by management's violation of the agreement

111 / Carscallen thesis, 147–50.

112 / 'Looking through the papers,' April 24, 1966. Newspapers critical of the producers included the *Vancouver Sun*, the Vancouver *Province*, the Saint John *Telegraph-Journal*, the *Hamilton Spectator*, *Le Soleil* of Quebec, the *Calgary Herald*, and columnists Charles Lynch and Philip Deane. More critical of CBC management were *L'Action* of Quebec, the *Ottawa Citizen*, the *Montreal Star*, *Le Devoir*, and columnist Peter Newman in the *Toronto Star*. Shaun Herron, of the *Winnipeg Free Press*, criticized both sides.

113 / *Debates*, April 19, 1966, 3977–9. The two referred to were Roy Faibish of Ottawa, and Patrick Watson. As president of the Association of Television Producers in 1964, Watson had submitted a memorandum to the Fowler committee that had been critical of CBC management.

not to breach the line of authority through the producer in hiring and firing program personnel.

The propriety of the 'Seven Days' producers conducting a campaign of agitation against their employers while still working for them was highly questionable. The fact that they were all contract employees, who had no guarantees that their employment would be extended, hardly changes the situation, for in fact the leading figures in the campaign had been working for the CBC for some period of time.

The CBC board met as scheduled in Halifax, heard a report on developments from the president, and discussed the memorandum from Haggan to Ouimet, dated April 14. They also reviewed a telegram from the Association of Television Producers and Directors, Toronto, which said:

The President has offered no cogent reasons, to us or the public, for repudiating the Department of Public Affairs, in the case of the Seven Days hosts.

This Association considers the President's action a contravention of the 1965 undertaking with respect to prior consultations with Producers about program matters. This contravention we view as an unacceptable threat to the responsible management of the CBC, and in effect a motion of want of confidence in the CBC's program and production staff. ...

We acknowledge the right of management to manage, but good management should find it possible to admit mistakes. There can be no peace nor can confidence in present Senior Management be established, unless prompt and positive remedial action is taken.[114]

Unless a satisfactory settlement was reached forthwith, the association said it would have to consider 'drastic measures,' including, if necessary, withdrawal of its members' services. In reply, the president promised that he would meet them within the next few days. The CBC directors also received telegrams from producers' associations in Ottawa and Winnipeg, supporting the Toronto producers and raising another grievance in respect to an Ottawa producer.

The directors met with Haggan on the morning of April 22, and with Douglas Leiterman in the afternoon, and afterwards prepared a news release confirming management's decisions with regard to 'Seven Days.' 'At the same time it [the board] observed that there had been a

---

114 / Dated April 19, 1966. The association in Toronto was not a legal bargaining unit and could not threaten a strike, but at most only a withdrawal of services as decided by each member. It soon became evident that a number of producers would refuse to take this step.

serious breakdown in formal communication between management and the producer of "Seven Days." Accordingly, the Board directed that steps be taken, at whatever levels necessary, to ensure effective communication between management and producers.'[115] The statement continued:

The Board asked that every effort be made to continue the improvement of the program, 'Seven Days.' It recognizes that this production is lively and provocative and has attracted a large following. The people involved in this program are hard-working and dedicated. A serious shortcoming of the program, however, has been its frequent departures from established corporation policy. ...

Finally, the Board stated the belief that the direct intervention of a Parliamentary Committee regarding a management decision had made more difficult its task and that of Management.[116]

The last paragraph was resented by several members of the parliamentary committee, and probably did not increase the chances that management would receive a favourable report.

While the broadcasting committee was holding its initial hearings in Ottawa, the producers' association in Toronto was trying to get the CBC president to relax his decision, but without success.[117] Another message was sent to Ouimet on April 27 threatening a withdrawal of services by Sunday, May 1, 'unless the CBC president takes action to eliminate the cause of the dispute.' Prime Minister Pearson, who met privately with members of the producers' association executive, offered to use his good offices to help in resolving the situation, and both sides agreed to meet with him. The 'strike' (or withdrawal of services) was off, and on May 1 the program was introduced by an announcer with these words: 'Ladies and gentlemen, through the good offices of the Prime Minister of Canada. ... This Hour *Has* Seven Days.'[118] Pearson asked Stuart Keate, publisher of the *Vancouver Sun*, to review the facts of the dispute and

115 / This was hardly a new criticism. The Fowler committee, looking back at the Glassco report, wrote: 'It was a 'paradox' that an agency engaged in communications seemed to have failed to perfect its internal communications.' *Fowler Report II*, 139.
116 / *1966 Proceedings*, 184.
117 / According to a member of the executive, the leaders of the producers' association considered it a handicap that the CBC president was also chairman of the board of directors. They thought that if a director who was not part of CBC management had been chairman, the board would have been more easily persuaded that the producers had a strong case.
118 / 'With thanks to the PM, Seven Days goes on,' *Globe and Mail*, May 2, 1966.

prepare a report. He was not appointed as an arbitrator, or even a conciliator.[119]

While CBC employees and managers continued to appear before the parliamentary committee, they were also being interviewed by Keate, who had not been appointed by order-in-council, had no specific powers, and was not paid for his services. Pearson received Keate's report on May 25, and its text was released May 27.[120]

Keate found that 'there have been mistakes on both sides of this debate.' The most valid criticism of 'Seven Days,' he suggested, was in respect of its interviewing techniques. Too often, its interviews 'descended to the level of a brutal, almost savage, inquisition.' There was an element of vanity in the program's performers, as manifest in their testimony before the House committee. And the producers had enjoyed wide latitude in the fifty programs presented, a latitude which was 'in the best CBC tradition of freedom.'

But his report, while finding fault with the producers, was tilted against management. Keate recalled that the Fowler Report had mentioned a 'smouldering dissatisfaction among producers.' The CBC board of directors must address itself to the personnel problem at the earliest opportunity. Some of the key executives had 'grown up in the age of radio,' perhaps understood television imperfectly, and were at or near retirement age. In the decision to drop the 'Seven Days' hosts, the line of authority had indeed been broken. The board's decision in Halifax to confirm management's decision was hard to understand, and lay at the root of the public protest. 'The Board's intransigent stand was an affront to an instinctive Canadian sense of fair play.'

Keate concluded his report with four recommendations: (1) at its end-of-month meeting in Ottawa, the CBC board should re-examine the basic questions of 'due process' and 'cogent reasons' as they applied to Watson and LaPierre, and issue an amplifying public statement thereon; (2) to help ease tensions, the House committee should now move to other considerations on its agenda; (3) the government should bring forward its White Paper as quickly as possible for consideration by the broadcasting committee; and (4) the producers' association should suspend their strike threat pending a procession through the foregoing procedures.

119 / *Ibid.*, 'Walkout is averted at CBC,' and 'Mediator Keate believes terms will go beyond Seven Days row.'

120 / *Debates*, May 25, 1966, 5510. The text of Keate's report is in the *Toronto Star*, May 27, 1966, 22–3.

But Keate also reported that 'on the re-opening of the case of the two hosts, the CBC will not negotiate.' This was a signal that, in reality, Keate's effort at mediation had failed.

When the CBC directors met on May 27, they discussed the statements made by Leiterman before the broadcasting committee (as well as the evidence of Marc Thibault)[121] and concluded that there were fundamental differences between their views and the corporation's stand that the CBC could not editorialize in controversial matters. They thought it would be naive to expect that the 'Seven Days' program could be continued with the same producers, but saw some possibility of reviving a magazine-type program through a merger of the news and current affairs sections.[122]

In a public release (May 27), the CBC directors promised the producers that 'no change in artists or performers will be made without full consultation with the Executive Producer and the Producer concerned,' and agreed that any departure from the above procedure would be subject to appeal to another level within the corporation. But so far as LaPierre and Watson were concerned, the board held to their decision not to renew their contracts as hosts. Each of them could continue to be employed in another capacity.[123] The directors also agreed that they would give consideration to Keate's suggestion that they appoint a vice-president of news and public affairs.

The Toronto producers' association, in a statement submitted to the broadcasting committee on May 30, reported that they had exhausted almost all possible avenues for resolution of the conflict. The 'intransigence' of the board of directors and of management had convinced them that any further trust in senior management would be misplaced. They looked to Parliament to restate the aims of public broadcasting when it gave consideration to the forthcoming White Paper. In the meantime, they could not withdraw their threat to withdraw services, since management had not shown a concern either for fair play or for professional respect in its dealings with producers.[124]

The broadcasting committee wound up its questioning of Alphonse

---

121 / The broadcasting committee heard evidence (May 12, 16, 17) from Claude Désorcy, producer, and Thibault, general supervisor of public affairs, that there were similar problems in the French network. Their evidence was countered (May 19) by Marcel Ouimet, general manager of the French network.
122 / Information from J.A. Ouimet, July 2, 1975.
123 / Statement reprinted in *1966 Proceedings*, 1096–7.
124 / *Ibid.*, 1090–5.

Ouimet on June 2, and turned to the preparation of an interim report. In the *Globe Magazine* (June 18), Norman Webster wrote that the hearings had indeed been rough on management:

The country's top television personalities and producers, criticizing their bosses, gave the performance of their lives – articulate, crusading, witty – and basked warmly in the committee's sympathy.

Program supervisors, theoretically the men in the middle, asked the committee for its protection, then delighted by promptly biting the heavy hand of head office. Management's men, precast as the heavies of the piece, came on strongly in their roles, and ran into a barrage of questions from hostile MP s.

But Webster could not predict the tenor of the report, because he said that the MP s who had shown themselves as critical of management did not constitute a majority of the committee. It was true that 'this group includes some of the more able MP s in the Commons – men such as the Liberals' Ron Basford and Robert Stanbury, the Conservatives' Gordon Fairweather and Lewis Brand, and the NDP's David Lewis.' But there would be dangers in a strong anti-management report, which might be embarrassing to the Liberal government, and in any case, 'Even some of those most incensed by Management's action in the Seven Days affair would be loath to establish a precedent of direct political interference in the CBC's internal affairs.'[125] Indeed, although Webster did not say so, the question might be asked why the 'Seven Days' producers were so quick to ask for parliamentary intervention. If it was wrong for government to interfere with programs they disliked, could one logically ask them to help sustain a program that the MP s favoured?

When the committee presented its report to the House on June 29, it proved to be highly critical of management, and by implication supported the stand taken by the producers and the two performers. The circumstances, the report said, were 'highly reminiscent of findings already made by previous enquiry groups, namely the Glassco Commission, the Fowler Committee on Broadcasting and the CBC President's Study Group as quoted in the Fowler Report.' The existing malaise was in no way limited to the 'Seven Days' issue, but pervaded the whole department of public affairs broadcasting.

To prevent such eruptions in the future, the committee recommended a collective agreement with producers, similar to that in Montreal, and

125 / 'A cool report in the offing on a hot issue.'

the setting up of a grievance procedure. It was wrong to try to run a radio or TV network in military fashion. 'Extreme nervousness or jumpiness on the part of management with regard to public reactions, and extreme touchiness or irritability on the part of creative personnel, spell the very formula of disaster.'

There was too much attempt at a 'remote control of programming.' The committee recommended that a senior vice-president responsible for programming and production should be located in Toronto and in Montreal.

On the question of program freedom, the committee expressed satisfaction that no evidence had been presented indicating that CBC management or program personnel had been subject to pressure from government or political parties. (Indeed, both management and the producers had insisted there had been none.) The committee also agreed with Ouimet that CBC personnel must not promote their own views in CBC programs. But, CBC neutrality in controversial matters should not be so scrupulous as to detract from its liveliness. Nor should performers be chosen for their blandness. 'What the CBC needs is the type of performers with strong individuality and personal opinions but who are aware of their own biases and are capable of keeping them in check.' The committee hoped that steps would be taken to ensure adventurous public affairs programming for the next season.[126]

The CBC directors were meeting in Ottawa when the broadcasting committee reported to the House. The government had not kept their numbers up to full strength: there were only six in addition to Ouimet and Briggs.[127] The director of news and public affairs in Toronto, William Hogg, had expressed a wish to be relieved of his duties. This, combined with the parliamentary committee's recommendation that a senior vice-president be located in Toronto, suggested that the board faced some ticklish problems regarding senior appointments. Furthermore, Ouimet had suggested in his evidence before the parliamentary committee that Haggan's position would need to be reviewed.[128] And there was still the question of whether to renew Leiterman's contract.

Walker had not made a good impression during the committee hear-

126 / *1966 Proceedings*, 1233–41.
127 / The part-time members were: Dr. James Beveridge, president of Acadia University, Wolfville, NS; David MacAulay, dean of men at Mount Allison University, Sackville, NB; E.B. Osler, director of a Winnipeg mortgage and trust firm; Dr. Stephanie Potoski, in medical practice at Yorkton, Sask.; John Prentice, president of a lumber company in Vancouver; and André Raynauld, an economist at the Université de Montréal.
128 / *1966 Proceedings*, 690, 735, 1068, 1088.

ings, and his mistake in short-circuiting the lines of authority was admitted. From time to time there were reports that some on the board of directors wanted him removed from office, but the majority apparently agreed with Ouimet that the principal causes of the trouble lay elsewhere.[129] After the directors met in Ottawa, June 27–30, nothing was said about any change in Walker's function, but it was announced that two senior vice-presidents would be placed at the earliest possible date in the two network centres of Toronto and Montreal.[130] (This transfer had been discussed previously by the board as a possibility, for example, on October 25, 1965, but the decision was taken only after the report of the broadcasting committee.)[131] When Ouimet announced the relocation of two vice-presidents, nothing was said about who would occupy the two positions, whether, for example, Walker and Marcel Ouimet would merely be transferred from Ottawa. Walker announced on the same day that Marce Munro would succeed W.H. Hogg in Toronto as director of news and public affairs, and let it be known that he himself was preparing to move to Toronto. There were reactions in both Toronto and Montreal among program personnel.

For its part, the 'Seven Days' unit responded with a statement by Leiterman that they could not work under Walker's direction, and that they were suspending all production activity in preparation for the fall.[132] Ouimet meanwhile was explaining that the new vice-presidential posts in Toronto and Montreal had been approved only a week before, and no specific appointments had yet been considered.[133] In a telephone conference with the other directors, it was agreed that Walker would not move to Toronto and that he would not be a candidate for the new vice-presidency position in Toronto.[134] (In the end, Ouimet and the board postponed the relocation of the general managers of the networks in Toronto and Montreal. New appointments were not made until after George Davidson had succeeded Alphonse Ouimet as CBC president. Well before this, in October 1966, H.G. Walker was appointed as the head of a project to advise Caribbean governments on broadcasting services and structures, and his assistant in Toronto, R.W. McGall, became acting general manager of the English network.)

129 / *Toronto Star*: 'CBC directors split,' May 27, 1966; 'Ouimet on CBC carpet for not firing Walker,' June 28, 1966.

130 / The announcement, July 5, was held until after the release of the government's White Paper on Broadcasting (July 4, 1966).

131 / Information from J.A. Ouimet, July 2, 1975.

132 / 'We'll all quit – 7-Days staff,' Toronto *Telegram*, July 6, 1966.

133 / *Ibid.*, 'The CBC situation is bizarre,' Bob Blackburn.

134 / 'CBC kills Walker shift as 7 Days men strike,' *Globe and Mail*, July 7, 1966.

In its meeting at the end of June, the CBC board also decided that Leiterman should be offered a contract to produce 'This Hour Has Seven Days' for the 1966–7 season, but subject to his written acceptance of corporation policies and direction. Management gave him a deadline of 4:00 PM, July 7, to sign this special agreement, and he would be expected to produce 'Seven Days' without the participation of Watson or LaPierre. Leiterman objected, arguing that his agreement to abide by corporation policies had always been part of his contract, but that any standard contract allowed the executive producer to choose his own employees.[135]

When Leiterman refused to meet the CBC's terms, Reeves Haggan transmitted to him the notice of his dismissal, and then submitted his own resignation. Haggan's resignation was followed by that of Watson and most of the contract employees who had been working on 'Document' and the summer replacement program 'Compass.' This spelled the end of 'Seven Days,' and left a widespread feeling that the CBC had abandoned its most provocative and hard-hitting television program through the ineptness or timidity of management. Certainly this was the conclusion of Haggan, who in a television interview with Douglas Fisher said:

I think they [management] feel ... that the CBC is best protected when it is least observed. My view is quite different and I think the CBC must be part of the life of the people. Now whether their feeling that everything should be kept quiet is engendered by fear of the politicians, I don't know. As you know, I was supervisor of Public Affairs in Ottawa for some years and in the position where the most immediate pressure from politicians comes. I never found it unhealthy or intolerable. ...

Seven Days in my view is, has been one of the most important things in the country primarily for this reason, that it speaks for an amorphous new Canada. A new Canada that isn't well understood, it speaks for it, it speaks to it. Now this new Canada is not something that everybody's going to like and that's why they don't like 7 Days, they don't like the new rising Canadianism and the entrenched old Canada must fight it. ...

I think Leiterman is the only authentic genius that I've known in my time ... an authentic genius in the field of communications. He is extremely difficult to work with but at the same time I must say stimulating to work with. ... He sees an objective and he goes straight to it and it is difficult to deflect him. But ... the cost

135 / 'Leiterman fired, Watson, two others quit – 7 Days kaput,' *Toronto Star*, July 8, 1966; 'Firing of Leiterman causes 10 to resign,' *Globe and Mail*, July 9, 1966. Christopher Young, editor of the *Ottawa Citizen*, reviewed the circumstances of the program's demise in 'Blood-letting at the CBC is management's failure,' July 9, 1966.

of putting up with a chap like Leiterman is nickels and dimes compared to the cost of losing him.[136]

But of course the 'Seven Days' tussle was not only a struggle within the CBC about program values. It was also a struggle over who would manage, who would make the most important decisions on behalf of the public corporation. It was even a struggle to influence the choice of the next generation of top executives. This is rather clear from the account given by Judy LaMarsh, the minister in office at that time. Her book describes meetings with Leiterman and Watson, kept secret from CBC management, and her feeling that Watson 'might soon become a senior officer of the Corporation.'[137]

Eight years later, Patrick Watson reflected on what was chiefly at issue in the 'Seven Days' dispute. 'What was at issue,' he said, 'was whether or not the people who ran the program Seven Days were going to allow themselves to be run by the management of the corporation. ... We ... wouldn't do what we were told, and had our own accounting system which was not the CBC accounting system, and really were creating an empire in a kind of counter-power centre within the CBC and that was intolerable to any management. ... I suggested myself as a possible president. ... Sure, I went down and lobbied on behalf of me ... in that case, the Secretary of State, Judy LaMarsh, and some of her colleagues in the cabinet. And I wrote up sort of a prospectus about how the CBC might be managed. ... I thought that it was in such a miserable state at that moment, that it really couldn't be done worse, and that it maybe ought to be done for a while by someone who understood programming and cared about programming.'[138]

The secretary of state arranged for Watson to be interviewed by the prime minister, but Watson never received an invitation to come into the CBC at the level of president or vice-president.

Changes were in the offing. At the same time the 'Seven Days' convulsion was over, the government produced its White Paper, the first step in the preparation of new broadcasting legislation.

136 / Interview on CJOH-TV, Ottawa, July 10, 1966. Haggan later joined the Department of External Affairs in Ottawa, then transferred to the Solicitor-General's Department as assistant deputy minister. Leiterman became an independent producer of television films, and then a operator of a cable television system. Watson, after producing a television series in New York, returned to Canada as an independent producer and an interviewer for the CBC.
137 / *Memoirs of a Bird in a Gilded Cage*, 251–8.
138 / CBC radio interview with Michael Enright, Nov. 19, 1974 (transcript provided by CBC).

12 THE WHITE PAPER AND THE 1967 BROADCASTING COMMITTEE

FROM JANUARY 1966 to the last months of the Pearson administration in 1968, the secretary of state and her department were engaged in an intensive effort to prepare new broadcasting legislation and to see it through the various stages of parliamentary consideration. This chapter will trace the government's procedure in reviewing the second Fowler report, and the representations made to it by the interested agencies and groups, leading to the production of a White Paper on broadcasting in July 1966. Before it could be referred to a committee of the House of Commons for review, other developments in broadcasting interposed themselves, suggesting some modifications in the government's plans even before drafting of the new legislation began – for example, the pressure to start colour television, to allow the CBC to consolidate its production facilities in Montreal, and to perpetuate the power of the cabinet to reverse or set aside licensing decisions of the BBG. Meanwhile, relations between the new secretary of state, Miss LaMarsh, and the CBC president and board of directors began to deteriorate, forcing the CBC to take quite unusual measures in its attempt to maintain its status and influence on developments. The parliamentary committee on broadcasting began its review of the White Paper in December 1966, hearing the same kinds of witnesses who had already presented their views to the cabinet, and, not surprisingly, its report in March 1967 was an endorsement of the policy announced by the government in the White Paper.

The legislative process will be described in chapter 13 – the drafting of the new broadcasting act, its consideration by the cabinet committee, the representations made to the ministers and the secretary of state's department by the CBC, and the debates in the House of Commons and Senate and the discussions in committee.

1 LaMarsh and the Cabinet Committee

As already described, the prime minister had announced the formation of the cabinet committee immediately after demoting Judy LaMarsh from her portfolio of minister of health and welfare to that of secretary of state. By taking the even more unusual step of designating himself as chairman of the committee, Pearson was signalling his intention to limit the control of policy formation that might be exercised by any one department or minister, and suggesting also that he would take a personal interest in the outcome. This procedure made it possible for group interests to circumvent the minister if they were not satisfied with the reception she or her department accorded their representations.

Judy LaMarsh was a tenacious minister, and took as seriously her responsibility for the drafting of new broadcasting legislation as she had shown in the drafting of the Canada Pension Plan. She was a person with her own firm ideas, and enjoyed the advantage of having in her department the two persons who now knew as much about broadcasting as any in the civil service – her undersecretary, Ernest Steele, and the recent secretary of the Fowler committee, Henry Hindley.

As time went on, Miss LaMarsh became increasingly resentful of the prime minister's role. In her memoirs, she complains that various ministers were assigned to the committee over the months it was in existence, that their attendance was irregular, and that the prime minister was not much more faithful in his own attendance.

He appeared for those sessions when some individual members of the public or broadcasting agencies were there to propose their briefs – I suppose to give them a sense that it was all under his own personal control. Several of those meetings occurred in his own office. With us, he saw members of the Board of both the C.B.C. and the B.B.G. He began to see the President and Chairman privately, without notifying me. ... He went so far as to interview my deputy with his special knowledge of the field derived from the Fowler Committee's investigations, not only without telling me but after cautioning the deputy not to tell me about it! ... I felt I was being undermined at every turn by the Prime Minister.[1]

As for the other ministers, LaMarsh makes particular mention of only one, Jack Pickersgill, the minister of transport. He was not only the most experienced, but had 'many friends in broadcasting and was always highly solicitous of the interests of his friends.'[2] Pickersgill's associations were especially close with the former president of the CAB, Don Jamieson, who before the end of 1966 joined Pickersgill as a Liberal member of Parliament from Newfoundland. As minister for the department licensing communications companies, including broadcasting sta-

1 / *Memoirs of a Bird in a Gilded Cage*, 260.
2 / *Ibid.*, 259.

tions and cable television systems, Pickersgill had more than a personal interest in the policy review that was under way.

In the spring of 1966, the cabinet committee had before it not only the Fowler Committee's report, but the comments on it submitted by the CBC and the CAB, as well as the memoranda transmitted more informally by the chairman of the BBG. With these documents, the files and records of the Fowler Committee, and the reports of the Troika, the cabinet committee might have proceeded without further consultations. Instead, each of the public agencies and the CAB were interviewed afresh by the ministerial committee: for example, the executive committee of CAB met with them on March 31.[3] The CBC president attended their meetings twice.[4] As for the BBG, Stewart's recollection is that he prepared internal documents on the Fowler Report, proposals for the White Paper, and draft legislation 'along the lines of the Australian Act.'[5] In Australia, the public broadcasting agency, the Australian Broadcasting Commission, was purely an operator of radio and television stations. The privately owned commercial stations were subject to the regulations of the Australian Broadcasting Control Board, appointed by the government. The Australians, therefore, had a dual system of broadcasting in which the public and private sectors were independent of one another.[6]

The CBC position had been outlined once again in its 'Comments ... on the Report of the Committee on Broadcasting, 1965,' and Ouimet presumably defended and enlarged upon that statement. He concurred with the Fowler Committee that the CBC 'must be paramount,' because of its national responsibilities. While private broadcasters could engage in all areas of broadcast interest – international, national, regional, provincial, and local – their primary responsibility to the public was the provision of community or local service. While each sector should provide access to

---

3 / The CAB General Newsletter, Jan. 17, 1966, reported that the CAB had been requested to make its views known to the cabinet committee, and had submitted documents to the secretary of state. It added, 'This material will now be useful to you in further briefing of all Federal M.P.'s from your area. Such briefing, it is felt, is best accomplished by personal meetings with each of these individuals.' Copy in E.A. Weir Papers, PAC MG30/DC4 (16).

4 / Information from Ouimet, who consulted minutes of the CBC board of directors, April 21, 1966.

5 / Letter from Stewart to the author, March 19, 1976.

6 / A comparison of the Australian and Canadian broadcasting structures is in W.H.N. Hull, "A Comparative Study of the Problems of Ministerial Responsibility in Australian and Canadian Broadcasting' (doctoral thesis, Duke University, 1959; University Microfilms, Ann Arbor, Michigan).

the audience for advertisers, this should not form a primary objective for the corporation, and the CBC directors again recommended a reduction in CBC commercial business.

The CBC strongly criticized the proposals for a small three or five-member regulatory board. It joined the BBG and CAB in expressing preference for a two-board system, but unlike the CAB it wanted the CBC to be under the authority of its own board, and the private sector to be under the authority of another board to be called the 'Private Broadcasting Authority.' But whichever choice was eventually to be taken, Ouimet urged that there should be 'a continuance of experience at both Board and senior Management levels.'[7]

In its statement addressed to the secretary of state early in 1966, the CAB asked for a 'continuation of an impartial agency of regulation' similar to the BBG, but advocated that it consist of only three full-time members. This view was reiterated in the brief presented to the cabinet committee, the CAB then suggesting that the part-time members be replaced by part-time advisers, whose function would be to 'bring in information' as representatives of the public.[8] In the CAB's lexicon, an authority of the type proposed by the Fowler Committee could not be 'impartial,' since it would have direct responsibility for the operations and performance of the CBC.

The CAB opposed granting the regulatory agency general powers to impose conditions of licence for individual stations, preferring that the governor in council retain final authority over licences. Then, as if to signal a mutual exchange with the CBC of support for each other's objectives, the CAB asked that the government decide in favour of two principles long advocated by the CBC: the financing of the CBC on a statutory five-year basis, and the provision of alternative television service in each community through the CBC 'and a privately owned station in each case.' The timing of the execution of this policy should be determined by the BBG.[9]

Fowler had met with Pearson and members of the cabinet committee (including Guy Favreau and John Turner) on February 3, urging that the

---

7 / 'Comments,' forwarded by CBC president to Secretary of State, Nov. 26, 1965, 3–10.
8 / The CAB's submission to the secretary of state was attached to a letter, T.J. Allard to LaMarsh, Jan 13, 1966; reported in *Canadian Broadcaster*, Feb. 3, 1966, 3. It also contained a draft act, and a comment that only 'comparatively minor modifications' were needed in the legislative and structural shape of Canadian broadcasting. The comment on the CAB's brief to the cabinet committee is by J.A. Pouliot, CAB president, 1966–7 *Proceedings*, Jan. 9, 1967, 1461.
9 / *Canadian Broadcaster* (Feb. 3, 1966).

government proceed as rapidly as possible. He followed up with a memorandum on February 8, recommending that the cabinet should go for the complete package – a White Paper, a new statute – and should clean up the whole business in a consistent way. He recognized that a bristling report might seem to offer difficulties, but added: 'We didn't create the problems.' Pearson replied that he was fully impressed with the importance of the broadcasting decisions, but cabinet must hear the views of the BBG, CBC, and in some way the CAB, so he could not 'get aboard your fast express.' Fowler wrote that there had been a sixteen-month investigation; they had already heard the views of the CBC, BBG, members of the CAB; there had also been the Troika report; consultation would cause confusion and delay; and he expressed some irritation that the process could go on for ever. He did not attend another meeting of the cabinet committee, nor did he see the minister (LaMarsh) subsequently.[10]

2   The White Paper

When LaMarsh tabled the White Paper on Broadcasting in the House of Commons on July 4, 1966, it became evident that the government was not prepared to revert to a one-board structure such as the Fowler Committee had recommended. The opposition to it was too overwhelming; only the Canadian Broadcasting League (and its affiliates) supported the proposal,[11] and that organization was too weak to overcome the combined opposition of the private broadcasters, the CBC, and the BBG. Apart from that, the government was probably looking for a compromise that could secure the support of many opposition members as well as its own supporters in the back benches. During the course of the

10 / Interview with Fowler, Jan. 27, 1976. LaMarsh wrote Fowler in March 1968, thanking him for his contribution to the development of the new legislation. In her *Memoirs*, LaMarsh wrote (p. 232) that Fowler, for a second time, had made 'an amateur but careful and intelligent appraisal of Canadian broadcasting.' She also added, with some degree of inaccuracy, that 'The Fowler report was written by Henry Hindley, one of Steele's senior assistants.' Hindley and each member of the committee wrote particular chapters, and shared in the editing.

11 / The league submitted a brief to the prime minister in April 1966, supporting a single system, a single authority, and most of the recommendations in the Fowler Report. It expressed disappointment in the performance of the BBG, and urged the strengthening of the role of the CBC and long-term financing on a statutory basis; Spry Papers. The Canadian Federation of Agriculture expressed a similar position in an open letter to the prime minister, Feb. 2, 1966.

cabinet committee's consultations, 'one of the largest Canadian private-station owners' told Spry that 'he had not bothered to read the [Fowler] report in full. He said, in effect, that it was perfectly clear that the situation, whatever sort of Board was set up, would remain for the private stations as it was before and they had nothing to be concerned about. In any event he saw no prospect of a single authority being accepted by the government or Parliament. As for CBC, it was going to get weaker and weaker and have more and more problems.'[12]

The White Paper emphasized the government's acceptance of the historic 'mandate' assigned to the CBC, suggested that the authority of the BBG should be strengthened, and accepted Fowler's idea that minimum standards of public-service programming and Canadian content should be determined by the BBG for private stations on an individual basis. But it specifically rejected the Fowler committee's recommendation for a single board:

The Canadian broadcasting system, comprising public and private sectors, must be regarded as a single system which should be regulated and controlled by a single independent authority. It is therefore proposed that the powers and authority of the Board of Broadcast Governors, which require extension and clarification, shall be applicable to all broadcasters alike, and that the Board itself shall be reconstituted. The Government does not concur in the recommendation of the Advisory Committee that the regulatory authority should be responsible for the management of the Canadian Broadcasting Corporation. However, the legislation will make it clear that the Corporation will be subject to the regulatory powers of the Board of Broadcast Governors in all matters affecting general broadcasting policy in Canada.[13]

If the White Paper did not accept Fowler's central recommendation, neither did it accept the recommendations of Ouimet and Stewart that there should be a dual system, each sector having its own authority. On this question of structure, the White Paper opted for the status quo, with incremental changes or improvements. In its broad outlines, the new set-up would more closely approximate the recommendations of Don Jamieson than those of his fellow-members of the Troika, Stewart and Ouimet.

On some other matters, the White Paper was more innovative. It accepted the recommendations of the BBG (and of Fowler) that community-antenna television systems (cable broadcasting) should be

12 / Spry Papers, Spry to E.A. Weir, April 27, 1966.
13 / Secretary of State, *White Paper on Broadcasting 1966*, 8.

treated as components of the national broadcasting system, subject to licensing, regulation and control by the BBG. Parliament would be asked to give guidance to the BBG aimed at preventing foreign control of broadcasting facilities (including cable systems), the domination of a local situation through multiple ownership, or the extension of chain ownership geographically 'in a manner that is not in the public interest.'

While Canadian experience had demonstrated the necessity for 'a broadcasting system that includes public and private elements,' the public element should predominate in policy areas where a choice between the two was involved. Almost for the first time, the government was willing to accept openly its responsibility for deciding the manner in which the public system should be extended. 'Since the coverage of the national broadcasting service must be provided by the public element, which is dependent on funds voted by Parliament, the physical structure of the system as a whole is a matter for the Government, which is responsible to Parliament, to decide.' This was the kind of declaration Stewart had long urged the government to make, but until then without success. Within the ministerial group, it was Pickersgill who was most insistent that the government must exercise control over the broadcasting system, and retain the formal powers necessary to do that.[14]

When it came to specifics, the government did not accept the recommendation that the CBC and private broadcasting should each be represented in any community that had an alternative television service. Rather, it leaned towards the recommendation of the Fowler Committee that CBC expansion be limited, but the White Paper did indicate exceptions: the government was willing to reserve channels for the CBC in four specific areas: Victoria; Saskatoon; Sudbury; and the Saint John – Fredericton area.[15] The CBC would be expected to provide television service in these locations initially by means of repeater stations. As a more general objective, the White Paper declared that all Canadians were entitled, 'subject only to practical considerations in the expenditure of public funds, to service in the Canadian official language that they habitually use.' This was part of the government's policy in respect to

14 / Interview with Henry Hindley, Ottawa, Aug. 25, 1976.
15 / In June 1963 the CBC had applied to the BBG for reservation of television channels in ten centres: Prince Edward Island, Saint John–Fredericton, an English-language channel in Sherbrooke, Trois Rivières, Sudbury, Port Arthur–Fort William, Regina, Saskatoon, Calgary, and Victoria. The BBG recommended approval for channel reservations at Saint John–Fredericton, Sudbury, and Saskatoon. BBG Annual Report, 1963–4, 8–9.

bilingualism, a concern which had prompted the government in 1963 to appoint a royal commission on bilingualism and biculturalism.

In order to exercise its responsibility for the structure of the system, the government would have authority under the new legislation to give formal directions to the regulatory authority.[16] Matters affecting programming would not be subject to such directions.

The BBG would assume full power to issue broadcasting licences, subject only to technical evaluation and certification by the Department of Transport, and to any formal direction issuing from the government in relation to the structure of the system. Licensing decisions could, however, be appealed to the cabinet. The BBG would also have full power to regulate networks, both public and private, and conditions of affiliation. It would be able to determine the programming standards for all stations on an individual basis, including those of the CBC. The board would not, however, be empowered to give directions, other than by generally applicable regulations or in the conditions of a licence, to any broadcaster in respect of specific programs. Finally, the BBG would be able to inflict monetary penalties for breaches of regulations, or suspend or revoke a licence when the conditions of a licence had not been observed, with provision for appeal to the courts on questions of law but not of fact.

The BBG was to have five rather than three full-time membrs, and up to seven part-time members. The CBC was to have a president, and an indeterminate number of part-time members 'chosen mainly but not exclusively for their knowledge and experience of management matters.' The board of directors would appoint a chief executive officer, subject to the approval of the governor in council.

The government accepted the Fowler Committee's recommendation that the CBC be financed by means of a statutory five-year grant. It also indicated that the CBC should seek to retain but not to increase its present 25 per cent share of the television advertising market and 4 per cent share of the corresponding radio market. The government also promised additional financial support for the CBC's northern service, the service for the armed forces overseas, and the shortwave international service.

The White Paper made no specific mention of the private television network, CTV. The Fowler Committee had recommended that it be

16 / This was a provision urged by Henry Hindley, who had had experience in a British crown corporation. He was aware that the BBC was subject to formal direction from the minister on program matters, a power that had never been applied to particular programs. Hindley considered that a governmental power to issue a formal direction provided an admirable safeguard. Interview, Aug. 25, 1976.

reorganized as a sort of public trust. Faced with financial collapse, the network company applied in February 1966 to transfer all its outstanding shares to the affiliated stations. Under the existing act, the BBG had entire authority to decide on this application and, ignoring Fowler's recommendations, it approved the transfer of CTV ownership to the member stations. As a condition imposed by the BBG, no station owner would be able to hold shares directly or indirectly in more than one CTV affiliate.[17] This was presumably to prevent control of the network falling to one of the wealthier stations, in particular, those in Toronto, Ottawa, or Montreal.

Fowler did not make any public comment on the government's response to his committee's report, but nine months later he wrote in private correspondence:

I am not entirely happy about the retention of the two boards for the reasons given in both reports that carry my name. It may be that it was too much to hope that the novel form of regulatory body we suggested would be acceptable. I foresee the possibility of some clashes between the two similar boards or the atrophy of one or other of them. But I don't think the two are completely impossible to make work. In any case, we seem to be stuck with them and should try to do so. ... If, by good luck, we get a strong, imaginative and articulate chairman, we might take off into a new era of Canadian broadcasting. I can't say I am confident that this will happen, but I have still some hope.[18]

By October 1966, the press was speculating about possible appointments to both the BBG and CBC, stimulated by interviews with Judy LaMarsh, who seemed to be 'talking freely about the problem of finding a successor or successors, and throwing names about quite indiscriminately.'[19] Ouimet had seen Pearson in March 1966 about the possibility of retiring, but agreed to Pearson's request that he stay on until there was new legislation. He confirmed his request in a letter dated June 17, and Pearson asked him not to make his wish public until the government announced its new policy. After Pearson returned from a commonwealth conference, Ouimet obtained Pearson's permission to write officially to request his release on the basis agreed upon, which he did on

17 / BBG announcement, March 4, 1966, following a public hearing in Ottawa, February 23.
18 / Fowler to Peers, April 3, 1967.
19 / Spry Papers, Peers to Spry, Oct. 31, 1966.

October 5, 1966. He still expected that it would only be a matter of a few months until the new legislation was enacted.[20]

3 Alternative Service: Politics as Usual

With the tabling of the White Paper in the Commons, the government announced through the minister of transport that it was lifting the freeze on establishment of alternative television service, and applications would be received for new locations except in the four places that were to be reserved for the CBC.[21] The BBG found the White Paper's statement on the provision of alternative television service 'singularly unclear,' and after its discussion of the lifting of the freeze in September, Stewart wrote the prime minister that the board would proceed with caution. The demand for a second service had already been stimulated by prospective applicants, but because of limitations of the market, it was probable that there would be 'no practical solution without the intervention of the CBC.' The BBG knew that if the existing private stations were to be disaffiliated from the CBC, they would not be able to survive and continue their local service without receiving network programs from the only source possible, namely the CTV network. And the board had no authority to require CTV to extend its service into small (and unprofitable) markets.[22]

The BBG's announcement of October 5, 1966, promised an intensive study of market areas in which only one service was being offered, and indicated that it would not be prepared to hear applications until at least February 1967. Even then, it would not make decisions which would 'prevent or seriously endanger the realization of the ultimate pattern of a CBC outlet and a private outlet wherever alternative service is available. It is the opinion of the Board that the best long-run pattern of alternative television service is a combination of a public broadcasting station (an outlet of the CBC carrying the CBC national network service) and a private broadcasting station (a privately owned station carrying the private network service). The White Paper does not exclude the ultimate establishment of such a pattern.'

Late in 1966, the CBC submitted an application for a television licence in Saskatoon. The application was heard by the BBG on April 25, 1967,

20 / Interview with Ouimet, July 2, 1975. Pearson's exchange of correspondence with Ouimet was tabled in the Commons on Oct. 7, 1966. *Debates*, 8437.
21 / *Ibid.*, July 5, 1966, 7187 (Pickersgill).
22 / Stewart MS, 85–6.

and recommended for approval. By the time the new legislation was proclaimed in March 1968, no action had been taken by the government on the board's recommendation. A Conservative member from Saskatoon, Dr. Brand, linked this inaction to a reported visit to the prime minister by the Liberal premier of Saskatchewan, Ross Thatcher. According to Brand, the premier 'discussed and made some sort of arrangement to allow a private station in Saskatchewan, incidentally a station which has some feeling for the present government, to put a satellite in the Saskatoon area, thus helping the private station out of an uneconomic situation.'[23]

Dr. Brand's interpretation may not be accurate in all its details, but it is not inconsistent with the account provided by Andrew Stewart:

As the White Paper had approved a CBC station in Saskatoon, it is difficult to understand why the Government did not proceed on the Board's recommendation. One complicating factor seemed to be the situation in Regina. In 1958 there was a private affiliate of the CBC operating in Regina [CKCK-TV]; and a private affiliate of the CBC operating in Moose Jaw [CHAB-TV]. The former was owned by the Siftons, the latter by the Moffat interests. In due course by extending the coverage of both stations through rebroadcasting stations ... and the affiliation of CHAB with CTV Network, alternative service was brought to the area. The Regina – Moose Jaw area was seen as a single market ... CKCK Regina continued to attract a larger audience than its competitor; but incurred heavy operating losses. Moose Jaw received substantial support from CTV Network, but remained a marginal operation. It was part of CBC's plan eventually to have its own outlet in the capital city of the Province; but the conditions in the market in 1967 were not such as to justify a third station. Although the CBC would have preferred Regina to Saskatoon, if a choice were necessary, it therefore chose to apply for Saskatoon. The owners of CKCK saw the way out of their problem through the CBC purchasing one of the stations in the area; but they did not wish to sell their station. They therefore mounted a campaign to have the CBC purchase CHAB, and to disaffiliate CKCK, which would permit them to affiliate with CTV Network. They appeared to have some support from Premier Thatcher of Saskatchewan. ... Thus the Regina–Moose Jaw situation was probably a factor in the Government's failure to proceed with the CBC station in Saskatoon.[24]

Pressures for a second service built up in other areas as well. In Lethbridge, a solution was found through an arrangement worked out

23 / *Debates*, Nov. 6, 1967, 3935.
24 / Stewart MS, 92–3. The CBC proceeded with the purchase of the Regina–Moose Jaw station, CHAB-TV, and did not establish its own station in Saskatoon until 1971.

between Selkirk Holdings (the licensee of stations in Calgary and Lethbridge) and Maclean-Hunter, the owner of the second private television station in Calgary, CFCN-TV. Southern Alberta was a rich enough area for private stations to provide alternative service to a smaller centre such as Lethbridge. But the problems were not as soluble in other cities demanding service from both networks, such as Brandon and Moncton. In each instance, CBC stations or rebroadcasting stations appeared to be necessary, and the government was not prepared to finance them. Stewart attended meetings of citizens in both cities, but could not promise any immediate action. The meeting in Moncton was almost the last function he performed as chairman. He comments that the Moncton *Transcript* reporter correctly summed up the situation: 'Two main problems are holding up the second service – lack of a commitment from the Federal Government to meet the costs required in setting up a CBC station in Moncton – CTV must approve Moncton Broadcasting Ltd's affiliation with the Network.'[25]

A more publicized example of the intertwining of broadcasting decisions and party politics occurred as a result of the attempt by the owners of CKVR-TV, Barrie, to move their station into the suburbs of Toronto. Toronto, the richest market in Canada, was already served by the CBC station, CBLT, the CTV affiliate, CFTO, and by the independent TV station in Hamilton, CHCH. So if the Barrie station penetrated the core of Toronto viewers, the city would have not just 'alternative service,' for which smaller centres were clamouring, but triple or quadruple choices, in addition to the programs of the three Buffalo stations serving as outlets for NBC, CBS, and ABC.

The original owner of CKVR-TV, Barrie, was Ralph Snelgrove, who was also the owner of a radio station in the same town. In 1965 he sold shares in his television station to two others who had extensive broadcasting interests: Allan Waters, owner of radio station CHUM, Toronto, and co-owner of CJCH in Halifax; and Geoffrey Stirling, owner with Don Jamieson of CJON and CJON-TV in St. John's, and owner in his own right of radio stations in Montreal and Windsor. Snelgrove, Waters, and Stirling each had a one-third interest in the television station in Barrie, and all had important connections in the Liberal party. Snelgrove indeed had twice been an unsuccessful Liberal candidate, most recently in 1963.[26]

It was obvious that the moving of the television transmitter from Barrie to Toronto would enormously increase the potential audience,

25 / Stewart MS, 107.
26 / *Debates*, Feb. 9, 1966, 977 (Reid Scott).

and thus the advertising rates for the station. John Diefenbaker said in the Commons that he had been told the value of the station 'would not be over $2.5 million as it is today,' but that the minute it was established in Toronto, the station would be worth $6 or $7 million.[27]

Pickersgill explained that the proposal was for Snelgrove Television to transfer the channel of the existing station at Barrie from 3 to 5, and to establish a new station on channel 3 in Toronto. He expressed the hope that it would be found possible to have a third television channel in Toronto, 'because I think it would provide employment for a good number of Canadians; it would provide for a lot of advertising being carried on a Canadian station instead of on the Buffalo stations.'[28] Diefenbaker countered that 'this thing is so smelly it requires no olfactory excellence in order to understand it. It has got all the appearances of a plan to make millions under cover of secrecy and concealment.'[29]

In March, Stewart advised the secretary of state that the CKVR application appeared to provide for a third Toronto station, which would be inconsistent with existing policy.[30] Snelgrove Television changed its application to provide merely for an increase in transmitter height (from 820 feet to 1267 feet), and its removal from Barrie to Palgrave, Ontario, about half-way between Barrie and Toronto.[31] This enabled the Department of Transport to forward the application to the BBG as a simple change in facilities. Nevertheless, the board recommended that the application be denied, concluding that 'the effect of the proposed change would be to establish CKVR-TV as a Toronto station,' and pointing out that the station's coverage would thereby be increased from 219,702 to 2,134,137 people. The BBG announced at the same time that it would be prepared to hear applications for 'third' stations in Montreal and Toronto after February 1967.[32]

The Toronto newspapers had led the opposition to the Barrie station's transfer, arguing that it was the Liberals' way of getting even for the awarding of the second television station licence to a Conservative newspaper, the *Telegram*. They also suggested that a station near Toronto using channel 3 would cause interference with the two Buffalo stations on channels 2 and 4. This was enough to bring all the MPs from Toronto under heavy pressure to block the move. According to Judy

27 / *Ibid.*, Feb. 10, 1966, 1009.
28 / *Ibid.*, 1001; Feb. 9, 1966, 980.
29 / *Ibid.*, Feb. 10, 1966, 1007.
30 / Stewart MS, 428.
31 / BBG Public Hearing, Nov. 15, 1966, 14.
32 / BBG announcement, Nov. 24, 1966. 7–8.

LaMarsh, the Liberal members from Toronto were almost unanimously opposed, including two cabinet ministers, Paul Hellyer and Mitchell Sharp.[33]

But Snelgrove, Waters, and Stirling were not to be put off so easily. Since the BBG was prepared to hear applications for another station in the Toronto area in 1967, in June of that year the trio renewed their application for a change in the antenna site. They were opposed by radio station CFRB, which hoped to establish a television station of its own; by Gordon Keeble, president of CTV; by Niagara Television (CHCH-TV, Hamilton); and by the Ontario Department of Education, which expressed concern about possible loss of a VHF channel for educational television.[34]

All the efforts were not directed at members of the board. Judy LaMarsh claims that she expended a great deal of ingenuity in *not* meeting the three applicants, 'or their swarming agents.' One of these she identified as Pat Lavelle, whom she did meet, and who 'spent more time in Ottawa lobbying the Cabinet over the Channel 3 licence than he had when he had been working full-time for [the Hon. Allan] MacEachen.' She added that both Waters and Stirling were 'old friends' of Jack Pickersgill.[35]

In the BBG's June meeting, there was apparently a hot debate, reflecting a division of opinion that had been manifest the previous year. This time there was a new member, Ian Stott from Nova Scotia, who had been appointed only a few days before the meeting of the board. The BBG approved the Snelgrove application in a split decision;[36] several newspapers (and later a member of Parliament from Nova Scotia) implied that the new member's vote had made the difference.[37]

LaMarsh says that one part-time member of the BBG told her that an assistant to Paul Martin (secretary of state for external affairs) had passed the word to members of the board that 'the Governors' (the government?) would be pleased to see the application approved. LaMarsh was horrified to learn of the BBG's decision, 'and sat back to await the arrival of the application from the Department of Transport.' But she learned that only the minister of transport's approval was needed for a change of location in the transmitter. The whole issue was

33 / *Memoirs*, 248.
34 / BBG Public Hearing, June 20, 1967, 84–181: 298–412.
35 / *Memoirs*, 247.
36 / *Ibid.*
37 / *Debates*, July 7, 1967, 2382 (D. MacInnis). Stewart himself opposed the majority decision; MS, 433.

creating such a political storm, however, that discussion by the full cabinet was inevitable, and the BBG's recommendation was not accepted.[38] The transmitter remained at Barrie, and Toronto did not get a third VHF station.[39]

LaMarsh believes that a lasting effect of the cabinet's 'reversal' of the BBG's recommendation was to change their earlier view, as expressed in the White Paper, that the BBG or its successor should have the final decision on such matters, 'with no right of appeal to the Cabinet' (*Memoirs*, p. 249). This is hard to reconcile with the actual text of the White Paper, which says on page 8: 'Licences will be issued on the authority of the Board itself, without reference, as at present, to the Governor in Council, but provision will be made for formal appeals to be made to the Governor in Council against decisions of the Board in the exercise of this power.' It is true, however, that the earliest drafts of the new legislation did not give the governor in council power to set aside the board's licensing decisions, whereas this power was included in the bill given first reading on October 17, 1967.

In the fall of 1966, the principal innovation for television viewers was the availability of Canadian television programs in colour. The Fowler committee had advised the governemnt to proceed with caution in authorizing conversion to colour telecasting, and the government decided that colour transmissions would begin in 1967, the year of the Canadian centennial. But it was awkward for the industry to introduce colour in the middle of a season, and on the advice of the BBG the starting date for regular colour transmissions was changed to September 1, 1966. Both networks began rapidly to convert their studios and mobile equipment to handle production in colour, and the CBC was authorized to install the necessary facilities in Montreal for the coverage of Expo 67.[40]

4 Review of the White Paper

Parliament resumed after its summer recess in 1966 on October 5, and on November 23 the White Paper on Broadcasting was referred to the

38 / *Memoirs*, 247–8. About this time, J.W. Pickersgill was succeeded as minister of transport by Paul Hellyer, Pickersgill leaving the government to become president of the new Canadian Transport Commission.
39 / Three UHF stations, including an educational television station, were licensed in Toronto after the CRTC succeeded the BBG as the regulatory authority.
40 / Stewart MS, 365–7; statement by LaMarsh, *Debates*, July 13, 1966, 7625–6.

standing committee. Gérard Pelletier, although he remained a member of the committee, stepped down as chairman because (we are told by Judy LaMarsh) he feared a conflict of interest since his wife did contract work as a writer for CBC programs.[41] The chairman was now Robert Stanbury, a lawyer from Toronto, who was a graduate in journalism and who had worked for both newspapers and radio stations before entering law school.[42] Another member of the committtee was Don Jamieson, who in a by-election held September 19 was elected as a Liberal member of Parliament for a Newfoundland constituency. Others in the committee with substantial broadcasting experience were Robert McCleave from Halifax, and L.R. (Bud) Sherman from Winnipeg, both Progressive Conservatives. There were twenty-five members of the committee, thirteen Liberals, nine Progressive Conservatives, two NDP, and one each for the Social Credit and Ralliement des Créditistes groups. The subcommittee on agenda and procedure (the standing committee) included the chairman and others, in the main, who supported a public service–social responsibility conception of broadcasting – Ronald Basford (Liberal), Gordon Fairweather (PC), and Robert Prittie (NDP).[43]

The committee's performance has been examined closely by Paul Thomas, of the University of Manitoba, who concluded that there was a low degree of partisanship involved in the committee's work. The divisions within the committee cut across party lines, and were based upon opposing views about the purposes of broadcasting. Thomas also suggests that the non-partisan atmosphere was due in part to the nature of the Conservative party's representation on the committee, in particular its leading spokesman and representative on the steering committee, Gordon Fairweather of New Brunswick.[44]

The hearings began on December 1 and concluded February 14, 1967 – fourteen hearings in all, compared with eighteen held to review the affair of 'Seven Days.' The future broadcasting policy was obviously the more important issue, and one might have expected its consideration to occupy more time, particularly since the White Paper had rejected the Fowler committee's main recommendations. Fowler himself was not

41 / *Memoirs*, 263.
42 / *Toronto Star*, Nov. 3, 1966.
43 / The term is used by Paul Thomas, in contradistinction to a 'commercial conception' of broadcasting supported by some other MPs. Thomas, 'The Role of Committees in the Canadian House of Commons, 1960–72' (doctoral thesis, University of Toronto, 1976), 193.
44 / *Ibid.*

called before the committee, as Sir John Aird and his fellow commissioners had been invited to appear before the first parliamentary committee on broadcasting in 1932.[45]

The committee was under some pressure to get through the hearings and bring in a report, so that the government could introduce the legislation that was already being drafted. The minister explained to the members, 'While we have been drafting legislation along the lines of the White Paper, it is far from locked up, and we do not intend to do that until we have had an opportunity to see the Committee's deliberations and to study them ourselves.'[46] It was fairly evident that the committee's work was intended, in the main, to provide further legitimacy to the policy decisions already taken by the government, rather than to contribute substantially to their development.

To a very considerable extent, the committee heard evidence from the same broadcasting interests who had already met with the cabinet committee during the preparation of the White Paper. There were few representations from the more general public. It would have been extraordinary, given these facts and the Liberal majority on the committee, if that body had not endorsed the White Paper in almost every respect.

Ten individuals or groups appeared as witnesses. J.A. Ouimet, and other members of the CBC board, appeared in three full sessions. Andrew Stewart and Pierre Juneau, from the BBG, appeared during two full sessions, and were questioned for only about three hours. The executive of the CAB appeared twice. Two guests from Great Britain appeared on February 2 and 3, Sir Hugh Greene of the BBC, and Sir Robert Fraser of the Independent Television Authority.

Other witnesses appeared only once: the executive of the National Community Antenna Television Association of Canada; the president and general secretary of the Association of Canadian Television and Radio Artists; the minister, Miss LaMarsh; and the only two organizations claiming to represent the wider 'public interest' in broadcasting policy, the Canadian Broadcasting League, and the Canadian Association for Adult Education.

Thomas has provided this assessment of the committee hearings:

The questioning was extremely uneven. There were trivial, time-consuming diversions, such as Mr. Johnston's (Social Credit–Okanagan) objections to the cancellation of the Canadian Broadcasting Corporation's program 'Butternut

45 / Peers, *Politics of Canadian Broadcasting*, 79.
46 / *1966–67 Proceedings*, 2035.

Square' and Mr. Ralph Cowan's (Liberal–York Humber) queries of the Director General of the British Broadcasting Corporation about the salaries paid to British footballers. By way of contrast, there were good, albeit brief, discussions of the commercial activities of the CBC, relations between the CBC and the regulatory agency, the Board of Broadcast Governors, and the problems posed for future broadcasting policy by the development of cable television. ... Few members, with the exception of the two New Democratic MPS, were prepared to criticize the performance of private broadcasters, although they had no difficulty finding fault with the CBC which received most of their attention. There were almost no challenges to the positions taken by the Canadian Association of Broadcasters, the lobbying arm of private broadcasting. The private sector's interests were also promoted by several MPS having backgrounds in commercial broadcasting. Most prominent of these were Mr. Don Jamieson (Liberal–Burin-Burgeo), a former president of the CAB, and Mr. Bud Sherman (PC–Winnipeg South), a former news announcer in private television. Both were hard in their questioning of CBC officials, but later asked leading questions seemingly designed to enable CAB officials to present their free-enterprise philosophy on broadcasting. There was no attention given to a possible definition of the role of the private sector in Canada's mixed broadcasting system.[47]

Thomas points out that during the final weeks of the committee's hearings, attendance averaged about ten members, but these were perhaps the most interested and best informed. Effective questioning was conducted by four Conservative members, Dr. Brand, Gordon Fairweather, Robert McCleave, and Bud Sherman; by two Liberals, Don Jamieson and Gérard Pelletier; and by Robert Prittie of the NDP.

The witness who made the most sustained effort to change the direction of the policy proposals in the White Paper was Alphonse Ouimet of the CBC. As the first witness, he presented a formal statement of comments on the White Paper, signed by each of the eleven CBC directors.[48]

The CBC's point of departure was the proposition that the single-system concept, which Ouimet said was an objective in the early days, had now been replaced in practice by two separate and highly self-sufficient operating systems – a public system and a private system. The intermeshing and interdependence of the public and private sectors, on which the one-system concept was based, was fast disappearing. 'In

47 / Thomas, 'The Role of Committees,' 311–2.
48 / *1966–67 Proceedings*, 1347–51. Signatories were J.M.R. Beveridge, W.E.S. Briggs, Maxwell Cohen, M.P. Hyndman, D.M. MacAulay, E.B. Osler, J.A. Ouimet, Dr. Stephanie Potoski, J.G. Prentice, André Raynauld, Dr. Leonard Roussel. The memorandum was dated Nov. 1, 1966.

radio the programming services of the CBC and its private station affiliates have reached the stage of major incompatibility because of differing concepts and needs. A similar development in television is inevitable.' The one-system concept had been outgrown and could not be effectively regained.[49]

Ouimet pointed out that in both Great Britain and Australia the public and private sectors were kept separate. In the latter country, the Australian Broadcasting Control Board was responsible for the general administration of the total structure and for the broad performance of the private sector. The Australian Broadcasting Commission, with its own board, had full responsibility and authority for ABC programming policies and operations. Each board reported separately to the Australian parliament.

Regarding the Australian pattern as simpler, less confusing, and more easily accountable, the CBC directors recommended that the BBG be given full authority for the planning and administration of the Canadian broadcasting structure, including licensing; for general broadcasting regulations; and for the general performance of the private sector.

Although the BBG would be responsible for licensing, Ouimet thought it should not have the power to impose individual conditions of licence for each CBC-owned station. That would involve the regulatory authority too much in the details of CBC operation, and would overlap the jurisdiction of the CBC's board of directors. The CBC should be subject only to the general regulations of the BBG, which would establish minimum standards for all stations. Otherwise, the CBC would take directions from its mandate, the goals of CBC that were to be set out in the new legislation.[50] Ouimet did concede that, in the present stage, the BBG should be concerned with the terms of affiliation between the CBC and its private affiliates. But probably within fifteen years, private affiliates would be unnecessary; the CBC could by then reach the public directly through the use of satellites.[51]

The CBC directors objected also that the CBC could not achieve the program goals set for it if the commercial formula proposed in the White Paper was implemented (25 per cent of all television advertising expenditure in Canada and 4 per cent of all radio advertising expenditures). They asked for a decreased commercial requirement, and a corresponding increase of public funds. As for coverage, they said that five million Canadians received only partial CBC service, and one million received

49 / *Ibid.*, 1348.
50 / *Ibid.*, 1349, 1354, 1362, 1376, 1384, 1386–7.
51 / *Ibid.*, 1359, 1378.

none. In addition to an accelerated coverage program, they asked for a policy of designating the CBC as the next licensee in areas served only by private stations.[52]

The CBC directors' criticism of the White Paper was made public about two weeks after an unsuccessful dinner meeting they had with Judy LaMarsh and the undersecretary of state, Ernest Steele. Although it lasted for five hours, Ouimet had the feeling that LaMarsh rather resented having to meet the directors' strongly held opinions on policy aspects of the White Paper. The vice-president, W.E.S. Briggs, whose term was up, was about to retire, and on another occasion Miss LaMarsh referred disparagingly to the directors' decision to appoint James Gilmore as acting vice-president.[53] In her view, Ouimet should have quit the CBC himself – she makes no reference to Ouimet's staying on at Pearson's request – and she had no confidence in the other directors, who she thought were dominated by the president. When Pearson insisted on reappointing some whose term of office expired, LaMarsh insisted that the order-in-council remove any reference to the secretary of state, and in her book she comments: 'So they stayed, rubber stamps to the end.'[54] With this feeling building up between the CBC directors and the minister, they decided to argue their case directly before other members of Parliament, and on February 9, 1967, they appeared as a body before the broadcasting committee. Stanbury, the chairman, commented, 'I am informed that this morning we are making some form of constitutional history in that this is the first time the full board of directors of any crown corporation has appeared before a Parliamentary committee.'[55]

On the face of it, the CBC directors in 1967 seemed a group of considerable merit. To take four examples: Maxwell Cohen was the dean of law at McGill University, and later became co-chairman of the Canada-US International Joint Commission. André Raynauld, director of the economics department at the University of Montreal, later became chairman of the Economic Council of Canada. Margaret Hyndman, a prominent Toronto lawyer, was former president of the International Business and Professional Women. John Prentice, an immigrant to Canada from Austria, was president of Canadian Forest Products Ltd. in Vancouver, and later became chairman of the Canada Council. The

---

52 / *Ibid.*, 1350–1, 1379–81.
53 / Interview with Ouimet, Aug. 6, 1975. But in her *Memoirs* (p. 273), LaMarsh writes that Gilmore was 'an exceptionally well-qualified and able man.'
54 / *Memoirs*, 242–4, 273.
55 / *1966–67 Proceedings*, 1975.

questioning of the directors in the committee showed that on most basic issues they were in agreement – for example, on preventing an overlap between the authority of the two boards, on assured longer-term financing for the CBC, on the desirability of shielding the CBC executive from too detailed or too frequent surveillance.[56] One of the directors, E.B. Osler of Winnipeg, was not in favour of having the chief operating officer (in the current set-up, the statutory vice-president) as a member of the board; rather, he should be appointed by the board and accountable to it.[57]

Andrew Stewart explained that the fifteen members of the BBG had decided 'not to attempt to express a collective judgment on the White Paper,' but had left it to the three full-time members (Stewart, Juneau, Sim) to assist the committee by answering questions.[58] Stewart's initial statement drew attention to parts of the White Paper that would need amplification or clarification in the terms of the legislation. In his second appearance, Stewart spoke for the three full-time members, generally in support of a more powerful BBG, as promised in the White Paper. The three members of the board were convinced that the board should have knowledge of the CBC's plans for expansion, and advise the government on them; and it would have to be involved in the plans for CBC budgets, at least so far as capital items were concerned.[59] And, countering the CBC's recommendation, they felt the BBG should have the power to impose conditions on any CBC licence. It would probably become necessary to establish different requirements for Canadian content is respect to CBC and private stations: 'If general regulations of a quantitative character are to be enacted by the board, the board should have the authority to establish the minimum at different levels for the public service and the private service and that in amending the regulations affecting one element, the board should be required to give consideration to the relationship with the regulations as they apply to the other element.'[60] Where Stewart drew the line was in the general responsibility for the nature of CBC programs. 'On balance, we think it would be preferable if the CBC directors were held responsible for the quality or public acceptability of their programs.'[61]

If the BBG appeared merely to assume that the basic policies had been

56 / *Ibid.*, 1995, 1998, 2013–15.
57 / *Ibid.*, 2019.
58 / *Ibid.*, 1401.
59 / *Ibid.*, 1427–30.
60 / *Ibid.*, 1431–3.
61 / *Ibid.*, 1432.

decided, and to suggest refinements, the CAB spokesman was affirmative and laudatory: the White Paper on broadcasting 'represents the most thoughtful and objective public statement on broadcasting so far produced.'[62] The CAB was even cautiously willing to accept the proposal for conditions of licence, which they had opposed when the Fowler Committee had advanced the idea. The president, Jean Pouliot, summarized the CAB's comments in these terms:

1. In view of the rapidly expanding and changing technology of broadcasting, there is urgent need for further formal consultations and agreements at the international level.
2. The impartial agency of regulation advocated by the White Paper, and with the structure it recommends, is the most practical and effective system for achieving objectives of public policy that appear to find general agreement.
3. The White Paper recommendations for extension of television broadcasting service are soundly based.
4. Conditions of licence, if adopted in the form recommended by the White Paper, should take into account all the factors we have mentioned and make due allowance for all of these. In the area of ownership, station's operating record should be the major factor taken into account by the Board of Broadcast Governors when assessment is being made of the public interest at the time of issue or renewal of a licence.
5. The recommendations of the White Paper on instructional television and those on community antenna television and related systems are sound and practical.
6. The White Paper's recommendations relative to the Canadian Broadcasting Corporation are in the main sound, although its recommendations concerning the CBC's commercial policy need clarification.
7. The political section (17) of the Broadcasting Act requires modification.
8. The position of broadcasting as an integral part of the press and the information agencies of Canada should be recognized clearly in any new legislation.[63]

There were two issues that the CAB thought needed further study. One was the matter of penalties for stations breaking regulations. Here they would have preferred the possibility of appealing a BBG decision to the courts on questions of fact as well as of law. The second issue was the proposal that the BBG become the licensing authority, with the right of appeal to the cabinet. On the whole, the CAB preferred the present arrangement, by which the BBG made recommendations to the Depart-

62 / *Ibid.*, 1450.
63 / *Ibid.*, 1451–2; written submission on 1543–52.

ment of Transport.[64] Pouliot also cautioned that in some cases the public interest, and the interest of a board of directors for the CBC, might differ. For example, the CBC might prefer to have a station in each city across Canada, whereas the public interest might require that service be given by an affiliated station.[65]

Following the CAB, the committee heard three other organized interest groups who had not achieved the degree of official recognition accorded the CAB: the National Community Antenna Television Association of Canada, the Canadian Broadcasting League, and the Association of Canadian Television and Radio Artists.

The National Community Antenna Television Association (later re-named the Canadian Cable Television Association) appeared before the committee for four hours, a longer period of time than had been given to the examination of the BBG. The association's position remained very much as it had been stated in previous inquiries presided over by the BBG (in 1960–1 and 1964).[66] In their appearance before the broadcasting committee in 1967, the cable operators maintained that a distinction must be maintained between transmission and reception, and that it would be dangerous to permit the same authority to control transmission (broadcasting) and that which may be received. The CATV industry was 'already more than adequately regulated under the Radio Act' by the Department of Transport. The public must have the unfettered right to listen to and view stations of their choice, and this right should be recognized in law.[67] The cable operators found a stout defender of their interests, in the committee and on the floor of the House of Commons, in Ralph Cowan, a Liberal from Toronto whose other chief concern was opposition to the CBC.

The Association of Canadian Television and Radio Artists (ACTRA), representing English-language performers and writers, had started a campaign over two years before to press for more emphasis on Canadian objectives for the broadcasting system, more Canadian programming, and more use of Canadian artists and writers. In 1964 the association had presented a forty-page brief to the Fowler Committee, in 1965 a brief to the minister of finance on methods of encouragement for the broadcast-ing industry, and in 1966 a brief to the secretary of state prior to the appearance of the White Paper.[68] As the newsletter of ACTRA

64 / *Ibid.*, 1452–3, 1469, 1484, 1500.
65 / *Ibid.*, 1484.
66 / Stewart MS, 338–9, 349–50.
67 / *1966–67 Proceedings*, 1621–2.
68 / *Ibid.*, 1717 (Henry Comor).

(November 1967) explained, 'These presentations were supplemented by personal contact with the Board of Broadcast Governors, many members of Parliament (particularly members of the Standing Committee on Broadcasting, Films and Assistance to the Arts) and to the Secretary of State and her staff.'

In its brief to the committee, ACTRA said that the broadcasting act should specify that Canadian broadcasting should be Canadian, that imported programs should be kept to a minimum. The CBC should be financed by a per-capita grant for five-year periods. The government should purchase all transmission facilities of CTV and its affiliated stations, and issue franchises to 'program producers.' The Canadian content requirements should be increased to 75 per cent for CBC, and 65 per cent for CTV and private television stations. Private broadcasters should be more strictly regulated.[69]

The Canadian Broadcasting League sent an eleven-member delegation representing a number of its constituent associations. David Kirk, of the Canadian Federation of Agriculture, was the chief spokesman. Other organizations represented included the Federated Women's Institutes, the Co-operative Union of Canada, the Canadian Labour Congress, the Consumers' Association of Canada, and various broadcasting and other unions.

The league recalled that it had never been convinced that two boards were necessary, and had always supported the one-board system. However, if that was not to be, the Board of Broadcast Governors must have real responsibility for the performance of all parts of the system:

In practice, the objectives of the Board and the CBC should not, in fact, be sharply different, and we think it is in the interests of the CBC that it have access to the support, encouragement and advice of the Board of Broadcast Governors. Here the principle already referred to, of the primacy of the public sector, comes very much into play. This principle should, if at all possible, be expressed in legislative terms. This, in our view, does not mean and should not mean that the Board of Broadcast Governors would have, or should accept, the role of review or decision-making on operational programming questions which are the responsibility of the CBC.[70]

The league supported statutory provision for the financing of the CBC, and the CBC's claim that the commercial targets mentioned in the White

69 / *Ibid.*, 1720, 1724–5.
70 / *Ibid.*, 1567.

Paper would make CBC programs too dependent on advertising.[71] But on the structural relationship between the CBC and the regulatory board, it seemed that the CBC's old allies had deserted it.

Indeed, the league vied with the Canadian Association of Broadcasters in its praise of the White Paper:

> If we read the Paper rightly, its intent is that a generous, and challenging mandate and responsibility be given to the broadcasting system in Canada, in all its parts, to serve Canada with devotion, with imagination and with continuing drive toward excellence – and with rigorous adherence to the principle of independence from political control or supervision in program content. This is what the Canadian Broadcasting League wants, and there is no doubt whatever in our minds that after all has been said, it is what the people of Canada want.[72]

To a practitioner of consensus politics, such as Prime Minister Pearson, the warm support of government policy in a contentious area, from two such diverse interests, must have been balm to his soul.

5 *Comparing the Canadian and British Systems*

The broadcasting committee had decided to invite appearances by representatives of the Australian Broadcasting Commission, the Australian Broadcasting Control Board, the British Broadcasting Corporation, and the Independent Television Authority of the United Kingdom. The Australians were unable to come to Canada, but in early February the committee met with Sir Hugh Greene, director-general of the BBC, and Sir Robert Fraser, director-general of ITA.

The impression that each of these men left with the committee was that the British system was much simpler than the Canadian, and they preferred it that way. A newspaper writer commented: 'Sir High and Sir Robert spoke with one voice: the British system works perfectly. The BBC and ITA are both run by Government-appointed boards, both directly responsible to the same Cabinet Minister (the Postmaster-

---

71 / *Ibid.*, 1568.

72 / *Ibid.*, 1566. A supporter of the original Canadian Radio League in 1932–6, E.A. Weir, submitted a written memorandum to the committee; *ibid.*, 1789–99. Weir, the author of *The Struggle for National Broadcasting in Canada*, also submitted (Feb. 25, 1966) a long memorandum to Judy LaMarsh commenting on the replies of the CBC and CAB to the Fowler Report (copy sent to the author). He supported Fowler's proposal for a one-board system.

General), and both totally independent of one another.'[73] The reporter's use of the phrase 'responsible to' the minister was not quite right, because as Sir Hugh Greene explained, the BBC Governors were regarded as 'trustees for the public, trustees for the nation,' whereas the CBC board of directors thought of themselves as trustees for Parliament.[74] The difference in concept arose from the ways in which the two corporations were financed. The BBC was financed by direct levies on the listeners and viewers, in the form of licence fees established for some period ahead. The CBC was financed by annual votes in Parliament. In each case, an annual report was submitted to Parliament, but the BBC did not have to appear before committees of the British house to account for its stewardship. Sir Hugh said that the individual political parties had committees on broadcasting and information, and he was invited from time to time to appear before such party committees. He added that one of the ways in which the BBC was most lucky was the infrequency of inquiries to which they were subjected. The last inquiry (the Pilkington inquiry, 1960) recommended that the BBC should be given a twelve-year charter. The charter would expire in 1976, so he did not expect another inquiry until 1972 or 1973.[75]

At that time, the BBC had a monopoly in radio, so the question of relating the two public authorities, BBC and ITA, presented itself only in television. Sir Robert Fraser explained:

In some way, strange as it may seem to you, the organization of British Broadcasting, the institutions of British Broadcasting, are extremely simple, unconfusing and also, I think, stale. ... The first thing that you notice ... is that you do not really come across a body with functions comparable to those of the Australian Broadcasting Board of Control or your own BBG. It is, directly you look at it, a rather simpler picture. You simply find that there are two absolutely independent self-contained broadcasting services ... two self-contained television authorities, independent of one another ... with no kind of institutional relationship between them. ... The members of the Independent Television Authority correspond to the Governors of the BBC, and these members have a total and exclusive responsibility for Independent Television and none for the BBC.[76]

Sir Robert Fraser said that of course in this description, there was a

73 / Bruce Lawson, ''Broadcasting: a (ahem) British view,' *Globe and Mail*, Feb. 11, 1967.
74 / *1966–67 Proceedings*, 1817.
75 / *Ibid.*, 1817, 1823–7, 1836.
76 / *Ibid.*, 1848–9.

missing link, and that was the postmaster general, who as the licensing authority had to approve the use of frequencies and the siting of transmitters:

> The authority is, in ministerial terms, the Postmaster General. Now, broadcasting is so much an interest of parliament and the cabinet as a whole that when one says 'the Postmaster General,' one is in a way using a piece of shorthand. Behind the decisions of the Postmaster General, in terms of broadcasting policy, there will, much more often than not, in fact be a decision of the cabinet and behind that of course, a decision of parliament. ... [So] you do find that at the centre of British broadcasting there is a very powerful central authority taking decisions which affect both the broadcasting authorities ... and you then have two services each self-contained with its own separate authority. ... And you therefore escape what I know has been a restless feature in the organization in Australian broadcasting and what I suspect as being perhaps a restless feature in the organization of Canadian broadcasting, namely the deadly problem of the distribution of powers and function between the public corporation ... and this other agency ... the BBG.[77]

The principal reason that the Canadian structure could not be so simple was, of course, that in Canada the public broadcasting corporation did not own all of its own distribution facilities (or lease them from the government, as in Australia). The case for a single board in Canada, or for a regulatory board with some authority over all stations, depended on the existence of private stations to help distribute the national programs of the CBC. Although Sir Robert Fraser tried not to give advice in the Canadian situation, he implied that if an authority was brought into being primarily to supervise the private sector, it should have as little to do as possible with the supervision of the public sector.[78]

The British system, as Sir Robert said, had its own illogical and untidy aspects. The act under which ITA operated was fairly detailed in setting out standards that should be applied to the programs received from the privately owned production companies: that they should provide information, education, and entertainment; that they were to be balanced; that the ITA should be impartial in controversial matters; that programs must not offend against public taste and decency; and that advertisements must not be misleading. In the case of the BBC, however, programming standards were mentioned only in the preamble of the charter, which spoke of the great value of broadcasting services 'as means of

77 / *Ibid.*, 1849.
78 / *Ibid.*, 1855.

disseminating information, education, and entertainment.' The other basic principles, such as impartiality, were to be found only in a published exchange of correspondence between the chairman of the BBC and the postmaster general.[79]

It emerged also that the postmaster general had different powers in relation to the BBC and ITA. Sir Robert Fraser explained that while the powers of the postmaster general (acting for the government) stopped with respect to the BBC when the area of major policy was exhausted, the full catalogue of his authority was very much more substantial under the detailed statute applying to ITA. Ordinarily, on matters such as the spacing of advertising periods, he accepted the practices that ITA itself developed. Sir Hugh Greene added that, under one clause in the licensing agreement with the BBC, the postmaster general had a reserve power allowing him to veto any particular program. He had never used that power, but when an MP wanted to object to a BBC program, he had to phrase the question in the form of, 'Will the Postmaster General stop the BBC from doing something?' The postmaster general then would reply, in time-honoured phraseology, 'No, sir.'[80]

Neither BBC nor ITA depended on American or other imported programs in anything like the proportion that was common in Canada. ITA was limited to accepting one program in seven from outside sources, and on the BBC's two television networks, 85 per cent of the programs were BBC productions.[81]

6 *The Committee's Report*

The questioning of the two British visitors was an educational experience for the Canadian members of Parliament, but it probably did not change their concepts of what was appropriate for the Canadian system. They could reason that the conditions in the two countries were so different. As one reporter wrote: 'There is no affiliate arrangement in Britain; there is no two-language problem; there is no commercial competition because the BBC has no commercials; there is no distance problems; there is no real threat of foreign domination of programming.'[82] It might have occurred to the MPs that the force of the testimony was to support Ouimet's views on the need for the CBC directors

79 / *Ibid.*, Fraser, 1858, 1860; Greene, 1829.
80 / *Ibid.*, Fraser, 1880–1, 1890–2; Greene, 1892–3.
81 / *Ibid.*, 1819.
82 / Lawson, *Globe and Mail*, Feb. 11, 1967.

to have more independence, but there were few signs that there would be any drawing back from the course set by the government's White Paper.

In the final hearing of the committee, the minister made an able presentation, outlining the government's position, with an emphasis on the single system and the rather wider powers that would be given the BBG. But she stressed that the BBG would have no right whatsoever to give directions to the CBC board concerning individual programs or concerning a series of programs. There would not be a diminution of the CBC board's responsibilities.[83] However, a few minutes later, she implied that if a member of Parliament objected to something that was on either CBC or CTV, she would say, 'get in touch with the BBG.' She added, 'Somebody will have to have some control over both systems. It cannot, by the very nature of parliament, be exercised by parliament. A minister cannot run the CBC or the private system, and it seems to us this is the only way for an expert board to run it. I mean, run it in this sense, not manage it.'[84] She had in mind that the CBC would report to the BBG, rather than reporting to Parliament as it had been doing, except that its five-year budget would go before the House.[85] Even there, she expected that the BBG would defend the CBC's estimates.[86]

The NDP member, Robert Prittie, showed that he had been influenced by the arguments of Ouimet and the other CBC directors: 'I would like to believe in the idea of a single system, but ... I find it very difficult to accept. The president of the CBC has said that within a very few years allocating a certain amount of money a year you could extend both the CBC television and radio service so that the Corporation would have very little need for affiliates. It seems to me that if this trend continues you will have two separate broadcasting systems.'[87] LaMarsh did not reply to this point specifically, but suggested that the BBG and the CBC would have to consult about some things, and that in the end the CBC would have to take direction from the BBG. The BBG would also have to be tougher in its regulation of the private stations.[88]

During a week in March, the committee held ten closed meetings to discuss a draft report prepared by the steering subcommittee, and amend it. On March 21, the chairman presented the committee's report to the House.

83 / *1966–67 Proceedings*, 2038.
84 / *Ibid.*, 2046.
85 / *Ibid.*, 2044.
86 / *Ibid.*, 2063.
87 / *Ibid.*, 2045.
88 / *Ibid.*, 2046, 2048.

The committee accepted the statement in the White Paper relating to objectives and general principles – that the airwaves are public property, that they must serve *Canadian* interests, that the system should include both public and private elements, in which the public element should predominate. The committee said it felt strongly that it was not a proper function of Parliament or the government to be involved in the programming or the day-to-day operation or supervision of the broadcasting system. And it wanted to see a clear, legislative declaration of the pre-eminence of the public sector.[89]

The committee accepted the proposal that the BBG should amplify the broad principles for Canadian broadcasting laid down by Parliament. But the CBC also needed a strong board of directors, which should take responsibility for its programming. Both the BBG and CBC should continue to report to Parliament annually, but a major parliamentary inquiry into broadcasting should not be necessary more than once every five years. Although the BBG and CBC should have discussions about the CBC's budget, the committee recommended that the BBG should *not* assume responsibility for the budget.[90]

On almost all of the succeeding sections of the White Paper, the committee expressed its concurrence, making only a few additional suggestions. It recommended that the legislative definition of the CBC's mandate include a clear recognition that the CBC was the principal agency for carrying out public policy through broadcasting (p. 2097). It suggested that the commercial target for the CBC needed reconsideration so as not to interfere with the carrying out of the CBC's mandate (p. 2099). It concurred with the proposal for a statutory five-year grant. As for the private sector, it cautioned against an undue concentration of ownership or control within broadcasting media (p. 2095). It concurred with the proposal that community antenna systems be treated as part of the broadcasting system, and be made subject to the jurisdiction of the BBG.

Robert Fowler, considering it an 'excellent report,' wrote that it had 'affirmed and even strengthened the White Paper. The committee reaffirmed the notion of a single system, under the supervision of the BBG, and wants the role of the CBC to be the primary one in the system.'[91] Gordon Fairweather, the broadcasting critic for the Progressive Conservatives, said in the House that 'it was not so much a party position that was taken ... but a position on the primacy of public broadcasting.'[92]

89 / *Ibid.*, 2088–9.
90 / *Ibid.*, 2090–2.
91 / Letter, Fowler to Peers, April 3, 1967.
92 / *Debates*, May 30, 1967, 727.

Heath Macquarrie, another Conservative member, thought the report demonstrated 'the value of the committee system in our House of Commons.'[93]

The government was not ready, however, to submit the legislation to the House until after the summer recess in 1967.

93 / *Ibid.*, 745.

13 THE BROADCASTING ACT, 1968

WHILE THE WHITE PAPER ON BROADCASTING was under review in and outside the House of Commons, other preparations were being made in the BBG and in the office of the secretary of state, particularly for a new federal agency to meet the demands for educational television. The man who was asked to plan this undertaking was Pierre Juneau, the newly appointed vice-chairman of the BBG. Judy LaMarsh had persuaded him to leave his previous post with the National Film Board in Montreal on the understanding, as she later wrote, 'that if he worked out well I would do my best to make him Chairman of the new board when it was appointed. ... This was my first step in my plan to bring qualified, non-partisan people to broadcasting. Juneau proved my faith in him many times over in the intensive work he did in the field of educational television, and he set out to expand the Board and the facilities and the personnel to provide the service which the new legislation would require.'[1] But the minister did not inform Stewart of this master plan.

Several provinces, particularly Ontario and Alberta, were pressing to establish educational television stations. The White Paper (p. 13) proposed a new federal organization licensed to operate facilities that would carry programs 'to meet the needs of the provincial educational system[s] as determined by the responsible provincial authorities.' This plan was conceived as a way of getting around the policy (in effect some twenty years) of not granting licences to provincial governments or agencies under their direct control.

In December 1966 the government formally asked the BBG to develop plans for educational television (ETV) within the authority of the existing legislation, and to get in touch with the provinces immediately interested.[2] The government also decided to create a company under Part II of the Canadian Corporations Act with power to construct, operate, and hold licences for transmission facilities for ETV. But the attempt to

1 / *Memoirs of a Bird in a Gilded Cage*, 245–6.
2 / *Debates*, March 22, 1967, 14325; BBG Annual Report, March 31, 1967, 37.

introduce the necessary expenditure item met with opposition in the House, and the estimate was withdrawn. Diefenbaker's interpretation was that the government had decided to bring in educational television 'by the back door through an estimate. We stopped that. I feel that it should be under the c.b.c. and there should not be another member of this vast, increasing family of bureaucracy.'³

Nevertheless, Juneau went ahead with drafting provisions for the setting up of a separate agency for educational broadcasting, which the BBG assumed would be included in the new act. However, uneasiness was expressed about the ETV proposals in the standing committee on broadcasting, particularly on the role of the provinces. Robert McCleave asked the minister, 'Would there be any safeguard that a provincial department of education, for example, would not be able to use such public facilities for propagandizing?'⁴ The committee also had before it the CBC's expressed opposition to the proposal in the White Paper: 'With respect to the operation of educational broadcasting, our present view is that it would be wasteful, impractical and unnecessary to establish a new federal agency as the operator of this public broadcasting service. We believe that, in the CBC, a suitable one already exists.' Having called attention to the corporation's long and successful history of school broadcasting, in co-operation with all the provinces, the CBC added: 'Looking ahead, it is our view that the establishment of a second federal operating body in broadcasting could lead to a conflict of program responsibilities between the two public operating agencies.'⁵ In adopting the proposal for a separate agency for educational broadcasting, the cabinet had accepted the advice of the BBG.⁶ It was obvious that the conflict between the CBC and the BBG, and the disparity in the views put before the government, had not yet ceased.

The standing committee agreed to postpone its hearings on educational broadcasting until the next year (1968), but cautioned against 'any departure from the long-standing policy that broadcasting licences not be granted to governments or to agencies under their direct control.'⁷

When a new session of Parliament opened on May 8, 1967, the speech from the throne hinted that there would be two bills, one for the 'better regulation and use of broadcasting privileges and responsibilities,' and a second for the provision of broadcasting facilities for educational pur-

3 / *Debates*, May 10, 1967, 45; Stewart MS, 327.
4 / *1966–67 Proceedings*, 2052.
5 / *Ibid.*, 1351; brief signed by the CBC board of directors.
6 / Stewart MS, 320, citing memorandum to the minister, May 12, 1966.
7 / *1966–67 Proceedings*, 2096; committee's report to the House, March 21, 1967.

poses.[8] At the end of May, the minister confirmed that there would be two pieces of legislation, both to be introduced in 1967, and that the main act would be sent for examination by the committee on broadcasting.[9] The latter intention was fulfilled, but the committee's hearings on educational broadcasting were not held until February 1968, after the committee had reported on the main bill and the act had received third reading. The Liberal leadership convention in March, and the dissolution of Parliament in April, prevented the hearings from being concluded, and the bill to establish a Canadian Educational Broadcasting Agency was introduced to the new Parliament on March 10, 1969, but not proceeded with. When the new secretary of state, Gérard Pelletier, announced the withdrawal of the government's plans for a federal television agency, he acknowledged that provincial opposition, led by the province of Quebec, was one reason for the decision.[10]

As well as initiating the plans for ETV that proved so abortive, the BBG made other moves to increase its influence and to meet the criticisms of it offered by the Fowler Committee. Its report had said that the BBG had 'failed to provide itself with a sufficiently large and diverse staff and facilities,' that it should review more carefully the program standards of individual stations, and conduct research into broadcasting developments and the social effects of radio and television.[11] In March 1966, there were only 42 persons on the staff of the BBG; the next year there were 72; and at the end of its life, on March 31, 1968, there were 123 positions, including the three full-time members.[12]

To put more information at its disposal, the board hired a firm of chartered accountants to review and analyse the financial operating results of the privately owned television stations and the CTV network.[13] And in March 1967 the full-time members of the board authorized appointment of a consultative committee on program policy, as an internal committee reporting to the BBG chairman. The committee was headed by Juneau, with Patrick Watson (of 'Seven Days' fame, now an independent broadcaster) as vice-chairman. Two of its members were drawn from private broadcasting – Stuart Griffiths, of CJOH-TV, Ottawa, and Jean-Paul Ladouceur, associated with CFTM-TV in Montreal. One

8 / *Debates*, May 8, 1967, 4.
9 / *Ibid.*, May 30, 1967, 729–30.
10 / 'Ottawa scraps education TV plan made obsolete by technology,' John Burns, *Globe and Mail*, Nov. 6, 1969.
11 / *Fowler Report II*, 114–16.
12 / Information from BBG Annual Reports.
13 / *1966–67 Proceedings*, 1402.

member was from the program staff of the CBC – Harry J. Boyle, appointed later as vice-chairman and subsequently chairman of CRTC, the commission superseding the BBG. The committee of eleven members[14] met periodically over the next year, reporting on March 15, 1968, three days before Stewart's resignation took effect. Stewart was not kept informed of the committee's deliberations, and cannot remember having seen the report. So if the work of the committee brought practical benefits, it was not to the BBG but to its successor organization.[15]

But the main task for 1967 was drafting the broadcasting act and seeing that it became law. Judy LaMarsh was determined that it should pass by the end of 1967, 'even though we planned a short House Session in 1967 because it was the Centennial year.'[16] The place to begin was in the special committee of the cabinet on broadcasting. LaMarsh did not wait for the report of the Commons standing committee on the White Paper, but plunged ahead.

I   *The Bill in Cabinet Committee*

From LaMarsh's statement to the Commons committee on February 14, 1967, it was obvious that the government was not about to accept the CBC's proposal for a wide separation between the CBC and the authority regulating private broadcasters, or the pattern of independence exemplified by the BBC and ITA in Britain. McCleave told her, 'We were much impressed by the British witnesses and it seems to me that they have found a method of co-existence, which removes a lot of the difficulties that come about perhaps by personality clashes, perhaps otherwise, between the BBG and the CBC.' LaMarsh replied: 'I would think that the government's views are pretty jelled; because, following all this [the Troika and the Fowler committee] there was a cabinat committee and then a full cabinet, and I think this system is the result of the cabinet's best judgment of what it would like to see enacted in legislation.'[17] So it was to be an integrated system, with the BBG having much wider respon-

14 / Others were: Soucy Gagné, Montreal; Donald Gordon, Waterloo; André Martin, Ottawa; Robert Russel, Montreal; and two members of the BBG's staff, Ross McLean and R.B. Chiasson.
15 / The report was in three volumes: Book I, The Immediate Problems; Book II, The Long-Term View; Book III, Appendices and Supplementary Reading. The reports have never been made public.
16 / *Memoirs*, 262.
17 / *1966–67 Proceedings*, 2054.

sibilities, even to the extent of indicating to the CBC what kind of programming it should carry in prime time, and making recommendations to the government about the size of the CBC's budget.[18]

That this was also the BBG's understanding at that time is indicated in a letter written by Dr. Stewart on February 17:

It seems to me that the design of the new legislation, as this is emerging, is to place the BBG in the position of a buffer between Parliament and the Government and the CBC. The BBG will perform the functions previously undertaken by Treasury Board in reviewing and approving the estimates or budget of the CBC. I am less clear as to the meaning of statements made about programming. It appears that if questions about CBC programming are raised in Parliament, they will be referred to the BBG.

I share some of your concern about the workability of such a plan; but is there any other plan that would appear to be more readily workable?[19]

It seems, however, that the minister was not reflecting accurately the contents of the draft proposals for legislation that were even then being discussed in the cabinet committee. According to a draft act, dated February 15, 1967, the CBC was to submit its five-year capital program to the minister and the president of the Treasury Board for transmission to cabinet; and it was also to submit a five-year operating budget for approval by the governor in council, followed by a tabling of the approved operating budget in Parliament. Nothing was said about any prior approval by the BBG, although it would have the authority 'from time to time and ... on request by the Governor in Council, after consultation with the Corporation, [to] make recommendations ... with respect to the financial needs of the Corporation.'[20]

There are at least five preliminary versions of the broadcasting act that finally was given third reading on February 7, 1968, and royal assent on March 7. Three versions were drafts prepared for the cabinet committee; then there was Bill C-163, given first reading on October 17, 1967; this was reprinted as amended and reported by the standing committee, in December; further amendments were adopted by the House of Commons prior to third reading, leading to the bill as enacted. LaMarsh recalls:

18 / *Ibid.*, 2061–2.
19 / Stewart to Bernard Trotter, Kingston.
20 / 'Memorandum of Legislative Proposals on Broadcasting,' mimeo, 31 pp.

The Broadcasting Act plodded through all stages of Cabinet Committee, and then on to the full Cabinet. That sentence is written quickly, but the legislation wasn't so quick in getting over the hurdles. By that time, in my Department at least (and probably many others, including the lawyers from the Justice Department who drafted, redrafted, and drafted yet again) we were sick to death of the whole matter and would gladly have forgotten it. The Bill was finally printed and ready for the Cabinet's consideration. When it arrived there, most of the ministers couldn't care less. They didn't read it and sat through explanation and discussion with their minds on other things in their own departments. Not so Maurice Sauvé [minister of forestry, whose wife was subsequently to become minister of communications], who was determined to show the scope of his knowledge and intelligence in broadcasting as well. At this late stage he came up with the idea of splitting the c.b.c. into programme-making and facilities-building halves and argued loud and long for it, blithely waving off the year and a half of Government study and work, its tabled White Paper, not to speak of the interminable and repeated prior investigations and reports from within and without the House. After he had had his lengthy say, the Bill as presented by [the Cabinet] Committee was approved.[21]

During the preparation of the first and subsequent drafts, the minister and her advisers (chiefly Ernest Steele and Henry Hindley) consulted or received representations from the bbg, the cbc, and some private broadcasters. LaMarsh says that the discussions with the bbg on details of the developing broadcasting act were conducted mainly with Dr. Stewart.[22] In a thesis written for Carleton University, Robert Nichols reports information from the parliamentary secretary to Miss LaMarsh that the government relied a good deal on the expertise of Don Jamieson during the preparation and passage of the broadcasting act, to the point that some resentment was expressed among other Liberal mps.[23] Alphonse Ouimet has mentioned that most of the cbc's communication was through Steele or Hindley; the minister was very busy in 1967 with centennial events, and also by this time relations between Ouimet and the minister were somewhat strained. When a more fundamental policy question arose, Ouimet sometimes wrote or saw the prime minister,

21 / *Memoirs*, 262–3.
22 / *Ibid.*, 246.
23 / 'Interest Groups and the Canadian Broadcasting System' (MA thesis, Ottawa, 1970), 60. The executive vice-president of the cab, Jim Allard, recalls being in touch with the cabinet committee on four or five occasions. Other than the formal meeting of the cab executive with the cabinet committee on March 31, 1966, these were probably informal discussions.

having inferred that there was very little communication between LaMarsh and Pearson.[24]

The draft act reproduced in February 1967 was similar in structure to Bill C-163 introduced into the House the following October. Part I outlined national broadcasting policy; Part II provided for the establishment of a board of broadcast governors (renamed in October the Canadian Radio Commission); Part III provided for the Canadian Broadcasting Corporation and its financial support; Part IV (left unfilled in the draft) was to outline necessary amendments in other acts such as the Radio Act in line with the new broadcasting act; and Part V dealt with transition and appeal. Our attention will be on the first three parts of the act, since the last two parts were, in the main, technical.

The principal differences between the February draft and the bill at first reading affected broadcasting policy, the BBG, and the CBC.

Broadcasting Policy

1. The draft had made no mention of the responsibility of Canadian broadcasters to provide for reasonable opportunity for the expression of conflicting views on matters of public controversy.
2. It was not as emphatic in stating that all stations should use *predominantly* Canadian resources.
3. It had not specified that the national broadcasting service (the CBC) should be extended to all parts of Canada as funds permitted, nor that one of its purposes was to contribute to the development of national unity and the expression of Canadian identity.
4. Nor was the statement included that in any conflict between the objectives of the national broadcasting service and the interests of private broadcasters, the former must prevail.

These four changes in Part I came from diverse sources. The phrase about 'reasonable opportunity for the expression of conflicting views on matters of public controversy' may well have been prompted by the report of the broadcasting committee following its review of the 'Seven Days' dispute.[25] The statement that all broadcasters should use 'pre-

24 / Ouimet interview, July 2, 1975. On January 31, 1967, Ouimet sent an aide-memoire to the prime minister (copy to the minister) outlining the CBC directors' views on four basic proposals of the White Paper, and on the organization and composition of the CBC board and executive. Ernest Steele (interview, Aug. 23, 1976) has commented that the head of an agency such as the CBC has every right to approach the prime minister directly if the minister is óccupied with other matters or is not receptive to the representations put forward by the agency on a change that may affect its future.
25 / Robert Nichols, 'Interest Groups,' 140.

dominantly Canadian resources' paralleled the objective stated in the 1958 act that the broadcasting service should be 'basically Canadian in content and character.' The statement that the national service should be extended to all parts of Canada is a reflection of a promise made in the White Paper (p. 9) that the government would give 'the highest priority to the extension of radio and television coverage' through the provision of funds to the CBC for this purpose. The objective set for the CBC of contributing to national unity came from the CBC's own conception of its mandate, quoted on page 124 of the Fowler Report: 'It should serve Canadian needs and bring Canadians in widely separated parts of the country closer together, contributing to the development and preservation of a sense of national unity. It must provide for a continuing self-expression of the Canadian identity.'[26] The fact that concern was often expressed in Parliament about the supposed separatist tendencies of the CBC's French network may well have increased the government's determination to have this objective spelled out in the act.

The principle that in any conflict between the objectives of the national service and the interests of private broadcasters the objectives of the national service must prevail had been stated in the Fowler report (p. 12) and restated in the White Paper, in the words (p. 7) 'the place of the public element should predominate in policy areas where a choice between the two is involved.' So the changes made in Part I during the summer months of 1967 did not represent anything new, but were rather a more complete spelling out of principles that had been accepted.[27]

Board of Broadcast Governors (Canadian Radio Commission)

The change in name of the regulatory agency was indicated in the second printed version of the draft bill (the end of August 1967); in the first printed draft (of June 1967), the name 'Board of Broadcast Governors' still appeared. The purpose of the change was ostensibly to adopt a name whose initials would be the same in English and French.[28] It may

26 / This statement in turn goes back to the speech delivered by Prime Minister Bennett while introducing the first broadcasting act to the House of Commons in 1932. He spoke of national broadcasting as 'the agency by which national consciousness may be fostered and sustained and national unity still further strengthened.' Peers, *The Politics of Canadian Broadcasting*, 101.

27 / The lack of this provision in the initial draft was noted by the CBC board of directors, which in a memorandum dated May 11, 1967, commented, 'The paramount role and position of the National Service in the Canadian broadcasting system is not stated and does not appear to have been taken into account.'

28 / During the summer of 1967 consideration was also given to changing the name of the CBC to 'Radio-Canada,' in both French and English. Interview, J.A. Ouimet, Oct. 22, 1975.

also have been a sign that the Liberal government wanted to dissociate itself from the BBG and the 1958 act passed by a Conservative administration.

The most important changes in this section of the act had the effect of reducing the authority of the regulatory body over the CBC. In the original draft, the BBG was to have all the authority over the CBC that it had over private licensees, and a few added responsibilities as well. The CBC was so alarmed on receipt of the legislative draft that the directors arranged a meeting in camera with the prime minister on May 11 to expressed their objections. They claimed that the authority vested in the BBG was so broad and complete as to make a CBC board of directors redundant within what was in effect a 'one-board' system. They said the legislation as worded would give the BBG almost total authority over the 'mix' and scheduling of CBC programs, well beyond the proposals of the White Paper which appeared to limit the regulatory authority of the BBG over CBC to matters of 'general broadcasting policy.' They objected specifically to a section of the draft bill which gave the BBG authority to 'regulate and control all aspects of the Canadian broadcasting system' (section 15). The CBC directors argued that the CBC could not serve two masters at the same time, the BBG first and Parliament second, yet the CBC was to continue reporting direct to Parliament (section 45). In order to continue their protests, and to suggest revisions, the CBC directors appointed a sub-committee consisting of Dean Cohen, Miss Hyndman, and Dr. Raynauld, with Ouimet as chairman. This group met with an interdepartmental committee of officials (from the Prime Minister's Office, the Secretary of State's Office, the Privy Council Office, and the Department of Justice) on May 30, May 31, and June 1.[29]

When a second version of the act appeared in June in printed form, Ouimet found that only one or two of the CBC's major recommendations had been adopted. One of these, already referred to, was in Part I – the clause that in any conflict, the objectives of the national system should prevail over the interests of the private element. The other changes had the effect of reducing the powers proposed for the BBG. In section 15, the general authority outlined for the BBG was not to 'regulate and control' all aspects of the Canadian broadcasting service, as in the earlier draft, but to 'regulate and supervise' all aspects. The board's power to regulate the 'scheduling of programs' had been changed to 'make regulations ... respecting scheduling policy' for any category of program. (In committee, this clause was deleted.)

The CBC made known its continued unhappiness with the draft legisla-

29 / Information from J.A. Ouimet, Oct 20, 1975.

tion, and Pearson thereupon arranged for Stewart, Ouimet, and Steele to meet early in July. On a number of points, Ouimet and Stewart were in agreement, and the further modifications in the bill reflected some of their common concerns.

The power of the board to revoke or suspend a licence issued to the corporation was removed in later drafts of the act. The authority of the board to recommend to the cabinet on the financing of the CBC was also removed. And important new provisions were added to two sections of the act regarding conditions attached to CBC licences. In essentials, these provisions remained in the final statute. Under section 17 (2), (3), (4), the BBG was to consult with the CBC about proposed conditions, and in case of dispute, the CBC could appeal to the minister for a written decision. Under section 24(2), a finding by the board that the CBC had violated a condition of licence was to be reported to the minister, who must table a copy of the report in Parliament.

The other major change in the bill pertaining to the regulatory board provided for the appeal of a licensing decision from the BBG to the cabinet. In the first three drafts, the cabinet could review any decision of the board regarding the issue, amendment, or renewal of a licence, and could ask the BBG to reconsider its decision, but the board's conclusion would then be final. In the fourth draft, and in the bill presented for first reading, the cabinet not only could refer back a licensing decision, but could set it aside, according to section 23(1). This change was prompted, not by a representation of the CBC, but (as Judy LaMarsh explains) because of the government's traumatic experience over the proposed location of the Barrie television station.

The Canadian Broadcasting Corporation

The several drafts did not vary much in their provisions for the structure, objects, and powers of the CBC, although some changes were made following the recommendations made by the CBC directors. In the earliest draft, the corporation was established for the purpose of operating *a* national broadcasting service; in subsequent drafts, the reference was to *the* national broadcasting service. In the first version of the bill, the corporation was not 'an agent of Her Majesty' except in acquiring or disposing of real property; in later versions, for all purposes of the act, the corporation was an agent of Her Majesty, and the CBC was also accorded the right to expropriate land, and to acquire or own subsidiary companies subject to the approval of the governor in council. Further, the bill now allowed the CBC to acquire real property up to a limit of

$250,000 without the approval of the government, rather than to a maximum of $100,000 as originally proposed.

It is evident that pressure from the CBC led to greater changes in successive drafts of the act than did representations from any other quarter, but of course it was the CBC that had been feeling most aggrieved.[30] The CAB, and even the chairman of the BBG, were generally content with the legislation as it emerged. Although the government paid some heed to the CBC's requests, it did not bend before a number of the representations put forward by Ouimet and his board. The CBC had suggested dropping reference to the 'single system'; this remained in the bill. The CBC wanted the removal of the provisions allowing conditions of licence for CBC stations; these remained, but with the possibility of appeal to the cabinet. The CBC asked for a statement to the effect that the public was better served by a combination of publicly owned and privately owned stations than by any other arrangement. The government did not commit itself to this. The CBC wanted a clause in the act that would ensure a measure of continuity in the membership of the board. This was not included. The CBC directors also urged a stricter limitation on the power of the permanent members of the BBG, or its executive committee, than was set out in the act, and a stipulation that new regulations should be preceded by public hearings. The only alteration was a provision that 'reasonable opportunity' would be afforded licensees and other interested persons to make representations with respect to proposed regulations. The CBC suggested that the BBG be required to establish a consultative committee with the CBC (as it had done on its own initiative previously). The act was silent on this. And for itself the CBC wanted the power to hold public consultations regarding the national service. The act made no such provision.[31]

2 *The LaMarsh–Ouimet Contretemps*

On the same day that LaMarsh moved second reading of Bill C-163, remarks that she made in a television interview reflecting on Alphonse

30 / E.S. Hallman, CBC vice-president (programming), wrote the author, Oct. 19, 1967, 'The President has had long discussions prior to the final formulation of this legislation in concert with Ernie Steele and Henry Hindley. Although I have not been able to make any personal judgment yet, he appears to be about 85% satisfied with the arrangements which are proposed.'

31 / Information about the CBC's requests from a memorandum drawn up by J.A. Ouimet (Ouimet Papers).

Ouimet and CBC management created an uproar in the press and in Parliament. Because this incident, combined with the legacy from 'Seven Days,' had an effect on the atmosphere in Parliament and the progress of the legislation, we shall refer to it before proceeding with a discussion of the bill as introduced, amended, and passed.

During the 'Pierre Berton Show,' taped some days in advance of the night it was shown (November 1, 1967), LaMarsh said, 'Quite frankly I think there is some rotten management in many places in the CBC and with a little better management ... there will be money at least for necessary things.'[32] On a CBC program the same night ('Twenty Questions'), in which she appeared with the Conservative MP Gordon Fairweather, she was asked whether she herself would like the top job in the CBC. LaMarsh answered, 'Yes, but I don't think it's in the cards.'[33]

In the interview with Pierre Berton, the minister also said that she had been told there were too many separatists in the French end of the CBC, and that the CBC might be obsolete in twenty years with satellite communication beaming world-wide programs to the home. She confirmed that Mavor Moore, a Toronto theatre producer, broadcaster, and journalist, was being considered for one of the top posts in the CBC or the regulatory commission.[34] On the other program, she admitted that the government was having difficulty filling the posts of president and executive vice-president in the CBC, and said that the CBC presidency was, in some ways, a bigger job than that of prime minister.[35]

The *Globe and Mail* wrote editorially (November 3):

Miss LaMarsh is almost in the position of the chairman of a board of directors who announces to the board that business is bad because management is rotten. A chairman who made this excuse would deserve to be fired.

There is one other reprehensible feature of this statement. It is a kick in the teeth to every single CBC employee with a management function (no small number, we understand). Whatever their weaknesses, they do not deserve to be subjected as a group to this kind of sweeping, non-specific insult.

When challenged in the House of Commons, LaMarsh refused to withdraw her charge, but Pearson made a point of inviting Ouimet and

---

32 / 'Nobody wants to run the CBC, LaMarsh tells Tory,' *Toronto Star*, Nov. 2, 1967.
33 / Roy Shields, *ibid*. Late in April 1967, LaMarsh had told the Liberal caucus, and confirmed to the press, that she did not intend to contest another election. Arthur Blakely, 'LaMarsh Hint of Retirement,' Montreal *Gazette*, April 22, 1967. A CP dispatch four days later confirmed her intention to retire from politics.
34 / *Globe and Mail*, Nov. 2, 1967.
35 / 'Nobody wants to run the CBC,' *Toronto Star*, Nov. 2, 1967.

James Gilmore to his office to thank them and their colleagues for the excellent coverage the CBC had given Expo '67 and the centennial celebrations, telling reporters that there were good and dedicated people within CBC management.[36]

It is ironic, and indicative of the minister's irresponsibility in making the 'rotten management' charge at this time, that 1967 had been a particularly active year for the CBC, and many thought one of its most successful. CBC networks had provided many hours of centennial programs and coverage of special events, including Expo '67 in Montreal. The domestic output for these purposes average four hours a day (radio and television, French and English) for 365 days, in addition to the programs beamed to overseas listeners by the CBC's international service. The centennial and Expo '67 programs attracted large audiences. The CBC had established in Montreal an International Broadcasting Centre and a Centennial Technical Centre to service all these operations, and had initiated colour television in time for the celebrations. This was also the year of the Pan-American games in Winnipeg, which for two weeks in mid-summer also received intensive coverage. Because of the centennial and Expo, the CBC produced more television and radio programs during 1967 than ever before.[37]

Even in an ordinary year, the amount of CBC production was prodigious. The need to operate in two languages, the demand for regional programming, and the proximity of the United States with its extended broadcast day, explained why so much production was necessary. Ouimet told the broadcasting committee in 1966 that the CBC was the largest producer of television programs in the western world. Its TV output exceeded that of the BBC, at least until the BBC obtained its second network. The CBC produced more French-language programs than were produced by ORTF (the television organization in France). And taking the CBC's French and English output together, 'it is larger by far than any of the American networks, whether it be N.B.C., C.B.S., or A.B.C.'[38]

Ouimet also stated that CBC programs were produced at a fraction of the cost of the programs produced in the United States or in England; they were produced with fewer staff, and with greater output per studio than any organization he had mentioned. 'C.B.C.'s output per man, per employee, is also the highest we know of: per dollar it is also the highest we know of.'

Indeed, through all the inquiries, and despite all the complaints that

36 / 'Judy repeats: CBC management rotten,' *ibid.*, Nov. 3, 1967.
37 / *CBC Annual Report, 1967–68,* 1–3.
38 / *1966 Proceedings,* 666.

were heard, no proof ever surfaced that the CBC was particularly 'extravagant' or 'inefficient.' There were certain inefficiencies built into the use of scattered and cheaply constructed production facilities in Montreal and Toronto, but these inefficiencies resulted not from a failure of management, but from an unwillingness of the government to provide capital for consolidation and renewal of plant.

After LaMarsh's outburst, Ouimet addressed a letter to her, asking her to substantiate her charges, and made the letter public:

Such accusations are capable of destroying public confidence in a national institution which must have the respect and confidence of the public it was created to serve. ...

If your charges are correct, they must be confined to those responsible and the corporation will take appropriate action.

If they are not justified, then the reputation of the corporation and its people must be cleared at the earliest possible moment. ... It is essential that the corporation be given all relative information which may be in your possession.[39]

LaMarsh told the House that the letter was arrogant, and that the head of an agency could not require anything of the minister or the government.[40] In her memoirs (p. 266) she explains that she was not in a position to affect day-to-day management decisions within the CBC. 'I had made no bones for months over the fact that I found the current management unsuitable. Had I had the full confidence of the Prime Minister, Alphonse Ouimet would by then have been long gone from office, and one already familiar with the C.B.C., who could have sliced away much of the deadwood ... would have been ensconced in the President's office. ... I had done everything possible short of resigning myself and denouncing my Leader, but it hadn't worked.' She added that she was even unable to find out from Pearson whether Andrew Stewart was to be replaced as the head of the BBG.

With the minister's refusal to substantiate her charges, either publicly or in private, the CBC directors had a telephone conference on November 9 and arranged to meet privately with the prime minister on November 12. Among themselves, they decided against any action of mass resignation, but prepared a statement for public release expressing their profound distress with the minister's statements:

These statements, coming during the debate on broadcasting legislation, have added to the climate of political attack and uncertainty that has enveloped the

39 / Quoted by Erik Nielsen, *Debates*, Nov. 3, 1967, 3882.
40 / *Ibid.*

CBC from time to time in past months. When to her charges against Management and the Directors, there has been added the silence of the Government itself on the propriety of her statements, the Directors as the public trustees for the Corporation feel it essential to speak out. ...

Parliament has always intended the Corporation to be free from governmental pressures and interference and to have the autonomy and freedom from political intervention that is so necessary for independent crown corporations in general and for the CBC, with its immense mass media responsibilities, in particular.

The Directors reject categorically Miss LaMarsh's sweeping allegations concerning 'rotten management' and related unsubstantiated statements as being utterly without practical value and gratuitously offensive. ... The Directors hope that Parliament will, in the course of adopting new broadcasting legislation, express confidence in the future of the CBC and in the devotion, dedication and competence of those who serve it.

In the face of a provocation that may have deserved the response of a mass resignation, the Directors have decided to carry on with their trust and to maintain the stability and continuity of the Corporation until the new legislation comes into effect and the new Board takes over. The Directors hope to bequeath to the new Board a viable and vigorous CBC whose role remains vital to Canada and Canadians.

The statement, released November 13, was signed by nine of the ten directors. (André Raynauld was not present at the meeting.)

About the same time, newspapers reported that the prime minister had selected the new team to head the CBC, and had secured their consent to serve as president and vice-president. Although there was no official confirmation, a number of reporters filled in rather complete background details on each of the men, suggesting that they had received a full briefing.[41] Dr. George Davidson, secretary of the Treasury Board and a long-time associate of Pearson in the federal civil service, was said to be the next president, and Dr. Laurent Picard, a management expert and director of l'Ecole des Hautes Etudes Commerciales, the next vice-president of the CBC.

The dispute raging between LaMarsh and the CBC directors gave the MPs plenty of opportunity to express their opinions in the debate on second reading of the broadcasting bill. When opposition speakers tried to learn details of her charges, she indicated that her information was second-hand, but that she would try to bring together those who had given her the information and 'the new management.'[42] She told another

41 / 'Davidson, Picard likely to get top two posts in CBC,' *Globe and Mail*, Nov. 14, 1967.
42 / *Debates*, Nov. 6, 1967, 3922.

questioner that what she had learned in the past two weeks was 'very much worse' than the general weaknesses described in the Glassco and Fowler reports.[43] However, if she were to disclose sources, 'no secretary of state hereafter would ever get any information about what was going on within the corporation.'[44]

John Munro, parliamentary secretary to the minister of manpower and immigration, and a former parliamentary secretary to LaMarsh, said of the CBC president: 'He has made mistakes during his presidency; he would be superhuman if he had not. ... But I know of no Canadian anywhere in this country who is more passionately and sincerely devoted to a simple love of Canada and the cause of national unity than this very honourable man. He is one of the few who can live in either a French or English Canadian atmosphere and feel at home. He has led the C.B.C. through its most difficult periods of development and adjustment to new circumstances. He has served with a modest integrity which I find superlative. Above all, he has been a committed devotee to the concept of public broadcasting and its responsibilities; he has given his life to a realization of that concept. We owe him a debt of gratitude which cannot be repaid in words.'[45]

But the vigour of the counter-attack by Ouimet and his fellow directors also brought expressions of support for the minister, especially from members who at other times had been most critical of the CBC. A Vancouver Liberal, Grant Deachman, thought that the CBC should be packed up, and 'we should establish a new Canadian educational television corporation in its place ... two E.T.V. networks, French and English, from coast to coast.'[46] The former Social Credit leader, Robert Thompson, of Red Deer, Alberta said: 'Canada's national broadcasting system has come under the influence of a few who are determined to undermine the morals, break down family units and, yes, even the political thinking of Canadians, not through the open forum of normal political activity but rather from inside the T.V. studio.'[47] Erik Nielsen, the Conservative member from the Yukon, complained: 'For months, Mr. Speaker, Canadians were treated over the C.B.C. to an unending parade of drug addicts, black power advocates, prostitutes, purveyors of filthy literature, Nazis and pseudo-Nazis. All of the scrapings and leavings of society sooner or later turned up on the C.B.C. No one in the

43 / *Ibid.*, Nov. 3, 1967, 3890.
44 / *Ibid.*, Nov. 6, 1967, 3923.
45 / *Ibid.*, Nov. 3, 1967, 3880.
46 / *Ibid.*, Nov. 6, 1967, 3955.
47 / *Ibid.*, 3979–80.

C.B.C. apparently was able to exercise any control over what went on.'[48] M.T. McCutcheon, an Ontario Conservative, said the basic issue was, 'How can we control and, yes, cut down on the woeful extravagance of this juggernaut? ... It has been said that no one should criticize this sacred cow. But now the minister has and she has been criticized for her actions. I do not agree too often with the minister on other things but in this regard I have to give her full marks.'[49] F.J. Bigg, a Conservative from Athabasca, said he had read in the *Ottawa Journal*, 'Judy Stands Alone in CBC Uproar.' 'I want to tell you right now, Mr. Speaker, that she does not. (Hear, hear.) She represents a great cross-section of the Canadian people and their thinking on this matter.'[50]

In general those MPs who were prominent supporters of the new Progressive Conservative leader, Robert Stanfield – like Gordon Fairweather, designated as broadcasting critic, and Gerald Baldwin, soon to become the party's House leader – were more restrained in their comments on the CBC and more critical of the minister than were some of the 'old guard,' who continued to hark back to the leadership of John Diefenbaker. Erik Nielsen was perhaps typical of this group, but L.R. Sherman of Winnipeg also expressed their sentiments, at least on broadcasting policy:

My views are not the same as many of my hon. friends on the Conservative benches. ... I find it extremely difficult to share the sense of outrage which some members of this chamber obviously feel over her recent and celebrated remarks. ... It appears to me the hon. lady was saying no more and no less than many of us have often said on this side of the house about the CBC, though perhaps she used different words. ...

Anyone who has watched the proliferation of C.B.C. employees, anyone who has watched the C.B.C.'s annual budget spiral up to $143 million this year, anyone who has taken the trouble to compare the methods by which a private broadcaster covers an event with the methods employed by the C.B.C., knows, Mr. Speaker, that there is some bad management in the C.B.C.[51]

Sherman supported the general terms of the new bill, but was dismayed by the provisions for increased fines on stations violating regulations. In voicing this criticism he was supporting representations being made to the government by the Canadian Association of Broadcasters.[52]

48 / *Ibid.*, Nov. 3, 1967, 3887.
49 / *Ibid.*, Nov. 6, 1967, 3980–1.
50 / *Ibid.*, 3993.
51 / *Ibid.*, Nov. 7, 1967, 4010.
52 / 'Threat of $100,000 fines assailed by broadcasters,' *Globe and Mail*, Nov. 1, 1967.

Their position was characterized by columnists Douglas Fisher and Harry Crowe as 'oddly cautious. ... Their long catalogue of minor criticisms seems to cover a determination not to block or slow up passage of the bill with a strong attack.'[53]

On November 8, the bill received second reading, and approval in principle. A Conservative amendment asking that the bill be sent back to the committee for study, which in effect would have killed the legislation, was defeated by a vote of 66 to 119. The bill was then referred to the broadcasting committee for detailed examination. The Conservatives had not won the support of members from any other party, although the Liberal maverick, Ralph Cowan, absented himself from the House.[54]

It was about this time that Ouimet telephoned the prime minister to set a definite date for his resignation. In a letter that followed, he recalled that fourteen months previously (and on several occasions since then) he had expressed the intention to return to a normal private life, but he had agreed to await the passing of new legislation. This had taken much longer than expected, but now, for personal reasons, Ouimet wanted to leave by December 15, by which time he would have completed thirty-three years of service with the CBC or its predecessor, the CRBC.

The prime minister replied that he was grateful for Ouimet's courtesy and consideration in postponing his retirement in view of the legislative developments, and thanked him for his 'untiring, unselfish and experienced service.'[55] Of Ouimet's thirty-three years in public broadcasting, fifteen had been spent as chief executive, either as general manager or as president of the corporation. These years saw the building and operation of one of the world's largest television systems, a more complete radio service, and a burgeoning northern service for communities in the Yukon, the Northwest Territories, and the northern areas of five provinces. Ouimet had contributed more to these enterprises than any other man.

Since the government was still not ready to announce that Davidson would be Ouimet's successor, and no statutory vice-president had replaced Briggs, the CBC directors appointed James Gilmore (formerly vice-president, planning) as acting president and chief executive officer. At the same time, the government announced that the annual budget of the CBC's international service, formerly handled as a separate item in

53 / Toronto *Telegram*, Nov. 3, 1967.
54 / *Debates*, 4055.
55 / CBC Toronto staff newsletter, Dec. 8, 1967.

the government's spending estimates, would be merged with the public grant to the national service.[56]

The minister was attempting to move the broadcasting legislation through its committee stages without delay, still in the hope that it might be given third reading before the end of 1967, or very early in 1968. On December 14, Pearson announced his own decision to retire from the leadership as soon as a national convention of the Liberal party could be organized to choose his successor.[57] The broadcasting legislation, however, was still one of his priorities.

3 *Amendments in Committee and the House*

The committee began its study of the bill on November 14, and submitted its report to the Commons on December 14. The report was given immediate consideration by committee of the whole, but their discussion was still in progress when Parliament adjourned for a month on December 21. The broadcasting committee held twelve meetings, with only government witnesses appearing before it: Judy LaMarsh, Ernest Steele, Henry Hindley, Fred Gibson who had drafted the legislation in the Department of Justice, and the deputy minister and two assistants from the Department of Transport. The steering committee again consisted of Robert Stanbury, committee chairman; Jean Berger, vice-chairman; Gordon Fairweather, Robert Prittie, and Alcide Simard (a Créditiste).

In analysing the broadcasting committee's proceedings at this stage, Paul Thomas concluded that the minister, Miss LaMarsh, showed a willingness to accept committee suggestions for improvements on points of detail, but not suggestions that would affect policy content. The changes in detail were on such points as pre-emption of time by the governor in council, the blackout on political advertising two days before an election, the limit of fines that could be imposed, and the size of the quorum for the executive committee of the new regulatory agency. But he points out that twenty-two of the twenty-six successful amendments were moved by Liberals, and seventeen of these were introduced by the minister's parliamentary secretary. Twelve amendments originating with the opposition parties were defeated, and most of

56 / E.J. Benson, president of the treasury board, *Debates*, Dec. 7, 1967, 5180; CBC staff newsletter, Toronto, Dec. 18, 1967.
57 / *Mike*, vol. 3, 309–10.

their successful amendments affected 'relatively unimportant details of the bill such as the title of the new regulatory agency, or were technical, correcting drafting errors, clarifying the original text without altering its substance, and bringing later parts of the bill into line with earlier parts which had been amended.'[58] Yet, Thomas concludes, the committee's work did not show a high degree of partisanship.

Two changes in the bill that went beyond the purely technical were these. In section 2, the final bill stated that the programming provided by each broadcaster should use predominantly Canadian *creative and other* resources. According to the minister, the italicized words were added as a result of a brief from the Association of Canadian Television and Radio Artists.[59] And in section 5, Part II, the committee substituted 'Canadian Radio-Television Council' for 'Canadian Radio Commission.'

When the report of the committee was before the House, Don Jamieson said that the bill was 'the best piece of broadcasting legislation we have had. It is far better than any of its predecessors.' He paid tribute to the former president of the CBC as a dedicated man who for his service to the Canadian people over many years deserved a great deal of credit. He added, 'I also want to say a few words of commendation, because they appear to be so rare these days, for the chairman of the Board of Broadcast Governors, and by and large for the actions of that board ... since it was established.' Its decisions had produced 'the best over-all system of broadcasting of any country of comparable size and geographic and language difficulties in the world.' He urged that the government retain the services of Dr. Stewart, at least during the transitional period.

He supported the provision in the bill that would bring cable broadcasting under the same kind of regulation as broadcasting stations. 'I think some form of integration between conventional broadcasting and cable systems is the answer if we are going to direct the whole of broadcasting.' But he believed the bill still had weaknesses. The provision for large fines for a breach of the regulations was unrealistic. And there were too many 'outs' for the CBC in its relations with the regulatory authority. It should be made subject to this authority 'in the same way as other broadcasters.'[60]

58 / Thomas, 'The Role of Committees,' 192–3. See also Thomas Hockin, 'The Advance of Standing Committees in Canada's House of Commons: 1965 to 1970,' *Canadian Public Administration* (Summer 1970).
59 / *Debates*, Jan. 24, 1968, 5928.
60 / *Ibid.*, Dec. 20, 1967, 5675–9.

On January 19, 1968, while Parliament was still in recess, Prime Minister Pearson announced the appointments of George Davidson and Laurent Picard as president and vice-president of the CBC, effective February 1. Pearson has referred to his difficulty in making these appointments:

I thought George Davidson, for many years a Deputy Minister and then Secretary of the Treasury Board, had the governmental background and organizational ability we needed. He had a broad understanding of human and social problems and, I felt, a real appreciation of the importance of broadcasting. The Minister did not agree. For that matter, neither did George Davidson. When he was approached at the very beginning of our search, he said: 'No. I'm not going to do it. I've had enough trouble in the Treasury Board. Why should I go from one frying pan into another fire?' But I finally persuaded him.[61]

But in others ways, Pearson's authority was beginning to seep from him. The Liberals' inattention became evident in February when, during Pearson's absence from the country, the government lost a vote on an important tax bill. The lack of unity and purpose in the Liberal ranks may have contributed to the slow progress of the broadcasting bill when the House resumed, an attempted filibuster by a dissident Liberal member, and finally the dropping of the government's plan for the five-year financing of the CBC.

When the House resumed its sittings on January 22, the broadcasting bill was still under consideration, and some of the debaters were particularly garrulous. There were the usual complaints about CBC programming, mainly on three counts: that it was anti-American and too critical of the United States' presence in Viet Nam; that too many programs were sex-oriented and immoral; and that the French network was promoting the cause of separatism in Quebec.[62] Aside from that, a majority of the Progressive Conservatives seemed to be in opposition to the plan to finance the CBC through five-year statutory grants, and they had vociferous support from Ralph Cowan (Liberal, York–Humber). Cowan had his own axe to grind, since he was determined to remove cable television from the definition of a 'broadcasting undertaking' (sections 2 and 3), and hence from regulation by the broadcasting authority. Their combined efforts brought such headlines as these: 'Broadcast bill battle rages on' (Toronto *Telegram*, January 25); 'Liberals out to foil

61 / *Mike*, vol. 3, 191.
62 / For example, *Debates*, 5796–8 (Caouette); 5825–7 (Stafford); 5866 (Patterson); 5979–80 (Smallwood); 6075–6 (Thompson); 6157 (Noble).

Cowan's filibustering' (*Telegram*, January 31); 'Trying to be helpful, MP s get nowhere on Broadcast Act' (*Globe and Mail*, February 1); 'Cowan caught out of House; 29 clauses pass' (*Globe and Mail*, February 2); 'Guillotine time only days away as broadcasting debate goes on' (*Globe and Mail*, February 3). At one point, Miss LaMarsh said of Gilles Grégoire, a member elected as a Créditiste but who had left his party to become a separatist, 'The hon. member apparently has nothing else to do than impede the business of the country. He has said clearly that it is his intention to destroy the country and he is now starting, with the assistance of the hon. member for York–Humber, to destroy parliament.'[63]

The government sought the cooperation of other parties in setting a time limit for debate, through use of the 'guillotine,' but finally decided instead to drop the five-year budgeting provision (section 47 of the bill before the House). The minister said that a separate bill to provide for the financing of the CBC on the basis of a formula would be introduced in the next session, but in the meantime, the CBC would continue to have its operating requirements met on an annual basis.[64] (At the time of writing, the CBC is still financed through annual appropriations.)

This was clearly the most important modification made in the government's bill. To respond part way to the private broadcaster's wishes, the maximum fine that could be levied on an erring station was changed from $100,000 to $25,000 for the first offence, and $50,000 for each subsequent offence. The title of the regulatory board became the 'Canadian Radio-Television Commission.' The clause setting forth the paramount position of the CBC in case of conflct with the private element was weakened slightly by substituting for the clause, 'the objectives of the national broadcasting service must prevail' the words, 'it shall be resolved in the public interest but paramount consideration shall be given to the objectives of the national broadcasting service.' The other changes were minor.

One of the amendments the government refused to consider was offered by Robert Prittie of the NDP. From the objectives assigned the CBC, section 2(g) (iv), he wanted to delete the phrase, 'contribute to the development of national unity.' He argued:

I am sure the present minister and the present government have no intention to

63 / *Ibid.*, Feb. 2, 1967, 6319. Earlier, when Cowan was complaining about the cost of the CBC, LaMarsh put $5.48 in an envelope, the annual per capita cost of the CBC, and said she would send it over to Cowan if he agreed to 'shut up about it' (6021).
64 / *Ibid.*, Feb. 5, 1967, 6391.

engage in the witch-hunt against the people employed in broadcasting. ... However, under certain conditions of management this could be done. ...

We might as well be frank about this. Where do these words come from? They are not in the previous broadcasting act. They result, I am sure, from the fact that members of the government caucus have said we must get at these separatists in Radio Canada at Montreal.[65]

The minister in rejecting the amendment recalled that the Association of Producers in Montreal had made similar objections in a telegram sent to her on October 26. She had replied by letter on November 9, and following that exchange of correspondence no further objection or complaint had been received.[66]

Following the government's concession in the matter of financing, the remaining clauses in the bill were quickly approved. After the minister moved third reading, Cowan moved to refer the bill back to committee to reconsider clause 28 (political broadcasts), but his motion was defeated 107 to 89.[67] The bill received third reading on February 7, with no recorded vote.[68]

On February 13 the bill was introduced in the Senate by Senator Keith Davey, who affirmed that in Canada public broadcasting and private broadcasting were each better off because of the existence of the other, and he said this after having spent eleven years at a private station in Toronto.[69] He explained the reason for including cable systems ('a broadcasting receiving undertaking') within the provisions of the act in this way: 'If a television advertiser is able to saturate a market by advertising on a station three – or four – hundred miles away, which then through community antenna television is seen in a particular area, that advertiser will not think it necessary, or essential or even desirable to buy radio and/or television advertising in the area which his message has reached by the community antenna system.'[70]

Senator Allister Grosart, a former advertising executive and national director of the Progressive Conservative party for five years, believed there was 'general agreement on this important bill.' It represented a 'sincere, thoughtful and thoroughgoing attempt to meet the problems

65 / *Ibid.*, Jan. 29, 1968, 6086. The 'national unity' phrase had actually been in the CBC's statement of its mandate.
66 / *Ibid.*, 6087.
67 / *Ibid.*, Feb. 7, 1968, 6468.
68 / *Ibid.*, 6471.
69 / Senate *Debates*, 821, 830.
70 / *Ibid.*, 823.

which have been created by the breakdown of control by Parliament, the Government, the B.B.G., and the C.B.C. management of both the expenditures and programming in one essential part of our broadcasting system, namely the public sector.'[71]

The bill was examined in the Senate committee on transport and communications, at which LaMarsh, Stewart, and the new president of the CBC, George Davidson, all appeared as witnesses. The CAB had submitted a written brief. Davidson attempted to secure an amendment favoured by both the CAB and the CBC, to remove one of the powers to be given the new regulatory authority, the CRTC. This power had been added to the bill in the House of Commons prior to third reading. To the clause in section 16 enabling the CRTC to make regulations respecting standards of programs, there had been added the words, 'and the allocation of broadcasting time for the purpose of giving effect to paragraph (d) of section 2.' The CAB and the CBC were concerned that this would allow the commission to get into the details of allocating specific times for particular programs; and this, Davidson said, could 'conceivably affect the ability of the corporation or of any broadcasting enterprise to schedule its own programs in a way that is going to make it possible for it to maintain a viable financial operation.'[72] Senator Grosart suggested that possibly the CAB and the CBC were too alarmed about that interpretation, and the government leader in the Senate, Senator Connolly, reported that the minister was not in favour of any deletion. The committee reported the bill without amendment.[73]

A Progressive Conservative senator, Jacques Flynn, wanted to delete section 2(i), a declaration that 'facilities should be provided within the Canadian broadcasting system for educational broadcasting.' He cited the declared opposition of Premier Johnson of Quebec to the proposed bill on educational broadcasting, on the grounds that education was a provincial responsibility, and that television was something in which Quebec had a special responsibility in safeguarding French cultural interests.[74] Senator Connolly argued that there must be a distinction between broadcasting transmission, which the courts had held to be a federal responsibility, and the preparation and use of educational pro-

---

71 / *Ibid.*, 857.

72 / Senate Standing Committee on Transport and Communications, *Proceedings*, Feb. 20, 1968, 55.

73 / Senate *Debates*, Feb. 20, 1968, 887.

74 / *Ibid.*, Feb. 26, 1968, 918. The text of Premier Johnson's letter was read by Senator Connolly, 920.

grams, which was a provincial responsibility if they sought to use it. In spite of this debate, the bill was given third reading without division.[75] The bill received assent on March 7, and was proclaimed April 1, 1968.

4 *Import of the Legislation*

Except for the inclusion of cable transmission systems as part of broadcasting, the Broadcasting Act of 1968 was essentially an improved version of the act passed in 1958. There had been only incremental changes in policy. The minister, Judy LaMarsh, while proud of her work, recognized the similarities with the 1958 act. In answer to a question from Senator Flynn, she said:

Before this the c.b.c. was set up and, as it were, created its own mandate. This bill for the first time tells the c.b.c. what Parliament expects it to do, the general terms of course. Section 15 charges the regulatory authority with seeing that the c.b.c. lives up to that mandate. The regulatory authority is, of course, charged with other responsibilities so far as the system as a whole is concerned. Then again, it places CATV as a broadcasting undertaking under that regulatory authority. I think that is substantially it.

She added that it might seem a lot of sound and fury 'for not much, but that "not much" is the whole kernel.'[76]

Robert Fowler had intended a more fundamental change, in recommending a single board that would supervise and take responsibility for the entire system, public and private, but as we have seen, opposition from political leaders, the CBC, the BBG, and the private broadcasters was too great for the central recommendation of the Fowler Committee to find acceptance. Other elements in the public did not understand what was at issue, and probably did not care very much. Once the government had settled on its policy – one in which the political risks were not great – the arguments were on refinements and points of detail. Only the CBC, in an effort to protect its partial autonomy, prompted very many changes of substance.

If the new act was in reality an improved version of the former act, some of the improvements were nevertheless substantial. Senator Grat-

75 / *Ibid.*, 926.
76 / Senate Standing Committee on Transport and Communications, *Proceedings*, Feb. 20, 1968, 43.

tan O'Leary said, 'This act on the whole is perhaps the best Broadcasting Act we have been able to get over these years.'[77] Prime Minister Pearson picked out these features as his government's accomplishments:

The principal element of our new policy was the statutory settlement that the airwaves are public property and that all those who use them constitute a single system, a distinctly Canadian broadcasting system in which we might ensure Canadian ownership and control of facilities and encourage Canadian creative talents and resources. I was quite pleased about the way it worked out and considered that the new Canadian Radio Television Commission, replacing the Board of Broadcast Governors, was an effective piece of machinery.[78]

The declaration in section 2 of the 1968 act that 'radio frequencies are public property' restored something that had been missing in the 1958 legislation, as E.A. Weir pointed out.[79] The act of 1936 had stated, 'no person shall be deemed to have any proprietary right in any channel heretofore or hereafter assigned, and no person shall be entitled to any compensation by reason of the cancellation of the assignment of a channel.' The private broadcasters had opposed such a stipulation. When Pearson read an article by Bernard Trotter discussing the 1958 omission, he mentioned to his aides that the point about the public nature of the airwaves should be included in the new legislation.[80]

The statement in the same section of the act that all broadcasting undertakings constitute a single system was intended to answer the objection (by Weir and others) that the existence of two boards, since 1958, had brought into being a dual system, one in which the private broadcasters had almost *carte blanche*, whereas the CBC was constrained by its mandate and its dependence on the government for annual appropriations. As we have seen, both Stewart and Ouimet had concluded that there was a logic in carrying this separation further, to the point of having two boards that would be almost independent of one another, but the government had set its face against this.

The primary objectives for the entire system were set out in 2(b) and 2(d):

(b) the Canadian broadcasting system should be effectively owned and con-

77 / Senate *Debates*, Feb. 26, 1968, 914.
78 / *Mike*, vol. 3, 190.
79 / *The Struggle for National Broadcasting*, 357.
80 / Steele to Trotter, Feb. 16, 1967.

trolled by Canadians so as to safeguard, enrich and strengthen the cultural, political, social and economic fabric of Canada;

(d) the programming provided by the Canadian broadcasting system should be varied and comprehensive and should provide reasonable, balanced opportunity for the expression of different views on matters of public concern, and the programming provided by each broadcaster should be of high standard, using predominantly Canadian creative and other resources.

The inclusion of these stated objectives for all broadcasters, not only the CBC, but private broadcasters and cable systems as well, was thought to give the new regulatory authority the direction it needed to impose standards and conditions of licence that would have some meaning. It would help redress the balance between the declining public component in the system and the burgeoning private elements, or so it was hoped by some of the supporters of public broadcasting. It would help maintain the existence of a broadcasting system intended to serve Canadian needs despite the influence everywhere of American television and films.

The decision to bring cable television under the control of the CRTC offered a measure of protection for conventional broadcasters, but was regarded also as a way of ensuring that Canadian programs would be available to more people. Before 1968, the emphasis in most cable systems was on importations of signals from the United States.

The declaration in section 2(e) that all Canadians were entitled to broadcasting service in English and French, as public funds became available, was new, although the CBC had proceeded on this assumption for over thirty years. But now the government was giving further impetus to the extension of the two language services.

In prescribing those aspects of policy in which the government should give direction, the 1968 act was both more explicit and more realistic than the act of 1958. Now it was contemplated that the government would issue formal directions to the CRTC on the number of channels to be used within a geographic area, to specify channels to be used for the CBC or any other special purpose, or to limit the classes of applicants to whom broadcasting licences might be issued (section 22). As before, the governor in council would make the appointments to the commission, and to the board of directors of the CBC. The government could, through notice, require stations to broadcast any program of 'urgent importance.' As we have seen, it could also refer a licensing decision back to the CRCT for reconsideration, or within sixty days set the decision aside (section 23).

The minister of transport (later, the minister of communications) was to continue regulating and controlling all technical matters with regard to the construction and operation of broadcasting facilities, and his certificate was required before any licence granted by the CRTC could take effect.

The secretary of state, on appeal of the CBC, was to have the power to override any condition the CRTC imposed on a CBC licence, but such a decision was to be published in the Canada Gazette and tabled in Parliament (section 17).

In Part II of the act, the powers of the Canadian Radio-Television Commission were stated more clearly and comprehensively than those of the BBG in the 1958 act. The executive committee of the commission was to consist only of the five full-time members. The ten part-time members were to be consulted before licensing decisions were made, but the executive committee had the responsibility for deciding on new licences, renewals, suspensions, and conditions of licence. The concentration of authority in the full-time members made it less likely that the board would be paralysed by differences or divisions, and also more probable that consistent standards would be applied. The making of general regulations was still to be the responsibility of the full board, but they were to act on the recommendation of the executive committee.

Private stations were given a number of guarantees of 'due process' with respect to hearings, advance notice, publication of notices and decisions, and licensing procedures. Appeals could still be made to the courts on questions of law. For an infraction of the regulations, licensees could still be fined on summary conviction, but the minimum fines were not specified as the Fowler report had recommended. Instead, the maximum fines were set at a fairly high figure.

The CBC retained many, but not all, of its former powers. The 1968 act stated categorically that the CRTC was to regulate and supervise *all* aspects of the Canadian broadcasting system, and the CRTC as the licensing authority could now impose conditions of licence on all stations or networks – although, as we have seen, the CBC could make an appeal to the minister if it thought the CRTC's decision unreasonable.

By terms of the 1958 act, the CBC could prevent an affiliated station from attaching itself to another network for a particular program or short series of programs. Under the act of 1968, only the CRTC could prescribe conditions for the operation of networks, although the CBC could still make operating agreements with private stations.

The CBC's board of directors was increased from eleven to fifteen members, including the president, and the president was to continue as the chief executive officer. But the vice-president specified in the statute was no longer to be a member of the board of directors. He was to be chosen by the board on the recommendation of the president, and with the approval of the governor in council.

Otherwise, the CBC's structure and powers were much as before. To its great disappointment, it would continue to depend on annual parliamentary appropriations. To supplement these, it would continue to sell advertising on its stations and networks. As before, the CBC's annual report would be submitted to the minister who in turn would table it in Parliament. A change had been made in its power to buy or lease real property: it could do this without the approval of the governor in council up to a limit of $250,000, rather than the former limit of $100,000.

5 Appointments to the CRTC and CBC

There remained only the appointments to the new commission and to the board of directors of the CBC.

Judy LaMarsh was determined to make a clean sweep, so that, except for her recent appointment of Pierre Juneau to the BBG, each board would start off with a fresh slate after the proclamation of the new act. She had not got the appointments she wanted to head the CBC – Prime Minister Pearson had insisted on making those appointments – but under the new arrangement, the vice-president, Laurent Picard, would not be a member of the board of directors. So there would be fourteen new appointments for the CBC, and probably the same number for the CRTC.

With George Davidson at the head of the CBC, the likelihood was that the chairman of the CRTC would be a French-Canadian, although some influential advisers like Don Jamieson were suggesting that Dr. Stewart be retained. When the new act was about to pass its final stage in the House, LaMarsh got a decision from Pearson that Stewart would be replaced, 'and that he was prepared to accept Pierre Juneau in his stead.'[81] On Febraury 23, she met with Dr. Stewart and explained the government's decision. Her reflections on the prime minister's role are bitter: 'I resented, and still do, the necessity to swing the axe at the last possible moment, when it might have been done with grace and some chance for Stewart to make his own plans to protect his pride, many months before. It was yet another of the instances when Pearson left the dirty work to someone else.'[82]

Stewart resigned as chairman of the BBG on March 18, and Juneau

81 / *Memoirs*, 275.
82 / *Ibid.*, 276.

became chairman of the board for the remainder of the month.[83] On April 1 he became chairman of the CRTC. The other four full-time members were: Harry Boyle, a program supervisor in CBC Toronto, vice-chairman; Pat Pearce, broadcasting columnist for the *Montreal Star*; Hal Dornan, former press secretary to the prime minister; and Réal Therrien, a Quebec City broadcasting and telecommunications consultant. Part-time members included: Helen James, who had long experience as a producer and program supervisor in the CBC; Gertrude Laing, member of the royal commission on bilingualism and biculturalism; Northrop Frye, a distinguished professor at the University of Toronto; Gilles Marcotte, head of the Canadian literature section of the University of Montreal; and Armand Cormier, an industrialist from Moncton, New Brunswick. Only one member of the BBG in addition to Juneau was reappointed to the CRTC: Dr. Gordon Thomas, a physician from St. John's, Newfoundland.

The CBC directors were not as well known as some of the CRTC appointments. They included, Beatrice R. Hayes, past president of the National Council of Women; Yves Ménard, a business man and former advertising executive; R.B. Wilson, former major of Victoria; A.F. Mercier, former president of The Canadian Press; and Una McLean Evans, an Edmonton alderman. None of the part-time directors had any experience with the CBC, and George Davidson had been president only for two months.

To complete the change in the cast of characters, Judy LaMarsh resigned as secretary of state on April 10, 1968, and Prime Minister Pearson left office on April 20. The new secretary of state was to be Gérard Pelletier, and Pierre Trudeau the successor to Pearson.

Another era had begun.

83 / The third full-time member of the BBG, David Sim, resigned on Feb. 29, 1968.

14 EVOLUTION OF THE BROADCASTING SYSTEM IN CANADA

By September 1968, television in Canada was sixteen years old. The rapid expansion of cable systems in the 1960s brought new problems to the fore, but policies to deal with them had to be formulated within the context of institutions and legislation already in place. This is still so. The structures and ways of thinking which had evolved not only in the television years but during the previous radio decades may themselves have to be changed if the needs of the 1980s are to be faced.

In 1968 radio broadcasting was entering its fiftieth year. The first radio station XWA (later CFCF), the station of the Canadian Marconi Company in Montreal, had gone on the air in 1919. From that year onward, Canadian governments had to formulate national policies to accommodate new means of communication and to try to ensure that radio, and later television, would serve the public interest. Although policy developed through a multitude of executive and administrative decisions, the most visible markers in the evolution of Canadian broadcasting policy were five acts: the Radiotelegraph Act of 1913, the Canadian Radio Broadcasting Act of 1932, the Canadian Broadcasting Act of 1936, the Broadcasting Act of 1958, and then the Broadcasting Act of 1968.

In making their policy decisions throughout those fifty years, governments (and the agencies created by government) had necessarily to weigh alternatives. The government could act through the state to provide broadcasting services directly to the Canadian public; it could rely on private owners to meet public demand through the operation of the market economy; it could strive to achieve national goals through the imposition of broadcasting standards and the regulation of broadcasters, especially if these broadcasters were private operators; or it could use some combination of these three devices.

Beginning with the royal commission appointed in 1928 (the Aird Commission), the country's national goals for broadcasting were examined and restated periodically – by prime ministers and other political leaders, by parliamentary committees, by regulatory agencies, by successive royal commissions and committees of inquiry. Essentially, from the 1930s on, the stated objectives remained fairly constant, if not too precise, and their formulation did not arouse much dissent. They were given their most succinct statement in section 2 of the broadcasting act of 1968 (see Appendix B). But from 1932 it had been clear that Canadians wanted a broadcasting system predominantly owned and operated by Canadians. They wanted a system that would provide as wide a choice of programs as was practical, and one that would allow for a free expression of differing views on matters of public concern. The system was to provide programs in English and French, and serve all communities of significant size with both national and local or regional programs. The programming was to be of 'high standard,' providing entertainment, information, and enlightenment, and be capable of serving a broadly educational function. Cultural disparities between larger and smaller communities were to be reduced, and communication between Canada's widely separated regions and among residents of diverse backgrounds and origins fostered. Broadcasting was to stimulate and encourage feelings of Canadian identity, but at the same time to provide a 'window on the world,' through information about the outside world, and through the importation of programs – mainly entertainment programs – made elsewhere in the two languages most commonly employed in Canada. The intention, finally, was to have a broadcasting system broadly accountable to public authority for its performance, but without direct political control of its programs. There was a further objective, one not often explicitly stated: radio and television were to serve a commercial purpose, through the advertising of goods and services.

Of course these are, in many ways, conflicting objectives. We have had to find ways of living with them, or of attempting to surmount the inherent contradictions. The choices were made more difficult by the north-south tug on our habits and predispositions, and through the very proximity of the United States. Nevertheless, general agreement on objectives was achieved because they reflected Canadian goals and aspirations. The declared national purpose of broadcasting was what reconciled proponents of commercial and public broadcasting, and produced at various times unanimity among political parties in Parliament.

But if there was general agreement on these objectives, there was none on institutional arrangements to give them effect. It was obvious that some arrangements would favour one objective more than another, that some policy decisions would benefit certain segments of the populations and be a cost to others. Those most immediately concerned – the broadcasters themselves, whether public or private – were especially quick to appraise policy changes, and often tried to influence the outcome to their own advantage. They had the resources and the access for day-to-day lobbying. But major changes had an impact on larger groups – the rural population, or the residents of large cities; French-speaking Canadians, or the people of the western provinces; those who wanted popular entertainment, or others who valued information programs or more serious drama and music; those who welcomed a large infusion of American programming, or those who resisted it; those who gave priority to commercial uses of the media, or those who emphasized its potential for public service; those who liked stations to serve their immediate and local interests, and those who wanted to learn what was going on in places remote from them. These groups were not so often heard from. They were most visible when formal occasions were provided, such as during the public hearings of a royal commission.

1 Choices Open to Government

Although there were a dozen choices of broadcasting structures that governments might have made (see Appendix A), the principal options fell into four categories: one system, public sector dominant; one system, parallel services (public and private), subject to one regulatory board; parallel systems, separately accountable; a market-oriented system, private sector dominant. The full range of these options was seldom elaborated, since most people took for granted that the political circumstances of the time severely limited the practical possibilities. But two additional options did seem real for a time. Before 1932, a fully commercial system existed, but that choice in reality disappeared in the early 1930s. At the other extreme, a system of complete public ownership was recommended in 1929, but never tried.

Of the four options listed above, the first, with a dominant public sector, was chosen in the years between 1932 and 1958: chosen, but never fully realized. The second option was recommended by public inquiries in 1957 and 1965, but the suggested concentration of authority in one board was rejected by two different governments. The third option, of parallel systems, now found in countries such as Great Britain and Australia, was advocated after 1963 by the president and board of directors of the CBC. To the present, the third option has not yet received serious consideration in Canada, though it may again arise. The system now operative is a variation of the second option, but as a result of technological and other developments it seems to be transforming itself into the fourth option – a system in which the commercial ethos is dominant.

The decisions made in 1932 and 1936 changed the system fundamentally from one in which privately owned stations were licensed, regulated, and controlled (very loosely) by a department of government, to a system in which a publicly owned agency became the regulatory authority in broadcasting and also the principal supplier of programs, distributed through its own and private stations. In other words, the system changed (or so it would seem from the legislation) from a market-oriented system, in which the private sector was dominant, to a system containing both public and private elements, but with the public sector dominant. In comparing the changes effected in the two years, 1932 and 1936, it appears that the more striking innovation, marking a shift away from the private component of the broadcasting structure, occurred in 1932, with the creation of the Canadian Radio Broadcasting Commission (CRBC). The legislation of 1936 remedied some of the weaknesses in the 1932 act, and established in the CBC an agency which was better able to win public support and legitimacy; but the 1936 legislation in most respects did not alter a fundamental decision that the earlier Conservative government had taken to charge the public broadcasting authority with the carrying out of national objectives and responsibilities. In so doing, the Canadian government was moving away from the North American model of broadcasting established in the United States towards a model introduced in Great Britain and adapted in some other countries of the Commonwealth, such as Australia and New Zealand.

The only other change of comparable magnitude was encompassed in the legislation enacted by a later Conservative government, that led by John Diefenbaker. The 1958 act revealed a governmental preference for establishing near-equality of status between private broadcasters and the national broadcasting agency, both of them made subject to regulation by a new public authority, the Board of Broadcast Governors. It was a shift to what was still being described as one system, but it incorporated parallel services, public and private, under one regulatory board, although a second board remained for the CBC, with more limited authority. To some degree, the 1958 legislation reversed the policy direction initiated in 1932, though it by no means went all the way in turning back the clock. The 1968 legislation refined and clarified the intent of the 1958 act, gave the regulatory board more scope and a new name, but it did not represent any fundamental policy departure from that introduced by the previous Conservative government.

Over the years there were modifications in policy that did not always coincide with statutory innovations or statutory amendments. Sometimes they came from government decisions to restrict budgets, advance loans, or change the basis of financing the agency engaged in public broadcasting, or they resulted from a decision to authorize new station licences, whether for the CBC or for private applicants. Sometimes they came from decisions of the controlling agency or the regulatory board–the Canadian Radio Broadcasting Commission, or the CBC, or later the BBG. Sometimes they resulted from a failure, possibly deliberate, to carry out or enforce provisions in the act currently in effect. Some changes resulted from claims advanced by private stations which were not challenged by the governing board or the political leadership within Parliament.

From the outset, the refusal of governments to fund the CRBC or the CBC so that it could establish stations in all provinces or regions affected the limits of policy choice, and tipped the balance from the public service towards the private stations. Financial limitations on the public network steadily increased the dependence of the entire system on commercial revenues and on programming that originated in the United States. All these modifications can be traced through a rapid survey of the principal developments in Canadian broadcasting from its inception in 1920.[1]

2 Before 1932

During the first twelve years of radio broadcasting, the Canadian system developed along the same lines as that in the United States. The radio stations were usually established by small interests, often individual owners, although sometimes by newspaper families or manufacturers of electrical equipment.[2] The stations were located principally in the more populous sections of the country, where residents were likely to have high levels of disposable income. The vast majority of stations broadcast in English. Regulation of stations under the Radiotelegraph Act by the Department of Marine and Fisheries was minimal. The elements of the population, therefore, who received few benefits from the system resulting from the policies then in effect included rural families, people living in remote areas, the smaller and poorer provinces such as the Maritimes, and the French-speaking population. It was to the advantage of all these

1 / Influences that can be identified and assessed as affecting the nature of policy developments at any particular time are listed in the Appendix.
2 / Peers, *Politics of Canadian Broadcasting*, 16–22.

people to secure a change in the prevailing patterns of ownership of broadcasting outlets. But even in the larger cities, there were other dissatisfactions. Network programming was beyond the resources of stations at that time, and increasingly Canadian stations sought program services that were becoming available from the United States. All these deficiencies, together with a fairly general unease with the quality of program service and the increasing stridency of radio advertising, led to the appointment of the Aird Commission in 1928. It was to recommend modifications to the system, and specifically to inquire into the desirability of adopting something like the British system, where the publicly owned BBC had a monopoly of radio services, and was financed from the proceeds of radio licence fees.

The Aird Commission recommended that a publicly owned system be instituted, to be financed mainly from licence fees or public subventions, but with some provision for what was called "indirect" advertising, so that Canadian companies would be able to advertise their wares. The commissioners stressed the informational and educational objectives of broadcasting, as well as the nation-building potential of the radio medium. They concluded that 'Canadian radio listeners want Canadian broadcasting,' and their recommendations were intended to make this goal possible.[3]

Although there were one or two hints in the Aird Report that a few local stations of low power might remain temporarily under private ownership, the commission's choice was clearly that of a publicly owned monopoly, in the manner of the BBC.

With delays in implementing the report, caused by an election and a change in government, followed by a constitutional challenge from the provice of Quebec, a new citizens' groups, the Canadian Radio League, was formed to campaign for governmental action on the commission's recommendations. To meet demands for local radio service in many small communities, and to make the choice of public ownership more palatable to the Conservative government of R. B. Bennett, the league emphasized the desirability of licensing 'small, short-range local radio broadcasting stations,' within the compass of a 'single national system.'[4] This was probably the genesis of the Canadian pattern of a mixed, publicly and privately owned system, governed by a single public authority.

3 / Royal Commission on Radio Broadcasting, 1929, *Report*, 6.
4 / On the efforts and impact of the Canadian Radio League, see Peers, *Politics of Canadian Broadcasting*, 64–8, 76, 89–94; and Margaret Prang, 'The Origins of Public Broadcasting in Canada,' *Canadian Historical Review*, XLVI (March 1965), 1–31.

Opinion was mobilized behind the efforts of the tiny Canadian Radio League, and the various counter-proposals advanced by private broadcasters lost out. Their recommendations, in their most persuasive form, called for a continued dominance of the system by privately owned stations, which would be enabled to provide a nation-wide network service by the grant of public subsidies.[5]

With the vigorous campaign of the Radio League, assisted by many established organizations and a large proportion of the country's newspapers, the Bennett government decided that it might be a popular move to establish a national instrument for the production of programs and their more complete distribution. The government had also become convinced that only a state-sponsored system could serve Canada's national interests, as distinct from local and commercial interests. The result was the appointment of a special House of Commons committee to advise the government, and the preparation of a bill introduced in Parliament in May 1932.

3 *The Legislation of 1932 and 1936*

As a result of the policy decision in 1932, the publicly owned component in Canadian broadcasting was clearly accorded the dominant position. The agency established, the Canadian Radio Broadcasting Commission, was both to regulate and control broadcasting in Canada, and to carry on the business of broadcasting (sections 8 and 9 of the act). The persons who stood to lose from this first major policy change were the owners of private stations in the major cities, who had looked forward to increasing the power and coverage of the stations, and their commercial revenues; the advertisers, who preferred a system run totally according to commercial principles; and American network and radio manufacturing interests, especially NBC-RCA, which by the late 1920s had established hegemony in American broadcasting, and which intended to extend its influence into Canada.

The CRBC, however, was not as strong as it looked on paper. The commission could not expropriate private stations without the concurrence of the government; and it was never given the funds to establish large regional stations such as the Aird Commission had recommended. A combination of the depression and obstruction offered by those opposed to the CRBC's establishment was nearly enough to cause the failure

5 / Peers, *Politics of Canadian Broadcasting*, 81–2, 94–5.

of the new experiment. Nevertheless, it established a few of its own stations, it provided a national radio program service, and in cities where it did not own stations, it distributed its network programs through private stations which in effect became network affiliates. Still, because of the CRBC's scanty revenues, at the end of its term in 1936 the public component was still a minor influence in the total broadcasting picture. The Radio Commission did not have as much independence from government as the Aird Commission had proposed, principally because of the government's unwillingness to give it adequate or guaranteed sources of funding.

In spite of its limited success, public broadcasting still had its proponents and allies. The Radio League was intermittently active behind the scenes, and it was still supported by important newspapers and editors, some of whom no doubt were influenced by the desire to restrain competitors for the advertising dollar. These allies were influential enough to induce the new Liberal government in 1936, and especially the prime minister, W.L. Mackenzie King, not to return control of broadcasting to a government department, or to allow private station owners unlimited scope for expansion. Instead, by the 1936 act, the new public agency, the CBC, was given greater powers and somewhat increased financial support. The corporation had the advantage of more independent financing through a statutory licence fee, and a more effective buffer between the broadcasting operation and the government through the device of the public corporation. It is noteworthy that the principal terms of the legislation were recommended to the government by the Canadian Radio League, and especially by its two most active members at this time, Alan Plaunt and Brooke Claxton. In opting for this structure, the prime minister was showing his support for the policy recommendations of the Aird Commission, and indeed he is quoted as saying, 'We want the Aird Report, and this is the Aird Report brought up to date.'[6] King in fact seems to have overruled his minister, C.D. Howe, who wanted the regulation of broadcasting to return to his department. Howe's preference was to assign the CBC a purely operational function, and not to have it exercise any control over the private stations.[7]

The licence fee that supported the CBC was still too low to enable it to carry out all the functions envisaged by the act. After a struggle with the resolute minister of transport, C.D. Howe, the CBC governors gained the backing of the prime minister for their plan to set up powerful regional transmitters in the prairies and in the Maritimes. These actions together

6 / *Ibid.*, 183.
7 / *Ibid.*, 171–4, 178, 183.

with an improved service for French Canada, consolidated the support the new broadcasting system was winning almost everywhere except in the wealthiest areas and the most populous urban centres, such as Toronto and Vancouver. In these centres, the private station owners and some of the business interests still thought they would have benefited more directly if the government were not committed to a national broadcasting service, supported as was the BBC in Great Britain, by licence fees.

The suspicion that many people had of government participation in communication services, and the fear of partisan influence in particular, convinced the King government to adopt another feature of the British system: that was, to transform the national agency into a full-fledged public corporation, whose decisions and operations would in the main be independent of the political executive – the cabinet. But the British influence was not strong enough to induce the government to set up a totally non-commercial system. Here the government was influenced by the existence of private stations that had been on the ground since the early 1920s. To have confiscated them, or legislated them out of existence, would have violated the prevailing norm in favour of private ownership, and deepened the fears of those who believed that any government involvement in the mass media was a danger to liberal democracy. The policy-makers were also aware that Canadian listeners had been much affected by American programs, the pattern of broadcasting in the United States, and the availability of programs at seemingly no cost to the listeners. Retaining some private ownership in Canadian broadcasting, and financing programs in part through commercial revenues, seemed an advantageous way of satisfying those listeners who liked the American pattern, and who wanted the Canadian stations to distribute American programs that were so well publicized. The fact that Canadian sponsors often sold or manufactured goods under the same brand names as in the United States, indeed were often branch plants of American firms, only increased the inducement not to cut all ties with the American radio networks and the system in operation in that country.

In wartime, radio provided a more efficient and pervasive means of national communication than Canada had ever had, and this confirmed the government's preference for an integrated broadcasting system, in which public and private stations co-operated, but a system, nevertheless, that placed the CBC in the leading position, and made the private stations subject to CBC regulation.

Towards the end of the war, however, the near-unanimous support in the House of Commons for the bill establishing the CBC began to crumble. The close relations that developed under wartime conditions between the government and the CBC impelled the main opposition party, the Progressive Conservatives, to advocate the partial restoration of the independent status of private stations, and to advocate that regulatory authority be removed from the CBC. This course had been urged on both political parties by the organization representing the majority of private stations, the Canadian Association of Broadcasters.

With the conclusion of the war, television developed rapidly in the United States, and soon had its impact on border areas in Canada, such as Toronto, Hamilton, Windsor, and Vancouver. The need to decide how television should be conducted in Canada, and whether it should be entrusted to the CBC, private enterprise, or some combination of the two, prompted the government to ask a royal commission to make recommendations on the matter, as well as on the controversial question of whether the CBC should continue to regulate the entire broadcasting system. Both the CBC and private industry had urged the government to authorize the introduction of television and because of the pressures arising from the American head start, the government made its initial decision before the royal commission could even start its hearings. Television would begin, initially with the CBC, in English and French. Later private stations would be authorized in cities where the CBC had not established its own television stations, but they would serve as outlets for the CBC's national service. The television service would follow the pattern in radio – partly state-supported, partly commercial; integrated by virtue of powers exercised by the CBC under the broadcasting act of 1936; and planned so that it would reach the largest possible share of the Canadian population in the shortest time. To achieve nearly complete national coverage, station duplication would be forbidden. Market forces would not be allowed to provide several stations in the most populous and richest areas while none served outlying or less populated regions. The cities with more than one domestic service would be those whose population distribution demanded both an English and a French-language station.

The availability of CBC network service to all television stations encouraged the establishment of stations in smaller centres, and the returns from sponsored programs on the CBC network augmented the private stations' revenues.

The government's 'single-station' policy for television was announced by the minister, Dr. McCann, but the architects of that policy were really the CBC and the royal commission of 1949–51 (the Massey

Commission). The CBC had held off recommending licences for private television applicants until the government had been persuaded to advance funds for two CBC television stations, and when it found out that the government was unwilling to commit itself much further, the CBC chairman and its general manager devised a way in which public and private stations could be linked together, and coverage rapidly expanded. This policy initiative was not, as in the 1930s, suggested from outside the public service. The questions to be solved were too technical for most laymen to deal with, and by now the CBC was expected to offer leadership even in policy questions that were the prerogative of the government. Within regular government departments, there were few if any who could match the experience or technical knowledge possessed by men in the CBC. Even within the informed public, many could not understand how the 'single service' principle would assist the rapid development of television across the nation. They did not realize that the CBC's own productions and its imported programs enabled marginally profitable private stations to survive. But most of the private broadcasters understood, and those that received television licences were prepared to co-operate in the integrated system.

Up to the time of the report of the Massey Commission in 1951, the system that had been established received fairly general support. Some of the private broadcasters were unhappy, and had associational support from various chambers of commerce and some newspapers, particularly those that had, or hoped to have, broadcasting interests. But at the public hearings of the royal commission, the preponderance of evidence was that most articulate Canadians approved of the radio services, the structures, and system of regulation then in existence.[8] The government acted with alacrity to endorse the main recommendations of the Massey Commission, to provide the CBC with a stable and somewhat more generous system of funding, and to enact a few amendments to the broadcasting act that would help assure the private stations that they were a recognized and permanent part of the broadcasting system.

4 After Television

With the arrival of television, the costs to the taxpayer, as well as the potential rewards to private investors, were much higher. The struggle between the proponents of a predominantly public system, and a system

8 / *Massey Report*, 28–9.

that was mainly commercial in emphasis and basis of support, was intensified. By this time the interest group that had been instrumental in promoting the changes of the 1930s, the Canadian Radio League, had gone out of existence. With legislation on the statute books seeming to offer assurance that the Radio League's objectives had been won, there seemed little reason for the organization to continue. Its views continued to be expressed by such national organizations as the Canadian Federation of Agriculture, the Canadian Congress of Labour, the Canadian Association for Adult Education, and other associations on a more intermittent or ad hoc basis, but these organizations had their own concerns that occupied most of their time and energy. It was mainly on formal occasions, such as before hearings of parliamentary committees or a royal commission, or in response to some assumed threat, that these organizations sought to intervene. The burden of speaking for the interests of the system fell more and more on the CBC itself, with the result that at times it acted, and was seen to act, as an institutional pressure group. Even so, it was restrained by its own wish not to become embroiled in political controversy, and by its desire not to offend the private stations with which it sought to maintain co-operative working relationships.

As for the government, its support of the system it had put in place, and for the CBC as the central institution in that system, weakened as the 1950s went on. The Liberal minister through whom the CBC reported, J.J. McCann, remained a firm supporter. On the whole, the government did not show signs of wanting to abandon the 'single system' it thought was in place, but it was uneasy about the heavy costs of television, and possibly about the degree of independence displayed by the CBC in its programming policies – expecially when, as during the pipeline debate, the Liberal party was very widely criticized, and appeared to be losing public support. The creation of the Fowler Commission in 1955 was intended to provide dispassionate advice on the level and form of financial support that should be extended to the CBC, and also to suggest a regulatory system that would reduce pressures from the private broadcasters and their allies without, presumably, abandoning the principles underlying the creation of the CBC, or the reliance on it as the primary source of Canadian programming. It is probably safe to conjecture that, if a Liberal government had remained in office after 1957, the modifications to the system recommended by the royal commission headed by Robert Fowler would have been adopted. One board would have governed the CBC and supervised the working relationships and operations of all parts of the system, public and private. Whether these changes would have been much more than cosmetic cannot be so safely conjectured.

In 1957, at the time the Liberal government was retired from office, the broadcasting system seemed to be performing many of the things expected of it. The system seemed, in fact, rather stable, although no one knew how and when an alternative television service would be delivered to Canadians. In areas served by only one channel, viewer dissatisfaction was beginning to be expressed. Another problem was for the CBC to keep pace with the increasingly professional, and costly, programs turned out by American networks and film suppliers; if this were not done, Canadian audiences would be drawn in increasing proportions to United States stations which were now accessible to more Canadian viewers. Canadian television had a late start, because of the reluctance of the government to incur the costs of programming and distribution. That was a handicap which the CBC and affiliated stations had a hard time overcoming. In several important areas, such as southern Ontario and British Columbia, patterns of viewing and audience attachments had already formed by the time Canadian stations came on the air.

But the Fowler Commission's investigation gave the Canadian system a generally good report. In spite of complaints publicized in several newspapers about CBC inefficiency and high costs, television service was being provided to viewers at a cost no higher than had been projected when television began. Coverage was growing by leaps and bounds. Within five years of television's inception, service was available to more than 80 per cent of Canadian households, and about 70 per cent of the homes had installed sets. French network service was available to 85 per cent of the French-speaking population, and the English network was scheduled for completion, from Victoria, British Columbia, to St. John's, Newfoundland, by the middle of 1959. Although viewers complained about individual programs, and not all tastes could be met in the hours available, surveys showed that viewership was high, that in most homes the sets were turned on about six hours a day, and that television had replaced almost every other recreational activity in the time and importance accorded to it.

Observers found that in Quebec, especially, television had an avid audience. The signs were that it was helping to give French-speaking Quebeckers a self-awareness and confidence greater than ever before. There were probably somewhat similar effects among English-speaking Canadians, but the results were diluted by the presence and popularity of United States originations, whether these were seen over American stations or on the English network of the CBC. (About 55 per cent of CBC network programs were Canadian productions, but the figure during the evening hours of prime time, when most of the audience was likely to be watching, was much lower.) Although some programs were carried on both the English and French networks – for example, 'The Plouffe Family ('La famille Plouffe'), 'Concert Hour' '(l'Heure du concert') and special events – in the main the programs were separate, and few did an adequate job of reflecting the life and interests of the other language group. It was therefore doubtful how well the CBC was meeting the expectation that it should contribute to a national awareness of Canada in all its parts. Radio did a better job in bringing contributions from all of Canada's regions than did television, but even in radio the language barrier was hard to overcome. It had been imagined that the pictorial qualities of television might help to bridge the gap, but they had failed to do so, whether because of lack of interest among the program personnel in each network, or because of costs, or as a result of more fundamental divisions that were an inescapable part of the Canadian reality.

The mixture of publicly owned and privately owned stations in the Canadian system was an untidy arrangement, and not all parts of the country received equal benefits from the publicly supported broadcasting service. But, considering the expanse of the country, the uneven distribution of population, and the length of time over which the national system had been operative in each medium, it can be said that the coverage and the quality of service were surprisingly good. There were few signs that any sizeable proportion of Canadians thought the costs too high, or that the public component in the system should be dismantled. Indeed, there seemed fairly general consensus that the mixed system was appropriate for Canada. There was a widespread predisposition in favour of private ownership in most business undertakings, but also a realization that a publicly supported broadcasting service was essential to ensure nation-wide distribution, program production in two languages, and programs of a quality that could withstand the competition from the United States.

Before 1958, the most vociferous opposition to the regime in Canadian broadcasting was expressed in the larger urban areas of English Canada, where Canadian programs competed with those spilling over the border from the United States. Some viewers resented paying for Canadian programs when they could see three American networks, or American programs on Canadian stations. These viewers were sometimes reminded by newspaper writers that their taxes were also helping to support French-language television, and costly services to outlying regions. Such dissatisfaction was fanned by a small number of private broadcasters, some of whom had been frustrated in their ambition to secure a television licence. They blamed both the CBC and the government's restrictive single-station policy, and demanded that television in lucrative markets be opened up to free enterprise, and the competitive commercial system.

The agitation was supported as a matter of principle by many station owners, and especially by those not yet in television. To them it seemed manifestly unfair that the CBC, in commercial business too, should operate stations and at the same time regulate private broadcasters who were in some respects competitors. The Progressive Conservative party had for some years past seen justice in the private stations' case. The Fowler Commission did not agree with the proposal for a regulatory board completely divorced from broadcasting operations, but conceded that some distance should be placed between the regulatory board and CBC's management. When the Progressive Conservatives came to power, the time was ripe for change, and the only question was the precise form that the change would take.

5 Policy Determination in 1958

It is remarkable how few of the previous changes in broadcasting policy were inspired within government departments. In most areas of public policy, the senior bureaucracy has a key role in selecting policy alternatives for ministers and the cabinet, sometimes in terms that almost guarantee a particular policy choice. This seems not to have been so usual in broadcasting matters. The recommendation that the government create a public broadcasting agency originated with a royal commission in 1929. In the 1930s, those who insisted that the issue be resolved were a voluntary group of citizen activists, under the leadership of the Canadian Radio League. Little has been disclosed about the way in which the first Radio Broadcasting Act of 1932 was formulated. Technically, it would have been prepared within the then Department of Marine. But there is little doubt that Prime Minister Bennett made the principal policy decisions, although he accepted suggestions from a parliamentary committee, and drew on the advice of his brother-in-law, W.D. Herridge.[9] In 1936, Prime Minister King decided to accept the suggestions of the Canadian Radio League on how the broadcasting act

9 / Peers, *Politics of Canadian Broadcasting*, 95–101.

should be changed, against the advice of the minister, C.D. Howe, and the department over which he presided. We know that the resulting legislation bears a strong resemblance to a draft bill prepared for the Radio League by Brooke Claxton (who later entered Parliament and became an assistant to Mackenzie King).[10]

The decision in 1937 to limit kilowatt power authorized for any private station was made by the minister on the recommendation of the CBC, and the gradual abandonment of that policy after 1949 was also the CBC's recommendation. The CBC on its own authority made impossible any future affiliations between private stations and United States networks, and in practice it also prevented the formation of a private radio network in Canada.

The introduction in 1951 of a statutory annual grant to supplement the CBC's revenue from the radio licence fee followed a recommendation of the Massey Commission, as did the decision to continue the CBC's regulatory powers under the 1936 act. Subsequently, the government rejected the CBC's advice to impose a television licence fee, and it abandoned the radio licence fee. The cabinet chose to finance the CBC through an excise tax and loans from the government to support television development.

The decision to initiate television in Canada was wrung from the cabinet after an intensive effort by the CBC, and the particular pattern of co-operative development involving private station licensees (the 'single-station' policy) was arrived at with the CBC's advice. The policy of limiting CBC stations to six production centres was taken by the cabinet, possibly on the advice of a few public servants surrounding the prime minister, such as J.W. Pickersgill.

It was generally expected that the next policy initiatives would be taken by the Liberal government on the recommendation of a third royal commission, the Fowler Commission of 1955–7. But the elections of 1957 and 1958 changed that. The new Conservative government would not have the same commitment to decisions taken in the past, and several options might be considered.

In fact, an interdepartmental committee which included the chairman of the CBC did recommend that the regulatory authority suggested by the Fowler Commission be established. Such an arrangement would have tended to preserve the single, mixed system of the past, and would have avoided the divided jurisdiction of two boards. The fact that the interdepartmental committee had been created informally at the suggestion

10 / *Ibid.*, 170–5, 182–6.

of the Conservative minister, George Nowlan, who placed a friend of his in charge of it, helped to ensure that the committee's recommendations would be supported by the minister. But Nowlan ran into opposition from other members of the cabinet, and the decision was finally taken to create two boards, one as the regulating authority, and the other as the directors of the Canadian Broadcasting Corporation. This was therefore a decision of the political executive, and very much in the spirit of Progressive Conservative party resolutions.

The secretary to the cabinet (the clerk of the privy council) undertook the task of preparing the new legislation, assisted by a law officer from the Department of Justice. Drafts of the legislation were discussed with the chairman and the general manager of the CBC, and their representations helped to preserve some of the CBC's powers and prerogatives, but there were ambiguities in the respective authority of the CBC and the new regulatory body, the Board of Broadcast Governors.

The 1958 act attempted to preserve one broadcasting system, but to establish as parallel and more nearly equal the public and private components. Equality had been the objective of the Canadian Association of Broadcasters, and their proposal for an independent regulatory board had been supported by the Conservatives in the interests of even-handed justice. As if to emphasize the equal roles of the public and private services, the only section of the act outlining the national objectives for broadcasting, section 10, applied these in the same terms to 'public and private broadcasting stations in Canada.' Part II of the act said that the CBC was established 'for the purpose of operating a national broadcasting service,' but this was the only specification of its special responsibilities. The safeguards placed in the act for the CBC – some authority over terms of network affiliation, direct reporting to Parliament – were in the act on the CBC's insistence.

By giving the new regulatory authority the name, Board of Broadcast Governors, as suggested in the Fowler report, the government hoped to increase support for its bill in Parliament. Indeed Nowlan's speech in the Commons implied that Fowler's principal recommendations were reflected in the legislation. The spokesmen for the Liberal opposition realized this was not so, but neither they nor the CCF members attempted to block the bill's passage.

Aside from the new regulatory structure, the creation of two boards, and the changed status of the CBC within the system, the principal innovations in 1958 were the decision to make the CBC dependent on an annual vote of funds by Parliament, and the specification that, in future, stations (with the exception of those few that were already foreign-owned) must have at least 80 per cent of their equity in Canadian hands. This ownership provision had been recommended by the Fowler Commission, and previously had been urged on the Liberal government by the CBC, without success. The decision to finance the CBC through annual appropriations ran directly counter to the Fowler Commission's recommendations.

To the policy decisions of 1958, we should add the later decision to authorize the licensing of second television stations in eight Canadian cities, since this step was implicit in the government's program for increasing competition and providing an alternative service. The other major decision in 1959, prescribing a minimum of Canadian content for all television stations, was taken by the BBG in consultation with the minister. The Fowler Commission had recommended that the regulatory board should insist that private stations employ more Canadian talent, but it had said that general regulations setting minimum standards would be less effective than requirements tied to individual licences.

In assessing effects of the policy shift in 1958–9, it is easier to identify the benefits than the costs. Obviously the private stations, or some of them, gained materially. They also gained status. The communities that were given second stations – eight of the larger Canadian cities – gained, in that viewers now had additional program choices. A larger percentage of programs were now financed by advertising, so business firms selling consumer goods may have gained, and advertising agencies and commercial representatives certainly did. Film suppliers and television production agencies in the United States benefited, because more US programs were needed to fill the greatly increased television time. Canadian production personnel, technicians, announcers, film editors, reporters, and news editors had increased opportunities for employment, though the statistics did not show comparable increases in amounts paid to Canadian performers such as singers, actors, and musicians. The 'second stations' were not ready to produce or distribute such expensive programming as the use of any sizeable amount of Canadian talent would entail.

The most noticeable costs were to the CBC. Its audiences were reduced, and it had to compete for advertising revenues in the country's largest cities. To meet such competition, it had to modify its programming not only to preserve its own revenues, but to satisfy the private affiliates. It lost in other ways: in the coverage of popular sports events, for example, such as Big Four football. It lost some of its direct contacts with the public, as its board no longer held public hearings and remained unknown to the vast majority of the public. More subtly, the character of its program mix gradually changed. This was hardly noticeable in any two successive years, but over a period of a decade, the CBC television schedules seemed to apply more commercial standards, the programs became less distinctive, were less likely to appeal to minority tastes, particularly in prime time.[11] Within CBC ranks, some program personnel seemed to lose sight of the special responsibilities that the CBC had been expected to carry out, and made their program decisions rather on the basis of what would attract the largest possible audiences, what would sell, or what was in fashion in New York and Hollywood. If this observation is valid, then the Canadian people as a whole may have been the losers, because in essence they were being offered less choice under the guise of more.

Certainly one result of the added second stations was an increase in the amount of viewing of American programs, as the Fowler Committee of 1965 discovered and pointed out.[12]

Some outside the CBC, including Liberal opposition spokesmen, argued that the removal of its statutory basis of funding made the CBC more vulnerable to political pressure. The corporation's insecurity had an important internal effect on program staff: to make them more suspicious of higher management, and to lessen the support that the president should have been able to take for granted. This factor, added to the almost continuous series of inquiries to which the CBC was subject, weakened the institution and diverted the attention of management. The frequent discussion and criticism of CBC programs in Parliament was hardly helpful. The Fowler Commission in 1957 had hoped this would decrease as a result of its recommendations. In fact, with a government that often seemed to act as if it were in opposition, and later with lack of a clear government majority in the House, parliamentary debate and argument, often on peripheral matters, increased. The Fowler Commission had said:

In the day-to-day matters of administration and broadcasting performance, we suggest with great respect that Parliament should consider how it can best exercise supervision of the broadcasting system. Perhaps the situation is covered by the old saying that if you keep a dog you should not try to do your own

11 / The effects of the changed regime on the broadcasting system by 1969 were assessed by the author in 'Oh say, can you see?' in *Close the 49th Parallel etc.*, ed. Ian Lumsden (Toronto, 1970), 135–56. For a somewhat similar assessment by a later president of the CBC, see the statement by A.W. Johnson, 'Touchstone for the CBC,' Ottawa, June 14, 1977.

12 / *Fowler Report II*, 34–5.

barking. ... However tempting it may be to raise questions as to particular programmes or activities of CBC in Parliament, the more effective and appropriate place to raise such questions is directly with the Board of Broadcast Governors.[13]

Of course, under the 1958 legislation the BBG did not have responsibility for CBC program decisions or for individual programs, unless they contravened one of the BBG's general regulations. And the CBC board of directors had insufficient prestige to encourage parliamentarians to refer all complaints to them.

The series of arguments between the BBG and the CBC arose partly from institutional biases, and partly from genuine ambiguities in the 1958 legislation. The BBG did not have the resources or experience of the CBC, and sometimes came out second best in such disputes. This probably encouraged the BBG to see itself as the protector of the private broadcasting interests, and particularly of CTV, a network that had been formed with the BBG's active encouragement. With the growing prosperity of the larger private stations, and the general satisfaction with their increased status, the stations were reasonably content with the regulatory system. The identification of the BBG with private broadcasting interests in the minds of some critical bystanders, and the suspicion that some of its members were sensitive to political pressures, guaranteed that when the Liberals came to power, some changes would be made. But whose advice would they follow?

6 *The Choices Confronting the Liberals after 1963*

The Pearson government had to reconcile its eventual policy choice with the party's historical position, as well as resolve the conflicting advice offered by close friends and associates. In opposition, the Liberals had been critical of the 1958 act, of the two-board concept, and of the performance of the BBG. Once in office, it seemed they might quickly introduce legislation to implement the recommendations of the Fowler report of 1957, which had served as the party's basis of attack on the Conservative government's bill in 1958. But in 1963, the choice was not so simple. For one thing, the party did not have a majority in the Commons. Perhaps they could count on the support of the NDP, but in 1958 Douglas Fisher, speaking for the small CCF group in the Commons,

13 / *Fowler Commission Report*, 128.

had announced his party's support for the Conservatives' bill. Then the fact that the BBG had been the controlling agency for five years also prevented any hasty move to dismantle it. Although the BBG had its critics, the chairman, who had been appointed for a term of seven years, was highly respected. He and the other members of the board possessed no operational experience in broadcasting, and were unlikely to be asked to take responsibility for CBC operations. But a request for their resignations would have been regarded as unfair, particularly among the private broadcasters and their allies. The organized broadcasters, through their association, the CAB, were at this time a considerable force in the country, and their president, Don Jamieson of St. John's, Newfoundland, had close connections with the Liberal party.

The new minister to whom broadcasting was assigned, the secretary of state, Jack Pickersgill, had argued Fowler's position in 1958, but even then there were signs that his support of it could be equivocal. In debate he explained, 'I have a predilection for the free play of economic forces; indeed I belong to a party which has this predilection. But ... there would be no distinctively Canadian content to radio broadcasting if it were left to undiluted commercial enterprise.' And although he felt there had been nothing wrong in principle or in practice with the regulation of private stations by the CBC board of governors, 'I must say I had a good deal of sympathy about employees of the C.B.C. exercising control over them.'[14] Pickersgill, Premier Smallwood, and Don Jamieson were close associates in Liberal party politics in Newfoundland, and since 1958 Pickersgill must have become well acquainted with the private stations' position.

On another front, the president of the CBC was 'going public' in promoting his view (and that of his board) that the CBC should, as soon as possible, distribute its national program service through its own facilities, thereby disentangling the private and publicly owned stations. A by-product of this separation would be to allow the BBG to concentrate on general regulations and the allocation of channels and licences to private stations. Such an option would be tantamount to abandoning the 'single system' concept that had originated with the Radio League in the early 1930s. Most of the CBC's customary supporters, however, refused to move from the 'single system' ideal, which had been reinforced by the Fowler Commission report, and it was unlikely that the Liberal leader would do so either. Pearson was an old friend not only of Fowler, but of Graham Spry, the repository of the Radio League tradition.

14 / *Debates*, July 15, 1958, 2252–3, 2255–6.

The CBC's proposal, if carried out, would create a simpler system, one that was easier to operate, and might also reduce the schizophrenic effect on the national program service of trying to fulfil two different sets of objectives – one set that was commercially appealing and rewarding to the private affiliates, and the other a set of public service objectives that historically had been assigned to the CBC. But the CBC president's advocacy did not amount to a sustained campaign, and did not find many allies outside the CBC. To some critics, the CBC's position looked merely like an attempt to escape any effective control. More substantively, there was the question of cost. No one knew how much additional money the public treasury would have to provide to enable the CBC to become less commercial, and to replace the private affiliates with CBC stations and transmitters. The CBC planners believed that, if the program were carried out gradually, the costs in any one year would not be large in relation to the CBC's total budget. That proposition could best be examined in a full and public inquiry. There was another difficulty that the CBC did not talk about. If the private sector became fully commercial, providing its own program mix and taking no CBC programs, it was at least doubtful that satisfactory standards could be maintained throughout the private system by regulation alone. Full competition between a publicly owned system that was held publicly accountable, and had varied responsibilities to discharge, and a private system that had only general regulations and minimum standards to observe, would give most of the advantages to the private operators. Great Britain, where the public service tradition in broadcasting was strong, had met this problem when introducing commercial television by creating a second *public* authority, the Independent Television Authority. The ITA not only set the standards and generally supervised the private television sector, but it selected the program companies that provided the commercial television service, it owned the facilities over which the commercially supported programs were broadcast, and it arranged that the production of news programs on ITV was handled by a non-profitmaking organization in which all the ITV program companies had shares.[15]

From the welter of options that were favoured by one group or another, the Liberal government decided that it would try to find a compromise by consulting the heads of the BBG, the CBC, and the CAB. But the 'Troika' committee could not agree on how the broadcasting system should be reconstituted. The president of the CBC, Alphonse Ouimet, and the chairman of the BBG, Andrew Stewart, came close to

15 / Independent Television Authority, *ITV 1972: Guide to Independent Television* (London, 1972), 9, 21.

agreement, but Don Jamieson was not persuaded that the CBC should be exempted from a degree of BBG control – the same degree of control it would exercise over the private stations. He became the champion of the 'single system,' in one sense at least. The recommendations of Ouimet and Stewart for a less commercial CBC, and a dual system not unlike that of Australia, were probably not to the government's taste. Even before the 'Troika' had concluded its deliberations, the government turned once more to Fowler for advice. His general position was known to them, and the government decided that the new committee Fowler headed need not engage in full public hearings, as the CBC had recommended. Pickersgill's successor as secretary of state, Maurice Lamontagne, wished his department to become a centre for co-ordinating the government's activities in cultural affairs, and to take a more active and positive role. Perhaps to encourage a continuing departmental function in establishing broadcasting policy, the minister appointed the undersecretary of state to the Fowler Committee, and an assistant in the department was made committee secretary.

The report of the Fowler Committee was forthright in recommending that there be a single system and one board as an authority over public and private broadcasters – as the royal commission had recommended in 1958. But by 1965 the situation had changed. The private stations were not unhappy with the existing regime, and the CBC resisted the return to one board, as the option furthest removed from the dual system it hoped to see established. As early as 1962, a Liberal party resolution had deleted reference to 'a single system,' and had emphasized instead, 'parallel development of both public and private initiative in broadcasting under an independent and truly non-partisan agency of control' – in effect, what the private broadcasters favoured.[16] The party resolution was one indicator that the government might be moving away from its 1958 position when its leaders were in opposition. Furthermore, Maurice Lamontagne, who likely would have fought for the Fowler Committee's recommendation, was no longer secretary of state, or even a member of the cabinet, after the election of 1965.

A cabinet committee, under the prime minister's chairmanship, was to take the main policy decisions, after listening to representations from the BBG chairman, the CBC president and board of directors, and the CAB. The cabinet's decision was not to abandon the 'single system,' to maintain two boards, to strengthen the regulatory board's powers as Fowler had recommended, and to delineate more precisely the responsibilities

16 / Bernard Trotter, 'Canadian Broadcasting Act IV: Scene '67, or Double Talk and the Single System,' *Queen's Quarterly* (Winter 1966), 461–82.

of the CBC and the objectives for broadcasting as a whole, in the hope that refurbishing the system established in 1958 would make it work better. Ouimet fought to keep the CBC's reporting line independent from the new regulatory authority (the Canadian Radio-Television Commission); the CBC was to continue reporting directly to Parliament. Assurances were also given that the CRTC would not oversee the CBC's operational decisions, although it would have the authority to review CBC licence applications.

Two new features of the 1968 act were of importance. Cable television was brought into the broadcasting system and made subject to the authority of the regulatory board. This meant that in future cable would not necessarily be, as it had been in the past, merely another means of importing and distributing American programs. The control of cable television by the broadcasting authority had been recommended for some years by the BBG, the CBC, and most private broadcasters. The other new feature was the assigning to the government of a greater role in broadcasting policy, and spelling this out in more specific terms. The government was to determine the classes of applicants to whom broadcasting licences should be granted; it was to issue directives to the CRTC regarding the reservation of channels for the CBC; it had the authority to require stations to broadcast programs that it deemed of urgent importance. The minister was also to adjudicate between the CRTC and the CBC if the CBC took exception to a condition of licence imposed by the CRTC. To exercise these powers intelligently, departments of government would need to develop more expert knowledge than they had commanded in the past. Government, it seemed, was about to augment its role in electronic communications, and wanted to establish this before provincial administrations claimed jurisdiction, either over educational television or wired systems.

The act also asserted a national policy that Canadians were 'entitled to broadcasting service in English and French as public funds became available.' The government was conscious of heightened French-Canadian nationalism in the province of Quebec, and was pursuing its program of recognizing the language rights of French-speaking Canadians in whatever province they resided. Similar concerns, and apprehension over separtist sentiment that was growing in Quebec, prompted the government to specify in the act that one of the CBC's purposes was to 'contribute to the development of national unity and provide for a continuing expression of Canadian identity.' For many years this had been included by the CBC in setting out its mandate, but it was significant that the government had now decided that the objective must be put formally into the governing legislation. A broadcasting organization's performance in realizing such an objective is hard to assess, and whenever Canadian unity was in jeopardy, the CBC was likely to come under critical attention.

Further evidence that nationalist concerns were more crucial than ever were in the declarations that the broadcasting system was to be effectively owned and controlled by Canadians (including cable television), and that the programs of each broadcaster should use 'predominantly Canadian creative and other resources.'

These policy decisions appeared to favour (1) the regulatory authority, given increased jurisdiction and somewhat increased powers; (2) Canadian capital that was interested in investing in cable and broadcasting stations; (3) smaller communities in both language groups, now given more assurance that the national services would reach them; (4) Canadian creative and performing talent, through increased emphasis on national objectives for broadcasting; and (5) existing television stations, less vulnerable to the unrestricted importation by cable companies of television signals from the United States.

The more clearly drafted legislation of 1968 brought an end to the series of confrontations that had been so characteristic of the period after 1958, and that factor alone had some benefits. The CBC and other broadcasters would have more time to get about their essential business of providing program services; they would spend less of their energies contending with parliamentary committees, the regulatory authority, or each other.

7 The Future

Even larger questions remained unsettled or unresolved. The decision in 1968 was essentially to continue with the structures that we had developed during the preceding forty years, but under the changed conditions of the 1970s these no longer seem adequate to the task of fulfilling the objectives laid down in the act. The challenges are from at least three sources: the new technologies, the ever-stronger influences on Canadian life emanating from the United States, and the provincial and other sectional impulses demanding greater local autonomy. For many years Canadians were served by a broadcasting system which was fashioned out of compromise, mainly a compromise between public and commercial broadcasting objectives. The same assumptions underlay the 1958 and 1968 acts, and most of the problems that had been troublesome after

1958 would persist. It was still believed that commercial and public service broadcasting were equally legitimate, that each would contribute similarly to national objectives, and that each should be given the same or nearly the same importance. After 1968, the regulatory board would again be in the position of protecting the private stations and networks it had authorized.[17] The private sector would still be unable or unwilling to use a preponderant amount of its funds to provide Canadian expression, and so to check the flood of images and words spilling into Canada from the United States.

To a degree, Canadians were lulled by the very successes of the broadcasting system that had been fashioned between 1932 and 1968. Though in some ways they had not realized the extent of their achievement, they had created a broadcasting service that was the envy of many other countries. But it was doubtful that the old system could survive without new decisions and new structures adapted to changed circumstances.

It is obvious that new technologies are forcing change – not only cable, but pay-TV, video recordings, and the possibility of international satellite penetration. But machinery alone need not dictate the pattern of change nor determine the purposes of the communications system. Advanced technologies can be used to realize our most important traditional objectives; they can give us the means to amplify Canadian expression.

The Canadian capacity in theatre, music, dance, literature, journalism, graphic arts and film, for instance, has grown enormously in one generation, partly as a result of the way radio and television developed across this country. Indeed, Canadian expression has expanded beyond the means of existing broadcasting organizations to display it, given the financial structures within the system, and the broadcasters' own assumptions about audience and profits. This new circumstance is another consideration compelling change.

Beyond questions of hardware and production capacity, are issues of national strategy. There have been increasing contradictions between the objectives declared by Parliament and the broadcasting pattern that has emerged in practice. If forty years ago we set up a system giving priority to broadcasting as a public service, over the years we have evolved a system increasingly concerned with commercial gain. The

17 / Robert E. Babe, 'Regulation of Private Television Broadcasting by the Canadian Radio-Television Commission: A Critique of Ends and Means,' *Canadian Public Administration* (Winter 1976), 552–86.

result has been a massive commitment of airtime to programs, many of them American, that are irrelevant to pressing Canadian needs. A clearer resolution of the old question is required: which tradition best serves the citizen. In the common interest, a new and better balance must be struck between the public and service principle, and the private and commercial. We can drift no longer.

BIBLIOGRAPHICAL NOTE

The main sources for this volume tracing broadcasting policy since the arrival of Canadian television are voluminous public documents: annual reports of the CBC and BBG, proceedings of parliamentary committees, the *Debates* of the House of Commons and Senate, the White Paper on Broadcasting in 1966, and successive broadcasting acts. Among other important public documents are the reports and records of the various public inquiries established to investigate Canadian broadcasting, especially the Massey Commission (the Royal Commission on National Development in the Arts, Letters and Sciences, 1949–51), the Fowler Commission (the Royal Commission on Broadcasting, 1957), and the Advisory Committee on Broadcasting (the Fowler Committee) of 1965. The records of these three inquiries are in the Public Archives of Canada, as are the records of the Royal Commission on Government Organization (the Glassco Commission), which in 1963 reviewed the organization of the CBC in Volume 4 of the Commission's report (*Special Areas of Administration*). The three-volume report in 1970 of the Special Senate Committee on Mass Media (the Davey Committee), although published after the period this book surveys, also contains a great deal of relevant information.

After its inception in 1958, the BBG published in multilith the records of its hearings, decisions, public announcements, and circular letters. These are on file in the library of the Canadian Radio-Television and Telecommunications Commission in Ottawa-Hull.

A diverse collection of records and documents, including CBC studies and reports, is in the archives of the CBC Historical Section in Ottawa. Among them, for example, are the first reports and television plans for Canada written by J. Alphonse Ouimet and other corporation employees. Some CBC records are at two other locations, particularly those relating to the program services of the English and French networks. These are in the CBC reference library in Toronto and in the CBC French network archives, Place Radio-Canada, Montreal. At all three locations are CBC publications, submissions to public inquiries, reports by the CBC research department, press clippings and summaries of press comment, selected correspondence and internal files, and books and articles on the general subject of broadcasting.

The Canadian Association of Broadcasters in Ottawa maintains a list of private and radio television stations and the dates they were licensed, but has few other documents that it makes public. The researcher trying to discover the CAB's positions on developing issues must have recourse to submissions made by the CAB to public inquiries, or to accounts appearing in the trade magazine *Canadian Broadcaster* (now published as *Broadcaster*). An assessment of the structure and regulation of Canadian broadcasting by Don Jamieson, president of the CAB for three years, is to be found in his book, *The Troubled Air* (Fredericton: Brunswick Press, 1966).

Private collections of papers have been an important source of information. One of the most extensive collections is that of J.A. Ouimet, arising from his career in public broadcasting. Although his records include minutes of the CBC board of directors and its committees during his term as president (1958–67), these minutes are not as yet open for inspection.

The papers of J.A. Corry in the library of Queen's University contain minutes of the CBC Board of Governors from 1950 to 1958. Other records at Queen's University include the papers of the historian, A.R.M. Lower, who was active in reviving the Canadian Radio League in the 1950s, and the papers of Grant Dexter, editor and Ottawa correspondent of the *Winnipeg Free Press*.

The founder of the Canadian Radio League, Graham Spry, has a large collection of documents and correspondence relating to broadcasting, including records of the league's revival after 1958 as the Canadian Broadcasting League. The papers of the veteran broadcaster, E.A. Weir, are in the Public Archives of Canada, as are those of Eugene Forsey, who was appointed to the Board of Broadcast Governors in 1958.

The chairman of the BBG, Andrew Stewart, kept few records, but soon after 1968 he wrote an account of his work in the BBG, producing a 434-page manuscript on which this volume has drawn heavily. A useful article on the regulatory performance of the BBG is Peter A. Grant, 'The Regulation of Program Content in Canadian Television,' in *Canadian Public Administration*, XI:3 (Fall 1968), 322–91.

Books dealing with the history of Canadian broadcasting include:

E.A. Weir, *The Struggle for National Broadcasting* (Toronto: McClelland and Stewart, 1965)

F.W. Peers, *The Politics of Canadian Broadcasting, 1920–1951* (Toronto: University of Toronto Press, 1968)

Albert A. Shea, *Broadcasting: The Canadian Way* (Montreal: Harvest House, 1963)

Broadcasting developments as seen by individual participants are reflected in several books of reminiscences:

Judy LaMarsh, *Memoirs of a Bird in a Gilded Cage* (Toronto: McClelland and Stewart, 1969)

J.A. Munro and A.I. Inglis, eds., *Mike: The Memoirs of the Rt. Hon. Lester B. Pearson*, vol. III (Toronto: University of Toronto Press, 1975)

Guy Parent, *Sous le règne des bruiteurs* (Montreal, Editions du Lys, 1963)

J.W. Pickersgill, *My Years with Louis St Laurent: A Political Memoir* (Toronto: University of Toronto Press, 1975)

Peter Stursberg, *Mister Broadcasting: The Ernie Bushnell Story* (Toronto: Peter Martin and Associates, 1971)

APPENDIX

1. *Range of Choices among Broadcasting Structures*

I / One system; public sector dominant
(a) complete public ownership, with the public agency guaranteed substantial independence from government
(b) the main facilities publicly owned; supplementary service through private stations, but with statutory recognition of the dominance of the public sector
(c) a dominant public broadcasting agency, with supplementary service from private stations, but with the operation of the public sector kept at arm's length from the regulatory body, in the interests of fairness to the private components of the system

II / One system: parallel services (public and private), under one regulatory board
(a) responsibilities of the two services similar, so that the public service can be partly commercial and have private affiliates
(b) the responsibilities of the two services different, with the private service commercial and the public service non-commercial

III / Parallel systems, separately accountable
(a) a public system, governed by its own board, and a private system, regulated by another public board
(b) a public system, governed by its own board, and a private system, using facilities owned by another public authority

IV / A market-oriented system: private sector dominant
(a) Most stations and networks privately owned, with a significant degree of regulation by a public authority
(b) Most stations and networks privately owned, with minimal regulation by a public authority, particularly in programming matters
(c) a system dominated by private stations, supplemented by publicly owned stations or program production services.

2. *Forces and Influences Affecting Broadcasting Policy*

I / *Environmental factors:*
Prevailing ideas and attitudes regarding
– desirable patterns of ownership
– the market system
– social purposes to be served by mass media
– role of political authorities in communications systems
International influences, from
– policy choices made elsewhere
– spillover effects of programs originated elsewhere
– presence in Canada of enterprises owned in other countries
Technological change, affecting
– costs, competition, potential distribution of services, and service choices available
Economic factors:
– size of national product, levels of prosperity
– means of securing revenues for broadcasting
– levels of taxation
– prevailing patterns in economic organization
Geographic and demographic factors:
– concentration or dispersal of population
– degree of urbanization
– clustering of audiences in regions or provinces
Cultural and linguistic influences; feelings of community as related to:
– principal languages spoken
– intensity of identification with localities and regions, the country as a whole, the North American continent, or a heritage derived from other lands

II / *Centres of political power or influence*
Cabinet and advisers:
– the prime minister and his principal associates
– government departments, senior civil servants
– inquiries and investigations: royal commissions, task forces, parliamentary committees
– party resolutions and commitments
Institutionalized agencies established by the state:
– programming agencies
– regulatory boards
Organized private interests
– clientele of regulatory agencies (private stations)

- associations of private broadcasters
- groups allied with private broadcasters
- potential competitors of licensed broadcasters
- interests in other media, especially newspapers
Organizations claiming to represent the public interest
- civic and educational groups
- mass-membership associations
- associations representing listeners and viewers
Other governments: the provinces

INDEX